I0896770

Handbook of Research on Social Marketing and Its Influence on Animal Origin Food Product Consumption

Diana Bogueva
Curtin University, Australia

Dora Marinova
Curtin University, Australia

Talia Raphaely
Curtin University, Australia

A volume in the Advances in Marketing, Customer Relationship Management, and E-Services (AMCRMES) Book Series

IGI Global
DISSEMINATOR OF KNOWLEDGE

Published in the United States of America by
IGI Global
Business Science Reference (an imprint of IGI Global)
701 E. Chocolate Avenue
Hershey PA, USA 17033
Tel: 717-533-8845
Fax: 717-533-8661
E-mail: cust@igi-global.com
Web site: http://www.igi-global.com

Library of Congress Cataloging-in-Publication Data

Names: Bogueva, Diana, 1974- editor. | Marinova, Dora, editor. | Raphaely, Talia, editor.
Title: Handbook of research on social marketing and its influence on animal origin food product consumption / Diana Bogueva, Dora Marinova, and Talia Raphaely, editors.
Description: Hershey, PA : Business Science Reference, [2018]
Identifiers: LCCN 2017032133| ISBN 9781522547570 (hardcover) | ISBN 9781522547587 (ebook)
Subjects: LCSH: Meat industry and trade--Environmental aspects. | Meat industry and trade--Social aspects. | Social marketing.
Classification: LCC HD9410.5 .S63 2018 | DDC 636.0068/8--dc23 LC record available at https://lccn.loc.gov/2017032133

This book is published in the IGI Global book series Advances in Marketing, Customer Relationship Management, and E-Services (AMCRMES) (ISSN: 2327-5502; eISSN: 2327-5529)

British Cataloguing in Publication Data
A Cataloguing in Publication record for this book is available from the British Library.

Advances in Marketing, Customer Relationship Management, and E-Services (AMCRMES) Book Series

Eldon Y. Li
National Chengchi University, Taiwan & California Polytechnic State University, USA

ISSN:2327-5502
EISSN:2327-5529

Mission

Business processes, services, and communications are important factors in the management of good customer relationship, which is the foundation of any well organized business. Technology continues to play a vital role in the organization and automation of business processes for marketing, sales, and customer service. These features aid in the attraction of new clients and maintaining existing relationships.

The Advances in Marketing, Customer Relationship Management, and E-Services (AMCRMES) Book Series addresses success factors for customer relationship management, marketing, and electronic services and its performance outcomes. This collection of reference source covers aspects of consumer behavior and marketing business strategies aiming towards researchers, scholars, and practitioners in the fields of marketing management.

Coverage

- Online Community Management and Behavior
- Text Mining and Marketing
- Mobile CRM
- Cases on CRM Implementation
- Customer Relationship Management
- Mobile services
- Telemarketing
- CRM in financial services
- Legal Considerations in E-Marketing
- Database marketing

IGI Global is currently accepting manuscripts for publication within this series. To submit a proposal for a volume in this series, please contact our Acquisition Editors at Acquisitions@igi-global.com or visit: http://www.igi-global.com/publish/.

The Advances in Marketing, Customer Relationship Management, and E-Services (AMCRMES) Book Series (ISSN 2327-5502) is published by IGI Global, 701 E. Chocolate Avenue, Hershey, PA 17033-1240, USA, www.igi-global.com. This series is composed of titles available for purchase individually; each title is edited to be contextually exclusive from any other title within the series. For pricing and ordering information please visit http://www.igi-global.com/book-series/advances-marketing-customer-relationship-management/37150. Postmaster: Send all address changes to above address.

Titles in this Series

For a list of additional titles in this series, please visit: www.igi-global.com/book-series

Digital Marketing Strategies for Fashion and Luxury Brands
Wilson Ozuem (University of Gloucestershire, UK) and Yllka Azemi (Indiana University Northwest, USA)
Business Science Reference • copyright 2018 • 460pp • H/C (ISBN: 9781522526971) • US $210.00 (our price)

Exploring the Rise of Fandom in Contemporary Consumer Culture
Cheng Lu Wang (University of New Haven, USA)
Business Science Reference • copyright 2018 • 300pp • H/C (ISBN: 9781522532200) • US $225.00 (our price)

Rethinking Market Research for Global Business Integration
Rajagopal (EGADE Business School, Tecnologico de Monterrey, Mexico)
Business Science Reference • copyright 2018 • 286pp • H/C (ISBN: 9781522527367) • US $235.00 (our price)

Driving Customer Appeal Through the Use of Emotional Branding
Ruchi Garg (BML Munjal University, India) Ritu Chhikara (BML Munjal University, India) Tapan Kumar Panda (BML Munjal University, India) and Aarti Kataria (Management Development Institute, India)
Business Science Reference • copyright 2018 • 366pp • H/C (ISBN: 9781522529217) • US $235.00 (our price)

Building Brand Equity and Consumer Trust Through Radical Transparency Practices
Elena Veselinova (Goce Delčev University of Štip, Macedonia) and Marija Gogova Samonikov (Goce Delčev University of Štip, Macedonia)
Business Science Reference • copyright 2018 • 392pp • H/C (ISBN: 9781522524175) • US $225.00 (our price)

Driving Traffic and Customer Activity Through Affiliate Marketing
Surabhi Singh (Jaipuria School of Business, India)
Business Science Reference • copyright 2018 • 233pp • H/C (ISBN: 9781522526568) • US $175.00 (our price)

Encouraging Participative Consumerism Through Evolutionary Digital Marketing Emerging Research and Opportunities
Hans Ruediger Kaufmann (University of Nicosia, Cyprus) and Agapi Manarioti (The Brand Love, Cyprus)
Business Science Reference • copyright 2017 • 222pp • H/C (ISBN: 9781683180128) • US $160.00 (our price)

Strategic Marketing Management and Tactics in the Service Industry
Tulika Sood (JECRC University, India)
Business Science Reference • copyright 2017 • 393pp • H/C (ISBN: 9781522524755) • US $210.00 (our price)

IGI Global
DISSEMINATOR OF KNOWLEDGE

701 East Chocolate Avenue, Hershey, PA 17033, USA
Tel: 717-533-8845 x100 • Fax: 717-533-8661
E-Mail: cust@igi-global.com • www.igi-global.com

To those who have been with us on this journey and to those whose world we are borrowing today.

List of Reviewers

Janet Bornman, *Curtin University, Australia*
Xiumei Guo, *Curtin University, Australia*
Nick Hardersen, *Oklahoma University, USA*
Amzad Hossain, *Curtin University, Australia & Rajshahi University, Bangladesh*
Silvia Lozeva, *Curtin University, Australia*
Nick Pendergast, *University of Melbourne, Australia*
Malte Roedl, *The University of Manchester, UK*
Krassi Rumchev, *Curtin University, Australia*
Kurt Schmidinger, *University of Vienna, Austria*
Kurt Seemann, *Swinburne University, Australia*
Vladislav Todorov, *University of Forestry, Bulgaria*
Jiuchang Wei, *University of Science and Technology of China, China*
Atiq Zaman, *Curtin University, Australia*
Jadwiga Ziolkowska, *Oklahoma University, USA*

List of Contributors

Table of Contents

Section 3
Case Studies in Social Marketing

Section 4
New Meat Plant-Based Products and Alternatives

Detailed Table of Contents

Human consumption of livestock remains a marginal issue in climate change debates, partly due to the IPCC's arbitrary adoption of 100-year global warming potential framework to compare different emissions, blinding us to the significance of shorter-term emissions, namely methane. Together with the gas it reacts to form - tropospheric ozone - methane has been responsible for 37% of global warming since 1750, yet its atmospheric life is just 10 years. Neglecting its role means overlooking powerful mitigation opportunities. The chapter discusses the role of livestock, the largest anthropogenic methane source, and the need to include reduced meat consumption in climate change responses. Looking beyond the conventional focus on the consumer, we point to some underlying challenges in addressing the meat-climate relationship, including the climate science community's reluctance to adopt a short-term focus in its climate projections. Policy options are presented.

Food waste is a major issue around the globe impacting food security, resource use, economic operations, and the environment. Meat waste, constituting approximately half of total annual meat production in the United States, is particularly relevant to address due to significant resource inputs used in livestock breeding and the meat production process. In this chapter, the authors monetize annual costs of natural resources including water, land, and energy, as well as emissions of methane and nitrous oxide embedded in wasted meat in the United States. Results indicate the total annual cost of $32-32.5 billion. The outcomes substantiate the need to reduce current levels of wasted meat in order to minimize economic, social, and environmental impacts on natural resources and make food and meat production more sustainable.

The application of antibiotics to livestock has become a serious global concern. The increasing demand for animal protein leads to a greater use of antibiotics in livestock production. This is contributing to a global scale-up in antibiotic consumption. This chapter analyses the use of antibiotics in animals and the emergence of antibiotics as a class of contaminants which pollute the natural environment and create antimicrobial resistance. The conclusion is that the current system is unable to withstand ethical health concerns.

This chapter discusses a South African supermarket's print advertisement promoting meat consumption for a national public holiday. Meat consumption is portrayed as symbolic of and necessary for cultural belonging, participation and celebration. It is used to maximise profits by maintaining the distance between consumers and the realities of the power and violence perpetrated against the sentient life from which the "culturally" commodified meat product is sourced. National Heritage Day celebrates the demise of South Africa's history of domination, exploitation and discrimination and its bright present and future. The case study however illustrates that the marketing of meat as a cultural commodity reinforces hegemonic control and is contrary to what Heritage Day represents. It indicates a dangerous dissonance that encourages and endorses domination and violence against animals. Whilst the case study focuses on South Africa, hegemonic influence through visual commodification and marketing of meat is apparent in most western societies.

This chapter describes how among vegetarian, vegan and animal advocates, it has been a common practice for many decades to cede the terms "meat" to livestock producers, and to ask people to sacrifice meat. Yet during those decades, global consumption of livestock products has exploded. People have often overlooked the fact that "meat" has been defined for centuries as an essential food that includes vegan versions, and plant-based meat has always been framed as equivalent or superior to animal-based meat. In fact, replacing animal-based foods with better alternatives is said to be the only pragmatic way to stop climate change quickly as needed. However, it is unlikely to happen through efforts to reduce meat consumption. It is much more likely to happen through efforts to disrupt meat production and consumption by making and marketing meat and other foods directly from plants.

Meat alternatives have been proposed as one solution to decrease meat consumption and thus its negative effects on individuals and the environment. Using three meat myths identified in literature on meat consumption—meat eating is normal, natural, and necessary—this chapter discusses how they emerge in six selected print adverts: (1) normal: dishes containing meat alternatives are portrayed as traditional, perpetuating normality; (2) natural: the myth that it is natural to eat meat is not explicitly opposed, but bypassed; (3) necessary: meat alternatives are portrayed as even more necessary for good health than

Preface

SOCIAL MARKETING AND ITS INFLUENCE ON ANIMAL-ORIGIN FOOD CONSUMPTION

Seemingly less serious to be considered a major problem, animal-origin food consumption is not any longer about cultural values and norms shaping the conventional western, and increasingly popular across the world, diet. It is about the profound impact animal agriculture and humanity's appetite for meat have on accelerating climate change, land degradation, water depletion, cruelty to animals, spread of non-communicable diseases and altering the natural balance of our planet whilst also harming our own human health. The role of social marketing is to be an eye-opener about these complex, persistent, multiple and concurrent harms and threats, all triggered by people's hunger for animal proteins and demand for them to be supplied. In fact, hardly anybody ever thinks about the entire cycle of impregnating animals, giving birth, raising and feeding the young ones, cleaning the excreta, prioritizing grains for food or feed, slaughtering, draining and directing the blood flows, when buying a steak or ordering a burger. In the previous centuries, it was socially acceptable for people to walk in the street with a cigarette between their fingers, now it is fully normal to have a takeaway coffee liquid based on milk in your hand. There is much more awareness about expensive meat cuts, food safety, transportation and storage of animal-based foods than there is about the harm they cause to human health, climate change and the wellbeing of all species on the planet. As human population numbers grew, their meat consumption exploded at an unprecedented rate (Raphaely & Marinova, 2016). The consumption of animal-origin foods is normalized as: this is the way things are.

Given the evidence we have, this has to change; but in addition to the inertia we call habit, people simply love the taste of animal flesh, other species' milk and dairy products. The change is a mammoth task requiring inventive and creative solutions. Irrespective as to whether people care about their individual personal health, pursuing reduction in the consumption of meat, dairy products and other animal-based foods is an urgent multifaceted issue because of the global priorities related to greenhouse gas emissions, biodiversity conservation, water use, land and soil pollution. The suite of approaches to influence people could vary from the simple encouragement to reduce meat consumption to more draconian governmental and institutional policies. One of them is marketing – a process which business commonly uses to introduce and promote its products. However, this needs to be a particular type of marketing, namely social and not-for-profit marketing (Elliott et al., 2014) which aims at changing consumers' behaviours for the common good and create value "for society at large" (Principles of Marketing, 2010). Rather than generating commercial profit for the marketer, social marketing relates to community wellbeing (Donovan & Henley, 2003). Although entirely human-centred, the benefits can flow to the more-than-human world when it targets behaviours related to the natural environment.

Preface

Since its emergence in the early 1970s, social marketing is recognised as an effective approach to persuading people to voluntary adopt healthy or prosocial behaviours for the benefits of the individuals and society (Andreasen, 1994; Kotler & Lee, 2008). Drawing on a wide range of social sciences – psychology, sociology, philosophy, policy, anthropology, ethnography, to name a few, social marketing is being widely used as an effective approach for developing programs to promote healthy behaviours (Coreil et al., 2001; Stead et al., 2007). Dedicated to solving public medical problems, social marketing has long become a recognisable part of the health domain (Ling et al., 1992). Since the introduction of the global sustainability agenda in the 1990s, human health is now seen as part of a healthy natural ecology and social marketing has been applied as a way to tackle environmental behaviours. For example, the Bangkok Charter for Health Promotion in a Globalised World (WHO, 2005) put forward that social marketing should target the social as well as environmental determinants of health and welfare.

In the last couple of decades social marketing has positively impacted on a long list of difficult public health, environmental protection and community mobilisation issues (Kotler & Lee, 2008), including: injury prevention, quitting tobacco use, heavy drinking, decrease in infant mortality, obesity, prevention of HIV/AIDS, immunisations, oral health, drink-driving, speeding, seatbelt use, waste reduction, recycling increase, energy and water saving, sunscreen use, organ and blood donation, voting, literacy, identity theft, child maltreatment etc., which has resulted in changing individual and community behaviour. Social marketing campaigns usually build their messages either soliciting positive emotions and motivation – "carrot approach", or by danger warning, threatening and creating fear (Stefan, 2012) – "stick approach". However, they can also target changes in social structures – at a social, physical and legislative environment level, which can help individuals achieve the desired behaviours (Donovan & Henley, 2010). This can include among others, access to sustainability education, nutritious and inexpensive plant-based food, public transport or affordable renewable energy options. Social marketing as an effective approach was also proposed for meat reduction to achieve health, animal welfare, climate change and environmental benefits (Bogueva et al., 2017).

The basic 4Ps – product, promotion, place and price, product-based (Wood, 2008) as well as the 4Cs – customer value, cost, communication and convenience, consumer-centric commercial marketing mixes (Lauterborn,1990) have played a significant role in social marketing. Other specific for social marketing frameworks have also been developed. For example, Donovan and Henley (2010) put forward an additional 4Ps, namely changes in: population prevalence of the undesired behaviour, products people consume or use, places where people live, work or recreate, and political structures that ensure equality and opportunity within society. Bogueva et al. (2017) developed a new sustainability-focussed approach for social marketing interventions around the 4Ss – sustainability or care for current and future generations, strength or the power and opportunity people have to arrest climate change and improve ecological health, self-confidence or the message that each person's actions matter, and sharing or the understanding that the planet is here to be shared with all other living creatures.

According to Kotler and Lee (2006, p. 3), the "genius of modern social marketing" is in managing the paradigm that helps achieve behavioural change. This book and its 41 contributors from 16 countries (representing all continents except Antarctica) help shape the current sustainability paradigm. Soft, passive, advisory, elaborative social marketing, midway, transitional social marketing and hard, aggressive, demanding, legislative, exigent social marketing are different ways to approach sustainability social marketing (Bogueva et al., 2017) based on the 4Ss.

There is no single solution to the problem of increasing consumption of meat and other animal-based foods. In 2014, the world population was 7.2 billion (PRB, 2016) and 70 billion animals, including birds, were slaughtered for human consumption (FAO, 2017). There was a further 29 billion livestock animals alive (FAO, 2017). This means that the planet needs to support 14 animals per every person alive, including providing enough oxygen and feed as well as dealing with the pollution and contamination from the 10 slaughtered animals per person. If the current trends do not change, the planetary tasks will only become overwhelmingly hard, if not impossible. Social marketing can help define, develop and deliver citizen-focussed and evidence-based programs and campaigns related to reduction in the consumption of animal-based foods. They can encourage individuals, social groups and society as a whole to accept a new behaviour (e.g. endorse plant-based alternatives), reject a potentially undesirable behaviour (e.g. stop consuming red meat) or modify a current behaviour (e.g. reduce the consumption of animal-based foods). Policy makers can incorporate such programs as plausible interventions in their strategic efforts to deal with climate change, improve population health or reduce the rate of biodiversity loss, for example.

The book's chapters are grouped in four sections. The first three broadly relate to the roles social marketing can play in facilitating desired behavioural changes for the common good as described by Donavan and Henley (2010), namely to educate, motivate and advocate. Hence, Section 1 deals with information about the reasons why we need social marketing; Section 2 provides approaches and tools to motivate and persuade consumers to change their behaviour; Section 3 offers case study examples of actions or the need for action within different national settings. The final Section 4 looks into the new plant-based alternatives to animal meat.

Section 1 presents relevant theories, models and evidence about the negative impacts from consuming animal-based foods. It aims to spread information, educate and equip the reader with the latest available scientific evidence in an objective and dispassionate way. Through a discussion of the role of various theories in understanding and changing behaviour, including carnism, the meat paradox, values-beliefs-norms and planned behaviour, and presenting rationalisations and mechanisms to achieve reduction, including community-based social marketing, Chapter 1, the psychology of meat consumption reveals many hidden aspects of the human psyche and its relationships to meat. Science-based evidence concerning animal foods, health and disease risks and solutions for reduction using plant-based and low animal-food diets are at the core of Chapter 2. The overlooked and often ignored relationship between human consumption and livestock as the largest anthropogenic methane source and contributor to climate change is debated in Chapter 3. It also examines the climate science community's reluctance to adopt a short-term focus in climate projections with possible policy options presented as solutions. Chapter 4 reflects on the vast economic and environmental costs of meat waste produced along the global food supply chain, especially in the United States. It argues that the food surplus used to protect the developed high-income countries from unexpected ecological disasters resulting from over-exploitation of resources could potentially be used in a wiser way if distributed to people on an adequate vegetarian diet. The harm caused to the natural environment and potentially human health through the development of antimicrobial resistance because of the widespread use of antibiotics for animals in sub-therapeutic doses is the central argument of Chapter 5. Chapter 6 examines the concept of speciesism – a prejudice concerning nonhuman animals, analogous to racism and sexism. It analyses the role of the mass media in perpetuating speciesist values and the urgent need for a paradigm shift.

The second section of the book includes research approaches, tools and mechanisms illustrating selected social marketing concepts with some examples provided about outcomes within a social marketing context. It goes a step further to providing information by attracting or imposing on the consumer better dietary options and different ways of perceiving meat. Chapter 7 discusses flexitarianism – a way to moderate the meat-centred western food culture, by using social marketing nudging interventions and proposing strategies for potentially successful implication. Given the fact that global demand for meat and meat products is on the increase and unregulated, Chapter 8 sees taxing meat and animal-origin products at a higher rate than other foods as a social marketing mechanism. This would reflect the disproportionately higher negative impacts on human health and the environment of meat production and consumption. Using script theory, Chapter 9 examines social networking sites (SNSs) as channels for implementing a mass dietary change in today's meat consumers' society away from animal foods. Flipping the script and creating mass change through social media can trigger the needed shift toward rejecting meat as being essential for the human diet. Solutions to problems and stereotypes associated with meat consumption can be solicited from male consumers as they generally have a higher intake of animal proteins. Chapter 10 reveals that there is potential for a change in perceptions about the link between meat and masculinity as contemporary males are now looking for healthier and environmentally more beneficial food options. Informed by the community activism work of popular action-oriented philosophers, Chapter 11 talks about influencing people through traditional wisdom to avoid unnecessary consumption of animal-origin food. Playing with the perception of meat being a luxury product, Chapter 12 investigates this concept amongst three generations of consumers. It discusses the emergence of new attitude towards meat as a luxury good rather than necessity in response to global efforts to slow down climate change and feed the world's population. Referring to well-known people who are now considered geniuses, Chapter 13 explores whether there is a relationship between genius, creativity and eating meat. It argues that such a link is non-existent given the fact that many geniuses rejected meat eating, and proposes social marketing techniques to utilise these personalities as role models for changing the current high dependence on meat.

Section 3 presents seven case studies from different geographical locations and advocates actions. Ideally action could start simply by restricting commercial advertising by the livestock and related industries. This however would require structural changes which we hope to see one day soon. In the meantime, other examples and analyses help outline the challenges present. Examining Turkey's first animal-origin food consumption campaign by Greenpeace Mediterranean in consideration with social marketing's basic concepts, problem definition, objectives, exchange, competition, audience segmentation and marketing mix, Chapter 14 focusses on understanding the NGO's techniques to affect animal-origin food consumption. It puts forward the power of the "brand attack" as a social marketing strategy. Chapter 15 investigates the dominance of the animal welfare ideology and the role it plays in the widespread consumption of animal-based products through marketing promotions, packaging and advertising using two Australian case studies. Using hindsight from Western meat production and consumption and their devastating consequences for humanity and the planet, Chapter 16 makes the case for the need of mechanisms in Nigeria to sustain the country's current predominantly plant-based diet with relatively low per capita meat intake and resist further westernisation. China's meat consumption has global implications and Chapter 17 specifically focusses on beef. Using netnography – a research method based on analysing the content of electronic message boards, the chapter identifies that short-term food safety issues are much more dominant for Chinese consumers than general understanding of the long-term impacts from a switch to beef as the meat of choice. A more sustainable diet model implemented in a residential college in Australia is described in Chapter 18. This community-based social marketing initiative evolved to become a deeply embedded component of the organisational identity. Chapter 19 analyses the trends in production and consumption for animal-based food products in Bulgaria and makes the case for social marketing based on the high consumption of processed meat and lack of dietary advice against this. The South African case study in Chapter 20 revolves around National Heritage Day celebrated with barbecued meat. A thorough analysis of the marketing dissonance is carried out emphasising that encouraging and endorsing domination and violence against animals convey other hegemonic symbolism that the country wants to leave behind.

The final section of the book illustrates alternatives and solutions beyond animal-based food consumption. Re-thinking meat – the title of Chapter 21, goes back to the centuries old definition of "meat" as the flesh of a fruit or vegetable. It makes the case that plant-based alternatives need to replace the main component of a western dish. According to Chapter 22, the marketing of meat alternatives should replicate in advertising the notion that plant-based meat is normal, natural and necessary. Based on the hypothesis of minimum energy, Chapter 23 puts forward the term "new meat" to describe options which do not involve livestock, outlines marketing strategies and makes policy suggestions.

Many recommendations and suggestions at the individual and social levels are contained in the book. It is a timely collection of 23 chapters multifarious in nature, but dedicated to finding solutions, focussing and illustrating the power of the social marketing methodology to promote sustainable behaviour and achieve a desirable social change. It is indeed time for social mobilisation described by McKee (1992) as the process which can bring together all allies to raise people's awareness and demand urgent changes. We believe the book as a step in this direction but it will be up to you, the readers, to become part of this social mobilisation and contribute to the process which will see reduction in the production and consumption of animal-origin food. Our 21st century calls for new paradigms and new ways of doing things. New meat is certainly one of them.

Diana Bogueva
Curtin University, Australia

Dora Marinova
Curtin University, Australia

Talia Raphaely
Curtin University, Australia

REFERENCES

Andreasen, A. R. (1994). Social marketing: Its definition and domain. *Journal of Public Policy & Marketing*, *13*(1), 108–114.

Bogueva, D., Marinova, D., & Raphaely, T. (2017). Reducing meat consumption: The case for social marketing. *Asia Pacific Journal of Marketing and Logistics*, *29*(3), 477–500. doi:10.1108/APJML-08-2016-0139

Bogueva, D., Raphaely, T., Marinova, D., & Marinova, M. (2017). Sustainability social marketing. In J. Hartz-Karp & D. Marinova (Eds.), *Methods for sustainability research* (pp. 280–291). Cheltenham, UK: Edward Elgar. doi:10.4337/9781786432735.00030

Coreil, J., Bryant, C. A., & Henderson, J. N. (2001). *Social and behavioural foundations of public health*. Thousand Oaks, CA: Sage.

Donovan, R., & Henley, N. (2003). *Social marketing: Principles and practice*. Melbourne, Australia: IP Communications.

Donovan, R., & Henley, N. (2010). *Principles and practice of social marketing: An international perspective*. Cambridge, UK: Cambridge University Press. doi:10.1017/CBO9780511761751

Elliott, G., Rundle-Thiele, S., & Waller, D. (2014). *Marketing* (3rd ed.). Milton, Australia: Wiley.

Food and Agriculture Organisation of the United Nations (FAO). (2017). *FAOSTAT*. Retrieved from http://www.fao.org/faostat/en/#data/QA and http://www.fao.org/faostat/en/#data/QL

Kotler, P., & Lee, N. (2008). *Social marketing: Influencing behaviours for good* (3rd ed.). Thousand Oaks, CA: Sage.

Lauterborn, B. (1990). New marketing litany: Four Ps passé: C-words take over. *Advertising Age, 61*(4), 26.

Ling, J. C., Franklin, B. A. K., Lindsteadt, J. F., & Gearon, S. A. N. (1992). Social marketing: Its place in public health. *Annual Review of Public Health, 13*(1), 341–362. doi:10.1146/annurev.pu.13.050192.002013 PMID:1599593

McKee, N. (1992). *Social mobilisation and social marketing*. Pennang, Malaysia: Southbound.

Population Reference Bureau (PRB). (2016). *World population data sheet 2014*. Retrieved from http://www.prb.org/Publications/Datasheets/2014/2014-world-population-data-sheet.aspx

Principles of Marketing. (2010). University of Minnesota Libraries Publishing. Retrieved from http://open.lib.umn.edu/principlesmarketing/

Raphaely, T., & Marinova, D. (Eds.). (2016). *Impact of meat consumption on health and environmental sustainability*. Hershey, PA: IGI Global. doi:10.4018/978-1-4666-9553-5

Stead, M., Gordon, R., Angus, K., & McDermott, L. (2007). A systematic review of social marketing effectiveness. *Health Education, 107*(2), 126–191. doi:10.1108/09654280710731548

Stefan, A. (2012). *Fear appeals in social marketing* [Thesis]. Aarhus University. Retrieved from http://citeseerx.ist.psu.edu/viewdoc/download?doi=10.1.1.471.9334&rep=rep1&type=pdf

Wood, M. (2008). Applying commercial marketing theory to social Marketing: A tale of 4Ps (and a B). *Social Marketing Quarterly, 14*(1), 76–85. doi:10.1080/15245000701856877

World Health Organization (WHO). (2005). *The Bangkok charter for health promotion in a globalized world*. Geneva, Switzerland: WHO. Retrieved from www.who.int/healthpromotion/conferences/6gchp/bangkok_charter/en/

Acknowledgment

We acknowledge the competent and skillful writing of all the 41 contributors to this book. Without your tireless work, submissions, revisions and individual inputs, this project would have not been accomplished. We are also thankful to all reviewers who provided timely and competent feedback which helped improve the quality of the final product.

Our thanks go to our loved ones who supported us in this journey. Lily, Alexander, Iavor, Ana, Mira, Nikolay, Daniel, Alex, Ariel and Roger, you are the inspiration behind our efforts and you give us hope for tomorrow.

Section 1
The Need for Social Marketing

Chapter 1
The Psychology of Meat Consumption

Iveta Šedová
Masaryk University, Czech Republic

Tereza Vandrovcová
University of New York in Prague, Czech Republic & Charles University, Czech Republic

ABSTRACT

This chapter starts with a brief outline of the historic development of the interspecies relationships and discusses the role of norms in changing behavior. Norms play a role in maintaining the ideology of carnism which enables people to eat the flesh of certain animals due to the invisibility of meat production and to the mechanisms of objectification, deindividualization and dichotomization of livestock. According to the meat paradox theory, people alleviate the unpleasant feelings about eating animal flesh by diminishing the minds of the eaten animals. The 4N (normal, natural, necessary and nice) rationalizations which justify eating meat in current society are also pointed out. Furthermore, the role of values, attitudes and different type of motivations are discussed. In conclusion, possible ways of employing community-based social marketing are offered.

INTRODUCTION

According to the Czech philosopher Kohák, the traditional European attitude dominated deeply over all other "non-European nations and nonhuman fellow creatures alike" (Kohák, 2000, p. 30). In the course of modern history, the European region has made a large progress in attitudes toward nonhuman animals. Over the last several centuries this attitude changed to being more compassionate.

The historian Thomas (1991) claims in his analysis that human attitudes to animals changed mostly because of two factors – the Enlightenment combined with urbanization. Serpell and Paul (2003, p. 134) explain that the migration of the European population into towns and cities helped distance people from any personal involvement "in the slaughter, subjugation or maltreatment of animals, and thus removed the need for belief systems designed to justify or reinforce such practices". The German sociologist

DOI: 10.4018/978-1-5225-4757-0.ch001

Norbert Elias (2006) also claims that the post-medieval European standards regarding violence against humans and nonhuman animals, as well as table manners, were gradually transformed. Throughout the history, together with the rise of civilization and evolution of good manners, people found it increasingly difficult to see a whole animal served on the table while eating (Elias, 2006). During medieval feasts, whole animals were served and cut on the table, but today the same picture often causes disgust (Elias, 2006, p. 193). Nowadays Europeans keep animals as members of their family, they admire wild animals and tend to understand that humans should protect endangered species (Franklin, 1999). According to Special Eurobarometer 442 (2015), the attitudes of Europeans toward nonhuman animals are generally positive and their concern for them is high.

At the same time, a vast majority of people consume large amounts of animal products, mostly from industrial-sized confined animal feeding operations where animals are treated more like units than individual living beings (Twine, 2010). Through excessive consumption of animal products people take part in unnecessary suffering and killing of sentient creatures (Pluhar, 2010) but also contribute to serious environmental threats (FAO, 2006; Thaler et al., 2013; Scarborough et al., 2014; Springmann et al., 2016).

How do people deal with this obvious paradox? What are the mechanisms which make it possible for them to love animals on the one hand and eat them on the other? How can it be the case that some environmentally aware people have no problem to save water, use public transportation instead of cars and sort their waste, but they keep eating meat despite the fact that it strongly contributes to environmental threats? What are possible ways of encouraging people to eat less meat and other animal products? This chapter aims to answer such questions by focusing on the psychology of meat eating.

THEORIES EXPLAINING MEAT CONSUMPTION

Current studies, concepts and theories on the issue of meat consumption are introduced below. They can inform possible ways for marketing campaigns to help people get their behavior in line with their attitudes.

Social Norms

Evidence shows that our behavior is to a large extent governed by social norms shared by society. Norms represent implied sets of rules or standards that determine appropriate or desirable behavior (Atkinson et al., 1995, p. 750; Myers & Twenge, 2016, p. 144) and reflect the group's accepted way of thinking, feeling or acting (Smith et al., 2014, p. 312).

Our behavior is also greatly influenced by a reference group, which consists of people "who portray standards with which to evaluate one's own attitudes, abilities, or current situation" (Koger & Winter, 2010, p. 100). In other words, it is a group of people that we identify with (Myers & Twenge, 2016, p. 257). For instance, students of environmental studies often conform to the social norms of their vegetarian and vegan fellow students and usually avoid meat when in their company as discovered in a Czech research project (Šedová et al., 2016). In some cases, the norms were so deeply internalized that the students felt guilty when shopping for meat even though none of their vegetarian friends could see them (Šedová et al., 2016).

In 1960s, Everett Rogers described the concept of "diffusion of innovation," a process by which an innovation is communicated through certain channels over time among the members of a social system (Rogers, 2010, p. 10). An innovation is an idea or practice perceived as new and diffusion is the process of information flow that brings new knowledge or ideas to another individual or group. According to this theory most individuals adopt new ideas not on the basis of scientific research, but through the subjective experience with this behavior in their peers.

Diffusion stems from the imitation of models of behavior observed in people who have already adopted the innovation. It is a social process (Rogers, 2010, p. 11-18). Based on this concept, flexitarianism, vegetarianism and veganism may spread in a similar way as fashion trends: when more and more of one's close peers become flexitarian, vegetarian or vegan, they set a social norm and the individual seeks to conform to it, reducing the consumption of animal products, as has been confirmed by recent research (Šedová et al., 2016).

In order to encourage dietary changes toward a plant-based diet, researchers recommend to establish an open and friendly social movement where people can get inspired without being threatened or mocked for holding a mainstream ideology. In the Czech Republic, the animal rights movement has good experience with hosting various community dinners, picnics or barbecues based on sharing plant-based food and meeting new people. One of the biggest obstacles to veganism, for example, are social pressures stemming from the fact that it seems unusual and outside the norm (Asher et al., 2014). Such events help to overcome this.

Another advantage of these events is that they are not too difficult to organize so they can be held even by a single person, which helps create local communities. These groups then can more easily organize other events. They can also provide local guides for people who want to reduce or eliminate their consumption of animal products and are lacking information about nutrition, vegan ingredients etc.

The Ideology of Carnism

Just as norms maintain racist ideology or gender discrimination in certain societies (Atkinson et al., 1995, p. 750), the ideology of carnism – eating certain animals deemed "normal", may be maintained through such norms. Melanie Joy (2011) describes carnism as a process that enables us to perceive animals as objects without a capacity for cognition or sentience, and it comprises of objectification, deindividualization and dichotomization. Rather than being intentional, these inner processes remain mostly unconscious, pertaining not so much to what we think as to how we think, while their potency dwells primarily in the coaction of all forces.

On a conscious level, people do not usually think about the categories of "edible" and "inedible" animals. We are not born with these schema, these social constructs are acquired during our lives. As children, most of us care about all animals without any difference, and we are even raised to love them. However, through socialization we learn cultural beliefs. We are taught that certain animals are edible and tasty, that it is better to become numb toward them and not to consider them as individualities (Cole & Steward, 2014).

Hence the reason why these schemas are formed is the fact that people usually love animals and, simultaneously, need to deal with the reality that they eat some of them. According to Joy (2011), the presence of confirmation bias can be detected in the effect the carnist schema has on people: what things we take into consideration, how we interpret them and whether we remember them. Such schema takes effect, for example, when we see footage from animal slaughter and after a short while we "forget" about it.

Cognitive Dissonance

One of the important traits of carnism is dichotomization which is the process of mentally putting animals into two opposing categories based on our beliefs about them. One of the reasons why we perceive eating "edible" animals as acceptable is a psychological phenomenon called the meat paradox. A psychological study by Steve Loughnan et al. (2010) included a series of experiments and came to the conclusion that people seem to alleviate unpleasant feelings about eating meat by diminishing the minds of animals which are eaten. That is why people tend to see farm animals as stupid, non-emotional and dirty withdrawing moral concerns from them which "leads to a reduction in the perceived capacity of meat animals to suffer" (Loughnan et al., 2010, p. 159). This finding coincides with the theory of cognitive dissonance (Festinger, 1962) – the mental stress or discomfort experienced by an individual who holds two contradictory beliefs, values or exhibits opposing behaviors. The inconsistency leads the person to try and reduce the dissonance.

Rothgerber (2014) applied the cognitive dissonance theory to the issue of meat consumption identifying eight mechanisms that people employ to reduce the discomfort they experience from eating animals. They include: avoidance – physical invisibility of factory farms, slaughter houses or not thinking about animal suffering; dissociation – using euphemistic labelling, e.g. meat is called "beef", not "cow" or "bull"; perceived behavioral change – "I don't eat meat so often"; denial of animal pain – "animals don't experience pain the way humans do"; denial of animal mind – "animals are lower in the hierarchy of species and have limited mental capacity"; pro-meat justifications – "I like eating meat" or "some animals are bred to be eaten"; reduction of perceived choice – "it is unhealthy to be vegans"; and behavioral change – e.g., going vegan (Rothgerber, 2014).

While behavioral change is the outcome any meat reduction campaigns are seeking to achieve through strengthening the cognitive dissonance, the other seven discomfort reduction mechanisms are undesired. It is therefore most effective when most or all seven are addressed and ruled out. It can be accomplished by pointing to the consciousness of animals and by increasing their moral value using videos of farm animals which show their individuality, emotionality and intelligence. At the same time. it is worth trying to weaken possible barriers by offering tasty plant-based alternatives, providing recipes, tips and also nutritional information.

Rationalizations

Pro-meat justifications are among the most elaborated mechanisms and form part of the rationalization process. Rationalization is a post-behavioral process through which a problematic behavior becomes less problematic for the person who displayed it (Beauvois and Joule, 1996). Joy (2011) noticed that people in modern society are conditioned by carnism to support meat consumption by three basic justifications – called 3Ns, which alleviate the moral discomfort: that eating other animals is (1) normal, (2) natural and (3) necessary.

The first rationalization – normal, is connected with the fact that the ideology of carnism has become normalized, and its tenets represent social norms which are followed because of the general tendency to conform (Asch, 1956). This social construction causes people to defend the status quo, just because the behavior was present in our society for a long time. The other rationalization – natural, stems from the belief that eating meat is natural and therefore justified, because humans have hunted and consumed animals for millennia, and because other animals do so too. Importantly, the third belief – necessary, creates unjustified reason that eating meat is necessary and that we cannot exist without it. In this day and age, we know that it is possible to survive and thrive without eating meat (Melina et al., 2016; Dietitians of Canada, 2014), but the system proceeds as if this myth were true (Joy, 2011).

A team of psychologists led by Jared Piazza from Lancaster University examined Joy's theory in research and suggested that people defend consuming animals by rationalizing their behavior using not only these three (3Ns) but four rationalizations (Piazza et al., 2015). They added a fourth category – that eating meat is nice – in other words, that it is delicious. Piazza et al. (2015) noted that this justification has been ignored in the past because it is so weak-seeming. That is, in most other contexts, we would not justify an otherwise morally problematic act by saying: "But it feels good!". However, they saw it as a common way to justify meat-eating and included it in the rationalization reasons (Piazza et al., 2015). Piazza et al. (2015) supported Joy's claim that rationalizations are effective for reducing guilt. They observed that necessary and nice may be the most useful variables for predicting differing dietary attitudes (Piazza et al., 2015, p. 125).

Based on these suggestions it might be crucial for any meat reduction activism to focus on disproving these two justifications. Regarding necessary it seems essential to disseminate information about the suitability of a plant-only diet which is the widespread consensus in public health (Melina et al., 2016; Dietitians of Canada, 2014). Also since meat is connected with masculinity (Adams, 2006), the "protein myth" also needs to be refuted. Regarding *nice* it might be useful to offer pleasant, high-quality plant-based substitutes, for example in the form of public stalls with free food-sampling. However, activists should presuppose that people might not be willing to try the food when it is labelled as "vegan".

An interesting experiment about the taste expectation of vegan products was conducted by the psychology student Santamaria (2015). She tested the strength of expectation confirmation and its effect on aversion to, or satisfaction with, plant-based food products with one hundred meat-eating participants recruited on the street. The author theorized that expectation confirmation will lead to dissatisfaction of meat-eaters with a plant-based food product. She purchased plant-based sausages mimicking a typical pork-based bratwurst called Tofurky. They were sliced, fried and offered to the participants with a purposely incorrect information. There were four plates labelled as A, B, C and D. Each participant was told they were different competing brands of sausage. First, they were comparing A and B and were told that these were two different types of pork-based sausage. After that, they were offered C and D and were told that C was pork-based sausage and D was a plant-based product. Santamaria (2015) concluded that the meat-eating participants had expectations that the vegan product would taste worse than the pork product. Based on this expectation, they actually perceived a lower quality of taste in the seemingly vegan product as compared to what they believed was a pork product (Santamaria 2015).

Values and Attitudes Towards Nonhuman Animals

Values represent the most central and relatively stable component of a personality, whereas beliefs, norms and attitudes are more easily subject to changes (Vaske & Donnely, 1999). Values may influence attitudes, norms and behavior (Steg & de Groot, 2012, p. 81-82). This also pertains to the relationship towards nonhuman animals. Attitudes refer to our evaluations and beliefs about a person, creature, place or event and they lead to a tendency for a certain behavior. To a certain degree, some attitudes are hereditary, whereas most psychologists agree that attitudes are primarily acquired by learning through experiences in a social context (Myers & Twenge, 2016, p. 110).

Attitude change may be much easier than permanent shift of every-day habits. Hormes et al. (2013) studied longitudinally the changes in dietary habits of psychology students who had read Michael Pollan's book *The Omnivore's Dilemma* (Pollan, 2006). The results confirmed short-term effects on the dietary habits of students who had read the book. When the students were surveyed one year later, it was found that most of the attitude and behavior changes relating to food consumption dissipated with time and that they reverted to their previous eating habits.

A relationship between attitude towards nonhuman animals and environmental concerns has also been noted. More often, people interested in environmental issues have a more positive attitude towards animals (see Pifer et al., 1994). This is a good predictor of values and can be used in pursuing reduction in the consumption of animal-based products.

Motivation for Vegetarian and Vegan Diet

Motivation represents one of the factors that influence behavior. The self-determination theory (Deci & Ryan, 1985) defines three basic types of motivation: intrinsic and extrinsic motivation and amotivation – the state of lacking control leading to a mindless, automated behavior, the consequences of which cannot be predicted by the person. Social conditions can nurture intrinsic motivation (for example, to adopt a different diet) and its internalization when promoting autonomy, competence and relatedness. On the contrary, this motivation can be undermined by conditions that control behavior and hinder perceived effectance (Ryan & Deci, 2000). Therefore, it is crucial that people are not forced to change but they perceive it as their own decision.

The psychologist Paul Rozin (2006) identifies three basic motives for choosing or refusing potential foods: sensory properties (taste, smell, appearance), effects of ingestion (repletion, nausea) and ideational concerns (having to do with the nature or origin of a food). Food choice is subject to biological – physiological reactions and brain processes, psychological – genetic predispositions, parental or peer influences, as well as beliefs about taste and health value, the individual's values related to ethical issues, price, conventions etc., sociological – demographic variables such as age or gender, as well as current fad movements like low-carb diet, and cultural factors – e.g. linked to tradition, ethnicity, religion etc. They all need to be considered in efforts to reduce the intake of animal-based foods.

Discrepancies Between Attitudes and Behavior

A lot of vegan campaigns focus on changing people's attitudes and expect to alter the behavior in favor of eating less animal products because of the cognitive dissonance effect (see above), but the situation is more complicated than that. As early as in the 1930s, the potential for discrepancy between attitudes and behavior was observed by LaPiere (1934). A meta-analysis of 47 studies examining the relationship of attitudes and actions was performed by Allan W. Wicker (1969). Factors postulated to cause discrepancies between attitudes and behavior are personal – other attitudes, competing motives etc., and situational – group pressure, norms, availability of alternative behavior, external events etc.

Just as attitudes can sometimes determine behavior, behavior can affect attitudes. People who are coaxed or coerced into a behavior that is against their beliefs avoided the resulting tension by altering their attitude (Myers, 2010, p. 118). It is therefore worthy to focus on changing the behavior even without the change of attitude. When an initiative like *Veganuary* (Tamplin, 2017) convinces meat-eaters to accept time-limited challenges to change the behavior, e.g. being a vegan for a month, it might be assumed that they will have more positive attitudes toward veganism at the end of the experiment.

Behavior Explaining Theory

In addition to value surveys, Schwartz (1977) formulated the norm-activation theory stating that altruistic behavior can be influenced by moral norms, once they become activated, bringing the awareness of consequences and ascription of responsibility into the situation. This theory might help us to better understand human attitude and behavior toward nonhuman animals. Often, people profess positive attitudes towards animals and an interest in animal welfare, but they still buy products that stand in sharp contrast to such statements. The reported reasons for such conduct are lack of information, unclear labelling of free-range animal products, low accessibility of animal-free products in common shops and the price barrier (Mayfield et al., 2007). These findings have been confirmed by research amongst meat-eating students of environmental studies and cultural and social ecology in the Czech Republic who declared their willingness to buy products from organic farms, and in fact were buying organic products minimally, mostly due to financial considerations (Šedová et al., 2016).

The Dutch researchers Berndsen and Van der Pligt (2003) examined factors that influence attitude toward meat consumption, inner beliefs, meat consumption itself and the tendency to reduce this consumption in the future. Their pilot study found that 69% of meat-eaters feel ambivalent when eating meat, whereas merely 4% of vegetarians feel ambivalent in relation to their meatless diet (Berndsen and Van der Pligt, 2003). Using research surveys that measured attitudes, current meat-eating habits, subjective norms etc. amongst students of psychology, the authors' hypothesis was confirmed: the stronger ambivalence towards meat consumption a person feels, the less positive attitude they have towards meat eating and the more often they associate it with negative emotions, morally unacceptable matters and negative factors concerning their health and the environment. These results show how important emotional beliefs are when regarded as an indicator of attitudes and ambivalence. This research suggests that the observed ambivalence about meat consumption can be an indicator of the current meat consumption habits: higher ambivalence is generally accompanied by lower meat consumption.

The norm-activation theory relates to the scope of justice theory (Opotow, 1990, 1994, 2001; Opotow & Weiss, 2000), stating that we decide who is to be included in the scope of our interest and deserves our help. After crushing an ant, we do not feel sorry, as it was outside our scope of justice (Winter and Koger, 2009). Scope of justice is a dichotomous concept as the other beings can only be either inside or outside of it. The borderline of each individual is influenced by the cultural or social conditions in which they grew up. Europeans or Americans might see the Japanese whale-hunting tradition as unacceptable (although not so long ago the U.S. was a major whale hunter), and vice versa, the eastern Buddhist tradition might hold the slaughter of factory-farm animals in Western countries as ethically intolerable (Opotow, 1990; Opotow, 1993). Pointing to the cultural differences and discussing their logic might help people to understand that their culture conditions them into eating the meat of certain animals but that the differences between edible and inedible animals (see carnism above) are not morally relevant.

Value-Belief-Norm Theory

To explain the behavior shift towards boycott of meat products, the value-belief-norm theory (VBN; Stern et al., 1999; Stern, 2000) can be applied. This theory claims that a personal moral norm is the fundamental premise for a pro-environmental behavior. As such it can also form a basis for positive attitude and behavior towards animals. This norm leads to awareness of consequences and subsequently to ascription of responsibility for the impacts that affect personal norms. When applied to the human–animal relations, these norms can manifest themselves as a pro-ethical attitude towards animals and eventually as a particular behaviour, e.g. animal rights activism, political support of animal interests or personal behavior. Thus, if people do not believe that they themselves can mitigate the negative consequences of their conduct, such as contributing to the practice of factory farming, it likely follows that they will not act in accordance with their attitudes and will keep consuming animal products.

The VBN theory has become a framework for research conducted by German scientists examining the demand for free-range meat (Uehleke & Hüttel, 2016). Their study assessed the willingness to pay for farm animal welfare labeled meat (from farms complying with more strict requirements) among respondents. Subjects were assigned to two groups: in one group they answered questions related to individual behavior – whether they would be willing to pay for more expensive meat coming from farms with animal welfare certificates; the other group was presented with a collective decision situation – whether they would vote in favor of improved farm animal conditions in a referendum, even though it would increase the price for meat. Two aspects from the VBN theory explaining pro-environmental decision-making were adopted in this study: ascription of responsibility (i.e. a subjective feeling about the personal responsibility for meat consumption) and personal norm (the extent of feeling a moral obligation to avoid consuming meat from conventional production). The ascription of responsibility had an effect in the collective, but not in the individual decision situation. Taste was an important indicator at the individual and income was important in the collective decision group. The results suggest that in an individual decision frame (purchasing meat), animal welfare is not a significant factor per se. Rather, it would be advisable to add claims about higher quality or better taste in addition to the label on animal welfare to induce a behavior shift (namely, reduction of meat consumption).

Kalof et al. (1999) examined the link between social structures (age, gender, education, race and rural childhood), individual social psychology (altruism, self-interest, traditionality and openness to change) and beliefs about the benefits of vegetarianism (for health, the environment, animals and world hunger), and self-reported vegetarianism. The authors used the VBN theory and adapted Schwartz's survey. The results show that none of the social structural variables had a direct influence on becoming vegetarian or vegan. Further, it was found that of the four above-mentioned psychological traits, only altruism and traditional values influenced the choice of giving up meat.

Theory of Planned Behavior

The theory of planned behaviour (TPB; Ajzen, 1991; Gifford 2007) is an updated version of the original theory of reasoned action, presented by Fishbein and Ajzen (1975) and based on the idea that a behavior is determined by a behavioral intention, which is influenced by the attitude towards the behavior and subjective norm, namely what one thinks significant others will think about his or her behavior. Ajzen (1991) extended these two components with a third one, perceived behavioral control, which is people's perception of their ability to perform a specific behavior, to form TPB, which says that a behavior intention is influenced by three determinants: perception of the behavior, perception of the expectations and attitudes of the others, and perception of one's ability to perform such behavior.

For instance, the TPB model was applied as a theoretical framework for research on fish consumption behavior in Belgium (Verbeke & Vackier, 2005). The research hypotheses predicted that attitude to meat consumption, subjective norms and perceived behavioral control have a positive impact on fish consumption decisions. Meat consumption is also greatly influenced by habit and taste. The results suggest that the most important drivers for eating fish are taste and believed health benefits of fish meat. Socio-demographic determinants also play a role in eating fish: women and elderly people with higher income had a greater fish consumption frequency. A higher intention to eat fish was observed in people who had higher education, but it had no effect on the amount of consumed fish. The authors proposed that attitude has an evaluative component (perceived costs and benefits) and an affective component (beliefs about positive and negative feelings derived from the behavior). Social norms could force people not to perform some behavior as intended, whereas moral norms can paradoxically lead to higher fish consumption (in relation to the negative impact of animal agriculture) due to the perceived positive health factor. This discrepancy could result in conflict between inner moral norms and external expectations and demands (social norms). Past experience and habit can be a predictor of later behavior.

The theory of planned behavior has also been applied in psychological research examining significant predictors of intention to follow meat, vegetarian or vegan diets (Povey et al., 2001). Questionnaires were used to uncover the most salient beliefs, behavioral intentions, attitudes, perceived behavioral control and subjective norms, self-identity and attitudinal ambivalence in different groups of respondents – meat eaters, meat avoiders, vegetarians and vegans. The study confirmed that attitude, subjective norms and perceived behavioral control are significant predictors of intention to follow a certain diet and of subsequent behavior (the participants had the most positive intentions and beliefs to follow their own type of diet), with the exception of vegetarian diet, where subjective norms had not been found to be significant (a possible explanation could be that the pressure from significant others is less important for vegetarians than for vegans or meat eaters). In general, subjective norms was found to be the weakest predictor of behavioral intention and attitude and perceived behavioral change had a stronger impact on behavioral intention.

Klöckner (2013) conducted a meta-analysis of 56 studies aimed at pro-environmental behavior and reported that apart from the variables mentioned above (the intention to act possibly being the strongest predictor), pro-environmental behavior can also be significantly predicted by habit. The habit strength is linked to intention, personal norms and perceived behavior control. Even when a person forms a behavioral intention, the strength of old habits or low perceived behavioral control might alter the resulting behavior. Habits are strong predictors for establishing a habitual behavior and need to be overcome if the shift towards pro-environmental behavior is to be permanent. Ouellette and Wood (1998) propose that adopting a healthier lifestyle should be accompanied by visible positive consequences of such a behavior and the new healthy behavior should be consistently repeated to yield new habits that can be performed automatically.

COMMUNITY-BASED SOCIAL MARKETING

As already stated, the choice of a particular diet is to some extent driven by our attitudes and values (Kalof et al., 1999), although these are not predictors of behavior *per se*. Social marketing attempts to guide people towards adopting a new attitude, value and subsequently behavior in order to offer a solution to social issues (Kotler and Roberto 1989). It can be defined as "the adaptation of commercial marketing technologies to programs designed to influence the voluntary behavior of target audiences to improve their personal welfare and that of the society of which they are a part" (Andreasen, 1994, p. 110). Social marketing adopts the strategy of marketing campaigns to achieve a greater social good. Thus, it can be an effective way to change dietary habits.

Community-based social marketing is based on the idea of social psychology that strategies to promote behavior change are most effective when they engage the whole community and involve direct contact with people. In contrast to information campaigns that utilize advertising, community-based social marketing proves to be a valuable behavior change tool. It involves five steps: selecting behaviors, identifying barriers and benefits, developing strategies, piloting and broadscale implementation, and evaluation (McKenzie-Mohr, 2013, pp. 8-10).

When considering to apply this knowledge in campaigns aimed to lower the consumption of animal products by the general public, it is necessary to choose the particular behavior, e.g. lowering the meat consumption, to identify barriers that prevent people from reducing the amount of meat in their diet – convenience, taste, fear of not getting enough nutrition etc., and benefits of a meat-free diet – getting the behavior in line with one's ethical and environmental values, health related benefits, discovering new kinds of food, saving money etc. As a result, it might be useful to organize for example plant-based food samplings at public places, small friendly gatherings like picnics where people can learn about the benefits of meat-free diet or bigger events like festivals with tasty food and informative lectures.

CONCLUSION

The historic development of interspecies' relationships since the beginning of the industrial revolution brought higher empathy toward nonhuman animals as well as increase of animal products consumption and intensification of animal husbandry. This has not only ethical but also severe environmental consequences. How to explain this obvious paradox?

One of the reasons is the social nature of humans and their tendency to conform to the norms of the others. Norms can determine appropriate or desirable behavior and reflect the group's accepted way of thinking, feeling or acting. The behavior is also influenced by a reference group.

The norms of the current society maintain the ideology of carnism, which Joy (2011) describes as a mostly unconscious process that enables people to perceive animals as objects without capacity for cognition or sentience. It is comprised of objectification, deindividualization and dichotomization. The central feature of this ideology is the dichotomization of animals into edible and inedible. It shows that people need to put animals into a special category in order to eat them without feeling guilt.

This situation creates cognitive dissonance that manifests itself in the context of meat consumption as the meat paradox. People seem to alleviate unpleasant feelings about eating meat by diminishing the minds of animals which are eaten. Any campaigns aiming at reducing the consumption of animal products can use this knowledge and point out animal consciousness, thus increasing the moral value of nonhuman animals. This may contribute to behavior change toward plant-based diet.

Besides diminishing the minds of the edible animals, people employ various culturally shared beliefs and rationalizations that eating meat is justifiable. Researchers identified four principal rationalizations described as the 4Ns: eating meat is normal, natural, necessary and nice. Because nice and necessary are the two rationalizations that predict dietary attitudes best, it is considered crucial to focus on disproving these two particular justifications.

Attitudes and behaviors are not always in line and factors that cause discrepancies are personal and situational. A positive attitude alone may not be potent enough to trigger a shift towards behavior that does not harm animals, such as avoiding the consumption of animal products that promote factory farming and slaughters. It seems therefore worthy to focus on changing the behavior even without the change of attitude because just as attitudes can sometimes determine behavior, the behavior can affect attitudes.

Altruistic behavior toward animals can be influenced by moral norms, once these norms become activated, bringing the awareness of consequences and ascription of responsibility into the situation. According to the value-belief-norm theory, personal moral norms can lead to an awareness of consequences and subsequently to ascription of responsibility for the negative impacts of the behavior but people need to believe that they themselves can mitigate these negative consequences. The theory of planned behavior is based on the idea that a behavior intention is determined by perception of the behavior, perception of the expectations and attitudes of the others, and perception of one's ability to perform such behavior.

Advocates for reduction in the consumption of animal-based foods may also draw on the possibilities for community-based social marketing. It attempts to guide people towards adopting a new attitude, value and subsequently behavior in order to offer a solution to social issues and it can be an effective way to change dietary habits. Based on the idea that strategies to promote behavior change are most effective when they engage the whole community, it involves direct contact with people. Such activities may include plant-based food samplings at public places, small friendly gatherings or bigger events like festivals with tasty food and informative lectures.

The issue of psychology of animal products eating is getting more attention in the recent decade as environmental threats by the livestock industry and the meat paradox are becoming increasingly visible. Psychological research helps to understand what are the factors that play the most important role in choosing to eat or not to eat animal products. Spreading this information among the lay public can assist people understand how culture conditions them into the feelings of cognitive dissonance and help them get their behavior in line with their inner feelings and positive attitudes toward nonhuman animals.

ACKNOWLEDGMENT

This chapter was written in collaboration with the Department of Environmental Studies, Faculty of Social Sciences, Masaryk University and was supported by a specific research Student Project Grant of Masaryk University No. MUNI/A/1190/2016.

REFERENCES

Adams, C. J. (2006). *The sexual politics of meat: A feminist-vegetarian critical theory*. New York, NY: Continuum.

Ajzen, I. (1991). The theory of planned behavior. *Organizational Behavior and Human Decision Processes*, *50*(2), 179–211. doi:10.1016/0749-5978(91)90020-T

Andreasen, A. R. (1994). Social marketing: Its definition and domain. *Journal of Public Policy & Marketing*, *13*(1), 108–114.

Asch, S. E. (1956). Studies of independence and conformity: A minority of one against a unanimous majority. *Psychological Monographs*, *70*(9), 1–70. doi:10.1037/h0093718

Asher, K., Green, C., Gutbrod, H., Jewell, M., Hale, G., & Bastian, B. (2014). Study of current and former vegetarians and vegans. *Faunalytics*. Retrieved from https://faunalytics.org/feature-article/hrc-study-of-current-and-former-vegetarians-and-vegans/

Atkinsonová, R. L., Atkinson, R. C., Smith, E. E., Bem, D. J., & Nolen-Hoeksema, S. (1995). Psychologie [Psychology]. Praha, Czech Republic: Victoria Publishing.

Beauvois, J. L., & Joule, E. V. (1996). *A radical dissonance theory*. London, UK: Taylor and Francis.

Berndsen, M., & Van der Pligt, J. (2004). Ambivalence towards meat. *Appetite*, *42*(1), 71–78. doi:10.1016/S0195-6663(03)00119-3 PMID:15036785

Cole, M., & Steward, K. (2014). *Our children and other animals: The cultural construction of human-animal relations in childhood*. Farnham, UK: Ashgate.

Deci, E. L., & Ryan, R. M. (1985). *Intrinsic motivation and self-determination in human behavior*. New York, NY: Plenum. doi:10.1007/978-1-4899-2271-7

Dietitians of Canada. (2014). *Healthy eating guidelines for vegans*. Retrieved from http://www.dietitians.ca/Downloads/Factsheets/Guidlines-for-Vegans.aspx

Elias, N. (2006). *O procesu civilizace: Sociogenetické a psychogenetické studie* [On the process of civilization: Sociogenetic and psychogenetic investigations]. Praha, Czech Republic: Argo.

Festinger, L. (1962). *A theory of cognitive dissonance* (Vol. 2). Stanford, UK: Stanford University Press.

Fishbein, M., & Ajzen, I. (1975). *Belief, attitude, intention, and behavior: An introduction to theory and research*. Reading, MA: Addison-Wesley.

Food and Agriculture Organization of the United Nations (FAO). (2006). Livestock's long shadow: Environmental issues and options. Rome, Italy: FAO. Retrieved from http://www.fao.org/docrep/010/a0701e/a0701e00.HTM

Franklin, A. (1999). *Animals and modern cultures: A sociology of human–animal relations in modernity*. London, UK: Sage.

Gifford, R. (2007). Environmental psychology: Principles and practice. Colville, WA: Optimal books.

Hormes, J. M., Rozin, P., Green, M. C., & Fincher, K. (2013). Reading a book can change your mind, but only some changes last for a year: Food attitude changes in readers of The Omnivore's Dilemma. *Frontiers in Psychology*, *4*, 778. doi:10.3389/fpsyg.2013.00778 PMID:24198795

Joy, M. (2011). *Why we love dogs, eat pigs, and wear cows: An introduction to carnism*. Berkley, CA: Conari press.

Kalof, L., Dietz, T., Stern, P. C., & Guagnano, G. A. (1999). Social psychological and structural influences on vegetarian beliefs. *Rural Sociology*, *64*(3), 500–511. doi:10.1111/j.1549-0831.1999.tb00364.x

Klöckner, C. A. (2013). A comprehensive model of the psychology of environmental behavior—A meta-analysis. *Global Environmental Change*, *23*(5), 1028–1038. doi:10.1016/j.gloenvcha.2013.05.014

Kohák, E. (2000). *Zelená svatozář: Kapitoly z ekologické etiky* (Green halo: Chapters in ecological ethics]. Praha, Check Republic: Slon.

Koger, S. M., & Winter, D. D. (2011). The psychology of environmental problems: Psychology for sustainability (3rd ed.). New York, NY: Psychology Press.

Kotler, P., & Roberto, N. (1989). *Social marketing. Strategies for changing public behavior*. New York, NY: Free Press.

LaPiere, R. T. (1934). Attitude versus action. *Social Forces*, *13*(2), 230–237. doi:10.2307/2570339

Loughnan, S., Haslam, N., & Bastian, B. (2010). The role of meat consumption in the denial of moral status and mind to meat animals. *Appetite*, *55*(1), 156–159. doi:10.1016/j.appet.2010.05.043 PMID:20488214

Mayfield, L. E., Bennett, R. M., Tranter, R. B., & Wooldridge, M. J. (2007). Consumption of welfare-friendly food products in Great Britain, Italy and Sweden, and how it may be influenced by consumer attitudes to, and behaviour towards, animal welfare attributes. *International Journal of Sociology of Agriculture and Food*, *15*(3), 59–73.

McKenzie-Mohr, D. (2013). *Fostering sustainable behavior: An introduction to community-based social marketing*. Gabriola Island, BC: New society publishers.

Melina, V., Craig, W., & Levin, S. (2016). *Position of the Academy of Nutrition and Dietetics: Vegetarian diets*. Retrieved from http://www.eatrightpro.org/~/media/eatrightpro%20files/practice/position%20and%20practice%20papers/position%20papers/vegetarian-diet.ashx

Myers, D. G., & Spencer, S. J. (2001). *Social psychology* (Canadian edition). Toronto, Canada: McGraw-Hill Ryerson.

Myers, D. G., & Twenge, J. M. (2016). *Social psychology* (12th ed.). New York, NY: McGraw-Hill.

Ouellette, J. A., & Wood, W. (1998). Habit and intention in everyday life: The multiple processes by which past behavior predicts future behavior. *Psychological Bulletin*, *124*(1), 54–74. doi:10.1037/0033-2909.124.1.54

Opotow, S. (1990). Moral exclusion and injustice: An introduction. *The Journal of Social Issues*, *46*(1), 1–20. doi:10.1111/j.1540-4560.1990.tb00268.x

Opotow, S. (1993). Animals and the scope of justice. *The Journal of Social Issues*, *49*(1), 71–85. doi:10.1111/j.1540-4560.1993.tb00909.x

Opotow, S. (1994). Predicting protection: Scope of justice and the natural world. *The Journal of Social Issues*, *50*(3), 49–63. doi:10.1111/j.1540-4560.1994.tb02419.x

Opotow, S. (2001). Reconciliation in times of impunity: Challenges for social justice. *Social Justice Research*, *14*(2), 149–170. doi:10.1023/A:1012888902705

Opotow, S., & Weiss, L. (2000). New ways of thinking about environmentalism: Denial and the process of moral exclusion in environmental conflict. *The Journal of Social Issues*, *56*(3), 475–490. doi:10.1111/0022-4537.00179

Pollan, M. (2006). *The omnivore's dilemma*. New York, NY: The Penguin Press.

Piazza, J., Ruby, M. B., Loughnan, S., Luong, M., Kulik, J., Watkins, H. M., & Seigerman, M. (2015). Rationalizing meat consumption. The 4Ns. *Appetite*, *91*, 114–128. doi:10.1016/j.appet.2015.04.011 PMID:25865663

Pifer, L., Shimizu, K., & Pifer, R. (1994). Public attitudes toward animal research: Some international comparisons. *Society & Animals*, *2*(2), 95–113. doi:10.1163/156853094X00126 PMID:11654358

Pluhar, E. B. (2010). Meat and morality: Alternatives to factory farming. *Journal of Agricultural & Environmental Ethics*, *23*(5), 455–468. doi:10.1007/s10806-009-9226-x

Povey, R., Wellens, B., & Conner, M. (2001). Attitudes towards following meat, vegetarian and vegan diets: An examination of the role of ambivalence. *Appetite*, *37*(1), 15–26. doi:10.1006/appe.2001.0406 PMID:11562154

Rogers, E. M. (2010). *Diffusion of innovations* (4th ed.). New York, NY: Simon and Schuster.

Rothgerber, H. (2014). Efforts to overcome vegetarian-induced dissonance among meat eaters. *Appetite*, *79*, 32–41. doi:10.1016/j.appet.2014.04.003 PMID:24727102

Rozin, P. (2006). The integration of biological, social, cultural and psychological influences on food choice. In R. Shepherd & M. Raats (Eds.), *Psychology of food choice* (Vol. 3, pp. 19–40). Oxfordshire, UK: CABI. doi:10.1079/9780851990323.0019

Ryan, R. M., & Deci, E. L. (2000). Self-determination theory and the facilitation of intrinsic motivation, social development, and well-being. *The American Psychologist*, *55*(1), 68–78. doi:10.1037/0003-066X.55.1.68 PMID:11392867

Santamaria, C. (2015). *Plant-based food experiment* (unpublished student research paper for the Social Psychology course). Psychology Department, University of New York in Prague. Retrieved from http://humanimal.cz/texty_soubory/plant-based_food_experiment-santamaria.pdf

Scarborough, P., Appleby, P. N., Mizdrak, A., Briggs, A. D. M., Travis, R. C., Bradbury, K. E., & Key, T. J. (2014). Dietary greenhouse gas emissions of meat-eaters, fish-eaters, vegetarians and vegans in the UK. *Climatic Change*, *125*(2), 179–192. doi:10.1007/s10584-014-1169-1 PMID:25834298

Serpell, J., & Paul, E. (2003). Pets and the development of positive attitudes to animals. In A. Manning & J. Serpell (Eds.), *Animals and human society: Changing perspectives* (pp. 127–144). London, UK: Taylor & Francis.

Smith, E. R., Mackie, D. M., & Claypool, H. M. (2014). *Social Psychology*. New York, NY: Psychology Press.

Special Eurobarometer 442. (2015). *Attitudes of Europeans toward animal welfare*. Brussels, Belgium: European Commission. Retrieved from http://ec.europa.eu/COMMFrontOffice/PublicOpinion/index.cfm/ResultDoc/download/DocumentKy/71348

Springmann, M., Godfray, H. C., Rayner, M., & Scarborough, P. (2016). Analysis and valuation of the health and climate change cobenefits of dietary change. *Proceedings of the National Academy of Sciences of the United States of America*, *113*(15), 4146–4151. doi:10.1073/pnas.1523119113 PMID:27001851

Steg, L., & de Groot, J. I. M. (2012). Environmental values. In S. D. Clayton (Ed.), *The Oxford handbook of environmental and conservation psychology* (pp. 81–92). Oxford, UK: Oxford University Press.

Stern, P. C., Dietz, T., Abel, T. D., Guagnano, G. A., & Kalof, L. (1999). A value-belief-norm theory of support for social movements: The case of environmentalism. *Human Ecology Review*, *6*(2), 81–97.

Stern, P. C. (2000). New environmental theories: Toward a coherent theory of environmentally significant behavior. *The Journal of Social Issues*, *56*(3), 407–424. doi:10.1111/0022-4537.00175

Šedová, I., Slovák, Ľ., & Ježková, I. (2016). Coping with unpleasant knowledge: Meat eating among students of environmental studies. *Appetite*, *107*, 415–424. doi:10.1016/j.appet.2016.08.102 PMID:27554181

Schwartz, S. H. (1977). Normative influences on altruism. *Advances in Experimental Social Psychology*, *10*, 221–279. doi:10.1016/S0065-2601(08)60358-5

Tamplin, H. (2016). *Veganuary campaign urges people to go vegan for a month*. Retrieved from http://metro.co.uk/2016/11/06/veganuary-campaign-urges-people-to-go-vegan-for-a-month-6238419

Thaler, S., Zessner, M., Mayr, M. M., Haider, T., Kroiss, H., & Rechberger, H. (2013). Impacts of human nutrition on land use, nutrient balances and water consumption in Austria. *Sustainability of Water Quality and Ecology*, *1-2*, 24–39. doi:10.1016/j.swaqe.2014.04.003

Thomas, K. (1991). *Man and the natural world: Changing attitudes in England 1500–1800*. London, UK: Penguin Books.

Twine, R. (2010). *Animals as biotechnology--ethics, sustainability and critical animal studies*. London, UK: Earthscan.

Uehleke, R., & Hüttel, S. (2016). The hypothetical free-rider deficit. In *The demand for farm animal welfare labeled meat*: *56th Annual Conference, Bonn, Germany, September 28-30*. German Association of Agricultural Economists (GEWISOLA). Retrieved from http://ageconsearch.umn.edu/record/244866

Vaske, J. J., & Donnelly, M. P. (1999). A value-attitude-behavior model predicting wildland preservation voting intentions. *Society & Natural Resources*, *12*(6), 523–537. doi:10.1080/089419299279425

Verbeke, W., & Vackier, I. (2005). Individual determinants of fish consumption: Application of the theory of planned behaviour. *Appetite*, *44*(1), 67–82. doi:10.1016/j.appet.2004.08.006 PMID:15604034

Wicker, A. W. (1969). Attitudes versus actions: The relationship of verbal and overt behavioral responses to attitude objects. *The Journal of Social Issues*, *25*(4), 41–78. doi:10.1111/j.1540-4560.1969.tb00619.x

Winter, D. D. N., & Koger, S. M. (2009). *The psychology of environmental problems*. Prague, Czech Republic: Portál.

KEY TERMS AND DEFINITIONS

Carnism: Prevailing ideology which conditions people to support the use and consumption of animal products, especially meat.

Cognitive Dissonance: The mental discomfort experienced by a person who simultaneously holds two or more contradictory beliefs, ideas or values.

Community-Based Social Marketing: The use of marketing techniques and strategies which engage the whole community and involve direct contact with people.

Rationalization: The action of attempting to explain or justify behaviour or an attitude with logical reasons, even if these are not appropriate.

Social Marketing: The use of commercial marketing approaches to guide people towards adopting a new attitude, value and subsequently behavior in order to find a solution to a social issue at the level of the individual or society; it is marketing for the greater good.

Social Norms: The rules of behavior considered acceptable in a group or society.

Veganism: A way of living which seeks to exclude, as far as possible and practicable, all forms of exploitation of, and cruelty to, animals for food, clothing or any other purpose.

Chapter 2
The Health Impact of Eating Foods of Animal Origin:
Evidence Regarding Animal Foods, Health, and Disease Risk

Kate Marsh
Northside Nutrition and Dietetics, Australia

Angela Saunders
Sanitarium Health and Wellbeing, Australia

Carol Zeuschner
Sydney Adventist Hospital, Australia

ABSTRACT

While foods of animal origin, including red meat, poultry, seafood, eggs and dairy foods, are good sources of protein and other nutrients including iron, zinc, calcium, vitamin B12 and omega-3 fatty acids, there is increasing evidence to suggest that regular consumption of animal foods may negatively impact health and disease risk. This chapter reviews the evidence linking high intakes of animal foods with chronic disease risk, particularly type 2 diabetes, cardiovascular disease and cancer, and discusses some of the possible mechanisms to explain the association between animal food intake and disease risk. The benefits of plant-based and low-animal food options as solutions to reducing these risks are also discussed, along with implications and recommendations for adopting such diets.

INTRODUCTION

It is well accepted that lifestyle factors, including diet, are a major contributor to chronic disease risk. While there is some controversy over what the optimal diet is for health, there is general consensus that the greatest benefits come from a diet which is based around plant foods (Katz & Meller, 2014).

DOI: 10.4018/978-1-5225-4757-0.ch002

Plant-based diets which exclude or contain low intakes of animal foods are associated with improved health outcomes (McEvoy et al., 2012). It is likely that these benefits are the result of both an increased consumption of plant foods and a reduced consumption of animal foods (Sabaté, 2003). Plant foods including fruits, vegetables, wholegrains, legumes and nuts are rich in dietary fibre, antioxidants and phytochemicals and increased intakes are associated with reduced disease risk. On the other hand, there are a number of nutrients and other compounds typically present in animal foods which may increase disease risk, including saturated fat, dietary cholesterol, animal protein, haem iron, Advanced Glycation End Products (AGEs) and nitrates and nitrosamines in processed and cooked meats.

This chapter:

- Reviews the evidence linking high intakes of animal foods with chronic disease risk, particularly type 2 diabetes, cardiovascular disease and cancer.
- Briefly discusses possible mechanisms to explain the association between animal food intake and disease risk.
- Discusses the benefits of plant-based diets as possible solutions to reducing the health risks associated with high intakes of animal foods.

BACKGROUND

Chronic diseases including heart disease, stroke, cancer and diabetes, are the leading causes of death and disability worldwide. According to the World Health Organisation (WHO, 2017), chronic diseases are responsible for around 70% of all deaths, globally.

Lifestyle factors, particularly diet, play a significant role in the development of chronic disease. In fact, diet-related chronic disease is one of the most preventable causes of morbidity and mortality worldwide. While there is some confusion among the public about what constitutes a healthy diet, research to date overwhelmingly supports the benefits of a largely plant-based diet (Katz & Meller, 2014).

Animal foods are promoted as important sources of iron, zinc, calcium, vitamin B12, protein and omega-3 fats, and concerns are raised regarding nutritional inadequacies when they are excluded from the diet. However, each of those nutrients are available from plant foods, with the exception of vitamin B12. Despite significant evidence showing health benefits of plant-based diets and negative health effects of diets high in animal foods, there continues to be a focus on what is 'missing' when animal foods are removed from the diet. Yet, particularly in the Western world, chronic disease is a much bigger contributor to morbidity and mortality than nutrient deficiencies. Furthermore, plant-based diets more closely match dietary recommendations for good health and prevention of chronic disease, and there is good evidence to show that plant-based diets containing little or no animal foods are associated with a reduced risk of chronic disease. The relationships between animal foods and chronic disease risk, the likely mechanisms underlying these relationships, and the reduction in chronic disease risk associated with diets low in animal foods are explored in this chapter.

A systematic search was conducted using the Medline database (www.pubmed.com; National Library of Medicine, Bethesda, MD) and Cochrane Reviews (www.cochrane.org/reviews; The Cochrane Collaboration) through to April 2017. Additional studies were obtained from reviewing the reference lists of other original studies and review papers. Due to the large number of studies, in most cases only the results of the most recent systematic reviews and meta-analyses have been included, along with other key papers where relevant and/or where a systematic review was not available.

ANIMAL FOOD INTAKE, HEALTH, AND CHRONIC DISEASE

Animal Protein

Animal protein itself has been associated with an increased risk of type 2 diabetes (Malik et al., 2016; Shang et al., 2016), and ischaemic heart disease (IHD) (Knight et al., 2003). Furthermore, animal-based low-carbohydrate diets are associated with a higher all-cause mortality, cardiovascular mortality and cancer mortality (Fung et al., 2010), and an increased risk of type 2 diabetes in men (de Koning et al., 2011) but not women (Halton et al., 2008). Vegetable-based lower carbohydrate diets, on the other hand, appear to be protective, suggesting it is the animal protein rather than a higher protein intake per se that is harmful (de Koning et al., 2011; Fung et al., 2010; Halton et al., 2008).

Red and Processed Meats

The greatest evidence for a link between animal foods and disease risk is for red and processed meats, with higher intakes positively associated with an increased risk of obesity (Rizzo et al., 2011; Rosell et al., 2006; Vergnaud et al., 2010), type 2 diabetes (Micha et al., 2013; Pan et al., 2013), coronary heart disease (Bernstein et al., 2010; Clifton, 2011; Micha et al., 2012; Micha et al., 2010), stroke (Chen et al., 2013; Kaluza et al., 2012), metabolic syndrome (Azadbakht & Esmaillzadeh, 2009; Babio et al., 2012; de Oliveira Otto et al., 2012) and some types of cancer, particularly colorectal cancer (Aune et al., 2013; Chan et al., 2011; Cross et al., 2007), independent of other lifestyle factors. All-cause mortality, and cardiovascular and cancer mortality, are also increased with higher intakes of meat, and in particular processed meat (Abete et al., 2014; Larsson & Orsini, 2014; Wang et al., 2015, 2016). A low meat intake, on the other hand, has been associated with an increased life expectancy, particularly with increasing duration of adherence (Singh et al., 2003).

The adverse effects of red meat on health appear to be related not just to saturated fat and cholesterol (as is commonly assumed), but to other substances present in meat, which may act synergistically in increasing disease risk (Kim et al., 2013). These include nutrients in meat (such as protein, amino acids, haem iron, L-carnitine and choline), substances produced during the processing and cooking of red meat (including heterocyclic amines, polycyclic aromatic hydrocarbons, nitrates, nitrites, nitrosamines and AGEs) and other components found almost exclusively in red meat such as NeuGc5 (Cross et al., 2010; de Oliveira Otto et al., 2012; Feskens et al., 2013; Micha et al., 2013). A detailed discussion of this area is beyond the scope of this chapter but can be found in previously published work (Marsh et al., 2016).

Poultry

There is evidence to show that long-term poultry intake increases the risk of hypertension even after controlling for other dietary factors that may influence hypertension (Borgi et al., 2015). A 2014 meta-analysis found that poultry intake was positively associated with oesophageal squamous cell carcinoma (Zhu et al., 2014), however, more recent research has found no association (Jiang et al., 2016). Unlike red meat and processed meats, it appears that poultry consumption has either no association or is negatively associated with cardiovascular disease (Battaglia Richi et al., 2015; Haring et al., 2014; Takata et al., 2013), type 2 diabetes (Battaglia Richi et al., 2015), some cancers (Carr et al., 2016; Dong & Wu, 2016; Farvid et al., 2014b; Lippi et al., 2016; Pham et al., 2014; Shi et al., 2015; K. Wu et al., 2016; Xu et al., 2013; Yoon et al., 2000; zur Hausen, 2012) and colorectal polyps (Yoon et al., 2000). In the Nurses' Health Study 2 adolescent intake of poultry was associated with a lower risk of both pre- and post-menopausal breast cancer (Farvid et al., 2014a). Other research has found no association (J. Wu et al., 2016) and there is some evidence of ethnic variances (Kim et al., 2016).

The mechanisms by which poultry consumption might increase the risk of hypertension are unclear but may relate to the formation of AGEs, acrylamides and heterocyclic amines, especially at high temperature cooking (Borgi et al., 2015). These compounds contribute to oxidative stress and inflammation by acting on receptors found in vascular tissue modulating vascular function and blood pressure homeostasis (Borgi et al., 2015).

Fish and Seafood

Fish and seafood have long been viewed as healthier alternatives to red meat, however, there are inconsistent reports regarding health benefits. Fish species, variable fat contents, processing and cooking methods, and the use of fish oil supplements provides challenges for finding dose-response relationships.

Fish intake significantly reduces the risk of coronary heart disease mortality, non-fatal myocardial infarcts, risk of stroke in middle-aged men and women and all-cause mortality (Kromhout & de Goede, 2014; Stradling et al., 2013; Zhao et al., 2016). However, this protective effect is non-linear with increasing fish intake providing only a marginal benefit (J. Zheng et al., 2012). There is evidence to suggest that fish intake is protective against some solid tumours such as lung cancer (Song et al., 2014), colorectal cancer (Lippi et al., 2016), oesophageal cancer (Salehi et al., 2013; Yu et al., 2014), hepatocellular cancer (Gao et al., 2015; Huang et al., 2015) as well as haematological cancers including multiple myeloma (Wang, Wu et al., 2015) and non-Hodgkin's lymphoma (Caini et al., 2016). However, these benefits are not found for other types of cancer (Bai et al., 2013; Bandera et al., 2007; Farvid et al., 2014b; Gathirua-Mwangi & Zhang, 2014; Jiang et al., 2014; Lee & Derakhshan, 2013; Wang, Wu, & Zhang, 2016). Evidence for a link between fish or seafood intake and the development of type 2 diabetes is inconsistent (Jafari et al., 2013; Patel et al., 2012; Zhou et al., 2012). The prevalence of type 2 diabetes relative to fish intake is higher in Western countries and lower in Asian countries (Kromhout & de Goede, 2014; Wallin et al., 2012; J.-S. Zheng et al., 2012). This divergence is likely to be multifactorial, but the presence of organic pollutants in fish may provide one reason for these variances (Marushka et al., 2017).

The mechanism by which fish and seafood provide protection against cardiovascular disease relates to omega-3 fatty acids, namely eicosapentaenoic acid (EPA), docosahexaenoic acid (DHA) and docosapentaenoic acid (DPA). These compounds are involved in regulating inflammation (including pro-inflammatory cytokines such as interleukin 6, tumor necrosis factor alpha and C-reactive protein), blood clotting and platelet aggregation, blood vessel contraction and dilation, muscle contraction and relaxation, hormone secretion, plasma membrane fluidity, and regulation of immune responses (Bonafini et al., 2015; Ellulu et al., 2015). Pollutants, toxins, viruses and parasites in waterways have contributed to safety concerns for fish and seafood intake (Oehlenschläger, 2012). Triphenyltin (TPT) contamination of waterways is a world-wide problem with concentrations in marine life higher than concentrations measured in the surrounding water (Yi et al., 2012). This is one of many persistent organic pollutants (POPs) which can bioaccumulate in fish and there are increasing concerns about the health risks of POPs, including their role as endocrine disruptors.

Eggs

Eggs have traditionally been limited in a heart healthy diet, but guidelines now emphasise a reduction in saturated and trans fats rather than dietary cholesterol to lower low density lipoprotein (LDL)-cholesterol levels (Eckel et al., 2013). However, eggs contain other components which may impact disease risk. A 2013 meta-analysis found an increased risk of diabetes and cardiovascular disease in those with the highest egg intakes, and for those already diagnosed with diabetes who ate the most eggs, risk of cardiovascular disease was greater compared to those without diabetes (Li et al., 2013). A second meta-analysis found a modest increased risk of type 2 diabetes (in US studies only) with consumption of three or more eggs per week (Djousse et al., 2016). In contrast, a more recent meta-analysis found no clear association between egg intake and coronary heart disease and a reduced risk of stroke with up to one egg per day (Alexander, Miller et al., 2016). Furthermore, in those following a low saturated fat diet, consumption of 6-12 eggs per week did not increase cardiovascular disease risk in individuals with type 2 diabetes (Richard et al., 2017). Consuming five or more eggs a week (compared with no eggs) has been associated with an increased risk of breast cancer (Keum et al., 2015) and egg consumption is also associated with advanced and fatal prostate cancers (K. Wu et al., 2016), and gastrointestinal cancers, particularly colon cancer (Tse & Eslick, 2014).

Eggs are a rich source of choline, an important nutrient, although high intakes may be associated with disease risk. For example, choline is highly concentrated in prostate cancer cells and blood concentrations of choline have been associated with an increased risk of prostate cancer (Richman et al., 2012). Choline kinase, an enzyme which breaks down choline, is elevated in colorectal cancer (Tse & Eslick, 2014), and high serum choline is also associated with increased risk of colorectal cancer (Guertin et al., 2017). Choline is converted to Trimethylamine N-oxide (TMAO) and higher consumption of egg yolks has been found to increase plasma and urinary concentrations of TMAO (Miller et al., 2014). Circulating TMAO levels are strongly associated with atherosclerosis (Velasquez et al., 2016) and colorectal cancer (Bae et al., 2014). However, conversion of choline to TMAO is dependent on gut bacteria and may explain the role of gut bacteria in metabolic and cardiovascular disease, particularly TMAO's inhibition of reverse cholesterol transport (Hansen et al., 2015) as well as TMAO's role in many genetic pathways implicated in cancer, particularly colorectal cancer (Xu et al., 2015). It is also unclear whether TMAO is a direct cause of, or a biomarker for disease (Cho et al., 2017).

Dairy Foods

Most Western dietary guidelines recommend dairy products as part of a well-balanced diet, particularly as a source of calcium and protein. However, there is increasing concern among consumers regarding the health effects of dairy consumption, reflected in the increasing popularity of plant-based milks, yoghurts and cheese. Worldwide sales of non-dairy milk alternatives more than doubled between 2009 and 2015 to $21bn, while milk consumption is declining (Financial Times, 2016).

While the nutrients found in dairy foods (apart from vitamin B12) can be obtained on a plant-based diet, there is little evidence for concern regarding consumption of dairy foods and chronic disease risk. A number of systematic reviews have been published over the past few years, showing no consistent association between milk and dairy food intake and mortality (Larsson et al., 2015), a neutral or reduced risk of type 2 diabetes (Gijsbers et al., 2016) and a reduced risk of cardiovascular disease, particularly stroke (Alexander, Bylsma, et al., 2016; Astrup et al., 2016; de Goede et al., 2016). Consumption of dairy foods is not associated with all-cancer mortality risk (W. Lu et al., 2016) and appears to be inversely associated with risk of colon cancer (Ralston et al., 2014). However, an increased intake of dairy foods and dairy calcium (but not supplemental or non-dairy calcium) is associated with an increased risk of, and mortality from, prostate cancer (Aune et al., 2015; W. Lu et al., 2016). Intake of dairy foods is inversely associated with weight gain and risk of obesity, including childhood obesity (Astrup et al., 2016; Lu et al., 2016).

The mechanisms responsible for the apparent protective effect of dairy foods are unclear. Although a source of saturated fat, the whole food matrix of dairy products (including the presence of probiotics, calcium, potassium, magnesium, riboflavin, vitamin B12, whey and casein) may partially mitigate the adverse metabolic effects usually associated with saturated fat (Alexander, Bylsma, et al., 2016). Yet replacement of dairy fat with PUFA vegetable fats or high-quality carbohydrates such as wholegrains is associated with reduced risk of cardiovascular disease, while the risk is higher when replaced with other animal fats (Chen et al., 2016). Fermented dairy products, including cheese and yoghurt, have been associated with a reduced risk of type 2 diabetes, cardiovascular disease and obesity, possibly related to their effect on the growth of beneficial microbiota and modulation of gut function (Gijsbers et al., 2016; Schwingshackl et al., 2016; Tapsell, 2015). However, it may be that those who eat fermented dairy foods also have an overall healthier eating pattern (Tapsell, 2015).

SOLUTIONS AND RECOMMENDATIONS

Health Implications of Diets Low in Animal Foods

While not everyone will choose to adopt a complete plant-based (vegan) diet, findings from the Adventist Health Study-2 suggest that any reduction in intake of animal foods and concomitant increase in intake of plant foods is likely to benefit our health. In a population of more than 73,000 men and women, health outcomes were compared for non-vegetarians, semi-vegetarians (those who ate meat, poultry or fish less than 1/week), pesco-vegetarians (those who ate fish but no other animal flesh), lacto-ovo vegetarians (those who ate eggs and dairy products but no animal flesh), and vegans (those who ate no animal products). Body mass index (BMI), and risk of diabetes and hypertension (even after controlling for weight) decreased incrementally from the non-vegetarians to vegans, as less animal foods were included in the diet (Orlich et al., 2013).

This is consistent with the findings of numerous studies showing that dietary patterns rich in plant foods and containing little or no animal foods, including vegetarian and vegan diets, Mediterranean diets, and the Dietary Approaches to Stop Hypertension (DASH) diet, are associated with reduced risk of chronic disease.

A vegetarian diet consists mostly of plant-based foods including fruit, vegetables, legumes, nuts, seeds and grains. The health benefits of vegetarian and vegan diets are strongly supported by research, particularly with respect to reducing chronic disease risk, including risk of cardiovascular disease, type 2 diabetes, metabolic syndrome, hypertension and obesity (Appleby et al., 2002; Orlich & Fraser, 2014; Rosell et al., 2006). While vegetarians generally have a lower BMI, and tend to be more health conscious than non-vegetarians, health outcomes remain better even when these factors are taken into account. Furthermore, several studies have shown increased longevity among vegetarians (Fraser & Shavlik, 2001; Singh et al., 2013) and vegan diets appear to offer additional protection for obesity, hypertension, TD2, and cardiovascular mortality (Le & Sabaté, 2014).

The Mediterranean diet is characterised by a high intake of fruits, vegetables, wholegrains, nuts and seeds. Fish, seafood, poultry, and eggs are consumed in moderation, while there is low consumption of dairy foods, red meat, processed meats and sweets. A meta-analysis of 36 prospective cohort studies demonstrated an 8% reduction in overall mortality (relative risk – RR, 0.92, 95% confidence interval –CI: 0.91-0.93), a 10% reduced risk of cardiovascular disease (RR 0.90, 95% CI: 0.87-0.92), and a 4% reduction in cancer incidence (RR 0.96, 95% CI 0.95-0.97) with a 2-point increase in adherence to the Mediterranean diet (Sofi et al., 2014). A second systematic review of 37 studies looking at the association between adherence to a Mediterranean diet and prevention of cardiodiabesity (incorporating type 2 diabetes, obesity, metabolic syndrome and cardiovascular disease) found that 33 of these studies provided strong evidence for an association between adherence to a Mediterranean diet and reduced risk of collective cardiodiabesity risk (Garcia-Fernandez et al., 2014).

The DASH diet is an eating pattern that encourages a higher intake of plant foods including fruits, vegetables, wholegrains, legumes and nuts, along with fat-free or low-fat dairy products. It restricts intake of red meat, sweets, added sugars, and sugar-sweetened drinks. In a meta-analysis of observational studies DASH-style dietary interventions were found to significantly reduce the risk of cardiovascular disease, coronary heart disease, stroke and heart failure (Salehi et al., 2013). A more recent systematic review of 20 studies found that the DASH diet resulted in significant reductions in cardiovascular risk factors including blood pressure and total and LDL cholesterol levels, with greater effects seen in those with an increased cardiometabolic risk (Siervo et al., 2015). Adherence to a DASH-style diet has also been associated with a lower risk of colorectal cancer (Fung et al., 2010) and oestrogen receptor-negative breast cancer in postmenopausal women (Fung et al., 2011).

Considering the current evidence supporting the benefits of a plant-based diet, why are more health professionals not recommending this type of eating plan? One barrier may be their belief that most people would not be willing to adopt such a diet. Yet the number of people voluntarily adopting a vegetarian or vegan diet is increasing and several intervention studies have found that vegetarian and vegan diets are well-accepted, and similar to that of control diets (Barnard et al., 2009; Barnard et al., 2004; Kahleova et al., 2011; Turner-McGrievy et al., 2015)

Meeting nutritional needs is also a commonly cited concern regarding diets that restrict animal foods. Yet, apart from vitamin B12, which must be supplemented on a strict plant-based (vegan) diet, and in some cases vitamin D and long chain essential fatty acids (DHA and EPA), diets based on plant foods can meet nutritional needs. This is supported by the American Academy of Nutrition and Dietetics, whose position paper on vegetarian diets states that, in addition to their health benefits, well planned vegetarian diets, including vegan diets, are nutritionally adequate and are appropriate for individuals during all stages of life (Melina et al., 2016). More details about meeting nutritional needs on a vegetarian diet can be found in previously published work (Reid et al., 2013).

FUTURE RESEARCH DIRECTIONS

High intakes of red and processed meats are consistently associated with an increased risk of chronic disease and mortality. However, the relationship between higher intakes of other animal foods (including poultry, fish and seafood, eggs and dairy foods) is less clear. While there appears to be some associations with these foods and certain disease states and/or in particular populations, more research is needed to confirm these findings and to elucidate the mechanisms underlying these associations.

In some cases, higher intakes of certain animal foods have been associated with a reduced disease risk, for example higher intakes of fish and dairy foods appear to protect against cardiovascular disease risk. Yet long term epidemiological studies have found that diets which exclude animal foods appear to confer the greatest health benefits with respect to reducing chronic disease risk and increasing longevity (Fraser, 2009; Le & Sabaté, 2014). It may be that while not all animal foods negatively impact health and disease risk per se, they instead replace plant foods in the diet, including legumes, wholegrains and nuts, which have been associated with reduced disease risk (Aune et al., 2016a, 2016b; Souza et al., 2015).

Despite the well-documented evidence for benefits of this type of eating plan, the number of people in Western countries who follow a plant-based diet is small. Further research is needed on raising awareness of the health implications of plant versus animal-based diets and factors preventing people from adopting a plant-based diet.

CONCLUSION

There is now significant evidence demonstrating an association between high intakes of red and processed meat, and chronic disease risk, and there are several plausible mechanisms to explain this association. The association between consumption of other animal foods and disease risk is less clear and further research is needed. However, diets low in animal foods are associated with improved health outcomes and reduced disease risk. In Western countries, plant-based diets low in animal foods may present a significant advantage over animal-based diets, not only for the environment but also for reducing chronic disease risk and increasing longevity.

ACKNOWLEDGMENT

We would like to acknowledge the valuable assistance of Shahna Van Eyssen, student at Avondale College of Higher Education, with the initial literature search.

REFERENCES

Abete, I., Romaguera, D., Vieira, A. R., Lopez de Munain, A., & Norat, T. (2014). Association between total, processed, red and white meat consumption and all-cause, CVD and IHD mortality: A meta-analysis of cohort studies. *British Journal of Nutrition, 112*(5), 762–775. doi:10.1017/S000711451400124X PMID:24932617

Alexander, D. D., Bylsma, L. C., Vargas, A. J., Cohen, S. S., Doucette, A., Mohamed, M., & Fryzek, J. P. et al. (2016). Dairy consumption and CVD: A systematic review and meta-analysis. *British Journal of Nutrition, 115*(4), 737–750. doi:10.1017/S0007114515005000 PMID:26786887

Alexander, D. D., Miller, P. E., Vargas, A. J., Weed, D. L., & Cohen, S. S. (2016). Meta-analysis of egg consumption and risk of coronary heart disease and stroke. *Journal of the American College of Nutrition, 35*(8), 704–716. doi:10.1080/07315724.2016.1152928 PMID:27710205

Appleby, P. N., Davey, G. K., & Key, T. J. (2002). Hypertension and blood pressure among meat eaters, fish eaters, vegetarians and vegans in EPIC-Oxford. *Public Health Nutrition, 5*(5), 645–654. doi:10.1079/PHN2002332 PMID:12372158

Astrup, A., Rice Bradley, B., Brenna, J., Delplanque, B., Ferry, M., & Torres-Gonzalez, M. (2016). Regular-fat dairy and human health: A synopsis of symposia presented in Europe and North America (2014–2015). *Nutrients, 8*(8), 463. doi:10.3390/nu8080463 PMID:27483308

Aune, D., Chan, D. S., Vieira, A. R., Navarro Rosenblatt, D. A., Vieira, R., Greenwood, D. C., & Norat, T. et al. (2013). Red and processed meat intake and risk of colorectal adenomas: A systematic review and meta-analysis of epidemiological studies. *Cancer Causes & Control, 24*(4), 611–627. doi:10.1007/s10552-012-0139-z PMID:23380943

Aune, D., Keum, N., Giovannucci, E., Fadnes, L. T., Boffetta, P., Greenwood, D. C., & Norat, T. et al. (2016a). Nut consumption and risk of cardiovascular disease, total cancer, all-cause and cause-specific mortality: A systematic review and dose-response meta-analysis of prospective studies. *BMC Medicine, 14*(1), 207. doi:10.1186/s12916-016-0730-3 PMID:27916000

Aune, D., Keum, N., Giovannucci, E., Fadnes, L. T., Boffetta, P., Greenwood, D. C., & Norat, T. et al. (2016b). Whole grain consumption and risk of cardiovascular disease, cancer, and all cause and cause specific mortality: Systematic review and dose-response meta-analysis of prospective studies. *BMJ (Clinical Research Ed.), 353*, i2716. doi:10.1136/bmj.i2716 PMID:27301975

Aune, D., Navarro Rosenblatt, D. A., Chan, D. S., Vieira, A. R., Vieira, R., Greenwood, D. C., & Norat, T. et al. (2015). Dairy products, calcium, and prostate cancer risk: A systematic review and meta-analysis of cohort studies. *The American Journal of Clinical Nutrition, 101*(1), 87–117. doi:10.3945/ajcn.113.067157 PMID:25527754

Azadbakht, L., & Esmaillzadeh, A. (2009). Red meat intake is associated with metabolic syndrome and the plasma C-reactive protein concentration in women. *The Journal of Nutrition, 139*(2), 335–339. doi:10.3945/jn.108.096297 PMID:19074209

Babio, N., Sorlí, M., Bulló, M., Basora, J., Ibarrola-Jurado, N., Fernández-Ballart, J., & Salas-Salvadó, J. et al. (2012). Association between red meat consumption and metabolic syndrome in a Mediterranean population at high cardiovascular risk: Cross-sectional and 1-year follow-up assessment. *Nutrition, Metabolism, and Cardiovascular Diseases, 22*(3), 200–207. doi:10.1016/j.numecd.2010.06.011 PMID:20875949

Bae, S., Ulrich, C. M., Neuhouser, M. L., Malysheva, O., Bailey, L. B., Xiao, L., & Caudill, M. A. et al. (2014). Plasma choline metabolites and colorectal cancer risk in the women's health initiative observational study. *Cancer Research*, *74*(24), 7442–7452. doi:10.1158/0008-5472.CAN-14-1835 PMID:25336191

Bai, H., Qian, Y., Shi, B., Li, G., Fan, Y., Wang, Z., & Liu, L. et al. (2013). The association between fish consumption and risk of renal cancer: A meta-analysis of observational studies. *PLoS One*, *8*(11), e81939. doi:10.1371/journal.pone.0081939 PMID:24312383

Bandera, E. V., Kushi, L. H., Moore, D. F., Gifkins, D. M., & McCullough, M. L. (2007). Consumption of animal foods and endometrial cancer risk: A systematic literature review and meta-analysis. *Cancer Causes & Control*, *18*(9), 967–988. doi:10.1007/s10552-007-9038-0 PMID:17638104

Barnard, N. D., Gloede, L., Cohen, J., Jenkins, D. J., Turner-McGrievy, G., Green, A. A., & Ferdowsian, H. (2009). A low-fat vegan diet elicits greater macronutrient changes, but is comparable in adherence and acceptability, compared with a more conventional diabetes diet among individuals with type 2 diabetes. *Journal of the American Dietetic Association*, *109*(2), 263–272. doi:10.1016/j.jada.2008.10.049 PMID:19167953

Barnard, N. D., Scialli, A. R., Turner-McGrievy, G., & Lanou, A. J. (2004). Acceptability of a low-fat vegan diet compares favorably to a step II diet in a randomized, controlled trial. *Journal of Cardiopulmonary Rehabilitation*, *24*(4), 229–235. doi:10.1097/00008483-200407000-00004 PMID:15286527

Battaglia Richi, E., Baumer, B., Conrad, B., Darioli, R., Schmid, A., & Keller, U. (2015). Health risks associated with meat consumption: A review of epidemiological studies. *International Journal for Vitamin and Nutrition Research*, *85*(1-2), 70–78. doi:10.1024/0300-9831/a000224 PMID:26780279

Bernstein, A. M., Sun, Q., Hu, F. B., Stampfer, M. J., Manson, J. E., & Willett, W. C. (2010). Major dietary protein sources and risk of coronary heart disease in women. *Circulation*, *122*(9), 876–883. doi:10.1161/CIRCULATIONAHA.109.915165 PMID:20713902

Bonafini, S., Antoniazzi, F., Maffeis, C., Minuz, P., & Fava, C. (2015). Beneficial effects of \$ω\$-3 PUFA in children on cardiovascular risk factors during childhood and adolescence. *Prostaglandins & Other Lipid Mediators*, *120*, 72–79. doi:10.1016/j.prostaglandins.2015.03.006 PMID:25834924

Borgi, L., Curhan, G. C., Willett, W. C., Hu, F. B., Satija, A., & Forman, J. P. (2015). Long-term intake of animal flesh and risk of developing hypertension in three prospective cohort studies. *Journal of Hypertension*, *33*(11), 2231–2238. doi:10.1097/HJH.0000000000000722 PMID:26237562

Caini, S., Masala, G., Gnagnarella, P., Ermini, I., Russell-Edu, W., Palli, D., & Gandini, S. (2016). Food of animal origin and risk of non-Hodgkin lymphoma and multiple myeloma: A review of the literature and meta-analysis. *Critical Reviews in Oncology/Hematology*, *100*, 16–24. doi:10.1016/j.critrevonc.2016.02.011 PMID:26921971

Carr, P. R., Walter, V., Brenner, H., & Hoffmeister, M. (2016). Meat subtypes and their association with colorectal cancer: Systematic review and meta-analysis. *International Journal of Cancer*, *138*(2), 293–302. doi:10.1002/ijc.29423 PMID:25583132

Chan, D. S., Lau, R., Aune, D., Vieira, R., Greenwood, D. C., Kampman, E., & Norat, T. (2011). Red and processed meat and colorectal cancer incidence: Meta-analysis of prospective studies. *PLoS One*, *6*(6), e20456. doi:10.1371/journal.pone.0020456 PMID:21674008

Chen, G.-C., Lv, D.-B., Pang, Z., & Liu, Q.-F. (2013). Red and processed meat consumption and risk of stroke: A meta-analysis of prospective cohort studies. *European Journal of Clinical Nutrition*, *67*(1), 91–95. doi:10.1038/ejcn.2012.180 PMID:23169473

Chen, M., Li, Y., Sun, Q., Pan, A., Manson, J. E., Rexrode, K. M., & Hu, F. B. et al. (2016). Dairy fat and risk of cardiovascular disease in 3 cohorts of US adults. *The American Journal of Clinical Nutrition*, *104*(5), 1209–1217. doi:10.3945/ajcn.116.134460 PMID:27557656

Cho, C. E., Taesuwan, S., Malysheva, O. V., Bender, E., Tulchinsky, N. F., Yan, J., & Caudill, M. A. et al. (2017). Trimethylamine-*N*-oxide (TMAO) response to animal source foods varies among healthy young men and is influenced by their gut microbiota composition: A randomized controlled trial. *Molecular Nutrition & Food Research*, *61*(1), 1600324. doi:10.1002/mnfr.201600324 PMID:27377678

Clifton, P. M. (2011). Protein and coronary heart disease: The role of different protein sources. *Current Atherosclerosis Reports*, *13*(6), 493–498. doi:10.1007/s11883-011-0208-x PMID:21912836

Cross, A. J., Ferrucci, L. M., Risch, A., Graubard, B. I., Ward, M. H., Park, Y., & Sinha, R. et al. (2010). A large prospective study of meat consumption and colorectal cancer risk: An investigation of potential mechanisms underlying this association. *Cancer Research*, *70*(6), 2406–2414. doi:10.1158/0008-5472.CAN-09-3929 PMID:20215514

Cross, A. J., Leitzmann, M. F., Gail, M. H., Hollenbeck, A. R., Schatzkin, A., & Sinha, R. (2007). A prospective study of red and processed meat intake in relation to cancer risk. *PLoS Medicine*, *4*(12), e325. doi:10.1371/journal.pmed.0040325 PMID:18076279

de Goede, J., Soedamah-Muthu, S. S., Pan, A., Gijsbers, L., & Geleijnse, J. M. (2016). Dairy consumption and risk of stroke: A systematic review and updated dose-response meta-analysis of prospective cohort studies. *Journal of the American Heart Association*, *5*(5), e002787. doi:10.1161/JAHA.115.002787 PMID:27207960

de Koning, L., Fung, T. T., Liao, X., Chiuve, S. E., Rimm, E. B., Willett, W. C., & Hu, F. B. et al. (2011a). Low-carbohydrate diet scores and risk of type 2 diabetes in men. *The American Journal of Clinical Nutrition*, *93*(4), 844–850. doi:10.3945/ajcn.110.004333 PMID:21310828

de Oliveira Otto, M. C., Alonso, A., Lee, D. H., Delclos, G. L., Bertoni, A. G., Jiang, R., & Nettleton, J. A. et al. (2012a). Dietary intakes of zinc and heme iron from red meat, but not from other sources, are associated with greater risk of metabolic syndrome and cardiovascular disease. *The Journal of Nutrition*, *142*(3), 526–533. doi:10.3945/jn.111.149781 PMID:22259193

Djousse, L., Khawaja, O. A., & Gaziano, J. M. (2016). Egg consumption and risk of type 2 diabetes: A meta-analysis of prospective studies. *The American Journal of Clinical Nutrition*, *103*(2), 474–480. doi:10.3945/ajcn.115.119933 PMID:26739035

Dong, Y., & Wu, G. (2016). Lack of association of poultry and eggs intake with risk of non-Hodgkin lymphoma: A meta-analysis of observational studies. *European Journal of Cancer Care*. doi:10.1111/ecc.12546 PMID:27405484

Eckel, R. H., Jakicic, J. M., Ard, J. D., Hubbard, V. S., de Jesus, J. M., Lee, I-M., … Yanovski, S. Z. (2013). 2013 AHA/ACC guideline on lifestyle management to reduce cardiovascular risk: A report of the American College of Cardiology/American Heart Association Task Force on Practice Guidelines. https://<ALIGNMENT.qj></ALIGNMENT>10.1161/01.cir.0000437740.48606.d1

Ellulu, M. S., Khaza'ai, H., Abed, Y., Rahmat, A., Ismail, P., & Ranneh, Y. (2015). Role of fish oil in human health and possible mechanism to reduce the inflammation. *Inflammopharmacology*, *23*(2-3), 79–89. doi:10.1007/s10787-015-0228-1 PMID:25676565

Farvid, M. S., Cho, E., Chen, W. Y., Eliassen, A. H., & Willett, W. C. (2014a). Adolescent meat intake and breast cancer risk. *International Journal of Cancer*, *136*(8), 1909–1920. doi:10.1002/ijc.29218 PMID:25220168

Farvid, M. S., Cho, E., Chen, W. Y., Eliassen, A. H., & Willett, W. C. (2014b). Dietary protein sources in early adulthood and breast cancer incidence: Prospective cohort study. *BMJ (Clinical Research Ed.)*, *348*, g3437. doi:10.1136/bmj.g3437 PMID:24916719

Feskens, E. J. M., Sluik, D., & van Woudenbergh, G. J. (2013). Meat consumption, diabetes, and its complications. *Current Diabetes Reports*, *13*(2), 298–306. doi:10.1007/s11892-013-0365-0 PMID:23354681

Financial Times. (2016). *Big business identifies appetite for plant-based milk*. Retrieved from https://www.ft.com/content/7df72c04-491a-11e6-8d68-72e9211e86ab

Fraser, G. E. (2009). Vegetarian diets: What do we know of their effects on common chronic diseases? *The American Journal of Clinical Nutrition*, *89*(5), 1607S–1612S. doi:10.3945/ajcn.2009.26736K PMID:19321569

Fraser, G. E., & Shavlik, D. J. (2001). Ten years of life: Is it a matter of choice? *Archives of Internal Medicine*, *161*(13), 1645–1652. doi:10.1001/archinte.161.13.1645 PMID:11434797

Fung, T. T., Hu, F. B., Hankinson, S. E., Willett, W. C., & Holmes, M. D. (2011). Low-carbohydrate diets, dietary approaches to stop hypertension-style diets, and the risk of postmenopausal breast cancer. *American Journal of Epidemiology*, *174*(6), 652–660. doi:10.1093/aje/kwr148 PMID:21832271

Fung, T. T., van Dam, R. M., Hankinson, S. E., Stampfer, M., Willett, W. C., & Hu, F. B. (2010). Low-carbohydrate diets and all-cause and cause-specific mortality: Two cohort studies. *Annals of Internal Medicine*, *153*(5), 289–298. doi:10.7326/0003-4819-153-5-201009070-00003 PMID:20820038

Gao, M., Sun, K., Guo, M., Gao, H., Liu, K., Yang, C., & Liu, N. et al. (2015). Fish consumption and n-3 polyunsaturated fatty acids, and risk of hepatocellular carcinoma: Systematic review and meta-analysis. *Cancer Causes & Control*, *26*(3), 367–376. doi:10.1007/s10552-014-0512-1 PMID:25534918

Garcia-Fernandez, E., Rico-Cabanas, L., Rosgaard, N., Estruch, R., & Bach-Faig, A. (2014). Mediterranean diet and cardiodiabesity. *Revista de Nutrição*, *6*(9), 3474–3500. PMID:25192027

Gathirua-Mwangi, W. G., & Zhang, J. (2014). Dietary factors and risk for advanced prostate cancer. *European Journal of Cancer Prevention, 23*(2), 96–109. doi:10.1097/CEJ.0b013e3283647394 PMID:23872953

Gijsbers, L., Ding, E. L., Malik, V. S., de Goede, J., Geleijnse, J. M., & Soedamah-Muthu, S. S. (2016). Consumption of dairy foods and diabetes incidence: A dose-response meta-analysis of observational studies. *The American Journal of Clinical Nutrition, 103*(4), 1111–1124. doi:10.3945/ajcn.115.123216 PMID:26912494

Guertin, K. A., Li, X. S., Graubard, B. I., Albanes, D., Weinstein, S. J., Goedert, J. J., & Sinha, R. et al. (2017). Serum trimethylamine n-oxide, carnitine, choline and betaine in relation to colorectal cancer risk in the Alpha Tocopherol and Beta Carotene Study. *Cancer Epidemiology, Biomarkers & Prevention, 26*(6), 945–952. doi:10.1158/1055-9965.EPI-16-0948 PMID:28077427

Halton, T. L., Liu, S., Manson, J. E., & Hu, F. B. (2008). Low-carbohydrate-diet score and risk of type 2 diabetes in women. *The American Journal of Clinical Nutrition, 87*(2), 339–346. PMID:18258623

Hansen, T. H., Gøbel, R. J., Hansen, T., & Pedersen, O. (2015). The gut microbiome in cardio-metabolic health. *Genome Medicine, 7*(1), 33. doi:10.1186/s13073-015-0157-z PMID:25825594

Haring, B., Gronroos, N., Nettleton, J. A., Wyler von Ballmoos, M. C., Selvin, E., & Alonso, A. (2014). Dietary protein intake and coronary heart disease in a large community based cohort: Results from the Atherosclerosis Risk in Communities (ARIC) Study. *PLoS One, 9*(10), e109552. doi:10.1371/journal.pone.0109552 PMID:25303709

Huang, R.-X., Duan, Y.-Y., & Hu, J.-A. (2015). Fish intake and risk of liver cancer: A meta-analysis. *PLoS One, 10*(1), e0096102. doi:10.1371/journal.pone.0096102 PMID:25615823

Jafari, T., Fallah, A. A., & Azadbakht, L. (2013). Role of dietary n-3 polyunsaturated fatty acids in type 2 diabetes: A review of epidemiological and clinical studies. *Maturitas, 74*(4), 303–308. doi:10.1016/j.maturitas.2013.01.008 PMID:23384976

Jiang, G., Li, B., Liao, X., & Zhong, C. (2016). Poultry and fish intake and risk of esophageal cancer: A meta-analysis of observational studies. *Asia Pacific Journal of Clinical Oncology, 12*(1), e82–e91. doi:10.1111/ajco.12114 PMID:23910094

Jiang, P., Jiang, Z., Shen, K., & Yue, Y. (2014). Fish intake and ovarian cancer risk: A meta-analysis of 15 case-control and cohort studies. *PLoS One, 9*(4), e94601. doi:10.1371/journal.pone.0094601 PMID:24732053

Kahleova, H., Matoulek, M., Malinska, H., Oliyarnik, O., Kazdova, L., Neskudla, T., & Pelikanova, T. et al. (2011). Vegetarian diet improves insulin resistance and oxidative stress markers more than conventional diet in subjects with Type 2 diabetes. *Diabetic Medicine, 28*(5), 549–559. doi:10.1111/j.1464-5491.2010.03209.x PMID:21480966

Kaluza, J., Wolk, A., & Larsson, S. C. (2012). Red meat consumption and risk of stroke: A meta-analysis of prospective studies. *Stroke, 43*(10), 2556–2560. doi:10.1161/STROKEAHA.112.663286 PMID:22851546

Katz, D. L., & Meller, S. (2014). Can we say what diet is best for health? *Annual Review of Public Health, 35*(1), 83–103. doi:10.1146/annurev-publhealth-032013-182351 PMID:24641555

Keum, N., Lee, D. H., Marchand, N., Oh, H., Liu, H., Aune, D., & Giovannucci, E. L. et al. (2015). Egg intake and cancers of the breast, ovary and prostate: A dose–response meta-analysis of prospective observational studies. *British Journal of Nutrition*, *114*(7), 1099–1107. doi:10.1017/S0007114515002135 PMID:26293984

Kim, A. E., Lundgreen, A., Wolff, R. K., Fejerman, L., John, E. M., Torres-Mejía, G., & Stern, M. C. et al. (2016). Red meat, poultry, and fish intake and breast cancer risk among Hispanic and Non-Hispanic white women: The Breast Cancer Health Disparities Study. *Cancer Causes & Control*, *27*(4), 527–543. doi:10.1007/s10552-016-0727-4 PMID:26898200

Kim, E., Coelho, D., & Blachier, F. (2013). Review of the association between meat consumption and risk of colorectal cancer. *Nutrition Research (New York, N.Y.)*, *33*(12), 983–994. doi:10.1016/j.nutres.2013.07.018 PMID:24267037

Knight, E. L., Stampfer, M. J., Hankinson, S. E., Spiegelman, D., & Curhan, G. C. (2003). The impact of protein intake on renal function decline in women with normal renal function or mild renal insufficiency. *Annals of Internal Medicine*, *138*(6), 460–467. doi:10.7326/0003-4819-138-6-200303180-00009 PMID:12639078

Kromhout, D., & de Goede, J. (2014). Update on cardiometabolic health effects of ω-3 fatty acids. *Current Opinion in Lipidology*, *25*(1), 85–90. doi:10.1097/MOL.0000000000000041 PMID:24345990

Larsson, S., Crippa, A., Orsini, N., Wolk, A., & Michaëlsson, K. (2015). Milk consumption and mortality from all causes, cardiovascular disease, and cancer: A systematic review and meta-analysis. *Nutrients*, *7*(9), 7749–7763. doi:10.3390/nu7095363 PMID:26378576

Larsson, S. C., & Orsini, N. (2014). Red meat and processed meat consumption and all-cause mortality: A meta-analysis. *American Journal of Epidemiology*, *179*(3), 282–289. doi:10.1093/aje/kwt261 PMID:24148709

Le, L. T., & Sabaté, J. (2014). Beyond meatless, the health effects of vegan diets: Findings from the Adventist cohorts. *Nutrients*, *6*(6), 2131–2147. doi:10.3390/nu6062131 PMID:24871675

Lee, Y. Y., & Derakhshan, M. H. (2013). Environmental and lifestyle risk factors of gastric cancer. *Archives of Iranian Medicine*, *16*(6), 358–365. PMID:23725070

Li, Y., Zhou, C., Zhou, X., & Li, L. (2013). Egg consumption and risk of cardiovascular diseases and diabetes: A meta-analysis. *Atherosclerosis*, *229*(2), 524–530. doi:10.1016/j.atherosclerosis.2013.04.003 PMID:23643053

Lippi, G., Mattiuzzi, C., & Cervellin, G. (2016). Meat consumption and cancer risk: A critical review of published meta-analyses. *Critical Reviews in Oncology/Hematology*, *97*, 1–14. doi:10.1016/j.critrevonc.2015.11.008 PMID:26633248

Lu, L., Xun, P., Wan, Y., He, K., & Cai, W. (2016). Long-term association between dairy consumption and risk of childhood obesity: A systematic review and meta-analysis of prospective cohort studies. *European Journal of Clinical Nutrition*, *70*(4), 414–423. doi:10.1038/ejcn.2015.226 PMID:26862005

Lu, W., Chen, H., Niu, Y., Wu, H., Xia, D., & Wu, Y. (2016). Dairy products intake and cancer mortality risk: A meta-analysis of 11 population-based cohort studies. *Nutrition Journal, 15*(1), 91. doi:10.1186/s12937-016-0210-9 PMID:27765039

Malik, V. S., Li, Y., Tobias, D. K., Pan, A., & Hu, F. B. (2016). Dietary protein intake and risk of type 2 diabetes in US men and women. *American Journal of Epidemiology, 183*(8), 715–728. doi:10.1093/aje/kwv268 PMID:27022032

Marsh, K., Saunders, A., & Zeuschner, C. (2016). Red meat and health: Evidence regarding red meat, health, and chronic disease risk. In T. Raphaely & D. Marinova (Eds.), *Impact of meat consumption on health and environmental sustainability* (pp. 131–177). Hershey, PA: IGI Global. doi:10.4018/978-1-4666-9553-5.ch008

Marushka, L., Batal, M., David, W., Schwartz, H., Ing, A., Fediuk, K., & Chan, H. M. et al. (2017). Association between fish consumption, dietary omega-3 fatty acids and persistent organic pollutants intake, and type 2 diabetes in 18 First Nations in Ontario, Canada. *Environmental Research, 156*, 725–737. doi:10.1016/j.envres.2017.04.034 PMID:28482294

McEvoy, C. T., Temple, N., & Woodside, J. V. (2012). Vegetarian diets, low-meat diets and health: A review. *Public Health Nutrition, 15*(12), 2287–2294. doi:10.1017/S1368980012000936 PMID:22717188

Melina, V., Craig, W., & Levin, S. (2016). Position of the Academy of Nutrition and Dietetics: Vegetarian Diets. *Journal of the Academy of Nutrition and Dietetics, 116*(12), 1970–1980. doi:10.1016/j.jand.2016.09.025 PMID:27886704

Micha, R., Michas, G., Lajous, M., & Mozaffarian, D. (2013). Processing of meats and cardiovascular risk: Time to focus on preservatives. *BMC Medicine, 11*(1), 136. doi:10.1186/1741-7015-11-136 PMID:23701737

Micha, R., Michas, G., & Mozaffarian, D. (2012). Unprocessed red and processed meats and risk of coronary artery disease and type 2 diabetes–an updated review of the evidence. *Current Atherosclerosis Reports, 14*(6), 515–524. doi:10.1007/s11883-012-0282-8 PMID:23001745

Micha, R., Wallace, S. K., & Mozaffarian, D. (2010). Red and processed meat consumption and risk of incident coronary heart disease, stroke, and diabetes mellitus: A systematic review and meta-analysis. *Circulation, 121*(21), 2271–2283. doi:10.1161/CIRCULATIONAHA.109.924977 PMID:20479151

Miller, C. A., Corbin, K. D., da Costa, K. A., Zhang, S., Zhao, X., Galanko, J. A., & Zeisel, S. H. et al. (2014). Effect of egg ingestion on trimethylamine-N-oxide production in humans: A randomized, controlled, dose-response study. *The American Journal of Clinical Nutrition, 100*(3), 778–786. doi:10.3945/ajcn.114.087692 PMID:24944063

Oehlenschläger, J. (2012). Seafood: Nutritional benefits and risk aspects. *International Journal for Vitamin and Nutrition Research, 82*(3), 168–176. doi:10.1024/0300-9831/a000108 PMID:23258397

Orlich, M. J., & Fraser, G. E. (2014). Vegetarian diets in the Adventist Health Study 2: A review of initial published findings. *The American Journal of Clinical Nutrition, 100*(Suppl. 1), 353S–358S. doi:10.3945/ajcn.113.071233 PMID:24898223

Orlich, M. J., Singh, P. N., Sabaté, J., Jaceldo-Siegl, K., Fan, J., Knutsen, S., & Fraser, F. et al. (2014). Vegetarian dietary patterns and mortality in Adventist Health Study 2. *JAMA Internal Medicine*, *173*(13), 1230–1238. doi:10.1001/jamainternmed.2013.6473 PMID:23836264

Pan, A., Sun, Q., Bernstein, A. M., Manson, J. E., Willett, W. C., & Hu, F. B. (2013). Changes in red meat consumption and subsequent risk of type 2 diabetes mellitus: Three cohorts of US men and women. *JAMA Internal Medicine*, *173*(14), 1328–1335. doi:10.1001/jamainternmed.2013.6633 PMID:23779232

Patel, P. S., Forouhi, N. G., Kuijsten, A., Schulze, M. B., van Woudenbergh, G. J., Ardanaz, E., & Wareham, N. J. et al. (2012). The prospective association between total and type of fish intake and type 2 diabetes in 8 European countries: EPIC-InterAct Study. *The American Journal of Clinical Nutrition*, *95*(6), 1445–1453. doi:10.3945/ajcn.111.029314 PMID:22572642

Pham, N. M., Mizoue, T., Tanaka, K., Tsuji, I., Tamakoshi, A., Matsuo, K., & Tanaka, K. et al. (2014). Meat consumption and colorectal cancer risk: An evaluation based on a systematic review of epidemiologic evidence among the Japanese population. *Japanese Journal of Clinical Oncology*, *44*(7), 641–650. doi:10.1093/jjco/hyu061 PMID:24842864

Ralston, R. A., Truby, H., Palermo, C. E., & Walker, K. Z. (2014). Colorectal cancer and nonfermented milk, solid cheese, and fermented milk consumption: A systematic review and meta-analysis of prospective studies. *Critical Reviews in Food Science and Nutrition*, *54*(9), 1167–1179. doi:10.1080/10408398.2011.629353 PMID:24499149

Reid, M. A., Marsh, K. A., Zeuschner, C. L., Saunders, A. V., & Baines, S. K. (2013). Meeting the nutrient reference values on a vegetarian diet. *The Medical Journal of Australia*, *199*(4 Suppl), S33–S40. PMID:25369927

Richard, C., Cristall, L., Fleming, E., Lewis, E. D., Ricupero, M., Jacobs, R. L., & Field, C. J. (2017). Impact of egg consumption on cardiovascular risk factors in individuals with type 2 diabetes and at risk for developing diabetes: A systematic review of randomized nutritional intervention studies. *Canadian Journal of Diabetes*, *41*(4), 453–463. doi:10.1016/j.jcjd.2016.12.002 PMID:28359773

Richman, E. L., Kenfield, S. A., Stampfer, M. J., Giovannucci, E. L., Zeisel, S. H., Willett, W. C., & Chan, J. M. (2012). Choline intake and risk of lethal prostate cancer: Incidence and survival. *The American Journal of Clinical Nutrition*, *96*(4), 855–863. doi:10.3945/ajcn.112.039784 PMID:22952174

Rizzo, N. S., Sabaté, J., Jaceldo-Siegl, K., & Fraser, G. E. (2011). Vegetarian dietary patterns are associated with a lower risk of metabolic syndrome: The adventist health study 2. *Diabetes Care*, *34*(5), 1225–1227. doi:10.2337/dc10-1221 PMID:21411506

Rosell, M., Appleby, P., Spencer, E., & Key, T. (2006). Weight gain over 5 years in 21,966 meat-eating, fish-eating, vegetarian, and vegan men and women in EPIC-Oxford. *International Journal of Obesity*, *30*(9), 1389–1396. doi:10.1038/sj.ijo.0803305 PMID:16534521

Sabaté, J. (2003). The contribution of vegetarian diets to health and disease: A paradigm shift? *The American Journal of Clinical Nutrition*, *78*(3 Suppl.), 502S–507S. PMID:12936940

Salehi, M., Moradi-Lakeh, M., Salehi, M. H., Nojomi, M., & Kolahdooz, F. (2013). Meat, fish, and esophageal cancer risk: A systematic review and dose-response meta-analysis. *Nutrition Reviews*, *71*(5), 257–267. doi:10.1111/nure.12028 PMID:23590703

Schwingshackl, L., Hoffmann, G., Schwedhelm, C., Kalle-Uhlmann, T., Missbach, B., Knüppel, S., & Boeing, H. (2016). Consumption of dairy products in relation to changes in anthropometric variables in adult populations: A Systematic review and meta-analysis of cohort Studies. *PLoS One*, *11*(6), e0157461. doi:10.1371/journal.pone.0157461 PMID:27310919

Shang, X., Scott, D., Hodge, A. M., English, D. R., Giles, G. G., Ebeling, P. R., & Sanders, K. M. (2016). Dietary protein intake and risk of type 2 diabetes: Results from the Melbourne Collaborative Cohort Study and a meta-analysis of prospective studies. *The American Journal of Clinical Nutrition*, *104*(5), 1352–1365. doi:10.3945/ajcn.116.140954 PMID:27629053

Shi, Y., Yu, P.-W., & Zeng, D.-Z. (2015). Dose–response meta-analysis of poultry intake and colorectal cancer incidence and mortality. *European Journal of Nutrition*, *54*(2), 243–250. doi:10.1007/s00394-014-0705-0 PMID:24788671

Siervo, M., Lara, J., Chowdhury, S., Ashor, A., Oggioni, C., & Mathers, J. C. (2015). Effects of the Dietary Approach to Stop Hypertension (DASH) diet on cardiovascular risk factors: A systematic review and meta-analysis. *British Journal of Nutrition*, *113*(1), 1–15. doi:10.1017/S0007114514003341 PMID:25430608

Singh, P. N., Sabaté, J., & Fraser, G. E. (2003). Does low meat consumption increase life expectancy in humans? *The American Journal of Clinical Nutrition*, *78*(3 Suppl.), 526S–532S. PMID:12936945

Singh, S., Singh, P. P., Roberts, L. R., & Sanchez, W. (2013). Chemopreventive strategies in hepatocellular carcinoma. *Nature Reviews. Gastroenterology & Hepatology*, *11*(1), 45–54. doi:10.1038/nrgastro.2013.143 PMID:23938452

Sofi, F., Macchi, C., Abbate, R., Gensini, G. F., & Casini, A. (2014). Mediterranean diet and health status: An updated meta-analysis and a proposal for a literature-based adherence score. *Public Health Nutrition*, *17*(12), 2769–2782. doi:10.1017/S1368980013003169 PMID:24476641

Song, J., Su, H., Wang, B., Zhou, Y., & Guo, L.-L. (2014). Fish consumption and lung cancer risk: Systematic review and meta-analysis. *Nutrition and Cancer*, *66*(4), 539–549. doi:10.1080/01635581.2014.894102 PMID:24707954

Souza, R. G. M., Gomes, A. C., Naves, M. M. V., & Mota, J. F. (2015). Nuts and legume seeds for cardiovascular risk reduction: Scientific evidence and mechanisms of action. *Nutrition Reviews*, *73*(6), 335–347. doi:10.1093/nutrit/nuu008 PMID:26011909

Stradling, C., Hamid, M., Fisher, K., Taheri, S., & Thomas, N. (2013). A review of dietary influences on cardiovascular health: Part 1: the role of dietary nutrients. *Cardiovascular & Hematological Disorders Drug Targets*, *13*(3), 1–34. PMID:24304234

Takata, Y., Shu, X.-O., Gao, Y.-T., Li, H., Zhang, X., Gao, J., & Zheng, W. et al. (2013). Red meat and poultry intakes and risk of total and cause-specific mortality: Results from cohort studies of Chinese adults in Shanghai. *PLoS One*, *8*(2), e56963. doi:10.1371/journal.pone.0056963 PMID:23451121

Tapsell, L. C. (2015). Fermented dairy food and CVD risk. *British Journal of Nutrition, 113*(S2), S131–S135. doi:10.1017/S0007114514002359 PMID:26148916

Tse, G., & Eslick, G. D. (2014). Egg consumption and risk of GI neoplasms: Dose–response meta-analysis and systematic review. *European Journal of Nutrition, 1*(7), 1581–1590. doi:10.1007/s00394-014-0664-5 PMID:24500371

Turner-McGrievy, G. M., Davidson, C. R., Wingard, E. E., Wilcox, S., & Frongillo, E. A. (2015). Comparative effectiveness of plant-based diets for weight loss: A randomized controlled trial of five different diets. *Nutrition (Burbank, Los Angeles County, Calif.), 31*(2), 350–358. doi:10.1016/j.nut.2014.09.002 PMID:25592014

Velasquez, M. T., Ramezani, A., Manal, A., & Raj, D. S. (2016). Trimethylamine N-Oxide: The good, the bad and the unknown. *Toxins, 8*(11), 326. doi:10.3390/toxins8110326 PMID:27834801

Vergnaud, A.-C., Norat, T., Romaguera, D., Mouw, T., May, A. M., Travier, N., & Peeters, P. H. et al. (2010). Meat consumption and prospective weight change in participants of the EPIC-PANACEA study. *The American Journal of Clinical Nutrition, 92*(2), 398–407. doi:10.3945/ajcn.2009.28713 PMID:20592131

Wallin, A., Di Giuseppe, D., Orsini, N., Patel, P. S., Forouhi, N. G., & Wolk, A. (2012). Fish consumption, dietary long-chain n-3 fatty acids, and risk of type 2 diabetes: Systematic review and meta-analysis of prospective studies. *Diabetes Care, 35*(4), 918–929. doi:10.2337/dc11-1631 PMID:22442397

Wang, W., Wu, Y., & Zhang, D. (2016). Association of dairy products consumption with risk of obesity in children and adults: A meta-analysis of mainly cross-sectional studies. *Annals of Epidemiology, 26*(12), 870–882.e2. doi:10.1016/j.annepidem.2016.09.005 PMID:27756684

Wang, X., Lin, X., Ouyang, Y. Y., Liu, J., Zhao, G., Pan, A., & Hu, F. B. (2015). Red and processed meat consumption and mortality: Dose-response meta-analysis of prospective cohort studies. *Public Health Nutrition, 19*(5), 1–13. PMID:26143683

Wang, X., Lin, X., Ouyang, Y. Y., Liu, J., Zhao, G., Pan, A., & Hu, F. B. (2016). Red and processed meat consumption and mortality: Dose–response meta-analysis of prospective cohort studies. *Public Health Nutrition, 19*(5), 893–905. doi:10.1017/S1368980015002062 PMID:26143683

Wang, Y.-Z., Wu, Q.-J., Zhu, J., & Wu, L. (2015). Fish consumption and risk of myeloma: A meta-analysis of epidemiological studies. *Cancer Causes & Control, 26*(9), 1307–1314. doi:10.1007/s10552-015-0625-1 PMID:26156047

World Health Organisation (WHO). (2017). WHO | *Noncommunicable diseases.* Retrieved from http://www.who.int/mediacentre/factsheets/fs355/en/

Wu, J., Zeng, R., Huang, J., Li, X., Zhang, J., Ho, J., & Zheng, Y. (2016). Dietary protein sources and incidence of breast cancer: A dose-response meta-analysis of prospective studies. *Nutrients, 8*(11), 730. doi:10.3390/nu8110730 PMID:27869663

Wu, K., Spiegelman, D., Hou, T., Albanes, D., Allen, N. E., Berndt, S. I., & Smith-Warner, S. A. et al. (2016). Associations between unprocessed red and processed meat, poultry, seafood and egg intake and the risk of prostate cancer: A pooled analysis of 15 prospective cohort studies. *International Journal of Cancer, 138*(10), 2368–2382. doi:10.1002/ijc.29973 PMID:26685908

Xu, B., Sun, J., Sun, Y., Huang, L., Tang, Y., & Yuan, Y. (2013). No evidence of decreased risk of colorectal adenomas with white meat, poultry, and fish intake: A meta-analysis of observational studies. *Annals of Epidemiology*, *23*(4), 215–222. doi:10.1016/j.annepidem.2012.12.016 PMID:23375344

Xu, R., Wang, Q., & Li, L. (2015). A genome-wide systems analysis reveals strong link between colorectal cancer and trimethylamine N-oxide (TMAO), a gut microbial metabolite of dietary meat and fat. *BMC Genomics*, *16*(Suppl. 7), S4. doi:10.1186/1471-2164-16-S7-S4 PMID:26100814

Yi, A. X., Leung, K. M. Y., Lam, M. H. W., Lee, J. S., & Giesy, J. P. (2012). Review of measured concentrations of triphenyltin compounds in marine ecosystems and meta-analysis of their risks to humans and the environment. *Chemosphere*, *89*(9), 1015–1025. doi:10.1016/j.chemosphere.2012.05.080 PMID:22704212

Yoon, H., Benamouzig, R., Little, J., François-Collange, M., & Tomé, D. (2000). Systematic review of epidemiological studies on meat, dairy products and egg consumption and risk of colorectal adenomas. *European Journal of Cancer Prevention*, *9*(3), 151–164. doi:10.1097/00008469-200006000-00002 PMID:10954254

Yu, X.-F., Zou, J., & Dong, J. (2014). Fish consumption and risk of gastrointestinal cancers: A meta-analysis of cohort studies. *World Journal of Gastroenterology*, *20*(41), 15398–15412. doi:10.3748/wjg.v20.i41.15398 PMID:25386090

Zhao, L.-G., Sun, J.-W., Yang, Y., Ma, X., Wang, Y.-Y., & Xiang, Y.-B. (2016). Fish consumption and all-cause mortality: A meta-analysis of cohort studies. *European Journal of Clinical Nutrition*, *70*(2), 155–161. doi:10.1038/ejcn.2015.72 PMID:25969396

Zheng, J., Huang, T., Yu, Y., Hu, X., Yang, B., & Li, D. (2012). Fish consumption and CHD mortality: An updated meta-analysis of seventeen cohort studies. *Public Health Nutrition*, *15*(4), 725–737. doi:10.1017/S1368980011002254 PMID:21914258

Zheng, J.-S., Huang, T., Yang, J., Fu, Y.-Q., & Li, D. (2012). Marine N-3 polyunsaturated fatty acids are inversely associated with risk of type 2 diabetes in Asians: A systematic review and meta-analysis. *PLoS One*, *7*(9), e44525. doi:10.1371/journal.pone.0044525 PMID:22984522

Zhou, Y., Tian, C., & Jia, C. (2012). Association of fish and n-3 fatty acid intake with the risk of type 2 diabetes: A meta-analysis of prospective studies. *British Journal of Nutrition*, *108*(03), 408–417. doi:10.1017/S0007114512002036 PMID:22857650

Zhu, H.-C., Yang, X., Xu, L.-P., Zhao, L.-J., Tao, G.-Z., Zhang, C., & Sun, X.-C. et al. (2014). Meat consumption is associated with esophageal cancer risk in a meat- and cancer-histological-type dependent manner. *Digestive Diseases and Sciences*, *59*(3), 664–673. doi:10.1007/s10620-013-2928-y PMID:24395380

zur Hausen, H. (2012). Red meat consumption and cancer: Reasons to suspect involvement of bovine infectious factors in colorectal cancer. *International Journal of Cancer*, *130*(11), 2475–2483. doi:10.1002/ijc.27413 PMID:22212999

KEY TERMS AND DEFINITIONS

Advanced Glycation End-Products (AGEs): AGEs are formed when foods high in fat and protein (particularly meat) are cooked at high temperatures resulting in the browning or charring of food.

Choline: A vitamin-like essential nutrient found mainly in animal foods including eggs, meat, poultry, fish and dairy foods.

Haem Iron: The form of iron found in animal products including red and processed meats, which is readily absorbed by the body; a catalyst or pro-oxidant in many cellular reactions, including the endogenous formation of n-nitroso compounds.

Persistent Organic Pollutants (POPs): Organic compounds that are resistant to environmental degradation, so which bioaccumulate, with potential negative impacts on health and the environment.

Saturated Fat (SF): A non-essential fatty acid found mostly in animal products, including red and processed meats and dairy, as well as coconut oil/milk, palm kernel oil and palm oil.

Trans-Fats: A non-essential fatty acid formed during the partial hydrogenation of vegetable oils to improve stability and shelf life; small amounts are naturally occurring in ruminant animals.

Trimethylamine-N-Oxide (TMAO): A toxic compound associated with increased cardiovascular disease risk, produced by the action of gut bacteria on L-carnitine and choline.

Chapter 3
Livestock's Near-Term Climate Impact and Mitigation Policy Implications

Gerard Wedderburn-Bisshop
Beyond Zero Emissions, Australia & Zero Emissions Byron, Australia

Lauren Rickards
RMIT University, Australia

ABSTRACT

Human consumption of livestock remains a marginal issue in climate change debates, partly due to the IPCC's arbitrary adoption of 100-year global warming potential framework to compare different emissions, blinding us to the significance of shorter-term emissions, namely methane. Together with the gas it reacts to form - tropospheric ozone - methane has been responsible for 37% of global warming since 1750, yet its atmospheric life is just 10 years. Neglecting its role means overlooking powerful mitigation opportunities. The chapter discusses the role of livestock, the largest anthropogenic methane source, and the need to include reduced meat consumption in climate change responses. Looking beyond the conventional focus on the consumer, we point to some underlying challenges in addressing the meat-climate relationship, including the climate science community's reluctance to adopt a short-term focus in its climate projections. Policy options are presented.

INTRODUCTION: A FRESH LOOK AT LIVESTOCK PRODUCTION AND CLIMATE POLICY

Enteric fermentation and manure from livestock are the largest source of methane (Ciais et al., 2013). Although methane is a highly significant greenhouse gas, it is marginal in mainstream climate change debates relative to CO_2 because of its ill-fit with dominant CO_2-centric greenhouse gas accounting methodologies. As a result, the climate change significance of livestock production – as well as other methane-producing processes such as amassing waste in landfill, fracking unconventional natural gas and burning biomass – has been under-recognised. A growing number of initiatives designed to reduce

DOI: 10.4018/978-1-5225-4757-0.ch003

meat consumption for climate change reasons are emerging, but these are predominantly run by non-governmental organisations and remain outside of mainstream policy. What is needed, we argue in this chapter, is far greater public awareness that choosing alternative proteins over red meat could slow down global warming by more than 15 years (Bryngelsson et al., 2017).

Why has the powerful role of methane and thus meat consumption in generating near-term climate change been neglected until late? One problem is the entrenched nature of livestock production and meat consumption in society (McGregor & Houston, 2017; Smil, 2013). Despite rising public awareness of the link between livestock and climate change, interlocking factors on both the production and consumption side mean that a large-scale shift towards a lower-meat diet is proving difficult. However, as indicated above, there is a further significant reason for meat consumption's neglect in climate change mitigation discussions: the seemingly mundane, technical question of greenhouse gas accounting protocols. Current protocols use CO_2 as the "standard" and an arbitrary 100-year period to assess the global warming significance of all greenhouse gases. While pragmatic, this approach downplays the importance of short-lived gases such as methane. It frames and filters our understanding of and responses to the climate change problem away from important methane-reduction measures, obscuring the need to radically reduce meat consumption. As we argue in this chapter, however, one immediate way of helping to rectify this blind spot in the climate change mitigation portfolio is to improve greenhouse gas accounting conventions.

The chapter begins with an overview of the relationship between livestock and climate change, highlighting the growing problem of livestock-based greenhouse emissions, notably short-lived or "near-term" ones. We then turn to the neglected issue of how such emissions are under-accounted in existing greenhouse emission accounting and policies and conceal the role of livestock in climate change. To end, some specific improvements to accounting for greenhouse emissions are suggested as one of many steps needed to address the issue of livestock's role in climate change.

CLIMATE CHANGE AND LIVESTOCK

Climate change is underway and accelerating. In 2015, Earth's average global surface temperature reached a full degree above the pre-industrial era (WMO, 2016). The period 2011 to 2015 was the warmest five year stretch on record. Extreme high temperatures are now 10 times more likely in places such as southern Europe, which by 2050 will face at least one severe climate hazard every year of the scale previously occurring once a century (Forzieri et al., 2016). Between 2011 and 2015 more than half the major extreme weather events were in part due to human-induced global warming (WMO, 2016). This includes droughts, floods and their complex flow-on effects, interacting with slower moving variables, multiplying other pressures and threatening numerous types of security. Temperatures may increase more rapidly in the future as major positive, reinforcing feedbacks in the Earth system lead to an amplification of climate change, potentially triggering abrupt shifts in climate conditions. Tipping points, causing abrupt and irreversible change, are increasingly acknowledged as a growing threat and reality (Kopp et al., 2016; Lenton et al., 2008). Forty-one cases of regional abrupt changes to ocean, sea ice, snow cover, permafrost and terrestrial biosphere have already been documented (Drijfhout et al., 2015). Alarmingly, many more are predicted for global warming even below 2°C. Tipping points include the melting of permafrost which is releasing trapped methane – a powerful greenhouse gas discussed further below – from newly exposed soil. The existence of such positive feedbacks (that is, climate change impacts that add to the level of global climate change) underlines the crucial importance of minimising climate change in the first place and as soon as possible.

In the international agreements about climate change action coordinated by the United Nations Framework Convention on Climate Change, 2°C of average global warming has been agreed upon as the "maximum" level that the world should collectively allow to occur, with warming beyond this level considered to be highly dangerous. With 1°C warming already breached, this underlines the need for strong and urgent mitigative action. At the same time, the so-called "guardrail" of 2°C average warming is no guarantee of safety. In fact, as low-lying states such as Pacific Islands and drought-affected sub-Saharan nations have tried to point out, given the already observable climate change effects such as loss of irrigation groundwater and continued crop failure, 2°C actually guarantees further serious impacts for many groups, species and parts of the world (Tschakert, 2015). Despite the array of consistent peer reviewed literature highlighting the significant negative impact that an average of 2°C will inflict (Jevrejeva et al., 2016; King et al., 2017; Knutti et al., 2016), the world is continuing to load the atmosphere with more and more greenhouse gases, placing us on a climatic trajectory that will far exceed the 2°C "guardrail" imperilling most species on the planet, including humans (García Molinos et al., 2016; Pacifici et al., 2017; Pecl et al., 2017). For these reasons, it is clear that the current framework for climate change mitigation is inadequate and new approaches are needed.

One sector that has conventionally been relatively overlooked in climate change mitigation efforts is Agriculture, Forestry and Other Land-Use (AFOLU). Reasons for this neglect are multiple. The sector is more heterogeneous and decentralised than many others, making emission measurement, regulation and collective action difficult. Its connection to atmospheric pollution is more variable, less visible and obvious than the energy sector where the iconic image of smoke stacks readily communicates the role of fossil fuel based energy generation in the causation of climate change. With agriculture and forestry's direct reliance on natural resources, and role in supporting global food security and many people's livelihoods, the main link emphasised between it and climate change has been the very real problem of its vulnerability to climatic impacts (Hughes et al., 2016). More recently, the positive role of soil and perennial plants in sequestering carbon from the atmosphere into the soil has gained in profile, thanks to the growing sense that deliberate negative emissions methods (which reduce atmospheric carbon concentrations directly) are needed in addition to efforts to stem the flow of further greenhouse gases into the atmosphere if the planet's climate is to have a chance of staying below 2°C average global warming (Gasser et al., 2015).

Although the focus on the AFOLU sector remains minimal compared to that on sectors such as energy and transport, there is growing awareness that climate mitigation in agriculture and forestry are vital in meeting the 2°C target. Even based on conventional 100-year greenhouse gas (GHG) accounting, the GHG emissions from the AFOLU sector represent approximately a quarter of global anthropogenic GHG emissions (10 to 12 $GtCO_2eq$, per year) and need to be halved by 2050 (P. Smith et al., 2016). A major source and driver of emissions in the AFOLU sector is the production of livestock.

Livestock production contributes to the climate change problem in multiple direct and indirect ways. To begin with, livestock production is the primary driver of deforestation, with 70% of the world's deforestation a result of stripping in order to grow animal feed and provide pasture (Stoll-Kleemann & Schmidt, 2017). Deforestation contributes to climate change by removing the carbon store of trees (that is, diminishing the capacity of the land to sequester carbon). During deforestation, vegetation is often burnt, returning much of the stored carbon to the atmosphere in forms including soot, discussed below (Arneth et al., 2017; van Marle et al., 2017). Deforestation also newly exposes soil, leading to potentially large fluxes in soil carbon loss over the long term (Arneth et al., 2017). Perhaps most significantly, deforestation for livestock production encourages and enables the breeding of more ruminant animals, namely cattle, sheep and goats, with such land either used to stock these animals directly or to produce feed (often involving the application of emission-intensive nitrogenous fertilisers) for livestock elsewhere. Such animals further contribute to climate change in three main ways: by directly releasing methane as a result of the enteric fermentation that their digestion involves ("cow burps"); by producing large amounts of manure that releases methane emissions as it decomposes; and by necessitating the use of emission-intensive (fossil-fuel based) processing, plastic packaging, refrigerated transportation and cooking in order for them or their milk products to be safely distributed and consumed.

Worsening the effect of these factors on the climate is the fact that global agricultural production is rising rapidly. Beef and milk production has doubled since the 1970s and pig and poultry production increased five times (FAO, n.d.). To try to manage the emerging collision between meat consumption and the climate, a range of technical solutions are being rolled out to reduce the emissions intensity of livestock production at different scales. These include efforts to cut the methane emissions of individual animals through measures such as oil-based feed supplements, and the use of selective breeding and hormone growth promotants (Prusty et al., 2017). At the farm system scale, mitigation options include capturing emissions from manure, often to turn into bioenergy, and efforts to reorganise farm logistics to avoid the production of unnecessary emissions (Rojas-Downing et al., 2017). All of these technical emission solutions are welcome, and some can produce co-benefts (Mottet et al., 2017). However, there has been limited adoption of such methods by producers (Eckard et al., 2010) and some of these approaches, such as feed supplements or manure management, raise new animal welfare concerns (Llonch et al., 2017) and/or are only feasible in intensive farming systems. Given that beef feedlots produce just 3.5% of Australian enteric fermentation emissions (DCCEE, 2012a), that leaves the larger issue of extensive (open pasture) livestock production, where feed supplements are problematic or not possible. Moreover, none of these approaches address the ongoing expansion of livestock production. Indeed, they are part of the 'sustainable intensification' paradigm that explicitly aims to increase agricultural production levels and productivity (McGregor & Houston, 2017).

To address climate change effectively, large demand-side reductions in livestock production are required (Herrero et al., 2016). This necessitates an approach that looks not just at emissions intensity per animal or farm but tackles the harder questions of overall production levels, consumer demand and systemic change (Bhopal et al., 2013; Cribb, 2010; Godfray et al., 2010; Ray et al., 2013; Schwarzer, 2012). In favour of a reduction in global meat consumption is the fact that such an achievement would help address the many other issues with livestock production related to their environmental, animal welfare and human health impacts (McGregor & Houston, 2017).

Environmental problems associated with livestock production include biodiversity loss, water pollution, air pollution, and land degradation (Pelletier & Tyedmers, 2010; Wiedemann et al., 2016). A recent assessment of the environmental costs of livestock production relative to the planet's environmental boundary conditions suggests that the livestock sector not only occupies 52% of 'humanity's suggested safe operating space for anthropogenic greenhouse gas emissions' but also contributes significantly to the transgression of other boundary conditions, including nitrogen, deforestation and fresh water consumption (Pelletier & Tyedmers, 2010, p. 18372).

Animal welfare concerns with livestock production are also numerous (Benson & Rollin, 2008). The sheer number of animals enrolled into the livestock production system means that care for individual animals is exceedingly difficult. More significantly, the commodification of production animals – that is, the treatment of them as units of production for sale, stripped of their existence as sentient beings of moral worth – means that efforts to consider their welfare above and beyond what is required by regulation or to win a "social licence" for the industry are discouraged (Wilkie, 2017). The prevalent productivist logic dictates that production levels must be maximised and this tends to encourage breeding, feeding and slaughtering regimes that trade off the welfare of individual animals (although if the true financial costs of animal welfare failures are accounted for, financial and ethical motivations can align) (Dawkins, 2017). However, growing public concern about the conditions in which many livestock animals live and die means that the social licence of many parts of the livestock industry is precarious (Martin & Williams, 2011). Indeed, Emel and Hawkins (2010) suggest industrial meat consumption and production have become sufficiently problematic that if government and industry support is withdrawn, these industries may be dismantled far quicker than supposed. Adding to the industry's issues is that climate change is already worsening animal welfare outcomes in the sector (e.g. in the form of droughts, floods, fires, extreme heat, and greater parasite and disease loads) and poses real constraints on the future viability of large scale livestock production (Fox et al., 2015; Nardone et al., 2010). Moreover, current methods for reducing greenhouse emissions from individual animals, namely those focused on increasing the production efficiency of each animal (Shields & Orme-Evans, 2015), impose new animal welfare concerns (Llonch et al., 2017), underlining further the need to breed fewer livestock in the first place.

Human healthwise, livestock production is less clearly a negative, but the current situation nevertheless presents some distinctive needs and opportunities for improvement. The main complexity is that meat intake can be an important source of protein for humans but such consumption is very unevenly distributed across the global population. Behind global averages in meat consumption – 117g per person per day in 2017, according to the Food and Agriculture Organisation of the United Nations (FAO, 2017) – lie huge variation and contrasting dietary problems. On the one hand, among many wealthy consumers the over-consumption of meat, amongst other food, is a major, growing health problem. In a study of diverse dietary interventions, for example Springmann et al. (2016) found that reducing red meat consumption had the most positive impact on health, responsible for up to 82% of avoidable deaths. On the other hand, for nearly a billion people worldwide, the under-consumption not over-consumption of protein is the main dietary concern. Large geographic discrepancies exist not in physical access but economic access to protein, pointing to broader inequalities and political economy problems to which centralised control of industrial scale, export oriented farming contributes. From a simple consumption perspective, an upshot is that the general mitigation of livestock emissions needs to simultaneously tackle overconsumption in some parts of the world and under-nutrition in other parts (Garnett, 2011; Liverman & Kapadia, 2010; Stehfest et al., 2009).

For this reason, the idea of "contraction and convergence" has been proposed, which aims to reduce overall consumption (contraction) while bringing the financial capacity of different groups to consume meat if they chose to into alignment (convergence). To this end, McMichael et al. (2007) proposed a working global consumption target of 90g of meat per person per day, down from the current average of 117g and shared more evenly than the current ten-fold variance between populations (McMichael et al., 2007). To achieve emissions reduction and health advantages, they note, only 50g per day of this meat should come from ruminant livestock. Since then, others, including the Australian National Dietary Guidelines, have recommended a maximum of 65g of red meat per person per day (or 455g per week) (NHMRC, 2013). Springmann et al. (2016) recommend red meat consumption be no more than to 42g per day. For most consumers in wealthy nations like Australia, these targets of 42g-65g of red meat per day represent a substantial reduction from current levels.

Consumers' awareness of food-climate impacts has been raised considerably in recent years. Campaigns include Meat-free Monday, Less Meat Less Heat, the Climatarian Diet and the US Environmental Working Group Meat Eaters' Guide, which vary in the extent to which they advocate for veganism, vegetarianism (of various types) or flexitarian (occasional meat) diets. Research initiatives around the food–climate relationship have also expanded, including groups such as the FAO, Oxford University's Food Climate Research Network, PBL Netherlands Environmental Assessment Agency, US thinktank Food Tank, the Barilla Center for Food & Nutrition, the Consultative Group on International Agricultural Research (CGIAR), City University London's Centre for Food Policy, Australia's Beyond Zero Emissions, and the UK's Eating Better alliance among others (Dibb & Fitzpatrick, 2014). Also, in some parts of the world (e.g. Denmark, Germany, China, UK), governments and public institutions are starting to push for lower meat consumption by issuing new dietary guidelines or removing meat from hospital menus. China, for example, which consumes more meat than any other country, albeit half as much meat per person as the USA, has embarked on a high-profile government-led campaign to reduce meat consumption by half.

Despite these efforts, livestock production and consumption continue to grow. At current rates livestock-related emissions are projected to rise at 1%–1.5% per year to 2050 (Herrero et al., 2016). It is clear that many significant barriers lie in the way of the necessary global reduction in livestock numbers. Some of these barriers are structural, such as the path dependencies embedded in the current "agro-industrial complex", including often highly vertically integrated agribusiness companies (Schewe & Stuart, 2017; Stuart & Schewe, 2016). Some are cultural and social, with meat consumption associated with status, Westernisation, masculinity and "proper family meals", among other things (Dibb & Fitzpatrick, 2014). As Cribb (2010, p. 193) suggests, if McMichael et al.'s target of 90g of meat per person per day were adopted, it would represent a 'profound shift in human tastes and sustainable consciousness'.

THE QUESTION OF GREENHOUSE GAS ACCOUNTING

What, then, can be done to encourage the shift away from livestock overproduction that climate safety demands? While the role of information in motivating and guiding decision-making should not be overstated or assumed – and there is much evidence to suggest that providing people with information about climate change science is vastly insufficient in triggering appropriate climate change responses (Dibb & Fitzpatrick, 2014) – the information that is available needs to present an accurate picture. At present, information about the contribution of livestock to climate change is arguably inaccurate, dangerously so, because it is obscured by a conventional, technical decision to rank the importance of different greenhouse gases according to a measure that overly focuses attention on CO_2 at the expense of other powerful near-term emissions, notably methane. As we now discuss, related disagreements and conflicts around greenhouse gas accounts (Ascui & Lovell, 2011) and, consequently, about what activities are most climate un-friendly, is one reason that a consistent method for weighing up the climate impact of foods has proven illusive and action on such impacts remains marginal.

At present, there is extreme variation in estimates of livestock greenhouse gas emissions. The FAO gives an estimate of 14.5% of global emissions (Gerber et al., 2013) and a review of 2005 agricultural emissions that allowed for certain associated processes of deforestation or foregone sequestration found livestock emissions to be between 12.7% and 17% of global emissions (P. Smith et al., 2016). In contrast, CGIAR found the global food system (mainly due to livestock) to be responsible for up to a third of global emissions (Vermeulen et al., 2012), and a World Watch report suggests that livestock production contributes a whopping 51% of global emissions (Goodland & Anhang, 2009). Some of the major reasons for this variation in estimates of the impact of livestock on climate change are whether deforestation, foregone sequestration (the opportunity cost of ruminant grazing vs vegetation growing and sequestering carbon), and livestock respiration (breathing out CO_2) are included or excluded. The highest of these estimates, the World Watch article, drew strong criticism for defining livestock respiration as an emission, but criticism of this component has diverted much-needed debate away from the important choice of 20-year greenhouse gas accounting vs 100-year accounting. Table 1 illustrates the component differences: deforestation and/or foregone sequestration; greenhouse gas accounting period; respiration and several other factors. We turn now to examine this neglected issue in more detail.

Table 1. Livestock emission estimates: components included/excluded in each

		FAO (2006) (Steinfeld et al., 2006)	**World Watch (2009) (Goodland & Anhang, 2009)**	**FAO (2013) (Gerber et al., 2013)**	**Herrero et al (2016) (LCA) (Herrero et al., 2016)**	**Beyond Zero Emissions (2015) (Wedderburn-Bisshop et al., 2015) ****
Livestock as % of Global Emissions		**18% (7,516 Mt CO_2-e)**	**51% (32,564 Mt CO_2-e)**	**14.5% (7,100 Mt CO_2-e)**	**13%-17% (5,600-7,500 Mt CO_2-e)**	**36% (GWP_{100}) 47%(GWP_{20}) (% of Australian Emissions)**
GHG accounting	20 years		✓			✓
	100 years	✓		✓	✓	✓
Included in calculation	Deforestation	✓	✓	✓*	✓	✓
	Foregone Sequestration		✓		✓	
	Respiration		✓			
	Livestock undercounting		✓			
	Additional livestock refrigeration / cooking / processing		✓		✓	
	Uncounted fish for feed		✓			
	Near-term emission carbon monoxide					✓*

* deforestation included: for crops - soybeans in Brazil and Argentina; for pasture - Latin America and Africa

** Australian national land use emissions study only, but uncounted carbon monoxide included

Accounting for Near-Term Emissions

Iconic graphical images of rising carbon dioxide concentrations in the atmosphere (Figure 1) now symbolise climate change. While useful in some ways, they have slipped from being a diagnosis of the problem to a prognosis of what needs to be done: progressively reduce carbon dioxide concentrations. It is indisputable that CO_2 emissions do need to be reduced, and that their major source – fossil fuels – therefore need to be effectively banned (Princen et al., 2015). Carbon dioxide has caused 55% of anthropogenic global warming to date (Table 2) and will need to be dealt with for coming centuries because it has a long atmospheric lifetime. Indeed, the atmospheric lifetime of CO_2 emissions is extreme. Although half of a given amount of atmospheric CO_2 is taken up in the ocean (mostly) and in land vegetation and soils within the first 30 years following its release, 1000 years later 20% of the original emission is still in the atmosphere (Archer et al., 2009). It is this long-lived tail that has many climate scientists most worried about the long-term future.

Without discounting the importance of this long-term outlook, the 45% of warming caused by other greenhouse gases (Table 2) is a dangerous blind spot in our current CO_2-centric policies. Overlooked are near-term emissions: those that exist in the atmosphere for shorter periods. Depending on their properties, emissions can last in the atmosphere from millennia (e.g. CO_2) to a few days (e.g. black carbon). Largely invisible in the conventional long-term measurement tools used in greenhouse gas accounting, are gases with lifetimes less than 100 years. Carbon monoxide and the derived gas tropospheric ozone, black carbon, and cooling emissions from nitrous oxides (NOx), sulphates and organic carbon are all

Figure 1. Mauna, Hawaii, CO_2 levels to 2015
Source: National Oceanic and Atmospheric Administration (NOAA) © 2015 NOAA. Used with permission

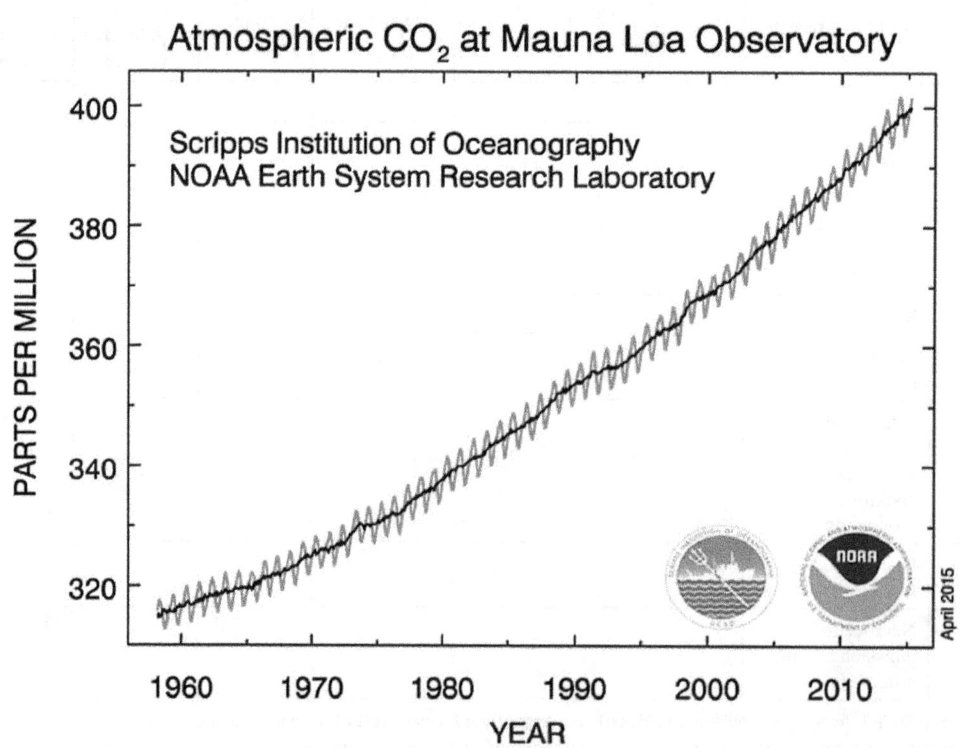

excluded from national and global inventories by the Intergovernmental Panel on Climate Change (IPCC) approach for their short-term nature, but also because of their variability, their regional (rather than global) impact and measurement difficulty when these conventions were first formalised. Although these short-lived emissions or "near-term climate forcers (NTCFs)" are largely naturally removed from the atmosphere within 10 years (Stocker et al., 2013), many have significant long-term impact. Table 2 lists the lifetime and warming impact of global emissions since 1750.

Once the importance of near-term climate forcers is recognised, a host of new emissions sources – outside the singular focus on fossil fuels – comes into view. We turn now to look at these forcers and their sources. The take home message is that near-term climate forcers, being precursors of tropospheric ozone, are predominantly from agriculture (Longmire et al., 2014). The relative greenhouse impact of agriculture is increased by the fact that some emissions from industry, notably fossil fuel combustion (nitrogen oxides –NOx, and sulphates – SO_2), actually have a slight cooling effect on the climate. In particular, livestock production is spotlighted as a major climate change issue.

Tropospheric Ozone

O_3(T), alone has caused 14% of warming since 1750, making it the third most important greenhouse gas (see Table 3.2). O_3(T) is not emitted —it is formed in a photochemical reaction between carbon monoxide (CO), nitrogen oxides (NOx) and volatile organic compounds (VOCs) including methane (Forster et al., 2007). It remains in the atmosphere for 4 to 18 days. The most effective means of reducing O_3(T) is to reduce CH_4, which is responsible for half of anthropogenic ozone production (Fowler,

Table 2. Emission-based global radiative forcing (RF) since 1750 showing the components included and excluded in UNFCCC GHG accounting rules

Emissions	Component Species	Included in UNFCCC Accounting	Atmospheric Lifetime	Global RF Since 1750 (W/m²)	Proportion of net Global RF From All Emissions Since 1750 (2.86 W/m²)
Long-lived gases	CO_2	Y	100-1000 years	1.56	55%
	CH_4	Y	10 years	0.86	30%
	Halocarbons	Y	600-3500 years	0.36	13%
	N_20	Y	100 years	0.16	6%
	HFCs	Y	1.4-270 years	0.02	1%
Short-lived gases	CO/VOC	N	Days-to-weeks	0.27	9%
	NOx	N	Days-to-weeks	-0.21	-7%
Aerosols	Black Carbon	N	3-8 days	0.44	15%
	Sulphates	N	Days-to-weeks	-0.4	-14%
	Organic Carbon	N	Days-to-weeks	-0.19	-7%
Tropospheric Ozone (produced from CH_4, CO, NOx, NMVOC emissions)	O_3(T)*	N*	4-18 days	0.39*	14%*

*Not an emission, included for comparison only. Radiative forcing from CH_4 and CO includes that caused by O_3(T).
Source: Adapted from Forster et al., 2007, Table 2.13

2008). Tropospheric ozone is detrimental to crop production. At atmospheric concentrations above 40 ppb, a level regularly recorded in many countries, tropospheric ozone also harms plants, reduces crop yields and slows forests' sequestration of atmospheric carbon (Ashmore, 2005). Wheat, rice, soybean and maize are all negatively impacted at these ozone concentrations, and crop damage is predicted to increase (Van Dingenen et al., 2009). This outlook will place further pressure on agricultural systems already impacted by climatic variables, soil salinity and pest and disease distributions.

Carbon Monoxide

CO, is an uncounted emission, since IPCC has excluded this from national and global inventories by convention. It has a regional rather than global impact, but has been responsible for 10% of global warming, so its omission results in significant under-reporting (Fry et al., 2012; Unger et al., 2008). It is created by incomplete combustion, the most common source being open agricultural fires. Although carbon monoxide emitted by industry is a key component of urban smog, most CO is emitted from biomass burning for pasture maintenance and deforestation fires (DCCEE, 2012b).

Black Carbon

BC, also known as soot, is produced from incomplete combustion of biomass, and lasts a few days in the atmosphere. Black carbon is the second greatest warming emission (not gas) after CO_2. A study by the Copenhagen Consensus Center calculated if programs to reduce open burning were implemented in Africa and South America these would provide a reduction of 80% of global black carbon emissions (Baron et al., 2009). Most BC comes from open fires, predominantly from agriculture (Bond et al., 2013). However, aerosols co-emitted with BC from open biomass burning may have a cooling effect, offsetting direct warming from BC (Bond et al., 2013). Data on BC and co-emitted aerosols is lacking, therefore the effects of these emissions are unknown, although they may potentially be a significant contributor to short-lived forcing. Because BC has caused 15% of human-caused warming, our understanding of this significant emission nationally would benefit from further research.

Methane

CH_4, is the most important of the near-term gases, second only to CO_2 for its global warming impact. If we include methane's 'downstream' products – notably the tropospheric ozone that it forms, we find that this gas has caused 37% of global warming since 1750 (Stocker et al., 2013). Methane has increased in atmospheric concentration by 260% since 1750, compared to the 40% increase in CO_2 (Blasing, 2013). Methane lasts only 10 years in the atmosphere, placing it in a uniquely powerful position to reduce warming in coming decades (Wedderburn-Bisshop et al., 2015). Methane atmospheric concentration is more than three times historic levels, and now rising at a record rate, pushing climate models into their highest temperature scenarios (Saunois et al., 2016). Methane's impact is now so great that the Earth will warm by 1.5°–2°C by 2050 whether or not CO_2 emissions are reduced (Howarth, 2014). Methane emissions from fossil fuel exploration and mining are now known to be up to twice that of current estimates (Schwietzke et al., 2016), however the recent surge is largely from livestock, with smaller contributions from fossil fuel use and wetlands (Saunois et al., 2016). The greatest anthropogenic methane source is enteric fermentation from ruminants and livestock manure (Ciais et al., 2013).

Overall, arbitrary adoption of 100-year accounting has strongly framed our response to global warming. The use of Global Warming Potential over 100 years – GWP_{100}, is an arbitrary compromise (Shine, 2012), not a 'gold standard' as many would believe. By IPCC convention, short-lived greenhouse gases are not reported in national inventories and the warming impact of methane is averaged over a period ten times its actual atmospheric life. Re-framing to examine near-term climate forcers not only improves our understanding of climate change, but challenges the extent, timing and targeting of our mitigation and adaptation responses.

Expanding the framing of GHG accounting to incorporate short-lived gases provides a more complete and sobering understanding of the climate change problem. It also reveals the importance of rethinking the timing of mitigation effort. Use of Global Warming Potential over 20 – year GWP_{20}. indicates that near-term warming from yearly non-CO_2 greenhouse gases in Australia is twice that of yearly CO_2 (see Figure 2, from an Australian study). Thus, over coming decades it is mitigation of CH_4 and CO (and likely black carbon) emissions that will have the greatest benefit (K.R. Smith et al., 2013; UNEP/WMO, 2011). That said, addressing longer-term warming remains critical. Twenty-year accounting is not appropriate for CO_2. Indeed even 100 years may be too short for CO_2, due to the 20% that still remains 1000 years after the emission. Sequestration of legacy carbon dioxide and drastic cuts in present-day CO_2 emissions remain essential.

The use of any timeframe is valid to discover the impact of emissions on a future climate stabilisation date (Manning & Reisinger, 2011), whether that be 1 year or 1000 years. The closer we are to that stabilisation date, GWP values for NTCFs rise rapidly, magnifying the importance of the shorter-term emissions. The use of GWP_{20} is therefore the most appropriate metric when assessing the warming impact of yearly emissions 20 years hence.

Figure 2. 2006-2010 Australian average annual emissions from agriculture (Mt.CO_2-e,) over 20 years (GWP_{20}) and 100 years (GWP_{100})
Source: Longmire et al., 2014 © 2014 Beyond Zero Emissions. Used with permission.

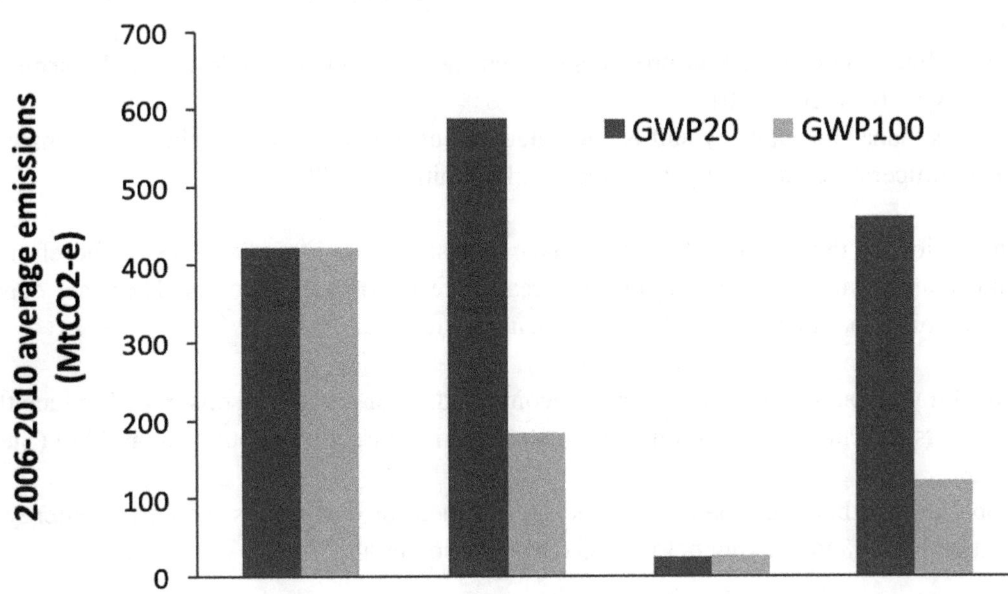

However, among climate scientists there tends to be resistance to shorter-lived greenhouse emissions being given importance as mitigation targets, partly because of scientific uncertainty about the relative importance of different gases, with debate as to whether the contributing effect of NTCFs, particularly methane, is over-valued (Shoemaker & Schrag, 2013). The primary reason for resistance is strategic: not wanting to distract from the fact that proposed NTCF mitigation will have little impact on peak (long-term) warming, and that future generations would have a more substantial long-term benefit if immediate reductions of CO_2 were implemented (Allen, 2015). It is true that cumulative atmospheric CO_2 is the overwhelming contributor to long-term warming (Allen et al., 2009), and that mitigating NTCFs without corresponding CO_2 controls will lead to far higher warming trajectories (Rogelj et al., 2014). Use of GWP_{100} may also suit political motives to focus attention on longer-lived fossil fuel emissions (Ascui & Lovell, 2011). There is however an urgent need – and opportunity – to help quell the climate crisis in coming decades by addressing NTCFs and realising the many co-benefits of doing so.

Possibilities for Positive Change

Near-term climate forcers offer transformative opportunities in the face of ineffective climate change action. In particular, methane can play a unique mitigation role (Stocker et al., 2013). As others have noted, there is an opportunity to develop 'short-term climate change mitigation policies that take advantage of the relatively short atmospheric lifetime of CH_4 of about 10 years, and the known technological and agronomical options available for reducing emissions' (Kirschke et al., 2013, p. 820) and make the most of 'methane's attractiveness as a cost-effective greenhouse reduction target' (Nisbet et al., 2014, p. 494). As we have pointed out, livestock production – which is the greatest source of not only methane but also tropospheric ozone (a 'downstream' product of methane and other gases), black carbon and carbon monoxide, is the sector whose transformation is most needed. Some of the enticing outcomes made possible by controlling livestock NTCF emissions are:

- Moderate methane reductions can slow global warming by 15 years and 0.5°C (UNEP/WMO, 2011).
- A global diet without ruminant products (no red meat or dairy) can slow global warming by 25 years (Bryngelsson et al., 2017).
- Cutting methane emissions by half is equivalent to cutting all carbon dioxide (CO_2) emissions for a global temperature target 45 years ahead (K.R. Smith et al., 2013).

Steep reductions in the major source of methane emissions, ruminant livestock, is therefore critical now that our planet is fast approaching or has already breached tipping points. There are compelling co-benefits in doing so. Financial and health co-benefits include:

- A global transition to a low meat-diet as recommended for health reasons would reduce the mitigation costs to achieve a 450 ppm CO_2-eq stabilisation target by about 50% in 2050 (Stehfest et al., 2009).
- A global diet without ruminant products (no red meat or dairy) cuts the cost of energy system mitigation by 25% for staying below 2°C (Bryngelsson et al., 2017).

- With healthy eating and energy intake, changes in mortality amount to US$21 trillion per year in 2050. For a vegan diet the benefit is US$30 trillion per year. This is 9% of expected GDP for healthy eating and 13% of GDP for a vegan diet (Springmann et al., 2016).
- Changes in the consumption of red meat, fruits, and vegetables and in total energy intake could result in reductions in total global mortality of 6–10%, compared with a reference diet in 2050. This estimate is likely an underestimate (Springmann et al., 2016).

CONCLUSION

An increasing number of studies have highlighted the near-term transformative impact of mitigating livestock emissions (Bryngelsson et al., 2017; Harwatt et al., 2017; K.R. Smith et al., 2013; Wedderburn-Bisshop et al., 2015). Although many reports and studies have urged policy action on livestock emissions (Briggs et al., 2013; Garnett, 2011; Herrero et al., 2016), little has been done (Bähr, 2015; Bailey et al., 2014; Wellesley et al., 2015). There are many reasons for this inaction: government reluctance to interfere with agriculture in the face of industry pressure and escalating climate change-related stresses; public resistance to government interference in what are (mis)understood to be individuals' personal food choices; and the risk that fully pricing emissions would make red meat unaffordable, with potentially regressive social outcomes if not managed well. All of these issues require serious attention and careful research. The particular sticking point we want to highlight in this chapter is the seemingly mundane but influential question of how different greenhouse gases are handled scientifically and institutionally, with flow on problems of inconsistent and inaccurate messaging about what is causing climate change. In order to support broader important policy measures such as properly pricing carbon and large-scale demand management in livestock consumption, there is a pressing need to alter national and IPCC greenhouse gas accounting protocols and inventories to better reflect the true impact of near-term as well as long-term gases. In particular, we suggest scientists and policy makers:

- **Include Near-Term Timelines:** In order to break the self-limiting framing imposed by 100-year accounting, and to re-frame the climate challenge in a new positive light, we urge that new IPCC inventories be published showing both 20-year and 100-year accounting. Use of GWP_{20} would provide policymakers with a clear picture of the relative importance of emissions of different gases as the world approaches the 2°C threshold.
- **Remove Net LULUCF Accounting:** Current 'net' accounting hides true deforestation emissions. We also recommend that deforestation be separated from 'land use' emissions and attributed to the activity responsible – in this case agriculture.
- **Publish True Sector Accounts:** Rather than delve into and sum obscure land use and agriculture categories, or attempting to separate stationary energy into industries, sector accounts would bring much needed transparency to national emissions.
- **Include Uncounted Emissions:** As the Australian study discovered, uncounted carbon monoxide and subsequent tropospheric ozone significantly skew results.

While seemingly small, technical and incidental, these measures would allow accurate, valuable information to be provided to consumers and others about the real impact of their choices. Although far from sufficient on its own, labelling foods with such information about different items' near-term climate impact may jolt some consumers into thinking again about their habitual consumption of meat. Imagine how you would respond if the next time you purchased a pack of red meat it bore a label clearly stating: "If you could slow down global warming by more than 15 years simply by choosing alternative proteins over red meat, what would you choose?". Regardless of your decision, the resultant dinner table conversation about livestock and climate may precipitate the broader social, institutional and political changes necessary to tackle this crucial part of the climate change crisis.

REFERENCES

Allen, M. (2015). *Short-lived promise? The science and policy of cumulative and short-lived climate pollutants (Oxford Martin Policy Paper)*. Oxford, UK: Oxford University. Retrieved from http://www.oxfordmartin.ox.ac.uk/publications/view/1960

Allen, M. R., Frame, D. J., Huntingford, C., Jones, C. D., Lowe, J. A., Meinshausen, M., & Meinshausen, N. (2009). Warming caused by cumulative carbon emissions towards the trillionth tonne. *Nature, 458*(7242), 1163–1166. doi:10.1038/nature08019 PMID:19407800

Archer, D., Eby, M., Brovkin, V., Ridgwell, A., Cao, L., Mikolajewicz, U., & Tokos, K. et al. (2009). Atmospheric lifetime of fossil fuel carbon dioxide. *Annual Review of Earth and Planetary Sciences, 37*(1), 117–134. doi:10.1146/annurev.earth.031208.100206

Arneth, A., Sitch, S., Pongratz, J., Stocker, B. D., Ciais, P., Poulter, B., & Zaehle, S. et al. (2017). Historical carbon dioxide emissions caused by land-use changes are possibly larger than assumed. *Nature Geoscience, 10*(2), 79–84. doi:10.1038/ngeo2882

Ascui, F., & Lovell, H. (2011). As frames collide. *Accounting. Auditing and Accountability, 24*, 978–999. doi:10.1108/09513571111184724

Ashmore, M. R. (2005). Assessing the future global impacts of ozone on vegetation. *Plant, Cell & Environment, 28*(8), 949–964. doi:10.1111/j.1365-3040.2005.01341.x

Bähr, C. C. (2015). Greenhouse gas taxes on meat products: A legal perspective. *Transnational Environmental Law, 4*(01), 153–179. doi:10.1017/S2047102515000011

Bailey, R., Froggatt, A., & Wellesley, L. (2014). *Livestock – climate change's forgotten sector: Global public opinion on meat and dairy consumption*. London, UK: Energy, Environment and Resources, Chatham House. Retrieved from http://www.chathamhouse.org/sites/files/chathamhouse/field/field_document/20141203LivestockClimateChangeBaileyFroggattWellesleyUpdate.pdf

Baron, R., Montgomery, W. D., & Tuladhar, S. (2009). *An analysis of black carbon mitigation as a response to climate change*. Washington, DC: Copenhagen Consensus Center. Retrieved from http://www.copenhagenconsensus.com/sites/default/files/ap_black_carbon_baron_montgomery_tuladhar_v.4.0.pdf

Benson, G. J., & Rollin, B. E. (Eds.). (2008). *The well-being of farm animals: Challenges and solutions.* Ames, IA: Blackwell Publishing.

Bhopal, V., Bola, G., Bottoms, I., Bromilow, J., Casson, L., & Hebditch, R. … Zeidler, M. (2013). *Zero carbon Britain: Rethinking the future.* Aberystwyth, UK: Centre for Alternative Technology. Retrieved from http://www.zerocarbonbritain.org/images/pdfs/ZCBrtflo-res.pdf

Blasing, T. J. (2013). *Recent greenhouse gas concentrations.* Oak Ridge, TN: Carbon Dioxide Information Analysis Centre; Retrieved from http://cdiac.ornl.gov/pns/current_ghg.html

Bond, T. C., Doherty, S. J., Fahey, D. W., Forster, P. M., Berntsen, T., DeAngelo, B. J., & Zender, C. S. et al. (2013). Bounding the role of black carbon in the climate system: A scientific assessment. *Journal of Geophysical Research, D, Atmospheres, 118*(11), 5380–5552. doi:10.1002/jgrd.50171

Briggs, A. D. M., Kehlbacher, A., Tiffin, R., Garnett, T., Rayner, M., & Scarborough, P. (2013). Assessing the impact on chronic disease of incorporating the societal cost of greenhouse gases into the price of food: An econometric and comparative risk assessment modelling study. *BMJ Open, 3*(10), e003543. doi:10.1136/bmjopen-2013-003543 PMID:24154517

Bryngelsson, D., Hedenus, F., Johansson, D. J. A., Azar, C., & Wirsenius, S. (2017). How do dietary choices influence the energy-system cost of stabilizing the climate? *Energies, 10*(2), 182. doi:10.3390/en10020182

Ciais, P., Sabine, C., Bala, G., Bopp, L., Brovkin, V., & Canadell, J. … Thornton, P.K. (2013). Carbon and other biogeochemical cycles. In *Climate Change 2013: The Physical Science Basis. Contribution of Working Group 1 to the Fifth Assessment Report of the Intergovernmental Panel on Climate Change.* Intergovernmental Panel on Climate Change (IPCC). Retrieved from https://www.ipcc.ch/pdf/assessment-report/ar5/wg1/WG1AR5_Chapter06_FINAL.pdf

Cribb, J. (2010). *The coming famine: The global food crisis and what we can do to avoid it.* Berkeley, CA: University of California Press.

Dawkins, M. (2017). Animal welfare and efficient farming: Is conflict inevitable? *Animal Production Science, 57*, 201–208.

Department of Climate Change and Energy Efficiency (DCCEE). (2012a). *Australian national greenhouse accounts national inventory report 2009.* Canberra, Australia: DCCEE. Retrieved from http://www.climatechange.gov.au/~/media/publications/greenhouse-acctg/national-inventory-report-2009-vol1.pdf

Department of Climate Change and Energy Efficiency (DCCEE). (2012b). *National inventory report (NIR) 2010 Australian national greenhouse accounts, The Australian Government: Submission to the United Nations Framework Convention on Climate Change.* Canberra, Australia: DCCEE. Retrieved from http://www.climatechange.gov.au/en/publications/greenhouse-acctg/national-inventory-report-2010.aspx

Dibb, S., & Fitzpatrick, I. (2014). *Let's talk about meat: Changing dietary behaviour for the 21st century.* Eating Better. Retrieved from http://www.eating-better.org/uploads/Documents/Let'sTalkAboutMeat.pdf?utm_source=FCRN+Mailing&utm_campaign=dc14cb3104-RSS_%2A%7CRSSFEED%3ADATE%3Aj+F+Y%7C%2A&utm_medium=email&utm_term=0_a29d7fdc4d-dc14cb3104-330057737

Drijfhout, S., Bathiany, S., Beaulieu, C., Brovkin, V., Claussen, M., & Huntingford, C. … Swingedouw, D. (2015). Catalogue of abrupt shifts in Intergovernmental Panel on Climate Change climate models. *Proceedings of the National Academy of Sciences* (pp. E5777–E5786).

Eckard, R. J., Grainger, C., & De Klein, C. A. M. (2010). Options for the abatement of methane and nitrous oxide from ruminant production: A review. *Livestock Science*, *130*(1), 47–56. doi:10.1016/j.livsci.2010.02.010

Emel, J., & Hawkins, R. (2010). Is it really easier to imagine the end of the world than the end of industrial meat? *Human Geographies*, *3*(2), 35–48.

Food and Agriculture Organisation of the United Nations (FAO). (2017). *Food outlook: Biannual report on global food markets*. Rome, Italy: FAO. Retrieved from http://www.fao.org/3/a-i7343e.pdf

Food and Agriculture Organisation of the United Nations (FAO). (n.d.). FAOSTAT Gateway. Retrieved from http://faostat3.fao.org/faostat-gateway/go/to/home/E

Forster, P., Ramaswamy, V., Artaxo, P., Berntsen, T., Betts, R., & Fahey, D. W. … Van Dorland, R. (2007). Changes in atmospheric constituents and in radiative forcing. In S. Soloman, D. Qin, M. Manning, M. Marquis, K. Averyt, & M.M.B. Tignor (Eds.), Climate change 2007: The physical science basis. contribution of Working Group I to the Fourth Assessment Report of the Intergovernmental Panel on Climate Change. Cambridge, UK: Cambridge University Press.

Forzieri, G., Feyen, L., Russo, S., Vousdoukas, M., Alfieri, L., Outten, S., & Cid, A. et al. (2016). Multi-hazard assessment in Europe under climate change. *Climatic Change*, *137*(1–2), 105–119. doi:10.1007/s10584-016-1661-x

Fowler, D. (2008). *Ground-level ozone in the 21st century: Future trends, impacts and policy implications. Science Policy Report 15/08*. London, UK: Royal Society. Retrieved from https://royalsociety.org/~/media/Royal_Society_Content/policy/publications/2008/7925.pdf

Fox, N. J., Davidson, R. S., Marion, G., & Hutchings, M. R. (2015). Modelling livestock parasite risk under climate change. *Advances in Animal Biosciences*, *6*(1), 32–34. doi:10.1017/S204047001400048X

Fry, M. M., Naik, V., West, J. J., Schwarzkopf, M. D., Fiore, A. M., Collins, W. J., & Zeng, G. et al. (2012). The influence of ozone precursor emissions from four world regions on tropospheric composition and radiative climate forcing. *Journal of Geophysical Research*, *117*(D7). doi:10.1029/2011JD017134

García Molinos, J., Halpern, B. S., Schoeman, D. S., Brown, C. J., Kiessling, W., Moore, P. J., & Burrows, M. T. et al. (2016). Climate velocity and the future global redistribution of marine biodiversity. *Nature Climate Change*, *6*(1), 83–88. doi:10.1038/nclimate2769

Garnett, T. (2011). Where are the best opportunities for reducing greenhouse gas emissions in the food system (including the food chain)? *Food Policy*, *36*, S23–S32. doi:10.1016/j.foodpol.2010.10.010

Gasser, T., Guivarch, C., Tachiiri, K., Jones, C. D., & Ciais, P. (2015). Negative emissions physically needed to keep global warming below 2 °C. *Nature Communications*, *6*, 7958. doi:10.1038/ncomms8958 PMID:26237242

Gerber, P. J., Steinfeld, H., Henderson, B., Mottet, A., Opio, C., & Dijkman, J. ... Tempio, G. (2013). *Tackling climate change through livestock: A global assessment of emissions and mitigation opportunities.* Rome, Italy: FAO. Retrieved from http://www.fao.org/docrep/018/i3437e/i3437e.pdf

Godfray, H. C. J., Beddington, J. R., Crute, I. R., Haddad, L., Lawrence, D., Muir, J. F., & Toulmin, C. et al. (2010). Food security: The challenge of feeding 9 billion people. *Science, 327*(5967), 812–818. doi:10.1126/science.1185383 PMID:20110467

Goodland, R., & Anhang, J. (2009). Livestock and climate change: What if the key actors in climate change are... cows, pigs and chickens? *World Watch Magazine*, November/December, 10-19. Retrieved from http://www.worldwatch.org/files/pdf/Livestock%20and%20Climate%20Change.pdf

Harwatt, H., Sabaté, J., Eshel, G., Soret, S., & Ripple, W. (2017). Substituting beans for beef as a contribution toward US climate change targets. *Climatic Change.* doi:10.1007/s10584-017-1969-1

Herrero, M., Henderson, B., Havlík, P., Thornton, P. K., Conant, R. T., Smith, P., & Stehfest, E. et al. (2016). Greenhouse gas mitigation potentials in the livestock sector. *Nature Climate Change*, *6*(5), 452–461. doi:10.1038/nclimate2925

Howarth, R. W. (2014). A bridge to nowhere: Methane emissions and the greenhouse gas footprint of natural gas. *Energy Science & Engineering*, *2*(2), 47–60. doi:10.1002/ese3.35

Hughes, L., Rickards, L. A., Steffen, W., Stock, P., & Rice, M. (2016). *On the frontline: Climate change & rural communities.* Sydney, Australia: Climate Council of Australia. Retrieved from https://www.climatecouncil.org.au/uploads/564abfd96ebac5cbc6cf45de2f17e12d.pdf

Jevrejeva, S., Jackson, L. P., Riva, R. E. M., Grinsted, A., & Moore, J. C. (2016). Coastal sea level rise with warming above 2°C. In *Proceedings of the National Academy of Sciences of the United States of America*, *113*(47), 13342–13347. doi:10.1073/pnas.1605312113 PMID:27821743

King, A. D., Karoly, D. J., & Henley, B. J. (2017). Australian climate extremes at 1.5°C and 2°C of global warming. *Nature Climate Change*, *7*(6), 412–416. doi:10.1038/nclimate3296

Kirschke, S., Bousquet, P., Ciais, P., Saunois, M., Canadell, J. G., Dlugokencky, E. J., & Zeng, G. et al. (2013). Three decades of global methane sources and sinks. *Nature Geoscience*, *6*(10), 813–823. doi:10.1038/ngeo1955

Knutti, R., Rogelj, J., Sedláček, J., & Fischer, E. M. (2016). A scientific critique of the two-degree climate change target. *Nature Geoscience*, *9*(1), 13–18. doi:10.1038/ngeo2595

Kopp, R.E., Shwom, R.L., Wagner, G., & Yuan, J. (2016). Tipping elements and climate–economic shocks: Pathways toward integrated assessment. *Earth's Future*, 4(8). doi:10.1002/2016EF000362

Lenton, T. M., Held, H., Kriegler, E., Hall, J. W., Lucht, W., Rahmstorf, S., & Schellnhuber, H. J. (2008). Tipping elements in the Earth's climate system. *Proceedings of the National Academy of Sciences of the United States of America*, *105*(6), 1786–1793. doi:10.1073/pnas.0705414105 PMID:18258748

Liverman, D., & Kapadia, K. (2010). Food systems and the global environment: An overview. In J. Ingram, P. Ericksen, & D. Liverman (Eds.), *Food Security and Global Environmental Change* (pp. 3–24). London, UK: Earthscan.

Llonch, P., Haskell, M. J., Dewhurst, R. J., & Turner, S. P. (2017). Current available strategies to mitigate greenhouse gas emissions in livestock systems: An animal welfare perspective. *Animal*, *11*(2), 274–284. doi:10.1017/S1751731116001440 PMID:27406001

Longmire, A., Taylor, C., & Wedderburn-Bisshop, G. (2014). *Land use: Agriculture and forestry discussion paper*. Melbourne, Australia: Beyond Zero Emissions; Melbourne Sustainable Society Institute. Retrieved from http://bze.org.au/land-use-agriculture-and-forestry/

Manning, M., & Reisinger, A. (2011). Broader perspectives for comparing different greenhouse gases. *Philosophical Transactions of the Royal Society A: Mathematical, Physical and Engineering Sciences*, *369*(1943), 1891–1905. doi:10.1098/rsta.2010.0349 PMID:21502165

Martin, P., & Williams, J. (2011). Renegotiating farmers' social licence. In *Defending the Social Licence of Farming: Issues, challenges and new directions for agriculture* (pp. 195–202). Melbourne, Australia: CSIRO Publishing.

McGregor, A., & Houston, D. (2017). Cattle in the Anthropocene: Four propositions. *Transactions of the Institute of British Geographers*, *6/30*. doi:10.1111/tran.12193

McMichael, A. J., Powles, J. W., Butler, C. D., & Uauy, R. (2007). Food, livestock production, energy, climate change, and health. *Lancet*, *370*(9594), 1253–1263. doi:10.1016/S0140-6736(07)61256-2 PMID:17868818

Mottet, A., Henderson, B., Opio, C., Falcucci, A., Tempio, G., Silvestri, S., & Gerber, P. J. et al. (2017). Climate change mitigation and productivity gains in livestock supply chains: Insights from regional case studies. *Regional Environmental Change*, *17*(1), 129–141. doi:10.1007/s10113-016-0986-3

Nardone, A., Ronchi, B., Lacetera, N., Ranieri, M. S., & Bernabucci, U. (2010). Effects of climate changes on animal production and sustainability of livestock systems. *Livestock Science*, *130*(1), 57–69. doi:10.1016/j.livsci.2010.02.011

National Health and Medical Research Council (NHMRC). (2013). *Australian Dietary Guidelines*. Canberra, Australia: NHMRC. Retrieved from https://www.nhmrc.gov.au/_files_nhmrc/file/publications/n55_australian_dietary_guidelines1.pdf

Nisbet, E. G., Dlugokencky, E. J., & Bousquet, P. (2014). Methane on the rise—again. *Science*, *343*(6170), 493–495. doi:10.1126/science.1247828 PMID:24482471

Pacifici, M., Visconti, P., Butchart, S. H. M., Watson, J. E. M., Cassola, F. M., & Rondinini, C. (2017). Species' traits influenced their response to recent climate change. *Nature Climate Change*, *7*(3), 205–208. doi:10.1038/nclimate3223

Pecl, G. T., Araújo, M. B., Bell, J. D., Blanchard, J., Bonebrake, T. C., Chen, I.-C., … Williams, S. E. (2017). Biodiversity redistribution under climate change: Impacts on ecosystems and human well-being. *Science*, 355(6332). doi:10.1126/science.aai9214

Pelletier, N., & Tyedmers, P. (2010). Forecasting potential global environmental costs of livestock production 2000-2050. *Proceedings of the National Academy of Sciences of the United States of America*, *107*(43), 18371–18374. doi:10.1073/pnas.1004659107 PMID:20921375

Princen, T., Manno, J., & Martin, P. (Eds.). (2015). *Ending the fossil fuel era*. Cambridge, MA: MIT Press. doi:10.7551/mitpress/9780262028806.001.0001

Prusty, S., Kundu, S. S., & Kumar Sharma, V. (2017). Nutrient utilization and methane emissions in Murrah buffalo calves fed on diets with different methanogenic potential. *Livestock Science*, *202*, 89–95. doi:10.1016/j.livsci.2017.05.023

Ray, D. K., Mueller, N. D., West, P. C., & Foley, J. A. (2013). Yield trends are insufficient to double global crop production by 2050. *PLoS One*, *8*(6), e66428. doi:10.1371/journal.pone.0066428 PMID:23840465

Rogelj, J., Schaeffer, M., Meinshausen, M., Shindell, D. T., Hare, W., & Klimont, Z., … Schellnhuber, H. J. (2014). Disentangling the effects of CO2 and short-lived climate forcer mitigation. In *Proceedings of the National Academy of Sciences* (Vol. 111, pp. 16325-16330).

Rojas-Downing, M. M., Nejadhashemi, A. P., Harrigan, T., & Woznicki, S. A. (2017). Climate change and livestock: Impacts, adaptation, and mitigation. *Climate Risk Management*, *16*, 145–163. doi:10.1016/j.crm.2017.02.001

Saunois, M., Jackson, R. B., Bousquet, P., Poulter, B., & Canadell, J. G. (2016). The growing role of methane in anthropogenic climate change. *Environmental Research Letters*, *11*(12), 120207. doi:10.1088/1748-9326/11/12/120207

Schewe, R. L., & Stuart, D. (2017). Why don't they just change? Contract farming, informational influence, and barriers to agricultural climate change mitigation. *Rural Sociology*, *82*(2), 226–262. doi:10.1111/ruso.12122

Schwarzer, S. (2012). *Growing greenhouse gas emissions due to meat production*. Geneva, Switzerland: UNEP Global Environmental Alert Service (GEAS). Retrieved from http://www.unep.org/pdf/UNEP-GEAS_OCT_2012.pdf

Schwietzke, S., Sherwood, O. A., Bruhwiler, L. M. P., Miller, J. B., Etiope, G., Dlugokencky, E. J., & Tans, P. P. et al. (2016). Upward revision of global fossil fuel methane emissions based on isotope database. *Nature*, *538*(7623), 88–91. doi:10.1038/nature19797 PMID:27708291

Shields, S., & Orme-Evans, G. (2015). The impacts of climate change mitigation strategies on animal welfare. *Animals (Basel)*, *5*(2), 361–394. doi:10.3390/ani5020361 PMID:26479240

Shine, K. P. (2012). The global warming potential—the need for an interdisciplinary retrial. *Climatic Change*, *96*(4), 467–472. doi:10.1007/s10584-009-9647-6

Shoemaker, J., & Schrag, D. (2013). The danger of overvaluing methane's influence on future climate change. *Climatic Change*, *120*(4), 903–914. doi:10.1007/s10584-013-0861-x

Smil, V. (2013). *Should we eat meat evolution and consequences of modern carnivory*. Chichester, UK: Wiley-Blackwell. doi:10.1002/9781118278710

Smith, K. R., Desai, M. A., Rogers, J. V., & Houghton, R. A. (2013). Joint CO_2 and CH_4 accountability for global warming. *Proceedings of the National Academy of Sciences of the United States of America*, *110*(31), E2865–E2874. doi:10.1073/pnas.1308004110 PMID:23847202

Smith, P., Nayak, D., Linthorst, G., Peters, D., & Bucquet, C. (2016). *Science-based GHG emissions targets for agriculture and forestry commodities*. University of Aberdeen, ECOFYS; PBL Netherlands Environmental Assessment Agency. Retrieved from http://www.pbl.nl/sites/default/files/cms/publicaties/pbl-2016-science-based-greenhouse-gas-emissions-targets-for-agriculture-and-forestry-commodities-2856.pdf

Springmann, M., Godfray, H. C. J., Rayner, M., & Scarborough, P. (2016). Analysis and valuation of the health and climate change cobenefits of dietary change. *Proceedings of the National Academy of Sciences of the United States of America, 113*(15), 4146–4151. doi:10.1073/pnas.1523119113 PMID:27001851

Stehfest, E., Bouwman, L., van Vuuren, D. P., den Elzen, M. G., Eickhout, B., & Kabat, P. (2009). Climate benefits of changing diet. *Climatic Change, 95*(1–2), 83–102. doi:10.1007/s10584-008-9534-6

Steinfeld, H., Gerber, P., Wassenaar, T., Castel, V., Rosales, M., & de Haan, C. (2006). *Livestock's long shadow: Environmental issues and options*. Rome, Italy: Food and Agriculture Organization of the United Nations; Retrieved from http://www.fao.org/docrep/010/a0701e/a0701e00.HTM

Stocker, T., Qin, D., Plattner, G.-K., & Tignor, M. (2013). *Climate change 2013, The physical science basis. Contribution of Working Group I to the Fifth Assessment Report of the Intergovernmental Panel on Climate Change*. IPCC. Retrieved from https://www.ipcc.ch/report/ar5/wg1/

Stoll-Kleemann, S., & Schmidt, U. J. (2017). Reducing meat consumption in developed and transition countries to counter climate change and biodiversity loss: A review of influence factors. *Regional Environmental Change, 17*(5), 1261–1277. doi:10.1007/s10113-016-1057-5

Stuart, D., & Schewe, R. L. (2016). Constrained choice and climate change mitigation in US agriculture: Structural barriers to a climate change ethic. *Journal of Agricultural & Environmental Ethics, 29*(3), 369–385. doi:10.1007/s10806-016-9605-z

Tschakert, P. (2015). 1.5°C or 2°C: A conduit's view from the science-policy interface at COP20 in Lima, Peru. *Climate Change Responses, 2*(1), 3. doi:10.1186/s40665-015-0010-z

Unger, N., Shindell, D., Koch, D., & Streets, D. (2008). Air pollution radiative forcing from specific emissions sectors at 2030. *Journal of Geophysical Research, 113*(D2), D02306. doi:10.1029/2007JD008683

United Nations Environment Program and World Meteorological Office (UNEP/WMO). (2011). *Integrated assessment of black carbon and tropospheric ozone: Summary for decision makers*. UNEP/WM. Retrieved from http://www.unep.org/dewa/Portals/67/pdf/Black_Carbon.pdf

Van Dingenen, R., Dentener, F. J., Raes, F., Krol, M. C., Emberson, L., & Cofala, J. (2009). The global impact of ozone on agricultural crop yields under current and future air quality legislation. *Atmospheric Environment, 43*(3), 604–618. doi:10.1016/j.atmosenv.2008.10.033

van Marle, M. J. E., Field, R. D., van der Werf, G. R., Estrada de Wagt, I. A., Houghton, R. A., Rizzo, L. V., & Tsigaridis, K. et al. (2017). Fire and deforestation dynamics in Amazonia (1973-2014). *Global Biogeochemical Cycles, 31*(1), 24–38. doi:10.1002/2016GB005445 PMID:28286373

Vermeulen, S. J., Campbell, B. M., & Ingram, J. S. I. (2012). Climate change and food systems. *Annual Review of Environment and Resources, 37*(1), 195–222. doi:10.1146/annurev-environ-020411-130608

Wedderburn-Bisshop, G., Longmire, A., & Rickards, L. A. (2015). Neglected transformational responses: Implications of excluding short lived emissions and near-term projections in greenhouse gas accounting. *The International Journal of Climate Change: Impacts and Responses*, *7*(3), 11–27.

Wellesley, L., Happer, C., & Froggatt, A. (2015). *Changing climate, Changing diets: Pathways to lower meat consumption*. London, UK: Chatham House Report. Retrieved from https://www.chathamhouse.org/sites/files/chathamhouse/publications/research/CHHJ3820%20Diet%20and%20climate%20change%2018.11.15_WEB_NEW.pdf

Wiedemann, S., McGahan, E., Murphy, C., & Yan, M. (2016). Resource use and environmental impacts from beef production in eastern Australia investigated using life cycle assessment. *Animal Production Science*, *56*(5), 882–894. doi:10.1071/AN14687

Wilkie, R. (2017). Animals as sentient commodities. In L. Kalof (Ed.), *The Oxford handbook of animal studies* (pp. 279–301). Oxford, UK: Oxford University Press.

World Meteorological Organisation (WMO). (2016). *The global climate in 2011-2015*. Geneva, Switzerland: WMO. Retrieved from http://ane4bf-datap1.s3-eu-west-1.amazonaws.com/wmocms/s3fs-public/1179_EN.pdf

KEY TERMS AND DEFINITIONS

Commodification: Turning of something which has an intrinsic value, such as natural resources, animals or human beings, into commodities. This includes treatment of sentient beings as units of production for sale, stripped of their existential value and moral worth.

Enteric Fermentation: The digestion process of multi-stomach ruminant animals (cattle, sheep, goats) that produces methane emissions.

Framing: The way different understandings of the world are shaped by social factors, including language, images, equations, maps and conventions.

Global Warming Potential (GWP): The radiative forcing (warming) of an emission relative to the radiative forcing of carbon dioxide for a given period. The Intergovernmental Panel on Climate Change (IPCC) lists GWPs of all greenhouse emissions for 20, 100 and 500 year periods.

Greenhouse Gas Accounting: A way of keeping an inventory and auditing of all gases causing a greenhouse effect generated by all sources, including business activities, organisations and individuals. It can be done on the basis of consumption or production. The period of accounting for the effect, for example over 20 or 100 years, influences the outcomes in terms of the contribution of the various greenhouse gases.

Mitigation: Actions directed towards reducing the impacts or severity of something. For example, climate change mitigation policy refers to policy actions to reduce the severity of impact of climate change.

Near-Term Climate Forcers (NTCFs): Greenhouse emissions with an atmospheric lifetime of 10 years or less; used interchangeably with short-term emissions. Methane, with a lifetime of 10 years, is classified by the IPCC as both a near-term and a long-term climate forcer.

Negative/Positive Feedback on Climate Change: Impacts on climate change which reduce/add to the level of global warming.

Chapter 4
Economic and Environmental Costs of Meat Waste in the US

Nicholas Hardersen
University of Oklahoma, USA

Jadwiga R. Ziolkowska
University of Oklahoma, USA

ABSTRACT

Food waste is a major issue around the globe impacting food security, resource use, economic operations, and the environment. Meat waste, constituting approximately half of total annual meat production in the United States, is particularly relevant to address due to significant resource inputs used in livestock breeding and the meat production process. In this chapter, the authors monetize annual costs of natural resources including water, land, and energy, as well as emissions of methane and nitrous oxide embedded in wasted meat in the United States. Results indicate the total annual cost of $32-32.5 billion. The outcomes substantiate the need to reduce current levels of wasted meat in order to minimize economic, social, and environmental impacts on natural resources and make food and meat production more sustainable.

INTRODUCTION

One-quarter to one-half of total agricultural production is wasted at different points along the global food supply chain each year, amounting to approximately 1.3 billion tons (Gustavsson et al., 2011; Kummu et al., 2012; Lipinski et al., 2013; Lundqvist et al., 2008). Regardless of the varying estimates in the literature, the amount of wasted food is substantial and directly translates into quantities of natural resources used for food production that are also wasted when food is discarded. The food waste problem and its impacts are discussed below followed by a closer exploration of animal husbandry and meat waste.

DOI: 10.4018/978-1-5225-4757-0.ch004

Food Waste Problem and Impacts on Natural Resources

Global food surplus, and particularly the surplus in high-income developed countries, has increased dramatically in the last few decades and is a root cause of food waste (Papargyropoulou et al., 2014). Agronomists recommend a food supply of 130 percent (2600 kcal/capita/day) to protect against unexpected environmental disasters as a result of resource overuse that may cause famine (Papargyropoulou et al., 2014). High-income developed countries regularly produce on average at least 1000 kcal/capita/day above the recommended food supply (1500 kcal/capita/day extra in the US), which could feed nearly 700 million people with an adequate vegetarian diet (Smil, 2004).

Both developed and developing countries generate large quantities of food waste, though they differ substantially in terms of where it occurs in the supply chain. Poor infrastructure for post-harvest storage, handling and distribution are the primary reasons why food is wasted in developing countries. On the contrary, in developed countries, while significant amounts of food are lost early in the supply chain due to out-grading from superficial appearance standards or unfavorable market conditions, negligent consumer behavior is responsible for the largest share of waste (Figure 1). According to Gustavsson et al. (2011), consumers in developed countries waste approximately 95-115 kg/capita/year, whereas consumers in developing countries waste only 6-11 kg/capita/year.

In the United States (US), since 1974 waste has increased by 50 percent along the food supply chain and amounted to losses of 1400 kcal/capita/day, or 150 trillion kcal/year in 2009 (Hall et al., 2009). In 2012, the US produced 518 billion pounds (or 235 billion kg) of food, of which 45 percent was lost or wasted (Toth & Dou, 2016). Consumers were responsible for 47 percent (i.e., 110 billion pounds) of wasted food, while retail was responsible for 19 percent (i.e., 45 billion pounds) (Toth & Dou, 2016). The total economic value of food waste at the retail and consumer level in the United States is worth a staggering \$165.6 billion, or \$390/capita/year (Buzby & Hyman, 2012). Over half of the total consumer

Figure 1. Food lost or wasted by region and stage in value chain, 2009 (percent of kcal lost and wasted)
Source: Lipinski et al. (2013) based on FAO (2011)

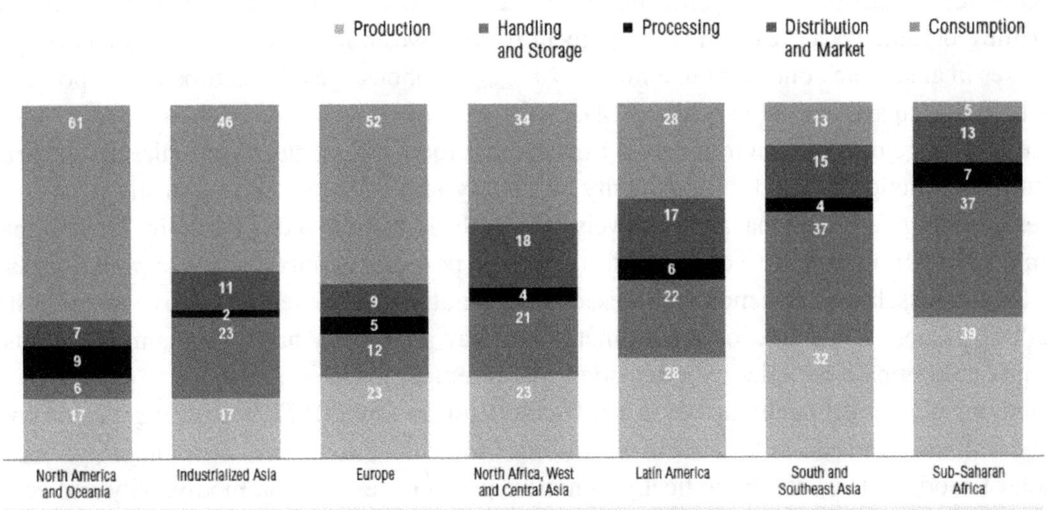

**For a more accurate representation see the electronic version.*

generated economic losses ($197/capita/year) was from meat waste. Wasting meat and meat products can have the most serious environmental impacts out of all food categories due to the resource-intensive nature of animal husbandry, which is the focus of this chapter and is discussed in the following sections.

Another major problem related to food waste regards the numerous implications for resource loss and environmental degradation. Food production covers 38 percent of global ice-free land area, of which 12 percent (1.53 billion ha) is devoted to crops and 26 percent (3.38 billion ha) is devoted to pastures (Foley et al., 2011). The total land area used to grow food that is eventually wasted equals 1.4 billion ha, or 30 percent of the global agricultural land (FAO, 2013). Toth and Dou (2016) estimated that 65 million acres of US cropland is embedded in food waste, while 40 million of these acres are used to grow crops for animal feed.

Other environmental impacts related to food waste regard application of artificial fertilizers, which can be beneficial for increasing crop yields initially, but over time its excessive use contributes to soil, water and air pollution (Sage, 2012). Uptake rates of fertilizers by plants are inefficient at approximately 40-50 percent, meaning that at least half of applied fertilizers are dispersed into the environment (Sage, 2012). Moreover, chemical runoff from fertilizers contributes to freshwater pollution in aquifers and surface bodies and is also the major cause of hypoxic zones found on coastlines around the world, and in the Gulf of Mexico in the US (Diaz & Rosenberg, 2008). Fertilizer use is also the major cause of nitrous oxide (N_2O) emissions, a greenhouse gas (GHG) 256 times more potent than carbon dioxide (CO_2). The US agriculture emits 318.4 million metric tons of N_2O each year from soil management (EPA, 2016). Considering that 45 percent of food in the US is wasted, 143.28 million metric tons of N_2O emissions result from waste each year (Toth & Dou, 2016).

In addition, one quarter of freshwater usage globally and in the US is embedded in food waste (Hall et al., 2009; Kummu et al., 2012; Toth & Dou, 2016). According to Toth & Dou (2016), 18 trillion gallons (or 68 trillion litres) of irrigation water in the US was used to grow wasted food in 2012, mostly in central and western regions where aquifers and surface water bodies are already used at unsustainable rates.

Moreover, greenhouse gas emissions occur at every stage of the food supply chain, from farm to fork and at disposal. Global annual emissions from food waste equal 3.3 Gt of CO_2 emission equivalent (FAO, 2013). One mitigation option to significantly decrease food waste emissions is to eliminate the practice of landfilling organic waste. Currently, 97 percent of food waste in the US is sent to landfill where it decomposes in anaerobic conditions to emit methane, a greenhouse gas 21-25 times more powerful than carbon dioxide (Papargryopoulou et al., 2014).

There is a range of other environmental impacts that food waste can cause indirectly as a result of agricultural production methods. Biodiversity and ecosystem services are two of the most important measures of ecological health that are negatively affected by industrialized agriculture. These impacts are occurring mainly from excessive chemical fertilizer and pesticide inputs that cause pollution, land-use change, habitat loss, large-scale monocultures, overexploitation, and generate invasive species (Steinfeld et al., 2006). Issues related to ecosystem functioning may potentially have serious implications in the future that could impact societies over extended spatio-temporal scales.

Monetizing ecological health however is difficult (Ziolkowska, 2017). Integrating its true costs into economic valuations needs to be prioritized in order to achieve long-term sustainability. Substantial reduction of food waste could theoretically minimize pressures exerted on biodiversity and ecosystem services. While recognizing the difficulty of quantifying economic and environmental impacts of food waste, following a study by Ziolkowska (2017), this research aims at monetizing food waste and resource losses related to animal and meat production in the US.

Impacts of Animal Husbandry and Meat Waste

By 2050, the world population is expected to reach 9 billion people, which will result in a 70-100 percent increase in food demand (Godfray et al., 2010). Global Gross Domestic Product (GDP) per capita is also expected to increase steadily at 2 percent/annum (Kearney, 2010). Rising incomes have been correlated with increasing meat consumption and decreasing consumption of staple crops at the same time (Bouwman et al., 2013; Kearney, 2010; McMichael et al., 2007; Steinfeld et al., 2006). China is a prime example of this transformation. Between 1963 and 2003 the GDP/capita increased from $74.3 to $1,288.6, while meat consumption increased by 349 percent in the same time frame (Kearney, 2010; World Bank, 2017). The average global increase in meat consumption during this time period has been much less drastic at 63 percent (Kearney, 2010), however, meat production is projected to more than double from 229 million tons in 1999/2001 to 465 million tons in 2050 (Steinfeld et al., 2006). The rapidly growing demand for meat will be met almost entirely through industrial livestock production systems, including concentrated animal feed operations (CAFOs), intensification of existing grazing systems, and spatial expansion of managed grazing systems largely in tropical forests (McAlpine et al., 2009; Naylor et al., 2005). Considering that one-third of global crop production is already fed to livestock, it should be expected that this pattern may intensify substantially in the future. Consequently, insuring food security for 9 billion people might prove to be very challenging due to limited resource availability.

Raising livestock for human consumption is a very resource-intensive process. This is true for both industrial and pasture systems, though pasture systems generally pose lower environmental impacts as they do not rely on growing crops for feed. Livestock production has been described as the "single largest anthropogenic user of land" and it occupies 3.73 billion hectares, or around 75 percent of global agricultural land (Steinfeld et al., 2006, p. xxi). Water requirements for livestock vary considerably among animals, though each animal has extremely high consumptive water use. In comparison to the water requirements for production of 1 kg of wheat (500-4 000 liters), producing 1 kg meat requires 5000-20000 liters (Lundqvist et al., 2008). Most of the water requirements to produce meat stem from the feed conversion efficiency of an animal, feed composition and origin of the feed (Mekonnen & Hoekstra, 2010). Around 18 percent of anthropogenic GHG emissions are attributable to livestock, of which most are methane and nitrous oxide emissions (McAlpine et al., 2009). Livestock contributes significantly to acidification and eutrophication of ecosystems from manure and soil management (Figure 2). They can also degrade soil through compaction and from overgrazing which eventually causes erosion. Producing meat is inherently inefficient due to poor feed conversion efficiencies, particularly in ruminants (Pimentel & Pimentel, 2008). Poor feed conversion efficiency means that more crops must be grown to produce the desired amount of protein, which translates to higher inputs of water, energy, and land. Beef is the most inefficient and resource-intensive animal to raise among all livestock categories and contributes the most to GHG emissions (de Vries & de Boer, 2010). According to Smil (2002), 89-97 percent of the gross energy content and 80-96 percent of total protein content in feed crops are not converted to edible protein and fat. Moreover, there is enough energy content in the 700 million tons of cereal and legumes fed to livestock each year to feed more than three billion people on a diet of corn, barley, sorghum and soy (de Vries & de Boer, 2010).

Also, the resource intensity and environmentally damaging aspects of livestock production raise important ethical questions about livestock breeding, meat consumption, living conditions and animal treatment. Questions are being raised about the legitimacy of animal production in the face of one billion people lacking food security as of today, while this number is anticipated to increase drastically by

Figure 2. Percentage of the overall national environmental burdens exerted by the individual animal categories
Source: Eshel et al. (2014)
Legend: Nr – reactive nitrogen fertilizer

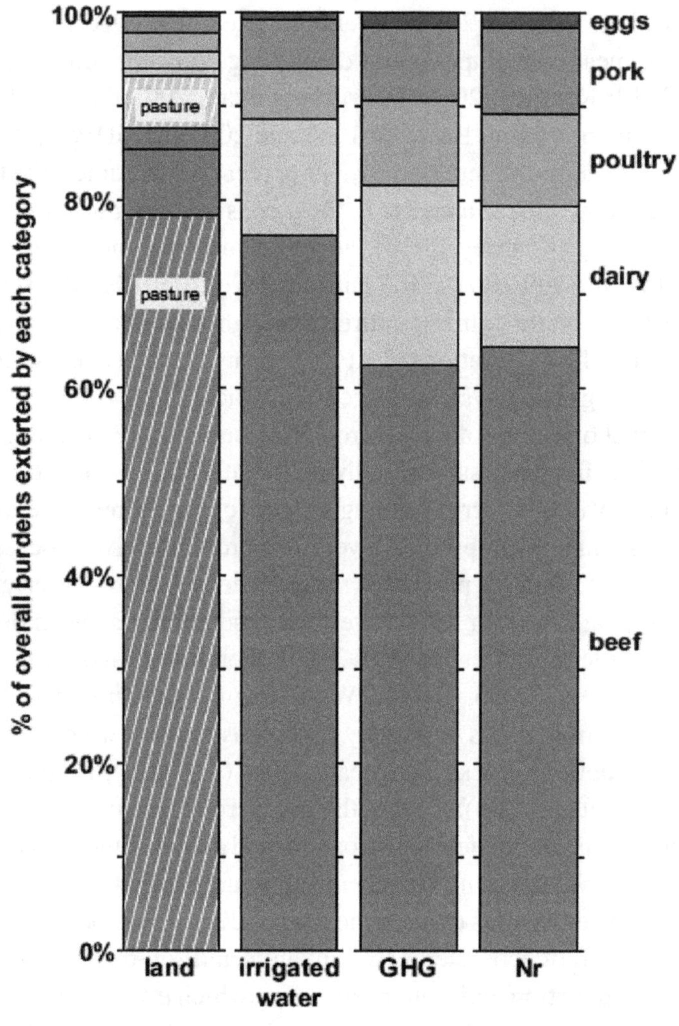

2050 due to increasing population (Pimentel & Pimentel, 2008; Smil, 2002). An additional 2.5 billion hectares would be required if the entire world population consumed 80 kg of meat/capita/year, which is the average intake of meat in a Western diet (Naylor et al., 2005). Although this scenario is unlikely to happen, a significant increase in meat consumption is expected (Keyzer et al., 2005), which will put substantially more pressure on resources and the environment.

A consequent question refers to ethical and moral aspects of wasting meat. According to Lipinski et al. (2013), of the 1.3 billion tons or 1.5 quadrillion kcal of food wasted each year, meat waste comprises 4% of total weight and 7% of total calories wasted. This means that 52 million tons or 105 trillion kcal of meat are wasted each year, which is equivalent to 16.8 percent of the total livestock production of 308.5 million tons in 2013 (FAO, 2014). Further, this equals 19 percent of total kcal available from meat (Lipinski et al., 2013). Although the proportion of meat waste is small compared to other food categories, meat requires significantly more resources to produce and causes significantly more environmental impacts than typical grains, fruit or vegetable crops (Pimentel & Pimentel, 2008). In developing countries meat is often lost or wasted in agricultural production due to high animal mortality rates from diseases and also due to poor infrastructure and distribution networks that fail to keep meat from spoiling (Gustavsson et al., 2011). In developed countries, consumption and retail stages of the food supply chain comprise approximately 50 percent of the total meat waste (Gustavsson et al., 2011). In the US, meat waste makes up 17.7 percent of the total food waste stream (Toth & Dou, 2016). As a percentage of total meat production, 41.5 billion pounds out of 83 billion pounds, i.e., 49.8 percent, were wasted in 2012 (Toth & Dou, 2016). In monetary values, in 2008, food loss of meat, poultry, and fish combined amounted to $66 231 million (41% of the total value of food loss in that year), while dairy product waste contributed by the additional 14% (Figure 3).

RESEARCH PURPOSE AND RELEVANCE

This chapter presents an economic cost analysis related to meat waste in the US. Wasted meat makes up 49.8 percent of the total meat production in the US (Toth & Dou, 2016). Meat waste surrounds two main issues: 1) resource use, environmental impacts and costs of raising livestock, and 2) economic and environmental impacts of wasting meat and meat products.

Figure 3. Different food groups' contribution to the total value of food loss ($165,579 million) in US in 2008
Source: Authors' presentation according to Buzby and Hyman (2012)

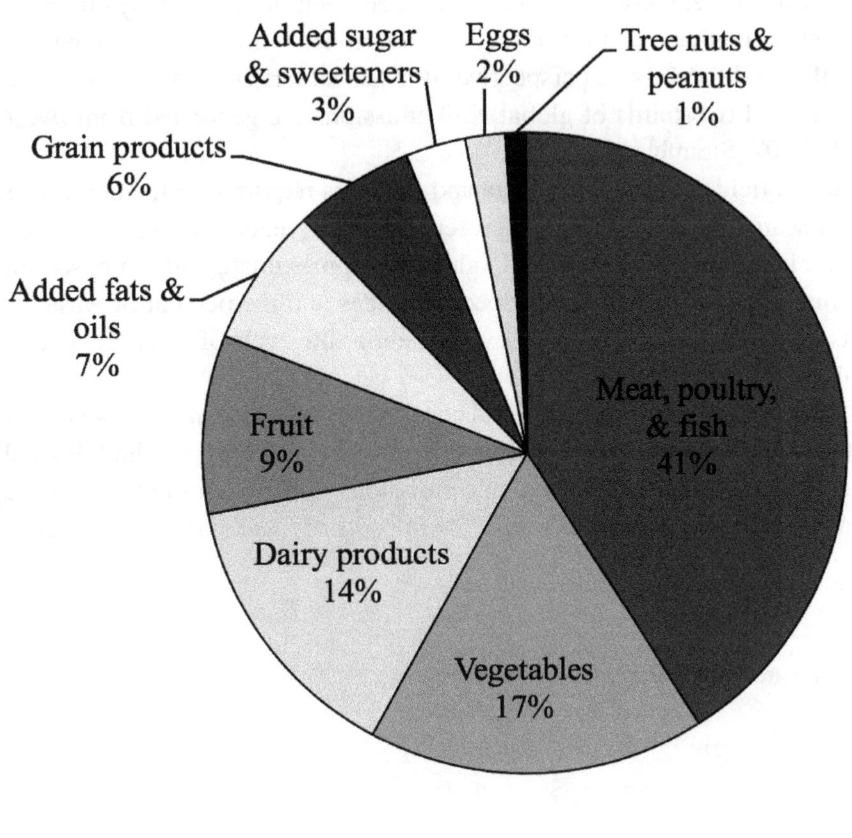

Livestock production is very resource intensive, particularly in terms of land, water and energy use (Eshel et al., 2014; Pimentel & Pimentel, 2008; Steinfeld et al., 2006). It is also the largest anthropogenic contributor to methane and nitrous oxide emissions, which are much more powerful GHGs than carbon dioxide. Wasting meat has high opportunity costs as these resources and money applied to meat production could be used in alternative ways to cope with other social issues, e.g. health problems caused by industrial agriculture.

While there is a common understanding about tremendous resource inputs for meat production, research quantifying those inputs and economic losses is still limited, as it is challenging at the same time due to data paucity. However, monetizing resource costs and GHG emissions associated with food waste that causes economic losses, environmental degradation and food insecurity may be a powerful tool for raising awareness, educating and incentivizing individuals, corporations, and governments to undertake actions towards reducing food waste (Ziolkowska, 2017).

Building on a study by Ziolkowska (2017) who quantified economic costs of the total food waste in the US, this chapter provides new insights into an economic analysis of resource and monetary losses caused specifically by meat waste.

METHODOLOGY AND DATA

For the presented analysis, a literature review on statistical specifications of meat waste and resource waste for meat production, has been conducted based on peer-reviewed journal articles, book chapters, and numerous reports from US Department of Agriculture (USDA), Environmental Protection Agency (EPA), and nonprofit organizations. Further, quantitative estimation of monetary costs related to meat waste and resource use for meat production was calculated, focused specifically on costs of energy, water and land use as well as methane and nitrous oxide emissions. While N_2O is not necessarily a relevant gas emitter from the total food waste perspective, it is particularly relevant to consider in calculations of meat waste as around two-thirds of global N_2O emissions are generated from livestock production (McMichael et al., 2007; Steinfeld et al., 2006).

As research in this field is still limited, data and statistics required for the analysis presented in this chapter have been scarce at times or they represent different years due to missing temporal analyses on this topic in the literature. The calculated values are approximate and are based on the amount of resources used/emissions generated, their respective prices and the percent of wasted meat within the US. These results do not represent total costs over the entire life cycle of meat production, consumption, and disposal which are much higher.

The analysis of monetary resource losses and costs associated with meat waste is based on the methodology presented by Ziolkowska (2017), while this study expands this methodological application by including nitrous oxide assessment and methane emissions in the meat pre-disposal stage. A series of equations presented below are used to calculate the impacts of meat waste on natural resources.

Water

The cost of wasted water was calculated as follows:

$$\text{Cost of water for meat production}(\$) = \text{price of water per acre}(\$ / ac) * \text{irrigated acres for feed crops and animal husbandry}(ac) \quad (1)$$

$$\text{Cost of wasted water in meat production}(\$) = \%\ \text{of wasted meat products} * \text{cost of water for meat production} \quad (2)$$

Only direct water costs were considered in this analysis, while water costs related to production factors were omitted here, as it would go beyond the scope of this study.

The total land area used for cropland in the US in 2013 was 408 million acres, of which 55.3 million acres were irrigated (USDA, 2014). Of the 55.3 million irrigated acres, 27 percent were used to grow feed crops, which equals 14.9 million acres (Eshel et al., 2014). For non-feed crop purposes, additional irrigation is required to raise livestock. In 2013, non-feed crop irrigation requirements equaled 7 480 247 acres and were as follows: 5 966 127 acres for beef cattle ranching and farming, 698 465 acres for cattle feedlots and 815 655 acres for all other animal specialties (USDA, 2014). Thus, the total irrigation requirements to raise livestock in 2013 were 22 380 247 acres. The price of water in 2008 was $26–$71 per acre (Ziolkowska, 2017), while the 'shadow price' of water was not considered (Ziolkowska, 2015), which would otherwise elevate the cost of water applied in this analysis. Two calculations were conducted to estimate the cost of wasted water, based on the minimum and maximum costs for water per acre in 2008 (rather than averaging the data) to provide a more detailed picture of the cost estimates.

Land

The cost of land use embedded in meat waste was calculated based on the following three equations to account for the different agricultural land uses and their differing prices per acre:

$$\textit{Cost of land use}(\$)[\text{irrigated cropland}] = \text{land rent}(\$) * \%\ \text{of wasted meat products} \quad (3)$$

$$\textit{Cost of land use}(\$)[\text{non - irrigated cropland}] = \text{land rent}(\$) * \%\ \text{of wasted meat products} \quad (4)$$

$$\textit{Cost of land use}(\$)[\text{pastureland}] = \text{land rent pastureland} * \%\ \text{of wasted meat products} \quad (5)$$

For equation 3, the total irrigated acres for feed crops (14.9 million acres) (Eshel et al., 2014) and acres for animal husbandry (7.5 million acres) (USDA, 2014) were summed up to a total of 22.4 million acres. The land rent for irrigated cropland in 2014 ranged from $64 to $405 per acre (USDA, 2015). To derive the total land rent for irrigated acres, the minimum and maximum land rent values were each multiplied by the total irrigated acres for livestock, and finally averaged.

In equation 4, non-irrigated acres for livestock production embedded in meat waste, the total irrigated acres for feed crops we subtracted from the total acreage used for crops and processed roughage that amounted to 0.6 million km^2 (148.2 million acres) annually from 2000 to 2010 (Eshel et al., 2014). Subtracting 14.9 million irrigated acres for feed crops from the total acreage used for crops and processed roughage (148.3 million acres) resulted in the total of 133.4 million non-irrigated acres. In 2014, the land rent for non-irrigated acres ranged from $14 to $206 per acre (USDA, 2015). Irrigated acres were calculated with the same methodological procedure as above, where the minimum and maximum land rent cost for non-irrigated acres were each multiplied by the total non-irrigated acres. Ultimately the values were averaged for clarity of the presented calculations and results and due to the fact that each equation relied on different land rent costs.

The annual land rent for pastureland in the US was $7.4 billion in 2014 (Ziolkowska, 2017). This calculation is based on an assumption that the majority of pastureland is used to raise livestock, though there might be slight deviations in terms of differing pastureland uses. This could arise from the emerging trend of agro-ecological farming methods that combine livestock and crop production. However, these types of land uses still remain marginal at this point in time. The annual land rent for pastureland, $7.4 billion, was multiplied by the percent of wasted meat in 2012, namely 49.8% (Toth & Dou, 2016).

Energy

The cost of lost energy from meat waste was calculated with the following equation:

$$\text{Cost of lost energy from wasted meat}(\$) = \sum \begin{bmatrix} \textit{energy lost}(BTU) * \% \text{ of energy source used} \\ *\text{price for energy source}(\$ / \text{million BTU}) \end{bmatrix} \quad (6)$$

Both direct and indirect energy costs from wasted meat were considered. Direct energy sources on farms in 2011 made up 66 percent of total energy use, while indirect sources represented 34 percent (Ziolkowska, 2017). The energy source estimates were derived from Miranowski (2002). Direct energy sources account for: 27 percent from diesel; 9 percent from gasoline; 5 percent from LP gas/propane; 4 percent from natural gas; and 21 percent from electricity. Indirect energy sources include: 28 percent for fertilizers production and 6 percent for pesticide production. The prices for energy sources were derived from Rapier (2010) and are as follows (in $/million BTU[1]): $15.49 for diesel; $17.81 for gasoline; $13.28 for LP gas/propane; $5.69 for natural gas; $26.31 for electricity; and $1.32 for coal. The amount of energy lost from wasted meat in the US in 2007 amounted to 972.1 trillion BTU (Cuéllar & Webber, 2010). This estimate includes energy used in production, transportation, handling and processing of meat. To calculate the cost of direct energy losses from meat waste, the percentage of energy from each source was multiplied by its corresponding price/million BTU and by the amount of energy lost due to meat waste. The estimates for the respective energy sources were further summed up to one final value.

Calculating the cost of energy loss from indirect energy sources involved the knowledge that a ton of artificial fertilizer requires 73 percent of natural gas and 27 percent of coal to produce (Kelischek, 2011). Accordingly, each of these values was multiplied by their corresponding prices/million BTU and by the amount of energy loss due to meat waste. Also in this case the estimates for the respective indirect energy sources were summed up to one final value.

Methane

The cost of methane from meat waste was calculated with the following two equations:

$$Cost\,of\,methane\,from\,wasted\,meat(\$)[pre-disposal] = carbon\,tax(\$/ton) * livestock\,CH_4\,emissions(MMT\,CO_2\,eq.) * \%\,of\,wasted\,meat\,products \quad (7)$$

$$Cost\,of\,methane\,from\,wasted\,meat(\$)[landfill] = carbon\,tax(\$/ton) * total\,US\,methane\,emissions(MMT\,CO_2\,eq.) * \%\,of\,methane\,from\,landfill(20\%) * \%\,of\,meat\,in\,total\,food\,waste\,in\,landfill(7.08\%) \quad (8)$$

In this analysis, a calculation of pre-disposal methane emissions was included due to the fact that almost all methane generated during agricultural production is attributable to livestock. However, landfill methane emissions are still important and necessary to consider in the analysis of food waste emissions. For both, equation 7 and 8, the carbon tax estimate implemented in British Columbia, Canada was included at \$23/ton (CAN \$30/ton) of CO_2 emission equivalent. As of 2012, this tax was the most stringent carbon tax in the western hemisphere (World Bank, 2016). In 2014, the US emitted 6870 million metric tons (MMT) of CO_2 equivalent (EPA, 2016). Methane emissions made up 11 percent of total emissions, which equals 775.7 MMT. Agriculture is responsible for 237.7 MMT, of which 225.5 MMT is generated during livestock production (164.3 MMT from enteric fermentation and 61.2 MMT from manure management) (EPA, 2016).

For equation 7, pre-disposal methane emissions, the hypothetical carbon tax was multiplied by total livestock methane emissions and the percent of wasted meat. Landfills are responsible for 20 percent of US methane emissions (EPA, 2016). Considering that 40 percent of landfill methane emissions are attributable to anaerobically decomposing food waste (Ziolkowska, 2017), and that meat makes up 17.7 percent of total food waste (Toth & Dou, 2016), meat waste is theoretically responsible for 7.08 percent of landfill methane emissions. This calculation does not consider the different carbon intensities of organic waste, which could theoretically slightly alter the estimates. To calculate the total cost of landfill methane emissions from wasted meat, the assumed carbon tax was multiplied by the total US methane emissions, the percent of methane from landfills, and the percent of landfill emissions from wasted meat.

Nitrous Oxide

The cost of N_2O emissions from meat waste was calculated with the following equation:

$$\begin{aligned}&\textit{Cost of nitrous oxide emissions from wasted meat}(\$) = \textit{carbon tax}(\$/\textit{ton})\\&\quad *\textit{total } N_2O \textit{ emissions from livestock}(MMT\, CO_2 eq.)\\&\quad *\%\textit{of wasted meat products}\end{aligned} \tag{9}$$

The US agriculture is responsible for 336 MMT of nitrous oxide emissions each year, of which 318.4 MMT come from soil management and 17.5 MMT from manure management (EPA, 2016). At the same time, 40 percent of US cropland is used for feed crops (Eshel et al., 2014), which translates to 127.36 MMT of N_2O from feed crops. Adding the N_2O estimates attributable to manure management and to cropland for feed crop production, the total of 144.86 MMT of N_2O was estimated that is attributable to livestock production. To calculate the cost of N_2O emissions from meat waste, the assumed carbon tax was multiplied by the total N_2O emissions from livestock and the percent of meat waste in the US.

RESULTS

The results of this analysis show that the total costs of meat waste in the US, under the assumption of this study, amount to a total of $32-32.5 billion per year (Table 1). Costs related to land use (including both cropland and pastureland costs) embedded in meat waste make up the biggest portion of economic losses and equal to $13.6 billion per year (Figure 4). Energy losses also represent an enormous cost of $13.1 billion per year.

The methane costs for pre-disposal livestock emissions amount to $3.1 billion per year, while landfill emissions cost $0.2 billion per year. Water was found to be the least costly resource, at $0.3-$0.8 billion per year. Ziolkowska (2017) found that water costs for all food waste were similarly the lowest in her study among different resources. However, she emphasized that water costs would be substantially higher if the true value of water as a resource was incorporated into valuations. The same could apply to all resources, particularly those used for food production. Lastly, nitrous oxide emissions from meat waste would cost approximately $1.7 billion per year based on the British Columbia carbon tax calculation of CO_2 equivalent emissions.

DISCUSSION

Based on the presented analysis, the US is losing substantial amounts of money (~$32 billion) annually due to meat waste. This estimated amount could be utilized to improve sustainability at different social, environmental or economic levels in the food production process. In addition, if resources and environmental impacts were valued for their true worth and costs to society, the presented results would fall much higher.

The vast amount of land being used to grow feed crops for livestock that is eventually wasted and the resulting costs have significant implications for several reasons. First, almost all land used to grow feed crops in the US is farmed industrially, which leads to harmful implications for the environment. Industrial agriculture negatively impacts ecosystems through overuse of fertilizers and pesticides, which consequently leads to water, air and soil pollution and degradation. Additionally, it fosters monocultures

Table 1. Costs related to meat waste by resource category

Resource	Cost of Meat Waste (Billion US$)
Water	0.3 – 0.8
Land Use (Cropland)	9.9
Land Use (Pastureland)	3.7
Energy	13.1
Methane Emissions (pre-disposal)	3.1
Methane Emissions (landfill)	0.2
Nitrous Oxide Emissions	1.7
Sum	**32 – 32.5**

Figure 4. Percent of costs related to meat waste by resource category

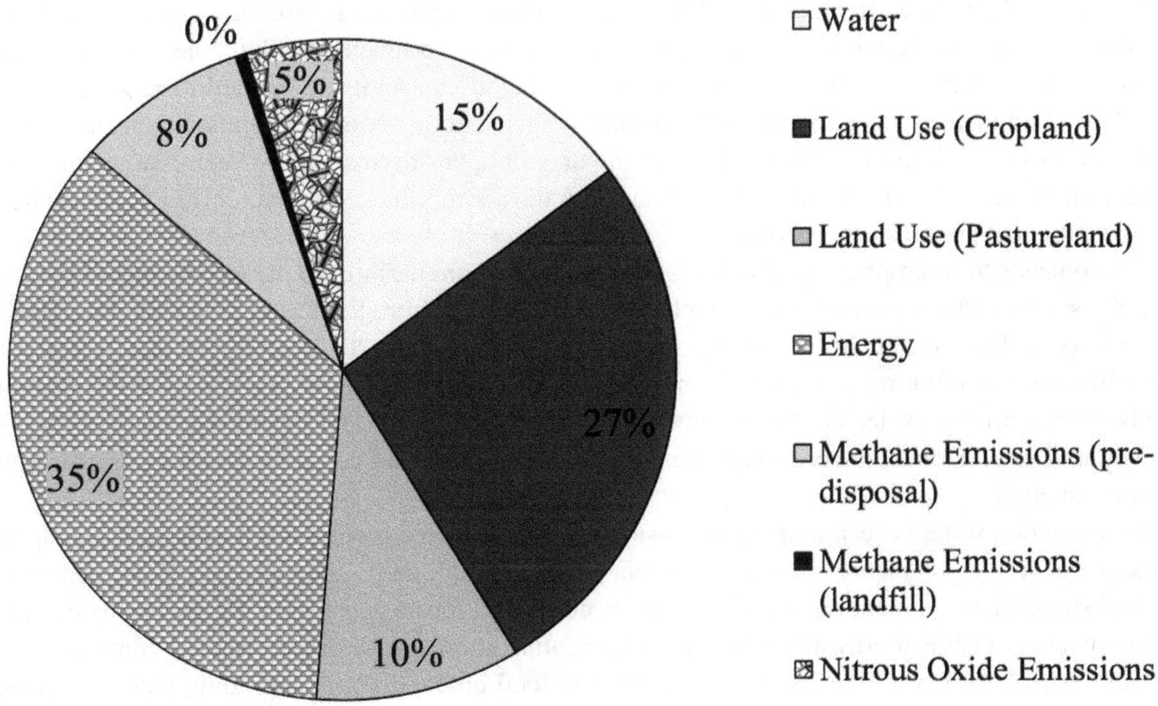

**For a more accurate representation see the electronic version.*

that impair biodiversity and deplete natural resources. Soil loss is one of the most pressing concerns for society's ability to produce sufficient amounts of food. Each year in the US, around 90 percent of cropland is losing soil at an average rate of 13 times faster than the estimated sustainable rate of 1 ton/ha/year (Pimentel & Pimentel, 2008). This development may lead to intensified land conversion into cropland in the future to compensate for the currently occurring losses, with amplified habitat and biodiversity declines. Cropland used to produce feed crops may lose even more topsoil each year than the average loss rates due to monocultures, abandonment of crop rotations, removal of tree shelter belts, leaving soil fallow without protective biomass cover and the use of heavy farm machinery (Pimentel & Pimentel, 2008).

Second, land used for feed crop production has very high opportunity costs, meaning that it has a very high alternative-use value and could be applied to grow crops for food production (including specialty crops like fruits and vegetables). Using land to grow food crops rather than feed crops would help provide calories to many more people. To put this in perspective, 45 million tons of plant protein is fed to livestock in the US each year, which produces only 7.5 million tons of animal protein for human consumption (Pimentel & Pimentel, 2008). In other words, it takes around 6 kg of plant protein to produce 1 kg of animal protein, while this plant protein could be utilized more efficiently to satisfy increasing food demands of the growing population.

Furthermore, unsustainable soil management, which often results from excessive fertilization of industrialized feed crops, is responsible for the majority of N_2O emissions from livestock production. Nitrous oxide emissions are miniscule in comparison to anthropogenic carbon dioxide emissions, but their global warming potential is 256 times as powerful, and thus needs to be seriously considered as efforts to mitigate GHG emissions across the world begin after the 2016 Paris Climate Agreement.

Demand for meat products is expected to increase rapidly by 2050 and consequently N_2O emissions will rise as well (Pelletier & Tyedmers, 2010). A carbon tax on polluters could be an effective measure to reduce N_2O emissions, while also raising revenues for the government. The hypothetical cost of N_2O emissions from meat waste, at $1.7 billion per year, is significant in itself. Wasted meat makes up almost half of all meat produced and thus the income from a carbon tax on N_2O emissions from all meat production would amount to around $3.4 billion per year. Considering that N_2O emissions are much more harmful than CO_2 emissions, the question about the appropriate carbon tax level might be a topic for scientific and political discussions.

It also needs to be emphasized that over-fertilization is more harmful to the environment than N_2O emissions alone. Plants only take up around half of the applied nitrogen fertilizers, while the remaining is dispersed into the environment (Sage, 2012). Bouwman et al. (2013) estimated that a surplus of 138 trillion grams of nitrogen is inputted into the environment every single year, far exceeding natural levels in the nitrogen cycle. The severe environmental consequences and potential economic costs of N_2O emissions underline the need to reduce feed crop cultivation and usage for livestock breeding and meat production.

Furthermore, water is becoming an increasingly scarce resource around the world and will only become scarcer as unsustainable water management practices continue (Lundqvist et al., 2008; Mekonnen & Hoekstra, 2010). As mentioned above, water is not priced for its true economic value as a resource and in many cases it is used without any regard for future stocks. When meat waste is combined with already unsustainable water management practices in food production, the unfolding picture becomes even more troubling in terms of sustainable resource allocation. Meat requires much more water than any other food produced, besides dairy, and approximately two-thirds (14.9 of 22.4 million acres) of the irrigation water requirements come from feed crop production (Eshel et al., 2014; USDA, 2014). Livestock conversion efficiencies from feed to protein are different for each animal but each species requires significant quantities. For example, feed and forage crops require 500-2000 l of water per kg of plant biomass produced, while producing 1 kg beef requires ~43 000 l of water, 43 times more water than 1 kg of grain (Pimentel & Pimentel, 2008).

In terms of energy use, industrial agriculture is a heavy user of fossil energy and a large portion of energy demand on farms comes from meat production. In fact, the agricultural stage of meat production requires 778 trillion BTU out of 1 270 trillion BTU from all food categories (Cuéllar & Webber, 2010). On average, 25 kcals of fossil energy are required to produce 1 kcal of animal protein, which is

10 times greater than the average energy requirements for grain protein (Pimentel & Pimentel, 2008). Other supply chain energy users, such as transportation, processing and handling, are similar in terms of overall energy use, but meat production is still a heavy energy user in all stages. It is implicit that lost energy from meat waste, at 49.8 percent of total production, is responsible for significant costs of $13.1 billion per year. Compared to the cost of lost energy from total food waste in Ziolkowska (2017), the lost energy from meat waste makes up slightly less than half of total economic losses ($13.1 billion out of $29.4 billion).

In regard to environmental impacts, landfill methane emissions from meat waste are insignificant compared to methane emissions generated during agricultural production that can be attributed to meat waste. Reducing meat waste (and in fact food waste in general) from landfills should be a primary goal of sustainable societies. Globally, ruminants are responsible for around 77 percent of livestock methane emissions from enteric fermentation (Herrero et al., 2013), while in the US they account for approximately 73 percent (EPA, 2016). Similarly, to nitrous oxide emissions, a higher pricing scheme for methane emissions than current carbon taxes could be considered.

The remainder of livestock methane emissions occurs mainly from manure management. Moreover, improper manure management also contributes to eutrophication, leaching of nitrates into groundwater, and excessively high nutrient levels in the soil that can volatize into nitrous oxides, nitrogen oxides, and ammonia which can ultimately cause acidification of ecosystems (Steinfeld et al., 2006). Switching from industrial livestock systems to pasture-based livestock systems, while simultaneously reducing meat production, could help mitigate this issue. Also, reducing consumption of ruminant meat from cows, goats, and sheep could significantly suppress methane emissions. Currently, the average American diet, including large quantities of meat, produces 1485 kg more of CO_2 emission equivalent than an average vegan or plant-based diet (Eshel & Martin, 2006). Educating societies about impacts of meat consumption on the environment could serve as a social marketing tool to influence people's behavior.

CONCLUSION

In this study, economic costs of meat waste in the US were quantified. The results show that meat waste generates substantial annual costs of $32-32.5 billion in regard to land, water, energy applied to produce meat as well as in methane and N_2O emissions. The estimates would most likely increase substantially if existing economic approaches of resources valuation and environmental impacts better represented resource values and were more accurately embedded in resource and product prices. It can be argued that this undervaluation is a root cause of modern environmental tragedies occurring across the world. The same can be stated about food waste and societal disconnect from food production. Considering food security as a granted right, missing understanding of food production and cultural/behavioral consumption habits lead to food waste as the ultimate result.

The solution to the food waste problem may rely on improving awareness specifically about monetary losses related to meat/food waste for consumers, businesses and governments, as they are the major decision-makers in implementing change on either household level or by means of legislative measures.

Policies incentivizing or dis-incentivizing certain food waste behaviors or else mandatory initiatives, e.g. citywide compost collection with penalties for non-compliance (as currently applied in Seattle, WA) could be one of possible actions in this direction. Also, educational programs, especially in schools, need to be enacted to create a notion about the need to reduce food/meat waste to limit unnecessary financial losses and to conserve natural resources at the same time.

ACKNOWLEDGMENT

This research was supported by the German Academy of Sciences Leopoldina.

REFERENCES

Bouwman, L., Goldewijk, K. K., Van Der Hoek, K. W., Beusen, A. H., Van Vuuren, D. P., Willems, J., & Stehfest, E. (2013). Exploring global changes in nitrogen and phosphorus cycles in agriculture induced by livestock production over the 1900-2050 period. *Proceedings of the National Academy of Sciences of the United States of America*, *110*(52), 20882–20887. doi:10.1073/pnas.1012878108 PMID:21576477

Buzby, J. C., & Hyman, J. (2012). Total and per capita value of food loss in the United States. *Food Policy*, *37*(5), 561–570. doi:10.1016/j.foodpol.2012.06.002

Cuéllar, A. D., & Webber, M. E. (2010). Wasted food, wasted energy: The embedded energy in food waste in the United States. *Environmental Science & Technology*, *44*(16), 6464–6469. doi:10.1021/es100310d PMID:20704248

de Vries, M., & de Boer, I. J. M. (2010). Comparing environmental impacts for livestock products: A review of life cycle assessments. *Livestock Science*, *128*(1–3), 1–11. doi:10.1016/j.livsci.2009.11.007

Diaz, R. J., & Rosenberg, R. (2008). Spreading dead zones and consequences for marine ecosystems. *Science*, *321*(5891), 926–929. doi:10.1126/science.1156401 PMID:18703733

Environmental Protection Agency (EPA). (2016). Inventory of US greenhouse gas emissions and sinks: 1990-2014. Washington, DC: EPA. Retrieved from https://www.epa.gov/sites/production/files/2016-04/documents/us-ghg-inventory-2016-main-text.pdf

Eshel, G., & Martin, P. A. (2006). Diet, energy, and global warming. *Earth Interactions*, *10*(9), 1–17. doi:10.1175/EI167.1

Eshel, G., Shepon, A., Makov, T., & Milo, R. (2014). Land, irrigation water, greenhouse gas, and reactive nitrogen burdens of meat, eggs, and dairy production in the United States. *Proceedings of the National Academy of Sciences of the United States of America*, *111*(33), 11996–12001. doi:10.1073/pnas.1402183111 PMID:25049416

Foley, J. A., Ramankutty, N., Brauman, K. A., Cassidy, E. S., Gerber, J. S., Johnston, M., & Zaks, D. P. M. et al. (2011). Solutions for a cultivated planet. *Nature*, *478*(7369), 337–342. doi:10.1038/nature10452 PMID:21993620

Food and Agriculture Organization of the United Nations (FAO). (2011). *Global food losses and food waste—extent, causes and prevention*. Rome, Italy: FAO.

Food and Agriculture Organization of the United Nations (FAO). (2013). *Food wastage footprint: Impacts on natural resources*. Summary Report. Retrieved from http://www.fao.org/docrep/018/i3347e/i3347e.pdf

Food and Agriculture Organization of the United Nations (FAO). (2014). *Animal Production and Health: Meat Consumption*. Agriculture and Consumer Protection Department. Retrieved from http://www.fao.org/ag/againfo/themes/en/meat/background.html

Godfray, H. C. J., Beddington, J. R., Crute, I. R., Haddad, L., Lawrence, D., Muir, J. F., & Toulmin, C. (2010). Food security: The challenge of feeding 9 billion people. *Science*, *327*(5967), 812–818. doi:10.1126/science.1185383 PMID:20110467

Gustavsson, J., Cederberg, C., Sonesson, U., van Otterdijk, R., & Meybeck, A. (2011). Global food losses and food waste: Extent, causes and prevention. *Food and Agriculture Organization of the United Nations*, *38*. doi:10.1098/rstb.2010.0126

Hall, K. D., Guo, J., Dore, M., & Chow, C. C. (2009). The progressive increase of food waste in America and its environmental impact. *PLoS One*, *4*(11), e7940. doi:10.1371/journal.pone.0007940 PMID:19946359

Herrero, M., Havlík, P., Valin, H., Notenbaert, A., Rufino, M. C., & Thornton, P. K., … Obersteiner, M. (2013). Biomass use, production, feed efficiencies, and greenhouse gas emissions from global livestock systems. *Proceedings of the National Academy of Sciences of the United States of America*, 110, 20888–20893. doi:10.1073/pnas.1308149110

Kearney, J. (2010). Food consumption trends and drivers. *Philosophical Transactions of the Royal Society of London. Series B, Biological Sciences*, *365*(1554), 2793–2807. doi:10.1098/rstb.2010.0149 PMID:20713385

Kelischek, N. (2011). Energy budget of nitrogen use in the United States. *Journal of Student Research in Environmental Science at Appalachian*, *1*(1), 32–35. Retrieved from http://pimlico.phys.appstate.edu/JSRESA/kelischek.1-1.pdf

Keyzer, M. A., Merbis, M. D., Pavel, I. F. P. W., & van Wesenbeeck, C. F. A. (2005). Diet shifts towards meat and the effects on cereal use: Can we feed the animals in 2030. *Ecological Economics*, *55*(2), 187–202. doi:10.1016/j.ecolecon.2004.12.002

Kummu, M., de Moel, H., Porkka, M., Siebert, S., Varis, O., & Ward, P. J. (2012). Lost food, wasted resources: Global food supply chain losses and their impacts on freshwater, cropland, and fertiliser use. *The Science of the Total Environment*, *438*, 477–489. doi:10.1016/j.scitotenv.2012.08.092 PMID:23032564

Lipinski, B., Hanson, C., Lomax, J., Kitinoja, L., Waite, R., & Searchinger, T. (2013). *Reducing food loss and waste* (Working Paper). World Resource Institute. Retrieved from http://pdf.wri.org/reducing_food_loss_and_waste.pdf

Lundqvist, J., De Fraiture, C., & Molden, D. (2008). *Saving water: From field to fork – curbing losses and wastage in the food chain. SIWI Policy Brief.* Stockholm, Sweden: Stockholm International Water Institute.

McAlpine, C. A., Etter, A., Fearnside, P. M., Seabrook, L., & Laurance, W. F. (2009). Increasing world consumption of beef as a driver of regional and global change: A call for policy action based on evidence from Queensland (Australia), Colombia and Brazil. *Global Environmental Change, 19*(1), 21–33. doi:10.1016/j.gloenvcha.2008.10.008

McMichael, A. J., Powles, J. W., Butler, C. D., & Uauy, R. (2007). Food, livestock production, energy, climate change, and health. *Lancet, 370*(9594), 1253–1263. doi:10.1016/S0140-6736(07)61256-2 PMID:17868818

Mekonnen, M. M., & Hoekstra, A. Y. (2010). The green, blue and grey water footprint of farm animals and animal products.: Vol. 1. *Main report*. Delft, the Netherlands: UNESCO. Retrieved from http://waterfootprint.org/media/downloads/Report-48-WaterFootprint-AnimalProducts-Vol1.pdf

Miranowski, J. (2002) Energy Consumption in U.S. Agriculture. Presentation for Farm Foundation. Retrieved from https://www.farmfoundation.org/projects/documents/miranowski.ppt

Naylor, R., Steinfeld, H., Falcon, Q., Galloway, J., Smil, V., Bradford, E., & Mooney, H. et al. (2005). Agriculture: Losing the links between livestock and land. *Science, 310*(5754), 1621–162. doi:10.1126/science.1117856 PMID:16339432

Papargyropoulou, E., Lozano, R., & Steinberger, K., J., Wright, N., & bin Ujang, Z. (. (2014). The food waste hierarchy as a framework for the management of food surplus and food waste. *Journal of Cleaner Production, 76*, 106–115. doi:10.1016/j.jclepro.2014.04.020

Pelletier, N., & Tyedmers, P. (2010). Forecasting potential global environmental costs of livestock production 2000-2050. *Proceedings of the National Academy of Sciences of the United States of America, 107*(43), 18371–18374. doi:10.1073/pnas.1004659107 PMID:20921375

Pimentel, D., & Pimentel, M. H. (2008). *Food, energy, and society* (3rd ed.). Boca Raton, FL: CRC Press.

Rapier. (2010, January 26). The price of energy. *Forbes*. Retrieved from https://www.forbes.com/sites/energysource/2010/01/26/the-price-of-energy/#25cf888f67b1

Sage, C. (2012). *Environment and food*. London, UK: Routledge.

Smil, V. (2002). Worldwide transformation of diets, burdens of meat production and opportunities for novel food proteins. *Enzyme and Microbial Technology, 30*(3), 305–311. doi:10.1016/S0141-0229(01)00504-X

Smil, V. (2004). Improving efficiency and reducing waste in our food system. *Environmental Sciences, 1*(1), 17–26. doi:10.1076/evms.1.1.17.23766

Spooner, B. (2016). Food Waste and Food Security in a Globalizing World. In *Food Waste Across the Supply Chain: A US Perspective on a Global Problem* (pp. 73–85). University of Pennsylvania.

Steinfeld, H., Gerber, P., Wassenaar, T., Castel, V., Rosales, M., & De Haan, C. (2006). *Livestock's long shadow: Environmental issues and options*. Rome, Italy: FAO.

Toth, J. D., & Dou, Z. (2016). Wasted food, wasted resources: Land, irrigation water, and nutrients associated with food wastage in the U.S. In Z. Dou, J. D. Ferguson, D. T. Galligan, A. M. Kelly, S. M. Finn, & R. Giegengack (Eds.), *Food waste across the supply chain: A US perspective on a global problem* (pp. 57–71). Ames, IO: Council for Agricultural Science and Technology.

United States Department of Agriculture (USDA). (2014). 2012 Census of Agriculture: Farm and Ranch Irrigation Survey 2013. USDA Census of Agriculture. Retrieved from https://www.agcensus.usda.gov/Publications/2012/Online_Resources/Farm_and_Ranch_Irrigation_Survey/

United States Department of Agriculture (USDA). (2015). 2014 Land values and cash rents: Cropland and pasture. National Agriculture Statistics Service (NASS) Highlights. Retrieved from https://www.nass.usda.gov/Publications/Highlights/2014_LandValues_CashRents/LVCR.pdf

World Bank. (2016). State and trends of carbon pricing. Washington, DC: World Bank Group. Retrieved from http://documents.worldbank.org/curated/en/598811476464765822/State-and-trends-of-carbon-pricing

World Bank. (2017). *GDP per capita (current US$)*. Retrieved from http://data.worldbank.org/indicator/NY.GDP.PCAP.CD

Ziolkowska, J. R. (2015). Shadow price of water for irrigation – a case of the High Plains. *Agricultural Water Management*, *153*, 20–31. doi:10.1016/j.agwat.2015.01.024

Ziolkowska, J. R. (2017). Economic and environmental costs of agricultural food losses and waste in the US. *International Journal of Food Engineering*, *3*(2), 140–145.

KEY TERMS AND DEFINITIONS

Agriculture: Science or practice of farming (soil cultivation for growing crops and grazing animals) to provide food, wool, and other products.

Animal Husbandry: The raising of any animal species to consume and/or utilize for various purposes.

Food Security: The state (of an individual or societies) of having a sufficient quantity of affordable and nutritious food.

Food Waste: The loss or wastage of edible food at any point in a food supply chain.

Livestock: Any living animal or group of animals used in animal husbandry to consume and/or use for various purposes.

Monetary Valuation: Assigning economic value and/or cost to a specific resource or product.

Natural Resources: Naturally occurring materials or substances that can be used for various purposes to gain specific benefits.

Sustainability: The ability to maintain environmental, social, and economic systems and capital indefinitely for the present generation to meet its needs without compromising the ability of future generations to meet their own needs.

ENDNOTE

[1] BTU – British thermal unit; 1 BTU = 1055 joules.

Chapter 5
Use of Antibiotics in Animals and Its Possible Impacts in the Environment

Jeeva M. Philip
Mahatma Gandhi University, India

Usha K. Aravind
Mahatma Gandhi University, India

Charuvila T. Aravindakumar
Mahatma Gandhi University, India

ABSTRACT

The application of antibiotics to livestock has become a serious global concern. The increasing demand for animal protein leads to a greater use of antibiotics in livestock production. This is contributing to a global scale-up in antibiotic consumption. This chapter analyses the use of antibiotics in animals and the emergence of antibiotics as a class of contaminants which pollute the natural environment and create antimicrobial resistance. The conclusion is that the current system is unable to withstand ethical health concerns.

INTRODUCTION

Humans have been using various pharmaceuticals for different therapeutic purposes since the mid-1800s. These diverse classes of pharmaceuticals include antibiotics, antipyretics, analgesics, antiepileptic drugs, antihistamines, antidepressants, β-blockers, non-steroidal anti-inflammatory drugs (NSAIDs), steroids, hormones and many others. However, from an environmental perspective, pharmaceuticals are indistinguishable from any other chemicals. At the end of 20th century with the development in analytical science, they emerged as micro-contaminants. At present, they are listed under the categories of emerging contaminants by the United States Environmental Protection Agency (USEPA). Emerging contaminants can be broadly defined as any synthetic or naturally occurring chemical or any microorganism that is

DOI: 10.4018/978-1-5225-4757-0.ch005

not commonly monitored but has the potential to enter the environment and cause known or suspected adverse ecological and/or human health effects (USGS, 2017). This includes personal care products, perfluorinated compounds, flame retardants, endocrine disrupting chemicals, plasticizers, industrial additives and agents, surfactants and pharmaceuticals. To date, many articles have reported the widespread occurrence of pharmaceuticals and their residues in surface waters, ground waters, wastewaters, sediments, sludge, animal manure and biota. Their concentration varies from picograms to micrograms levels.

Antibiotics are one of the important classes among the emerging contaminants. For instance, occurrence of antibiotics was determined in the effluents from hospitals, residential facilities and dairies, municipal wastewater, influent and effluent of a wastewater treatment plant (WWTP) and surface waters in New Mexico (Brown et al., 2006). Presence of antibiotics was detected in three hospital effluents, five WWTPs, six rivers and a drinking water storage catchment within watersheds in South–East Queensland, Australia (Watkinsona et al., 2009). Significant levels (μg/l) of pharmaceuticals that include antibiotics, estrogens, non-steroidal anti-inflammatory drugs (NSAIDs), beta-blockers and lipid regulators were frequently detected in the urban regions of Taiwan's surface waters (Lin & Tsai, 2009). The occurrences of pharmaceuticals belonging to predominant therapeutic classes was detected in surface water, suspended solids and sediments in the Ebro river basin in Spain (da Silva et al., 2011). Presence of sulfonamides was found in two ground waterbodies in Catalonia indicated manure contamination from livestock veterinary practices (García-Galán et al., 2010). Despite this, limited information exists on the impacts of antibiotics on the environment.

GLOBAL ANTIMICROBIAL CONSUMPTION IN LIVESTOCK

The increased demand for animal protein that leads to greater use of antibiotics in livestock production is considered one of the trends contributing to a global scale-up in antibiotic consumption. This trend began just after the Second World War when there was a lack of good quality feed (Aarestrup, 2012). Antibiotic consumption in livestock worldwide is twice that of humans (Aarestrup, 2012; WHO, 2012). For instance, in the United States ~80% of the nation's annual antibiotic consumption accounted for antimicrobial use in animals (CDDEP, 2015; Van Boeckel et al., 2015).

In a study conducted to analyze antimicrobial consumption in livestock production, Van Boeckel et al. (2015) estimated that the global average annual consumption of antimicrobials per kilogram of animal produced was 45 mg/kg, 148 mg/kg and 172 mg/kg for cattle, chicken and pigs respectively. On the basis of this baseline data, the study estimated that between 2010 and 2030, the global consumption of antimicrobials in food animal production will increase by 67%, i.e. from 63,151 ± 1,560 tonnes to 105,596 ± 3,605 tonnes. Two thirds (66%) of this global increase is attributed to the increase in the number of animals raised for food production. The remaining third (34%) results from the shift toward intensive production systems in middle-income countries where antimicrobials are used routinely in sub-therapeutic doses for disease prevention and growth promotion, rather than for disease treatment. The study also reported that the five countries with the largest shares of global antimicrobial consumption in food animal production in 2010 were China (23%), the United States (13%), Brazil (9%), India (3%), and Germany (3%). If current trends continue, by 2030 this ranking is projected to be China (30%), the United States (10%), Brazil (8%), India (4%), and Mexico (2%). This means, by 2030 antimicrobial use in livestock production in Brazil, Russia, India, China and South Africa (BRICS) will increase by 99% which is seven times the projected population growth in this group of countries.

SOURCES OF PHARMACEUTICALS IN THE ENVIRONMENT

Pharmaceuticals enter the environment via various pathways. They include point sources, such as effluent releases from pharmaceutical production plants, hospitals and WWTPs, and non-point sources, such as urban runoff, disposal of unused and expired medicines, human and animal excreta, leakage from septic systems, landfill leachates, manure applications, agricultural runoff, discharges from poultry, aquaculture and livestock production. Compared to human use, currently antibiotics are intensively used in poultry, swine and cattle to promote growth and prevent diseases.

It was reported that worldwide in 2010, at least 63,200 tonnes of antibiotics were consumed by livestock which is expected to be more than all human consumption (Van Boeckel et al., 2015). By 2030, this figure is projected to rise by two-thirds to 105,600 tonnes to meet the demands of a projected 8.5 billion human population. In addition, approximately 75% of the antibiotics administered to feedlot animals were estimated to be excreted into the environment. Consequently, significant amounts of the antibiotics used in animals eventually find their way into the environment, particularly in surface and ground water, sediment and in soil.

Pharmaceutical Production Plants

Discharges from pharmaceutical production plants are generally assumed to be minimal because of the existing good manufacturing practice regulations in each country. However, studies from Asian countries revealed that this could be a relevant source that may release pharmaceuticals in concentrations 10-1000 fold higher than generally measured in WWTP effluent samples. In 1993 using a spectrophotometric method, Bisarya and Patil (1993) determined high concentration of salicylic acid (2270 ppm) in the effluent of an aspirin plant in Bangalore, India. Similarly, series of studies from Hyderabad, India, revealed that drug manufacturers have become a point source of active pharmaceutical ingredients (APIs) contamination in local environments (Fick et al., 2009; Kristiansson et al., 2011; Larsson et al., 2007; Rutgersson et al., 2014). Patancheru, near Hyderabad is an important hub for the world's bulk drug production and features a huge number of industries (nearly 90 bulk drug manufacturers) clustered in a limited area. Effluents from these drug manufacturers are being treated at Patancheru Enviro Tech Ltd. (PETL), an effluent treatment plant in Patancheru which receives approximately 1,500 m^3 of wastewater per day. Occurrences of high concentrations of APIs were reported in the PETL effluent sample in which ciprofloxacin, an antibiotic-fluoroquinolone, exhibited the highest level (up to 31 mg/l) ever detected in the environment (Rutgersson et al., 2014). In 2006, release of estrogens from a plant producing contraceptives was reported in China (Cui et al., 2006). Steroid estrogens, such as estrone (E1), 17β-estradiol (E2), estriol (E3), and 17α-ethynylestradiol, were determined in the effluent at the ng/l level.

Sparse information is available on the potential releases from production plants in developed countries. In a study conducted in Taiwan, diclofenec concentrations exceeded 20μg/l in the effluent of a WWTP that received pharmaceutical formulation facilities discharge (Lin et al., 2008). Another study from Taipei district of Taiwan also demonstrated significant discharge of pharmaceuticals from drug production facilities into surface waters (Lin & Tsai, 2009). Similarly, the results of a study conducted in New York indicated that the concentrations of pharmaceuticals for WWTPs receiving substantial discharges from pharmaceutical formulation facilities can exceed 1000 μg/l (Phillips et al., 2010). Production wastewater samples of a veterinary pharmaceuticals industry in an eastern European country also showed the presence of pharmaceuticals such as enrofloxacine, sulfamethazine, sulfadiazine and sulfaguanidine (Babić et al., 2006).

Wastewater Treatment Plants

Wastewater treatment plants are considered as a significant source of pharmaceuticals into the environment. So far, strategies for wastewater treatment have hardly focused on the elimination of trace organic pollutants like pharmaceuticals. They are partially or incompletely removed during treatment and are often discharged into surface waters. This may also contaminate drinking water in areas where surface waters are used. Several studies referred WWTPs as the sources of pharmaceuticals in surface water. For instance, the Yamuna river in India which receives the sewage from a treatment plant located at Okhla, Delhi, exhibited the presence of antibiotics such as ampicillin, ciprofloxacin, gatifloxacin, sparfloxacin and cefuroxime (Mutiyar & Mittal, 2014). Results of a study conducted in 59 wadeable headwater streams in the highly urbanized Piedmont ecoregion of the southeastern United States confirm that WWTPs are important sources of in-stream pharmaceutical contamination (Bradley et al., 2016).

A Canadian study demonstrated that wastewater discharges into surface waters have the potential to contaminate downstream sources of drinking water with drugs of abuse like cocaine, benzoylecgonine, morphine, acetylmorphine, dihydrocodeine, acetylcodeine, oxycodone etc. (Rodayan et al., 2016). Another study conducted in Calgary city in Alberta, Canada also mentioned that the drug residues in downstream surface water could be associated with incomplete removal of pharmaceuticals during the treatment process (Chen et al., 2015). Antibiotics were found in the Chaobai river in Beijing, China which receives effluent from a WWTP, with concentrations ranging from 0-41.8 ng/l (Chunhui et al., 2016). The study also concluded that WWTPs discharges are a dominant point-source input of antibiotics into rivers. Similarly, a study conducted in northeast Spain showed that WWTP effluents are major contributor of pharmaceuticals in the river (da Silva, et al., 2011). Occurrence of pharmaceuticals was determined in WWTP effluents as well as river water samples collected from downstream.

Runoff

Runoff includes diffuse sources of pharmaceuticals input and is a major pathway for environmental pollution, particularly in agricultural areas. Due to rain after the application of manure to agricultural land, runoff is an important contributor for the input of veterinary pharmaceuticals into surface waters. A high percentage of pharmaceuticals consumed by humans and animals are excreted as parent compounds or as metabolites via urine and faeces. Consequently, they enter the wastewater through the sewage systems and may end up in the environment.

Pharmaceuticals such as carbamazepine, gemfibrozil, carisoprodol were identified in agricultural runoff from fields irrigated with waste water (Pedersen et al., 2005). The high concentrations of pharmaceuticals found in the Sindian and Dahan rivers of Taiwan demonstrated the impact of urban drainage – waste effluents from hospitals, households and pharmaceutical production facilities (Lin & Tsai, 2009). Comparable pharmaceutical concentrations and detections at sites with and without permitted wastewater discharges demonstrate the importance of non-WWTP sources and the need for broad-scale mitigation (Bradley et al., 2016).

Aquaculture

Antimicrobial agents and antiparasitics are used extensively in intensive aquaculture for the treatment and prevention of bacterial infections, sea lice infestations, furunculosis etc. Antibiotics have been used mainly for therapeutic purposes and as prophylactic agents. Tetracyclines (oxytetracycline, chlortetracycline, tetracycline), quinolones (oxolinic acid, sarafloxacin), fluoroquinolones (flumequine, enrofloxacin), aminopenicillins (amoxycillin, ampicillin), amphenicols (chloramphenicol, florfenicol), aminoglycosides (streptomycin, neomycin), nitrofurans (furazolidone, nitrofurantoin), macrolides (erythromycin), sulfonamides (sulfamerazine, trimethoprim) etc. are the common antimicrobial drugs used in aquaculture. The main routes of administration are immersion therapy, medicated feed and occasionally by injections. If the antibiotic treatment is achieved by medicated baths and medicated food, there is high probability for antibiotics to enter the environment. Fishes do not effectively metabolize antibiotics which are therefore released into the environment via urine and faeces and/or as unused medicated food.

Studies indicate that 70-80% of the antimicrobials used in aquaculture end up in the environment (Hektoen et al., 1995; Samuelsen et al., 1992). This may lead to the development of a reservoir of antimicrobial-resistant bacteria and resistance genes in aquatic environments. Oxytetracycline and quinolones, such as oxolinic acid, sarafloxacin and flumequine, were reported to be very persistent in the sediment (Hektoen, et al., 1995).

Livestock Production

Antibiotics used in commercial livestock production (cattle, swine and poultry) can be categorized as therapeutic, metaphylactic, prophylactic and sub-therapeutic (FAO, 2011). Therapeutic use corresponds to the treatment of existing infections. Metaphylaxis is a term used for group-medication procedures (whole flock or herd) that aim to treat sick animals while also medicating others in the group to prevent the spreading of disease. Therapeutic and metaphylactic treatments usually occur at high doses for a relatively short period of time. Prophylactic use means the treatment of individuals or groups with low, sub-therapeutic doses of antibiotics in feed or drinking water to prevent the development of infections. The treatment can be over a period of several weeks, sometimes longer. In sub-therapeutic use, antibiotics are given to animals in their feed at very low doses nominally to increase their growth-rate and productivity. Such treatment is continuous and can last for a large part of the animal's life.

The most controversial of these uses is sub-therapeutic use, because it does not serve to maintain the health of the livestock but to stimulate quicker growth and maximize profits. Antimicrobial drug classes and active ingredients approved by the US Food & Drug Administration (FDA) for use in food-producing animals that were actively marketed in 2015 include aminocoumarins (novobiocin) aminoglycosides (dihydrostreptomycin, gentamicin, hygromycin B, neomycin, spectinomycin) amphenicols (florfenicol), cephalosporins (ceftiofur, cephapirin), diaminopyrimidines (ormetoprim), fluoroquinolones (danofloxacin, enrofloxacin), glycolipids (bambermycins), ionophores (laidlomycin, lasalocid, monensin, narasin, salinomycin), lincosamides (lincomycin, pirlimycin), macrolides (erythromycin, gamithromycin, tildipirosin, tilmicosin, tulathromycin, tylosin, tylvalosin), penicillins (amoxicillin, ampicillin, cloxacillin, penicillin) pleuromutilins (tiamulin), polymyxins (polymyxin B), polypeptides (bacitracin), quinoxalines (carbadox), streptogramins (virginiamycin), sulfonamides (sulfadimethoxine, sulfamerazine, sulfamethazine, sulfaquinoxaline) and tetracyclines (chlortetracycline, oxytetracycline, tetracycline) (FDA, 2016). These antibiotics are administered either orally or by injection. Most of the antibiotics administered by oral route are not completely absorbed in the gut, resulting in the excretion of the parent compounds and their metabolites via the urine and faeces (Seo et al., 2007). The excretion rate varies depending on the antibiotic properties.

It has been estimated that as much as 90% of some of the antibiotics administered to feedlot animals could be excreted into the environment as parent compound (Kumar et al., 2005). These are often released either directly or indirectly into the aquatic environment through runoff or by the application of manure in the agricultural fields. They may also leach into groundwater and move through the environment. Poultry manure and sewage treatment plants are the potential sources of tetracycline antibiotics detected in the sediment samples of two rivers on the eastern shore of the Chesapeake Bay, an estuary in the US states of Maryland and Virginia (Simon, 2005). Manure contains significant amounts of antibiotics which may persist in soil after land application. Continuous application of animal manure to agricultural land can lead to the accumulation of antibiotics in the soil which may adversely affect its ecosystems. Based on the excretion rate and degree of sorption to soil solids, after manure application on agricultural land, seventeen veterinary antibiotics active ingredients were classified as "high priority" in terms of the potential to reach the environment (Seo et al., 2007).

IMPACTS OF PHARMACEUTICALS ON THE ENVIRONMENT

All pharmaceuticals have a specific mode of actions and may probably exert some effects on terrestrial and aquatic ecosystems once they enter into the environment. One of the clearest cases of pharmaceuticals causing population-level effects is the collapse of vulture populations occurred in south Asia (Green et al., 2004; Prakash, 1999; Prakash et al., 2007; Prakash et al., 2003; Risebrough, 2004). Rapid population decline in the three species of vulture (Gyps bengalensis, Gyps indicus and Gyps tenuirostris) was reported due to consumption of carcasses of livestock treated with diclofenac, a widely used veterinary medicine in India and Pakistan. Diclofenac causes renal failure and visceral gout (accumulation of uric acid throughout the body cavity following kidney malfunction) in vultures that lead to their mortalities.

Antibiotics are biologically active in nature and usually very soluble with low biodegradability (Wollenbergera et al., 2000). These properties pose a potential for bioaccumulation and persistence in the environment. The fate and transport of antibiotics in the environment primarily depend on the physical and chemical processes of sorption, leaching and degradation – the three important processes in the soil-water systems (Sarmah et al., 2006). These processes in-turn depend on the physico-chemical properties of the antibiotics, such as their molecular structure, size, shape, solubility, speciation and hydrophobicity. Sorption is the amount of antibiotics adsorbed per gram of soil. Most of the sorption studies reveal that although the majority of the antibiotics used in animal production are strongly sorbed to soil and clay particles, they may still be biologically active and can influence the selection of antibiotic resistant bacteria in the terrestrial environment.

Antibiotics entered into the environment may interact with the soil solid phase and undergo microbial transformation (Jechalke et al., 2014). This biotransformation may result in retransformation of metabolites into the parent compound, e.g. sulfonamides. Only less than 2% of the added compounds undergo mineralization. Photo-degradation, an alternative pathway of pharmaceutical degradation is also limited by poor light penetration. However, surface runoff and particle-facilitated transport may disperse them in the environment. Only few antibiotics such as the sulfonamides undergo leaching into the groundwater. Hence, when manure is applied, the largest fraction of most antibiotics is usually retained in the surface soil. The excreted compounds via urine and faeces can be adsorbed, leached, bio-accumulated, degraded through biotic or abiotic processes, and in some cases, may revert back to the parent compound (Sarmah et al., 2006).

Emergence of Antibiotic Resistance Bacteria/Genes

The widespread use of antibiotics in livestock production leads to the emergence of antimicrobial resistant bacteria and genes (ARGs) in the environment. Nowadays, the infections caused by antibiotic-resistant bacteria are increasing and are a major public health issue around the world. The major threat is that these resistance genes in a bacteria genome may shift to mobile genetic elements such as integrons, plasmids and transposonsable elements and are horizontally transferred to bacteria adapted to soil or other habitats that may support their environmental transmission (Heuer et al., 2011). Therefore, ARGs are also considered emerging contaminants as once they are integrated in successful gene-transmission elements, they can persist and spread even in the absence of antibiotics (Coutinho et al., 2013; Martinez, 2009; Sanderson et al., 2016; Zhu et al., 2013).

Mobile integrons are bacterial genetic elements which are efficient tools for bacterial adaptation and play a significant role in antibiotic resistance (Stalder et al., 2012). The persistence of glycopeptide-resistant enterococci in Danish pig herds after the ban of glycopeptides was mentioned as the genetic link between ermB and vanA and as a consequence of coselection by the continued use of macrolides (tylosin) for treatment and growth promotion (Aarestrup, 2000). Enterococcus faecium isolated from conventional and ecological poultry farms in Denmark exhibited resistance to glycopeptides such as vancomycin and avopracin (Aarestrup, 2009).

Wind-dispersed particulate matter from feed yards also harbours antibiotics and ARGs. A study conducted in the central plains of the United States found that particulate matter generated at beef cattle feed yards contains distinct communities of bacteria, antibiotics and antibiotic resistance gene sequences (McEachran et al., 2015).

The usage of antibiotics in livestock also promoted the development and abundance of antibiotic resistance in manure. Concentrations of antibiotics in manure can be very stable or even increase due to retransformation of metabolites back to the parent compound. Application on agricultural fields of such animal manure carrying drug-resistant bacteria leads to the dissemination of antibiotic resistance genes. It has been identified that animal wastes (e.g. manure, poultry litter and slurry) are the main vectors of dissemination of mobile integrons in soil (Stalder et al., 2012). The application of the organic manure and wastewater on agricultural land significantly causes a spread of antibiotic resistance genes to bacterial population in soil and produced vegetables (Oluyege et al., 2015). In Madrid, Spain, gram-negative bacteria isolated from cattle manure samples exhibited antimicrobial resistances to tetracycline (66.7%), sulphamethoxazole (55.6%), ampicillin (52.4%), cephalothin (46.0%), chloramphenicol (44.4%), nalidixic acid (39.7%) and trimethroprim-sulphamethoxazole (33.3%) (Carballo et al., 2013). Extended-spectrum beta-lactamase (ESBL)-producing E. coli isolated from pig farm samples (manure and compost) and soil treated with pig manure in the rural region of Tai'an, China showed multiple drug resistance to 14 antibiotics commonly used in the local clinics (Gao et al., 2015). Similarly, abundance of ARGs was found in manure and compost collected from large-scale swine farms and soil receiving manure compost in three Chinese provinces including Beijing, Zhejiang and Fujian (Zhu et al., 2013).

Impacts on Plants

Several pharmaceuticals may also be taken up by plants but their concentrations in plant tissues are commonly so small but sufficient to induce phytotoxic effects (Jechalke et al., 2014). Plant uptake of pharmaceuticals may occur when treated wastewater is reused for irrigation, by the application of animal manure and sewage sludge on agricultural land and irrigation using surface water that receives wastewater effluent, sewer overflow and runoff from livestock production sites. Antibiotics in the soil may affect plant development indirectly by disrupting soil communities (Carvalho et al., 2014). The decline in the number of soil bacteria leads to a lack of food for soil fauna (protozoa, nematodes, micro arthropods) which finally slows down soil functions like decomposition, denitrification and nutrient cycle.

The uptake of five antibiotics (chlortetracycline, monensin, sulfamethazine, tylosin and virginiamycin) by 11 vegetable crops (spinach, lettuce, cabbage, carrot, radish, onion, garlic, tomato, green bell pepper, sweet corn and potato) in two different soils fertilized with raw versus composted turkey and hog manures or inorganic fertilizer were analysed (Kang et al., 2013). Almost all vegetables showed some uptake of antibiotics from manure treatments with antibiotic concentrations <10 µg/kg fresh weight. This concentration would not pose any health risks based on the standards for maximum residue levels in animal tissues (2-1200 µg/kg) and acceptable daily intake (levels that can be ingested daily over a lifetime without any health risks, which is 10-30 µg/kg for the selected compounds in the study) unless one is allergic to that particular antibiotic.

Impacts on Aquatic Environment

Antibiotics administered to livestock can reach the aquatic environment as parent compounds or as metabolites by the application of manure or slurry on agricultural fields or by pasture-reared animals excreting directly on the land, followed by surface runoff or leaching in deeper layers of earth. The presence of antibiotics in the aquatic environment can lead to the development and spread of antimicrobial-resistant bacteria and resistance genes. Such genes can be disseminated by horizontal gene transfer to other bacteria and ultimately reach human pathogens. Some compounds are persistent in sediments and can therefore affect the microbial community near aquaculture sites. For instance, quinolones remain active in sediments for prolonged periods of time as they are not readily biodegradable. Antibiotics may also affect the composition of the phytoplankton, zooplankton community and even the diversity of populations of larger animals because of their toxicity to microorganisms. Potential alterations in the diversity of the marine micro-biota caused by antibiotics may alter the homeostasis of the marine environment and affect complex forms of life including fish, shellfish, marine mammals and human beings.

The presence of antibiotic residues in the aquatic environment may cause reproductive and other adverse effects on early life stages of different aquatic organisms. Results of the chronic toxicity test of antibiotics such as oxytetracycline, sulfadiazine, tetracycline and tiamulin, which are used both therapeutically and as growth promoters in intensive farming, showed reproductive effects (EC50) on the freshwater crustacean Daphnia magna in the range of 5 to 50 mg/l (Wollenbergera et al., 2000). Also, the no-observed-effect concentration (NOEC) of oxolinic acid was 0.38 mg/l in the reproduction test which indicates that this substance which is commonly used as feed additive in fish farms has a potential to cause adverse effects on the aquatic environment.

EXISTING CONTROL MEASURES AND REGULATIONS

Legal and regulatory efforts are taken in some regions of the world in order to reduce the animal antibiotic use as growth promoters as it provides no health benefit to the animals but accelerates antibiotic resistance. The first nation that prohibited the use of antibiotic growth promoters in animal feed was Sweden in 1986 (Castanon, 2007). Later, all other member-states of the European Union prohibited the use of certain antibiotics in animal feedstuffs on their territories. Avoparcin was banned in Denmark (May 20, 1995) and Germany (January 19, 1996), spiramycin was prohibited in Finland (January 1, 1998) and virginiamycin was prohibited in Denmark (January 15, 1998) (Castanon, 2007). The prohibition of these antibiotics is based on the evidence of antibiotic resistant bacteria/genes as well as their clinical importance in human medicine. As a result of these national initiatives, the European Union banned all use of avoparcin (April 1, 1997), spiramycin, virginiamycin (June 30, 1999) and bacitracin zinc (1998) (Castanon, 2007). Finally, in 2003, the European Union regulation declared that most antibiotics would no longer be allowed as feed additives as of January 1, 2006 (CDDEP, 2015). This is to combat the dangerous trend of human infection with strains of bacteria that are resistant to those antibiotics. As a result, between 2014 and 2015, overall sales of antibiotics for food-producing animals in UK decreased by 10% from 62 mg/kg to 56 mg/kg and if this trend continues, UK will achieve its 50 mg/kg target by 2018 (VMD, 2015).

The Danish government banned the application of a growth promoter called avoparcin in livestock in 1995 as a result of the studies showing the relationship between its use and the widespread occurrence of avopracin resistant bacteria. Soon after the ban on avoparcin, the Danish Integrated Antimicrobial Resistance Monitoring and Research Programme – the first comprehensive surveillance system, was established to monitor the use and health effects of antibiotics in livestock (Aarestrup, 2012). This collaboration between veterinarians and human-disease epidemiologists monitors antimicrobial usage and resistance in animals, food products and humans in Denmark. The government issued legislation in 1995 preventing veterinarian doctos from profiting from selling antibiotics to farmers, another key step that most countries have not yet taken (Aarestrup, 2012). This legislation made a huge impact on the overuse of antibiotics in livestock. The Danish government banned another growth promoter – virginiamycin, in 1998 as scientists found more instances of antibiotic resistance. In 1998 and 2000 respectively, the Danish poultry and pig industries voluntarily stopped all use of antibiotics for growth (Aarestrup, 2012). The Danish agriculture ministry began issuing warning letters as 'dubbed yellow cards' to the pig farmers who had the highest consumption of antibiotics per pig produced (Aarestrup, 2012). This has led to almost 25% reduction in antibiotic use for therapy since 2010.

There exists a debate that the agricultural industry will collapse without the use of antibiotics. However, Danish studies showed that long-term swine productivity and kilograms of chickens produced per square metre were not affected by a ban on the use of antimicrobial growth promoters (Aarestrup et al., 2010; Emborga et al., 2001).

The US FDA issued voluntary guidelines in 2011 and 2013 for the producers of veterinary drugs added to water or feed, with the aim of eliminating the use of medically important antibiotics as growth promoters by the end of 2016 (CDDEP, 2015). The FDA's Center for Veterinary Medicine (CVM) prohibited the use of enrofloxacin in poultry in 2005 due to the development of fluoroquinolone-resistant Campylobacter species in poultry which may transfer to humans and cause infections in them. In 2012, CVM issued an order prohibiting the extralabel use of cephalosporin drugs (excluding cephapirin) in cattle, swine, chickens and turkeys considering the human health risk associated with cephalosporin-resistant strains of certain bacterial pathogens.

The Canadian government implemented a voluntary strategy similar to the effort by FDA in 2014. In Australia, some antibiotic growth promoters are banned (fluoroquinolones, avoparcin, virginiamycin, etc.) and nearly all veterinary antibiotics can only be sold on a prescription. Three non-European members of OECD – Mexico, South Korea and New Zealand, have banned all use of antibiotic growth promoters, but the drugs are still authorized in Japan, among other countries. Antibiotic growth promoters are not banned in most non-OECD countries which are major meat (poultry, pig and cattle) producers, including Argentina, Indonesia, Philippines and BRICS (Laxminarayan et al., 2015).

CONCLUSION

It is now well proven that extensive use of antibiotics and other medicines in livestock subsequently leads to various environmental and potential health risks. The health risks from these drugs in biological systems are not fully known and are only evolving. However, on the basis of the available data, it can be concluded that the use of these drugs needs to be controlled. It is also clear from the above descriptions that the concern about antibiotic resistance in humans may not be purely from excessive intake of antibiotics by them. There are other channels, such as the one from soil and water potentially of livestock origin, which also contribute to this phenomenon.

There is definitely a concern about overuse of antibiotics in livestock with a view to prevent diseases. The different aspects of the fate of such antibiotics in the environment detailed in this chapter hints at strictly restricting the antibiotic use. However, mere regulations may not always work as there are several incidences where one cannot fully rule out antibiotic use against potential illness in livestock. A complete rethinking of livestock production is needed and it is high time that we look for other options.

REFERENCES

Aarestrup, F. (2012). Get pigs off antibiotics. *Nature*, *486*(7404), 465–466. doi:10.1038/486465a PMID:22739296

Aarestrup, F. M. (2000). Characterization of glycopeptide-resistant enterococcus faecium (GRE) from broilers and pigs in Denmark: Genetic evidence that persistence of GRE in pig herds is associated with coselection by resistance to macrolides. *Journal of Clinical Microbiology*, *38*, 2774–2777. PMID:10878086

Aarestrup, F. M. (2009). Occurrence of glycopeptide resistance among enterococcus faecium isolates from conventional and ecological poultry farms. *Microbial Drug Resistance (Larchmont, N.Y.)*, *1*(3), 255–257. doi:10.1089/mdr.1995.1.255 PMID:9158784

Aarestrup, F. M., Jensen, V. F., Emborg, H. D., Jacobsen, E., & Wegener, H. C. (2010). Changes in the use of antimicrobials and the effects on productivity of swine farms in Denmark. *American Journal of Veterinary Research*, *71*(7), 726–733. doi:10.2460/ajvr.71.7.726 PMID:20594073

Babić, S., Mutavdžić, D., Ašperger, D., Horvat, A. J. M., & Kaštelan-Macan, M. (2006). Determination of veterinary pharmaceuticals in production wastewater by HPTLC-Videodensitometry. *Chromatographia, 65*(1-2), 105–110. doi:10.1365/s10337-006-0109-2

Bisarya, S., & Patil, D. (1993). Determination of salicylic acid and phenol (ppm level) in effluent from aspirin plant. *Research and Industry, 38*, 170–172.

Bradley, P. M., Journey, C. A., Button, D. T., Carlisle, D. M., Clark, J. M., Mahler, B. J., & VanMetre, P. C. et al. (2016). Metformin and other pharmaceuticals widespread in wadeable streams of the southeastern United States. *Environmental Science & Technology Letters, 3*(6), 243–249. doi:10.1021/acs.estlett.6b00170

Brown, K. D., Kulis, J., Thomson, B., Chapman, T. H., & Mawhinney, D. B. (2006). Occurrence of antibiotics in hospital, residential, and dairy effluent, municipal wastewater, and the Rio Grande in New Mexico. *The Science of the Total Environment, 366*(2-3), 772–783. doi:10.1016/j.scitotenv.2005.10.007 PMID:16313947

Carballo, M., Esperón, F., Sacristán, C., González, M., Vázquez, B., Aguayo, S., & Torre, A. (2013). Occurrence of tetracycline residues and antimicrobial resistance in gram negative bacteria isolates from cattle farms in Spain. *Advances in Bioscience and Biotechnology, 4*(2), 295–303. doi:10.4236/abb.2013.42A040

Carvalho, P. N., Basto, M. C. P., Almeida, C. M. R., & Brix, H. (2014). A review of plant–pharmaceutical interactions: From uptake and effects in crop plants to phytoremediation in constructed wetlands. *Environmental Science and Pollution Research International, 21*(20), 11729–11763. doi:10.1007/s11356-014-2550-3 PMID:24481515

Castanon, J. I. R. (2007). History of the use of antibiotic as growth promoters in European poultry feeds. *Poultry Science, 86*(11), 2466–2471. doi:10.3382/ps.2007-00249 PMID:17954599

Center for Disease Dynamics, Economics & Policy (CDDEP). (2015). State of the world's antibiotics, 2015. Washington, DC: CDDEP.

Chen, M., Cooper, V. I., Deng, J., Amatya, P. L., Ambrus, D., Dong, S., & Patel, J. et al. (2015). Occurrence of pharmaceuticals in Calgary's wastewater and related surface water. *Water Environment Research, 87*(5), 414–424. doi:10.2175/106143015X14212658614199 PMID:26460461

Chunhui, Z., Liangliang, W., Xiangyu, G., & Xudan, H. (2016). Antibiotics in WWTP discharge into the Chaobai River, Beijing. *Archives of Environmental Protection, 42*(4). doi:10.1515/aep-2016-0036

Coutinho, F. H., Pinto, L. H., Vieira, R. P., Martins, O. B., Salloto, G. R. B., & Santoro, D. O. … Cardoso, A.M. (2013). Antibiotic resistance in aquatic environments of Rio de Janeiro, Brazil. In I. Ahmad, & M.A. Dar (Eds.), Perspectives in water pollution (pp. 1-22). Rijeka, Croatia: InTech.

Cui, C. W., Ji, S. L., & Ren, H. Y. (2006). Determination of steroid estrogens in wastewater treatment plant of a controceptives producing factory. *Environmental Monitoring and Assessment, 121*(1-3), 409–419. doi:10.1007/s10661-005-9139-8 PMID:16758282 da Silva, F. B., Jelic, A., López-Serna, R., Mozeto, A. A., Petrovic, M., & Barceló, D. (2011). Occurrence and distribution of pharmaceuticals in surface water, suspended solids and sediments of the Ebro river basin, Spain. *Chemosphere*, *85*(8), 1331–1339. doi:10.1016/j.chemosphere.2011.07.051 PMID:21880345

Emborga, H., Ersbøll, A. K., Heuera, O. E., & Wegenera, H. C. (2001). The effect of discontinuing the use of antimicrobial growth promoters on the productivity in the Danish broiler production. *Preventive Veterinary Medicine*, *50*(1-2), 53–70. doi:10.1016/S0167-5877(01)00218-5 PMID:11448495

Fick, J., Söderström, H., Lindberg, R. H., Phan, C., Tysklind, M., & Larsson, D. G. J. (2009). Contamination of surface, ground, and drinking water from pharmaceutical production. *Environmental Toxicology and Chemistry*, *28*(12), 2522–2527. doi:10.1897/09-073.1 PMID:19449981

Food and Agriculture Organization of the United Nations (FAO). (2011). *Antibiotics in farm animal production: Public health and animal welfare*. Rome, Italy: FAO.

Food and Drug Administration (FDA). (2016). *2015 Summary Report on antimicrobials sold or distributed in for use in food-producing animals*. Department of Health and Human Services. Retrieved from https://www.fda.gov/downloads/ForIndustry/UserFees/AnimalDrugUserFeeActADUFA/UCM534243.pdf

Gao, L., Hu, J., Zhang, X., Wei, L., Li, S., Miao, Z., & Chai, T. (2015). Application of swine manure on agricultural fields contributes to extended-spectrum β-lactamase-producing Escherichia coli spread in Tai'an, China. *Frontiers in Microbiology*, *6*, 1–7. doi:10.3389/fmicb.2015.00313 PMID:25926828

García-Galán, M. J., Garrido, T., Fraile, J., Ginebreda, A., Díaz-Cruz, M. S., & Barceló, D. (2010). Simultaneous occurrence of nitrates and sulfonamide antibiotics in two ground water bodies of Catalonia (Spain). *Journal of Hydrology (Amsterdam)*, *383*(1–2), 93–101. doi:10.1016/j.jhydrol.2009.06.042

Green, R. E., Newton, I. A. N., Shultz, S., Cunningham, A. A., Gilbert, M., Pain, D. J., & Prakash, V. (2004). Diclofenac poisoning as a cause of vulture population declines across the Indian subcontinent. *Journal of Applied Ecology*, *41*(5), 793–800. doi:10.1111/j.0021-8901.2004.00954.x

Hektoen, H., Berge, J. A., Hormazabal, V., & Yndestad, M. (1995). Persistence of antibacterial agents in marine sediments. *Aquaculutre*, *133*(3-4), 175–184. doi:10.1016/0044-8486(94)00310-K

Heuer, H., Schmitt, H., & Smalla, K. (2011). Antibiotic resistance gene spread due to manure application on agricultural fields. *Current Opinion in Microbiology*, *14*(3), 236–243. doi:10.1016/j.mib.2011.04.009 PMID:21546307

Jechalke, S., Heuer, H., Siemens, J., Amelung, W., & Smalla, K. (2014). Fate and effects of veterinary antibiotics in soil. *Trends in Microbiology*, *22*(9), 536–545. doi:10.1016/j.tim.2014.05.005 PMID:24950802

Kang, D. H., Gupta, S., Rosen, C., Fritz, V., Singh, A., Chander, Y., & Rohwer, C. et al. (2013). Antibiotic uptake by vegetable crops from manure-applied soils. *Journal of Agricultural and Food Chemistry*, *61*(42), 9992–10001. doi:10.1021/jf404045m PMID:24106840

Kristiansson, E., Fick, J., Janzon, A., Grabic, R., Rutgersson, C., Weijdegard, B., & Larsson, D. G. et al. (2011). Pyrosequencing of antibiotic-contaminated river sediments reveals high levels of resistance and gene transfer elements. *PLoS One*, *6*(2), e17038. doi:10.1371/journal.pone.0017038 PMID:21359229

Kumar, K., Gupta, C. S., Chander, Y., & Singh, A. K. (2005). Antibiotic use in agriculture and its impact on the terrestrial environment. *Advances in Agronomy*, *87*, 1–54. doi:10.1016/S0065-2113(05)87001-4

Larsson, D. G., de Pedro, C., & Paxeus, N. (2007). Effluent from drug manufactures contains extremely high levels of pharmaceuticals. *Journal of Hazardous Materials*, *148*(3), 751–755. doi:10.1016/j.jhazmat.2007.07.008 PMID:17706342

Laxminarayan, R., Van Boeckel, T., & Teillant, A. (2015). *The economic costs of withdrawing antimicrobial growth promoters from the livestock sector* (Vol. 78). Paris, France: OECD Publishing. doi:10.1787/18156797

Lin, A. Y., Yu, T., & Lin, C. (2008). Pharmaceutical contamination in residential, industrial, and agricultural waste streams: Risk to aqueous environments in Taiwan. *Chemosphere*, *74*(1), 131–141. doi:10.1016/j.chemosphere.2008.08.027 PMID:18829065

Lin, A. Y. C., & Tsai, Y. (2009). Occurrence of pharmaceuticals in Taiwan's surface waters: Impact of waste streams from hospitals and pharmaceutical production facilities. *The Science of the Total Environment*, *407*(12), 3793–3802. doi:10.1016/j.scitotenv.2009.03.009 PMID:19345984

Martinez, J. L. (2009). Environmental pollution by antibiotics and by antibiotic resistance determinants. *Environmental Pollution*, *157*(11), 2893–2902. doi:10.1016/j.envpol.2009.05.051 PMID:19560847

McEachran, A. D., Blackwell, B. R., Hanson, J. D., Wooten, K. J., Mayer, G. D., Cox, S. B., & Smith, P. N. (2015). Antibiotics, bacteria, and antibiotic resistance genes: Aerial transport from cattle feed yards via particulate matter. *Environmental Health Perspectives*, *123*, 337–343. PMID:25633846

Mutiyar, P. K., & Mittal, A. K. (2014). Occurrences and fate of selected human antibiotics in influents and effluents of sewage treatment plant and effluent-receiving river Yamuna in Delhi (India). *Environmental Monitoring and Assessment*, *186*(1), 541–557. doi:10.1007/s10661-013-3398-6 PMID:24085621

Oluyege, J. O., Oluwaniyi, T. T., & Ijasan, O. C. (2015). Composition of antibiotic resistant bacteria from irrigated vegetable farmland. *Journal of Microbiology Research (Rosemead, Calif.)*, *5*(5), 161–168.

Pedersen, J. A., Soliman, M., & Suffet, I. H. (2005). Human pharmaceuticals, hormones, and personal care product ingredients in runoff from agricultural fields irrigated with treated wastewater. *Journal of Agricultural and Food Chemistry*, *53*(5), 1625–1632. doi:10.1021/jf049228m PMID:15740050

Phillips, P. J., Smith, S. G., Kolpin, D. W., Zaugg, S. D., Buxton, H. T., Furlong, E. T., & Stinson, B. et al. (2010). Pharmaceutical formulation facilities as sources of opioids and other pharmaceuticals to wastewater treatment plant effluents. *Environmental Science & Technology*, *44*(13), 4910–4916. doi:10.1021/es100356f PMID:20521847

Prakash, V. (1999). Status of vultures in Keoladeo national park, Bharatpur, Rajasthan, with special reference to population crash in Gyps species. *Journal of the Bombay Natural History Society*, *96*, 365–378.

Prakash, V., Green, R. E., Pain, D. J., Ranade, S. P., Saravanan, S., Prakash, N., & Cunningham, A. A. et al. (2007). Recent changes in populations of resident *Gyps* vultures in India. *Journal of the Bombay Natural History Society*, *104*, 129–135.

Prakash, V., Pain, D. J., Cunningham, A. A., Donald, P. F., Prakash, N., Verma, A., & Rahmani, A. R. et al. (2003). Catastrophic collapse of Indian white-backed *Gyps bengalensis* and long-billed *Gyps indicus* vulture populations. *Biological Conservation*, *109*(3), 381–390. doi:10.1016/S0006-3207(02)00164-7

Risebrough, R. W. (2004). Population collapses of three species of *Gyps* vultures in the Indian Subcontinent: An overview. In R. D. Chancellor & B. U. Meyburg (Eds.), *Raptors worldwide* (pp. 197–214). Budapest, Hungary: WWGBP/MME.

Rodayan, A., Afana, S., Segura, P. A., Sultana, T., Metcalfe, C. D., & Yargeau, V. (2016). Linking drugs of abuse in wastewater to contamination of surface and drinking water. *Environmental Toxicology and Chemistry*, *35*(4), 843–849. doi:10.1002/etc.3085 PMID:26190693

Rutgersson, C., Fick, J., Marathe, N., Kristiansson, E., Janzon, A., Angelin, M., & Larsson, D. G. et al. (2014). Fluoroquinolones and qnr genes in sediment, water, soil, and human fecal flora in an environment polluted by manufacturing discharges. *Environmental Science & Technology*, *48*(14), 7825–7832. doi:10.1021/es501452a PMID:24988042

Samuelsen, O. B., Torsvik, V., & Ervik, A. (1992). Long-range changes in oxytetracycline concentration and bacterial resistance towards oxytetracycline in a fish farm sediment after medication. *The Science of the Total Environment*, *114*, 25–36. doi:10.1016/0048-9697(92)90411-K PMID:1594922

Sanderson, H., Fricker, C., Brown, R. S., Majury, A., & Liss, S. N. (2016). Antibiotic resistance genes as an emerging environmental contaminant. *Environmental Reviews*, *24*(2), 205–218. doi:10.1139/er-2015-0069

Sarmah, A. K., Meyer, M. T., & Boxall, A. B. A. (2006). A global perspective on the use, sales, exposure pathways, occurrence, fate and effects of veterinary antibiotics (VAs) in the environment. *Chemosphere*, *65*(5), 725–759. doi:10.1016/j.chemosphere.2006.03.026 PMID:16677683

Seo, Y., Choi, J., Kim, S., Min, H., & Jung, Y. (2007). Prioritizing environmental risks of veterinary antibiotics based on the use and the potential to reach environment. *Korean Journal of Soil Science and Fertility*, *40*(1), 43–50.

Simon, N. S. (2005). Loosely bound oxytetracycline in riverine sediments from two tributaries of the Chesapeake Bay. *Environmental Science & Technology*, *39*(10), 3480–3487. doi:10.1021/es049039k PMID:15952351

Stalder, T., Barraud, O., Casellas, M., Dagot, C., & Ploy, M.-C. (2012). Integron involvement in environmental spread of antibiotic resistance. *Frontiers in Microbiology*, *3*, 1–14. doi:10.3389/fmicb.2012.00119 PMID:22509175

United States Geological Survey (USGS). (2017). Contaminants of emerging concern in the environment. *Environmental Health – Toxic Substances Hydrology Program*. Retrieved from http://toxics.usgs.gov/investigations/cec/index.php

Van Boeckel, T. P., Brower, C., Gilbert, M., Grenfell, B. T., Levin, S. A., & Robinson, T. P., … Laxminarayan, R. (2015). Global trends in antimicrobial use in food animals. *Proceedings of the National Academy of Sciences of the United States of America*, *112*, 5649-5654. doi:10.1073/pnas.1503141112

Veterinary Medicines Directorate (VMD). (2015). UK veterinary antibiotic resistance and sales surveillance report. Surrey, UK: VMD. Retrieved from https://www.gov.uk/government/uploads/system/uploads/attachment_data/file/582341/1051728-v53-UK-VARSS_2015.pdf

Watkinsona, A. J., Murbyd, E. J., Kolpine, D. W., & Costanzof, S. D. (2009). The occurrence of antibiotics in an urban watershed: From wastewater to drinking water. *The Science of the Total Environment*, *407*(8), 2711–2723. doi:10.1016/j.scitotenv.2008.11.059 PMID:19138787

Wollenbergera, L., Halling-Sùrensenb, B., & Kusk, K. O. (2000). Acute and chronic toxicity of veterinary antibiotics to Daphnia Magna. *Chemosphere*, *40*(7), 723–730. doi:10.1016/S0045-6535(99)00443-9 PMID:10705550

World Health Organization (WHO). (2012). The evolving threat of antimicrobial resistance: Options for action. Geneva, Swizerland: WHO.

Zhu, Y.-G., Johnson, T. A., Su, J.-Q., Qiao, M., Guo, G.-X., & Stedtfeld, R. D., … Tiedje, J.M. (2013). Diverse and abundant antibiotic resistance genes in Chinese swine farms. *Proceedings of the National Academy of Sciences of the United States of America*, *110*, 3435-3440. doi:10.1073/pnas.1222743110

KEY TERMS AND DEFINITIONS

Antibiotics: Medicines used to treat infections or diseases caused by bacteria; referred also as antibacterials.

Antimicrobial Resistance: The ability of a bacteria to stop an antimicrobial, such as antibiotic, to work against it.

Growth Promoter: Application of medication to stimulate growth.

Metaphylaxis: Mass application of medication to a group of animals to prevent or minimise disease outbreaks.

Pharmaceutical: Related to medicinal drugs or a medicinal drug.

Prophylactic: Application of medicine or other actions intended to prevent a disease.

Sub-Therapeutic Dose: A dose of medicine that is less than the amount required for treating a disease.

Wastewater Treatment Plant: A plant which treats wastewater and sewage by eliminating contaminants with the aim of the treated water to be safely disposed in the natural environment.

Chapter 6

It's the Speciesism, Stupid!

Animal Abolitionism, Environmentalism, and the Mass Media

Paula Brügger
Santa Catarina Federal University, Brazil

ABSTRACT

In a time of intense instrumentalization of life, nature becomes a mere factory from which natural resources are withdrawn. This system is causing immense social, ethical and environmental impacts, and livestock raising is at the core of these problems. The concept of speciesism – a prejudice concerning nonhuman animals, analogous to racism and sexism – is paramount in this realm. This chapter analyses the role of the mass media in perpetuating speciesist values and the urgent need for a paradigm shift. A genuine concern about the future of the planet and nonhuman animals involves questioning our speciesism and our narrow instrumental and economic paradigms.

INTRODUCTION

We live in a time of intense instrumentalization of life. The paradigm still dominant in the Western culture has helped to weave a concept of nature as a set of instruments for the human species. A consequence is that out of the three pillars underlying sustainability the economic one becomes prevalent in its "green" version. Markets for environmental commodities and payment for environmental services are mechanisms born in this context. The quest to tackle the climate change problem via a carbon market is probably the most emblematic example.

Although the climatic issue is a real question to be faced, other problems associated with the so-called "Anthropocene" (Lewis & Maslin, 2015; Zalasiewicz, 2015) are equally or even more severe. Extensive destruction and degradation of habitats – main causes for biodiversity loss, are primary cases requiring urgent attention.

DOI: 10.4018/978-1-5225-4757-0.ch006

Rockström et al. (2009, p. 472), for example, proposed nine "Earth-system processes and its associated thresholds which, if crossed, could generate unacceptable environmental change". Their analysis shows that "three of these processes – climate change, rate of biodiversity loss and interference with the nitrogen cycle – have already transgressed their boundaries" (Rockström et al., 2009, p. 475) and the rate of loss of biodiversity, terrestrial and marine, appears as the most critical, since the border for a safe range of operation is already far exceeded (see also WWF, 2016).

Likewise, according to the 2016 Living Planet Report (WWF, 2016, p. 3), "species populations of vertebrate animals have decreased in abundance by 58 per cent between 1970 and 2012". Although climate change is a significant menace, the most common threat to declining animal populations is the loss and degradation of their habitat (WWF, 2016).

It is also paramount to focus on a specific group of vertebrates – mammalians. Smith et al. (2016, p. 101) point out that there has been "a fundamental shift from a world dominated by wild animals to one largely composed of humans and their livestock". This transition in the biosphere has a number of important implications in terms of ecosystem functions. As the megafauna animals (including elephants, rhinoceroses, giraffes, hippopotamuses, lions, bears, elks, wild buffaloes etc.) have been important ecosystem engineers, "there is an urgent need to understand in a holistic way just how ecosystems may ´unravel´ with their decline or extinction" (Smith et al., 2016, p. 107). Smith et al. (2016) evaluate several proposals of "rewilding", but in order to look at this issue through a genuinely holistic perspective, one must investigate the underlying context. In this case, the historical, economic, political and cultural causes of such decline must be taken into account, along with a critical analysis of the dominant solutions that prevail today, which are market-based and extensively dominated by a chrematistic view.

Aristotle, in his book "*Politics*" (see Aristotle, 1999), explained the difference between economics and chrematistics or wealth getting. The first is concerned with the material supply of the *oikos* (the family, house or family property) or the *polis* (the city, city-state or body of citizens) while the latter, even being part of the economy, is essentially an acquisitive technique. Aristotle also made explicit that chrematistics can become unnatural, breaking all limits, and anticipated that the accumulation of wealth would end up destroying the good way of living (Rossi & Tierno, 2009).

Indeed, the financialization of nature has many problems. New technologies, for example, may turn innocuous the value of an "ecosystem service". Silvertown (2015) cites the case of a species of bats whose "service" concerning cotton productivity was almost wiped out by the introduction of a transgenic technology, combined with a fall in the price of that commodity in the market. He enumerates several other problems concerning the concept of ecosystem services, including "make-believe" fictitious markets. According to him, the dominant way of envisaging our dependence upon the existence and functioning of the environment through monetization devalues nature and provides power to political-economic systems that are at the very basis of the current environmental crisis, such as the neoliberal ideology. Silvertown (2015) also stresses that anthropocentrism lies at the core of the problem of monetization of ecosystem services.

This ethical and moral problem that resides in our relationship with nature, occurs because in industrial societies we have created a very peculiar relationship with technology, taking technical advances as if they were the development tout court. Postman (1993) states that there is a supremacy of technology over all other things, created throughout the history of the Western world, culminating in what he calls technopoly. The idea of technopoly involves a belief in progress, standardization, and superior machine efficiency with respect to humans. Postman (1993) says that because the changes wrought by technology are subtle, they are also wildly unpredictable. He argues that "embedded in every tool is an ideological bias, a predisposition to construct the world as one thing rather than another, to value one thing over another" (Postman, 1993, p. 13). In essence, Postman (1993) highlights the role technology plays in dealing with nature and on how we relate to each other.

The inconsistency subjacent to technical, instrumental and marketing approaches orients us towards the ethical field. Furthermore, the fact that there is now a mammalian biomass consisting predominantly of humans and their farm animals, is the strongest testament that we urgently need to address a matter directly associated with ethics: the presence of animal products in human diet. A key concept in this context is that of speciesism.

SPECIESISM AS A MORAL QUESTION

The term speciesism was originally coined by Richard Ryder in the 1970s, in an analogy to racism and sexism which are also prejudices based on morally irrelevant differences. Ryder (2005, n.p.) argues that because animals suffer pain and distress similarly to humans, our concern for others should be "extended to any ´painient´ – pain-feeling – being regardless of his or her sex, class, race, religion, nationality or species". To him, painience is the only convincing basis for attributing rights or interests to others. Many qualities and moral principles, such as inherent value, justice, freedom, or equality have been proposed over the centuries, but these are mere stepping stones to the ultimate good – happiness – which is made easier by "freedom from all forms of pain and suffering" (Rider, 2005, n.p.). Humans, being related to all other animals through evolution, have no moral grounds to justify exploitation and oppression of nonhuman species.

Nonhuman animals are indeed victims of countless atrocities: they are exploited and killed by the food, clothing and pharmaceutical industries; in religious or "cultural" practices; for "entertainment"; in war experiments, etc. The list is virtually endless. In these different contexts, they are subjected to a variety of forms of torture: they are injured, burned, mutilated, beaten; they suffer partial or total deprivation of liberty; they are injected with toxic substances or forced to ingest them; they are subjected to extreme environmental conditions, restrictive diets and many other perversities. Such a morally repugnant treatment is aggravated by the fact that we currently have an expressive amount of studies of highly qualified researchers about sentience and consciousness in animals.

The recognition of the existence of an emotional life in animals is not a recent fact. According to Bekoff (2007), Charles Darwin was the first scientist to take seriously the study of emotions in animals and described more than twenty different kinds[1]. Darwin postulated that emotions evolved, both in animals and humans, for the purpose of strengthening the social bonds of those living in groups. He believed that emotions connected us with the rest of our community and with the rest of the biosphere. Darwin also supported the theory that even animals without language are capable of reasoning. In other words, it is possible to find the roots of human intelligence and emotions in other animals (Bekoff, 2007).

Bekoff (2007) points out that it is ´bad biology´ not to recognise the existence of emotions, empathy and moral behaviour in animals. He cites countless studies that attest the ability of animals to experience not only the relatively simple emotional states of joy, anguish or fear, but also to establish complex rules of social coexistence, display behaviours related to mourning, honour, empathy and justice. Many mammals also demonstrate the ability to reflect on future events (Bekoff, 2007). Even in animals considered more distant from us, such as fish, there is evidence of capacity to feel pain and fear. Bekoff (2007) highlights the importance of the precept of the ´benefit of the doubt' as a way to halt speciesist attitudes.

Balcombe (2010, p. 88), who endorses basically the same arguments about fish and other nonhuman species, states that the question today is "no longer whether animals think, but what they think". It is therefore essential that we understand that animals are intelligent (and think) to the extent of their needs. Countless reports attest the intelligence, sentience and richness of the social life of animals such as birds, amphibians and reptiles. Balcombe (2010) also defends the thesis that morality did not originate in humans and that the evolution of sentience was a crucial mutation that affected all animals in biological history. Another thought provoking question he raises is the hypothesis that animals without a rich cognitive life may experience even more suffering, due to a reduced ability to anticipate its end.

In 2012, a group of outstanding neuroscientists affirmed that "humans are not unique in possessing the neurological substrates that generate consciousness" (Cambridge Declaration on Consciousness, 2012, n.p.). All mammals, birds and many other creatures – for example, octopuses – possess the neurological substrates associated with conscious states and the capacity to exhibit intentional behaviours (Cambridge Declaration on Consciousness, 2012). It turns unequivocal, therefore, that there are no longer any arguments left to justify the treatment of animals as human properties (Francione, 2004). Although only a fraction of the animal kingdom is mentioned in the Cambridge Declaration on Consciousness, mammals and birds constitute the majority of the 70 billion animals raised and slaughtered for human consumption every year and many more are exploited and killed for other animal products.

Irrespective as to whether this is a legal issue, it is disturbing to think that people in industrial societies do not need any of these products for survival, or to promote a good physical or mental health (Craig & Mangles, 2009). Paradigm changes however are slow. They encounter innumerous obstacles of juridical, political, economic, philosophical, psychological and even religious nature (Wise, 2004).

The debate around speciesism could be extended to much wider frontiers, but this is not the main purpose of this chapter. Nevertheless, it is paramount to make a brief reflection on what could be called "selective speciesism". In this nuance of speciesism, instead of a total and generic dichotomy between us, humans – holders of absolute moral value, and other animals whose value is only instrumental, moral value is attributed to some species, but not to others. This is certainly the most prevalent and diffused modality of speciesism because its moral and cognitive incongruity finds a safe place in our everyday practices. Depending on the species in question, selective speciesists see the very same treatments given to some animals as good (or acceptable), while to others as abhorrent. However, such judgments are inextricably linked to cultural perceptions and personal tastes, not to scientific evidence about sentience, affectivity or cognition, for example. An emblematic instance of this "moral schizophrenia" (Francione, 2000) is the difference of status between pets, such as dogs and cats, and other mammals. The former – recipients of moral considerations, are treated as family members. However, other mammals, many of which with equivalent cognitive, social and affective abilities and behaviours as, for example, dogs, are simply part of abstract collectives called "herds". Pigs fit very well in this category of second-class animals who are not considered "subjects of a life", as proposed by Regan (2004). They are only numbers in a statistic panel, and treated as if each individual did not have a personality, temperament, peculiar way of being and, worse, as if they were not capable of suffering.

Some species, apparently, ascend to the status of holders of moral consideration without being companion animals. This is the typical case of endangered species. However, the extension of some moral consideration to these animals is mainly due to their potential instrumental value as "genetic banks", as maintainers of biodiversity, as an environmental service. This presumed upgrade of status happens often as the result of campaigns led by environmental organizations that, moreover, do not share the abolitionist point of view and remain at the level of a traditional deep ecology within which the value of each individual is not considered (Brügger, 2013, p. 130). We should, in reality, rename this perspective as shallow ecology, in spite of its concern regarding "animals".

The unlimited instrumentalization of everything also explains what might be called "intraspecific selective speciesism". This is the case of pure breed animals who are fabricated to be desired, sold, and who are potentially more likely to be loved and well cared for than those "un-pedigreed" of the same species. Nonetheless, even these manufactured lives are not free from abandonment or ill-treatment. If they lose or do not exhibit the qualities (instrumentalities) for which they were designed – such as company, hunting, guarding etc. – or if the interest from the human part ceases (the motives can be the most futile), they run the risk of being discarded as worthless objects, passing into the category of second-class animals. Indeed, there is a rather nefarious consistency in all this: if they were "invented" to be marketed, and to serve a purpose, they are not seen as lives, but as products that can be returned or withdrawn. There are also conflicts of interest that trigger selective speciesist attitudes, such as those in which animals are used for ritualistic, scientific, or "cultural" purposes, among others. Selective speciesists filtrate species, breeds, situations, goals and contexts, all depending on their personal interests or the interests of a particular group.

There are many theories that aim at constructing ethically sound relationships with nonhuman animals, either or not based on rights, as well as many ways to defend their interests, such as laws and public policies. However, in order to achieve a genuine shift of paradigm we need a new education, one that exposes the connections between the pillars of our Western culture – dominated by an instrumental, mechanistic and speciesist paradigm – and our present environmental, social, economic, political and ethical crisis. Are the most important formal and informal institutions of our society – schools and the media – embracing this perspective?

EDUCATION AND ROLE OF THE MEDIA

Formal education and the mass media could promote a revolution of unimaginable proportions disseminating the animal abolitionist ideology. Nevertheless, schools and the mass media play the role of reproducing and legitimizing dominant worldviews. Speciesism is no exception to the rule: in addition to the usual programming, TV commercials flood us daily with unrealistic images and messages about animals. A strong indication of this are the numerous publicity spots that show animals helping housewives to prepare their own cadavers for dinner (Brügger, 2008). Although this is not what Oliviero Toscani meant with the title of his book "*Advertising is a carrion that smiles at us*"[2] (in SALESmanago, 2015), this is literally the case in contexts that display images of smiling cows or happy pigs.

The more subtle "animal harming" advertisements cover a vast category of all kinds of pervasive propaganda which aims at luring people to acquire things they do not need. Good examples are the ostensive selling of new cell phones whose components are directly destroying the habitat of gorillas, besides the future of children, or advertisements which show beautiful – and supposedly healthy – people wearing fancy white milky moustaches, or fashionable leather items, to mention only a few. In these universes, where skies are eternally blue and people always cheerful, a whole chain of suffering and cruelty towards animals, environmental destruction, and (often) degrading jobs, is appropriately concealed. It is pathetic to think that none of these products are indispensable to promote a good living. Instead, it is all about profit, sheltered by hedonism, indifference and selfishness. Many of these egocentric values have a very narrow connection with the maintenance of a certain (hegemonic) order.

Belloni (1994) affirms that communication, as a typical phenomenon of economic globalization, has invaded all sectors of social life with messages and contents that trivialize violence and promote the emergence of a culture of consumerism and narcissism. She also points out that communication as a social phenomenon arose in the 1970s – when Western economies began to restructure – and flourished in the following decade, in a period of economic, cultural and social reorganization of the developed world. It is in this historical moment that transnational corporations gained power aiming at the domain of the geoeconomy in order to create a global culture to provide the inputs for the production of material and symbolic goods through this world-communication. This phenomenon was, in its basic idea, predicted by some philosophers:

The products indoctrinate and manipulate; they promote a false consciousness which is immune to its falsehood. And as these beneficial products become available to more individuals in more social classes, the indoctrination they carry ceases to be publicity; it becomes a way of life (…), and as a good way of life, it militates against qualitative change (Marcuse, 1968, p. 12).

The media use art, politics, religion and philosophy to create commercials, "bringing these realms of culture to their common denominator – the commodity form" (Marcuse, 1968, p. 61). According to Marcuse (1968, p. 64), "the new totalitarianism manifests itself precisely in a harmonizing pluralism, where the most contradictory works and truths peacefully coexist in indifference". Isn't that exactly the case of those commercials which show cheerful chickens selling poultry, and happy cows selling beef or milk?

Western mass media accomplish this kind of (economic and ideological) goal because communication is "event-oriented and superficial; does not report the underlying structure, historical contexts or long-term implications; simplifies issues and has little tolerance for uncertainty, ambiguity or complexity" (Meadows, 1991, p. 75). Overwhelmingly, advertising is involved with the economic interests of large groups, markets and consumers worldwide.

There is also no neutrality in the selection of the contents that compose news or entertainment programs, among others. In the environmental field, for instance, Meadows (1991, p. 76) says that one hears about "industries that create jobs for workers", but not about "workers who generate profits for the industries". Neutrality is also greatly impaired if we think that headlines such as "Environmental license is denied because of an endangered reptile" could be replaced by "Greed jeopardizes the last specimens of an endemic species". The facts *per se* may be the same, but the way they are reported can vary greatly. This happens because "the assumptions which guide journalists' choices about worthiness, and how newsworthy events will be reported, are not haphazard" (Schlechtweg, 1996, p. 258).

In this sense, Friedman (1991) comments that an increasing number of people think that journalists should become more educators than mere providers of information. The two are however inseparable. There is no such a thing as sheer information. A dialectical relationship lies between "mere informative" content and the formation of values and worldviews (Brügger, 2008, p. 158). The discussion on the issue of neutrality versus advocacy in journalism is not new (see, for instance, Chapman et al., 1997), but very little progress has been made in this subject.

Impartiality – in the strictest sense of the term – is impossible even in formal school education, although many journalists and teachers have such a conviction (Brügger, 2008). Educating journalists in science could help, but improving technical and scientific knowledge alone, will not resolve a problem that has ethical and epistemological roots. It is a "rancid" trait of our culture, dominated by a blind faith in science and technology, the belief that objectivity, in general, and of course, in journalism, could be achieved only through science knowledge. This condition is necessary, but we need a wider, systemic view on that subject.

Let's retrieve the argument that technology shapes our relationship with the environment. Thinking about how one significant change generates a total transformation, Postman (1993, p. 18) says that "in the year 1500, fifty years after the printing press was invented, we did not have old Europe plus the printing press. We had a different Europe. After television, the United States was not America plus television; television gave a new coloration to every political campaign, to every home, school, church, and industry". This is pretty much what Marshall McLuhan (1964) meant by his famous "the medium is the message". Nowadays, the world of television is characterized by its "emphasis on imagery, narrative, presentness, simultaneity, intimacy, immediate gratification, and quick emotional response" (Postman, 1993, p. 16).

Perhaps for these reasons television exerts a particularly pernicious form of symbolic violence. To Bourdieu (1997, p. 22), one of its most striking features is the tacit complicity of those who suffer it and those who exert it, insofar as they are unaware of exerting or suffering this sort of violence. In line with Schlechtweg (1996), Bourdieu (1997) also affirms that journalists operate a selection and a construction, in the search of the sensational, the spectacular. Television invites dramatization in a twofold sense: it puts an event in images on the scene and exaggerates its importance, gravity and its dramatic and tragic features. This requires the use of extraordinary words. Paradoxically, the world of images is dominated by words. Photographs are nothing without the subtitles which tell us what must be read (Bourdieu, 1997).

In fact, despite the sensation of experiencing a world dominated by images and sounds, we live in an increasingly "written" world. What is opposed to a written world is not virtual images and sounds, but the oral one. The universe of orality is the realm of the bards' songs, the rustling of the seagulls' wings, the whispering of the wind and all sounds, pictures and events that are never repeated in the same way again. Although the world of television may be dominated by images, it is still a "written" world because of its unstoppable reproducibility. Any material which allows an eternal come-and-go, the possibility of repeating the same experience *ad infinitum*, in a perfect control of the pace and "thickness" of time is a written one (Brügger, 2008, p. 173). In this aspect, books are less "written", less reified than television: they allow imagination to wander wider, to roam more freely, less tied to preformed images, sounds and rhythms.

This possibility of re-playing everything turns the mass media into a huge repository of ideas that shape concepts such as what animals are or what the environment is. There is a saying: "a lie told a thousand times becomes the truth". Either through its direct or latent content, the diverse hegemonic values of our society are created, replicated and disseminated in these indefatigable machines, regardless of whether or not they are supported by reliable evidences.

Two studies conducted in a mainstream Brazilian TV channel (Brügger, 2013; Brügger, 2016) revealed a total lack of the so proclaimed impartiality and the presence of extremely speciesist values, transmitted via latent content. The two reinforced the merely instrumental value of nonhuman animals and all selective forms of speciesism quoted previously. One of them, an entertainment program, begins with the phrase "It´s information with fun!", that is, the selected topics – including those on animals – cannot have a critical bias or be tedious. This may launch disastrous miseducational consequences, since it becomes a form of incidental learning. The most prominent case was an episode on veganism which showed rescued animals living in a sanctuary. A poor (and even wrong) translation, allied with a narrative that emphasized the pragmatic/aesthetic aspects of the theme – in the detriment of the ethical ones – cooled down any possibility of a genuine debate, by obliterating the core of the matter: animal abolitionism (Brügger, 2013).

Similarly, the analysis of a documentary theoretically dedicated to the memory of a famous lion cowardly murdered, Cecil[3], disclosed elements that were silenced or appeared in an incipient manner, such as the cruelty and violence subjacent to the practice of hunting and its moral dimension (Brügger, 2016). The program – whose title was "Lion hunt in Zimbabwe, stirs the world" – assigned substantial time to biodiversity, a digressive issue in that context, and treated the abhorrent practice of hunting nearly exclusively from its technical and legal dimensions. It also conceded more space to defenders of spurious ideas such as "sustainable hunting", downgrading nonhuman animals to sheer provisions or objects of entertainment. As Schlechtweg (1996, p. 258) states, "by closely attending to the verbal and visual elements of the televisual text, it is possible to tease out the assumptions, and the unifying logic, that shape its content". In this case, a speciesist background totally obfuscated the efforts to honour Cecil.

Hunting can never be sustainable if we add an ethical dimension to the tripod of sustainability. However, even though a traditional conservationist lens there may be miscalculations regarding quotas of animals that can be "harvested", besides social and economic problems. These and other issues were brilliantly discussed by the dissonant voice of a member of the NGO "Born Free", who is also professor of zoology at Oxford University. However, his participation was brief, considering the relevance of the topics he addressed, and his arguments were very much beclouded by other supposedly neutral, but in fact pro-hunting testimonies.

Schlechtweg (1996, p.258) argues that: "Mapping the media's interpretive frameworks is a useful exercise because it can help explain why some aspects of a news story receive attention while others are neglected". Furthermore, presenters often speak lightly, without any idea of the difficulty and the gravity of what they evoke and of the responsibilities they incur when doing this before thousands of viewers (Bourdieu, 1997). In the program about Cecil, there is a scene that illustrates this well, although subtly: during an interview concerning "killing quotas" for seals in Namibia, the reporter smiles as she hears the World Wild Fund for Nature (WWF) members discourse about the subject. The acceptance of these abominable licenses to murder animals that are not in extinction is an example that, devoid of instrumental value as "genetic banks", these creatures are obliged to serve other instrumental purposes, such as protein sources, objects of learning, research etc.

Other aspects of these two programs could enrich this debate even further. Notwithstanding this, the crucial issue is that, if even in cases like the assassination of Cecil, the mass media fail in addressing the core of the matter – our speciesist prejudice – let alone will it be capable of presenting any kind of educative content about climate change or biodiversity loss, deflagrated by the animal protein sector. It is theoretically easier to do a good job on subjects that gather a great deal of consensus concerning the existence of cruelty, like hunting, than on those not considered cruel by most people, as domestication.

The silence surrounding the livestock sector is not only due to a speciesist background. In many countries livestock raising, transgenic grains, antibiotics, pesticides and other products that integrate mega production chains with severe social and environmental externalities, are directly linked to hegemonic political and economic powerful clusters (Brügger, et al., 2016). Fighting this makes the task even harder.

EPILOGUE: IT'S THE SPECIESISM, STUPID!

The current forms of protecting the environment and animals – legislation, public policies, education – rooted in the impersonal category of "fauna", have resulted in being deficient and poor. Technical approaches have been proving inadequate and even detrimental. The dominant environmental education has left a debit balance for perpetuating speciesism and false dilemmas such as "progress" (crude economic growth is the appropriate term) versus conservation. Curricula of journalism are, as so many other areas, marked by an instrumental rationality within which lies the unlimited commodification of nature, regardless of the suffering imposed to human and nonhuman animals. Instrumental rationality is the background upon which each living being ceases to exist as an end in itself, to be reduced to a mere resource. These questions point to the need for changes in the education of media professionals. Speciesist ideas do not match the ideal of exemption of values discussed before and, worse, they are usually anchored in personal preferences and cultural anachronistic beliefs.

Popper (in Popper and Condry, 1995) emphasized that civilization consists essentially in reducing violence. This is its main function and also the goal we aim when trying to raise the level of civility in society.

As children most of us were taught that cows give us milk, meat and leather; chickens provide us with poultry and eggs, sheep hand out their wool and so on. However, animals do not give us any of these things. All these body parts, secretions or "products" are ripped off from them under torture and death. In the beginning of times these processes were probably less painful, but Masson (2014, p. 4) argues that it was precisely "the domestication of animals that has brought to the fore a latent cruelty in humans".

With or without feelings towards animals, it is unmistakable that our speciesist prejudice is at the forefront when it comes to the destruction of the living conditions on the planet. Embracing animal rights will not solve everything because it is impossible to live without some kind of impact. Besides, many impacts are not a consequence of our speciesism and are motivated by sheer economic factors.

"It's the economy, stupid!" was a phrase that became notorious because it pointed, theoretically, to the importance of this sector in promoting the success of a presidential candidacy. Nonetheless, this exclamation should be rephrased to "It's the chrematistics stupid!" according to Aristotle´s arguments.

For those who have a wider concept of the economy and a genuine concern about animals and the future of our planet, the exclamation is: It's the speciesism, stupid! If at least the industrialized world were adept of veganism, our debt towards the animals who share the planet with us today could almost be zeroed. Our impact on future generations of human and nonhuman animals would also be greatly reduced. And the entire biosphere would dramatically benefit by this single ethical ecological change.

REFERENCES

Aristotle. (1999). *Politics* (B. Jowett, Trans.). Kitchener, ON: Batoche Books. (Original work published 4th century BC). Retrieved from http://socserv2.mcmaster.ca/~econ/ugcm/3ll3/aristotle/Politics.pdf

Balcombe, J. (2010). *Second nature: The inner lives of animals*. New York, NY: Palgrave Macmillan.

Bekoff, M. (2007). *The emotional lives of animals: A leading scientist explores animal joy, sorrow, and empathy – and why they matter*. Novato, CA: New World Library.

Belloni, M. L. (1994). A mundialização da cultura. *Sociedade e Estado*, *9*(1/2), 35–53.

Bourdieu, P. (1997). *Sobre a televisão* (M. L. Machado, Trans.). Rio de Janeiro, RJ: Jorge Zahar.

Brügger, P. (2008). Os novos meios de comunicação: Uma antítese da educação ambiental? In C. Loureiro, P. Layrargues, & R. Castro (Eds.), *Educação ambiental: Repensando o espaço da cidadania* (4th ed., pp. 143–177). São Paulo, SP: Cortez.

Brügger, P. (2013). Especismo na TV: Um olhar abolicionista sobre o programa "Pelo Mundo". *Brazilian Animal Rights Journal, 8*(13), 121–165. doi:10.9771/rbda.v8i13.8638

Brügger, P. (2016). Educação e televisão: O leão Cecil no programa Sem Fronteiras, Globo News. *Brazilian Animal Rights Journal, 11*(21), 169–199. doi:10.9771/rbda.v11i21.16504

Brügger, P., Marinova, D., & Raphaely, T. (2016). Animal production and consumption: An ethical educational approach. In T. Raphaely & D. Marinova (Eds.), *Impact of meat consumption on health and environmental sustainability* (pp. 295–312). Hershey, PA: IGI Global. doi:10.4018/978-1-4666-9553-5.ch017

Cambridge Declaration on Consciousness. (2012). Retrieved from http://fcmconference.org/img/CambridgeDeclarationOnConsciousness.pdf

Chapman, G., Kumar, K., Fraser, C., & Gaber, F. (1997). *Environmentalism and the mass media: The North-South divide*. London, UK: Routledge. doi:10.4324/9780203443514

Craig, W., & Mangles, A. (2009). Position of the American Dietetic Association: Vegetarian diets. *Journal of the American Dietetic Association, 109*(7), 1266–1282. doi:10.1016/j.jada.2009.05.027 PMID:19562864

Francione, G. (2000). *Introduction to animal rights: Your child or the dog?* Temple, PA: Temple University Press.

Francione, G. (2004). Animals: Property or persons? In C. Sunstein & M. Nussbaum (Eds.), *Animal rights: Current debates and new directions* (pp. 108–142). New York, NY: Oxford University Press.

Friedman, S. M. (1991). Two decades of the environmental beat. In C. I. LaMay & E. E. Dennis (Eds.), *Media and the environment* (pp. 17–28). Washington, DC: Island Press.

Lewis, S., & Maslin, M. (2015). Defining the Anthropocene. *Nature, 519*(7542), 171–180. doi:10.1038/nature14258 PMID:25762280

Marcuse, H. (1968). *One-dimensional man: Studies in the ideology of advanced industrial society.* Boston, MA: Beacon Press.

Masson, J. M. (2014). *Beasts: What animals can teach us about the origins of good and evil.* New York, NY: Bloomsbury.

McLuhan, M. (1964). *Understanding media.* London: Routledge.

Meadows, D. (1991). Changing the world through the information sphere. In C. Lamay & E. Dennis (Eds.), *Media and the environment* (pp. 67–79). Washington, DC: Island Press.

Popper, K., & Condry, J. (1995). *Televisão: Um perigo para a democracia* (M. Carvalho, Trans.). Lisboa, Portugal: Gradiva.

Postman, N. (1993). *Technopoly: The surrender of culture to technology*. New York, NY: Vintage Books/ Random House.

Regan, T. (2004). *Empty cages: Facing the challenge of animal rights*. Lanham, MD: Rowman & Littlefield Publishers.

Rockström, J., Steffen, W., Noone, K., Persson, A., Chapin, F. S. III, Lambin, E. F., & Foley, J. A. et al. (2009). A safe operating space for humanity. *Nature*, *461*, 472–475. doi:10.1038/461472a

Rossi, M. A., & Tierno, P. (2009). A dimensão econômica da teoria política aristotélica. *Lua Nova*, *77*(77), 179–204. doi:10.1590/S0102-64452009000200006

Ryder, R. (2005). All beings that feel pain deserve human rights - Equality of the species is the logical conclusion of post-Darwin morality. *The Guardian*. Retrieved from http://www.guardian.co.uk/uk/2005/aug/06/animalwelfare

SALESmanago. (2015). *Advertising: the smiling carrion? How Oliviero Toscani Destroyed 5 Foundations of Marketing*. Retrieved from http://blog.salesmanago.com/marketing-automation-2/advertising-the-smiling-carrion-how-oliviero-toscani-destroyed-5-foundations-of-marketing/

Schlechtweg, H. P. (1996). Media frames and environmental discourse: The case of "Focus: Logjam". In J. Cantrill & C. Overac (Eds.), *The symbolic Earth: Discourse and our creation of the environment* (pp. 257–277). Lexington, KY: The University Press of Kentucky.

Silvertown, J. (2015). Have ecosystem services been oversold? *Trends in Ecology & Evolution*, *30*(11), 641–648. doi:10.1016/j.tree.2015.08.007 PMID:26437632

Smith, F. A., Doughty, C. E., Malhi, Y., Svenning, J.-C., & Terborgh, J. (2016). Megafauna in the Earth system. *Ecography*, *39*(2), 99–108. doi:10.1111/ecog.02156

Wilks, J. (2011). *Animal rights and 19th century antivivisection – was Charles Darwin the catalyst?* Retrieved from https://makinghistoryatmacquarie.wordpress.com/2011/11/22/animal-rights-and-19th-century-antivivisection-was-charles-darwin-the-catalyst/

Wise, S. (2004). Animal rights, one step at a time. In C. Sunstein & M. Nussbaum (Eds.), *Animal rights: Current debates and new directions* (pp. 19–49). New York, NY: Oxford University Press.

World Wild Fund for Nature (WWF). (2016). *Living planet report 2016; Summary*. Gland, Switzerland: WWF. Retrieved from: http://awsassets.panda.org/downloads/lpr_living_planet_report_2016_summary.pdf

Zalasiewicz, J. (2015). Epochs: Disputed start dates for Anthropocene. *Nature*, *520*, 436. doi:10.1038/520436b

KEY TERMS AND DEFINITIONS

Animal Abolitionism: Animal rights advocacy opposing the use or property of animals under any circumstances.

Anthropocene: According to some scientists, the current geological age whose characteristics are highly influenced by human activities.

Anthropocentrism: A philosophical view that makes humans most significant by putting them at the centre of all events.

Chrematistic: Related to wealth creation as measured in money.

Environmental Services: Natural ecosystem processes that ensure water purification, climate balance, soil fertility etc, safeguarding the sustainability of all forms of life on Earth; they also provide "products" such as food, natural remedies, fibers, fuels etc.

Mammalian: Belonging to the class Mammalia which refers to "mammals" – vertebrate animals who possess hair and mammary glands with nutritional functions when the females have young; examples include dogs, lions, giraffes and humans.

Neoliberal Ideology: A worldview which endorses privatisation of all goods and services, seeks deregulation of markets and sees competition as a strong trait of human relations.

Speciesism: A belief that humans are superior to nonhuman animals; a form of prejudice, analogous to racism and sexism, based on morally irrelevant differences.

ENDNOTES

1 Although Charles Darwin's work represented a paradigm shift for his time, it did not serve as the basis for the animal rights movement (Wilks, 2011).

2 Reference to Toscani's book "*La pub est une charogne qui nous sourit*", first launched in 1995.

3 See, for instance, https://www.cbsnews.com/pictures/cecil-the-lion-killed-by-hunter/

Section 2

Social Marketing Tools, Mechanisms and Approaches

Chapter 7
Flexitarianism and Social Marketing:
Reflections on Eating Meat in Moderation

Hans Dagevos
Wageningen University and Research, The Netherlands

Machiel J. Reinders
Wageningen University and Research, The Netherlands

ABSTRACT

Society increasingly expresses concerns about the meat-centred food system, there is an increasing choice of plant-based meat substitutes and a growing amount of food consumers abstain from eating meat for several days per week (i.e., flexitarianism). However, consumers differ in their engagement regarding meat consumption moderation, leading to different transition routes of reducing meat consumption. Social marketing strategies are relevant when it comes to this transition and can be divided along a spectrum from light ("education") to heavy ("law"). In the middle of this spectrum, nudging may be typified as aiming to unconsciously change behaviour by intervening in the context of consumption. This chapter presents two field experiments showing how these unconscious behavioural interventions could offer opportunities to effectively reduce meat consumption. Despite the promising contributions of these nudging interventions, a sustainable transition towards less meat consumption also requires changes in both prevalent consumers' mind-set and consumer culture.

Changes in consumer behaviour and food consumption will be needed, with the need to shift the dietary balance to one with a higher proportion of plant foods relative to animal foods. (Mason & Lang, 2017, p. 2-3)

DOI: 10.4018/978-1-5225-4757-0.ch007

INTRODUCTION

This chapter reflects on several prospects for a transition to more sustainable diets generally, with special attention to moderation of our meat consumption. The topic cannot be taken for granted given the circumstances that animal-based consumption patterns and practices are both deeply rooted in multiple socio-cultural ways and continuously cultivated by massive advertising and promotion – making meat the easy choice, and facilitating many consumers to choose one of their most desired food categories. Rather than reconciling ourselves to the fact that the omnipresent meat-centred food consumer culture will and should last forever, this chapter tries to find holes in the stronghold of meat hegemony. The following section examines a few of these cracks in our meat-heavy diet as default foodstyle. It reflects on flexitarianism, dynamics in the world of meat replacements, and rising consumer concerns about the sustainability of the food system as we know it in general and contemporary meat intake levels specifically. The next section is devoted to various modes of meat reduction against the backdrop of social marketing and the emerging field of nudging. Nudging interventions are introduced by presenting some of their merits as well as by positioning them next to other intervention instruments. Pivotal to the section to follow are two recent field experiments applying nudging with a focus on reduction of meat consumption. In the closing section we briefly discuss the potential of flexitarianism, consumer concerns, meat-alternative product innovations and nudging strategies in the transition of moderating meat consumption.

ANTICIPATIONS OF A TURNING TIDE?

The arising flexitarianism, availability of meat alternatives and increasing concerns linked to livestock industry's impact on sustainability, human and animal welfare are manifestations of a turning tide in people's diets. They are discussed in turn below.

Arising Flexitarianism

What immediately comes to mind when we start reflecting on (a possible) transition in meat consumption, is the advent of the flexitarian. Flexitarianism means meat reduction on a part-time basis, that is, eating meat occasionally without abandoning meat totally – in contrast to vegetarians and vegans. This flexitarianism has been "detected" in recent years and is appointed as food trend of the year 2017, according to, for example, Whole Foods (Hosie, 2016; Whole Foods Market, 2017). At the same time, the topicality of meat reduction is confirmed by the recent launch of the cognate term "reducetarian" (Kateman, 2017).) Although it is unknown how many flexitarians already existed in the second half of the previous century, scholarly attention to meat reduction practices in the last few years provides evidence that flexitarianism constitutes a genuine food consumer segment. As yet, empirical studies from various countries find that a considerable amount of food consumers regularly abstain from eating meat for several days per week (see Dagevos, 2016, pp. 237-238 or Verain et al., 2015, pp. 211-212 for references).

Such results suggest fertile grounds for a growing normalisation of low and no meat consumption patterns. However, prudence is in order because a gradual normalisation of flexitarianism in terms of a socially accepted mind-set and interesting topic for media-attention does not automatically result in a drastic fall in meat demand figures. On a global level, this is certainly not the case. Meat production and consumption are rising and it is expected that this trend will go on for the coming decades. It appears to be almost a "worldwide law" that as soon as people become wealthier, they yearn for consuming more meat. From this perspective, it is surprising that with respect to the meat market in some affluent countries the end phase of the lifecycle of this "meatification of diets" is discussed in terms of "peak meat" (see Dagevos, 2016; Mathijs, 2015; Spiller & Nitzko, 2015).

Current meat consumption figures in the Netherlands are an example of this tendency. In retrospect, and after a slowly but gradually decreasing meat consumption level during the '10s, we may suggest cautiously that in 2010 peak meat has been reached. After being largely stable during 1990-2010 on a level of more than 40 kg of meat consumed on average per person a year, since 2011 the line of 40 kg has been passed and a yearly decrease of about half a kilogramme has turned into a level of 37.7 kg of meat consumed in 2015.

Meat Alternatives

A second reflection on moderating meat consumption addresses the growing interest of food consumers to embrace more vegetable-based dishes. This offers a promising opportunity for meat replacements. While the market shares of meat alternatives remain hitherto marginal in comparison to the magnitude of the meat market, plant-based analogues are sold in increasing amounts and via an increasing number of supermarkets, online outlets as well as restaurants and other places to eat. The target group of this meat alternative market is a wider range of consumers than just vegetarians and vegans – important as they are for the market of meat-free products – and includes also flexitarians as well as meat lovers (see e.g. Apostolidis & McLeay, 2016). Although it can be learned from studies focused on meat replacement (e.g. Hartmann & Siegrist, 2017; Hoek et al., 2011) that consumer reluctance to buy and eat meat substitutes originates from such factors as product unfamiliarity, food neophobia, perceived quality, price and healthiness of meat-free alternatives, or resistance to a less meat-based foodstyle, further improvements in the sensory quality and ease of use of substitutes will be helpful to overcome practical obstacles like taste, appearance, and fitting into a "normal" meal. The same accounts for marketing efforts which provide consumers with tempting opportunities to taste and try meat substitutes (promotion, special offers). All this could have stimulating effects on making plant-based meat-alternative products more accessible to both vegetarians and (meat-eating) flexitarians.

On the whole, the flexitarian trend is, in principle, supportive to plant-based foods because of food consumers' search for meat alternatives in practicing their reduced meat foodstyle. Flexitarianism thus potentially contributes to the market penetration of newly-manufactured vegetarian and vegan food products. Whether or not these foods are framed as meat replacements (see further Sexton, 2016), a promising outlook for the market of "alternative protein products" is encouraged by the continuous innovation process meat alternatives are going through at present. The quality of vegan meat replacements on the food market of today is unprecedentedly high and more improvements are on their way in the foreseeable future. Rising product quality and rising volumes of the next generation meat analogues will be advantageous to both consumer appreciation and competitive pricing – it goes without saying that the latter is an important condition for the further growth of the meat analogues market which, in turn, is helpful in making the plant-based choice an easier choice.

Concerns

Reflections upon a transition in meat consumption should also include a growing and more society-wide awareness that food systems as we know them are more or less harmful in sustainability, health as well as animal welfare and food security aspects. To a smaller or larger extent professionals, practitioners, politicians or the general public express concerns and create debate about the dominant food system and its performance. In this respect, critics argue, for example, that the food system is unsatisfactory or even unsuccessful considering its negative environmental impact, its global and non-transparent supply chains (controlled by a select group of stakeholders), its proliferation of agriculture and food culture as monoculture, its violation of animal welfare, or its incapacity to make food equally available and affordable to everyone. Environmental and socio-economic "collateral damage" marks the dominant food paradigm as unsustainable over time and socially unjust, according to those who are concerned. In addition to this, negative health consequences can be added as soon as we think of the costs – economically, and simultaneously personally and culturally in terms of decreasing quality of life – of food-related diseases, such as overweight and obesity, type II diabetes and cardiovascular diseases.

From a perspective of environmental stewardship as well as human health, the current high levels of meat production and consumption are problematic. Much scholarly evidence has been compiled in recent years confirming that animal-based diets generally and the overconsumption of (red) meat particularly suffer from this double burden (see e.g. Hallström et al., 2015 or Van Dooren et al., 2017, to refer only to two studies in this body of literature). Against this backdrop of health, environmental and animal welfare concerns, it is hardly surprising to read in contemporary scholarly papers sentences such as: "Meat eating is a practice that in recent years has become subject of criticism" (Piazza et al., 2015, p. 115); "High levels of meat consumption are increasingly criticised for ethical, environmental, and social reasons…" (Apostolidis & McLeay, 2016, p. 74), or: "Meat production and consumption are increasingly contested…" (Mathijs, 2015, p. 115).

Professional health councils and nutrition experts not only broadly agree on the sustainable and health benefits of diets less centred on animal-based foods (meat, fish, eggs and dairy products) and more on plant-based food products (vegetables, fruits, pulses or nuts), but also make efforts to inform the general public about this by communicating the "win-win" message that foods that are best for your personal health are generally consistent with diets with lower environmental impact on the planet. In practice, there seems to be ample reason to communicate this message because much improvement can be made in this respect as consumer studies frequently conclude that awareness is relatively low with respect to the environmental impact of meat (Bogueva et al., 2017; Hartmann & Siegrist, 2017; Hoek et al., 2017a; Macdiarmid et al., 2015; Pohjolainen et al., 2016; Wellesley et al., 2015). In principle, informing food consumers about the ecological burden of meat is beneficial to fuel public awareness and enhance consumer understanding that however complex the food system may be, they can simply choose to make a reduction in their personal meat consumption in order to change their food choices in more healthy and sustainable directions. Generally, eating less meat has significant impact on a reduction of our personal ecological footprint[1].

The Health Council of the Netherlands (2011) can be credited for a pioneering advisory report published in 2011 in which it was clearly stated that an increase in plant-based food consumption and a decrease in animal product (over)consumption result in healthier eating and a more sustainable diet for people and the planet. While making a concrete, quantified, reduction in meat consumption is no part of the dietary guidelines, the overall message of the Dutch dietary guidelines is in favour of a more plant-based diet.

A similar conclusion in favour of a diet higher in plant-based foods and lower in animal-based foods for health and environmental reasons was drawn by the Scientific Advisory Committee of the 2015 U.S. Dietary Guidelines (DHHS/USDA, 2015), but eventually did not hold in the dietary guidelines of the U.S. (see also Mason & Lang, 2017; Sachs, 2017). All in all, evidence-based policymaking corresponding to the available scientific proof is still hard to find (Dagevos & Voordouw, 2013; Wellesley et al., 2015; Wynes & Nicholas, 2017). Recent exceptions to the rule of ignoring the health and sustainable advantages of eating less meat, is governmental attention in Sweden and China are devoted to encouraging consumers to eat less meat. In other countries such as Germany, Brazil, the UK or the Netherlands, national dietary guidelines refer to sustainability and food choices in general without a specific and direct recommendation to cut on meat. Meanwhile, scholarly attention to sustainable diets based less on meat and more on plant protein within the context of healthiness from a personal to a planetary scale, continues to grow (see e.g. Aschemann-Witzel, 2015; Hoek et al., 2017a, 2017b; Mason & Lang, 2017; Mertens et al., 2016; Meybeck & Gitz, 2017; Van Loo et al., 2017; Verain et al., 2017).

SOCIAL MARKETING AND MODES OF MEAT MODERATION

Another reflection on meat moderation is not so much about tendencies at the demand or supply-side of the food market, but rather about modes of change – more specifically: change in meat consumption behaviour and patterns. It is common knowledge that our food consumption behaviour is notoriously difficult to change, particularly when substantial change from the conventional is involved. It is in this respect that it is useful to fall back on a contribution made by Bill Hopwood and colleagues (2005) in which they offer three different modes of change ranging from modest to fundamental and transformative change, coined respectively status quo, reform, and transformation (see also Peattie & Collins, 2009). In retrospect, it is realised that the categorisation of routes of transition in meat consumption which was introduced some years ago (De Bakker & Dagevos, 2012) is in fact closely related to – and subconsciously inspired by – the arrangement of Hopwood et al. (2005) on different approaches to sustainability (see also Dagevos & Voordouw, 2013; Dagevos, 2016; Verain et al., 2015).

Appetite for Change

These three pragmatic approaches which were provided to engage consumers as allies in meat reduction differ in consumers' appetite for change towards a low or non-meat food consumption pattern. The lowest degree of consumer desire to reduce meat consumption is labelled as the transition route of "sustainability by stealth". Here consumers are more passive food purchasers and not actively reducing their meat consumption. A solution to involve consumers is to make plant-based equivalents of animal products more accessible and attractive to them. Consumers are more likely to accept low meat or meat-free meal options which are not noticeably different from the foods they are used to eat. The second strategy, termed "moderate involvement," takes a somewhat more radical stance in comparison to the incremental position of sustainability by stealth. Moderate involvement is about consumers who are more active in making food choices targeted on reducing their meat consumption. They are more inclined to support and normalise more meat-free and low-meat meals. Being familiar with a flexitarian diet, they neither fully eschew meat nor fully rationalise meat consumption as normal, natural and necessary (Piazza et al., 2015). The final destination of the third route of "cultural change" is a more disruptive and paradigmatic shift in the existing meat-centric food culture. This pathway leads to values and lifestyles encouraging cutting down on meat practices or even giving up our meat-heavy foodstyles entirely, and taking environmental, health and animal-welfare issues profoundly into account when making food choices. As this consumer-oriented approach has been adopted and applied by other researchers (see Apostolidis & McLeay, 2016; Sage, 2014; Schösler et al., 2012; Vanhonacker et al., 2013), it is more widely acknowledged that distinct consumer groups vary in their engagement regarding meat consumption moderation in the wider perspective of making sustainable and healthy food choices.

Simultaneously it is realised that discussions about strategies and their effectiveness with respect to lower meat intake levels are not easily settled. It is in this respect that the subdiscipline of social marketing – central to this book – has a contribution to make. That is, generally social marketing stands for making the role of marketing beneficial to social goals and better social outcomes. Consequently, social marketing is about triggering behavioural change for the personal and common good. Traditionally, it is characteristic for social marketing to focus on issues in the personal health field, such as obesity and overweight or alcohol and tobacco abuse (see e.g. Peattie & Peattie, 2009; Wymer, 2010). In the course of time, environmentally-oriented social marketing with a focus on sustainable production practices and sustainable consumption patterns has evolved. It goes without saying that both traditions are directly relevant when it comes to meat consumption and its reduction – although to the best of our knowledge the issues of eating meat and flexitarianism are not explicitly addressed in social marketing studies (which adds to the value and uniqueness of this book's point of view).

Nudging

More specifically, however, social marketing is interested in what means to deploy in order to gain intended ends. Social marketing strategies could be divided along a spectrum ranging from education and information campaigns to financial incentives and regulatory measures. This brings the tripartite classification of education, marketing and law by Michael Rothschild (1999) to mind. In terms of the so-called intervention ladder that reaches from providing information to choice editing and choice encouraging as relatively informal form of influencing behavioural choice ("education"), to more invasive forms in the sense of steering and elimination of particular choices ("law"), the middle part of this ladder contains a concept that has gained much popularity in recent years: nudging (Thaler & Sunstein, 2008).

In Rothschildian terms nudging may be typified as a social marketing strategy that aligns with "marketing". On the one hand, nudges aim to change behaviour but do not forbid or exclude undesirable behavioural choices ("law"). On the other hand, nudges do more than providing information ("education"), particularly by intervening in the conditions of consumption – the choice architecture, to use jargon – through which the accessibility, availability, acceptability or attractiveness of behavioural options change. Nudging interventions are not about "hard" financial incentives or regulatory mechanisms, and as such, are a "soft" category of social marketing. This adjective implies no disqualification of nudging, but rather refers to one of its merits. That is, because nudging in principle does not exclude any options or significantly change their economic incentives it is an acceptable and attractive behavioural intervention method for both policy makers and companies. Nudges aim to change behaviour "in the right direction" but do not forbid undesirable behaviour. Such features of nudges leave the "sacrosanct" freedom of choice intact while being simultaneously facilitatory instead of nannying or authoritarian – as in the case of information campaigns or the use of law[2]. As a result, policy makers increasingly implement these techniques in their policy making (e.g. the UK Behavioural Insights Team, 2017). Also, the food service business is gathering interest in nudging experiments, and findings of the effectiveness of such behavioural interventions in altering food choices are appearing in scientific journals (see e.g. Bucher et al., 2016; Filimonau et al., 2017; Velema et al., 2017).

Nudging has additional advantages. First, nudging is demand-oriented. It concentrates on consumption. This is not self-evident given the long and strong tradition that concentrates first and foremost on technological progress in terms of improving the efficiency of food production. The technological efficiency is a prevailing supply-side response to solve problems, provide prosperity or boost sustainability in the world of food. Nudging, however, accords with the opinion that also demand-side changes supporting a sustainable diet transition are necessary in helping to make the food system as a whole more sustainable. Another merit of nudging intervention is that it focuses on changing the food or shopping environment. In this respect nudging takes it seriously that our behavioural choices are highly influenced by the environment – the "decision context" – in which we make these choices. Although nudging concentrates primarily on physical aspects of situational circumstances, and how small the intervention into this infrastructure of consumption may be, nudging rightly targets on the environment as behavioural determinant. This focus on situational factors is all the more important given the fact that many of our food consumption choices are made quickly (Cohen & Babey, 2012) and without much cognitive information processing and conscious deliberation (Johnson et al., 2012). Eating decisions are often driven by sights, smells, rumble in the stomach, or power of habit. When food choices are, in large part, a consequence of automatic responses to contextual food cues, then "law" and "education," which largely rely on cognition, are not the only or best ways to change people's behaviour. An appropriate remark in this respect has been made by Brian Wansink and colleagues (2009, p. 167) when they point out that it is often "easier to change their [consumers'] environment, then to change their mind".

FIELD EXPERIMENTS APPLYING MEAT NUDGES

In this section we present two field experiments with nudging. They show how these unconscious behavioural interventions could offer opportunities to effectively reduce meat consumption by making the flexitarian choice the default option.

Nudging Smaller Meat Portions in Restaurants

First, we present an unconscious behavioural intervention that examined the effects of modified portion sizes of meat (and vegetables) during the main dish in a real-life restaurant setting (Reinders et al., 2017). The idea behind this experiment is that people tend to increasingly consume their meals out-of-home, for example in cafeterias and restaurants. As a consequence, both increasing and reducing intake (large portions) of meat may also be associated with out-of-home consumption (Dagevos & Voordouw, 2013). Such observations imply that restaurants could play an important role in scaling down meat consumption. Additionally, food interventions could have the greatest impact when they are conducted in "limited access" sites such as restaurants, as opposed to supermarkets or grocery stores, as it is easier in these settings to change the choice architecture – i.e., manoeuvre customers towards making healthier choices (Zandstra et al., 2002).

One of the instruments that these "limited access" sites can use to reduce meat consumption is portion size modifications. When people are served larger portions, they eat more compared to when smaller portions are offered (Steenhuis et al., 2010; Vermeer et al., 2014). Reduced portion sizes not only result in reduced intake, but also in reduced plate waste (Freedman & Brochado, 2010). This previous experimental evidence suggests that modifying portion size can be potentially effective in decreasing meat consumption in restaurants.

The field experiment by Machiel Reinders and colleagues took place during May 2015 in three restaurant locations of a major restaurant chain in medium-sized cities in the Netherlands. This chain was selected because its restaurants receive guests from all population layers. A cross-over design was used in which the three participating restaurants were randomly assigned to a sequence of an intervention or control condition. In the intervention period, portion sizes of meat on plates of the main dishes were reduced by on average 12.5 percent and simultaneously portion sizes of vegetables on plates of the main dishes were doubled (150 grams of vegetables instead of 75 grams). In the control period, portion sizes of the main dishes were kept as usual. In total, 1,006 observations and questionnaires were included, 536 in the control condition and 470 in the intervention condition. People that took part in the experiment were unaware of this.

The results of the experiment showed that meat consumption was significantly lower during the intervention period (M = 183.1 grams) than during the control period (M = 211.1 grams). In addition, total vegetable consumption (including side dishes) was significantly higher during the intervention period (M = 178.0 grams) than during the control period (M = 137.0 grams). Furthermore, although participants evaluated the amount of meat lower in the intervention period compared to the control period, satisfaction with the restaurant visit did not differ during the intervention and control periods. Satisfaction with the main dish was significantly lower during the intervention period than during the control period, but the scores indicate that participants were still (very) satisfied with their main dish. Moreover, no complaints from guests were received during the intervention period. These results suggest that portion size could significantly affect meat consumption, while leaving satisfaction largely unaffected. The findings seem to be consistent with an earlier field study by Nicole Diliberti et al. (2004), in which no differences in satisfaction were found between restaurant meals with a higher and lower portion size. This is all the more an interesting finding given the fact that in restaurants hedonic goals are salient (i.e., people commonly go to a restaurant for hedonic reasons and not for health reasons), and generally unhealthy products are preferred when hedonic goals are salient (Raghunathan et al., 2006). Unknowingly decreasing meat portions on plates (and simultaneously increasing vegetables portions) thus does not disturb these hedonic goals in such a way that satisfaction is affected.

In summary, Reinders et al. demonstrate that unknowingly decreasing meat portions in combination with increasing vegetables portions decreased the amount of meat eaten in favour of the amount of vegetables consumed. Besides, despite the changes in portion sizes participants remained satisfied with their restaurant visit and main dish. The findings of this study imply that modifications of portion sizes of meat in restaurants could offer opportunities to effectively limiting meat consumption. By the same token, by serving more vegetables and less meat in their restaurants, restaurant owners could play an important role in promoting meat-reduced meal options, and thereby contribute to a consumption cultural normalisation process of eating meat in moderation.

Nudging à la Carte

The results obtained by the just-mentioned intervention study are consistent with other findings in the new field of nudging. Nudging studies applying default-based interventions learn that changing the default can have both motivational influence as well as actual impact on consumer choice. This promising effectiveness of nudge strategies has been demonstrated with respect to the enhancement of healthier choices (Arno & Thomas, 2016; Reisch et al., 2017). The potential that nudges hold for sustainable consumer behaviour generally and lower meat consumption choices specifically, is addressed by Matthias Lehner et al. (2016) and Victoria Campbell-Arvai and colleagues (2014) respectively. In line with the aforementioned intervention study by Reinders et al., the latter also concentrates on meat consumption choice offering meat-free meal options. This study too concludes that food service managers of dining halls or cafeterias could play their part in steering consumers towards more pro-environmental and/or healthier food choices, i.e. a meat-free menu option in this study, by "placing unhealthier or less environmentally 'friendly' food options in a slightly less convenient position" (Campbell-Arvai et al., 2014, p. 465).

Proceeding further into the foodsteps of Wansink's earlier nudging experiments in out-of-home contexts (see e.g. Wansink, 2006), the recent experiments conducted by Campbell-Arvai et al. and Reinders et al. have been supplemented by a meat-oriented nudging experiment by Christina Gravert and Verena Kurz (2017). In Gravert and Kurz's study entitled "Nudging à la carte" the menu is rearranged in favour of a vegetarian dish option instead of a meat meal option. Likewise, this field experiment demonstrates that a considerable amount of consumers are willing to opt for a vegetarian choice as a result of changing the default option.

The researchers changed the framing of different options of three dishes (meat, fish and a vegetarian dish) in a restaurant located in Gothenburg, Sweden with the intervention period lasting for three weeks in May 2016. Customers of this restaurant were randomly presented a lunch menu offering a meat and a fish dish while a vegetarian dish was not directly displayed on the menu but was offered upon request. The other menu was almost the opposite, and offered a vegetarian dish and a fish dish spelled out on the menu while a meat dish was not mentioned on the menu but only noted that an option containing meat was available on request. In both menus the fish dish was presented as second with the lunch options for the meat and vegetarian dish as the first on each of the different menu designs. This experiment of rearranging the menu shows that a meat/fish menu results in consumer choices for meat and fish dish in more than 95 percent of the total orders and hardly for the vegetarian option (2 to 4 percent). As soon as the vegetarian/fish menu was given to the customers, the meat option dropped to 10-25 percent during the three weeks of the intervention and the vegetarian dish was opted for in 10-23 percent in the intervention period (fish was chosen in more than 60 percent of the total orders).

This simple and subtle choice editing in which the menus are rearranged without banning meat or changing prices, resulted into an increase in vegetarian dishes and a decrease in the share of meat dishes. In sum, the study by Gravert and Kurz provides another example of a small behavioural intervention with substantial effects on consumer choice. Consequently, this experiment adds to the development of a body of knowledge of intervention studies in real-life settings where consumers are nudged to eat low or non-meat meals. It confirms that nudges can be a promising tool with respect to eating meat in moderation.

IN CLOSING: A FEW QUALIFICATIONS

In addition to product innovations in meat substitutes and food consumer concerns about environmental, animal and human welfare of common production and consumption practices in the current food system, also nudge intervention studies are contributing to our reflections on moderation in meat consumption. However hopeful these prospects are, they may also be put into perspective.

Meat-Eating Culture and Cutting Down on Meat

With respect to flexitarianism and the food market for low or non-meat products, we should realise that despite today's presence of less meat-based foodstyles and slowly falling meat consumption levels in parts of the developed world, we are persistent meat eaters fueling the rising meat consumption levels on a global scale. At the same time, in most parts of the world a meat-eating consumer culture ("a carnivorous culture") remains dominant that is not in favour of a transition towards meat consumption reduction. In other words, the 4Ns of meat consumption still prevail: choosing and eating meat is considered natural, normal, necessary, and nice (Piazza et al., 2015). This also resonates in consumer acceptance of "new proteins" such as algae or insects, and plant-based meat replacements generally. Although the outlook for the meat alternative market is positive, it is anything but self-evident that food consumers in large numbers are going to adopt such products – notwithstanding the "flexible" attitude of meat-reducing consumers.

A qualification may also be made with respect to the meat reducing effect of consumer concerns and (scholarly) consensus about negative impacts of meat production and consumption in terms of personal and planetary health. Besides that, science runs ahead of society with respect to overcoming the reluctance or resistance to a "cutting down-strategy" in order to reduce adverse side effects of meat production and consumption, it should also be realised that even when consumers become or are more aware of these meat-related issues this information is often of limited value with respect to substantial and sustainable behavioural change.

Consumer Engagement and Consumers' Environment

The latter brings us to our final qualification regarding nudges. Despite the suitability of nudging interventions in the field of meat reduction, possible doubts could be raised about the long-term behavioural effects of nudging as well as about its persuasiveness. Nudges subtly steer consumers to certain behavioural options without limiting their freedom of choice. It is, however, questionable whether this libertarian paternalism of changing the decision context without eliminating options is appropriate to realise a transition in limiting meat consumption to such an extent that meat intake levels – at least – fall within environmental boundaries and meet dietary guidelines. Nudging strategies have started to provide proof of motivational influence and impact on food choices, but nudging interventions are primarily focused on behavioural "change by stealth, not tackling consumer consciousness or choice reduction" (Mason & Lang, 2017, p. 19). Nudging, therefore, is close to the transition route of sustainability by stealth (De Bakker & Dagevos, 2012). Characteristic of this pathway is the relatively limited level of consumer involvement. This relates to a comment by Lehner et al. (2016, p. 176) that nudges "do not actively engage the public in debating patterns and levels of consumption".

Put differently, nudging is no part of the transition route of cultural change. In this route, it is acknowledged that sustainable transition demands more than (incremental) changes in individual choice through changing the choice architecture, but is about changing power relations profoundly (see also Fuchs et al., 2016), adopting a consumer ethics of enough, and an economy of sufficiency. In such a situation of systematic change, a significant and lasting reduction in meat consumption is driven by turning the above-cited remark by Wansink and colleagues about changing consumers' environment and their mind upside down. Now it is rather claimed: "The best interventions will certainly be those that seek to change minds alongside changing contexts" (Paul Dolan et al., quoted in Lehner et al., 2016, p. 176). Put differently and more specifically to curbing meat consumption: "If we want to make more radical cuts to our meat habit, we need to flip our mind-set around" (Wilson, 2017, p. 149).

REFERENCES

Apostolidis, C., & McLeay, F. (2016). Should we stop meating like this? Reducing meat consumption through substitution. *Food Policy*, *65*, 74–89. doi:10.1016/j.foodpol.2016.11.002

Arno, A., & Thomas, S. (2016). The efficacy of nudge theory strategies in influencing adult dietary behaviour: A systematic review and meta-analysis. *BMC Public Health*, *16*(1), 1–11. doi:10.1186/s12889-016-3272-x PMID:27475752

Aschemann-Witzel, J. (2015). Consumer perception and trends about health and sustainability: Trade-offs and synergies of two pivotal issues. *Current Opinion in Food Science*, *3*, 6–10. doi:10.1016/j.cofs.2014.08.002

Behavioural Insights Team. (2017). In partnership with Cabinet Office. Retrieved from http://www.behaviouralinsights.co.uk

Bogueva, D., Marinova, D., & Raphaely, T. (2017). Reducing meat consumption: The case for social marketing. *Asia Pacific Journal of Marketing and Logistics*, *29*(3), 477–500. doi:10.1108/APJML-08-2016-0139

Bucher, T., Collins, C., Rollo, M. E., McCaffrey, T. A., De Vlieger, N., Van der Bend, D., & Perez-Cueto, F. J. A. et al. (2016). Nudging consumers towards healthier choices: A systematic review of positional influences on food choice. *British Journal of Nutrition*, *115*(12), 2252–2263. doi:10.1017/S0007114516001653 PMID:27185414

Campbell-Arvai, V., Arvai, J., & Kalof, L. (2014). Motivating sustainable food choices: The role of nudges, value orientation, and information provision. *Environment and Behavior*, *46*(4), 453–475. doi:10.1177/0013916512469099

Cohen, D. A., & Babey, S. H. (2012). Contextual influences on eating behaviours: Heuristic processing and dietary choices. *Obesity Reviews*, *13*(9), 766–779. doi:10.1111/j.1467-789X.2012.01001.x PMID:22551473

Dagevos, H. (2016). Exploring flexitarianism: Meat reduction in a meat-centred food culture. In T. Raphaely & D. Marinova (Eds.), *Impact of meat consumption on health and environmental sustainability* (pp. 233–243). Hershey, PA: IGI Global. doi:10.4018/978-1-4666-9553-5.ch012

Dagevos, H., & Voordouw, J. (2013). Sustainability and meat consumption: Is reduction realistic? *Sustainability: Science, Practice, and Policy*, *9*, 60–69.

De Bakker, E., & Dagevos, H. (2012). Reducing meat consumption in today's consumer society: Questioning the citizen-consumer gap. *Journal of Agricultural & Environmental Ethics*, *25*(6), 877–894. doi:10.1007/s10806-011-9345-z

De Boer, J., & Aiking, H. (2017). Pursuing a low meat diet to improve both health and sustainability: How can we use the frames that shape our meals? *Ecological Economics*, *142*, 238–248. doi:10.1016/j.ecolecon.2017.06.037

Department of Health and Human Services/Department of Agriculture (DHHS/USDA). (2015). *Scientific report of the 2015 dietary guidelines advisory committee*. Washington, DC. First print, February. Retrieved from https://ods.od.nih.gov/pubs/2015_DGAC_Scientific_Report.pdf

Diliberti, N., Bordi, P. L., Conklin, M. T., Roe, L. S., & Rolls, B. J. (2004). Increased portion size leads to increased energy intake in a restaurant meal. *Obesity Research*, *12*(3), 562–568. doi:10.1038/oby.2004.64 PMID:15044675

Filimonau, V., Lemmer, C., Marshall, D., & Bejjani, G. (2017). 'Nudging' as an architect of more responsible consumer choice in food service provision: The role of restaurant menu design. *Journal of Cleaner Production*, *144*, 161–170. doi:10.1016/j.jclepro.2017.01.010

Freedman, M. R., & Brochado, C. (2010). Reducing portion size reduces food intake and plate waste. *Obesity (Silver Spring, Md.)*, *18*(9), 1864–1866. doi:10.1038/oby.2009.480 PMID:20035274

French, J. (2011). When nudging is not enough. *Journal of Social Marketing*, *1*(2), 154–162. doi:10.1108/20426761111141896

Fuchs, D., Di Guilio, A., Glaab, K., Lorek, S., Maniates, M., Princen, T., & Røpke, I. (2016). Power: The missing link in sustainable consumption and absolute reductions research and action. *Journal of Cleaner Production*, *132*, 298–307. doi:10.1016/j.jclepro.2015.02.006

Graham, T., & Abrahamse, W. (2017). Communicating the climate impacts of meat consumption: The effect of values and message framing. *Global Environmental Change*, *44*, 98–108. doi:10.1016/j.gloenvcha.2017.03.004

Gravert, C., & Kurz, V. (2017). Nudging à la carte: A field experiment on food choice. Working Paper in Economics, No. 690. Gothenburg, Sweden: University of Gothenburg, Department of Economics.

Hallström, E., Carlsson-Kanyama, A., & Börsjesson, P. (2015). Environmental impact of dietary change: A systematic review. *Journal of Cleaner Production*, *91*, 1–11. doi:10.1016/j.jclepro.2014.12.008

Hartmann, C., & Siegrist, M. (2017). Consumer perception and behaviour regarding sustainable protein consumption: A systematic review. *Trends in Food Science & Technology*, *61*, 11–25. doi:10.1016/j.tifs.2016.12.006

Health Council of the Netherlands. (2011). *Guidelines for a healthy diet: The ecological perspective*. The Hague, the Netherlands: Health Council of the Netherlands. Retrieved from https://www.gezondheidsraad.nl/sites/default/files/201108E.pdf

Hoek, A. C., Luning, P. A., Weijzen, P., Engels, W., Kok, F. J., & De Graaf, C. (2011). Replacement of meat by meat substitutes: A survey on person- and product-related factors in consumer acceptance. *Appetite*, *42*, 265–272. doi:10.1016/j.appet.2003.12.003 PMID:21315123

Hoek, A. C., Pearson, D., James, S. W., Lawrence, M. A., & Friel, S. (2017a). Shrinking the food-print: A qualitative study into consumer perceptions, experiences and attitudes towards healthy and environmentally friendly food behaviours. *Appetite*, *108*, 117–131. doi:10.1016/j.appet.2016.09.030 PMID:27686818

Hoek, A. C., Pearson, D., James, S. W., Lawrence, M. A., & Friel, S. (2017b). Healthy and environmentally sustainable food chpoices: Consumer responses to point-of-purchase actions. *Food Quality and Preference*, *58*, 94–106. doi:10.1016/j.foodqual.2016.12.008

Hopwood, B., Mellor, M., & O'Brien, G. (2005). Sustainable development: Mapping different approaches. *Sustainable Development*, *13*(1), 38–52. doi:10.1002/sd.244

Hosie, R. (2016). Flexitarianism predicted as key food trend for 2017. *The Independent*, 9 December. Retrieved from http://www.independent.co.uk/life-style/food-and-drink/flexitarianism-predicted-as-key-food-trend-for-2017-vegetarian-less-meat-a7465156.html

Johnson, E. J., Shu, S. B., Dellaert, B. G. C., Fox, C., Goldstein, D. G., Häubl, D. G., & Weber, E. U. et al. (2012). Beyond nudges: Tools of a choice architecture. *Marketing Letters*, *23*(2), 487–504. doi:10.1007/s11002-012-9186-1

Kateman, B. (Ed.). (2017). *The reducetarian solution: How the surprisingly simple act of reducing the amount of meat in your diet can transform your health and the planet*. New York, NY: TarcherPerigee.

Lehner, M., Mont, O., & Heiskanen, E. (2016). Nudging – a promising tool for sustainable consumption behaviour? *Journal of Cleaner Production*, *134*, 166–177. doi:10.1016/j.jclepro.2015.11.086

Macdiarmid, J. L., Douglas, F., & Campbell, J. (2015). Eating like there's no tomorrow: Public awareness of the environmental impact of food and reluctance to eat less meat as part of a sustainable diet. *Appetite*, *96*, 487–493. doi:10.1016/j.appet.2015.10.011 PMID:26476397

Mason, P., & Lang, T. (2017). *Sustainable diets: How ecological nutrition can transform consumption and the food system*. London, UK: Earthscan.

Mathijs, E. (2015). Exploring future patterns of meat consumption. *Meat Science*, *109*, 112–116. doi:10.1016/j.meatsci.2015.05.007 PMID:26002118

Mertens, E., Van 't Veer, P., Hiddink, G. J., Steijns, J. M. J. M., & Kuijsten, A. (2016). Operationalising the health aspects of sustainable diets: A review. *Public Health Nutrition*, *20*(04), 739–757. doi:10.1017/S1368980016002664 PMID:27819199

Meybeck, A., & Gitz, V. (2017). Sustainable diets within sustainable food systems. *The Proceedings of the Nutrition Society*, *76*(01), 1–11. doi:10.1017/S0029665116000653 PMID:28195528

Peattie, K., & Collins, A. (2009). Guest editorial: Perspectives on sustainabel consumption. *International Journal of Consumer Studies*, *33*(2), 107–112. doi:10.1111/j.1470-6431.2009.00758.x

Peattie, K., & Peattie, S. (2009). Social marketing: A pathway to consumption reduction? *Journal of Business Research, 62*(2), 260–268. doi:10.1016/j.jbusres.2008.01.033

Piazza, J., Ruby, M. B., Loughnan, S., Luong, M., Kulik, J., Watkins, H. N., & Seigerman, M. (2015). Rationalizing meat consumption: The 4Ns. *Appetite, 91*, 114–128. doi:10.1016/j.appet.2015.04.011 PMID:25865663

Pohjolainen, P., Tapio, P., Vinnari, M., Jokinen, P., & Räsänen, P. (2016). Consumer consciousness on meat and the environment – Exploring differences. *Appetite, 101*, 37–45. doi:10.1016/j.appet.2016.02.012 PMID:26873454

Raghunathan, R., Naylor, R. W., & Hoyer, W. D. (2006). The unhealthy – tasty intuition and its effects on taste inferences, enjoyment, and choice of food product. *Journal of Marketing, 70*(4), 170–184. doi:10.1509/jmkg.70.4.170

Reinders, M. J., Huitink, M., Coosje Dijkstra, S., Maaskant, A. J., & Heijnen, J. (2017). Menu-engineering in restaurants: Adapting portion sizes on plates to enhance vegetable consumption – a real life experiment. *The International Journal of Behavioral Nutrition and Physical Activity, 14*(1), 1–11. doi:10.1186/s12966-017-0496-9 PMID:28424081

Reisch, L. A., Sunstein, C. R., & Gwozdz, W. (2017). Viewpoint: Beyond carrots and sticks: Europeans support health nudges. *Food Policy, 69*, 1–10. doi:10.1016/j.foodpol.2017.01.007

Rothschild, M. L. (1999). Carrots, sticks and promises: A conceptual framework for the management of public health and social issue behaviors. *Journal of Marketing, 63*(4), 24–37. doi:10.2307/1251972

Sachs, J. (2017). The meat lobby, the politicians, and U.S. nutrition. In B. Kateman (Ed.), *The reducetarian solution: How the surprisingly simple act of reducing the amount of meat in your diet can transform your health and the planet* (pp. 103–106). New York, NY: TarcherPerigee.

Sage, C. (2014). Making and un-making meat: Cultural boundaries, environmental thresholds and dietary transgressions. In M. K. Goodman & C. Sage (Eds.), *Food transgressions: Making sense of contemporary food politics* (pp. 181–203). Farnham, UK: Ashgate.

Schösler, H., de Boer, J., & Boersema, J. J. (2012). Can we cut out the meat of the dish?: Constructing consumer-oriented pathways towards meat substitution. *Appetite, 58*(1), 39–47. doi:10.1016/j.appet.2011.09.009 PMID:21983048

Sexton, A. (2016). Alternative proteins and the (non)stuff of "meat". *Gastronomica, 16*(3), 66–78. doi:10.1525/gfc.2016.16.3.66

Spiller, A., & Nitzko, S. (2015). Peak meat: The role of meat in sustainable consumption. In L.A. Reisch & J. Thøgersen (Eds.), Handbook of research on sustainable consumption (pp. 192-208). Cheltenham: Edward Elgar.

Steenhuis, I. H., Leeuwis, F. H., & Vermeer, W. M. (2010). Small, medium, large or supersize: Trends in food portion sizes in the Netherlands. *Public Health Nutrition, 13*(06), 852–857. doi:10.1017/S1368980009992011 PMID:19912675

Thaler, R. H., & Sunstein, C. R. (2008). *Nudge: Improving decisions about health, wealth, and happiness*. New Haven, CT: Yale University Press.

Van Dooren, C., Douma, A., Aiking, H., & Vellinga, P. (2017). Proposing a novel index reflecting both climate impact and nutritional impact of food products. *Ecological Economics*, *131*, 389–398. doi:10.1016/j.ecolecon.2016.08.029

Van Loo, E. J., Hoefkens, C., & Verbeke, W. (2017). Healthy, sustainable and plant-based eating: Perceived (mis)match and involvement-based consumer segments as targets for future policy. *Food Policy*, *69*, 46–57. doi:10.1016/j.foodpol.2017.03.001

Vanhonacker, F., Van Loo, E. J., Gellynck, X., & Verbeke, W. (2013). Flemish consumer attitudes towards more sustainable food choices. *Appetite*, *62*, 7–16. doi:10.1016/j.appet.2012.11.003 PMID:23195711

Velema, E., Vyth, E. L., & Steenhuis, I. H. (2017). Using nudging and social marketing techniques to create healthy worksite cafeterias in the Netherlands: Intervention development and study design. *BMC Public Health*, *17*(1), 1–9. doi:10.1186/s12889-016-3927-7 PMID:28077114

Verain, M., Dagevos, H., & Antonides, G. (2015). Flexitarianism: A range of sustainable food styles. In L. A. Reisch & J. Thøgersen (Eds.), *Handbook of research on sustainable consumption* (pp. 209–223). Cheltenham: Edward Elgar. doi:10.4337/9781783471270.00023

Verain, M. C. D., Sijtsema, S. J., Dagevos, H., & Antonides, G. (2017). Attribute segmentation and communication effects on healthy and sustainable consumer diet intentions. *Sustainability*, *9*(5), 1–19. doi:10.3390/su9050743

Vermeer, W. M., Steenhuis, I. H., & Poelman, M. P. (2014). Small, medium, large or supersize?: The development and evaluation of interventions targeted at portion size. *International Journal of Obesity*, *38*, 13–18. doi:10.1038/ijo.2014.84 PMID:25033959

Wansink, B. (2006). *Mindless eating: Why we eat more than we think*. New York, NY: Bantam Books.

Wansink, B., Just, D. R., & Payne, C. R. (2009). Mindless eating and healthy heuristics for the irrational. *The American Economic Review*, *99*(2), 165–169. doi:10.1257/aer.99.2.165

Wellesley, L., Happer, C., & Froggatt, A. (2015). *Changing climate, changing diets: Pathways to lower meat consumption*. London, UK: Chatham House.

Whole Foods Market. (2017). *Whole Foods Market serves up top 10 trends for 2017*. Retrieved from http://media.wholefoodsmarket.com/news/whole-foods-market-serves-up-top-10-trends-for-2017

Wilson, B. (2017). Wisdom from Margaret Mead. In B. Kateman (Ed.), *The reducetarian solution: How the surprisingly simple act of reducing the amount of meat in your diet can transform your health and the planet* (pp. 148–150). New York, NY: TarcherPerigee.

Wymer, W. (2010). Rethinking the boundaries of social marketing: Activism or advertising? *Journal of Business Research*, *63*(2), 99–103. doi:10.1016/j.jbusres.2009.02.003

Wynes, S., & Nicholas, K. A. (2017). The climate mitigation gap: Education and government recommendations miss the most effective individual actions. *Environmental Research Letters*, *12*(7), 1–10. doi:10.1088/1748-9326/aa7541

Zandstra, E. H., Stubenitsky, K., De Graaf, C., & Mela, D. J. (2002). Effects of learned flavour cues on short-term regulation of food intake in a realistic setting. *Physiology & Behavior*, *75*(1-2), 83–90. doi:10.1016/S0031-9384(01)00647-3 PMID:11890956

KEY TERMS AND DEFINITIONS

Flexitarianism: Reducing or abstaining from eating meat for several days per week.

Foodstyle: Preferred eating lifestyle and habits; it can describe eating choices, such as flexitarian, vegetarian, vegan or meat-rich diet.

Nannying: Providing excessive protection and help to the extent that this prevents the person/s from being independent.

Nudging: Interventions which aim at producing positive behavioural change without banning or excluding unfavourable choices.

Paternalism: A system which regulates the behaviour and supplies the needs of those under its control to the extent that they are not in a position to control matters affecting them individually and in relation to other individuals and the system itself.

Peak Meat: Observed and projected long-term decline in meat consumption following an extended period of growth.

Reducetarian: A person reducing their consumption of meat.

Social Marketing: Making the role of marketing beneficial to social goals and better social outcomes.

ENDNOTES

1 More specifically we should always realise that both the sort of meat (animal type) and production method (livestock system) generate substantial differences in terms of land, water or energy use as well as greenhouse gas emissions.

2 Other drawbacks attached to information and law are also that the latter often do not fit into a neo-liberal way of thinking (French, 2011), while information often proves to have limited impact on behavioural change. In the field of food, this is, for example, illustrated by a minority of consumers eating fruit and vegetables according to dietary guidelines in spite of public awareness campaigns and advertising campaigns to encourage the consumption of fruit and vegetables. Furthermore, with respect to (reducing) meat consumption and the issue of communication/framing, see also two recent studies by De Boer and Aiking (2017) and by Graham and Abrahamse (2017).

Chapter 8
Taxing Meat and Animal Food Products

Dora Marinova
Curtin University, Australia

Talia Raphaely
Curtin University, Australia

ABSTRACT

This chapter develops the argument for taxing meat and animal-based products higher than other foods because of their negative effects on both human health and the environment. This includes a disproportionately higher contribution to climate change compared to plant-based options. With the taxation system serving as a mechanism for revenue collection and distribution, it is important to make transparent the reasons for taxing animal foods as well as the services and facilities which will benefit from the increased government proceeds. The example of goods and services tax (GST) in Australia is used to estimate the additional state revenue that can be collected through taxing meat. Taxing also acts as a social marketing mechanism to push consumption away from animal based food products and towards better dietary choices.

INTRODUCTION

Taxation systems serve one main goal - namely to raise revenue for services provided by governments (Gans et al., 2014). Closely linked to this fiscal purpose of taxation is the use of the raised revenue to lessen income and wealth distribution inequality within society (Cox et al., 2009). This is why some refer to taxation as a "tax and transfer system" (Commonwealth of Australia, 2009). There are many principles how taxation levels should be determined and what activities should be supported with the tax revenue. For example, the Australian Council of Social Services states that taxes should be: adequate in order to provide the needed revenue; equitable in distributing public support between low, middle and high-income earners in a way that improves and maintains good living standards for all; and economically efficient by differentiating between various forms of income and activities (ACOSS, 2013).

DOI: 10.4018/978-1-5225-4757-0.ch008

Among the multitude of activities on which taxes can be collected – also described as bases for taxation – private consumption is of a particular interest when it comes to food. Although the main principle for consumption taxes is that they should be broad and simple, provisions are made for the existence of specific taxation to "efficiently address social or economic costs – such as taxes on tobacco, alcohol… and environmental costs" (Commonwealth of Australia, 2009, p. xviii). According to OECD (2015, p. 25), pricing mechanisms such as taxes encourage actions to reduce environmental damage "at least cost".

Every true economist would argue that introducing a tax on purchasing a particular product does not change the demand curve but only pushes it towards making the prices higher allowing for more revenue to be collected (see Figure 1). In this respect taxes per se are not a mechanism for social marketing as they are not aimed at shifting demand or changing social preferences. The relationship between taxes and human behaviour however is more complex. When consumers are required to pay a higher price for the same product after the introduction of a tax (E1 in Figure 1), they start reconsidering their purchasing behaviour. Consequently, a new equilibrium point between demand and supply (E2 in Figure 1) is established at a higher price and lower quantity of demand (Gans et al., 2014).

As in the case of tobacco or alcohol, taxation sends clear signals that there are costs to be borne by society for which the individual consumers should pay. This makes the taxation process transparent and leaves it to consumers to decide whether to continue with a particular behaviour or change their choices to products that are not singled out as being particularly costly to society. When given such a transparency role, taxation becomes a mechanism for social marketing. Overall, it is highly likely that with the introduction of a tax the new equilibrium between demand and supply will result in lower quantities sold at a higher price (see point E2 in Figure 1).

Figure 1. Changes in demand and supply following a new tax
E – equilibrium point between supply and demand; E1 – equilibrium point between demand and supply after the introduction of a new tax; E2 – equilibrium point after shift in demand in response to the new tax

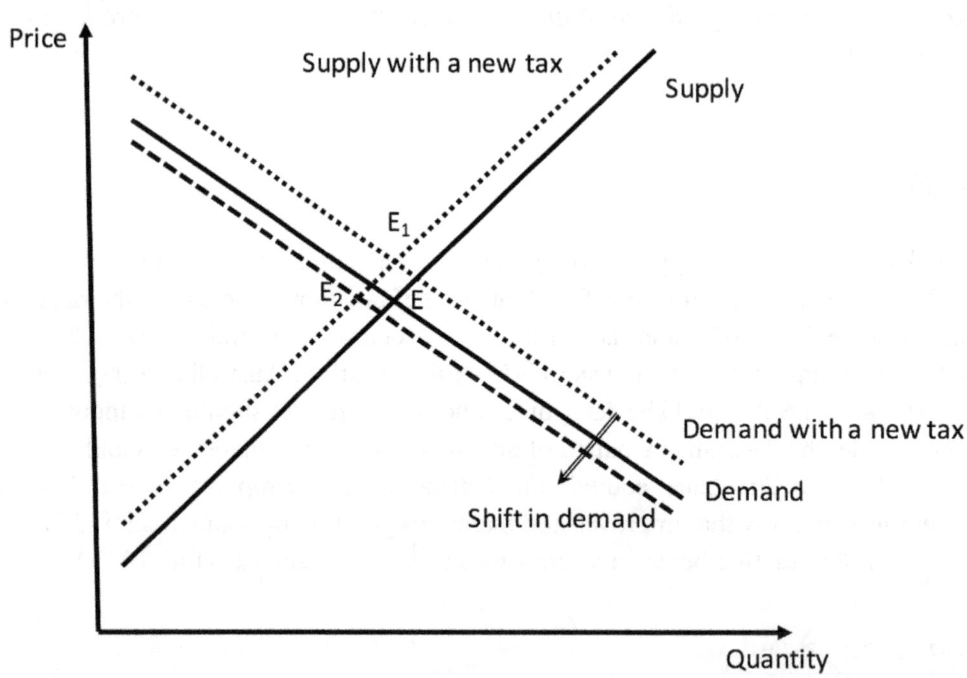

This chapter explains the need for taxes on meat and animal-based foods in order to first, increase the revenue raised to compensate for public health and environmental costs; and second, decrease the consumption of such products and eliminate some of the negative consequences associated with them. After discussing taxes on food and presenting an international overview, it examines the case of Australia where there have been calls for reforming the Goods and Services Tax (GST) to generate more revenue for the government and deal with current and projected budget deficits. Estimates of the potential GST returns from meat consumption in Australia are given. The chapter concludes with analysis of the transparency role of taxation as a powerful social marketing tool in triggering behavioural changes for the greater common good.

TAXING FOOD

In February 2017, the German Minister for the Environment imposed a ban on serving meat and fish at official public functions because of the negative environmental impacts of these types of food (Huggler, 2017). The scientific evidence about meat's contribution to climate change, environmental deterioration, biodiversity loss and increasing burden on the public health system is clear and categorical (e.g. Raphaely & Marinova, 2016). Many non-government organisations (NGOs) and civil society bodies have long been calling for changes in human diets away from animal-based products, promoting vegetarianism – eliminating all meat, chicken and fish from the human diet, flexitarianism – flexible vegetarianism, more specifically defined as reduction in meat consumption to the dietary limits set by reputable health organisations (Raphaely & Marinova, 2016), and veganism – eliminating all animal-based foods from a person's diet. When faced with the challenges of run-away climate change and other environmental problems, banning certain products, and particularly discouraging certain food choices, from human use may seem like a benevolent ecofascism. However, this is not an easy political or governmental agenda on any level. Eating foods from animal origin may be a matter of life or death, survival or starvation in many impoverished places around the globe. In wealthier parts of the world, people not only feel attached to particular food preferences but also consider them to be their human right. The choice for animal-based foods is often an expression of improved income capacity, living standards and quality of life. Banning such foods can be met with opposition, ridicule, disbelief and protests. This explains why the bold decision of the German Minister for the Environment is seen as controversial and also why prestigious and influential bodies, including national governments, the Lancet Commission on Health and Climate Change (Watts et al., 2015) and the Intergovernmental Panel on Climate Change (IPCC) conference of the parties' (COP) meetings (McMahon, 2016), stay away from restricting the consumption of foods from animal origin unless they are prepared to face political suicide.

At the same time, national and international health authorities issue warnings and recommendations regarding healthy dietary intakes. All of these recommendations are based directly on the impact of food choices on individual and public health. None are explicitly linked to the enormous negative impact animal-based foods have on the planet and its ecological systems. For example, in relation to red meat, the World Cancer Research Fund sets a public health goal of no more than 300 g of unprocessed, lean cooked meat per week (WCRF/AICR, 2007); the Australian National Health and Medical Research Council similarly limits the intake of red meat to a maximum of 455 g per person per week (NHMRC, 2013), UK Standing Advisory Committee on Nutrition – to a maximum of 490 g cooked meat per day (SACN, 2011) and China advises 280-525 g of all meat per person per week (FIA Communications, 2016).

This is primarily because red meat is now recognised as being probably carcinogenic (Group 2A) by the World Health Organisation (WHO, 2015) based on the evidence from "more than 800 epidemiological studies that investigated the association of cancer with consumption of red meat or processed meat in many countries, from several continents, with diverse ethnicities and diets" (Bouvard et al., 2015, p. 1599). Consumption of processed red meat, on the other hand is categorised as definitely carcinogenic to humans (Group 1) and it is explicitly recommended that it should not be consumed.

Notwithstanding this, governments have another safer and effective approach to the sensitive issue of food through their fiscal power and authority to raise and distribute revenue via the taxation system. They have used this power differently around the world.

Most European countries apply a Value Added Tax (VAT) on all foodstuffs (European Commission, 2017). Zero VAT rate however is applied to some foods and drinks intended for human consumption in Ireland (with the exception of alcohol and processed foods), Malta (except for pre-cooked dishes and highly processed foods) and UK (except for alcohol and processed foods). Super-reduced tax rates of less than 5% apply for food products in Spain, France, Italy and Luxemburg (European Commission, 2017). In Australia most foods, including beverages and ingredients for beverages, are exempt from the Goods and Services Tax (GST) with only processed foods and meals prepared for consumption being GST-taxable (ATO, 2016). Most jurisdictions in the USA exempt food from the State Sales Tax (Money-Zine, 2017). Overall, it appears that food has a special tax status, including tax-exempt status, in many parts of the world.

Regardless of the level of tax charged (or not charged) on food, taxation systems universally fail to distinguish between the origin of the nutrient matter contained in food, namely whether it is animal, plant or other (e.g. synthetic). Put simply, currently taxes do not reflect the differences between animal- and plant-based foods and do not make transparent the varied societal and environmental costs associated with their consumption. If we accept that taxes, as well as revenue collection, also result in shifts in the demand curve encouraging or discouraging certain behaviours, then the question arises why meat and animal-based products are taxed (or exempted) at the same rate as fruits, vegetables, pulses, nuts, grains, oilseed crops, tubers and other foods of plant origin. Such tax and transfer systems ignore the fact that not all food is created and consumed equally.

The production and consumption of animal-based foods imposes disproportionately high environmental burdens on society. Compared with plant-based options, meat has higher greenhouse gas emissions per unit of nutritional value (Doran-Browne et al., 2014), as well as excessively higher water and land impacts (Eshel et al., 2014). Such direct negative environmental consequences also have indirect but significant negative human health impacts. Also, because of its connection to cancer risks, red meat in particular is enforcing higher costs on national healthcare systems. Furthermore, all intensive livestock production is associated with use of antimicrobials applied "prophylactically amongst healthy animals, to stop the development of an infection within a flock or herd, or simply for growth promotion, to speed up the pace at which animals gain weight" (Review on Antimicrobial Resistance, 2015, p. 1) which threatens society with the potential loss of antibiotics for human treatment (Raphaely et al., 2016).

Despite this strong and conclusive evidence, governments continue to treat animal-based food in an equal manner to other plant-based foodstuffs by charging the same level of tax and often offering reduction and even exemption from any tax. This sends the wrong message to the consumers – that all foods can and should be considered equally in terms of production and consumption – and hides the true environmental and public health costs of individual and collective dietary choices. Tax revenue is used (among other things) to support public health care and to fund government-backed environmental initiatives. Given that animal-based foods compromise both public health and the environment, it surely follows such choices be taxed accordingly.

CALLS FOR TAXING MEAT

Ideas about and calls for taxing meat have emerged from various parts of the globe. The main justification for what might be considered a controversial approach by government is because of the environmental, social and economic costs imposed by meat intake. With all trends showing rapidly increasing human consumption of animal-based products – overall and on a per capita base (e.g. Raphaely & Marinova, 2016), the urgency for government intervention through taxes is again justified based on the ecological and health damage. For example, the proposal for greening the tax system of the Netherlands included a recommendation for introducing "a tax on meat or animal feed that ensures that the harmful impacts of meat consumption, many of them outside the Netherlands, are passed on to Dutch consumers" (Blom et al., 2010, p. 8). From a climate change perspective, Ripple et al. (2014) point out that the urgently needed large-scale dietary change will not happen without incentives, such as implementing a tax proportionate to livestock's greenhouse gas emissions which would push up prices and modify consumer demand. This call for taxation is supported by high profile scientists, such as the former Chair of the UN Intergovernmental Panel on Climate Change and the economist Lord Stern (Vaughan, 2013) as well as civil society groups, such as People for the Ethical Treatment of Animals (PETA, 2017). In the same vein, the Danish Council of Ethics considers climate change to be an ethical problem and also recommends the introduction of a tax on beef which has the highest negative impact (Withnall, 2016).

Although falling short of explicitly arguing for taxing meat production or consumption, the 2016 UNEP analysis of the food systems and national resources includes the need to review the tax regime (UNEP, 2016, p. 29). One of its twelve critical shifts towards resource-smart food systems states: "Re-orient away from resource-intensive products such as meat" (UNEP, 2016, p. 31). Governments have a role to play, particularly in affluent sections of society in any country, to transition to lower consumption of animal-based products because of disproportionately higher environmental costs and undermining of public health (UNEP, 2016).

Another important consideration is the threat of antibiotic resistance (Review on Antimicrobial Resistance, 2015; Raphaely et al., 2006) due to widespread and large use of antimicrobials in livestock husbandry. People enter directly in contact with animals, drug-resistant strains can be passed to humans through the food chain and the animal excretion of unmetabolised active ingredients causes "the environment to be tainted with antibiotics, providing further opportunities for exposure to bacteria and creating additional selective pressure that leads to the development of drug resistance" (Review on Antimicrobial Resistance, 2015, p. 1). Hence suggestions are made to tax meat which contains antibiotics (Giubilini, 2017). On the revenue raising side of the argument (Raphaely & Marinova, 2015) and given the large government budget deficits in countries, such as USA, Japan, UK, Australia and even China and most of Latin America (CountryEconomy, n.d.), taxing meat can help improve the balance between state revenues and expenditures.

At the other end of the spectrum, most debates about diets free of animal-based products are usually framed around ethical values and availability of choice. Only recently have they begun to be linked to awareness of inherent and pervasive oppression, sexism, nationalism, power and privilege in a capitalist system that commodifies humans and animals (Tsampiras & Overy, 2016). Introducing appropriate taxes on meat and food products of animal origin offers a direct contribution to making transparent the significant, yet still hidden, environmental and public health costs associated with their consumption. Such taxation can also play an indirect role in preparing the grounds for a quiet ethical revolution against the currently institutionalised forms of speciesism and enslavement of the animal world (Singer, 2009; Florit & Sbardelati, 2016; Tsampiras & Overy, 2016).

Despite governments still being reluctant to make the first step with the use of the tax and transfer system towards such an ethical revolution, research evidence has started to emerge that there is enough support from broader civil society across the globe. A 2015 study by the Royal Institute of International Affairs Chatham House and Glasgow University shows that the public expects the government to take a lead in curbing the unsustainable consumption of meat and that governments overestimate the risk of public backlash (Wellesley et al., 2015). According to the research covering a survey in 12 countries (Brazil, China, France, Germany, India, Italy, Japan, Poland, Russia, South Africa, UK and USA) and focus groups in Brazil. China, UK and USA: "approaches such as taxation do risk public resistance, but… this would be short-lived, particularly if people understood the policy rationale" (Wellesley, 2015, p. vii). This is seen as a win-win situation.

Consumption of red meat on a per capita basis, and in particular beef which has the heaviest environmental footprint, may have plateaued and may even be on the decrease in the developed countries, including USA, Australia, Canada, EU and overall in OECD (see Figure 2). In fact, we may have already witnessed the peak beef phenomenon – in 1995 for EU countries, 2003 for OECD and 2007 for the world overall (see Figure 2). This change however is not enough given the rising beef consumption in the developing and emerging economies of Asia, Africa and Latin America. Moreover, per capita consumption of poultry is steadily increasing in all areas of the world (see Figure 3). This type of meat is also strongly associated with intensive farming and high use of antibiotics and all the related human and environmental negative consequences.

In order to deal with the environmental devastation and stretched public health resources, the decline in the preferences for beef must be much faster than the voluntary trends experienced so far in some parts of the world. Arresting the burgeoning demand for poultry is another major environmental, public health and ethical priority. Using taxation, governments can facilitate and speed up a transition to diets healthier for the planet and its human inhabitants. A study by Oxford University's Future of Food program modelled the taxes on greenhouse gas emissions associated with different food commodities required to combat climate change whilst also being a health-promoting policy for most low- and middle-income countries where obesity and malnutrition are on the rise (Springmann et al., 2017). It shows that beef, milk, lamb and poultry, for example, require surcharges of 40%, 20%, 14% and 8% respectively to mitigate their contribution to climate change. Such taxes are likely to decrease the demand for beef by 13%, milk by 7%, lamb by 5% and poultry by 2% (Springmann et al., 2017). The study further makes the point that any emissions-related taxes need to be combined with subsidies for healthy foods, such as fruit and vegetables, as well as compensation for the poor and socially weak within society to ensure equitable outcomes for all. Earlier modelling studies of the climate change–human health co-benefits through taxing food have included scenarios in which all raised revenue is passed on to the British consumer (Briggs et al., 2013 and 2016) although in practice such an approach is highly unlikely.

Figure 2. Annual per capita beef consumption [kg]
Data source: OECD, 2017

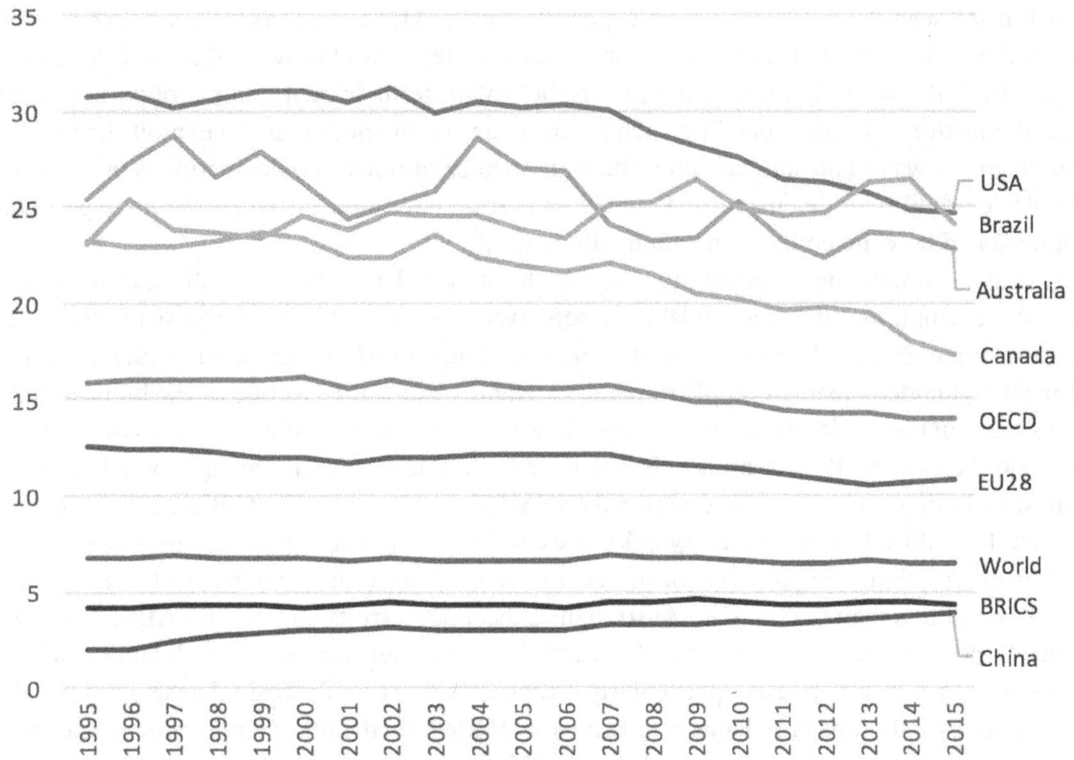

Figure 3. Annual per capita consumption of poultry [kg]
Data source: OECD, 2017

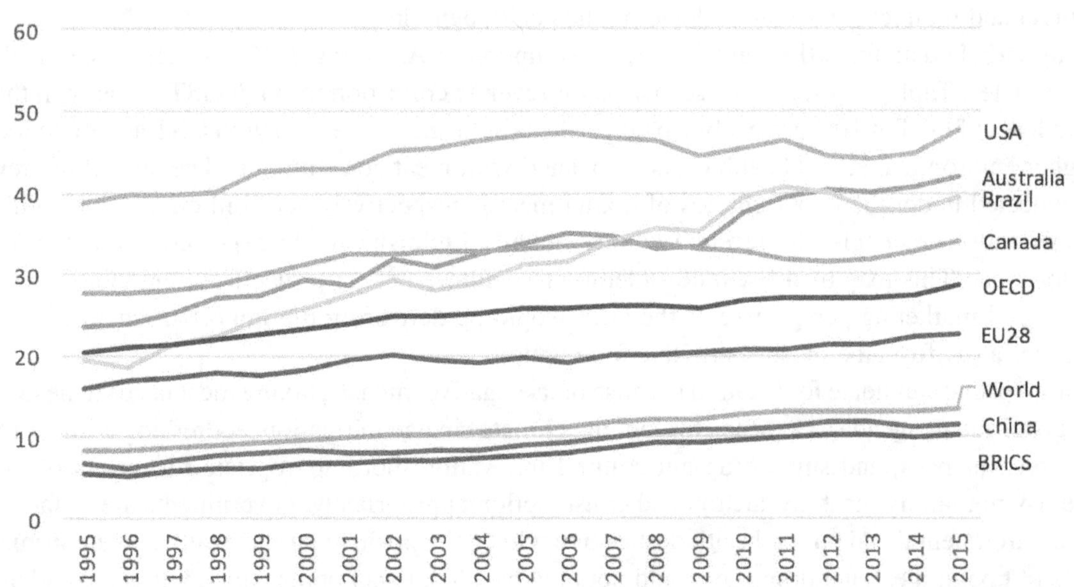

GENERAL SALES TAX ON MEAT SOLD IN AUSTRALIA

Taxation is often seen as a blunt instrument which does not tackle the reasons for a certain behaviour and arguments that taxes aimed at changing consumption interfere with human rights are frequently heard (Lane, 2014). Although individuals have the "right" to abuse their own bodies (often at the expense of the public health system), expanding such an argument to an entitlement to exploit the global commons of clean air, water and soil, and thus abuse the bodies of other people as well as other species no longer holds credibility or defensibility. People however do have the right to know why a particular tax is introduced and how the collected revenue will be used.

In Australia, introducing an equal tax, such as the standard 10% GST, on all fresh food, which is currently tax-exempt, would understandably be perceived as serving the only purpose of revenue raising for the government budget. Most importantly, this would maintain the current unhealthy overconsumption of meat and underconsumption of fruit and vegetables. Australia has one of the highest individual intakes of meat in the world, including beef, poultry, pig, lamb and mutton (refer also to Figures 2 and 3) with Australians currently consuming almost twice the amount stated as the maximum limit in dietary guidelines, including national and international (NHMRC, 2013 and WCRF/AICR, 2007). On the other hand, Australians do not meet the dietary guidelines as far as fruit and vegetables are concerned. In fact, only 4% of the Australian population consumes the recommended daily amounts of vegetables, beans and legumes and less than one in three Australians eats enough fruits and grains (ABS, 2016). From a public health perspective, consumption of foods, such as fruit, vegetables, beans, legumes, wholegrain seeds and nuts, should not be taxed, particularly if those revenues are destined for the public health sector – eating such foods already reduces healthcare costs! Meat on the other hand, directly and indirectly increases the burden on the health system because of its connection with cancer risks and ominous environmental outcomes. In 2015, the Lancet Commission (Watts et al., 2015) recognised climate change as the greatest threat to human health and the livestock sector is a leading contributor to greenhouse gas emissions. A reduction in meat consumption encouraged through differential taxation would thus have both direct and indirect environmental and public health benefits.

Using OECD data for 2015 annual meat consumption in Australia, 2017 population size and meat price estimates, Table 1 presents two scenarios for revenue collection through GST – one with the current flat level of GST at 10% applicable to all products sold and the second with GST at 15% to indicate the higher environmental and health costs associated with meat consumption. The annual tax revenue to be collected under the two scenarios of taxing meat is respectively A$2 billion and A$3 billion. If economists are correct, this GST revenue would gradually diminish with the expected shift in the demand curve for meat. This may be a fiscal consideration for future budget projections, but is not a concern from a social marketing perspective as the GST would be delivering the important change in dietary preferences away from the most destructive food options.

Being a prime candidate for taxation because of its negative impacts, taxing meat needs to be included on the government agenda as a means for funding climate change mitigation, addressing climate-related health consequences, and supporting agricultural innovation more appropriate for an era of climate change. By not taxing meat production and consumption appropriately, governments are in fact subsidising environmental and public health destruction. Given the positive public health and environmental benefits of taxing meat, not doing so would not only be a lost fiscal opportunity, but we would also be letting down our health, the environment and life on Earth.

TAX AS A SOCIAL MARKETING TOOL

For any tax to act as a social marketing tool in changing "people's behaviour for the benefit of individuals and society as a whole" (NSMC, 2011, n.p.), it is important for the government to be transparent in both: (1) why the tax is introduced; and (2) how the collected revenue is used. In 2011, Denmark introduced the world's first tax on fat which was applied to products containing more than 2.3% saturated fat, including meat and dairy (BBC News, 2012). The tax which did not have broad political support was abolished a year later as part of the negotiations of the country's minority government. Most importantly, however, the government did not make it transparent how the raised revenue was used.

In this day and age, any government, when introducing a new tax and when transferring the raised revenue, needs to work together with the public and broader civil society. Deliberative democracy methods (e.g. Hartz-Karp & Weymouth, 2017), such as participatory budgeting (e.g. Allegretti & Hartz-Karp, 2017), can be used to co-design, co-implement and co-create the required social change. Research already confirms that people across the globe are prepared to accept taxes when they understand the rationale (Wellesley, 2015) and when the government is transparent and involving in the budget process (Allegretti & Hartz-Kart, 2017).

The magnitude of the threats and challenges surrounding climate change are beyond the capacity of any institution or national government, were it to act alone without the support of its constituency and the global community. Taxing meat and animal products offers opportunities for united global action in the pursuit of a better future for life on this planet, starting from the countries which have the greatest responsibility for the current situation of environmental destruction and public health negligence. As a social marketing tool, a tax on meat has the following benefits:

- It makes it transparent that some food choices are less desirable and those who opt for them should pay higher prices to compensate for environmental, social and public health costs;
- It encourages people to seek alternatives based on simple economic rationality and promotes behavioural shifts;
- The collected tax revenue can be channelled to compensate for the higher costs associated with meat production and consumption;
- It offers the opportunity to engage in a transparent way with the wider public on a journey of healing the diseases stemming from the overuse of natural resources and abuse of species;
- It builds trust in the global community for a more ethical approach to life and responsibility for current and future generations.

CONCLUSION

Economists have long directed fiscal policies towards shaping the demand and supply for goods and services based on existing priorities through the tax and transfer system. We deliberately chose not to explicitly distinguish between production and consumption taxes as ultimately all costs get transferred to the consumer.

Research shows that people react more to changes in price than information promoting health and sustainable actions contained in labels and logos (de Jonge et al., 2015; Hoek et al., 2016). The idea about taxing the consumption of meat and animal products is not new. Its time however has come! Society is

Table 1. Potential tax revenue from meat sold in Australia

Meat	Price per kg [A$]	Price per kg GST @ 10% [AUD]	Price per kg GST @ 15% [AUD]	Average Consumption [kg per Person per year] 2015 OECD Carcass Data	Average Consumption [kg per Person per Year] 2015 Retail Weight	Total Consumption [kg]	Total Revenue [A$]	GST Revenue @ 10% [A$]	GST Revenue @ 15% [A$]
Beef and veal	17	18.56	19.40	22.8	16.0	390 mln	6.5 bln	658 mln	987 mln
Lamb and mutton	14	15.17	15.86	7.4	6.5	160 mln	2.2 bln	220 mln	330 mln
Pork	14	15.93	16.65	20.3	15.8	386 mln	5.6 bln	559 mln	838 mln
Chicken	6	6.15	6.43	42.0	37.0	903 mln	5.0 bln	505 mln	757 mln
TOTAL	–	–	–	92.5	75.3	1,838 mln	19.4 bln	**2 bln**	**3 bln**

Data sources: OECD, 2017 and ABS, 2017. Meat prices are estimated using information from https://www.harrisfarm.com.au/pages/meat-prices-find-out-how-much-meat-costs.

ready for it and most importantly, climate change and other environmental priorities require us to act urgently. Compared to technological innovation and the need to shift technology trajectories away from fossil fuels, introducing a new tax is a relatively simple exercise which does not require investments and new scientific discoveries. What it needs is public support facilitated by transparency on the part of government regarding why the tax is introduced and how the revenue raised will be used.

Compared to many of the other social marketing methods described in this book, taxation is not a voluntary act. Shifting consumer preferences however is a voluntary act when choice exists. A deferential tax on food leaves the power with the individual to make the transition to a new ethical ground and become part of the new quiet revolution.

REFERENCES

Allegretti, G., & Hartz-Karp, J. (2017). Participatory budgeting: a methodological approach to address sustainability challenges. In J. Hartz-Karp & D. Marinova (Eds.), *Methods for sustainability research* (pp. 203–216). Cheltenham, UK: Edward Elgar. doi:10.4337/9781786432735.00024

Australian Bureau of Statistics (ABS). (2016). *Australian Health Survey: Consumption of food groups from the Australian Dietary Guidelines, Australia 2011-12* (Catalogue number 4364.0.55.012). Canberra, Australia: ABS. Retrieved from http://www.ausstats.abs.gov.au/ausstats/subscriber.nsf/0/12E8766EBAB492B0CA257FAF001A3CFD/$File/43640do002_20112012.pdf

Australian Bureau of Statistics (ABS). (2017). *Population clock*. Retrieved from http://www.abs.gov.au/ausstats/abs%40.nsf/94713ad445ff1425ca25682000192af2/1647509ef7e25faaca2568a900154b63?OpenDocument

Australian Council of Social Services (ACOSS). (2013). *Tax reform: purpose, principles and process*. Strawberry Hills, Australia: ACOSS. Retrieved from http://www.acoss.org.au/wp-content/uploads/2015/06/Tax_reform_ACOSS_August_2013.pdf

Australian Taxation Office (ATO). (2016). GST status of food items. Australian Government. Retrieved from https://www.ato.gov.au/business/gst/in-detail/your-industry/food/gst-food-guide/?anchor=H4#H4

Blom, M., Schroten, A., de Bruyn, S., & Rooijers, F. (2010). *Limits to green? Greening tax system in the Netherlands*. Delft, the Netherlands: CE Delft. Retrieved from http://www.ce.nl/publicatie/limits_to_green_elements_of_a_green_tax_system/1026

Bouvard, V., Loomis, D., Guyton, K. Z., Gross, Y., El Ghissassi, F., Benbrahim-Tallaa, L., & Straif, K. et al. (2015). Carcinogenicity of consumption of red and processed meat. *The Lancet Oncology*, *16*(16), 1599–1600. doi:10.1016/S1470-2045(15)00444-1 PMID:26514947

Briggs, A. D. M., Kehlbacher, A., Tiffin, R., Garnett, T., Rayner, M., & Scarborough, P. (2013). Assessing the impact on chronic disease of incorporating the societal cost of greenhouse gases into the price of food: An econometric and comparative risk assessment modelling study. *BMJ Open*, *3*(10), e003543. doi:10.1136/bmjopen-2013-003543 PMID:24154517

Briggs, A. D. M., Kehlbacher, A., Tiffin, R., & Scarborough, P. (2016). Simulating the impact on health of internalising the cost of carbon in food prices combined with a tax on sugar-sweetened beverages. *BMC Public Health*, *16*(107), 1–14. PMID:26837190

Commonwealth of Australia. (2009). *Australia's future tax system*. Canberra, Australia: Attorney-General's Department. Retrieved from https://taxreview.treasury.gov.au/content/downloads/final_report_part_1/00_AFTS_final_report_consolidated.pdf

CountryEconomy. (n.d.). *Government budget deficit*. Retrieved from http://countryeconomy.com/deficit

Cox, M. S., McLure, C. E., & Neumark, F. (2009). Taxation. In *Encyclopaedia Britannica*. Retrieved from https://www.britannica.com/topic/taxation

de Jonge, J., van der Lans, I. A., & van Trijp, H. C. (2015). Different shades of grey: Compromise products to encourage animal friendly consumption. *Food Quality and Preference*, *45*, 87–99. doi:10.1016/j.foodqual.2015.06.001

Doran-Browne, N. A., Eckard, R. J., Behrendt, R., Ross, S., & Kingwell, R. S. (2015). Nutrient density as a metric for comparing greenhouse gas emissions from food production. *Climatic Change*, *129*(1-2), 73–87. doi:10.1007/s10584-014-1316-8

Eshel, G., Shepon, A., Makov, T., & Milo, R. (2014). Land, irrigation water, greenhouse gas, and reactive nitrogen burdens of meat, eggs, and dairy production in the United States. In *Proceedings of the National Academy of Sciences of the United States of America*, *111*(33), 11996–12001. doi:10.1073/pnas.1402183111 PMID:25049416

European Commission. (2017). *VAT rates applied in the Member States of the European Union*. Retrieved from http://ec.europa.eu/taxation_customs/sites/taxation/files/resources/documents/taxation/vat/how_vat_works/rates/vat_rates_en.pdf

Florit, L., & Sbardelati, C. (2016). Intensive speciesism regions in Brazil: Ethical and social stains in territories supplying global meat markets. In T. Raphaely & D. Marinova (Eds.), *Impact of meat consumption on health and environmental sustainability* (pp. 277–294). Hershey, PA: IGI Global. doi:10.4018/978-1-4666-9553-5.ch016

Food Industry Asia (FIA) Communications. (2016). *New Chinese dietary guidelines: A reference for industry*. Retrieved from https://foodindustry.asia/new-chinese-dietary-guidelines-a-reference-for-industry

Gans, J., King, S., Stonecash, R. E., Byford, M., Libich, J., & Mankiw, N. G. (2013). *Principles of economics* (6th ed.). South Melbourne, Australia: Victoria Cengage Learning.

Giubilini, A. (2017). Why we should tax meat that contains antibiotics. *The Conversation*. Retrieved from https://theconversation.com/why-we-should-tax-meat-that-contains-antibiotics-75721

Hartz-Karp, J., & Weymouth, R. (2017). Deliberative democracy – democratic renewal capable of addressing sustainability. In J. Hartz-Karp & D. Marinova (Eds.), *Methods for sustainability research* (pp. 113–128). Cheltenham, UK: Edward Elgar. doi:10.4337/9781786432735.00017

Hoek, A. C., Pearson, D., James, S. W., Lawrence, M. A., & Friel, S. (2017). Healthy and environmentally sustainable food choices: Consumer responses to point-of-purchase actions. *Food Quality and Preference*, *58*, 94–106. doi:10.1016/j.foodqual.2016.12.008

Huggler, J. (2017). Discord in Angela Merkel's government after environment ministry bans meat at official functions. *The Telegraph*, 21 February. Retrieved from http://www.telegraph.co.uk/news/2017/02/21/discord-angela-merkels-government-environment-ministry-bans/

Lane, A. (2014). *A taxing approach to choice: How behavioural taxes deliver perverse outcomes*. Institute of Public Affairs. Retrieved from https://ipa.org.au/portal/uploads/IPA_Paper-A_taxing_approach_to_choice-Feb_2014.pdf

McMahon, J. (2016). Paris Agreement portends a reckoning for meat and dairy. *Forbes*. Retrieved from https://www.forbes.com/sites/jeffmcmahon/2016/01/01/paris-agreement-will-impact-meat-and-dairy/#3106b4cc446b

Money-Zine. (2017). 2017 *State Sales Tax Rates*. Retrieved from http://www.money-zine.com/financial-planning/tax-shelter/state-sales-tax-rates/

National Health and Medical Research Council (NHMRC). (2013). *Australian dietary guidelines*. Canberra, Australia: NHMRC and Department of Health and Ageing, Australian Government.

National Social Marketing Centre (NSMC). (2011). *What is social marketing?* Retrieved from http://www.nsmcentre.org.uk/content/what-social-marketing-1

BBC News. (2012, November 10). *Denmark to abolish tax on high-fat foods*. Retrieved from http://www.bbc.com/news/world-europe-20280863

Organisation for Economic Co-operation and Development (OECD). (2015). *Towards green growth? Tracking progress. Four years of the Green Growth Strategy*. Paris, France: OECD Green Growth Studies; doi:10.1787/9789264234437-

Organisation for Economic Co-operation and Development (OECD). (2017). *Meat consumption (indicator)*. doi: Retrieved from https://data.oecd.org/agroutput/meat-consumption.htm10.1787/fa290fd0-en

People for the Ethical Treatment of Animals (PETA). (2017). *Tax meat*. Retrieved from http://www.peta.org/features/tax-meat/

Raphaely, T., & Marinova, D. (2015). Here's an idea to chew over: GST reform should add meat to the tax buffet. *The Conversation*. Retrieved from https://theconversation.com/heres-an-idea-to-chew-over-gst-reform-should-add-meat-to-the-tax-buffet-45160

Raphaely, T., & Marinova, D. (2016). *Impact of meat consumption on health and environmental sustainability*. Hershey, PA: IGI Global. doi:10.4018/978-1-4666-9553-5

Raphaely, T., Marinova, D., & Marinova, M. (2016). Antibiotics and the livestock sector. In T. Raphaely & D. Marinova (Eds.), *Impact of meat consumption on health and environmental sustainability* (pp. 178–200). Hershey, PA: IGI Global. doi:10.4018/978-1-4666-9553-5.ch009

Review on Antimicrobial Resistance. (2015). *Antimicrobials in agriculture and the environment: Reducing unnecessary use and waste*. Retrieved from https://amr-review.org/sites/default/files/Antimicrobials%20in%20agriculture%20and%20the%20environment%20-%20Reducing%20unnecessary%20use%20and%20waste.pdf

Ripple, W. J., Smith, P., Haberl, H., Montzka, S. A., McAlpine, C., & Boucher, D. H. (2014). Ruminants, climate change and climate policy. *Nature Climate Change*, *4*(1), 1–4.

Scientific Advisory Committee on Nutrition (SACN). (2010). *Iron and health*. London, UK: TSO. Retrieved from https://www.gov.uk/government/uploads/system/uploads/attachment_data/file/339309/SACN_Iron_and_Health_Report.pdf

Singer, P. (2009). Animal liberation: The definitive classic of the animal movement (updated ed.). New York, NY: HarperCollins.

Springmann, M., Mason-D'Croz, D., Robinson, S., Weibe, K., Godfray, H. C. J., Rayner, M., & Scarborough, P. (2017). Mitigation potential and global health impacts from emissions pricing of food commodities. *Nature Climate Change*, *7*(1), 69–76. doi:10.1038/nclimate3155

Tsampiras, C., & Overy, N. (2016). Why cutting meat from your diet could be a revolutionary act. *The Conversation*. Retrieved from https://theconversation.com/why-cutting-meat-from-your-diet-could-be-a-revolutionary-act-69904

United Nations Environment Program (UNEP). (2016). Food systems and natural resources. A Report of the Working Group on Food Systems of the International Resource Panel. Retrieved from https://www.dropbox.com/sh/bhhivquadq7ycnd/AAAIl8mVW9GCiOyGwk71At_ra?dl=0&preview=UNEP_Food+systems+and+natural+resources_summary_web.pdf

Vaughan, A. (2013, December 20). Tax meat to cut methane emissions, say scientists. *The Guardian*. Retrieved from https://www.theguardian.com/environment/2013/dec/20/tax-meat-cut-methane-emissions-scientists

Watts, N., Adger, W. N., Agnolucci, P., Blackstock, J., Byass, P., Cai, W., & Costello, A. et al. (2015). Health and climate change; policy responses to protect public health. *Lancet, 386*(10006), 1861–1914. doi:10.1016/S0140-6736(15)60854-6 PMID:26111439

Wellesley, L., Happer, C., & Froggatt, A. (2015, November). *Changing climate, changing diets: Pathways to lower meat consumption*. Chatham House Report. Retrieved from https://www.chathamhouse.org/sites/files/chathamhouse/publications/research/CHHJ3820%20Diet%20and%20climate%20change%2018.11.15_WEB_NEW.pdf

Withnall, A. (2016, April 27). Denmark Ethics Council calls for tax on red meat to fight 'ethical problem' of climate change. *The Independent*. Retrieved from http://www.independent.co.uk/news/world/europe/denmark-ethics-council-calls-for-tax-on-red-meat-to-fight-ethical-problem-of-climate-change-a7003061.html

World Cancer Research Fund and American Institute for Cancer Research (WCRF/AICR). (2007). *Food, nutrition, physical activity and the prevention of cancer: a global perspective*. Washington, DC: AICR.

World Health Organisation (WHO). (2015). *Q&A on the carcinogenicity of the consumption of red meat and processed meat*. Retrieved from http://www.who.int/features/qa/cancer-red-meat/en/

KEY TERMS AND DEFINITIONS

Antimicrobial Resistance: The ability of microbes, such as bacteria, viruses and parasites, to resist the effect of treatment with antibiotics, antivirals and antimalarials.

Carcinogenic: A property of a substance to cause cancer.

Demand–Supply Equilibrium: A state in which demand and market supply are in balance generating a stable price.

Flexitarianism: Decrease in meat consumption to a level which is not higher than the limit recommended by reputable dietary guidelines.

Peak Beef: A peak in beef consumption in a region after which the amount of beef per person declines.

Social Marketing: An activity that aims at behavioural change for the broader social good.

Speciesism: A philosophic view which espouses the idea that humans have greater moral rights than non-human animals.

Tax: State revenue collected on a compulsory basis and used to support activities or provision of facilities by government.

Chapter 9
Flipping the Script:
Creating Mass Change Through Social Networking Sites

Jessica Campbell
University of Central Florida, USA

ABSTRACT

This chapter proposes to "Flip the Script" of the prescribed diet in USA today that primarily revolves around eating meat. The consumerization of the consumption of meat is pervasive in this country, and individuals are culturally constructed to believe animal proteins are essential to the human diet. Using script theory, this chapter examines social networking sites (SNSs) as channels for implementing a mass dietary change in today's society, that which excludes meat. Script theory determines that individuals use instrumental knowledge of how to understand, react, and respond to situations that are repeatedly encountered. Being ideal spaces for initiating social changes, SNSs replicate real-life situations and are platforms, whereby messages can be shared, promoted, and exchanged in a global networked public.

INTRODUCTION

The consumption of meat has become a habitual practice in the United States. Stemming from the Second Industrial Revolution (Boundless, n.d.) in the nineteenth century, when society turned to capitalist modes of production, meat became a commodity—filling up U.S. dinner plates. While meat was consumed prior to the Industrial Revolution, it was only afforded by the elite and wealthy, therefore making it more popular and desired once it became cheaper. Marx (1867, p. 27) states:

A commodity is, in the first place, an object outside us, a thing that by its properties satisfies human wants of some sort or another. The nature of such wants, whether, for instance, they spring from the stomach or from fancy, makes no difference.

DOI: 10.4018/978-1-5225-4757-0.ch009

In a capitalist society, Marx maintains that people desire commodities simply because of the value that has been attached to them. Today, meat and other animal products are a large part of the Standard America Diet or SAD (USDA, n.d.). Nowhere is the commodification of products and items of desire more visible than in the U.S. with factory farms killing millions of animals to produce cheap meat. A powerful influence on individuals' conception of meat are the dominant industries that have profited from humans' consumption of animal products, including the livestock, food, and pharmaceutical industries. These profitable businesses invest many dollars into marketing and advertising of their products, which fuels existing consumer behavior and the mass desire to eat meat.

Scientific evidence has proven that the consumption of meat is damaging to the human body and causes diseases (Marcus, 1998). Furthermore, the production of animals for human consumption is, and will continue to be, environmentally devastating. Factory farming not only produces large concentrates of pollutants, but also uses up natural resources, such as land and water (Marcus, 1998). Yet, despite this evidence, most individuals blindly consume meat and believe that it is an essential part of the human diet. Numerous researchers have studied the psychological and social dynamics of the consumption of meat, as well as methods of changing individuals' dietary habits (Delahoyde & Despenich, 1994; Lucan et al., 2012). However, there have been no successful solutions to altering society's meat-eating mentality or to creating omnipresent behavior modifications. Thus, the question remains: How does one shift the social norm of meat consumption in a society whose thought processes and behaviors are governed by dominant power structures (media and advertising) and (constructed) habitual forces?

The purpose of this chapter is to approach social networking sites (SNSs) as networked publics for the construction of new social norms that censor the consumption of meat and reconfigure dietary practices which eliminate the eating of meat and establish the new standard script for eating in the U.S. Script theory, borrowed from the cognitive sciences, is used as a theoretical lens to understanding social media as agents of change. Applying script theory to endemic health and social problems has limitedly been studied (Enticott & Vanclay, 2011) and is a novel approach to mass social change.

This chapter discusses the stages of "Flipping the Script" of the SAD. First, embedding immersive experiences within SNSs is projected to expose individuals to the realities of the consumption of meat and to introduce new ways of thinking. Once engaged with the media and rhetoric of meat consumption, individuals will be motivated and compelled to participate in causal challenges and perform new behaviors and activities that are propagated through online sociality. Lastly, the reproduction of real-life social change will occur in online spaces as individuals reinforce one another's newly formed dietary behaviors and the script for eating, which eliminates meat, will become the new social norm.

Despite technology's role in solving human problems of efficiency and survival, many times technology creates more problems, such is the case with the mass consumption and consumerization of meat. That said, this chapter proposes to "Flip the Script" of technology's role in promoting the consumption of meat and use it to encourage meat-free diets and prescribe the new script for eating in the U.S. Due to the popularity of SNSs, they effectively facilitate simulation enabling individuals to freely learn, communicate, and practice target behaviors. This chapter presents a new method of creating nationwide awareness of the detrimental impacts of meat consumption and proposes challenges that include education and incentives which drive healthy consumer behaviors and enable individuals to create new habits excluding the consumption of animal proteins. Users will regain a sense of control of their food choices. Correspondingly, as individuals perform repetitious behaviors, new healthy habits will be established, transforming their actions in real life. Social media platforms effectively serve as simulation sites for practicing and exhibiting real-world behavior, beliefs, and self-control, thus, act as agents for creating revolutionary changes in the nation's dietary habits and social norms.

BACKGROUND

The consumption of meat is rooted in individuals' construction of their identity and social behaviors, and is governed by several factors. From the day humans are born they are constructed by social status, demographics, religion, and by what they encounter and experience as they formulate their behaviors and beliefs. The proliferation of information today has only exacerbated humans' need to selectively filter information and apply past knowledge to navigate new experiences. Humans use cognitive blueprints, called scripts, when encountering familiar, constructed social situations. Following the repeated confrontation with similar and shared experiences, humans are able to interact and behave automatically, unaware that their behaviors are governed by unconscious scripts. According to Schank and Abelson (1977, p. 16), scripts represent what results in the primitive actions humans use to react to different situations. Scripts encompass the actors, interactions, dialogue and behaviors that have been socially standardized for any particular situation and form the basis of one's memory (Schank & Abelson, 1977, p. 19). Socially constructed scripts, in effect, enable humans to multitask and reserve mental power. These scripts are what people do or expect automatically in situations that are frequently encountered and similarity shared with others. That said, scripts are flexible and able to be updated or changed (Enticott & Vanclay, 2011, p. 294). They are powerfully influenced by one's social experiences and individuals learn through their social interactions.

The agribusiness has profited from meat marketing and advertisements that socially construct individuals into believing meat consumption is necessary and a standard practice. Saturated with advertisements and the media promoting meat consumption, individuals have become constructed to believe that animal products are essential to the human diet. After being exposed to the rhetoric of meat media, experiencing social situations where others are eating animal-based foods, and repeatedly participating in such consumption, individuals unconsciously ingrain the meat-eating script and use it to navigate other similar experiences and social interactions. Essentially, eating meat has become the script for the hegemonic diet in the U.S. today, the SAD—in which it is the predominant food consumed at any meal.

The consumption of meat is almost an inborn practice in North American society today. Because individuals are born into families where meat forms the basis of every meal, they become instilled with the notion that eating animal flesh is a part of everyday life. Humans' knowledge of what it means to eat is used to navigate almost every situation where one eats or anticipates eating, such as: when grocery shopping for a meal, one will purchase meat; when cooking a meal, one cooks meat; and when dining out, one orders and consumes a dish with meat. Scripts are the prescribed knowledge and behaviors that individuals use to interpret and respond to events they have been through many times (Schank & Abelson, 1977, p. 37). Today, eating meat is the script for the SAD.

Individuals behave and respond to environmental stimulants and in different social situations based on their socially constructed script for that particular situation. Goffman (1959, p. 22) observed that individuals habitually perform a certain role with specific behaviors and this performance occurs within a particular setting in front of particular observers. Thus, explain Schank and Abelson (1977, p. 19), rather than assimilate or learn the details of restaurant etiquette, memory simply points to one's internal restaurant script and only attends to the stimulants that diverge from the script. Individuals recognize the waitress or waiter based on her or his uniform and dialogue, and they perform in their role as the diner, and, as such, order and eat a dish with meat. Because we live in a society of consumption, eating meat and other like-dietary practices have become the script for the U.S. diet—the food not of choice, but configured as a way of life through sociality and the construction of one's identity.

Humans' use of scripts to navigate social situations and new experiences essentially impresses conformity. Because scripts are socially constructed and hegemonically used in everyday life, those that do not ingrain the socially accepted norms of behavior into their memory and practice are systematically called attention to or not accepted. Additionally, because scripts largely reside in one's unconscious memory and are automatically drawn on when encountering particular situations, which "Fit the Script," individuals are not even aware of their own conformity. For example, on Twitter, one can show they like another user's post by clicking on the heart icon. Posts that receive a high volume of "Likes" gain a higher status on individual users' news feeds, which express popularity (Fendley, 2015). Individuals interpret the post as being popular because of its "Like" status and automatically "Like" the post because their script for popularity and recognition on Twitter includes "Liking" all popular posts. Individuals embed scripts and conform to the socially constructed, hegemonic norms of behavior crafted by the knowledge and information shared in social interactions.

THE OMNIPRESENCE OF SOCIAL NETWORKING

The speed and scope at which information is shared and exchanged today allow technology to perpetuate and heighten individuals' ability to embed specific knowledge about how to interpret certain situations and fashion automatically used scripts for understanding and behaving in reoccurring experiences. Meat rhetoric is pervasive—it is in magazines, as advertisements; it is in books, as the food pyramid; it is in the media, as television commercials endorsing lunch meat—and it has saturated the dialogue of social situations (grocery shopping, cooking meals, and dining out). "Factory farming," states Baur (2008, p. 8), "is a huge part of the problem. Baur (2008, p. 8) describes how the agribusiness spends enormous amounts of money to create positive feelings about eating meat as consumers are subject to persistent advertisements featuring actors, musicians, and other celebrities endorsing their animal food products. It is nearly impossible for individuals to sidestep the notion that eating meat is normal. Thus, eating meat has become the prescribed script for the SAD and is referenced when individuals encounter a situation where they are going to eat or anticipate eating. Humans save on mental capacity and assimilate more knowledge by employing scripts, which are natural and primal ways of behaving, responding, and mentally processing information. Scripts enable humans to quickly filter the vast information they are flooded with and attend to only that which is necessary or new and provide the directions for behaving and reacting accordingly.

In order to create mass shifts in paradigmatic thinking and social norms, one must first be capable of transmitting messaging to the targeted wide-scale audience, acquire mass acceptance of new constructs, and instill habitual behaviors. Given the pervasiveness of SNSs and online sociality today, social networking sites are a unique space to instigate behavior change. Many individuals are deeply engaged with social media and connect, congregate, and share information and knowledge in these networked publics. Therefore, the ability to engage with a multifarious audience, implant the seeds of new constructs, and reconfigure the standard North American script of the essentialness of eating meat, will facilitate mass social change. That said, mass social change and paradigm shifts do not occur overnight or rapidly. This approach will be a slow progression as individuals first become accepting of new perspectives, participate in behavioral changes, and establish new scripts for habitual eating.

Social networking has penetrated online sociality as one of the most influential drivers of the construction of moral norms, individuals' identities, and self-representation both in online environments and in real-life. These platforms not only have a facilitating role in online sociality, but are integral to most individuals' day-to-day interactions with both known friends and unknown connections. There are many possibilities for why individuals maintain multiple online profiles across many different SNSs, but online sociality is salient in most individuals' lives. Van Dijck (2013, p. 12) explains that users value the human connectedness that SNSs offer. Other scholars, such as Turkle (2011, p. 11), remark how digital communication platforms are substitutes for face-to-face connections. Individuals consciously create their online presence—essentially "branding" their persona on the various social networking they select to participate in. They consciously self-stage themselves and measure their popularity by their online manifestation (van Dijck, 2013, p. 202). Boyd (2014, pp. 77-99) and van Dijck (2013, pp. 12-18) express the rhetoric that is embedded in the architecture of SNSs and technologically inscribed on their users. In fact, the networking facilitation that is controlled by these platforms and social practices are mutually constitutive (van Dijck, 2013, p. 6).

Considering the invasiveness of SNSs in individuals' everyday existence and performance, they become a unique, effective, and viable space for which to craft and execute social change. First, SNSs marshal a global network of users, therefore, congregate a wide mass, multifarious audience in one digital space for which communication and rhetoric can be presented. A 2016 survey of Americans' social media use reflects that seven-in-ten Americans utilize at least one social networking platform to connect with others, engage with news content, and share information (PewResearchCenter, 2017). Social media platforms comprise of two of the most critical factors when striving to change individuals' perspectives and behaviors on a wide scale basis: rhetoric is communicated and a large audience is able to be reached via one online channel.

Social networking also enables the mass sharing and distribution of rhetorical media. Many users and scholars alike have voiced concern over platforms' policing of content using built-in algorithms that filter social media. The most "Liked," "Shared," and "Reacted to" posts get pinned to the top of networked users' feeds and timelines further establishing popular media as a dominant rhetoric. However, the visibility that popular media attain demands users' attention and instigates social engagement and familiarity with messages. Individuals are more likely to simulate the ideas and behaviors that their friends convey and perform. Being visible means being relevant in one's networked public, which prompts users to continue to share the posts that are popular, thereby, furthering online visibility. Furthermore, some individuals are so impressionable and moldable that they willingly "jump on the bandwagon" of popular belief. When striving to enact new concepts and ideas, the legislation of popular subject matter that algorithms perform is beneficial if that content presents the immersive experiences that impact users emotionally and can become assimilated into their acquired knowledge and information.

The agency with which users are able to craft their own profile is debatable and overtly complex and depends on the platform owner. However, despite the agency implications of users' ability to craft their own profile, they are motivated and constructed by the SNS and by the networking interactions they share with others on the site. The standardization of profile display and the implicit and explicit conformity rules of conduct that SNSs govern call to question users' agency in identity formation, activities performed, and communications exchanged. Van Dijck (2013, p. 31) describes how the visible interface—that which users see—translates coded information which directs specific user actions. Settings, and chiefly, defaults, automatically channel user behavior, for which they have little or no control. In fact, platform owners can change defaults without users being aware of it, and, "if changing a default takes effort, users are more likely to conform to the site's decision architecture"– states van Dijck (2013, p. 32). For example, one change Facebook implemented in 2015 was the Dynamic Type, which is a larger text size. According to Facebook (2015), this change was to enhance the readability for those with vision impairments as a key part of helping the world become connected. The platform owners established this new default, and despite some people's dislike, it remained a default that users were unable to change. However, the rule that a post with 35 characters or fewer appears in the interface as large text can be leveraged by individuals to gain visibility. If an individual wants to call attention to her- or himself, they can simply post a text message that appears in the large text, which is more easily read than the smaller version. Van Dijck (2013, p. 33) informs that the platform's implicit participation (coding and design) enforces its usage.

This implicit and explicit conformity expressed in the online exchanges on social media can be leveraged to create behavior change. Social media platforms congregate a mass audience of users with shared interests, thereby effectively enable messages to become infiltered throughout the networked public and make it possible to create mass shifts in perspectives and circumscribe new dietary habits.

EMBEDDING IMMERSIVE EXPERIENCES

Assumingly, individuals are compelled to eat meat due to their script for the SAD. Because most individuals employ their script for eating, which includes eating animal flesh, they may not be aware of or consciously consider other ways of eating or other diets. This may be because they have never encountered an alternate experience of eating that did not include meat nor become informed and acknowledge another way for experiencing the practice of consuming food (that which does not include meat). Humans can apply their scripts to online situations, such as understanding and interpreting the rhetoric of factory farming and intensive meat consumption. There are communities and online publics which do share and exchange information on dietary practices that do not include meat and inform of factory farming, the cruel treatment and killing of animals, and the environmental destruction that occurs in the agribusiness, but unless individuals search for such information or alternative methods of behavior, they are likely to not become informed of these practices. "The first special mechanism must be able to recognize that a script – a standard event sequence – has been mentioned," state Schank and Abelson (1977, p. 38). Embedding immersive experiences that showcase graphic images and videos of factory farms within social media effectively gains users' attention. It benefits from increased visibility when individuals use the activities of online society to promote the images and videos within networked publics. Individuals will be exposed to and be able to create new scripts for understanding and responding to the rhetoric of factory farming and intensive meat consumption.

For instance, if just one individual shares a video from Farm Sanctuary (2017), the video could potentially go viral if users within the networked public "Liked," "Shared," and "Reacted to" the post. As online sociality guides one's construction of their identity and embedded scripts, establishing the Farm Sanctuary video as dominant rhetoric will inform the public on factory farming and the horrific treatment of animals and compel them to consider other methods of eating that do not include meat. Individuals will be more likely to consider eating a diet free of meat due to its online popularity.

Scripts are organized by the linking of episodes in a sequence of actions to be executed when encountering well-known, defined situations (Schank & Abelson, 1977, p. 41). While scripts have no mechanism for handling novel situations that do not "Fit the Script," they do allow for the replacement of objects within the script. Thus, even though individuals' prescribed script for eating in the U.S. includes meat, this can easily be replaced. To "Flip the Script" of eating meat, in the U.S., individuals can replace the animal foods in their script with vegetables and grains, which can be shared and knowledge exchanged via social media along with the immersive experiences of factory farms. Additionally, much like the way in which humans organize the episodes of scripts, SNSs afford connectedness. As individuals share the links which direct to the images, videos, and websites that regard factory farming, vegan, and vegetarian diets, connections among networked publics and individuals' multiple SNSs will be created, thus, engaging and appealing to the global audience required to create mass social change. The role that technology plays in our shared experiences and everyday life makes it an ideal vehicle for which to construct and distribute new messages for social change.

CREATING MOTIVATION THROUGH ONLINE SOCIALITY

In order to begin to form new habits, one must first practice the behaviors of that habit. That said, in order to participate in new behaviors, one must be motivated either intrinsically or extrinsically. Along with willingness, the most significant factor to prompting individuals to change their behaviors and social constructions is motivation. Online sociality, which is largely governed and guided by SNSs, renders them as ideal spaces for implementing motivational and conformist strategies that result in widespread behavior modifications and permanent changes in individuals' scripts for normative behaviors. Schank and Abelson (1977, p. 16-17) describe scripts as episodic memories of one's life, which are organized as sequences of events that occur in time and space. Thus, as individuals encounter a similar event or activity, they retrieve the episode of their memory that most closely resembles the new experience and use their knowledge of that episode to contend with the new experience. The formation of one's identity on social media constructs individuals' episodic memory and scripts as they conform to the SNSs' profile construction rules, default settings, and interaction activities.

Once individuals become informed of the cruel treatment of animals and become aware of new foods with which to replace the meat in their script for eating, they will be more willing to accept a new method of eating. Tomkins (1962, p. 27, 29) suggests that evolution has constructed a human to have a primal desire for the preservation of life and to reproduce, the need to socialize and to interact with other humans, and the need for exploration and novel experiences. Human experience is constructed and created based on these evolutionary constructs. Individuals' afferent and efferent systems are in constant operation as information and stimuli enter through the afferent system and individuals' respond to that information through their efferent system using blueprints—scripts—for how they are to respond based on that situation.

In effect of humans' basic needs of survival, socialization, and novelty, they are motivated by two innate systems: the drive system and the affect system. The drive system is based on biological factors required by the human body to maintain homeostasis—those which are required for survival. This includes the need to eat, sleep, reproduce, and defecate as basic biological necessities required for the preservation of life and to duplicate. Humans automatically execute these behaviors unconsciously, as inborn scripts for survival. For example, humans do not have to think about breathing, they simply do.

The drive system, however, can be made conscious when an individual's homeostatic level reaches a threshold that is diminishing to one's survival. For instance, if an individual has been submerged and cannot breathe, she or he will immediately become aware that one of their primary, basic needs is not being met, and she or he will be motivated to act in order to reach their biological level of homeostasis once again.

That said, the drive system is secondary to the affect system. Most of the motivational power of the drive system comes from the affect system as it is simultaneously activated when the drive system is (Tomkins, 1962, p. 22). The affect system is based on humans' experience of pain and pleasure. For instance, the pleasure of eating and the pain of hunger motivate a human to eat. While this is based on biological factors, what individuals eat is primary aesthetic and constructed by social norms and affect. Tomkins (1962, p. 19) states: "The individual can be consciously aware of his own reports, whether they are constructions from memory, or his constructions guided by an external source". As such, like the drive system, humans employ scripts for how to react to stimuli in their environment. Humans learn to respond to similar situations and stimulations with the behaviors that previously gained them positive affect or enabled them to escape a negative feeling (Tomkins, 1962, p. 44). They passively behave in an effort to maximize pleasure and avoid pain.

There are several means by which humans' affect system is mobilized that establish SNSs as successful platforms for generating social change. First, as Tomkins (1962, p. 23) indicates, there are numerous stimulants for any one affect, as well as numerous means for diminishing the affect. Considering SNSs' media extravaganza that is posted, displayed, and shared within networked publics, users are likely to stumble upon sites or content that generate an emotional reaction which produces a behavior. According to Tomkins (1962, pp. 22-23), the positive or negative status of an individual's response is irrelevant to the attempt to control the situation that caused the affect. The graphic images and videos of factory farms will likely generate a negative response for most individuals. In effect, individuals will be prompted to share the post with their network—perhaps even going outside of the borders of the particular SNS it was published on and posting the content in other environments. Users wish to trigger the same response in other humans—thus satisfying both their own novelty and social needs as well as those same needs of others. Additionally, SNSs' enhanced visibility fuels the social change effort.

Facebook, Twitter, and other SNSs govern individuals to drive popularity and content visibility by, "Liking," "Sharing," "Commenting," and even adding an emotional reaction. Not only are individuals engaging in an activity that is based on the affect system, but they are simultaneously receiving validation for their behaviors when other users repost or respond to the content they post. If a user posts a video of a pig being cruelly and inhumanly treated at a factory farm, which can be easily performed from the Farm Sanctuary (2017) website, that user is expressing their intolerance for factory farming and what could be assumed their practice of a meat-free diet. The user who posted the content receives validation for their thoughts and behaviors, as well as a positive affect from the online socialization. Users who share or comment on the video are both experiencing affect through participating in the online socialization and recognition of the content. An essential aspect of being human is the constant strive to duplicate oneself in space and time (Tomkins, 1962, p. 7). Social networking platforms afford users this space and time for which to continuously reproduce oneself, not only in the multiple SNSs that exist today, but through mediated achievements of SNSs. Boyd (2014, p. 11) explains that the persistence, visibility, spreadability, and searchablity of social media both facilitate and construct online sociality. These four unique qualities of SNSs present an opportunity to create social change and challenge the status quo diet centered on meat in the U.S. and beyond.

Additionally, individuals use others' behaviors and recommendations as motivational information for decision making. Users are more likely to blindly accept the recommendations of others and perform as others do. When assimilating new into existing information, Manthiou et al. (2016, p. 364) suggest that external information helps direct users in their decision-making process. In fact, users will actually ask others in their networked publics for advice on their anticipated performance. After being informed of factory farming and the cruel treatment of animals and willing to practice a diet free of meat, individuals may ask their connections on SNSs if they should, "Go vegan?" – state Manthiou et al. (2016, p. 364): "In such a case, an external information search (e.g. ask for suggestion from others) would be necessary for the further decision-making process". Not only does this posted question gain the user attention, but the positive response from others merely builds the user's motivation for eating a vegan diet and may motivate others to adopt such a diet.

Motivation for eating a diet free of meat comes from stimulating individuals' drive and affect systems, which is performed through the posting of rhetorical content. The mass sharing and distribution of rhetorical content afforded by SNSs enables individuals to become aware of new experiences and react based on their prescribed scripts or by mimicking other' reactions in their networked publics. All SNSs incorporate their own language for sharing content, commenting, and reacting to others' content. The lack of face-to-face communication performed on SNSs affords anonymity, which enables individuals to react more strongly than they would in the similar real-life situation. "We perform different roles at different times in different situations in society," concurs Dawson and Phelan (2016, p. 3). However, by experimenting with strong reactions and behaviors that occur through the online SNS language exchanged, individuals may feel more comfortable to practice the same behaviors in real-life. Language varies depending on the social situations and the purpose, but reflects both the speaker's identity and the social and cultural constructs of a society (Dawson & Phelan, 2016, p. 3). Analyzing the media rhetoric surrounding bullying and how it is constructed on social media sites, Boyd (2014, p. 133) describes: "The visibility and persistence of networked publics may enable larger audiences to witness acts of bullying". Boyd (2014, p. 133) continues: "These same affordances create novel opportunities for people to intervene". Saturating networked publics with images and videos of the cruel treatment of animals raised as meat products makes visible the real-life occurrence and enables individuals to step in, speak out, and express their dislike, which will reinforce the elimination of eating meat in one's diet. The rhetorical language used in the conversation that results from immersive experiences of factory farms motivates individuals to react strongly and execute the real-life practice of a diet free of meat.

Tomkins (1962, p. 22) depicts how the affect system is able to disregard and even impede the drive system by being activated independently or by due to individuals' learned or unlearned behaviors. In different social situations, humans are biased to react to stimuli and behavior in certain ways, as well as capable of learning new constructs and new ways to behave in those situations (Tomkins, 1962, p. 22). For instance, if an individual is out dining with friends and the majority eats a dish with meat, yet one orders a vegan meal, the person may conform to the dominant social behavior. Yet he or she may also learn that eating vegan is acceptable in that situation and may be biased toward making such a choice in another similar social situation due to their learning an alternate way to behave. Likewise, in SNSs, when challenges pressure individuals to react based on their biases towards a particular behavior, the construction of a new behavior, a new practice of eating a diet free of meat, individuals will be able to learn the new script for eating and be able to employ it when their drive for eating is stimulated.

In these situations, humans are inhibiting their drive system through their affect system. Their drive system may be prescribing them to eat meat, yet their affect system is more powerful in enabling them to employ their newly constructed script for eating, that which is learned through the SNSs' challenge and executed upon stimulation of their basic need to eat. With repetition, this instrumental behavior will become an automatic, scripted behavior and successfully instill individuals with the new meat-free eating behavior—the goal of the social change.

In addition, the affect system can be stimulated through a variety of external factors and humans are able to increase pleasure and avoid pain in many ways. The drive system has a limited number of reactions that humans can perform in order to satisfy basic needs: eating, sleeping, having sex, urinating, and defecating. Conversely, the affect system enables humans to experience and react to stimuli through numerous social satiations and numerous learned and unlearned behaviors. If the affect reaction is motivating to an individual, the stimulant that articulates the affect system will become a motivating factor for that individual to continue the performance of the behaviors that stimulate their affect system. As individuals take on the challenge of eating a diet free of meat and subsequently post their successes on SNSs, they will not only receive positive affect stimulation from others' "Likes" and "Reactions," but will also receive the positive affect from gaining visibility and attention from participating in the online challenge. Due to the shared challenges and motivating responses and visibility, individuals will be motivated to continue their behavior of eating a meat-free diet and continue to post their successes—thus increasing the stakes in the challenge, the visibility of the new script, and the hegemony of the new social norm.

COMPLETE BEHAVIOR MODIFICATION

The final step to complete, permanent behavior modification occurs through the maintenance of the new behavior. Once individuals are continuously practicing the behavior of eating a meat-free diet, this will have essentially become the new script for the practice of eating, and the social change of "Flipping the Script" of the SAD will have occurred. Individuals' scripts become innate and executed unconsciously when stimulated. Complete behavior modification occurs naturally as individuals repeat the same behaviors in similar situations. Affect acts as a general-purpose amplifier of humans' motivation for performing and repeating behaviors; thus, the performance of a behavior that intensifies the affect system increases the likelihood that behavior will become assimilated in one's memory. Following the repetition of the behavior and accompanying affect, that behavior and knowledge of the situations will construct individuals' scripts—the knowledge and behaviors that one uses to understand and respond in reoccurring social situations.

CONCLUSION

Social networking sites are effective agents of social change because they represent real-life social exchanges, are socially constructed, and compel individuals to perform using unconscious scripts. The evolution of the social experience of immersive meat rhetoric, the participation in the execution of the behavior of eating a meat-free diet, and the perpetuation of this behavior will successfully change the dominant behavior of the consumption of meat in our society.

It was technology that transformed our society into one of consumption via the ability to rapidly produce and sell products, which initiated the agribusiness and the factory farming practice of raising and killing animals for human consumption. However, just as technology created the mass social change of capitalism, it can also create the mass social change of the SAD to that of a diet that excludes the consumption of meat. Yet, it is important to note that technology merely reproduces that which occurs in real-life and actually makes it more visible. The concerns of factory farming and over-consumption are real, and the only way to begin to create social change is if we first express these real-life issues to people. Community networks and connectivity, combined with the conformity prescribed on SNSs, make them an effective medium for transferring meat rhetoric and motivating individuals to implement new standards of behaviors. The question of concern is: How does one shift the omnipresent social norm of meat consumption in a society whose diet is scripted by the dominant power structures of the agribusiness and the perpetual behavior of eating meat? This chapter proposed using SNSs as agents of changing the SAD via the communication, social practice, and "Flipping the Script" of the standard American dietary preferences to a meat-free diet. The proposed agent of social change is complex, volatile, and remains a fruitful area for the progression of ideas, online sociality, and connectivity. Further research can explore individual SNSs' effectiveness for behavior modification and the extent that natural individual tendencies has on social media presence and script creation.

REFERENCES

Baur, G. (2008). *Farm sanctuary: Changing hearts and minds about animals and food*. New York, NY: Simon & Schuster.

Boundless. (n.d.) *Second Industrial Revolution*. Retrieved from https://www.boundless.com/definition/second-industrial-revolution/

Boyd, d. (2014). *It's complicated: The social lives of networked teens*. New Have, NY: Yale University Press.

Dawson, H. C., & Phelan, M. (Eds.). (2016). *Language files material for an instruction to language and linguistics* (12th ed.). Columbus, OH: The Ohio State University.

Delahoyde, M., & Despenich, S. C. (1994). Creating meat-eaters: The child as advertising target. *Journal of Popular Culture*, *28*(1), 135–149. doi:10.1111/j.0022-3840.1994.2801_135.x

Enticott, G., & Vanclay, F. (2011). Scripts, animal health and biosecurity: The moral accountability of farmers' talk about animal health risks. *Health Risk & Society*, *13*(4), 293–309. doi:10.1080/13698575.2011.575456

Facebook. (2015, 6 November). Facebook Accessibility (Facebook message). Retrieved from https://www.facebook.com/accessibility/posts/997008960342829

Farm Sanctuary. (2017). *Farm sanctuary*. Retrieved from https://www.farmsanctuary.org/

Fendley, S. (2015, 3 November). What does the Twitter heart mean? *ClearPivot*. Retrieved from https://www.clearpivot.com/blog/what-does-the-twitter-heart-mean

Goffman, E. (1959). *The presentation of self in everyday life*. New York, NY: Anchor Books.

Lucan, S., Barg, F., Karasz, A., Palmer, C., & Long, J. (2012). Concepts of healthy diet among urban, low-income, African Americans. *Journal of Community Health*, *37*(4), 754–762. doi:10.1007/s10900-011-9508-x PMID:22101636

Manthiou, A., Kang, J., Chiang, L., & Tang, L. (2016). Investigating the effects of memorable experiences: An extended model of script theory. *Journal of Travel & Tourism Marketing*, *33*(3), 362–379. doi:10.1080/10548408.2015.1064055

Marcus, E. (1998). *Vegan: The new ethics of eating*. Ithaca, NY: McBooks Press.

Marx, K. (1887). Capital: A critique of political economy (Vol. 1, F. Engels Ed., S. Moore, & E. Aveling, trans.). Moscow, Russia: Progress Publishers. (Original work published 1867).

Pew Research Center. (2017, January 12). *Social media fact sheet*. Retrieved from http://www.pewinternet.org/fact-sheet/social-media/

Schank, R., & Abelson, R. (1977). *Scripts plans goals and understanding: An inquiry into human knowledge structures*. Mahwah, NJ: Lawrence Erlbaum Associates.

Tomkins, S. S. (1962). Affect imagery consciousness (Vol. 1). New York, NY: Springer.

Turkle, S. (2011). *Alone together: Why we expect more from technology and less from each other*. New York, NY: Basic Books.

United States Department of Agriculture (USDA). (n.d.) ChooseMyPlate.gov. Retrieved from https://www.choosemyplate.gov/

Van Dijck, J. (2013). *The culture of connectivity: A critical history of social media*. New York, NY: Oxford University Press. doi:10.1093/acprof:oso/9780199970773.001.0001

KEY TERMS AND DEFINITIONS

Affect System: The evolutionary mechanism that urges humans to perform the behaviors and respond to environmental stimuli in ways which will increase or gain them positive feelings and decrease or avoid negative feelings; for example, a woman is likely to continue to wear her hair down instead of up if she receives positive affirmations from individuals in her environment.

Consumerization: Refers to society's need to purchase or somehow gain access to a product or service considered a commodity simply because of the need to purchase or gain access to it; for instance, meat has become a commodity in the U.S. today because individuals believe it is essential to the human diet and purchase and eat it regularly.

Drive System: The evolutionary, physical mechanism that urges humans to perform the behaviors required for their survival and to duplicate themselves in time and space; these drives include hunger (sustenance), tiredness (sleep), and sex (reproduction).

Farm Factory: An intensive form of modern farming, whereby animals are mass-produced and killed to be sold for human consumption; factory farms are large facilities, whereby livestock are routinely mistreated; harmed; injured; starved; injected with medicines and hormones to combat disease and for rapid growth; artificially inseminated; dragged; overheated, and cruelly treated in more industrial-style like methods prior to their being killed.

Motivation: The abstract force that compels humans to perform, act, or do that which they desire; motivation can be intrinsic, such as an individual taking a class to simply learn a new skill, or extrinsic, such as an individual taking a class because she or he will get paid more at her or his workplace after taking the class.

Paradigm: An exemplar prototype of a law, theory, or application that is widely known, believed, and accepted to be the best or most popular of its kind; for example, Facebook may be widely known to be the paradigmatic SNS.

Script: The knowledge stored in an individual's memory that is unconsciously used to understand, react, and behave in repeatedly encountered real-life social situations; scripts are stimulated when an individual encounters the situation that which has been repeatedly experienced.

Social Networking Site (SNS): An online/digital platform whereby individuals congregate to communicate, share information, photos, videos, and links, and can respond to each other via a constructed lexicon comprised of symbols ("Like" button) and icons (emoji).

Stimulant: An environmental element or dynamic that affects another environmental element or dynamic, usually causing a reaction from that which it affects; for example, the environmental stimulus of a baby crying may cause a mother to behave in nurturing ways towards the baby; the environmental stimulus of cold weather may cause individuals to dress in warm clothing.

Chapter 10
What Is More Important: Perception of Masculinity or Personal Health and the Environment?

Diana Bogueva
Curtin University, Australia

Dora Marinova
Curtin University, Australia

ABSTRACT

The unnecessary question what a man is without his masculinity, is deeply ingrained into the socially established norms of strength, power, virility and machoism. Although the traditional male masculinity stereotype and its association with meat consumption are still undisputable for many "real" men, there is indication about a shift toward a new modern evolutionary masculinity which reflects more sustainability values. The chapter explores this based on a survey of Sydney men. It reveals the influence of new factors, such as environmental, health and animal welfare concerns, which shape the concept of the masculine. Meat-eating men will experience increasing pressure to defend their traditional masculinity. The Sydney study also explores the factors likely to influence Australian men to replace a meat-centred diet with more plant-based alternatives.

INTRODUCTION

Manliness (of old English origin) describes a set of traits, abilities, attributes and qualities which characterise the male human species, whilst masculinity (of Latin origin) is the property of manifesting these features (English Oxford Living Dictionaries, 2017). Although these two terms are intertwined, masculinity – that is, the manifestation of manliness, is much more affected by social factors and practices.

The relationship between man, meat and masculinity has manifold meanings and for centuries has represented a socially acceptable norm about male self-perception and identity. Currently, the list of prevailing hegemonic masculinity characteristics in western countries includes: heterosexuality, power, physical strength, toughness, aggression, decision-making, independence, dominance, authority, asser-

DOI: 10.4018/978-1-5225-4757-0.ch010

tiveness, courage, rationality, emotional stoicism, muscularity and prowess, adventurous spirit, initiative, self-confidence, work supremacy, financial independence, virility, playboy behaviours and violence (Fiddes, 1994; Austin, 2008; Van Hoven & Hopkins, 2009; Bogueva & Phau, 2016; Kahn, 2011; Reeser, 2010; Pease, 2010; Hearn et al., 2013).

Masculinity is also determined by biological and presentation factors. In the past male emperors, sages and leaders of yore had attributes like facial hair – a style also popular nowadays for many celebrities. Beards have been associated with high testosterone, virility, leadership and power (Schiebinger, 1993; Withey, 2015). The upper class male aristocracy in 16th-17th century Europe enjoyed the privilege of eating meat abundantly as well as "manly" attributes, including wearing high-heal shoes and wigs (Zevallos, 2014), which are no longer considered such. Socially-defined signs of power, rank and prestige change over time and, for example, high-heel shoes now symbolise femininity (Zevallos, 2014). What this chapter explores is whether the connection between meat and masculinity is also evolving.

MEAT AND MANLINESS

Meat, and especially red meat, is an archetypical masculine food (van den Wijngaard, 1997) embedded in the western construction of masculinity (De Boer, 2006; Rothgerber, 2012; Rozin et al., 2012). The contemporary male meat consumption behaviour is equated and effectively wrapped under the pretext of traditional masculinity traits aimed at positioning men at the top of the social and animal hierarchy. Historically a scarce resource attributable to the privileged rich as a means of demonstrating authority and wealth, meat has become a highly palatable food associated with strength, virility, blood, masculinity and tangibly represents human power over the rest of the natural world (Fiddes, 1991; Kubberød et al., 2002; Stibbe, 2004; Ruby & Heine, 2011). The deeply believed link between meat and masculinity is traced back to ancient times with Aristotle stating: "other animals exist for the sake of man" (in Fiddes, 1994, p. 276). In the 1840s meat gained a scientific status with the popularised 'protein myth' and the notion that animal food is more nutritious than plants as it can replenish muscular strength (Fiddes, 1994).

According to Lupton (1996), the type of food men prefer to eat is a central part of their subjective identity, sense of self and experience of macho embodiment. Attempts to usurp the western menu consisting of a piece of flesh from warm-blooded animal plus a piece of vegetable, usually potato or pumpkin, and gravy (Lupton, 1996; Murcott, 1982:203; Douglas and Gross, 1981, p. 6-8), could cause serious social disharmony and instability (Lupton, 1996). Manly foods are not a necessary part of the male nourishment and physiological need to eat, but a major aspect of the socio-cultural environment where they belong or with which they identify.

While there is a shared culture across the western world considering meat as normal, natural, necessary and nice – the 4Ns (Piazza et al, 2015), it is particularly perceived as a masculine food (Willard, 2006) and masculinity is performed through meat-eating (and macho behaviour) for the approval and recognition by other men. When men consume meat in public places, such as steak houses, strip clubs or around the BBQ, they validate their manhood and self-comfort about being a man (Rothgerber, 2012). "Meat eating is an act of a self-definition as a privileged (male-identified) human" gaining strength from consuming strong animals, such as bulls and cows, as vegetables represent passivity (Adams & Calarco, 2016, p. 34). Men often emphasise meat while women minimise meat, displaying gender individualities (van den Wijngaard, 1997).

Food marks boundaries not only between cultures, geographic regions, social classes, rituals, traditions, religious, life stages, but also in the perception of manliness. It is also gendered, that is masculine – men eat meat, and feminine – women eat vegetables (Adams & Calarco, 2016, p. 34). Vegetarians and other non-orthodox eaters are treated with disguised suspicion because they challenge the western "society's basic cosmology" where taste is culturally conditioned and governed by patterned rules (Fiddes, 1994).

In addition to the social framing of the link between meat and masculinity, other factors are shaping the consumption of animal-based foods in the 21st century. Being highly inefficient use of natural resources, including phosphorus (White & Cordell, 2015), current and future expansion of meat consumption is incompatible with the projected world population growth and the rocketing appetite for animal foods, especially in countries transitioning to more prosperous economies (Roberts, 2008; McMichael & Bambrick, 2005; York & Gossard, 2004; Bogueva et al., 2017). Considered a dietary norm for men across the globe, increasing and excessive meat consumption in response to hegemonic masculinity traits is contributing to detrimental ecological impacts directly linked with livestock, including climate change. Furthermore, meat's association with cancers and unnecessary use of antibiotics is causing public health concerns. The abundant scientific evidence is supported by strong arguments for reduction in the intake of animal-based products by researchers (Pimentel & Pimentel, 2003; Goodland & Anhang, 2009; Garnett, 2014; Raphaely & Marinova, 2016; Springmann et al., 2016) and prestigious international bodies (UN, 2015; WHO, 2015).

Against this up-to-date understanding of the pitfalls in linking masculinity with meat consumption, it is probably time to abandon this myth the way society ditched male high-heel shoes as impractical. The problem however is disproportionately more complex as not doing so challenges the health of any life on our planet the way we know it today. Interventions and methodologies for sustainability social marketing (Bogueva et al., 2017) are needed to create ways for overcoming people's, and specifically men's, addiction to meat or their ignorance about its destructive impacts.

This however is not an easy task. The remainder of the chapter examines men's attitudes about the importance of their perceptions about masculinity, and its social norms of machoism, bravery, virility and stamina, against environmental and health concerns. Understanding what drives men in their food choices can help target better any efforts to restrain the escalating problems associated with meat consumption.

SYDNEY SURVEY

An online survey was conducted in Sydney, Australia in 2017 with 545 male participants aged 18 to 57 years about the symbolism of meat, their perceptions about the link between meat and human health and any factors that could influence a change in consumption patterns. The survey was statistically representative of the total Sydney population at a 95% confidence level with a 4% error of margin (or confidence interval). Below are the description of the sample and discussion of the results.

Sample Description

Six hundred people – 150 from four age groups (born 1960-1969, 1970-1979, 1980-1989 and 1990-1999), were invited to participate in the survey. The overall response rate was 91% with two age groups providing a complete 100% response (see Table 1). Although the overwhelming majority of the participants

Table 1. Sydney men's survey sample

Age Group by Year Born	Number of Respondents	Percentage
1960-1969	117	21%
1970-1979	150	28%
1980-1989	150	28%
1990-1999	128	23%
Total:	545	100%

– 512 (94%) are meat-eaters (seven or 1% of whom have chosen to eat only white meat), the sample also comprises 32 (6%) vegetarians and one (0.2%) vegan.

Results

The participants were asked what is their main association with meat (refer to Figure 1). As expected, the majority of them – 58% (317), linked meat to manliness, namely: symbol of strength and masculinity for 32% (175), human power over animals for 16% (88) and being the "real" food for 10% (54). Similar justification of meat consumption is reported by other researchers showing it is human fate to eat animals as they are lower in the food hierarchy chain (Rothgerber, 2012) and a meal is not considered real unless it contains meat (Sobal, 2005).

A second group of participants – 17% (93) associate meat with being an attractive dietary option, namely: prestigious and luxury food for 9% (49), nutritious healthy food for 5% (27), food rich in protein and iron for 3% (15) and food related to the Australian identity for 0.4% (2). They represent popular-held beliefs about the nutritional value of meat without explicit awareness of the health and environmental dangers triggered by excessive consumption.

The most interesting is the third group of participants – 25% (135), for whom meat is associated with negative impacts and who are aware of the need to limit its intake, namely negative environmental effects for 19% (103), animal suffering for 5% (25) and moderate consumption because of potential risks for 1% (7). This group manifests a change in the awareness pattern among the Sydney male population with a quarter of the participants associating meat with worrying concerns about human, animal and planetary wellbeing.

When asked directly about meat's effect on human health (see Table 2), the majority of the participating males – 52% (286), do not see any negative impacts. They take meat for granted without any concerns about impacts on men's masculinity or health. The remaining 48% (259), however, are of the opinion that meat should either be consumed in moderation or not at all, namely: 20% (109) believe that eating up to 100g per week is good for human health, 14% (74) believe that excessive consumption causes disease and another 14% (76) that meat is bad for human health. Combined these results illustrate clearly the fact that a large section of men worries about health implications associated with eating meat. This is a shift away from the traditional masculinity traits of strength, toughness and stoicism regarding men's own health towards more self-conscious awareness.

The research results suggest emerging understanding of masculinity which rejects the old social norms and establishes a pathway for changing meat consumption behaviours based on healthier and more sustainable food choices. Referring to a similar trend, another research points out that men are now

Figure 1. Opinions about what red meat symbolises

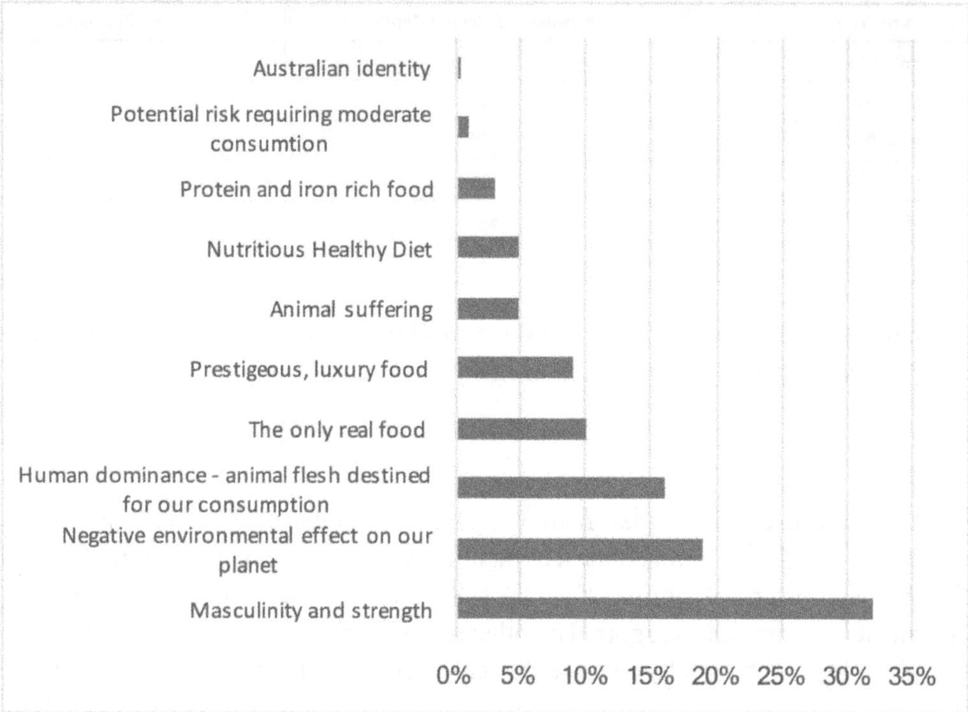

Table 2. Meat and health

Options	Number of respondents	Percentage
Meat consumption has nothing to do with health and health related issues	286	52%
Eating meat in moderation up to a maximum of 100g - 2-3 times a week is good for your health	109	20%
Excessive meat consumption - 300-500g and above daily causes disease	74	14%
Eating meat is bad for your health	76	14%
TOTAL	545	100%

building their identity through becoming healthier, exercise conscious, prioritising family, putting children before work, appreciating a more equal social position for women, being open to new experiences and overall enjoying happiness over more traditional signs of power, virility and success (Connelly, 2016). This emerging trend of health self-consciousness and family values is an important influential factor for Australian male meat consumers that could become a driving force towards reduction in meat intake. It should be vigorously explored by marketers and producers of plant-based alternatives as a start of a substantial move towards eating less or no meat to achieve more sustainable consumption for human, planetary and animal wellbeing benefits.

Further interesting results are generated by the question about factors that can influence men to reduce their meat intake (see Table 3). Health-related factors are the most influential for the Sydney men, namely: personal health for 58% (317), dietary requirements for 51% (280) and health problems of relatives/friends for 21% (117). Environmental reasons are also a highly ranked factor with 40% (216) of the men indicating that they will respond to them. Animal welfare is an influential factor for 34%

Table 3. Factors that could influence men to reduce meat consumption (multiple choice)

Factor	Number of Respondents	Percentage
Personal health problems	317	58.2%
Dietary requirements	280	51.4%
Environmental reasons	216	39.6%
Marketing campaigns	193	35.4%
Animal welfare	186	34.1%
Relative/friend health problems	117	21.5%
Peer pressure	114	20.9%
Government (Federal, State) regulations	106	19.4%
Vegetarianism/veganism	36	6.6%
Other factors	31	5.7%

(186) of the Sydney male respondents. Of interest are also external factors that can push men's dietary choices towards meat reduction – marketing campaigns are likely to influence 35% (193) of them; peer pressure will have an impact on 21% (114) and government regulations on 19% (106). Understanding better vegetarianism and veganism will influence only 7% (36) of the Sydney men.

These results manifest that the new contemporary masculinity concept places under threat the old-school masculine identity passed through generations, from father, grandfathers and beyond. Coupled with proper social marketing messages about health, the natural environment and animal wellbeing, this new trend can lead to individual meat consumption behaviour changes.

Restricting red meat consumption to the limit put forward by the Australian health authorities, namely no more than 455g/week of cooked red meat (NHMRC, 2013; van Dooren & Kramer, 2012) and adopting more sustainable plant-based diets (Audsley et al., 2009; van Dooren & Kramer, 2012; Bogueva et al., 2017) will be positive for the environment, producing less greenhouse gas emissions compared to current levels of intake and will also lower the risk of chronic and non-communicable diseases (Pan et al., 2012), including diabetes (Feskens et al., 2013; Li et al., 2014; Micha et al., 2010), various types of cancer (WCRF/AICR, 2007; Giles et al., 1997; Bosland et al., 1999), stroke and other hearth disease (Dauchet et al., 2005, 2006, 2009; Greger, 2010; Micha et al., 2010). As voluntary dietary alterations, men can choose fluctuating the frequency of meat consumption or retaining the typical meal patterns, but opting to reduce the meat portions.

DISCUSSION

Health perception usually carries varieties of complexities linked with dietary types and strong masculinity appearance. They are difficult to define as often males treat their health-related symptoms in the traditional masculinity way of considering them as effeminate quality (Reeser, 2010; Devaney, 2005). A man is also seen not as masculine if he suffers from illnesses related to his manly attributes like prostate (Reeser, 2010). With 1 in 7 men diagnosed with prostate cancer during his lifetime (AIHW, 2017), awareness about the link between meat and cancer is essential.

Environmental considerations are already affecting Sydney men's meat consumption and this is likely to expand in the future. A radical alteration in western diets towards severe cuts in meat consumption can help curb the world's huge and increasing appetite for meat (Bogueva et al., 2017) to avoid devastating climate change to which agricultural livestock is contributing significantly (Bailey et al., 2014; Hedenus et al., 2014; Raphaely & Marinova, 2016; Stehfest et al., 2009). Climate change requires urgent action from consumers, producers and introduction of government policies. As the Sydney men's survey shows, the first steps are changing the notion about responsible consumption and no longer being ignorant about the carbon footprint of food.

Depersonalising and deidentifying ourselves with animal cruelty and slaughter remove the relation with meat production in our contemporary world. A large share of the Sydney participants pointed out animal welfare as a potential factor for swaying their attitude against meat consumption.

Masculinity norms are influenced by peer pressure reflecting socially recognised men-related beliefs, expectations and values (Mahalik et al., 2003). Friends' peer pressure encourages diverse degrees of decision-making from benign types such as choosing hair styles, clothes, music, TV shows, electronic games to moral, values and belief-based challenging decisions as body piercing, bodybuilding steroids (Sagoe, 2014) and fuelling addiction to tobacco (Conrad et al., 1992; Turner et al., 2004; Walsh & Tzelepis, 2009), illegal drugs (Jaslow, 2012; Palmqvist & Santavirta, 2006; Karvelas, 2012; King, 2009) and alcohol as part of being a masculine macho (Iwamoto and Smiler, 2013, King 2009). The mass media are a most powerful conveyor of these masculine socio-cultural needs (Palmqvist & Santavirta, 2006) and can also influence meat consumption directions based on peer pressure.

Government regulations at a federal, state or local level is another change factor. Being influential in regards to tobacco smoking behaviour change through taxing cigarettes, banning advertising, plain packaging, setting age limits for purchases, smoking ban in workplaces, airplanes, bars and restaurants, government restrictions played role in encouraging smokers to abandon their habits. Effective regulation could be put in place for meat consumption in a similar way through policies regarding food labelling, advertising and the supply of environmentally friendly food data (Pollard et al., 2013).

Vegetarianism and veganism as a factor influencing changes in meat consumption remain least influential. Although men are becoming more conscious about their own health and the environment, there is still a long way to go before fully restraining the deeply-rooted social masculinity traits and start accepting as normal, natural, necessary and nice (Piazza et al, 2015) vegetarian or vegan food. An Indiana Earlham College study in USA found that men abstaining from meat because of personal choice, physical, health problems or love for animals are alleged to be less masculine (Thomas, 2015). However, research by the University of Harvard shows men who consume higher quantities of processed meat to be 30% less manly based on sperm count (Mendes, 2017). Furthermore, research shows that vegan men have higher levels of testosterone (Allan et al., 2000), a less intense and more pleasant and attractive scent compared to meat consumers' hedonistic body odour (Havlicek & Lenochova, 2006) and less erectile dysfunctions (Greger, 2013). It is likely that in the future these positive scientific findings about the benefits of excluding meat from the male diet may start having a stronger impact on those concerned about their health and sexual attractiveness.

IS MASCULINITY UNDER THREAT?

The societal pressure on men to be always masculine with optimal physical and well-defined muscular body image pitched to them and intensified by popular culture, other men, women, the media, advertising, marketing, magazines and social interaction with others (Parasecoli, 2006; Crawshaw, 2007) is massive. Faced with this, men unconsciously and habitually continue to consume animal-based nutrients and meat proteins in their strive for strength and muscle building to prove and improve their masculinity. The hegemonic notion of masculinity and the muscular body ideal is claimed by fitness and men's health magazines as something that is mass-attainable and instrumental to achieving good health (Parasecoli, 2006). It is an imperative physical manifestation of men-gendered specific masculine traits and performances (Bennett & Gough, 2012; Gill, 2005; Nash & Phillipov, 2014; Gattario et al., 2015).

In the pursuit of being perceived as macho, men naturally distance themselves from practices considered feminine (Gough & Conner, 2006; Nash & Phillipov, 2014), such as being on a diet, skipping meals, avoiding social spaces where food is consumed (Gough, 2007; Contois, 2013) or eating vegetables (Adams & Calarco, 2016). The male aversion to ordering anything different than meat off a menu is a result of social policing fear of being ridiculed and seen weak by other men because of considering vegetables deemed as not as manly and acceptable choice as eating a steak for instance (Nash & Phillipov, 2014; Oliffe et al., 2015). These old-fashioned norms about masculinity however could be changed as the Sydney men's study reveals – the male participants are open to embrace new consumption behaviour, including when challenged in relation to concerns about health, animal welfare and the environment. Also, there are numerous examples of leading world athletes, including bodybuilders, who exhibit muscles, strength, agility, speed and tenacity, and are vegetarian or vegan – Carl Lewis, Mac Danzic, Mike Tyson, to mention a few names (The Richest, 2017).

The old-fashioned, stereotypical views of masculinity clash with the modern-day manifestation of manliness. In addition to social perceptions (as was the case with high-heel shoes and wigs) and physical power (as was the case with chasing wild animals), environmental, health and compassion considerations coupled with technological and scientific advances are shaping masculinity in new directions as indicated in the Sydney men's survey. Men are searching for their new role in modern society (McAllister, 2009). Characteristics, such as gentle nature, not being bound by manliness, lack of aggression in romance, seeing women as equal and avoiding causing pain (Morioka, 2013), are defining a new category of men in Japan (referred to as the "herbivore men"). Contemporary men are evolving by transforming their attitude and perceptions with more respect not only toward the other gender, but also to other sentient beings and the surrounding environment.

The introduction of plant-based options offered as a healthy fashionable trend and more amenable to men can respond to the sustainability priorities and the shift towards new social and environment values within society. Men were introduced to stylish grooming products, including perfumes, moisturisers, hair colouring, beard caring products, oils, moustache waxes, intimate hair removal, depilation tools and anti-aging creams (Fury, 2016), there is surely the possibility to create the seeds of a mass acceptance of plant-based foods as being good for human health and the environment revolutionising the new masculinity perception.

CONCLUSION

With the Sydney survey we tried to answer the question as to what is more important for the contemporary Australian men – the existing perceptions of masculinity as they relate to the consumption of meat or personal health and environmental wellbeing. Although the majority of men still support the prevailing opinion about the place and role of meat in their diets, there are categorical new signs which indicate that a shift towards healthier and more sustainable food choices is possible.

Rather than juxtaposing these two concepts, it is time to bring them together in a new way which redefines masculinity in response to the current sustainability, climate change and health priorities. Social marketing, education, mass media – there are many channels that can be used to facilitate this process of transformation. It will free up men to demonstrate their true masculinity in making the best food choices for all.

ACKNOWLEDGMENT

The authors acknowledge the contribution of an Australian Government Research Training Program Scholarship in supporting this research.

REFERENCES

Adams, C. J., & Calarco, M. (2016). Derrida and the sexual politics of meat. In A. Potts (Ed.), *Meat culture* (pp. 31–53). Leiden, UK: Brill. doi:10.1163/9789004325852_003

Allan, N. E., Appleby, P. N., Davey, G. K., & Key, T. J. (2000). Hormones and diet: Low insulin-like growth factor-I but normal bioavailable androgens in vegan man. *British Journal of Cancer*, *83*(1), 95–97. PMID:10883675

Audsley, E., Brander, M., Chatterton, J., Murphy-Bokern, D., Webster, C., & Williams, A. (2009). How low can we go? An assessment of greenhouse gas emissions from the UK food system and the scope to reduce them by 2050. *WWF-UK*. Retrieved from https://dspace.lib.cranfield.ac.uk/handle/1826/6503

Austin, D. W. (2008). Hyper-Masculinity and Disaster: Gender Role Construction in the Wake of Hurricane Katrina. *Allacademic*. Retrieved from http://www.allacademic.com/meta/p241530_index.html

Australian Institute of Health and Welfare (AIHW). (2017). *Cancer in Australia 2017*. Canberra, Australia: AIHW. Retrieved from http://www.aihw.gov.au/WorkArea/DownloadAsset.aspx?id=60129559144

Bailey, R., Froggatt, A., & Wellesley, L. (2014). *Livestock – Climate Change's Forgotten Sector: Global Public Opinion on Meat and Dairy Consumption*. Chatham House, Energy, Environment and Resources. Retrieved from https://www.chathamhouse.org/sites/files/chathamhouse/field/field_document/20141203LivestockClimateChangeForgottenSectorBaileyFroggattWellesleyFinal.pdf

Bennett, E., & Gough, B. (2012). In pursuit of leanness: The management of appearance, affect and masculinities within a men's weight loss forum. *Health, 17*(3), 284–299. doi:10.1177/1363459312454149 PMID:22815334

Bogueva, D., Marinova, D., & Raphaely, T. (2017). Reducing meat consumption: The case for social marketing. *Asia Pacific Journal of Marketing and Logistics, 29*(3), 477–500. doi:10.1108/APJML-08-2016-0139

Bogueva, D., & Phau, I. (2016). Meat myths and marketing. In T. Raphaely & D. Marinova (Eds.), *Impact of meat consumption on health and environmental sustainability* (pp. 264–276). Hershey, PA: IGI Global. doi:10.4018/978-1-4666-9553-5.ch015

Bosland, M. C., Oakley-Girvan, L., & Whittemore, A. S. (1999). Dietary fat, calories and prostate cancer risk. *Journal of the National Cancer Institute, 91*(6), 489–491. doi:10.1093/jnci/91.6.489 PMID:10088612

Connelly, T. (2016, July 22). New man about town – "Traditional masculinity is dead", says new research. *The Drum*. Retrieved from http://www.thedrum.com/news/2016/07/22/new-man-about-town-traditional-masculinity-dead-says-new-research

Conrad, K., Flay, B., & Hill, D. (1992). Why children start smoking cigarettes: Predictors of onset. *British Journal of Addiction, 87*(12), 1711–1724. doi:10.1111/j.1360-0443.1992.tb02684.x PMID:1490085

Contois, E. J. H. (2013). *Gender and dieting. Encyclopedia of Food and Agricultural Ethics*. Springer. doi:Retrieved from https://link.springer.com/referenceworkentry/10.1007/978-94-007-6167-4_472-1#page-1 doi:10.1007/97894-007-6167-4_472-1

Crawshaw, P. (2007). Governing the healthy male citizen: Men, masculinity, and popular health in Men's Health magazine. *Social Science & Medicine, 65*(8), 1606–1618. doi:10.1016/j.socscimed.2007.05.026 PMID:17628269

Dauchet, L., Amouyel, P., & Dallongeville, J. (2005). Fruit and vegetable consumption and risk of stroke: A meta-analysis of cohort studies. *Neurology, 65*(8), 1193–1197. doi:10.1212/01.wnl.0000180600.09719.53 PMID:16247045

Dauchet, L., Amouyel, P., & Dallongeville, J. (2009). Fruits, vegetables and coronary heart disease. *Nature Reviews. Cardiology, 6*(9), 599–608. doi:10.1038/nrcardio.2009.131 PMID:19652655

Dauchet, L., Amouyel, P., Hercberg, S., & Dallongeville, J. (2006). Fruit and vegetable consumption and risk of coronary heart disease: A meta-analysis of cohort studies. *The Journal of Nutrition, 136*, 2588–2593. PMID:16988131

De Boer, J. (2006). Socio-cultural potential. In H. Aiking, J. de Boer, & J. Vereijken (Eds.), *Sustainable protein production and consumption: Pigs or peas?* (pp. 103–110). Dordrecht, the Netherlands: Springer.

Devaney, E. (2005). A plan for men's health. *Mid Western Health Board*. Retrieved from http://www.lenus.ie/hse/handle/10147/45737

Douglas, M., & Gross, J. (1981). Food and culture: Measuring the intricacy of rule system. *Social Sciences Information. Information Sur les Sciences Sociales, 20*(1), 1–35. doi:10.1177/053901848102000101

English, O. L. D. (2017). *Dictionary*. Oxford University Press. Retrieved from https://en.oxforddictionaries.com

Feskens, E. J. M., Sluik, D., & van Woudenbergh, G. J. (2013). Meat consumption, diabetes, and its complications. *Current Diabetes Reports*, *13*(2), 298–306. doi:10.1007/s11892-013-0365-0 PMID:23354681

Fiddes, N. (1991). *Meat: A natural symbol*. London, UK: Routledge.

Fiddes, N. (1994). Social aspects of eating meat. *The Proceedings of the Nutrition Society*, *53*(02), 272–280. doi:10.1079/PNS19940032 PMID:7972141

Fury, A. (2016, January 14). Men's grooming is now a multi-billion pound worldwide industry. *The Independent*. Retrieved from http://www.independent.co.uk/life-style/fashion/features/mens-grooming-is-now-a-multi-billion-pound-worldwide-industry-a6813196.html

Garnett, T. (2014). Changing what we eat: A call for research and action on widespread adoption of sustainable healthy eating. *Food Climate Research Network*. Retrieved from http://www.fcrn.org.uk/sites/default/files/fcrn_wellcome_gfs_changing_consumption_report_final.pdf

Gattario, K. H., Frisén, A., Fuller-Tyszkiewicz, M., Ricciardelli, L. A., Diedrichs, P. C., Yager, Z., & Smolak, L. (2015). How is men's conformity to masculine norms related to their body image? Masculinity and muscularity across Western countries. *Psychology of Men & Masculinity*, *16*(3), 337–347. doi:10.1037/a0038494

Giles, G., & Ireland, P. (1997). Diet, nutrition and prostate cancer. *International Journal of Cancer. Supplement*, *10*(S10), 13–17. doi:10.1002/(SICI)1097-0215(1997)10+<13::AID-IJC5>3.0.CO;2-C PMID:9209014

Gill, R., Henwood, K., & McLean, C. (2005). Body projects and the regulation of normative masculinity. *Body & Society*, *11*(1), 37–62. doi:10.1177/1357034X05049849

Goodland, R., & Anhang, J. (2009). Livestock and climate change: What if the key actors in climate change are … cows, pigs, and chickens? *World Watch*, November/December. Retrieved from http://www.worldwatch.org/files/pdf/Livestock%20and%20Climate%20Change.pdf

Gough, B. (2007). "Real men don't diet": An analysis of contemporary newspaper representations of men, food and health. *Social Science & Medicine*, *64*(2), 326–337. doi:10.1016/j.socscimed.2006.09.011 PMID:17070972

Gough, B., & Conner, M. T. (2006). Barriers to healthy eating among men: A qualitative analysis. *Social Science & Medicine*, *62*(2), 387–395. doi:10.1016/j.socscimed.2005.05.032 PMID:16011867

Greger, M. (2010). Eliminating the #1 cause of death. *NutritionFacts.org*. Retrieved from https://nutritionfacts.org/video/eliminating-the-1-cause-of-death/

Greger, M. (2013). Survival of the firmest: Erectile dysfunction and death. *NutritionFacts.org*. Retrieved from https://nutritionfacts.org/video/survival-of-the-firmest-erectile-dysfunction-and-death/

Havlicek, J., & Lenochova, P. (2006). The effect of meat consumption on body odour attractiveness. *Chemical Senses*, *31*(8), 747–752. doi:10.1093/chemse/bjl017 PMID:16891352

Hearn, J., Blagojević, M., & Harrison, K. (Eds.). (2013). *Rethinking transnational men: Beyond, between and within nations*. London: Taylor & Francis.

Hedenus, F., Wirsenius, S., & Johansson, D. J. A. (2014). The importance of reduced meat and dairy consumption for meeting stringent climate change targets. *Climatic Change*, *124*(1-2), 79–91. doi:10.1007/s10584-014-1104-5

Iwamoto, D. K., & Smiler, A. P. (2013). Alcohol makes you macho and helps you make friends: The role of masculine norms and peer pressure in adolescent boys' and girls' alcohol use. *Substance Use & Misuse*, *48*(5), 371–378. doi:10.3109/10826084.2013.765479 PMID:23421386

Jaslow, R. (2012, August 22). Survey: "Digital peer pressure" fuelling drug, alcohol use in high school students. *SBS News*. Retrieved from http://www.cbsnews.com/news/survey-digital-peer-pressure-fueling-drug-alcohol-use-in-high-school-students/

Kahn, J. S. (2011). Feminist therapy for men: Challenging assumptions and moving forward. *Women & Therapy*, *34*(1-2), 59–76. doi:10.1080/02703149.2011.532458

Karvelas, P. (2012, December 26). Peer pressure key to drug use. *The Australian*. Retrieved from http://www.theaustralian.com.au/news/health-science/peer-pressure-key-to-drug-use/news-story/8bf6a201c01e365c31c5b8dc8ea0c8a7

King, L. (2009, December 30). *Peer pressure is what made me use drugs and alcohol*. Drugfree.org. Retrieved from https://drugfree.org/parent-blog/peer-pressure-is-what-made-me-use-drugs-and-alcohol/

Kubberød, E., Ueland, O., Rodbotten, M., Westad, F., & Risvik, E. (2002). Gender specific preferences and attitudes towards meat. *Food Quality and Preference*, *13*(5), 285–294. doi:10.1016/S0950-3293(02)00041-1

Li, M., Fan, Y., Zhang, X., Hou, W., & Tang, Z. (2014). Fruit and vegetable intake and risk of type 2 diabetes mellitus: Meta-analysis of prospective cohort studies. *BMJ Open*, *4*(11), e005497. doi:10.1136/bmjopen-2014-005497 PMID:25377009

Lupton, D. (1996). *Food, the body and the self*. London, UK: Sage.

Mahalik, J. R., Locke, B. D., Ludlow, L. H., Diemer, M. A., Scott, R. P. J., Gottfried, M., & Freitas, G. (2003). Development of the conformity to masculine norms inventory. *Journal of Men and Masculinity*, *4*(1), 3–25. doi:10.1037/1524-9220.4.1.3

McAllister, P. (2009). *Manthropology: The science of the inadequate modern male*. Sydney, Australia: Hachette Australia.

McMichael, A., & Bambrick, H. (2005). Meat consumption trends and health: Casting a wider risk assessment net. *Public Health Nutrition*, *8*(04), 348–356. doi:10.1079/PHN2005742 PMID:15975177

Mendes, J. (2017, June 23). *Eating bacon shown to reduce sperm in man*. Virility protocol. Retrieved from http://virilityprotocol.com/bacon-shown-reduce-sperm-men/

Micha, R., Wallace, S. K., & Mozaffarian, D. (2010). Red and processed meat consumption and risk of incident coronary heart disease, stroke, and diabetes mellitus: A systematic review and meta-analysis. *Circulation, 121*(21), 2271–2283. doi:10.1161/CIRCULATIONAHA.109.924977 PMID:20479151

Morioka, M. (2013). A phenomenological study of "Herbivore Men". *The Review of Life Studies, 4*, 1–20.

Murcott, A. (1982). The cultural significance of food and eating. *The Proceedings of the Nutrition Society, 41*(2), 203–210. doi:10.1079/PNS19820031 PMID:7111265

Nash, M., & Phillipov, M. (2014). Introduction to the special issue. Eating like a "man": Food and the performance and regulation of masculinities. *Women's Studies International Forum, 44*, 205–208. doi:10.1016/j.wsif.2014.03.007

National Health and Medical Research Council (NHMRC). (2013). Australian Dietary Guidelines. Canberra, Australia: NHMRC. Retrieved from https://www.eatforhealth.gov.au/sites/default/files/files/the_guidelines/n55_australian _dietary_guidelines.pdf

Oliffe, J. L., Bottorff, J. L., Sharp, P., Caperchione, C. M., Johnson, S. T., Healy, T., & Errey, S. et al. (2015). Healthy eating and active living: Rural-based working men's perspectives. *American Journal of Men's Health*. doi:10.1177/1557988315619372 PMID:26669775

Palmqvist, R., & Santavirta, N. (2006). What friends are for: The relationship between body image, substance use, and peer influence among Finnish adolescents. *Journal of Youth and Adolescence, 35*(2), 203–217. doi:10.1007/s10964-005-9017-2

Pan, A., Sun, Q., Bernstein, A. M., Schulze, M. B., Manson, J. E., Stampfer, M. J., & Hu, F. B. et al. (2012). Red meat consumption and mortality: Results from 2 prospective cohort studies. *Archives of Internal Medicine, 172*(7), 555–563. doi:10.1001/archinternmed.2011.2287 PMID:22412075

Parasecoli, F. (2006). Feeding hard bodies: Food and masculinities in men's fitness magazines. *Food & Foodways, 13*(1-2), 17–37. doi:10.1080/07409710590915355

Pease, B. (2010). *Undoing privilege: Unearned advantage in a divided world*. London, UK: Zed Books.

Piazza, J., Ruby, M. B., Loughnan, S., Luong, M., Kulik, J., Watkins, H. N., & Siegerman, M. (2015). Rationalising meat consumption: The 4Ns. *Appetite, 91*, 114–128. doi:10.1016/j.appet.2015.04.011 PMID:25865663

Pimentel, D., & Pimentel, M. (2003). Sustainability of meat-based and plant-based diets and the environment. *The American Journal of Clinical Nutrition, 78*, s660–s663. PMID:12936963

Pollard, C. M., Daly, A., Moore, M., & Binns, C. W. (2013). Public say food regulatory policies to improve health in Western Australia are important: Population survey results. *Australian and New Zealand Journal of Public Health, 37*(5), 475–482. doi:10.1111/1753-6405.12128 PMID:24090332

Raphaely, T., & Marinova, D. (Eds.). (2016). *Impact of meat consumption on health and environmental sustainability*. Hershey, PA: IGI Global. doi:10.4018/978-1-4666-9553-5

Reeser, T. W. (2010). *Masculinities in theory: An introduction*. Chichester, UK: Wiley- Blackwell. doi:10.1002/9781444317312

Roberts, P. (2008). *The end of food*. New York, NY: Houghton Mifflin Harcourt.

Rothgerber, H. (2012). Real men don't eat (vegetable) quiche: Masculinity and the justification of meat consumption. *Psychology of Men & Masculinity*, *14*(4), 363–375. doi:10.1037/a0030379

Rozin, P., Hormes, J. M., Faith, M. S., & Wansink, B. (2012). Is meat male? A quantitative, multi-method framework to establish metaphoric relationships. *The Journal of Consumer Research*, *39*(3), 629–643. doi:10.1086/664970

Ruby, M. B., & Heine, S. J. (2011). Meat, morals and masculinity. *Appetite*, *56*(2), 447–450. doi:10.1016/j.appet.2011.01.018 PMID:21256169

Sagoe, D. (2014). *Anabolic steroid use is not just about bodybuilding*. The Conversation. *Health & Medicine*, *15*(July). Retrieved from http://theconversation.com/anabolic-steroid-use-is-not-just-about-bodybuilding-29180

Schiebinger, L. (1993). *Nature's body: Gender in the making of modern science*. Boston, MA: Beacon Press.

Sobal, J. (2005). Men, meat, and marriage: Models of masculinity. *Food & Foodways*, *13*(1-2), 135–158. doi:10.1080/07409710590915409

Springmann, M., Godfray, H. C. J., Rayner, M., & Scarborough, P. (2016). Analysis and valuation of the health and climate change cobenefits of dietary change. In *Proceedings of the National Academy of Sciences of the United States of America*, *113*(15), 4146–4151. doi:10.1073/pnas.1523119113 PMID:27001851

Stehfest, E., Bouwman, L., van Vuuren, D. P., den Elzen, M. G. J., Eickhout, B., & Kabat, P. (2009). Climate benefits of changing diet. *Climatic Change*, *95*(1–2), 83–102. doi:10.1007/s10584-008-9534-6

Stibbe, A. (2004). Health and the social construction of masculinity in "Men's health" magazine. *Men and Masculinities*, *7*(1), 31–51. doi:10.1177/1097184X03257441

The Richest. (2017). *Top 10 vegetarian or vegan athletes*. Retrieved from http://www.therichest.com/sports/other-sports/top-10-vegetarian-or-vegan-athletes/

Thomas, M. (2015). Are vegans the same as vegetarians? The effect of diet on perceptions of masculinity. *Appetite*, *97*, 79–86. doi:10.1016/j.appet.2015.11.021 PMID:26593101

Turner, L., Mermelstein, R., & Flay, B. (2004). Individual and contextual influences on adolescent smoking. *Annals of the New York Academy of Sciences*, *1021*(1), 175–197. doi:10.1196/annals.1308.023 PMID:15251888

United Nations (UN). (2015). Transforming our world: The 2030 Agenda for Sustainable Development. Retrieved from https://sustainabledevelopment.un.org/post2015/transformingourworld

van den Wijngaard, M. (1997). *Reinventing the sexes: the biomedical construction of femininity and masculinity (Race, gender, and science)*. Bloomington, IN: Indiana University Press.

van Dooren, C., & Kramer, G. (2012). Food patterns and dietary recommendations in Spain, France and Sweden: Healthy people, healthy planet. *LiveWell for life*. Retrieved from http://www.livewellforlife.eu/wp-content/uploads/2012/05/LiveWell_A4-Food-Patterns-Report_web.pdf van Hoven, B., & Hopkins, P. (2009). Masculinities. In R. Kitchin & N. Thrift (Eds.), *International Encyclopedia of Human Geography* (pp. 492–496). Oxford, UK: Elsevier. doi:10.1016/B978-008044910-4.00970-6

Walsh, R., & Tzelepis, F. (2007). Adolescents and tobacco use: Systematic review of qualitative research methodologies and partial synthesis of findings. *Substance Use & Misuse*, *42*(8), 1269–1321. doi:10.1080/10826080701204904 PMID:17674235

White, S., & Cordell, D. (2015). Global phosphorus security – diet, sustainability and food for thought. In K. Soeters (Ed.), *Meat the future: How cutting meat consumption can feed billions more* (pp. 75–86). Amsterdam, the Netherlands: Nicholaas G Pierson Foundation.

Willard, B. E. (2006). The American story of meat. *Journal of Popular Culture*, *6*, 105–118.

Withey, A. (2015, December 23). Beards, masculinity and history. Dr Alan Withey blog. Retrieved from https://dralun.wordpress.com/2015/12/23/beards-masculinity-and-history/

World Cancer Research Fund and American Institute for Cancer Research (WCRF/AICR). (2007). Food, nutrition, physical activity, and the prevention of cancer: A global perspective. Retrieved from http://www.aicr.org/assets/docs/pdf/reports/Second_Expert_Report.pdf

World Health Organization (WHO). (2015). Q&A on the carcinogenicity of the consumption of red meat and processed meat. Retrieved from http://www.who.int/features/qa/cancer-red-meat/en/

York, R., & Gossard, M. (2004). Cross-national meat and fish consumption: Exploring the effects of modernization and ecological context. *Ecological Economics*, *48*(3), 293–302. doi:10.1016/j.ecolecon.2003.10.009

Zevallos, Z. (2014, November 28). *Sociology of gender*. The Other Sociologist. Retrieved from https://othersociologist.com/sociology-of-gender/

KEY TERMS AND DEFINITIONS

Animal Welfare: Consideration about the conditions in which animals live.

Health Consciousness: Behaviour and attitude which considers health considerations in a person's diet or lifestyle.

Macho: A man who is explicitly proud of his masculinity.

Manliness: A set of traits, abilities, attributes and qualities which characterise the male human species.

Masculinity: Manifestation of manliness.

Vegan: Related to a person, diet and lifestyle that voluntary excludes animal-based products.

Vegetarian: Related to a person or diet that voluntary excludes meat and meat-based products.

Chapter 11
The Baul Tradition in Bangladesh:
Sustainability Activism for a Meatless Dietary Culture

Amzad Hossain
Rajshahi University, Bangladesh

Sayedul Islam Montu
Curtin University, Australia

Md Abul Azad
Curtin University, Australia

ABSTRACT

Humans' foremost desire is to achieve longevity through a healthy body and mind. The Baul philosophers of Bangladesh fulfil this sustainability desire through meatless diets and esoteric physio-spiritual practices. Their mission in life is to pursue voluntary community activism and social sustainability marketing by promoting the sermon of simplicity and that eating meat destroys longevity, personal and environmental health. This chapter analyses the role the Bauls play in guiding the Bangladesh population and counteracting western influences. It uses quotes from the oral wisdom of the Baul songs and orations included by UNESCO as part of the global intangible heritage of humanity.

INTRODUCTION

At 3.3 kg per person per year (0.9 kg beef, 1.2 kg sheep and 1.3 kg poultry), Bangladesh has the second lowest per capita meat consumption in the world (OECD, 2017). With 1.1 percent of its adult population being obese, Bangladesh is also the second (after Ethiopia) least obese country on the globe (The GBD 2015 Obesity Collaborators, 2017). This is compared to 33 percent obese adult population in USA where the annual per capita meat consumption is 97.1 kg, 26.8 percent obesity and 94.8 annual per capita meat

DOI: 10.4018/978-1-5225-4757-0.ch011

consumption in Australia, and 1.9 percent obesity and 3.1 kg annual per capita meat consumption in neighbouring India (OECD, 2017; The GBD 2015 Obesity Collaborators, 2017).

With the improvement in living standards, however, meat is increasingly seen as a desirable food choice in Bangladesh, particularly for the wealthier urban dwellers. Not surprisingly, there is also mounting evidence that in Bangladesh obesity "is alarmingly high and on rise amongst certain groups, particularly amongst urban children from affluent households" (Rahman et al., 2014, n.p.). The nutritional changes also explain, at least partially, the recent increases of overweight and obese adult population in Bangladesh associated with higher morbidity and mortality as well as risk of developing non-communicable diseases, such as diabetes and cardiovascular disease (Biswass et al., 2017). Westernisation of both, Bangladeshi culture and diet (Hossain, 2016), plays a major role in fueling these new emerging trends.

Are there any forces which can counteract the course of events in Bangladesh and is this country going to succumb to the global influences of unhealthy diets? Is there any hope to preserve the good aspects of Bangladeshi culture while achieving improvements in the quality of life of its people?

Among other things, Bangladesh is renowned for the unorthodox devotional tradition of its Baul philosophers, recognised by UNESCO (2008) as part of the intangible global cultural heritage. Influenced by Hinduism, Buddhism, Bengali, Vasinavism and Sufi Islam, the Bauls spread their wisdom through songs and public orations attended by numerous followers in rural and urban gatherings as well as through television and more recently, the social media. This chapter explores the role of the traditional community activism of the Bauls for maintaining the low-meat diet of the people in Bangladesh. Some background information about the Bauls is provided first and then their role in community marketing is explained.

INTRODUCING THE BAUL TRADITION OF BANGLADESH

The Bauls (also known as Baul Fakirs) "belong to a devotional tradition influenced by Hinduism, Buddhism, Bengali, Vasinavism and Sufi Islam, but yet distinctly different from them" (UNESCO, 2008, n.p.). There are both male and female Bauls and they do not identify with any specific religion, caste system, temples or sacred places (Tagore, 1970). By nature, the Bauls are singing mendicants, mystics, saintly and poetic thinkers. They are mostly unlettered, yet full of poetic, musical and philosophical talents. The Bauls are seen as being at the root of Bengali culture with influence over large sections of the Bangladesh population (UNESCO, 2008). As a tradition in the Bengali cultural context, the Bauls are unique in volunteering for socio-religious syncretisation in the culturally pluralistic country.

The significance of the Bauls and their role have been acknowledged by many, including Dimock (1966), Bhattacarya (1971), Haq (1975), Dasgupta (1976), Rajneesh (1977), Uddin (1978), Mitra (1979), Karim (1980), McDaniel (1989), to name a few. In 2003, UNESCO (2008) proclaimed the Bauls as representatives of the global intangible cultural heritage of humanity for their life philosophy and contribution to sustainability. The Bauls manifest their excellent aptitudes and charisma for guiding people towards individual, social, cultural, economic and ecological sustainability by using discourses, mostly in terms of spontaneous songs, which reveal traditional beliefs and practices, spiritual experience, cultural and geo-environmental conditions. They are truly soul-stirring and take the listeners closest to nature and the divine.

The Bauls prefer to live in poverty-like conditions. They deliberately possess nothing beyond the bare necessities because of socio-religious and spiritual mysticism grounds. Glimpses of Baul literature or Baul mysticism reveal a mystical undercurrent in Bengali religiosity (Hossain, 1995).

Being the spokespersons and reflectors of the Bengali folk philosophy, the Bauls show how the unlettered and economically poor folks of Bangladesh can maintain their physical health by adhering to esoteric physio-spiritual philosophy and practices, which they call 'Deha Sadhana' or body contemplation (Dasgupta, 1976). The Deha Sadhana of the Baul Fakirs suggests that the Bengalis are keen to keep themselves in sound health, full of energy and vigour to extend their spiritual attachment to and adoration of God in their own body and heart. Furthermore, the Baul gurus observe body-energy conservation practices through contemplation and mysticism (McDaniel, 1989).

The Bauls are socially recognised as the mystic volunteers who live pro-environmental lives. Most Bauls do not consume animal products and observe asceticism. They are well respected by people, though jealously disrespected by some of the religious leaders and the elite because of their social activism against unsustainability, which is often labelled as heretic. Yet, due to the present ecological degradation and high illiteracy rates in Bangladesh, NGOs and government agencies value the Bauls as the best of all social and environmental facilitators, educators and animators. For example, the media of Bangladesh frequently invite Bauls from different parts of the country to present in radio and television programs dedicated to environmental ethics, agriculture, fishing, food habits, population control, morality, schooling, general education and ecological literacy.

Mujtaba and Musavi (2000, p. 47) explain that all naturalists acquire wisdom for modest living from the manifestations of how every other species adapts to the natural conditions of life. The Bauls respect nature and live as naturalists to account for the planet's limits. Guided by the Bauls and traditional sustainability accounting, the people of rural Bangladesh look not only for what harvest the current season will bring but also how to sustain the productivity of the land for future yields. It is in this context that in recent years villagers have changed their practices away from the discredited methods of the Green Revolution that leads to planetary death (Shiva 2005). Small-scale and organic farming which supports biodiversity and does not exploit nature's fertility beyond restoration are now preferred and practiced.

The Bauls are also increasingly focusing on supporting a meatless dietary culture, firmly stressing that meat eating is the root of all livability evils on earth (Hossain, 2016). To them, the degrading sustainability of the planet is primarily linked to humans' indiscriminate consumption of meat. Baul guru Aziz Shah Fakir[1] sees voluntary hunger or fasting combined with a plant-based diet as the panacea for healthy lives and longevity. Harun Baul[2] sings: "Eating meat destroys longevity, social values die, and punishment awaits hereafter"[3]. He describes his activism to establish a meatless dietary culture as for the sake of both, human and planetary health. All Bauls stress that the meatless dietary culture is a vital life-support element for holistic sustainability.

THE BAULS' INFLUENCE IN BANGLADESH

Hundreds of disciples of the Bauls all over Bangladesh visit the gurus regularly to receive their reflective teachings on doing good deeds for spiritual contentment, maintaining healthy dietary practice to live longer, be kind to all living beings in nature and live a simple life with minimal possessions with a small ecological footprint. The Bauls' discourses emphasise a modest simple lifestyle with voluntary hunger and food abstinence as a way to achieve healthy lives, longevity and happiness. Their personal lifestyle, teachings and age-long traditions reject Western type consumerism and encourage voluntary simplicity.

According to Elgin (2010), purposeful simplicity is a means for spiritual satisfaction and liberation. It "fosters a sense of personal empowerment, creative engagement, and opportunity" (Elgin, 2010, p. 19). This also resonates with Princen's (2005) logic of sufficiency in relation to material possessions whilst enriching the non-material dimensions of life. Voluntary simplicity and sufficiency refer to finding the levels of consumption and possession that are truly satisfactory and provide the optimal management of resources, including food, from a sustainability point of view. Simplicity in what we eat and avoiding meat consumption are echoed as a matter of ethics by Singer and Mason (2006).

The Baul activism promotes this view effectively because their discourse is inherently dynamic and charismatic. It is comprised of spontaneous revelations in the form of new songs, wisdom and folkloric aspects, including stories, fables, proverbs, traditional beliefs and practices, myths, tales and legends (JBPV's Blog, 2009). The Baul discourse also uses Khonar Bachan, i.e. the verses of Khona (Jalil, 1993) – a mythical woman. Her verses are the most basic guidelines for traditional agriculture, social life, cooking, food habits and seasonal climatic conditions. The Bauls largely use the guidance of the Khona to tell people about things in everyday life, including fears, hopes, dreams and rules.

Hence, the Bauls' discourse is a body of blended experience, wisdom and belief creating the lore that is integrally linked to the folk people's lives (Hossain & Marinova, 2006) with which they can associate. The Bauls' charismatic art of delivery makes it easy for people to memorise and apply their teachings in daily life. Pastoral people are informed about seasonality of sustainable agricultural production, harvest management and guided in dietary consumption. The Baul view of meatless dietary patterns as the basis for longer life-span is confirmed in numerous scientific studies across Europe and North America (e.g. Singh et al., 2003). A transition to plant-based diets is described as a nutritional "paradigm shift" (Sabaté, 2003) which improves health and helps fight non-communicable diseases, such as cancer (Samraj et al., 2015). Using folklore as a vehicle of ethnological wisdom in Bangladesh (Islam, 1985), the Bauls explain the meatless dietary culture is an easy one-stop solution that the world needs to maintain public health and for avoiding the existential threats of acute hunger, climate change and environmental deterioration.

The Bauls' community activism is a way of social marketing (Wymer, 2010). It targets individuals and helps safeguard public concerns related to personal health, food availability, global warming and ecological decline against powerful Western interests, upstream causes of commercialism (Wymer, 2011) and negative social structural influences (Goldberg, 1995). The Bauls' communitarian approach based on wisdom, art and charisma, invokes positive responses from the rural people of Bangladesh to reconcile their simple livelihood impacts on the natural environment. All messages are communicated orally because most rural people are formally uneducated. It is a social practice that touches millions of people every day and allows learning from the past and practicing for the present (Khan et al., 2015).

PROMOTING THE FUNCTIONAL PHILOSOPHY OF A FLEXITARIAN DIETARY CULTURE

According to Nuttal (2007), philosophy cannot be understood only as an activity (rather than a subject of learning), neither as a conceptual analysis (thinking about how we think). Philosophy, however, has very distinctive functions within society (Nuttal, 2007) as: metaphysics – the nature of reality, epistemology – how we create knowledge, and moral and political stances – how we conduct ourselves in the world. The strength of the Baul philosophers is in the third aspect of philosophy – the behaviour of the followers, which is the foundation of their community activism. Hence, through folklore and art, the Bauls convey functional philosophic messages, including promoting plant-based diets.

The functional philosophy of a meatless diet can be succinctly summarised as: "Eating meat is eating death, not life" (Webb, 1998, p. 73). Simplicity and sufficiency are at the core of the Bauls' eating philosophy, insights on life and messages to leave a better world for future generations. The Bauls administer vital roles in nurturing a minimal food-print for people in respect to their dietary intake and food harvesting in order to fit within the changing cultural, demographic, socio-economic and ecological dynamics of the country. In essence, they encourage a dietary lifestyle which includes meat only in the absence of other food options and occasionally for particular social and religious ceremonies, such as weddings and animal sacrifice (Hossain, 2016). In fact, the above is one of the possible definitions of flexitarianism – the current dietary style encouraged in the West (Raphaely and Marinova, 2014; Dagevos, 2016), which aims at eliminating meat in favour of plant-based options.

The sustainability-oriented Baul tradition of Bangladesh maintains that eating meat destroys human longevity and if this is disregarded, nature can retaliate. According to the vegan Baul guru Aziz Fakir, ceremonial meat consumption, which is inherently infrequent, is socially needed and ecologically permissible. The main food consumption, however, should be plant-based.

In this day and age, the culture of Bangladesh, similar to many other eastern traditions, is being eroded under the strong influence of western-type high consumption of meat. Globalisation is inflicting powerful and aggressive commercial interests for profit making on other cultures, including manipulating and changing food habits. The powerful West is corrupting the traditional flexitarianism of Bangladesh by imposing foreign values (Brenkert, 2008) which lead to increasing the amount of livestock production and unfairly promoting meat consumption. Livestock marketers see meat as a means of profiteering and promote its consumption as a "healthy" diet and a sign of civilisational advancement. Little attention is given to the social, cultural and environmental costs this involves. The world is yet to accept that without drastically reducing the use of animal products in the human diet, the achievement of the global Sustainable Development Goals (SDGs) will remain a mission impossible.

With their functional philosophy, the Bauls of Bangladesh act as a strong counterforce and community activism aimed at preserving the public goods and benefits. Lalon Fakir's song says:

Do not proceed through conjectural path. It has fatal pitfalls.

Identifying a sustainable path, proceed diligently.

Intention results in right or wrong.

Sail on a boat of commitment, and go ahead to overcome adversities.

Lalon says, you can then accomplish your goal![4]

CONCLUSION

The ever-increasing production and consumption of meat worldwide are challenging humanity's prospects for sustainable development and combatting climate change (Raphaely & Maronova, 2016). Livestock puts a large burden on the planet's resources by consuming 27 percent of the global water, 70 percent of all agricultural land, 30 percent of the land surface of the planet, and is also an inefficient way to produce food – an average of 25 kcal of fossil energy is required to produce 1 kcal of animal protein (Hoekstra, 2013). The SDGs aimed at dealing with poverty, hunger, health, water, energy, life and resources on land, ecosystems, climate change etc. are all compromised by the expanding human obsession with animal-based food.

Besides, countries such as Bangladesh, in recent years, have introduced western types of food outlets based on meat and other processed items through global brands like McDonalds, KFC and Subway. The impacts of the gradual westernisation of the Bangladesh diet are starting to appear with increasing levels of obesity and non-communicable diseases. Most importantly, the ecology of the country (and for that matter, also the globe) cannot support its population on a meat-based diet.

"Eat to live, but not live to eat" is the philosophical baseline for promoting the traditional meatless dietary culture in Bangladesh. Through their tireless activism and devotion to doing good, the Baul philosophers play a vital role in community marketing. They have millions of followers who are influenced by their wisdom and charisma. This is a strong example of social marketing based on higher moral grounds and activism against the global push for increased meat consumption in Bangladesh. A song of Baul Bijoy Sarkar calls for a religious sermon and behaviour: "We are obliged to leave this beautiful Earth, keeping the Earth unharmed". The Baul sustainability activism brings rays of hope for positive results for those who live now and those who will be born tomorrow.

ACKNOWLEDGMENT

The second and third author acknowledge the contribution of an Australian Government Research Training Program Scholarship in supporting this research.

REFERENCES

Bhattacarya, U. (1971). *Banglar Baul o Baul gaan*. Kolkata, India: Oriental Book Company.

Biswas, T., Garnett, S. P., Pervin, S., & Rawal, L. B. (2017). The prevalence of underweight, overweight and obesity in Bangladeshi adults: Data from a national survey. *PLoS One*, *12*(5), e0177395. doi:10.1371/journal.pone.0177395 PMID:28510585

Brenkert, G. G. (2008). *Marketing ethics*. Oxford, UK: Blackwell Publishing.

Dagevos, H. (2016). Exploring flexitarianism: Meat reduction in a meat-centred food culture. In T. Raphaely & D. Marinova (Eds.), *Impacts of meat consumption on health and environmental sustainability* (pp. 233–243). Hershey, PA: IGI Global. doi:10.4018/978-1-4666-9553-5.ch012

Dasgupta, S. (1976). *Obscure religious cults*. Kolkata, India: Firma KLM.

Dimock, E. C. Jr. (1966). *The place of the hidden moon*. Chicago, IL: The University of Chicago.

Elgin, D. (2010). Voluntary simplicity: Toward a way of life that is outwardly simple, inwardly rich (2nd rev. ed.). New York, NY: Harper.

Goldberg, M. E. (1995). Social marketing: Are we fiddling while Rome burns? *Journal of Consumer Psychology*, *4*(4), 347–370. doi:10.1207/s15327663jcp0404_03

Haq, M. E. (1975). *A history of Sufi-ism in Bengal*. Dhaka, Bangladesh: Asiatic Book Society of Bangladesh.

Hoekstra, A. Y. (2013). *The water footprint of modern consumer society*. London, UK: Earthscan from Routledge.

Hossain, A. (1995). *Mazar culture in Bangladesh* [PhD thesis]. Perth, Australia: Murdoch University.

Hossain, A. (2016). Sustainable food consumption: A mission almost impossible because of the West. In T. Raphaely & D. Marinova (Eds.), *Impact of meat consumption on health and environmental sustainability* (pp. 255–263). Hershey, PA: IGI Global. doi:10.4018/978-1-4666-9553-5.ch014

Islam, M. (1985). *Folklore, pulse of the people: in the context of Indic folklore*. New Delhi, India: Naurang Rai Concept Publishing Company.

Jalil, A. (1993). *Diverse aspects of folk literature (in Bangla)*. Dhaka, Bangladesh: Bangla Academy.

JBPV's Blog. (2009). *Folklores – the heart of Bangladeshi culture and heritage (Part One)*. Retrieved from https://jbpv.wordpress.com/2009/10/17/folklores-the-heart-of-bangladeshi-culture-and-heritage/

Karim, A. (1980). *The Bauls of Bangladesh*. Kushtia, Bangladesh: Lalon Academy.

Khan, M., Hossain, A., & Marinova, D. (2015). Traditional sustainability accounting principles in Bangladesh. *World Journal of Social Sciences*, *5*, 201–210.

McDaniel, J. (1989). *The madness of the saints: Ecstatic religion in Bengal*. Chicago, IL: University of Chicago Press.

Mitra, S. K. (Ed.). (1979). *Lalon Fakir: Kabi a kavya*. Kolkata, India: Pustak Bipani.

Mujtaba, S., & Musavi, L. (2000). *God and his attributes: Lessons on Islamic doctrine* (H. Algar, Trans.). Potomac, MD: Islamic Education Centre.

Nuttal, J. (2007). *An introduction to philosophy*. Cambridge, UK: Polity Press.

Organisation for Economic Co-operation and Development (OECD). (2017). *Meat consumption (indicator)*, doi: Retrieved from https://data.oecd.org/agroutput/meat-consumption.htm10.1787/fa290fd0-en

Princen, T. (2005). *The logic of sufficiency*. Cambridge, MA: MIT Press.

Rahman, S., Islam, M. T., & Alam, D. S. (2014). Obesity and overweight in Bangladeshi children and adolescents: A scoping review. *BioMed Central (BMC). Public Health*, *14*, 70. doi:10.1186/1471-2458-14-70 PMID:24450958

Rajneesh, B. (1977). *The beloved: Songs of the Baul mystics* (Vol. 1). Pune, India: Rajneesh Foundation.

Raphaely, T., & Marinova, D. (2014). Flexitarianism: A more moral dietary option. *International Journal of Sustainable Society*, *6*(1/2), 189–211. doi:10.1504/IJSSOC.2014.057846

Raphaely, T., & Marinova, D. (Eds.). (2016). *Impacts of meat consumption on health and environmental sustainability*. Hershey, PA: IGI Global. doi:10.4018/978-1-4666-9553-5

Sabaté, J. (2003). The contribution of vegetarian diets to health and disease: A paradigm shift? *The American Journal of Clinical Nutrition*, *78*(Suppl.), 502S–507S. PMID:12936940

Samraj, A., Pearce, O. M. T., Läubli, H., Crittenden, A. N., Bergfeld, A. K., & Banda, K. … Varki, A. (2015). A red meat-derived glycan promotes inflammation and cancer progression. *Proceedings of the National Academy of Sciences of the United States of America*, 112, 542-547. doi:10.1073/pnas.1417508112

Shiva, V. (2005). *Earth democracy: Justice, sustainability and peace*. Cambridge, UK: South End Press.

Singer, P., & Mason, J. (2006). *The ethics of what we eat: Why our food choices matter*. New York, NY: Rodale.

Singh, P. M., Sabaté, J., & Fraser, G. E. (2003). Does low meat consumption increase life expectancy in humans? *The American Journal of Clinical Nutrition*, *78*(suppl), 526S–532S. PMID:12936945

Tagore, R. (1970). *The religion of man*. London, UK: Allen & Unwin.

The GBD 2015 Obesity Collaborators. (2017). Health effects of overweight and obesity in 195 countries over 25 years. *The New England Journal of Medicine*, 377, 13-27.

Uddin, M. (1978). *Hara moni* (Vol. 7). Dhaka, Bangladesh: Bangla Academy.

United Nations Educational Scientific and Cultural Organization (UNESCO). (2008). *Baul songs*. Retrieved from http://www.unesco.org/culture/ich/RL/00107

Webb, S. H. (1998). *On God and dogs: A Christian theology of compassion for animals*. Oxford, UK: Oxford University Press.

Wymer, W. (2010). Rethinking the boundaries of social marketing: Activism or advertising? *Journal of Business Research*, *63*(2), 99–103. doi:10.1016/j.jbusres.2009.02.003

Wymer, W. (2011). Developing more effective social marketing strategies. *Journal of Social Marketing*, *1*(1), 17–31. doi:10.1108/20426761111104400

KEY TERMS AND DEFINITIONS

Bangla: The language spoken in Bangladesh.

Bauls: Mystic minstrels who live in Bangladesh and West Bengal, India and spread their wisdom through songs and charismatic discourses. They are included in UNESCO's Representative List of the Intangible Cultural Heritage of Humanity.

Flexitarianism: A predominantly plant-based diet which allows sporadic meat consumption when other options are not available and also during religious celebrations.

Functional Philosophy: A branch of philosophy which focusses on the moral and political stances guiding how people conduct themselves in the world.

Naturalist: An adherent to a lifestyle in respect and close to nature.

Sufficiency: Condition, quantity or quality that is adequate for human wellbeing.

Sustainable Development Goals: A global sustainability agenda for 2016–2030 adopted by the United Nations; it includes 17 goals, namely: no poverty; no hunger; good health, quality education; renewable energy; good jobs and economic growth; innovation and infrastructure; reduced inequalities; sustainable cities and communities; life below water; life on land; peace and justice; and partnerships for the goals.

ENDNOTES

1 Aziz Shah Fakir (106 years old) lives in Charaikole village of Kushtia district in Bangladesh.

2 Harun Baul of Choraikole, Kumarkhali, Kushtia – a poet-philosopher-singer, was one of the disciples of Baul guru Aziz Shah Fakir. He never went to school but learnt informally to read and write in simple Bangla. His sustainability views are published by Amzad Hossain under the caption "I'm Harun Baul Speaking" (http://baulism.blogspot.com.au/2012/04/im-harun-baul-speaking-9.html).

3 Khele mansho; ayu hoy dhongsh, somaj hoy nosto ar porokale kosto (in Bangla).

4 Jeo na andaji pathe, o mon rasana.Kupanke kupanche pole, praan bachbe na. Pather parichoy kare,Jao na maner sandeh mere,Laav lokshan buddhir dare Jabe jana.Anurag tarani choroDhar chine ujan dhoroLalon bole karte paro mul sadhana (in Bangla).

Chapter 12
Is Meat a Luxury?

Diana Bogueva
Curtin University, Australia

Dora Marinova
Curtin University, Australia

Ian Phau
Curtin University, Australia

ABSTRACT

Once perceived as a nutritional and occasional bonus, meat has now daily presence in the affluent West, serving human appetite for food. Although meat is not a product typically associated with luxury, its large ecological footprint poses the question whether it is time to challenge consumers' perception about animal-based proteins. The purpose of this chapter is to gain a perspective on how consumers respond to the idea of meat being a luxury product. A 2017 Sydney study investigated the concept of luxury meat and meat consumption amongst three generations – Xers, GenY and GenZ. It shows the emerging meaning of luxury goods related to meat that is sustainable, healthy and socially responsible, in response to climate change and feeding the world's population. The Sydney evidence also suggests meat is no longer essential for human health. A shift towards plant-based and new meat alternatives can create more compassionate and environmentally responsible choices.

The monopolising eater of animal flesh would no longer destroy his constitution by eating an acre at a meal. Percy Shelley, A Vindication of Natural Diet (1813)

INTRODUCTION

The concept of luxury has had various descriptions throughout the years (Hennings et al., 2013a and b). According to the French fashion icon Coco Chanel: "Luxury is a necessity that begins where necessity ends" (in Husic & Cicic, 2009, p. 235). This famous quote refers to a particular life style described by the Oxford Latin Dictionary (1992, p. 30) as "extravagant living, (over)-indulgence". Similarly, luxury

DOI: 10.4018/978-1-5225-4757-0.ch012

is defined as enlightening, providing extra pleasure and flattering simultaneously all senses and is "the appendage of the ruling classes" (Kapferer, 1997, p. 253). Luxury provides numerous forms of physical and psychological values (Wiedman et al., 2007). The Merriam-Webster dictionary (2009, n.p.) explains luxury as "a condition of abundance or great ease and comfort" or "something adding to pleasure or comfort but not absolutely necessary". Phau and Prendergast (2000) suggest that luxury brands evoke exclusivity, high brand awareness and perceived quality, and consequently attract customer loyalty. The qualities of: (1) life style; (2) abundance and access; (3) pleasure; and (4) loyalty, are major characteristics associated with luxury. What this chapter does is look at meat through the lens of luxury.

Meat's four luxury characteristics differ in a historical perspective – they manifest differently in the past, the present and the future. Whilst in the past availability and economic affordability determined meat's luxury status, its environmental and public health impacts combined with ethical considerations are likely to influence its future. A diet with high meat intake has a much bigger environmental footprint – in relation to greenhouse gas emissions and climate change (Hedenus et al., 2014), biodiversity loss, land and water use (Marinova & Raphaely, 2017), peak phosphorus (White & Cordell, 2015), as well as serious negative consequences for public health (Marsh et al., 2016). Nevertheless, the global population continues to expand its per capita meat supply and consumption (Raphaely & Marinova, 2016) augmenting the need to understand the link with luxury.

The consumption of meat also differs across geographies and nations. In the West nowadays meat is a daily nutritional source and not considered a luxury food while in cuisines like Korean, Bangladeshi or Ethiopian, it is more like a seasoning rather than main meal (Kaye, 2014; Smith, 2017). Environmental and animal rights groups (e.g. Animal Liberation Front, 2006) on the other hand argue that meat should be treated as a luxury because of livestock welfare and ecological considerations. A shift to seeing meat as a luxury in the West, can also potentially help preserve and reaffirm the traditional diets in the developing world which are generally healthier and rely more on plant-based products. The aim of this chapter is to unpack the four luxury characteristics of meat in order to encourage a new attitude and behavioural changes towards reduction in the consumption of animal-based products.

MEAT AND LUXURY IN THE PAST

With industrialisation and economic development, meat has obtained an established presence for the mass-market consumers in the affluent Western countries as well as for those with higher incomes in the burgeoning economies of the developing world. This is a very new situation compared to meat's previous status of rarity, exclusiveness and prestige in the past. Meat throughout human history was perceived as uncommon luxury symbolising unrestrained pleasure, power, dominance, virility, status and pure manliness. It was surrounded by many prohibitions, taboos, understanding for dominance and social hierarchy and meat myths (Fessler & Navarrete, 2003; Rozin et al., 2012; Dhont et al., 2014; Bogueva & Phau, 2016).

Life Style

In the olden times of ancient places such as Greece, Rome, Sparta and Egypt, meat – including beef, pork, sausages and poultry, was solely enjoyed by the wealthiest people in society (Fresco, 2016; Toussaint-Samat, 2009; Stambaugh, 1988). The best and most uncommon meat was usually devoured by rich people. In the ancient Roman city meat "was scarce except at sacrifices and the dinner parties of the rich" (Stambaugh, 1988, p. 148). Fresco (2016, p. 121) succinctly summarises meat as a life style luxury stating that "a rich person eats meat; an even richer person eats the best, most uncommon meat".

Heroes, fighters, warriors and athletes were also privileged in ancient societies. They preferred consuming meat, and specifically red meat, because of the belief it was giving them the courage and strengths needed to defeat the enemies, battle opponents and maintain their glory, dignity and reputation (Nenova, 2015). The famous distinct "black broth" of the Spartans was a pork stew made with pig legs, blood and vinegar and itself required exceptional bravery to be consumed (Nenova, 2015; Flacelière, 2002). Olympic athletes who previously ate dried fruits, grains and cheese, turned to meat in the 3rd century (Grivetti & Applegate, 1997). Eating meat, as well as drinking wine, was believed to give them competitive advantage (Grivetti & Applegate, 1997).

Meat was strongly associated with social and physical power. However, Fresco (2016) points out that refusal to eat meat was used as an expression of rejection of power. The Pythagorean sect in ancient Greece was vegetarian in protest to the ruling state (Fresco, 2016).

Abundance and Access

Prior to industrial farming of both, crops for feed and animals for slaughter, access to meat was restricted because it was simply not available in the quantities required for it to be the main part of every meal. In historical periods of famine, associated with plagues, cholera and other epidemic diseases, droughts, frosts, floods and further climatic and geological events, wars, revolutions, blockades and governance failures (The Free Library, 2004), supply of food, and particularly meat, was highly restricted (Ó Gráda, 2009). During the two World Wars meat like many other foods was difficult to obtain and became a wartime necessity. Rationing was widely introduced to manage shortages and control civilian consumption with equitable distribution of food which was often barely edible (Lee, 2014). People in Europe and to some extent in the United States and Australia experienced meatless years as meat was shipped to feed the soldiers at the frontline (Sundin, 2011; BBC, 2014; Australian War Memorial, n.d.). Internal animal organs such as hearts, livers, tripe, tongue and kidneys, were introduced as a mainstream part of dining (Romm, 2014).

In the last 55 years however, things drastically changed and meat became the norm, very affordable for many. Worldwide meat consumption surged from 61 g per person per day (Sans & Combris, 2015) or 21.7 kg per person per year in 1961 to 96 g per person per day or 34.3 kg per person per year in 2017 (OECD, 2017). In the most developed countries, animal protein intake now exceeds nutritional needs (Sans & Combris, 2015). There meat has become a food in abundance, easily accessible affordable luxury offering gastronomic comfort.

Pleasure

Luxury is an indulgence which generates physical, mental or emotional pleasure. For meat eaters, the sensation of eating this food is described as "mouth-watering", "delicious", "more than simple enjoyment. It's like orgasm" (Bogueva et al., 2017, p. 485, 486, 488). Silverstein and Fiske (2003, p.1) depict meat as a new luxury belonging to a class of premium highly desirable goods to which consumers are attached on an emotional level perceiving them to be of higher levels of quality, taste and aspirational achievement compared to the alternatives. In fact, humans are the only animal which eats not just to satisfy energy and nutritional needs, but for pleasure (Fresco, 2016). Throughout human history, abundance of meat has been a symbol of "lavish hospitality" (Fresco, 2016, p. 103).

Loyalty

The loyalty of consumers to meat is demonstrated in their attachment to and explicit preference of this kind of food over other vegetarian and vegan options. Whilst meat intake has been on a constant increase to reach unhealthy levels in Western diets (Marsh et al., 2016), consumption of fruits and vegetables is significantly below recommended daily doses. In fact, in 2010 Greece was the only developed country where the average consumption of vegetables, including legumes, was at the recommended level (Micha et al., 2015). No developed country had average consumption of fruit at the recommended level (Micha et al., 2015). This loyalty to meat also expands to people getting out of poverty in the emerging economies where traditional diets rich in plant-based nutrients are gradually replaced by animal proteins. Consumers seem unconscious about how their daily food reaches their plates (Fresco, 2016) and the environmental and health consequences of their loyalty to meat.

MEAT AND LUXURY TODAY

In order to understand the link between meat and luxury today, a survey was conducted in Sydney, Australia in 2017. Being Australia's largest city and one of the world's most liveable urban environments (Arlington, 2016), Sydney is representative of a wealthy economy characterised with a predominantly western type of diet which has embraced the multi-cultural nature of the Australian society (Wells, 2015). Any insights from Sydney can be extrapolated to many other Australian cities as well as affluent western societies.

The anonymous, randomly selected representative sample included 1100 participants – 545 males and 555 males representing three generations of consumers – Generation X or Xers (born between 1965 to 1976), Millennials or Generation Y (born between 1977 to 1995) and adult Centennials or Generation Z or iGen (born between 1996 and 1999). Although sociologists and psychologists assign different influences, core values and characteristics to these three generations (McCrindle Research, 2012; Centre for Generational Kinetics, 2016; Generational Differences Chart, n.d.), what was of interest in this survey was for these adults to be in full or part-time employment imposing less financial restrictions on their dietary choices.

Following ethics approval obtained from Curtin University, the survey was sent to 1500 people. The 73% response rate was high and indicated interest and engagement with the topic. Table 1 shows the survey participants by generation. The Millennials engaged strongly with the issue as indicated by their high response rate of 99.6% and overall large representation in the survey sample at 45%. Generation X and the Centennials were respectively represented at 32% and 23% (see Table 1).

In Australia, consumption of meat, and especially red meat, is very popular (Bogueva et al., 2017) and with 93 kg per year per person, the country had one of the highest per capita rates in the world in 2016 (OECD, 2017). The popularity of meat is also manifested in Sydney. Almost 80% (875 people) of the participant sample included meat in their diet (see Table 2) with the remaining 20% being either vegetarian or piscetarian (eating fish but not poultry, red or game meat). This is in line with the 2016 Roy Morgan Research poll which reports that 14.4% of the Sydney residents eat an almost vegetarian diet.

Table 1. Sydney survey participants by generation, 2017

Year Born	Generation	Number of Participants	Percentage of Total Sample
1965 – 1976	Generation X	354	32%
1977 – 1994	Millennials	498	45%
1995 – 1999	Centennials	248	23%
Total		1100	100%

Table 2. Profile of the participants per generation groups

Generation	Meat Eaters (%)	Non-Meat Eaters (%)	Meat Perceived as Luxury (%)
Generation X	291 (82%)	63 (18%)	247 (70%)
Millennials	418 (77%)	124 (23%)	384 (71%)
Centennials	166 (81%)	38 (19%)	151 (74%)
Total	875 (80%)	225 (20%)	782 (71%)

A large share of the Sydney respondents – 71% (or 782 people), across the three generational groups described meat as a luxury product (see Table 2). It appears that the younger people are, the more likely they are to see meat as a luxury with 74% of the Centennials agreeing with this statement (see Table 2). The reasons behind this are described below.

Life Style

Climate change and other environmental concerns are influencing people's life style in Australia. This large continent is exposed to the effects of more aridity, heavier rainfalls and record high temperatures and combinations of these extreme weather events (Bao et al., 2017). Sydney is already experiencing such changes and environmental considerations are increasingly shaping the city dwellers' attitudes as demonstrated with adoption of renewable energy and more sustainable transport options. However, despite the confirmed scientific evidence and a lot written about livestock's impact on greenhouse gas emissions and the ecology (e.g. Raphaely & Marinova, 2016), the link between maintaining the current livability and life style of Sydney and meat consumption is yet to be widely understood. Less than a third of the Sydney participants, namely 28% (refer to Table 3), see meat as an environmentally expensive dietary option which could potentially seriously impact on their wellbeing. On the other hand, there seems to be a trend of younger generations being more aware of the heavy environmental footprint of meat (see Table 4).

Furthermore, meat consumption has been associated with health risks. Processed meat is Group 1 carcinogenic and red meat is Group 2A probably carcinogenic (WHO, 2015). The use of antibiotics in industrial chicken factories poses threats to the development of widespread antimicrobial resistance (Review of Antimicrobial Resistance, 2015). Again, only a small share of the survey participants, namely 9% (see Table 3), realised that consuming meat is optional for human health and in fact, larger quantities and particular meats can be detrimental and negatively impact on life style. Education and social marketing (Bogueva et al., 2017) are most needed to inform better the Sydney public.

Table 3. Is this a reason for meat to be perceived as a luxury product?

Reasons	Yes, i.e. Luxury (%)	No, i.e. Non-Luxury (%)
Eating meat is rare and exclusive	69 (6%)	1031 (94%)
Meat conveys a special social status of prestige and prosperity	80 (7%)	1020 (93%)
Meat is optional for human health	102 (9%)	998 (91%)
Meat is environmentally expensive	309 (28%)	791 (72%)
Meat is sustainably produced	514 (47%)	586 (53%)
Meat has expensive premium cuts	589 (54%)	511 (46%)

Table 4. Environmental aspects of meat

Generation	Meat Needs to be Sustainably Produced to be a Luxury (% of Generation Respondents)	Meat is Environmentally Expensive Luxury (% of Generation Respondents)
Gen X	91 (25.7%)	65 (18.3%)
Millennials	306 (56.4%)	177 (32.6%)
Centennials	118 (57.8%)	67 (32.8%)

Abundance and Access

Almost all Sydney participants, namely 94%, did not consider meat to be a rare and exclusive food and 93% did not associate it with social status of prestige or prosperity (see Table 3). This is a big change from previous times and/or other places where meat is not as widely affordable. Industrial farming combined with increased purchasing capacity has contributed to this widespread attitude. Compared to traditional diets and other not as wealthy societies, the abundance and easy access to livestock meat products in Sydney are turning what used to be an exclusive and luxury product to an everyday option with many seeing this change as improvement in living standards (Bogueva et al., 2017). In other words, the desire for luxury foods based on animal proteins has triggered industrial livestock farming which has made meat accessible and affordable and hence no longer perceived as a luxury. To paraphrase Chanel Coco, meat has become a necessity where the necessity for meat had ended.

Pleasure

The Sydney participants were asked to describe in their own words when and why meat could be considered a luxury. Many used explanations that evoke the sense of pleasure from consuming meat (see Table 5). Descriptions, such as: "Gourmet… meat is luxurious", "Meat shows good social standing" clearly indicate feelings of comfort and enjoyment when eating meat. There were a few voices, however, which argued that for food to be pleasurable, it doesn't need to contain animal-based ingredients. For example: "vegan dishes… are just as filling" and "Meat is so bad… we are all guilty of eating it" (see Table 5).

Table 5. Descriptions of meat as a luxury product in the words of Sydney participants

The way meat is cooked and presented make it look luxurious.
Gourmet, rare meat is luxurious.
Good meat is a premium product that needs hips of water, good food and space to produce.
It depends on the animal, cut, grade and recipe; e.g. rump steak vs traditional beef wellington
Quality and preparation of meat is important when dining to know you will receive good meal.
Meat is expensive and shows good social standing.
Meat is expensive nowadays especially when compared to most vegetarian/vegan dishes that are just as filling.
As a vegan the amount of harassment, ridicule and judgement I get from meat-eaters is astounding. It really confronts them to have someone around them be vegan.
Meat is so bad sustainability-wise to produce and we are all guilty for eating it.

Loyalty

When meat is largely available and accessible in affluent societies such as Australia, USA or Western Europe, its status as a luxury food is manifested by the consumption of either very expensive cuts or from organically raised animals. More than half of all Sydney participants – 54%, were of the opinion that the expensive premium cuts explain the meat's status as a luxury product. The Sydney sample was also divided in its perception of the link between sustainably produced meat and luxury – 47% thought that this was the case while 53% disagreed. In other words, consumers' loyalty to meat persists in this day and age but there is a shift in their attitude to luxury related not to meat in general, but to the more expensive meats.

The sustainably produced meat is an emerging new meaning of luxury in response to environmental awareness. When this becomes reflected in consumer behaviour, meat consumption around the globe, including in Australia, will drastically reduce as there is not enough available agricultural land on the planet to raise livestock organically for the current levels of animal protein intakes. A study by Erb et al. (2016) modelled whether the world's estimated population of 9.6 billion by 2050 can be fed without expanding the currently used agricultural land in order to arrest deforestation and avoid further environmental harm. It concludes that only 15% of the 2050 world population would be able to be fed on a Western-type meat-based diet compared to everybody on an organic vegan diet. For those whose loyalty to meat is likely to continue in a world of high environmental consciousness, the concept of organic meat as a luxury will be further reinforced.

MEAT AND LUXURY IN THE FUTURE

Luxury is rooted in human culture and possesses special attributes including premium price, unique ownership, a degree of craft, high level of quality, strong aesthetics and positive social perception. As our value systems develop and change, things that were once acceptable as luxury objects, such as elephant ivory, rhinoceros horns, lion heads, crocodile and tiger skins, are no longer seen as such and the practices which allowed them to exist are often subjected to strong moral judgements and rejected as things of the past not acceptable in the future. With society embracing environmental and sustainability values at large, there is ample evidence that industrially produced livestock meat, and in fact any animal meat, may soon become an outdated way to feed a hungry global population. Although there is a long way to go before this becomes a reality, the climate change imperatives combined with the planet's ecological limits are already imposing the need for a social transformation towards predominantly plant-based diets. Social marketing is urgently needed to counteract the existing trends and facilitate such a shift (Bogueva et al., 2017).

Life Style

Contemporary luxury is extremely difficult to define beside the basic consensus that it is an expenditure beyond what is considered necessary (Godart & Seong, 2014). Understanding luxury is even more challenging with marketing and advertising efforts consistently targeting a broad mass-consumer market as distinctive to images of rarity and exclusivity (Kapferer & Bastien, 2010). The Greek philosopher Plato (482 BC–348 BC) explained luxury as scarcity, a battle over highly desirable resources and hence, at the root of wars and conflicts; those who are successful obtain high social status and associated life style (in Godart and Seong, 2014). According to Godart and Seong (2014), there are two fundamental philosophical positions associated with luxury and they are likely to persist into the future. The first is that originating from the French philosopher Voltaire (1694–1778) for whom luxury is joy and a stimulus for economic development; the French philosopher Rousseau (1712–1778), on the other hand, sees luxury as detrimental not only because it causes conflicts but also because it detracts from more meaningful pursuits (in Godart & Seong, 2014). Within the new culture of sustainability, developments around food are likely to exhibit both philosophical views.

As with clothes, food will "not only be the vehicle for more respect for the environment and social development, but it will also be synonym of culture, art and innovation" (Gardetti & Justo, 2017, p. 347). This creative and entrepreneurial aspect is most needed in opening up and developing the market of new meats (Schmidinger et al., 2018). Organically and sustainably produced meat is also part of the solution of maintaining the current life style food choices and culture through innovative environmentally friendly approaches. At the other end of the spectrum are reclaiming and resurrecting the meaning of "meat" as the flesh of fruits and vegetables – the most common objection to the efforts to create new plant-based alternatives and analogues to animal proteins, including lab meat.

Abundance and Access

The pursuit of luxury places an individual at the top of the social hierarchy and can be desirable if seen as part of improving the overall quality of life. However, as meat's ecological footprint uses scarce resources, generates high levels of greenhouse gas emissions, causes deforestation, land misuse, fresh water depletion and biodiversity loss, the increase in the global demand for animal products combined with population growth, the price of meat will naturally raise restricting its abundance and access. Climate change fluctuations, including extreme temperatures, droughts and floods, will disproportionately affect livestock production. Furthermore, grain as animal feed will continue to compete with food for human consumption raising moral concerns about justice and equity. Western consumers will also start feeling the environmental price as they start competing with wealthy elites from developing countries such as China who are not far behind in following the meat indulgence steps (Bogueva et al., 2017). Meat is unlikely to remain a viable luxury food option on the supply side of the global economy, particularly if government subsidies are withdrawn (Shapiro, 2016).

From a demand perspective, meat and animal products are also likely to face decreased popularity. As the results from the Sydney survey show, the younger generations of Millennials and Centennials are conscientiously evolving through a different mindset, more environmental awareness and perhaps not as easily deceived by the livestock industry's marketing campaigns. These generations are increasingly becoming more aware of the environmental havoc caused by animal agriculture, intense meat farming and the gruesome process of transforming animals in the slaughterhouses into food. They embrace technology and have information on their fingertips, including when actively searching for answers, participating in social media, freely discussing issues they are passionate about. Opinionated, health conscious and knowledgeable, these generations are likely to want to avoid the causes (e.g. cancer, obesity, diabetes, heart disease and stroke) killing their parents and grandparents through better nutritional choices. They also care for the future of the planet and will have to deal with the environmental consequences of the previous generations. It will come as no surprise if they are willing to embrace the new meat alternatives and a more plant-centric way of eating making smart environmental and health choices. These new generations are also more spiritual (Robey-Graham, 2008) and highly likely to be more compassionate to other living animals compared to the individualist and self-absorbed baby boomers (Robey-Graham, 2008) and the conservative traditionalist silent generation borne prior to the end of World War Two (Generational Differences Chart, n.d.).

Pleasure

A modern socio-economic trend amongst the mass middle-market consumers is the "new luxury" (Silverstein & Fiske, 2003) described with terms, such as true luxury, masstige, premium, ultra-premium, opuluxe, casual luxury, accessible luxury, hyperluxury and meta luxury (Kapferer & Bastien, 2009). Instead of being unreachable, luxury is becoming more accessible to many. Consumers are accountable for democratising the access to the luxury market (Tsai, 2005) and conquering the perception of prosperity (Schwartz, 2002). In wealthy societies, consumers who have surmounted the phase of securing basic survival and comfort, are seeking expansion of pleasure (Patrick & Hagtvedt, 2015, p. 269).

Food is part of this new luxury market. Represented by advertising images, symbols and luxury brands (Chevalier & Mazzalovo, 2012; Freire, 2014), the food industry and fine dining are penetrating the emotions and experiences of consumers, reflective of the changing nature of their needs and preferences (Danziger, 2005). With the transition to a more sustainable way of living, meat is unlikely to be able to keep its position of pleasure and will be replaced by other more sophisticated plant-based food products. In fact, meat-free options are becoming the new luxury offering colour, flavour, texture and sensational taste in fine dining and in response to the increasing prevalence of climatarian, flexitarian, vegetarian and vegan dietary styles in Australia (Roy Morgan Research, 2016) and across the globe (Cormack, 2016).

Loyalty

Although "organic agriculture has an untapped role to play when it comes to the establishment of sustainable farming systems" (Reganold & Wachter, 2016, n.p.), those loyal to meat as food will have to drastically reduce its consumption within the context of environmental and sustainability priorities. This will be in line with dietary recommendations (e.g. WCRF/AICR, 2007; SACN, 2011; NHMRC, 2013; NHMRC, 2016; FIA Communications, 2016) which restrict the intake of red meat because of health reasons, including its link to cancer. Poultry consumption would similarly have to be reduced as the current methods for industrial production of chicken meat is threatening the availability of antibiotics for human use (Review of Antimicrobial Resistance, 2015). Realistically, humanity is unlikely to give up livestock meat completely. However, the only place such meat is likely to have in people's diet is as an occasional luxury product and something that is neither necessary nor good for human health.

CONCLUSION

Luxury and sustainability are not a usual pair you expect to find combined in the same sentence as they describe largely different concepts. Symbolising prosperity, power, social status (Kapferer & Bastien, 2010) and a highly desirable luxury product in the past, meat nowadays has become the norm and affordable to many due to economic development, higher incomes and the industrial farming practices of the livestock industry. Meat is no longer perceived as a luxury and the production methods, shear volume of livestock animals, resources they use and associated greenhouse gas emissions make it also unsustainable.

The four characteristics of luxury, namely life style, abundance and access, pleasure and loyalty, and their association with meat, have changed drastically throughout the years in response to the broader socio-economic, cultural and environmental contexts. So has the luxury market which has become more democratised and embraced new luxury products, including foods. The Sydney survey shows that firstly, people perceive as luxury only particular types of meat, namely organic and sustainably produced as well as expensive cuts and gourmet meats; and secondly, that there is lack of understanding about the environmental and health impacts of meat production and consumption with the younger generations being relatively more aware of the problems.

Deep values like environmental, social and animal welfare issues can be encompassed by consumer aspirations in luxury products (Bendell & Kleanthous, 2007). According to Hashmi (2017), currently there is a shift in the luxury realm and consumers from all walks of life "are increasingly concerned about social and environmental issues, and prefer ethical and green products that reflect their own values and beliefs" (Hennigs et al., 2013, p. 25). This is the case with meat where consumers are now either looking for organic and sustainable products or shifting altogether towards plant-based options. The new luxury mass market which reflects improved prosperity and quality of life, will continue to include food but with dominating sustainability and climate change concerns it is very likely that livestock meat will soon be replaced as a desirable product by non-animal based options which reflect the art, creativity and innovation in dealing with the challenges of feeding a healthy global population. This will bring the new luxury consumption in line with the sustainability imperatives.

ACKNOWLEDGMENT

The first and second author acknowledge the contribution of an Australian Government Research Training Program Scholarship in supporting this research.

REFERENCES

Animal Liberation Front. (2006). *Meat-eating is an unsustainable luxury*. Retrieved from http://www.animalliberationfront.com/Practical/Health/MeatNotSustainable.htm

Arlington, K. (2016, August 18). Why The Economist says Sydney is no longer one of the world's 10 most liveable cities. *The Sydney Morning Herald*. Retrieved from http://www.smh.com.au/nsw/the-heightened-perceived-threat-of-terrorism-affects-sydneys-liveability-20160817-gqv8kf.html

Australian War Memorial. (n.d.). Rationing of food and clothing during the Second World War. Retrieved from https://www.awm.gov.au/articles/encyclopedia/homefront/rationing

Bao, J., Sherwood, S. C., Alexander, L. V., & Evans, J. P. (2017). Future increases in extreme precipitation exceed observed scaling rates. *Nature Climate Change*, *7*(2), 128–132. doi:10.1038/nclimate3201

BBC. (2014). Life on the front line. World War I. Retrieved from http://www.bbc.co.uk/schools/0/ww1/26247563

Bendell, J., & Kleanthous, A. (2007). *Deeper luxury*. London, UK: WWF-UK.

Bogueva, D., Marinova, D., & Raphaely, T. (2017). Reducing meat consumption: The case for social marketing. *Asia Pacific Journal of Marketing and Logistics*, *29*(3), 477–500. doi:10.1108/APJML-08-2016-0139

Bogueva, D., & Phau, I. (2016). Meat myths and marketing. In T. Raphaely & D. Marinova (Eds.), *Impact of meat consumption on health and environmental sustainability* (pp. 264–276). Hershey, PA: IGI Global. doi:10.4018/978-1-4666-9553-5.ch015

Centre for Generational Kinetics. (2016). *An intro to generations*. Retrieved from http://genhq.com/faq-info-about-generations/

Chevalier, M., & Mazzalovo, G. (2012). *Luxury brand management: A world of privilege* (2nd ed.). Singapore: John Wiley & Sons. doi:10.1002/9781119199168

Cormack, L. (2016, June 5). Australia is the third-fastest growing vegan market in the world. *The Sydney Morning Herald*. Retrieved from http://www.smh.com.au/business/consumer-affairs/australia-is-the-thirdfastest-growing-vegan-market-in-the-world-20160601-gp972u.html

Danziger, P. N. (2005). *Let them eat cake: Marketing luxury to the masses—as well as the classes*. Chicago, IL: Dearborn Trade Publishing.

Dhont, K., Hodson, G., Costello, K., & MacInnis, C. C. (2014). Social dominance orientation connects prejudicial human–human and human–animal relations. *Personality and Individual Differences*, *61-62*, 104–108. doi:10.1016/j.paid.2013.12.020

Erb, K.-H., Lauk, C., Kastner, T., Mayer, A., Theurl, M. C., & Haberl, H. (2016). Exploring the biophysical option space for feeding the world without deforestation. *Nature Communications*, *7*, 11382. doi:10.1038/ncomms11382 PMID:27092437

Fessler, D. M. T., & Navarrete, C. D. (2003). Meat is good to taboo: Dietary proscriptions as a product of the interaction of psychological mechanisms and social processes. *Journal of Cognition and Culture*, *3*(1), 1–40. doi:10.1163/156853703321598563

Flacelière, R. (2002). *Daily life in Greece at the time of Pericles*. London, UK: Phoenix Press.

Food Industry Asia (FIA) Communications. (2016). *New Chinese dietary guidelines A reference for industry*. Retrieved from https://foodindustry.asia/new-chinese-dietary-guidelines-a-reference-for-industry

Freire, N. A. (2014). When luxury advertising adds the identitary value of luxury: A semiotic analysis. *Journal of Business Research*, *67*(12), 2666–2675. doi:10.1016/j.jbusres.2014.04.004

Fresco, L. O. (2016). *Meat necessity and luxury, hamburgers in paradise: The stories behind the food we eat*. Princeton, NJ: Princeton University Press. doi:10.1515/9781400873319

Gardetti, M. A., & Justo, R. (2017). Sustainable luxury fashion: The entrepreneurs' vision. In M. A. Gardetti (Ed.), *Sustainable management of luxury* (pp. 347–360). Singapore: Springer. doi:10.1007/978-981-10-2917-2_16

Generational Differences Chart. (n.d.). *West Midland Family Center*. Retrieved from http://www.wmfc.org/uploads/GenerationalDifferencesChart.pdf

Godart, F., & Seong, S. (2014). Is sustainable fashion possible? In M. A. Gardetti & A. L. Torres (Eds.), *Sustainability luxury: Managing social and environmental performance in iconic brands* (pp. 12–27). Sheffield, UK: Greenleaf Publishing. doi:10.9774/GLEAF.9781783530625_3

Gráda, Ó. C. (2009) Famine: A short history, Princeton, NJ: Princeton University Press.

Grivetti, L., & Applegate, E. A. (1997). From Olympia to Atlanta: A cultural-historical perspective on diet and athletic training. *The Journal of Nutrition*, *127*(5), 860S–868S. PMID:9164253

Hashmi, G. (2017). Redefining the essence of sustainable luxury management: The slow value creation model. In M. A. Gardetti (Ed.), *Sustainable management of luxury: Environmental footprints and eco-design of products and processes* (pp. 4–27). Singapore: Springer Nature. doi:10.1007/978-981-10-2917-2_1

Hedenus, F., Wirsenius, S., & Johansson, D. J. A. (2014). The importance of reduced meat and dairy consumption for meeting stringent climate change targets. *Climatic Change*, *124*(1–2), 79–91. doi:10.1007/s10584-014-1104-5

Hennigs, N., Wiedmann, K. P., Klarmann, C., & Behrens, S. (2013b). Sustainability as part of the luxury essence: Delivering value through social and environmental excellence. *Journal of Corporate Citizenship*, *52*(11), 25–35. doi:10.9774/GLEAF.4700.2013.de.00005

Hennings, N., Wiedmann, K. P., & Klarmann, C. (2013a). Consumer value perception of luxury goods: A cross cultural and cross industry comparison. In K. P. Wiedmann & N. Hennings (Eds.), *Luxury marketing: A challenge for theory and practice* (pp. 77–100). Gabler, Germany: Springer. doi:10.1007/978-3-8349-4399-6_5

Husic, M., & Cicic, M. (2009). Luxury consumption factors. *Journal of Fashion Marketing and Management, 13*(2), 231–245. doi:10.1108/13612020910957734

Kapferer, J. N. (1997). *Strategic brand management: Creating and sustaining brand equity long term* (2nd ed.). London, UK: Kogan Page.

Kapferer, J. N., & Bastien, V. (2009). The specificity of luxury management: Turning marketing upside down. *Journal of Brand Management, 16*(5/6), 311–322. doi:10.1057/bm.2008.51

Kapferer, J. N., & Bastien, V. (2010). *The luxury strategy: Break the rules of marketing to build luxury brands*. London, UK: Kogan Page.

Kaye, L. (2014, 29 October) Should we view meat as a luxury? Triple Pundit: People, Planet, Profit. Retrieved from http://www.triplepundit.com/2014/10/meat-as-a-luxury/

Lee, A. (2014, 28 August) The battle to feed Tommy: New exhibition looks at the diet of a WW1 soldier. *Express*. Retrieved from http://www.express.co.uk/news/world-war-1/502452/The-Battle-to-feed-Tommy-The-diet-of-a-WW1-soldier

Marinova, D., & Raphaely, D. (2017) Impact of vegetarian diets on the environment. In W. Craig, W. (Ed.), Vegetarian nutrition and wellness (forthcoming). Boca Raton, FL: CRC Press/Taylor and Francis.

Marsh, K., Saunders, A., & Zeuschner, C. (2016). Red meat and health: Evidence regarding red meat, health, and chronic disease risk. In T. Raphaely & D. Marinova (Eds.), *Impact of meat consumption on health and environmental sustainability* (pp. 131–176). Hershey, PA: IGI Global. doi:10.4018/978-1-4666-9553-5.ch008

McCrindle Research. (2012). Generations defined. Retrieved from http://mccrindle.com.au/resources/Generations-Defined-Sociologically.pdf

Merriam-Webster. (2009), Luxury. Retrieved from http://www.merriam-webster.com/dictionary/luxury

Micha, R., Khatibzadeh, S., Shi, P., Andrews, K. G., Engell, R. E., & Mozaffarian, D. (2015). Global, regional and national consumption of major food groups in 1990 and 2010: A systematic analysis including 266 country-specific nutrition surveys worldwide. *BMJ Open, 5*(9), e008705. doi:10.1136/bmjopen-2015-008705 PMID:26408285

National Health and Medical Research Council (NHMRC). (2013). *Australian dietary guidelines*. Canberra, Australia: NHMRC and Department of Health and Ageing, Australian Government.

Nenova, S. (2015). *Ancient meals and eating habits*. Part 1 Greeks. Retrieved from http://www.ancientworldalive.com/single-post/2015/06/03/Ancient-meals-and-eating-habit-Part-1-Greeks

Organisation for Economic Cooperation and Development (OECD). (2017). *Meat consumption (indicator)*. Retrieved from; doi:10.1787/fa290fd0-

Oxford Latin Dictionary. (1992). Oxford, UK: Oxford University Press.

Patrick, V. M., & Hagtvedt, H. (2015). Luxury branding. In D. J. MacInnis, C. W. Park, & J. W. Priester (Eds.), *Handbook of Brand Relationships* (pp. 267–280). New York, NY: Routledge.

Phau, I., & Prendergast, G. (2000). Consuming luxury brands: The relevance of the "rarity principle". *Journal of Brand Management*, *7*(5), 366–375. doi:10.1057/bm.2000.26

Raphaely, T., & Marinova, D. (Eds.). (2016). *Impact of meat consumption on health and environmental sustainability*. Hershey, PA: IGI Global. doi:10.4018/978-1-4666-9553-5

Reganold, J. P., & Wachter, J. M. (2016). Organic agriculture in the 21st century. *Nature Plants*, *2*(2), 15221. doi:10.1038/nplants.2015.221 PMID:27249193

Review on Antimicrobial Resistance. (2015). *Antimicrobials in agriculture and the environment: Reducing unnecessary use and waste*. Retrieved from https://amr-review.org/sites/default/files/Antimicrobials%20in%20agriculture%20and%20the%20environment%20-%20Reducing%20unnecessary%20use%20and%20waste.pdf

Robey-Graham, A. K. (2008). Generational comparisons and contrasts chart. Retrieved from http://www.napavalley.edu/people/jhall/Documents/Generational%20Chart.pdf

Romm, C. (2014). The World War II campaign to bring organ meats to the dinner table. *Atlantic (Boston, Mass.)*, *25*(September). Retrieved from https://www.theatlantic.com/health/archive/2014/09/the-world-war-ii-campaign-to-bring-organ-meats-to-the-dinner-table/380737/

Roy Morgan Research. (2016). The slow but steady rise of vegetarianism in Australia. Retrieved from http://www.roymorgan.com/findings/vegetarianisms-slow-but-steady-rise-in-australia-201608151105

Rozin, P., Hormes, J. M., Faith, M. S., & Wansink, B. (2012). Is meat male? A quantitative multimethod framework to establish metaphoric relationships. *The Journal of Consumer Research*, *39*(3), 629–643. doi:10.1086/664970

Sans, P., & Combris, P. (2015). World meat consumption patterns: An overview of the last fifty years (1961-2011). *Meat Science*, *109*, 106–111. doi:10.1016/j.meatsci.2015.05.012 PMID:26117396

Schmidinger, K., Bogueva, D., & Marinova, D. (2018this volume). New meat without livestock. In D. Bogueva, D. Marinova, & T. Raphaely (Eds.), *Social marketing and its influence on animal-based products*. Hershey, PA: IGI Global.

Schwartz, J. (2002, December 16). Supersize American dream: Expensive? I'll take it. *The New York Times*, 8.

Scientific Advisory Committee on Nutrition (SACN). (2010). *Iron and health*. London, UK: TSO. Retrieved from https://www.gov.uk/government/uploads/system/uploads/attachment_data/file/339309/SACN_Iron_and_Health_Report.pdf

Shapiro, P. (2016). Feasting from the federal trough: how the meat, egg and dairy industries gorge on taxpayer dollars while fighting modest rules. In T. Raphaely, & D. Marinova (Eds), Impact of meat consumption on health and environmental sustainability (pp. 244-254). Hershey, PA: IGI Global. doi:10.4018/978-1-4666-9553-5.ch013

Silverstein, M. J., & Fiske, N. (2003). *Trading up: The new American luxury*. New York, NY: Portfolio Penguin Group.

Smith, O. (2017, 14 May) Revealed: The nation that eats the least meat per capita. *The Telegraph*. Retrieved from http://www.telegraph.co.uk/travel/maps-and-graphics/world-according-to-meat-consumption/

Stambaugh, J. E. (1988). *The ancient Roman city*. Baltimore, MD: Johns Hopkins University Press.

Sundin, S. (2011). Make it do – meat and cheese rationing in World War II. WWII novels by Sarah Sundin. Retrieved from http://www.sarahsundin.com/make-it-do-meat-and-cheese-rationing-in-world-war-ii-2/

The Free Library. (2004). *Famines through history*. Scholastic, Inc. Retrieved from https://www.thefreelibrary.com/Famines+through+history-a0114325996

Toussaint-Samat, M. (2009). *A history of food*. Chichester, UK: John Wiley & Sons.

Tsai, S. (2005). Impact of personal orientation on luxury-brand purchase value. *International Journal of Market Research*, *47*(4), 429–454.

Wells, K. (2015). *Australian food and drink*. Australian Government. Retrieved from http://www.australia.gov.au/about-australia/australian-story/austn-food-and-drink

White, S., & Cordell, D. (2015). Global phosphorus security – diet, sustainability and food for thought. In K. Soeters (Ed.), *Meat the future: How cutting meat consumption can feed billions more* (pp. 75–86). Amsterdam, the Netherlands: Nicholaas G. Pierson Foundation.

Wiedmann, K. P., Hennigs, N., & Siebels, A. (2007). Measuring consumers' luxury value perception: A crosscultural framework. *Academy of Marketing Science Review*, *7*(7), 333–361.

World Cancer Research Fund and American Institute for Cancer Research (WCRF/AICR). (2007). *Food, nutrition, physical activity and the prevention of cancer: A global perspective*. Washington, DC: AICR.

World Health Organisation (WHO). (2015). Q&A on the carcinogenicity of the consumption of red meat and processed meat. Retrieved from http://www.who.int/features/qa/cancer-red-meat/en/

KEY TERMS AND DEFINITIONS

Centennials: Generation Z or iGen, people born between 1996 and 1999.

Generation X: Xers, people born between 1965 to 1976.

Life Style: The way a person lives, including the objects and services s/he consumes.

Loyalty: Support, allegiance or attachment demonstrated towards a particular person, place, organisation or objects.

Luxury: A perceived necessity in excess of normal necessities which makes us feel better.

Millennials: Generation Y, people born between 1977 and 1995.

New Meat: Plant-based alternatives to animal products, including the flesh of fruits and vegetables.

Chapter 13
Genius, Creativity and (Not) Eating Meat

İsmail Hakkı Tekiner
Istanbul Gelişim University, Turkey

Ahmad Ni'matullah Al-Baarri
Diponegoro University, Indonesia

Diana Bogueva
Curtin University, Australia

ABSTRACT

A major hypothesis argues that the dietary shifts of the proto-humans towards animal proteins enabled humans to develop large brains as well as build planning, cooperating, socializing, exploring and creative skills, related to food techniques, including using fire, cooking, fermentation, agriculture and animal domestication. Many million years later, human population has drastically increased and livestock has grown even faster creating unprecedented global environmental, climate change and health challenges. This chapter asks whether animal meat continues to be essential for human nutrition. It refers to prominent people in human history considered geniuses because of their creative and intellectual abilities. It explores whether there is a link between genius, creativity and eating meat and answers this in the negative based on well-known geniuses who have negated the meat-eating diet. Social marketing can anchor some of its techniques in using such personalities as role models for changing the current high dependence on meat.

INTRODUCTION

The modern human brain is the largest and most complex organ among the living primates. Constituting only about 2 percent of the human body, the brain is responsible for all body functions (NMNH, 2017). The major causes for the physical growth and creativity of the human brain have been of boundless research interest.

DOI: 10.4018/978-1-5225-4757-0.ch013

A major hypothesis about the evolution of the human brain relates to dietary shifts in the human nutrition (Schoenemann, 2006). According to the anthropologists (Joyce, 2010), the proto-humans started consuming a diet rich in animal proteins, especially meat, with the use of fire and cooking. Animal protein from the meat initially provided sufficient nutrition and energy for the physical growth of the human brain. Subsequently, the increased brain size positively influenced the development of intelligence, and hereby enabled humans to plan, cooperate and socialize (Smil, 2013). Although anthropology tells us something about the positives of eating meat linked to physical growth and the relative size of the human brain, it does not convey anything about creativity and talent We do not know whether eating meat has contributed to the development of exceptional intellectual, creative, knowledge and wisdom abilities and talents associated with being a genius. There are also some other major dietary shifts in the human evolution, including cooking, fermenting, plant growing, animal domestication and agriculture (Luca et al., 2010).

According to Dunn (2012) from the Scientific American, human ancestors were nearly all vegetarians, and the human digestive systems evolved as the practices of growing, producing, processing and preparing food developed. The gut microbiota seems to have evolved too and in fact varies according to the adopted food practices. For instance, some populations in Japan have bacteria in their guts allowing them to break down seaweed – a foodstuff popular for them and not so common in other places (Dunn, 2012).

Humans evolved with eating meat (Gupta, 2016), supplied with no guaranteed luck by male hunter-gatherers, but also with good quantities of fruits, vegetables, roots, seeds and nuts collected by females. Later agriculture allowed the ploughing of the land to produce crops, followed by domestication of animals. Although meat does provide some valuable micronutrients and essential fats, according to Prof. Peter Ungar it is carbohydrates, not meat that fuel the human brain (in Despain, 2012). He also explains: "The hominin lifestyle is more about a broadened niche than meat per se… Lots of people live in lots of places because they can find something to nourish themselves… Western Australian aboriginals did quite well without lots of meat" (Ungar in Despain, 2012).

The evolution came after the discovery of fire, which enabled humans to cook their meat to increase its digestibility, making it more tender, tastier and even reducing the risk of infection (Ali, 2015, p. 25). Actually, cooking or heat treatment was more important than meat for the evolution of the human brain. According to Herculano-Houzel (2012, p. 10667), "the advent of the ability to control fire to cook foods, which increases enormously the energy yield of foods and the speed with which they are consumed…, may have been a crucial step in allowing the near doubling of numbers of brain neurons that is estimated to have occurred between *H. erectus* and *H. sapiens*". The use of fire freed up time from chewing to obtain the daily calorific intake, which humans used to their advantage developing remarkable cognitive abilities (Herculano-Houzel, 2012).

Cooking starch-rich vegetables and grains – that is digestible carbohydrates, was necessary in human evolution "to accommodate the increased metabolic demands of a growing brain… cooked starch, a source of preformed glucose, greatly increased energy availability to human tissues with high glucose demands, such as the brain, red blood cells, and the developing fetus" (Hardy et al., 2015, p. 252). Based on these findings, the researchers point out: "'Eating meat may have kick started the evolution of bigger brains, but cooked starchy foods together with more salivary amylase genes made us smarter still" (in Millner, 2015)

Controversially, according to Rettner (2009), there are three other hypotheses trying to explain why human brains today are so big: climatic changes, ecological shifts away from the equator with less parasite exposure and social competition. Of the three hypotheses, recent studies suggest that social competition for scarce resources may be the major cause. In any case, the issue remains a matter of debate.

According to Prof. Hurlbut from California University, people with bigger brains are not necessarily smarter than those with smaller brains (in Hirshon, 2017). There is only weak correlation between brain size and intelligence. Hirshon (2017) compares the size of the brain of Anatole France (a French author who won the 1921 Nobel Prize in Literature) and that of Jonatan Swift (the author of "Gulliver's Travels") which was twice bigger despite both of them being extremely talented. Besides size, a range of other factors, such as density of nerve cells per area, nutrition quality and environmental stimulation, probably contribute to how well a brain functions (Hirshon, 2017).

However, humans are both biological organisms and social beings in interaction with their environment (Bubolz & Sontag, 1993). We may ask ourselves whether eating meat is still necessary for the proto-humans' 21st century descendants. If we look at the history's pages, we find many outstanding people who did not consume meat. For instance, the inventor Nikola Tesla advised: "practically abstain from meat… Stay away from acid, keep a vegetarian diet" (Wrots, 2016). Many people regarded as geniuses were vegetarians, including Leonardo da Vinci, Gandhi, George Bernard Shaw, the Nobel Prize-winning mathematician Norbert Wiener, Isaac Newton and Albert Einstein (Weiner, 2016).

TRACING THE HISTORY OF EATING MEAT

There is no doubt that animal meat has played an important role in human evolution and survival. The proto-humans were eating roots, wild berries, fruits, vegetables and nuts to stay alive. By adding animal flesh to their diet, they were able to reduce the energy required for the foraging of vast land areas in search of food. According to the evolutionary biologists Zink and Lieberman (2016), *H. erectus* started consuming a much more calorie-rich diet with animal proteins which resulted in the need for less chewing cycles and total masticatory force. This meant a significant saving in time and calorie-burning effort for the early humans (Kluger, 2016).

In the opinion of the evolutionary anthropologist Aiello (in Ireland, 2008), there is evidence in the fossil record for a human animal-based diet, such as animal bones from 2.5 million years ago with cut marks thought to be from the earliest stone tools and species of first hominids who had strong jaws and molar-like teeth (Ireland, 2008). Meat was plentiful on the African savannah in East Africa, where the humans first evolved, and then dispersed outwards (Maslin et al., 2015). This is where meat stepped. Another set of nutrients came from seafood, such as fish and shellfish, which provided dietary sources of omega-3 fatty acids for humans' brains (Mouritsen, 2016). According to Aiello (1997), animal-based proteins are only one aspect of the brain evolution. Other contributing factors include terrestriality with large group sizes, bipedalism freeing the forelimbs, more complex foraging behaviour, adaptation to climatic variability, necessity for behavioural flexibility and social intelligence (Aiello, 1997).

Later, environmental constraints related to high population densities coupled with traditional and cultural adaptations often linked to religious commandments and economic affordability made meat a relatively rare food in rural societies (Smil, 2013). Within the second half of the 19th century, industrialization and urbanization resulted in more frequent meat eating in Europe and North America followed by Asia and Latin America as part of the post-World War II modernization (Smil, 2013). The year 1959 was a turning point in population growth when the number of people on the planet reached 3 billion and was set to double to 6 billion in the next 40 years (Smithsonian, 2010). Meat production and consumption however more than tripled between 1961 and 2001 – increasing from 71 to 232 million tonnes (FAOSTAT, 2017).

This enormous raise in meat production and consumption is adversely influencing all aspects of human life and humanity's long-term survival prospects. It is contributing to global greenhouse gas emissions, land and water pollution and depletion, biodiversity loss, antimicrobial resistance, and is also negatively impacting on human health (Raphaely & Marinova, 2014 and 2016). Irrespective as to what role meat played millions of years ago in human evolution, humanity is now faced with unprecedented challenges to reduce and even eliminate meat consumption in order to deal with climate change and safeguard the planet's ecosystems. Environmental values and priorities dictate a new understanding – to the one evolutionists, biologists and anthropologists hold, of the role of meat in human diets.

However, is reducing or eliminating meat from people's diet going to impact on human creativity and intellectual abilities? We answer this negatively by looking back in history at exceptional minds who were vegetarian and achieved extraordinary heights in creativity, innovation, versatility and human brilliance. These geniuses were able to set their marks in human evolution in all walks of life and represent role models that social marketing can use to send the message that remarkable human performance does not have to rely on meat intake. Many of the examples we use are people who have lived in times when there was much less pressure to conserve the planet's ecosystems and climate change was yet to be defined as an existential threat to humanity. In their decision to abstain from meat, these geniuses were guided by other priorities and values, such as respect for non-human animals, rejection of violence and desire to live long, happy and healthy lives. Irrespective as to what the reasons for these outstanding people were to be vegetarian, the message of this chapter is that this did not impact on their creativity and exceptional talents. It is time to put the role of meat in human evolution aside and face the reality of the 21st century which requires urgent responses to climate change and preserving the planet's ecosystems.

THE GENIUS MINDS

What characterizes the geniuses' exceptional minds? It is a combination of creativity, curiosity, attentiveness to everything, natural abilities and brilliance. The historian McMahon (2013) describes the genius as a misfit, martyr, loner and rebel but also hard-working individual. Using the remark of one of these geniuses – Thomas Edison: "Genius is 1 percent inspiration and 99 percent perspiration" (The Phrase Finder, 2017). First used two-thousand years ago by the Roman author Plautus, the word genius described individuals "who possess rare and special powers: the power to create, redeem and destroy; the power to penetrate the fabric of the universe; the power to see into the future or to see into our souls" (McMahon, 2013, p. xix). The English Oxford Living Dictionaries (2017) define genius as those, who are exceptionally intelligent, have exceptional creativity or other natural ability or are simply very clever. Geniuses have made many of the great discoveries and developments in the sciences and the arts (Barker, 1998).

What makes a person a genius is a very complex matter which has something to do with genetics, education and training, personality, psychology and perhaps diet, the food that fuels the greatest mercurial minds. The foods humans consume play a crucial role for the healthy brain functions, encouraging memory, learning and creativity. In fact, the microbiome of the guts influences all organ systems of the body, including the brain (Korn, 2014). Many geniuses specifically preferred plant-based food. The list includes Pythagoras, Isaac Newton, Leonardo da Vinci, Nikola Tesla, Albert Einstein, Thomas Edison, Franz Kafka, Leo Tolstoy, Benjamin Franklin all of whom claimed to be vegetarian. To this list can also be added more contemporary prominent vegetarian geniuses such as Steve Jobs (Apple Computer) and Steven Hawking (the famous paraplegic physicist).

Being fervent about vegetarianism, some of these great minds have expressed their personal reasons for the chosen diet: "Vegetarianism has a powerful influence upon the mind and its action, as well as upon the health and vigour of the body. Until we stop harming all other living beings, we are still savages" –Thomas Edison, and "Nothing will benefit human health and increase chances for survival of life on Earth as much as the evolution to a vegetarian diet" – Albert Einstein (Florida News Group, n.d.). Nikola Tesla who shifted gradually away from a meat diet wrote regarding the physical and moral benefits of vegetarianism: "It is certainly preferable to raise vegetables, and I think, therefore, that vegetarianism is a commendable departure from the established barbarous habit. That we can subsist on plant food and perform our work even to advantage is not a theory, but a well-demonstrated fact" (Tesla, 1900, p. 180).

GENIUSES' EATING SECRETS

There are many complex factors, including neurological (Oikkonen et al., 2016, Jauk et al.,2015; Ridley, 2010; Mayseless et al., 2015; Falk et al., 2013; Shi et al., 2017), psychological such as mental disorders and dyslexia (Heilman, 2016; Leutgeb et al., 2016; Andreasen, 2011; Kéri, 2009; Zhang et al., 2016), genetic (Dietrich, 2014; Borreli, 2016; Kéri, 2009; Oikkonen et al, 2016; Zabelina et al., 2016; Reuter, 2006; Mayseless et al., 2013), education and training (Rettner, 2009; Shamay-Tsoory et al., 2011; Sun et al, 2016), which distinguish the genius brain from the ordinary normal human brain. Is diet also a significant factor for being a genius?

It is known that the best brain-boosting foods are vegetables or plant-based products including blueberries, avocados, beetroot, broccoli, celery, coconut oil, dark chocolate, extra virgin olive oil, walnuts, green leafy vegetables and herbs (Bailey, 2013). The same plant-rich food formula appears to have worked for many of the world geniuses (Ahn, 2014). Scientific studies show correlation between eating vegetables and fruits and higher IQ (Alleyne, 2011), connection between a country's level of chocolate consumption and its per capita number of Nobel laureates (Messerli, 2012) and a link between the plant pigment lutein in leafy green vegetables and healthy brain aging (Breyer, 2016).

The greatest minds needed and were stimulated by certain foods and drinks to keep them in shape, awake and inspired. What you eat has a profound influence on brain function, one of the greatest genius of all time Da Vinci said (Gelb, 2000). Some of the world geniuses have quite attained taste and unusual dining habits. They used nicotine, caffeine, cocoa and alcohol to start and end the day. Beethoven ("Only the pure of heart can make a good soup"[1]), Victor Hugo ("First it was necessary to civilize man in relation to man. Now it is necessary to civilize man in relation to nature and the animals"[2]) and Balzac ("Great love affairs start with Champagne and end with tisane"[3]) consumed too many cups of coffee a day. Tolstoy ("As long as there are slaughterhouses, there will be battlefields"[2]), Gustav Mahler ("You will appreciate how full I am of this idea [vegetarianism] when I tell you that I expect it to work the regeneration of mankind"[4]), Jean-Paul Sartre ("Man is condemned to be free; because once thrown into the world, he is responsible for everything he does"[5]) and Mark Twain ("Whenever you find yourself on the side of the majority, it's time to pause and reflect"[6]) ate too many eggs (Weiner, 2016). Picasso ("An idea is a point of departure and no more. As soon as you elaborate it, it becomes transformed by thought"[7]) consumed mineral water, milk, vegetables, fish, rice pudding and grapes. Tesla ate fresh vegetables, fish and meat sparingly and rarely till he totally removed the latter two from his diet (Ahn, 2014). Benjamin Franklin ("Flesh eating is unprovoked murder"[2]) ate many apples and cranberries but was also extremely fond of pickles (Franklin & Marshall College, 2008).

These notable geniuses respected the benefits of their meat-free lifestyle, they were analyzing the essence of the food they consumed. Nikola Tesla believed longevity has very much in common with controlling passions and appetites, saying humans are overeating especially the wrong kind of food. Potatoes for Tesla were among his preferred food: "Potatoes are splendid, and should be eaten at least once a day. They contain valuable mineral salts and are neutralizing" (Wrots, 2016). Although adopting vegetarianism in his late ages, Albert Einstein appears to have supported it throughout all his life, writing to Max Kariel in 1953: "I have always eaten animal flesh with a somewhat guilty conscience" and later with quite an enlightenment: "Vegetarian food leaves a deep impression on our nature. If the whole world adopts vegetarianism, it can change the destiny of humankind" (Calaprice, 2010).

The foods and drinks the exceptional minds preferred to consume are loaded with nutrients which positively affect the cognitive functions: flavonoids in cocoa, green tea, wine (higher in red wine) and dark chocolate, vitamin D in milk and cereal grains, combination of vitamins C, E and carotene in citrus fruits, vegetables, nuts, peanuts, olives, choline in egg yolks and lettuce, calcium, zinc and selenium in milk, beans, nuts, almonds, whole grains, nuts, cereals and eggs (Gómez-Pinilla, 2008). Steve Jobs existed primarily on dates, almonds, lots of carrots and weeks of fasting (Weiner, 2016).

Excessive meat consumption is not neutral for the human brain and can cause severe problems. The saturated fat consumption associated with red meat might trigger negative changes in the cognitive function of the human brain, damaging its memory (Sifferlin, 2012, Health & Fitness Advisory, 2013). A study suggests that high intake of omega-6, which is found in red meat and dairy is positively associated with cognitive impairment and brain allergies (Melendez, 2010, p. 24-25). One further study refers to the danger of Mad Cow Disease (21st century) and the sheep Scrapie disease (in the 1700s) affecting human brain (Cox, 2002) questioning whether or not they can be transmitted to humans as seen in the Creutzfeldt-Jakob degenerative disease, affecting the brain and neurological system. Processed meat can induce memory loss and increase Alzheimer's disease (Wegerer, 2014) in a similar way as a diet high in grilled and well-done meat can impact brain health and cause dementia and Alzheimer's (Pollack, 2015).

Against this background, the question that arises is actually not whether excluding meat from human diet would impact on creativity and intellectual capacities but whether we still need to eat meat. This is particularly relevant to situations where people have a choice and consuming animal proteins is not a matter of survival or death.

DO WE STILL NEED TO EAT MEAT?

It is difficult to argue that there is a secret link between genius, creativity and not eating meat. We have selectively chosen exceptional personalities who have excluded animal flesh from their diets on their own volition. These examples show that meat is not necessarily a brain food. A large group of world geniuses turned into vegetarianism and affirmed its advantages not only from a compassion and morality point, but because of realizing that abstaining from meat is good for human health, body and brain, for the animals and the planet as a whole. Their geniality helped them to see this (Elephant Journal, 2011; Turner, 2012). Several more quotes in support of this position:

Our task must be to [widen] our circle of compassion to embrace all living creatures and the whole of nature in its beauty[8] *– Albert Einstein*

The greatness of a nation can be judged by the way its animals are treated[9] *– Mahatma Gandhi*

A man can live and be healthy without killing animals for food; therefore, if he eats meat, he participates in taking animal life merely for the sake of his appetite. And to act so is immoral[2] *– Leo Tolstoy*

Global warming could be controlled if we all became vegetarians and stopped eating meat… giving up pork chops, lamb cutlets and chicken burgers would do more for the environment than burning less oil and gas[10] *– Alan Calverd, British physicist*

Eating meat might be what fueled human brains million years ago. However, humankind's historic evolution does not take into consideration the devastating impacts on the environmental and human health presently faced. Today, 70 billion animals are slaughtered every year to be consumed by 7 billion humans (Bogueva & Phau, 2016). Global meat production has expanded more than fourfold in the last five decades and continues to rise to a new peak, according to the United Nations Food and Agriculture Organization (FAO) (Renner, 2015, p. 56), due to consumers' growing purchasing power, urbanization and changing diets. Limiting the environmental and health impacts caused by meat production and consumption worldwide involves not only knowledge of how much meat people eat, but also about the meat type consumed. Most low-income and developing countries are at various points along the rapidly ascending phase of their meat consumption growth curves, but some are already approaching the upper bend (Kearney, 2010), including China (Bogueva et al., 2017).

Today, a meat-rich diet may not always be good for the modern humans and their brains. The adoption of uniformed excessive meat consumption habits (Ali, 2015, p.9) and modern livestock production are posing an unprecedented threat to the limited resources of the planet as well as human health (Raphaely & Marinova, 2016). The long-term consumption of meat is associated with an increased risk of mortality, cardiovascular disease, colorectal cancer and type-2 diabetes, in both men and women because chronic high protein intake, the studies suggest, may result in digestive, renal and vascular abnormalities (Wu, 2016). It is clear that we no longer need to eat meat.

THE HUMAN PRICE OF MEAT-PRODUCTION SYSTEMS

The discussion over the human desire for meat foments all kinds of passion. However, the environmental and human health related facts are hard to ignore (Kaye, 2014). Shall we see the enormous cost of excessive meat production and consumption on the survival of life on Earth, their contributions to environmental crises such as climate change and biodiversity loss, and human health? If not restrained, by the middle of the 21st century, unnecessary meat production and consumption will continue to pose a threat to the biosphere's integrity. The expanded farming operations, extensive conversion of tropical forests into new pastures and mass-scale feed industry will trigger serious concerns, related to the gaseous emissions from livestock, water depletion and degradation from fertilizers-manure and other agrochemicals, land misappropriation and deprivation, biodiversity and rapid species loss (FAOSTAT, 2003; Smil, 2013; Raphaely & Marinova, 2014).

According to the statistical facts given by Wolchover (2012), OSU (2012) and USGS (2016), there is excess water-depletion and pollution in meat production (1,890 litres for 450 grams of chicken meat production and 1,750 litres for 113 grams of hamburger beef production). More than 400 different gases are released in the air from factory livestock facilities and in the US, "animal feeding operations annually produce about 100 times more manure than the amount of human sewage sludge processed in US municipal wastewater plants" (Grace Communications Foundation, 2017).

Cattle consume 17 times more grain calories than they produce as meat calories (Eshel et al., 2014). People in India consume about 200 kilograms of grain per person each year (Brown, 2009). At that level of consumption, the total current grain harvest could support 10 billion people on the planet (Brown, 2009). On the other hand, in the US people consume 800 kilograms of grain per person each year, including for food and animal feed with livestock eating much of it. At that level of consumption, the Earth can support only 2.5 billion people creating world hunger, starvation and food-related conflicts. These facts can no longer be ignored, given that agriculture is the sector with the highest greenhouse gas emissions on a 20-year horizon (IPCC, 2014).

Furthermore, in the last 60 years food-producing animals massively consume most of the antibiotics manufactured (100,000–200,000 tonnes per year) across the world (Tekiner & Özpınar, 2016). The World Health Organization defined antimicrobial resistance (AMR) as "biohazard", and declared that AMR is present in every country (WHO, 2016). The repeated preventative overuse of antibiotics can develop antibiotic resistance in the bacteria and in the environment. This continued evolution limits the ability to treat bacterial infections. The A "worst-case" scenario for AMR suggests that by 2050 cumulative global economic losses would reach $120 trillion and 444 million adults would have died or not been born (RAND Corporation, 2016).

Sixty percent of all known infectious diseases are zoonotic in origin, and 75% of the new human pathogens reported in the past 25 years originated in animals (Tomley & Shirley 2009). Animal husbandry is an important source of zoonotic and foodborne disease agents that spread from pigs, poultry, cattle and other livestock, by direct contact or through the environment. In 2015, WHO estimates the median global number of foodborne illnesses and deaths at 349 405 380 and 187 285, respectively (WHO/FDBERG, 2015). Food allergy is also a major health problem across the world with 200 to 250 million people suffering globally (Pawankar, 2014). At least thirty percent of the food allergens originate from food animals, leading to 60 to 75 million suffering from animal origin related allergenic cases (Pawankar, 2014; Bøgh & Madsen, 2016).

Reducing meat production will have many benefits for all people who inhabit our planet. The geniuses of the past were able to perceive this. Nowadays this has become a global agenda for all. Together with other priorities, only through drastic reductions in meat consumption will we be able to achieve United Nations' Sustainable Development Goals 2 No Hunger and 3 Good Health for all.

CONCLUSION

In the William Shakespeare's *Twelfth Night* comedy, one of the not so wise personalities Sir Andrew reasons his lack of intelligence with his diet: "But I am a great eater of beef, and I believe that does harm to my wit"[9] (Act I, Scene III). Leaving the Elizabethan age common belief that eating too much meat makes you a meat-head (Despain, 2012) aside and the Shakespeare's mockery, it is difficult to link the expansion of the human brain with one particular food or a food preparation method. Similarly, there is not a single food which can be given the status of evoking creativity and geniality.

The matter is too complex and whether there is a secret link or not between genius, creativity and (not) eating meat is likely to remain debatable. What this chapter showed is that excluding meat from human diet does not affect intellectual capacities and human brilliance. It is profoundly clear the dietary habits of the exceptional minds, mostly vegetarianism, deserve great attention, because these geniuses could see beyond the mundane habits of the present into the future.

"We are all born ignorant, but one must work hard to remain stupid"[2] – Benjamin Franklin's words are a call against ignorance. It is a statement that given the evidence about the destruction caused by meat production and consumption to the planet, its climate, species and people, continuing to be ignorant equals sheer stupidity. And you do not need to be a genius to understand this.

REFERENCES

Ahn, K. (2014). *What geniuses actually eat?* Retrieved from https://food-hacks.wonderhowto.com/how-to/real-brain-food-what-geniuses-actually-eat-part-1-0156531/

Aiello, L. C. (1997). Brains and guts in human evolution: The expensive tissue hypothesis. *Brazilian Journal of Genetics*, *20*(1), 141–148. Retrieved from http://www.scielo.br/scielo.php?script=sci_arttext&pid=S0100-84551997000100023 doi:10.1590/S0100-84551997000100023

Ali, S. M. (2015) *Meat: The opium of the 21st century* (2nd rev. ed.). Hamburg, Germany: Books on Demand.

Alleyne, R. (2011, February 8). Food for thought – diet does boost your intelligence. *The Telegraph*. Retrieved from: http://www.telegraph.co.uk/news/health/news/8308726/Food-for-thought-diet-does-boost-your-intelligence.html

Andreasen, N. C. (2011). A journey into chaos: Creativity and the unconscious. *Mens Sana Monographs*, *9*(1), 42–53. doi:10.4103/0973-1229.77424 PMID:21694961

Bailey, C. (2013, June 6). 9 brain foods that will improve your focus and concentration. A life of productivity. *A Life of Productivity*. Retrieved from http://alifeofproductivity.com/9-brain-foods-that-will-boost-your-ability-to-focus/

Barker, P. (1998). Creativity and psychic distress in artists, writers and scientists: Implications for emergent models of psychiatric nursing practice. *Journal of Psychiatric and Mental Health Nursing*, *5*(2), 109–117. doi:10.1046/j.1365-2850.1998.00103.x PMID:9661412

Bøgh, K. L., & Madsen, C. B. (2016). Food allergens: Is there a correlation between stability to digestion and allergenicity? *Critical Reviews in Food Science and Nutrition*, *56*(9), 1545–1567. doi:10.1080/10408398.2013.779569 PMID:25607526

Bogueva, D., Marinova, D., & Raphaely, T. (2017). (forthcoming). Red meat consumption and social marketing interventions promoting appetite for change. *International Journal of Food Engineering*, *3*(2).

Bogueva, D., & Phau, I. (2016). Meat myths and marketing. In T. Raphaely & D. Marinova (Eds.), *Impact of meat consumption on health and environmental sustainability* (pp. 264–276). Hershey, PA: IGI Global. doi:10.4018/978-1-4666-9553-5.ch015

Borreli, L. (2016, April 18). Mind wandering origins: Creative thinking is influenced by family genes, personality traits. *Medical Daily*. Retrieved from http://www.medicaldaily.com/creative-thinking-personality-traits-mind-wandering-family-genes-382323

Breyer, M. (2016, December 15). Eating this is linked to brain health and intelligence in older adults. *Tree Hugger*. Retrieved from https://www.treehugger.com/health/eating-linked-brain-health-and-intelligence-older-adults.html

Brown, L. (2009). *Plan B 4.0: Mobilizing to save civilization*. New York, NY: W.W. Norton & Company.

Bubolz, M. M., & Sontag, M. S. (1993). Human ecology theory. In P. G. Boss, W. J. Doherty, R. LaRossa, W. R. Schumm, & S. K. Steinmetz (Eds.), *Sourcebook of family theories and methods: A conceptual approach* (pp. 419–448). New York, NY: Plenum Press. doi:10.1007/978-0-387-85764-0_17

Calaprice, A. (2010). *The expanded quotable Einstein*. Retrieved from https://ivu.org/history/northam20a/einstein.html

Cox, P. (2002). *You don't need meat*. New York, NY: St. Martin's Press.

Despain, D. (2012, December 2). Why you can all stop saying meat eating fueled evolution of larger brains right now. *Evolving Health*. Retrieved from: http://evolvinghealthscience.blogspot.com.au/2012/12/why-you-can-all-stop-saying-meat-eating.html

Dietrich, A. (2014). The mythconception of the mad genius. *Frontiers in Psychology*, *5*, 79. doi:10.3389/fpsyg.2014.00079 PMID:24616710

Dunn, R. (2012). *Human ancestors were nearly all vegetarians*. Retrieved from https://blogs.scientificamerican.com/guest-blog/human-ancestors-were-nearly-all-vegetarians

Elephant Journal. (2011). The world's greatest geniuses are vegetarians! Retrieved from https://www.elephantjournal.com/2011/02/the-worlds-greatest-geniuses-are-vegetarians/

English Oxford Living Dictionaries. (2017). *Definition of genius in English: Genius.* Retrieved from https://en.oxforddictionaries.com/definition/genius

Eshel, G., Shepon, A., Makov, T., & Milo, R. (2014). Land, irrigation water, greenhouse gas, and reactive nitrogen burdens of meat, eggs, and dairy production in the United States. *Proceedings of the National Academy of Sciences of the United States of America, 111*(33), 11996–12001. doi:10.1073/pnas.1402183111 PMID:25049416

Falk, D., Lepore, F. E., & Noe, A. (2013). The cerebral cortex of Albert Einstein: A description and preliminary analysis of unpublished photographs. *Brain, 136*(4), 1304–1327. doi:10.1093/brain/aws295 PMID:23161163

FAOSTAT. (2003). *Global and regional food consumption patterns and trends.* Retrieved from http://www.fao.org/docrep/005/AC911e/ac911e05.htm

FAOSTAT. (2017). *Livestock primary.* Food and Agriculture Organization of the United Nations. Retrieved from http://www.fao.org/faostat/en/#data/QL

Florida News Group. (n.d.). *Eminent scientists and inventors on vegetarianism.* Vegetarian Era. Retrieved from http://www.godsdirectcontact.org/eng/news/160/vg5.htm

Franklin & Marshall College. (2008). *Franklin's favorite foods.* The Benjamin Franklin Tercentenary. Retrieved from http://www.benfranklin300.org/etc_article_foods.htm

Gelb, M. J. (2004). *How to think like Leonardo da Vinci: Seven steps to genius every day.* New York, NY: Bantam Dell.

Gómez-Pinilla, F. (2008). Brain foods: The effects of nutrients on brain function. *Nature Reviews. Neuroscience, 9*(7), 568–578. doi:10.1038/nrn2421 PMID:18568016

Grace Communications Foundation. (2017). *Waste management.* Retrieved from http://www.sustainabletable.org/906/waste-management

Gupta, S. (2016). Brain food: Clever eating. *Nature, 531*(7592), S12–S13. doi:10.1038/531S12a PMID:26934519

Hardy, K., Brand-Miller, J., Brown, K. D., Thomas, M. G., & Copeland, L. (2015). The importance of dietary carbohydrate in human evolution. *The Quarterly Review of Biology, 90*(3), 251–268. doi:10.1086/682587 PMID:26591850

Health & Fitness Advisory. (2013). Is red meat bad for your brain? Retrieved from http://www.fitnessadvisory.org/2013/09/04/is-red-meat-bad-for-your-brain/

Heilman, K. M. (2016). Possible brain mechanisms of creativity. *Archives of Clinical Neuropsychology, 31*(4), 285–296. doi:10.1093/arclin/acw009 PMID:27001974

Herculano-Houzel, S. (2012). The remarkable, yet not extraordinary, human brain as a scaled-up primate brain and its associated cost. *Proceedings of the National Academy of Sciences of the United States of America, 109*(Suppl. 1), 10661–10668. doi:10.1073/pnas.1201895109 PMID:22723358

Hirshon, B. (2017). *Big heads*. American Association for the Advancement of Science (AAAS). Retrieved from http://sciencenetlinks.com/science-news/science-updates/big-heads/

Intergovernmental Panel on Climate Change (IPCC). (2014). Climate change 2014: Synthesis report. Fifth Assessment Report. Retrieved from http://www.ipcc.ch/report/ar5/syr/

Ireland, C. (2008). Eating meat led to smaller stomachs, bigger brains. *Harvard Gazette*, 3 April. Retrieved from http://news.harvard.edu/gazette/story/2008/04/eating-meat-led-to-smaller-stomachs-bigger-brains/

Jauk, E., Neubauer, A. C., Dunst, B., Fink, A., & Benedek, M. (2015). Gray matter correlates of creative potential: A latent variable voxel-based morphometry study. *NeuroImage*, *1*(111), 312–320. doi:10.1016/j.neuroimage.2015.02.002 PMID:25676914

Joyce, C. (2010). Food for thought: Meat-based diet made us smarter (Special series: The human edge). *NPR*. Retrieved from http://www.npr.org/2010/08/02/128849908/food-for-thought-meat-based-diet-made-us-smarter

Kaye, L. (2014). Should we view meat as a luxury? *Triplepundit*. Retrieved from http://www.triplepundit.com/2014/10/meat-as-a-luxury/

Kearney, J. (2010). Food consumption trends and drivers. *Philosophical Transactions of the Royal Society of London. Series B, Biological Sciences*, *365*(1554), 2793–2807. doi:10.1098/rstb.2010.0149 PMID:20713385

Kéri, S. (2009). Genes for psychosis and creativity: A promoter polymorphism of the neuregulin 1 gene is related to creativity in people with high intellectual achievement. *Psychological Science*, *20*(9), 1070–1073. doi:10.1111/j.1467-9280.2009.02398.x PMID:19594860

Kluger, J. (2016). Sorry vegans: Here's how meat-eating made us human. *Time*. Retrieved from http://time.com/4252373/meat-eating-veganism-evolution/

Korn, C. (2014, October 16). How gut bacteria ensure a healthy brain – and could play a role in treating depression. *The Conversation*. Retrieved from https://theconversation.com/how-gut-bacteria-ensure-a-healthy-brain-and-could-play-a-role-in-treating-depression-33041

Leutgeb, V., Ille, R., Wabnegger, A., Schienle, A., Schöggl, H., Weber, B., & Fink, A. et al. (2016). Creativity and borderline personality disorder: Evidence from a voxel-based morphometry study. *Cognitive Neuropsychiatry*, *21*(3), 242–255. doi:10.1080/13546805.2016.1182904 PMID:27174566

Luca, F., Perry, G. H., & Di Rienzo, A. (2010). Evolutionary adaptations to dietary changes. *Annual Review of Nutrition*, *30*(1), 291–314. doi:10.1146/annurev-nutr-080508-141048 PMID:20420525

Maslin, M. A., Shultz, S., & Trauth, M. H. (2015). A synthesis of the theories and concepts of early human evolution. *Philosophical Transactions of the Royal Society of London. Series B, Biological Sciences*, *370*(1663), 20140064. doi:10.1098/rstb.2014.0064 PMID:25602068

Mayseless, N., Eran, A., & Shamay-Tsoory, S. G. (2015). Generating original ideas: The neural underpinning of originality. *NeuroImage*, *116*, 232–239. doi:10.1016/j.neuroimage.2015.05.030 PMID:26003860

Mayseless, N., Uzefovsky, F., Shalev, I., Ebstein, R. P., & Shamay-Tsoory, S. G. (2013). The association between creativity and 7R polymorphism in the dopamine receptor D4 gene (DRD4). *Frontiers in Human Neuroscience*, *7*, 502. doi:10.3389/fnhum.2013.00502 PMID:23986684

McMahon, D. M. (2013). *Divine fury: A history of genius*. New York, NY: Basic Books.

Melendez, S. (2010). *How to strengthen your brain*. Griffin, GA: Melendez Publishing International.

Messerli, F. H. (2012). Chocolate consumption, cognitive function, and Nobel laureate. *The New England Journal of Medicine*, *367*(16), 1562–1564. doi:10.1056/NEJMon1211064 PMID:23050509

Millner, J. (2015, September 23). The secret to man's intelligence? POTATOES: Humans evolved large brains because our ancestors ate starchy carbohydrates. *Daily Mail Australia*. Retrieved from http://www.dailymail.co.uk/sciencetech/article-3189454/The-secret-man-s-intelligence-POTATOES-Humans-evolved-large-brains-ancestors-ate-starchy-carbohydrates.html#ixzz4qTO6KgWA

Mouritsen, O. G. (2016). Deliciousness of food and a proper balance in fatty acid composition as means to improve human health and regulate food intake. *Flavour (London)*, *5*(1), 1. doi:10.1186/s13411-016-0048-2

National Museum of Natural History (NMNH). (2017). *Brains*. Retrieved from http://humanorigins.si.edu/human-characteristics/brains

Oikkonen, J., Kuusi, T., Peltonen, P., Raijas, P., Ukkola-Vuoti, L., Karma, K., & Järvelä, I. et al. (2016). Creative activities in music--a genome-wide linkage analysis. *PLoS One*, *11*(2), e0148679. doi:10.1371/journal.pone.0148679 PMID:26909693

Oregon State University (OSU). (2012). *Trophic issues*. Retrieved from http://people.oregonstate.edu/~muirp/trophic.htm

Pawankar, R. (2014). Allergic diseases and asthma: A global public health concern and a call to action. *The World Allergy Organization Journal*, *7*(1), 12. doi:10.1186/1939-4551-7-12 PMID:24940476

Pollack, H. (2015). Ordering your steak well-done can impact your brain health. *Munchies*, 9 April. Retrieved from https://munchies.vice.com/en_us/article/ypxbe5/ordering-your-steak-well-done-can-impact-your-brain-health

RAND Corporation. (2016). *The global economic costs of antimicrobial resistance*. Retrieved from https://www.rand.org/blog/2016/05/the-global-economic-costs-of-amr.html

Raphaely, T., & Marinova, D. (2014). Flexitarianism: A more moral dietary option. *International Journal of Sustainable Society*, *6*(1/2), 189–211. doi:10.1504/IJSSOC.2014.057846

Raphaely, T., & Marinova, D. (Eds.). (2016). *Impact of meat consumption on health and environmental sustainability*. Hershey, PA: IGI Global. doi:10.4018/978-1-4666-9553-5

Renner, M. (2015). Peak meat production strains land and water resources. Vital Signs: The trends that are shaping our future, 22. The Worldwatch Institute. Retrieved from http://www.worldwatch.org/peak-meat-production-strains-land-and-water-resources-1

Rettner, R. (2009). *Why are human brains so big?* Live Science. Retrieved from: https://www.livescience.com/5540-human-brains-big.html

Reuter, M., Roth, S., Holve, K., & Hennig, J. (2006). Identification of first candidate genes for creativity: A pilot study. *Brain Research, 1069*(1), 190–197. doi:10.1016/j.brainres.2005.11.046 PMID:16403463

Ridley, L. (2010). What's inside the brain of a genius? *BBC Science Focus Magazine*. Retrieved from http://www.sciencefocus.com/feature/tech/whats-inside-brain-genius

Schoenemann, P. T. (2006). Evolution of the size and functional areas of the human brain. *Annual Review of Anthropology, 35*(1), 379–406. doi:10.1146/annurev.anthro.35.081705.123210

Shamay-Tsoory, S. G., Adler, N., Aharon-Peretz, J., Perry, D., & Mayseless, N. (2011). The origins of originality: The neural bases of creative thinking and originality. *Neuropsychologia, 49*(2), 178–185. doi:10.1016/j.neuropsychologia.2010.11.020 PMID:21126528

Shi, B., Cao, X., Chen, Q., Zhuang, K., & Qiu, J. (2017). Different brain structures associated with artistic and scientific creativity: A voxel-based morphometry study. *Scientific Reports, 21*, 42911. doi:10.1038/srep42911 PMID:28220826

Sifferlin, A. (2012, May 21). Fat in red meat and butter may hurt your brain. *Time Magazine*. Retrieved from http://healthland.time.com/2012/05/21/fat-in-red-meat-and-butter-may-hurt-your-brain/?iid=hl-main-lede#ixzz1vWWNx67G

Smil, V. (2013). Should humans eat meat? [Excerpt]. *Scientific American*. Retrieved from https://www.scientificamerican.com/article/should-humans-eat-meat-excerpt/

Smithsonian. (2010). *Milestones in human evolution*. Newsdesk: Newsroom of the Smithsonian, Retrieved from http://newsdesk.si.edu/factsheets/milestones-human-evolution

Sun, J., Chen, Q., Zhang, Q., Li, Y., Li, H., Wei, D., & Qiu, J. et al. (2016). Training your brain to be more creative: Brain functional and structural changes induced by divergent thinking training. *Human Brain Mapping, 37*(10), 3375–3387. doi:10.1002/hbm.23246 PMID:27159407

Tekiner, İ. H., & Özpınar, H. (2016). Occurrence and characteristics of extended spectrum beta-lactamases-producing Enterobacteriaceae from foods of animal origin. *Brazilian Journal of Microbiology, 47*(2), 444–451. doi:10.1016/j.bjm.2015.11.034 PMID:26991276

Tesla, N. (1900, June). The problem of increasing human energy. *The Century Illustrated Monthly Magazine*. Retrieved from https://books.google.com.au/books?id=v-GZLL15Pb4C&printsec=frontcover&source=gbs_ge_summary_r&cad=0#v=onepage&q&f=false

The Phrase Finder. (2017). *The meaning and origin of the expression: Genius is one percent inspiration, ninety-nine percent perspiration*. Retrieved from https://www.phrases.org.uk/meanings/genius-is-one-percent-perspiration-ninety-nine-percent-perspiration.html

Tomley, F. M., & Shirley, M. W. (2009). Livestock infectious diseases and zoonoses. *Philosophical Transaction of the Royal Society B, 364*(1530), 2637–2642. doi:10.1098/rstb.2009.0133 PMID:19687034

Turner, S. (2012). What did Einstein, Gandhi & Benjamin Franklin all have in common? *Elephantjournal.com*. Retrieved from https://www.elephantjournal.com/2012/02/what-did-einstein-gandhi-benjamin-franklin-all-have-in-common/

United States Geological Survey (USGS). (2016). The water content of things: How much water does it take to grow a hamburger? Retrieved from https://water.usgs.gov/edu/activity-watercontent.php

Wegerer, J. (2014, January 2). Nutrition and dementia: Foods that may induce memory loss & increase Alzheimer's. *Alzheimers.net*. Retrieved from http://www.alzheimers.net/2014-01-02/foods-that-induce-memory-loss/

Weiner, E. (2016). *Gastronomy of genius: History's great minds and the foods that fueled them*. NPR. Retrieved from http://www.npr.org/sections/thesalt/2016/03/11/469543237/the-gastronomy-of-genius-food-and-drink-that-inspired-great-minds

Wolchover, N. (2012). Will people really be forced to stop eating meat? *Livescience.com*. Retrieved from http://www.livescience.com/22814-meat-eating-vegetarianism.html

World Health Organization & Foodborne Disease Burden Epidemiology Reference Group (WHO/FDBERG). (2015). *WHO estimates of the global burden of foodborne diseases: Foodborne disease burden epidemiology reference group 2007-2015*. Retrieved from http://apps.who.int/iris/bitstream/10665/199350/1/9789241565165_eng.pdf?ua=1

World Health Organization (WHO). (2016). *Antimicrobial resistance*. Retrieved from http://www.who.int/mediacentre/factsheets/fs194/en

Wrots, C. (2016). What do geniuses eat? Here's Nikola Tesla's diet. *Onedio*. Retrieved from https://onedio.co/content/heres-genius-inventor-nikola-teslas-nutrition-diet-11938

Wu, G. (2016). Dietary protein intake and human health. *Food & Function, 7*(3), 1251–1265. doi:10.1039/C5FO01530H PMID:26797090

Zabelina, D. L., Colzato, L., Beeman, M., & Hommel, B. (2016). Dopamine and the creative mind: Individual differences in creativity are predicted by interactions between dopamine genes DAT and COMT. *PLoS One, 11*(1), e0146768. doi:10.1371/journal.pone.0146768 PMID:26783754

Zhang, L., Qiao, L., Chen, Q., Yang, W., Xu, M., & Yao, X. (1532). … Yang, D. (2016). Gray matter volume of the lingual gyrus mediates the relationship between inhibition function and divergent thinking. *Frontiers in Psychology, 7*. doi:10.3389/fpsyg.2016.01532

Zink, K. D., & Lieberman, D. E. (2016). Impact of meat and Lower Palaeolithic food processing techniques on chewing in humans. *Nature, 531*(7595), 500–503. doi:10.1038/nature16990 PMID:26958832

KEY TERMS AND DEFINITIONS

Animal Protein: Protein present in animal tissues.

Brain: An organ inside the skull which controls thought, memory, feelings and activity.

Creativity: Tendency to generate or recognize ideas, alternatives or possibilities that may be useful in solving problems, communicating with others, and entertaining others and ourselves.

Genius: A person with exceptional intellectual or creative power or other natural ability.

Health: A person's mental or physical condition; also, the state of being free from illness or injury.

Nutrition: The process of providing or obtaining the food necessary for health and growth.

Vegetarian: A person who does not eat meat, fish and other animal products, especially for moral, religious, environmental or health reasons.

ENDNOTES

1 Quote cited from https://www.goodreads.com/author/quotes/40589.Ludwig_van_Beethoven
2 Quotes cited from https://veganrabbit.com/quotes-about-veganism-activism-and-animal-rights/
3 Quote cited from https://www.brainyquote.com/authors/honore_de_balzac
4 Quote cited from https://ivu.org/history/europe19b/mahler.html
5 Quote cited from https://ivu.org/people/quotes/freedom.html
6 Quote cited from https://thefriendlyfig.com/2015/02/19/inspirational-vegan-quotes/
7 Quote cited from https://www.brainyquote.com/authors/pablo_picasso
8 Quote cited from https://www.brainyquote.com/quotes/quotes/a/alberteins122243.html
9 Quote cited from https://veganrabbit.com/quotes-about-veganism-activism-and-animal-rights/
10 Quote cited from https://phys.org/news/2005-07-global-vegetarian.html

Section 3
Case Studies in Social Marketing

Chapter 14
The Social Marketing Campaign by Greenpeace Mediterranean Against Broiler Chicken Consumption

B. Pınar Özdemir
Ankara University, Turkey

ABSTRACT

Turkey's first encounter with social marketing began in the 1960s from which time the field has been dominated by public institutions, although during the 1990s non-governmental organisations started running some social marketing campaigns. This chapter analyses Turkey's first campaign concerning animal products for human consumption called "We Don't Swallow!" which was undertaken by an environmental non-governmental organisation (NGO) called Greenpeace Mediterranean. The campaign is analysed in terms of the basic concepts of social marketing (problem definition, objectives, exchange, competition, audience segmentation and marketing mix). An attempt is made to establish an understanding of how a NGO sought to affect its target audience's behaviour in relation to the origin of the meat they consumed. The chapter considers how "brand attack" works as a social marketing strategy and explores the possibilities that new communication technologies offer for social marketing.

INTRODUCTION

This chapter is about Greenpeace Mediterranean's "We Don't Swallow!" campaign which started in May 2016 and was the first social marketing campaign to be carried out in Turkey about the origin of animal products for human consumption. It differs from other social marketing campaigns in that country in its use of a "brand attack" strategy which centres on encouraging the target audience to stop consuming specific brands of chicken that are intensively raised by the broiler industry. The study focuses on the campaign's problems, objectives, exchange promises, competition circumstances, audience segmentation and marketing mix following a general overview of broiler chicken production and consumption in Turkey.

DOI: 10.4018/978-1-5225-4757-0.ch014

The broiler industry is of significant importance to the Turkish economy. As of 2014 the revenue from the broiler industry was US$4.5 billion with domestic poultry production, consumption and especially export having witnessed an increase compared to previous years (Duyum, 2016). With chicken and egg production totaling 1.9 million and 16.5 billion tonnes respectively, Turkey is the largest producer of poultry meat and the third largest egg producer in Europe (Aksoy, 2014). Poultry production has increased considerably due to contracted-out farming and the establishment of large-scale integrated facilities initiated in the late 1980s (Sariozkan et al., 2009). In Turkey, the production and consumption of poultry are mostly based on chicken which constitutes the major part of the meat diet. In 2014 meat consumption per capita was 35 kilograms per year of which only 13 kilograms was red meat. According to the 2015 data from the Turkish Statistical Institute (TUİK), more than one billion chickens were slaughtered in Turkey, meaning that every 35 seconds a chicken was killed, a number that had multiplied five times since 1995 (Sik, 2016). While chicken consumption in Turkey was close to the world average between 1980 and 2010, it rose to above average after 2010, something which a sector report published by the Turkish Ministry of Food, Agriculture and Livestock correlated to the rise in the price of red meat. As the report explains: "The shortfall in protein emerged in Turkey due to the high production costs of red meat and the economic crises which consumers have tried to balance by the consumption of chicken and turkey meat" (TEPGE, 2014, p. 14).

Debates about industrial agriculture and industrial livestock emerged in Turkey in the 2000s as the increase in livestock production became apparent. In 2004 the famous sports commentator, Erman Toroglu, stated during a media interview that he did not consume chicken meat because he believed "all chickens are fed on artificial grains and antibiotics" (Pamir, 2004). This interview triggered a wide-scale public debate that has continued to take place every so often in Turkey despite the regular and systematic public relations efforts of the broiler chicken producers. The main axis of this debate centres on food safety with reference to the use of hormones, antibiotics and genetically modified grains and oilseeds in broiler chicken production, a concern that has also created a foundation for organic chicken production and consumption. Research conducted in 2015 concluded that the majority of Turkish consumers were aware of the term genetically modified organisms (GMO) and had some fears about genetically modified food (GMF) believing that they were carcinogenic to humans. They also expressed concern about the increasing risk that natural foods might be disappearing (Tas et al., 2015). However, Turkey's domestic consumption of organic products is still at a very early stage and demand for them is mostly concentrated in metropolitan areas such as İstanbul and Ankara with the main motivation for their consumption being health and environmental benefits (Ergin & Sacmaci, 2011).

BACKGROUND

Social marketing can be defined as the use of marketing principles and techniques for social change. In their ground-breaking article Kotler and Zaltman (1971, p.5) stated that "social marketing is the design, implementation, and control of programs calculated to influence the acceptability of social ideas and involving considerations of product planning, pricing, communication, distribution and marketing research". Social marketing came into being when it was realised that it is not enough just to provide information to change people's minds (Maio et al., 2007). The emphasis on behavioural change is important in social marketing and is focused on a number of areas: changing an individual's undesirable behaviours; changing the products used by the public that impact on health and wellbeing; making changes in areas where people live, work and play so as to reduce damage and support wellbeing; and changes in the political structures that protect equality of access and opportunity in society (Donovan & Henley, 2010, p. 17). Manoff (1985) states that in developing countries like Turkey social marketing may also involve the introduction of new products (e.g. oral rehydration salts), the modification of existing ones (e.g. iodized salt) and the promotion of structural change in existing institutions (e.g. food stamps, hospital practices) as well as behavioural change. During the last seventy years, various types of social marketing have been used all over the world to promote traffic safety, tobacco control, drug prevention, childhood immunizations, improved nutrition and diet, environmentally friendly behaviour as well as the reduction in infant mortality (Smith, 2006).

Social marketing in Turkey started to be employed in the 1960s around the issue of birth control as was the case in many other developing countries. The main users of social marketing became public institutions, especially the Ministry of Health, whose main goal was to improve public health. More recent social marketing campaigns have focused on hand washing, anti-obesity and tobacco control. Whilst social marketing campaigns carried out by NGOs are not as common, since in Turkey these organisations are still in their infancy compared to developed countries, the number of NGOs has increased progressively throughout the 2000s along with their reach and the issues they focus on (Keyman, 2006). These largely centre around issues of social solidarity and services and much less rarely on policy change and advocacy issues. More than 18% of the associations in Turkey are made up of mosque societies that aim to improve religious services, 14.3% are sports clubs, 13.7% are benevolent societies, 9.5% are development and housing associations and 10% are professional solidarity organisations (TÜSEV, 2011). Only a very few NGOs engage in advocacy activities that focus on issues such as women's rights, environmental problems, human rights, consumer rights, and student and youth issues (TÜSEV, 2011).

GREENPEACE MEDITERRANEAN'S "WE DON'T SWALLOW!" CAMPAIGN

In a country like Turkey where advocacy movements are not that common, Greenpeace Mediterranean is one of the leading and best known environmental NGOs. Greenpeace Mediterranean has been an active and reasonably successful NGO since 1992 in Turkey and on its website, describes its areas of work as concerns with climate change, forests, oceans, agriculture, toxic pollution and nuclear power (Greenpeace Mediterranean, 2017a). Its successful campaigns include the 2011 "How Many Centimetres is Yours?" which sought to change the size of fish that can be legally caught signed by about 750,000 people and the 2012 "We Won't Eat It!" campaign to get well-known companies to withdraw their proposals for GMO imports into Turkey with the active participation of 326,591 people (Greenpeace Mediterranean, 2017b).

The subject of this current study analysed using the basic concepts of social marketing (problem definition, objectives, exchange, competition, audience segmentation and marketing mix) is the "We Don't Swallow It!" campaign started by Greenpeace Mediterranean in 2016 in Turkey which focuses on the broiler chicken industry. It can be clearly designated as a social marketing campaign within the framework proposed by the prominent social marketing researcher Alan Andreasen (2002) and complying with his six social marketing benchmark criteria: (i) the campaign aims for an attitude change; (ii) it is based on formative research; (iii) it uses segmentation/targeting/tailoring to select a group and during the design of the intervention; (iv) the design focuses on the creation of attractive and motivational exchanges with the target audience; (v) a traditional marketing mix is used instead of just advertising or communications; and (vi) it pays due regard to the competition that the desired behaviour faces and strategies are employed to minimize this competition.

Problem Definition

In May 2016, Greenpeace Mediterranean held a press conference to announce the focus of its new social marketing campaign by presenting the report "Consuming the World: Livestock Industry with a Focus on Poultry Farming". This report explains why chicken must be regarded as an industrial product and outlines the three main problems created by broiler chicken production: (i) climate crisis; (ii) deforestation and loss of biodiversity; and (iii) food safety. The report suggests that the vast increase in poultry production and consumption that Turkey had witnessed over the last 10 years could not have been achieved through a sustainable production model that allows for both the wellbeing of people and animals (Sik, 2016).

According to the report, animal abuse along with threats to people's health and the environment is what lies beneath Turkey's high chicken production and consumption figures and that the most important issue the broiler industry faces is its contribution to climate change as a result of the production of methane and nitrous oxide gases. These are greenhouse gasses that negatively affect the energy balance in the earth's atmosphere by trapping heat which may result in atmospheric warming (Dunkley, 2014). In addition, the broiler industry also leads to deforestation and damage to meadows and grasslands as industrial-scale breeding requires industrial-scale forage production, and to meet this need rainforests are exploited and turned into fields to plant chicken feed like soy and corn. The campaign itself focused specifically on another aspect of broiler production – the threat to food safety, which according to the NGO's analysis can be classified under three categories. First is the microbiological risk as broiler chicken production creates a suitable environment for the growth of many harmful organisms and the possibility of contamination. The second is the chemical risk arising from antibiotic residues in the industry's various products and as the report points out while there are 15,000 poultry houses in Turkey there is no data on how antibiotic-based compounds are used in the broiler industry. Third is the waste created by the industry which results in water pollution. There is no independent establishment to regularly check the broiler industry in Turkey in accordance with the quality criteria set by the Ministry of Environment and Urbanization (Sik, 2016).

Objectives

Kotler and Lee (2008) outline three types of objectives in a social marketing campaign: behavioural, informational and belief. Compared to other campaigns such as health improvement, tobacco control or injury prevention, the objective of the Greenpeace Mediterranean's social marketing campaign was rather more complicated since it asked consumers to reduce their consumption of broiler chickens not only because of the possible effect that their intake has on human health but also by highlighting the adverse effects that the industry has on animal welfare and the environment. Its aim was to produce change in the broiler industry so as to create less harm to animals and the environment as well as human health by reducing the consumption of broiler chickens. Thus in terms of the three objectives it can be said that: the behavioural objective of the "We Don't Swallow!" campaign was to get the target audience to cease broiler chicken consumption and instead buy organically raised products; while the informational objective was to let the target audience know that the broiler industry is harmful to both the environment and human health as well as animals; and the belief objective was to get the target audience to believe that the broiler industry can change its methods through consumer power.

If successful, the designated behavioural objective of the Greenpeace Mediterranean campaign would have a high impact potential since if the target audience aggregately avoided broiler chicken consumption then the industry would feel under pressure to improve its practices. In this sense the means of achieving the behavioural objective was easily outlined as it required a simple, clear and well-defined act from their target audience: do not consume broiler chicken; if you want to eat chicken then eat organic ones (Dinç, 2017). Equally, the actual achievement of the behavioural objective could be easily gauged by measuring the amount of increase in organic chicken sales and the decrease in industrial chicken purchases.

Informational objectives are those relating to statistics, facts and other information that the target audience might find persuasive. In the case of the Greenpeace Mediterranean campaign, most of this information was conveyed to its target audience in an engaging way by the use of various examples, images and animations; for example: "While a 36-week old chick was 300 g in 1936, it is now 2.5 kilos" and "The living space of a broiler chicken is smaller than A4 paper". Finally with regard to the campaign's belief objectives, Greenpeace Mediterranean clearly outlined a number of ways by which the target audience could support the campaign, such as reducing the consumption of animal protein, avoiding industrial chicken and meat producers, preferring products raised in more natural and sustainable environments, getting parents to put pressure on school managers to provide organic products in school canteens and cafeterias, getting employees to pressure their employer to provide organic products in workplace dining halls and cafeterias, avoiding places that served broiler chicken while eating outside of the home, and establishing a community agriculture group or consumer cooperative or participating in an existing one (Dinç, 2017).

Exchange

According to Kotler (1972), the core concept of marketing is the transaction, that is an exchange of values between two parties, where the consumer needs to be offered something beneficial to incentivise change in their behaviour. As Smith (2000, p. 13) points out, "the central problem of any social marketing program is to establish what exchange is likely to satisfy both the marketer's (public health, education, environmental) needs and enough consumers' wants to produce a societal benefit". In terms of Exchange Theory, it means that if the social marketer can "demonstrate that the perceived benefits...outweigh the perceived costs of its purchase, voluntary adoption by the consumer is most likely" (Maibach, 1993 in Hastings & Saren, 2003, p. 30). In the case of the Greenpeace Mediterranean's campaign this exchange could be defined in the following way: given that broiler chicken consumption is harmful to the environment, human health and animal welfare, in exchange for your support for this campaign, both your health will improve and you will do something good for the environment and animal welfare. Thus, both the needs of Greenpeace Mediterranean – to change the nature of chicken production, and the needs of the consumer – healthier eating, saving the environment, could be met.

Competition

Social marketers must be aware of the competition (Andreasen, 1995) since they are dealing with voluntary behaviour and the fact that their customers always have a choice. Customers, therefore, have buyer power and that means competition is inevitable (Hastings, 2003). The analysis for the "We Don't Swallow!"

campaign showed that the competition in the field was fierce. First of all, there was serious competing behaviour in favour of broiler chicken consumption. Broiler chicken meat is both easily accessible and easy to cook as well as being a popular food in Turkey. People's consumption choices are likely to be affected by those they spend time with and if their friends and family consume broiler chicken then it makes them more likely to resist calls to move away from consuming this product.

However, the fiercest opponents of the campaign, and hence important competitors influencing consumer behaviour and attitudes, came from the poultry industry itself. The industrial poultry producers had encouraged consumer demand through competitive behaviour amongst themselves with regard to development, branding and promotion, while the Association for Industrial Poultry Producers (the BESD-BİR) had directly countered negative messages regarding the broiler industry. The Association has developed good relations with the Ministry of Food, Agriculture and Livestock and was occasionally invited to take part in commissions working on poultry production undertaken by the Ministry. Furthermore, the Association works with a professional public relations firm and social media agency. They define any negative views about broiler chicken production as "information pollution" and one of their main goals has been to deal with this "pollution" (BESD-BİR, 2015).

The BESD-BİR places great importance on media relationships and encourages reporters to check their website or directly visit the Association before reporting any news item about the industry. People and institutions that wish to see the production facilities are given tours organised by the Association along with a presentation about the industry with the opportunity to ask questions. To achieve media visibility, the Association arranges interviews for its advisory board members with various media channels and in 2015 it placed 120 advertisements covering ten distinctive messages in twenty different newspapers. The main message of these adverts was that broiler chicken production in Turkey is no different from Europe's and that people can safely consume these products (BESD-BİR, 2015).

Another competitor is the "Healthy Chicken Information Platform" made up of the companies which between themselves produce 85% of the chicken meat in Turkey: Banvit, Şenpiliç, Erpiliç, Lezita, Keskinoğlu, Gedik and CP (Sağlıklı Tavuk Bilgi Platformu, 2016). One of the founding aims of the platform as stated on their website is "correcting wrong perceptions of the public regarding the industry caused by claims with no scientific basis, helping professionals convey true and reliable information to the consumers to prevent information pollution" (Sağlıklı Tavuk Bilgi Platformu, 2016). There is also information about broiler chicken production, articles on the correlation between white meat and a healthy lifestyle, recipes featuring chicken, as well as published articles and reports.

Audience Segmentation

It is vital for a social marketer to know the values of the target audience if they want their efforts to succeed. The rationale is that by subdividing a large heterogeneous audience into smaller more homogeneous groups social marketers can make better decisions as to which group or groups to target (Maibach et al., 1996; Forthofer & Bryant, 2000).

Greenpeace Mediterranean conducted research before determining its target audience and benefited from establishing some segmenting criteria. While its Campaign Manager, Nejat Tarık Dinç, did not directly share the results of this research, he did outline what was taken into consideration while segmenting the audience (Dinç, 2017). The primary target audience was attitudinally segmented in terms of attitudes toward broiler chicken consumption. If an audience's existing values, beliefs and preferences are opposed to the overarching goal of a campaign, then these place important limits in reaching this section of the audience (Corner & Randall, 2011). Changing already existing negative attitudes towards a product or issue is always easier than changing neutral or positive ones and, on this basis, Greenpeace Mediterranean prioritized consumers who already had some worries about consuming broiler chicken. Demographic criteria were also used to segment the target audience as younger and well-educated people in cities make up Greenpeace Mediterranean's primary target audience. In any social marketing campaign, motives and likely benefits also have to be considered in determining the target audience and in the case of the "We Don't Swallow!" campaign these centred around issues of health. The campaign promised a significant benefit in giving up eating broiler chicken to people who cared about their health. With the message that if you avoid eating broiler chicken you will contribute to your health, the campaign specifically targeted people who cared about their health and wished to maintain a healthy diet, especially parents responsible for their children's diet. When it came to psychological segmentation which involves dividing the target audience according to their values, attitudes, personality characteristics, interests and lifestyles, Greenpeace Mediterranean took into account the transformation that had taken place in urbanised, and especially upper-class, consumer lifestyles in Turkey from the 2000s onwards. Now, being healthy and fit, taking care of oneself, and being concerned about certain social causes are far more "trendy" than in previous periods and this became one of the criteria that the campaign considered when segmenting the target audience (Dinç, 2017).

Marketing Mix

Product

The first P of marketing is product which traditionally has been perceived as something tangible but in social marketing the concept of product is extended beyond the tangible to include ideas and behaviour change (MacFadyen et al., 1999). Three stages must be taken into consideration when developing a product in social marketing: core product, actual product and augmented product. Kotler and Lee (2008) explain that the core product is the benefit the audience wants and expects in exchange for performing the desired action. In the case of the "We Don't Swallow!" campaign the Greenpeace Mediterranean team asked the question "what potential benefits should we stress?" and after reviewing the benefits that would arise from the desired change in behaviour were able to define the core product (benefit) as "better health, better environment and better animal welfare" (Dinç, 2017). The second stage according to Kotler and Lee (2008) is the actual product which is defined in terms of the specific behaviour that will influence the target audience to "buy" or in the case of the "We Don't Swallow!" campaign "not buy" broiler chicken meat. Finally, Kotler and Lee (2008) define the augmented product as the additional product elements sustaining behavioural change which in the case of the campaign was the information that told the target audience about the harm caused by the broiler chicken industry to human health, the environment and animal welfare.

The product that the campaign was promoting was fairly complex when compared to the product of many other social marketing campaigns. While there are several economic benefits arising from the broiler industry, there are also many negative outcomes and the target audience, therefore, was expected to access and understand complicated information about a wide range of issues related to broiler chicken production, including antibiotic use in chickens, genetically modified organisms and climate change. Greenpeace Mediterranean used memorable statistics and simplifying visuals to overcome this potential problem. The campaign's product was not only complex but also controversial. Industrialisation of livestock production, especially white meat production, is a contentious issue. There is a substantial audience in Turkey who thinks that the campaign regarding broiler chicken consumption was a blow to one of Turkey's growing industries, one that is of economic benefit to the country. Compared to this perceived benefit, Greenpeace Mediterranean's "product" offered a relatively weak personal benefit and in addition the individual may well believe that their actions will have little impact on broiler chicken sales or that the industry will react to reduced sales by lowering prices to lure back customers. To overcome this problem, Greenpeace Mediterranean emphasised the concept of synergy and reminded the target audience that by working together they could produce an effect greater than the sum of their individual efforts. Successes in previous campaigns were proof of this.

Price

The second P of marketing is price which refers to the cost exchanged for the promised benefits. Social marketing has taken the idea of price beyond monetary value to include psychological, social, geographic and other rewards and costs that arise from engaging in particular behaviours (Lefebvre & Flora, 1988). Also, as Weinstein (1988) points out, costs in social marketing are generally short-term and certain while benefits are long-term and less certain resulting in a target audience less willing to pay the cost. An evaluation in terms of the price of Greenpeace Mediterranean's social marketing campaign presented consumers with both monetary and non-monetary costs. The campaign asked the target audience who wanted to eat chicken to stop consuming cheap broiler meat and buy much more expensive organic products, a change in their usual buying habits. However, even if the target audience were to accept this monetary cost, they would still have additional non-monetary costs because organic goods are not that common in Turkey, unlike in many industrialised countries, and therefore people would have to devote extra time and effort to find them.

One of the things that had to be considered in relation to the psychological price of the campaign was the possible suspicion among consumers whether the messages about using organic instead of industrial products were true or not. Consumers might ask whether industrial poultry is truly bad or is this something concocted by organic chicken producers to scare people and sell more of their products. Another psychological price that was especially applicable to women arose from the fact that the duties of shopping for food and keeping a balanced budget primarily falls upon them. However, this was not necessarily an unbearable cost for all women as researchers have shown that many consumers are willing to pay more in Turkey for goods certified as organic instead of their conventional alternatives (Akgungor et al., 2010; Gunduz & Bayramoğlu, 2011).

Place

Place in social marketing is "where and when the target market will perform the desired behaviour, acquire any related tangible object and receive any associated services" (Kotler & Lee, 2008, p. 247). Even though Greenpeace was not offering a tangible physical product it still had a product that it needed to convey (the campaign message) and for reasons that will be discussed in the next section chose social media and social networking sites as the best channels of distribution to "move" the product from the producer to the consumer.

Promotion

In many ways promotion is the most visible and most important P in social marketing. Promotion is concerned with communications that are designed and delivered to inspire the target audience to action (Kotler & Lee, 2008, p. 268). Greenpeace's promotional message was clear: don't consume broiler chicken meat but eat organic products instead. After determining the key message, Greenpeace selected a number of key facts and information to emphasise in their promotion. As mentioned above, the main motivation of Greenpeace during the planning of the campaign was the broiler industry's adverse effects on climate change. However, as the Campaign Manager Nejat Dinç explained, the research conducted with the target audience suggested that Turkish consumers were unlikely to reduce their broiler chicken consumption because of concerns about this issue. For this reason, the consequences of the intensive farming methods used to raise broiler chicken which required the application of antibiotics and the poor conditions in which the chickens were raised were highlighted in the campaign in terms of their effects on human health and animal welfare (Dinç, 2017). The campaign, therefore, needed to communicate to the public a belief that broiler chicken meat is harmful to humans, the environment and the chickens themselves and as a result persuade consumers to turn to organic products instead of broiler chickens.

The campaign had a simple, original, and catchy title: Yutmayız! The idiom is a homophone borrowed from Turkish slang and literally means "We don't swallow it!". However, it can also mean "We don't believe it!" and therefore in a semiological sense it suggested that broiler chicken meat should not be consumed, while at the same time voicing the worries and suspicions surrounding broiler production. Drawing on this, Greenpeace Mediterranean, which as a NGO is very aware of the power of visual imagery, adopted the image of a half antibiotic pill/half chicken to support the slogan of the campaign (see Figure 1).

In 2012 Greenpeace Mediterranean had run a very successful "We Don't Eat It" campaign about genetically engineered food for which they had used a "brand attack" strategy (Ozdemir, 2012). Given its success they decided to follow a similar path for the current campaign by targeting Turkey's biggest broiler chicken producers. However, this time Greenpeace Mediterranean was forced to design its own social marketing campaign and run its own online promotion phase because the public relations, adver-

Figure 1. "We Don't Swallow!" campaign logo

tising and media agencies which had collaborated with Greenpeace Mediterranean during its previous campaigns did not want to work for them this time, largely for fear of damaging their existing relationships with the broiler industry. This challenge led Greenpeace Mediterranean to concentrate its efforts on the power of social media as had been done in the earlier 2012 "We Don't Eat It" campaign.

Boyd and Ellison (in Ozdemir, 2012) define social networking sites as the latest online communication tool that allows users to create a public or semi-public profile and to create and view their own as well as other users' online social networks. According to Dinç (2017), Greenpeace Mediterranean identified Facebook and Twitter, which are the most popular networking sites in Turkey, as the main domains of the campaign. There are 46.28 million active internet users in Turkey (Kemp, 2016) and, according to 2015 statistics, 39 million have Facebook accounts (Business HT, 2015), while according to the latest available statistics, 9.6 million people in Turkey are active on Twitter (Koca, 2013) which is a micro blogging service that enables people to share short textual messages or tweets with other participants. Greenpeace Mediterranean at the time of writing had 1.6 million followers on Facebook and 465,000 followers on Twitter.

Greenpeace Mediterranean first created a micro website (yutmayiz.org) to secure the campaign's promotion process. The opening page of the website (which is banned at the time of writing) had a 1 minute and 45 seconds long animation about antibiotic use in the broiler industry and the poor living conditions of the animals. It also contained the following text:

The dinner table is the most important meeting place where we gather with our friends and family. The broiler industry wants to conquer this seat of honour; however it does not deserve this place. By thinking only about the profit it will gain from our table, it harms our health and the environment, and it abuses the animals. As long as they are not produced in a healthy and environmentally friendly way we do not invite them to our table. We do not swallow!—neither their excuses nor their products. (Dinç, 2017).

The website also called on the target audience to sign a petition against broiler chicken producers.

Considering that in their everyday life individuals encounter many messages through their use of social media, it is crucial in any social marketing campaign to attract and engage people's attention. For its new campaign, Greenpeace had a relatively powerful position in this regard because it already had a massive cyber activist following (Ozdemir, 2012) and throughout the campaigning process news, articles and links posted on the yutmayız.org website was shared on Facebook. Greenpeace also directed users to the site under the Yutmayız! and Yutmadıksoruyoruz hash tags on Twitter and extended the impact through tweets that were accumulated in the Yutmayız! hash tag pool. Another promotional tool used by Greenpeace Mediterranean was its mailing lists with its e-mail list having over 800,000 subscribers (Dinç, 2017). On 25 May 2016, during the first month of the campaign, e-mails were sent with the title "You should watch this animation" with a link to the video on the micro website; and in subsequent emails during the following weeks Greenpeace invited consumers not to eat broiler chicken meat. Each e-mail also had a link to the petition.

Soon after the campaign began, the major companies responsible for the production of broiler chicken, Banvit, Beypiliç, Keskinoğlu and Şenpiliç, went to court requesting that Greenpeace Mediterranean shut down yutmayiz.org. The case was successful and access to the website was prohibited in May 2016. As a result, Greenpeace Mediterranean opened another website, yutmayiz2.co. but one of the largest broiler chicken producers in Turkey and among those targeted by the website, Keskinoğlu Poultry, sued Greenpeace claiming that its registered brand and logo were being used by the campaign without authorisation and that Greenpeace's accusations were inaccurate and damaging to their commercial activities as well as harming the reputation of its brand and products (Ocak, 2017). This case hardened Greenpeace's promotion strategy and they changed the campaign's title to "The Egg Has Knocked on the Door" (a Turkish idiom meaning it is now the eleventh hour and the time to act is just about to run out). The new communication strategy asked consumers to directly question the broiler chicken producers on a number of different issues rather than simply asking people to cease broiler chicken consumption:

We were all preoccupied with the broiler industry's procedures that threaten health and the environment. That is why "We Don't Swallow!" was created and why we have demanded along with tens of thousands of people transparency from the poultry industry and its positive transformation. While we expected an answer from brands, instead we received warnings and then our website was blocked. Not long after we heard the news that changed the entire course of our campaign: Keskinoğlu sued Greenpeace. By suing us, Keskinoğlu took on everyone who wanted to sit at their dinner table in peace. We await clear answers from 8 different brands to our crucial questions. All of these brands are members of the "Healthy Chicken Platform". We expect a promise from these 8 companies and before them from all the poultry industry to transform any procedures that threaten the environment and human life. Then we can comfortably sit at the dinner table together (Greenpeace Mediterranean, 2017c).

Greenpeace made it easy for consumers to send questions to the eight broiler chicken producers concerning antibiotics, GMOs, pesticides, waste and animal welfare. For example, by clicking on the "animal rights" button, the e-mail below would be sent using the person's own e-mail address to the producer that they had chosen:

Dear Authorised Person at X,

What is the physical size of each coop used by subcontractor farmers? How many chicks are contained in in [sic] these coops over recent years? What is the average number of chicken [sic] per coop during the last three years? (Greenpeace Mediterranean, 2017c).

By pressing the "antibiotics" button the following message would be sent:

Dear Authorised Person at X,

What amount [sic] prophylactic drugs (some of which are antibiotics) named below have been used in the last 5 years?

In this way, Greenpeace encouraged the target audience to not only quit using their products but also to directly put pressure on the producers. At the time of writing in August 2017, 10,667 e-mails have been sent to broiler companies from the target audience (Greenpeace Mediterranean, 2017c).

CONCLUSION

Social marketing campaigns in Turkey are generally carried out by public institutions and usually focus on health issues like obesity. However, Greenpeace Mediterranean has for the first time in Turkey created a campaign about a different aspect of nutrition and has encouraged people to think about the consequences of their dietary choices for the environment and animal welfare rather than just their health. Greenpeace Mediterranean chose to undertake a risky campaign about a product that is complex, where the price is high and promotion hard but still managed to find a place in the hectic agenda of Turkey in 2016 at a time when there has been an attempted coup and a debate about a change in the presidential system. Given the context, the campaign's strategy was quite daring particularly as social marketing in Turkey has not as a whole directly targeted those institutions which some see as responsible for encouraging unhealthy eating habits. Yet Greenpeace Mediterranean decided to adopt a "brand attack" strategy, especially in the promotional stage of its campaign, that sought to get consumers to think critically about the activities and claims made by the producers of broiler chickens, diminishing the public's trust in them and denting the industry's prestige.

Unlike non-governmental organizations, the government's social media campaigns do not suffer greatly from a lack of visibility since current laws require government social marketing messages to be aired on TV for free and thanks to their large budgets, campaign messages also find a place in newspapers, magazines and billboards. It is much harder for NGOs to get their campaign messages into circulation. For this reason, Greenpeace Mediterranean's "We Don't Swallow!" campaign is important as it demonstrates that a social media campaign can be successfully undertaken without the use of conventional media. It also shows how with the help of new communication technologies, NGOs can create effective social media campaigns with low budgets and use their supporters as campaign multipliers.

The "We Don't Swallow!" campaign has now been running for a year and given its complex task of transforming consumer habits it is too short a time to judge how successful the campaign has or will be. However, the broiler chicken industry's reaction to it and the continuing level of support given to it by Greenpeace and its members surely show that the campaign is on the right track.

REFERENCES

Akgungor, S., Miran, B., & Abay, C. (2010). Consumer willingness to pay for organic food in urban Turkey. *Journal of International Food & Agribusiness Marketing*, *22*(3-4), 299–313. doi:10.1080/08974431003641455

Aksoy, T. (2014). Turkish organic poultry sector: General evaluation and lessons from successful practices. *Paper presented at the Practitioners' Track, IFOAM Organic World Congress 2014, 'Building Organic Bridges.'* Retrieved from http://orgprints.org/24161/

Andreasen, A. R. (1995). *Marketing social change: Changing behaviour to promote health, social development, and the environment.* San Francisco, CA: Jossey-Bass.

Andreasen, A. R. (2002). Marketing social marketing in the social change marketplace. *Journal of Public Policy & Marketing*, *21*(1), 3–13. doi:10.1509/jppm.21.1.3.17602

Beyaz Et Sanayıcılerı ve Damızlıkçıları Bırlığı Derneğı (BESD-BİR). (2015). *Olağan genel kurul toplantısı sunumu* [Presentation of 17th Ordinary General Assembly Meeting] Retrieved from http://www.besd-bir.org/assets/documents/SaitKocaGKSUNUMU.pdf

Business, H. T. (2015). Kaç kişi Facebook'ta? [How many people are on Facebook?]. Retrieved from http://www.businessht.com.tr/teknoloji/haber/1123980-kac-kisi-facebookta

Corner, A., & Randall, A. (2011). Selling climate change? The limitations of social marketing as a strategy for climate change public engagement. *Global Environmental Change*, *21*(3), 1005–1014. doi:10.1016/j.gloenvcha.2011.05.002

Dinç, N.T. (2017, June 3). Personal interview.

Donovan, R. J., & Henley, N. (2010). *Principles and practice of social marketing: An international perspective*. Cambridge, UK: Cambridge University Press. doi:10.1017/CBO9780511761751

Dunkley, C. S. (2014). Global warming: How does it relate to poultry? *Caes.uga*. Retrieved from https://secure.caes.uga.edu/extension/publications/files/pdf/B%201382_4.PDF

Duyum, S. (2016). *Turkey: Poultry and poultry products semi-annual*. Global Agricultural Information Network (GAIN) Report TR-6014. Retrieved from https://gain.fas.usda.gov/Recent%20GAIN%20Publications/Poultry%20and%20Poultry%20Products%20Semi-Annual_Ankara_Turkey_3-23-2016.pdf

Ergin, E. A., & Ozsacmaci, B. (2011). Turkish consumers' perceptions and consumption of organic foods. *African Journal of Business Management*, *5*(3), 910–914.

Forthofer, M. S., & Bryant, C. A. (2000). Using audience-segmentation techniques to tailor health behavior change strategies. *American Journal of Health Behavior*, *24*(1), 36–43. doi:10.5993/AJHB.24.1.6

Greenpeace Mediterranean. (2017a). *Biz kimiz?* [Who are we?]. Retrieved from http://www.greenpeace.org/turkey/tr/about/

Greenpeace Mediterranean. (2017b). *Başarılar* [Success stories] Retrieved from http://www.greenpeace.org/turkey/tr/about/history/basarilar/

Greenpeace Mediterranean. (2017c). *Acil cevap bekleniyor* [Urgent reply expected]. Retrieved from https://imza.greenpeace.org/yumurtakapi

Gunduz, O., & Bayramoglu, Z. (2011). Consumer's willingness to pay for organic chicken meat in Samsun province of Turkey. *Journal of Animal and Veterinary Advances*, *10*(3), 334–340. doi:10.3923/javaa.2011.334.340

Hastings, G. (2003). Competition in social marketing. *Social Marketing Quarterly*, *9*(3), 6–10. doi:10.1080/15245000309109

Hastings, G., & Saren, M. (2003). The critical contribution of social marketing: Theory and application. *Marketing Theory*, *3*(3), 305–322. doi:10.1177/147059310333005

Kemp, S. (2016). *Digital in 2016*. Retrieved from https://www.slideshare.net/wearesocialsg/digital-in-2016

Keyman, F. (2006). *Türkiye'de sivil toplumun serüveni: İmkânsızlıklar içinde bir vaha* [Adventure of civil society in Turkey? An oasis in impossibility]. Ankara, Turkey: Sivil Toplum Geliştirme Merkezi Yayınları.

Koca, A. (2013). Türkiye'deki Twitter kullanıcılarının sayısı 9.6 milyona ulaştı [Twitter users in Turkey reached 9.6 million]. Retrieved from http://webrazzi.com/2013/02/12/twitter-turkiye-istatistikleri-2013/

Kotler, P. (1972). A generic concept of marketing. *Journal of Marketing*, *36*(2), 46–54. doi:10.2307/1250977

Kotler, P., & Lee, N. (2008). *Social marketing: Influencing behaviors for good* (4th ed.). Thousand Oaks, CA: Sage.

Kotler, P., & Zaltman, G. (1971). Social marketing: An approach to planned social change. *Journal of Marketing*, *35*(3), 3–12. doi:10.2307/1249783 PMID:12276120

Lefebvre, R. C., & Flora, J. A. (1988). Social marketing and public health intervention. *Health Education Quarterly*, *15*(3), 299–315. doi:10.1177/109019818801500305 PMID:3056876

MacFadyen, L., Stead, M., & Hastings, G. (1999). A synopsis of social marketing. Institute for Social Marketing. Retrieved from http://www.qihub.scot.nhs.uk/media/162221/social_marketing_synopsis.pdf

Maibach, E. W., Maxfield, A., Ladin, K., & Slater, M. (1996). Translating health psychology into effective health communication: The American Healthstyles Audience Segmentation Project. *Journal of Health Psychology*, *1*(3), 261–277. doi:10.1177/135910539600100302 PMID:22011991

Maio, G. R., Verplanken, B., Manstead, A. S., Stroebe, W., Abraham, C., Sheeran, P., & Conner, M. (2007). Social psychological factors in lifestyle change and their relevance to policy. *Social Issues and Policy Review*, *1*(1), 99–137. doi:10.1111/j.1751-2409.2007.00005.x

Manoff, R. K. (1985). *Social marketing: A new imperative for public health.* New York, NY: Praeger.

Ocak, H. (2017). "Greenpeace'e tavuk davası" [Chicken case to Greenpeace]. Cumhuriyet. Retrieved from http://www.cumhuriyet.com.tr/haber/cevre/656945/Greenpeace_e_tavuk_davasi.html

Ozdemir, B. P. (2012). Social media as a tool for online advocacy campaigns: Greenpeace Mediterranean's anti genetically engineered food campaign in Turkey. *Global Media Journal*, *5*(2), 23–39.

Pamir, B. (2004). Ben kesinlikle tavuk yemem [I definitely do not eat chicken] Retrieved from http://arsiv.sabah.com.tr/2004/11/01/gun101.html

Sağlıklı Tavuk Bilgi Platformu. (2016) Platform hakkında [About the platform]. Retrieved from http://www.sagliklitavuk.org/platform-hakkinda

Sariozkan, S., Yalcin, C., Cevger, Y., Aral, Y., & Sipahi, C. (2009). The financial impacts of the avian influenza outbreaks on Turkish table egg producers. *World's Poultry Science Journal*, *65*(01), 91–96. doi:10.1017/S0043933909000075

Sik, B. (2016). Dünyayı tüketmek: Kümes hayvancılığı odağında endüstriyel hayvancılık sektörü [Consuming the world: Livestock industry with a focus on poultry farming]. Retrieved from http://www.greenpeace.org/turkey/Global/turkey/report/2016/dunyayi-tuketmek.pdf

Smith, W. A. (2000). Social marketing: An evolving definition. *American Journal of Health Behavior, 24*(1), 11–17. doi:10.5993/AJHB.24.1.3

Smith, W. A. (2006). Social marketing: An overview of approach and effects. *Injury Prevention, 12*(Suppl. 1), i38–i43. doi:10.1136/ip.2006.012864 PMID:16788110

Tarimsal Ekonomi ve Politika Geliştirme Enstitüsü (TEPGE). (2014). *Ürün raporu: Kümes hayvancılığı* [Product report: Poultry farming]. Retrieved from http://arastirma.tarim.gov.tr/tepge/Lists/Haber/Attachments/18/KANATLI_URUN_RAPORU_2014.pdf

Tas, M., Balci, M., Yüksel, A., & Sahin Yesilçubuk, N. (2015). Consumer awareness, perception and attitudes towards genetically modified foods in Turkey. *British Food Journal, 117*(5), 1426–1439. doi:10.1108/BFJ-01-2014-0047

Türkiye Üçüncü Sektör Vakfı (TÜSEV). (2011). *Türkiye'de sivil toplum: Bir dönüm noktası* [Civil society in Turkey: A turning point]. İstanbul, Turkey: TÜSEV Yayınları.

Weinstein, N. D. (1988). The precaution adoption process. *Health Psychology, 7*(4), 355–386. doi:10.1037/0278-6133.7.4.355 PMID:3049068

KEY TERMS AND DEFINITIONS

Broiler Chickens: Domesticated chickens bred and raised industrially specifically for meat consumption. Serious concerns about animal welfare, impacts on human health and the natural environment are raised about the methods used by the broiler industry among others for species selection, artificial insemination, feeding, living conditions, slaughter, contamination and antimicrobial use.

Greenpeace Mediterranean: Established in 1995 as a separate foundation under the banner of Greenpeace, Greenpeace Mediterranean in a non-government organisation active in Turkey, Israel, Lebanon, Jordan and Egypt, with the aim to change attitudes and behaviours in order to protect the natural environment and promote peace.

Homophone: Two or more words with the same pronunciation but different meaning or spelling.

Market Segmentation: The process of dividing potential consumers into groups based on different characteristics.

Marketing Mix: A set of tools/words used by marketing to convey and pursue specific objectives. Examples include 4Ps (product, price, promotion, and place), 4Cs (consumer, cost, communication, convenience) and 4Ss (sustainability, strength, self-confidence and sharing).

Organic Product: A product produced using farming methods which rely on naturally occurring substances and methods for increasing soil fertility, including natural living conditions and feed for livestock.

Social Media: Communication-based technologies which allow the creation and sharing of information through computer or mobile phone networks as well as the establishment of virtual communities. Examples include Facebook, Twitter, Instagram and LinkedIn.

Chapter 15
The Role of the Ideology of Animal Welfare in the Consumption and Marketing of Animal-Origin Products

Nick Pendergrast
University of Melbourne, Australia

Sarah McGrath
Independent Researcher, France

ABSTRACT

This chapter investigates the dominance of the animal welfare ideology and the role it plays in the widespread consumption of animal-origin products. Animal welfare ideology promotes the humane use and slaughter of non-human animals. This chapter includes a literature review on the dominance of the animal welfare perspective. It also analyses how this ideology is reflected and promoted in the marketing of animal-origin products. This is done by exploring the packaging and advertising of the company Harvey Fresh as well as the role of the accreditation of the government-funded non-profit organisation the Royal Society for the Prevention of Cruelty to Animals (RSPCA) in Australia. Their marketing and accreditation are linked to the dominance of the animal welfare perspective and the widespread consumption of animal-origin products.

INTRODUCTION

This chapter investigates the dominance of the animal welfare ideology and the role it plays in the widespread consumption of animal-origin products. Animal welfare ideology promotes the humane use and slaughter of non-human animals.[1] How this ideology is reflected and promoted in the marketing of animal-origin products is also investigated. The focus is on animal consumption in the Western world, as there are great similarities between Western countries such as Australia, New Zealand, the United States and Canada when it comes to attitudes and practices towards non-human animals (White, 2009,

DOI: 10.4018/978-1-5225-4757-0.ch015

p. 97). In order to explore this issue, the authors draw on advertising promoting the consumption of animal-origin products, a wide range of academic literature and interviews conducted by them. This includes an interview with Australian ethicist Peter Singer, who is often referred to as the "father" of the animal advocacy movement (Bourke, 2009, p. 136).[2] Singer's book *Animal Liberation* was first published in 1975 and led to an 'organizational explosion' in groups advocating for animals (Beers, 2006, p. 3).

The first section of this chapter draws on this interview with Singer and a wide range of academic literature to give an overview of the dominance of the animal welfare perspective. After this literature review, the authors link the dominant ideology to the marketing of animal-origin products. This is done by exploring the packaging and advertising of the company Harvey Fresh and the government-funded non-profit organisation the Royal Society for the Protection of Animals (RSPCA) in Australia. An analysis is conducted to investigate the role of the ideology of animal welfare in their marketing. The objectives of this chapter are to: give an overview of the literature on the dominance of the animal welfare perspective; explore how this ideology is reflected in the marketing of animal-origin products; and examine the role this ideology and marketing play in the widespread consumption of animal-origin products.

BACKGROUND: THE DOMINANCE OF THE ANIMAL WELFARE PERSPECTIVE

The idea of animal welfare came about with the realisation that animals' physical and emotional well-being is important, not just their productivity for human ends (Bourke, 2009, p. 132). Cary Williams (2012, p. 12) explains that 'both animal rights and animal welfare advocates agree that animals should be protected, and that animals are sentient creatures'. This sentience refers to non-human animals as conscious beings capable of experiencing suffering and pleasure, rather than objects (Munro, 2012, p. 169; Freeman, 2013, p. 98). These ideologies however vary greatly in the protection that should be granted to non-human animals as a result of their sentience. Animal rights are related to challenging the human-animal boundary and contesting the concept of other animals being here for humans to use and slaughter; regardless of how "humanely" or otherwise this is done (Cherry, 2010, p. 458; Williams, 2012, pp. 13-14). The focus of animal welfare is on working for better treatment of other animals used and slaughtered for human ends (Beers, 2006, pp. 3-4; Singer, 2012, interview).

According to an animal welfare approach, when humans use other animals for their own ends, they have a duty to provide the following five freedoms for animals: 'to be free from thirst and hunger; to have adequate shelter; to be kept free from pain, injury and disease; to be permitted to express normal behaviours (by providing sufficient space); and to be free from fear or distress' (Bourke, 2009, p. 132). Despite the widespread acceptance of the idea of animal welfare in attitudes and legislation, these freedoms are not necessarily guaranteed for animals, who continue to be routinely crowded, confined, and harmed. The animal welfare approach, which opposes "unnecessary" suffering to the animals used by humans, assumes that animal pain and suffering can be acceptable, as long as humans believe the pain and suffering caused is "reasonable" or "necessary". Even when the five freedoms are ensured, animal welfare ideology gives animal lives no value at all, and it totally accepts their slaughter and use, while facilitating and regulating the process (Bourke, 2009, p. 133; Taylor, 2005, p. 47; Signal & Taylor, 2006, p. 266).

Animal welfare is an integrationist approach to understanding and addressing humans' relationship with non-human animals (O'Sullivan, 2006, p. 3; Signal & Taylor, 2006, p. 266; Munro, 2012, p. 170; Williams, 2012, p. 46; Freeman 2013, p. 108). Integrationist refers to working to speed up progressive gains within the current system, rather than seeking to destroy the existing system which has led to inequality (Wallerstein 2003, pp. 653, 658). The animal welfare approach accepts and promotes the idea of non-human animals being used for human ends in most cases, as long as certain safeguards are put in place to offer some protection for these animals (Francione, 1996, p. 1; Bourke, 2009, pp. 132-133). It also accepts the current property status of non-human animals (where they are considered merely property under the law) and speciesism (discrimination based on species) but attempts to place constraints on how this property may be treated and limit the damage caused by speciesism through animal welfare regulations (White, 2009, p. 97; Francione, 1996, p. 10; Best & Nocella, 2004, p. 26; Beers, 2006, pp. 3-4; Munro, 2012, p. 170).

In *Animal Liberation*, Singer (1975) drew on liberation sociology to understand that through "othering", dominant groups assume their interests are more important than those of the oppressed group. This fundamental dynamic is useful in understanding racism and sexism, as well as speciesism (Wicks, 2004, p. 269; Singer, 2012, interview). Non-human animals are sentient, meaning that they have interests - for example, an interest in avoiding suffering. The wide prevalence of speciesism means their interests are denied on the basis of their species (Wicks, 2004, p. 269). Singer's notion of animal liberation and discussion of speciesism were a strong influence in the more widespread adoption of an animal rights ideology that contested human-imposed hierarchies (Beers, 2006, p. 3).

These views challenged long held values related to the animal welfare ideology, which was, and remains, focused on limiting the harm caused by the lower place in the hierarchy of living beings ascribed to non-human animals (Beers, 2006, pp. 3-4; Singer, 2012, interview). While there had been individuals advocating for vegetarianism and against vivisection (experimentation on live animals) since the 1800s, before the 1970s, a more radical movement with a significant animal rights component did not exist. The idea of animal welfare has been in existence for the last few hundred years, whereas animal rights theory only emerged in the late 1970s (Francione, 1996, p. 1; Singer, 2012, interview; Beers, 2006, pp. 3-4). Before this time, most animal advocacy organisations were traditional animal welfare organisations like the RSPCA, as well as cat and dog societies (Singer, 2012, interview; Leneman, 1999, p. 219).

Welfarists not only accept human supremacy over all other animals but also uphold hierarchies amongst non-human animals: while all animals deserve ethical consideration, some are given more than others (Beers, 2006, p. 3; Munro, 2012, p. 170). For example, 'the family companion animal, they contend, unquestionably earns a higher place on the pyramid than a cow or pig' (Beers, 2006, p. 3). Cherry (2010, p. 458) explains that in Western culture, cats and dogs are seen as 'symbolically unfit for consumption', in contrast to other animals socially constructed as "food animals". The dominant ideology of animal welfare does not challenge these social constructions.

Animal welfare has been taught to children in schools from as early as the 1940s (Beers, 2006, p. 148) and could be classified as the 'default' position in society, or 'the status quo position' (White, 2009, p. 97). In Western countries at least, it is widely viewed as a 'moderate and respectable' position (Francione, 1996, p. 163) and is accepted by 'almost everyone' (Francione, 1996, p. 1). This includes a large majority of citizens (Sankoff, 2009, p. 9; Freeman, 2013, p. 108) and even those who directly use and kill other animals for purposes such as food or experimentation (Francione, 1996, p. 1; Garner, 2006, p. 161).

Surveys have shown that ninety-five percent of Canadians 'agree that animal suffering and pain should be reduced as much as possible' (World Society for the Protection of Animals, 2011) and over ninety-three percent of Australians have some level of concern about farm animal welfare (Taylor & Signal, 2009, p. 354). In a survey of 2000 Australians, ninety-three percent of people either agreed or strongly agreed with the statement that it is: 'Quite acceptable to eat meat so long as animals are reared and killed humanely' (Franklin, 2007, p. 22). Surveys have also indicated that approximately ninety percent of people in the United States (Kline et al., 2012) and eighty-six percent of Australians are happy to pay more for animal-origin products to ensure that animals are raised humanely (Taylor & Signal, 2009, p. 351). Such surveys clearly demonstrate the widespread acceptance of the ideas of the humane use and slaughter of other animals, as well as a common desire to improve conditions for animals within this framework.

Even though there is variation in the degree of concern for animal welfare (Taylor & Signal, 2009, p. 355), it is clear that most people's views, including those involved in using and killing animals, are consistent with the ideology of animal welfare: that is, they consider it acceptable for humans to use other animals, as long as their wellbeing is considered (Signal & Taylor, 2006, p. 266). This plays a central role in the widespread consumption of animal-origin products. This is because those concerned about animal welfare will strive to consume "humane" animal-origin products, however defined, rather than no animal-origin products.

As is discussed later in the chapter, there are different forms of animal-origin product consumption that can put into practice varying levels of animal welfare. For example, some people may consume any animal-origin product available, as they will consider any product humane based on animal welfare regulations enforced by the government. Others will strive for higher levels of animal welfare by choosing animal-origin products that claim to provide this. Still others will only purchase products which have been approved by certain certification schemes that they believe make the humane label more meaningful. Whatever the case, individuals put the ideology of animal welfare into practice by consuming "humane" animal-origin products, however defined, just as others put into practice animal rights on the individual level by rejecting the consumption of animal-origin products altogether (Francione, 2010, pp. 64-65, 71). The following analysis explores the way in which this dominant animal welfare ideology is drawn on and promoted in the marketing of animal-origin products.

ANIMAL WELFARE AND THE MARKETING OF ANIMAL-ORIGIN PRODUCTS

The widespread concern for animal welfare outlined above has led to a growing desire for consumers to choose animal welfare-friendly products (Harper & Makatouni, 2002, p. 288; María, 2006, p. 256; Schröder & McEachern, 2004, pp. 168-169). This increased consumer concern about farm animal welfare is primarily in reaction to the intensification of agricultural animal production, widely referred to as "factory farming" (Harper & Makatouni, 2002, pp. 287-288). The increased consumption of free-range eggs and other animal-origin products marketed as having higher animal welfare standards is part of a broader movement of ethical consumption. This movement is all about consuming products that have less impact on humans, other animals and the environment (Harper & Makatouni, 2002, pp. 288-289; Schröder & McEachern, 2004, p. 169).

The increasing focus of consumer solutions to social problems, where society is shaped by 'the consumer's economic vote', can be linked to the growing dominance of neoliberalism (free market capitalism) (Wrenn, 2011, pp. 17-19). There are many barriers to ethical consumption serving as a means of political activism (Wrenn, 2011, pp. 17-19). The higher cost for products associated with higher animal welfare standards is a significant barrier to people consuming these products. While individuals often express a willingness to pay more for products associated with higher animal welfare standards (Harper & Makatouni, 2002, pp. 287-289; Taylor & Signal, 2009, p. 351), in practice this is not necessarily the case (María, 2006, p. 256). Other barriers include the disconnection between consumption and production, with a lack of information about the treatment of animals involved in the production process, which leads to widespread confusion about the actual level of animal welfare in products marketed as more animal-friendly. An example of such confusion is consumers equating organic and free-range animal-origin products (Harper & Makatouni, 2002, pp. 287-289).

In order to explore some of these issues associated with animal welfare and the marketing of animal-origin products, the focus here is on the company Harvey Fresh and the government-funded not-for-profit organisation the Australian Royal Society for the Prevention of Cruelty to Animals (RSPCA). Harvey Fresh was originally an Australian owned company until it was acquired in 2014 by Parmalat Australia (Harvey Fresh, n.d.a), a subsidiary of Parmalat Group, a company listed on the Italian stock exchange with market capitalisation of approximately 2.7 billion Australian dollars (Parmalat, 2016). Parmalat Group is controlled by the Lactalis Group, the largest dairy group in the world with operations in forty-three countries worldwide, their products being sold in over 140 countries (Lactalis, n.d.). In the case of Harvey Fresh, the company branding strategy appears to be strongly geared toward promoting itself as a Southwest Australian brand and company (Harvey Fresh, n.d.a). Harvey Fresh's animal-origin products are cow's milk and other dairy products such as cheese, cream and custard (Harvey Fresh, n.d.b). The Harvey Fresh core function in this supply chain is primarily that of processing, packaging, and brand management, with the milk used by Harvey Fresh originating from farmers with supply contracts with the company (Pancia, 2017).

The RSPCA is an animal welfare organisation and charity (RSPCA, 2017a). The organisation has been operating in Australia since 1871, founded because of concerns regarding the welfare of horses in the state of Victoria (RSPCA, 2017b). Since 1981, the organisation has operated under company status as RSPCA Australia (RSPCA, 2017b). The organisation obtains funding through donations from the public, fundraising, grants, and business partnerships to run its programs and finance operations (RSPCA, 2017a). The RSPCA has over ten corporate supporters and also receives government funding (RSPCA, 2012a and 2012b). The organisational mission of the RSPCA is 'to prevent cruelty to animals by actively promoting their care and protection' (RSPCA, 2017a). As stated on the company website (RSPCA, 2017a), the organisational strategies to meet this mission are enforcing existing animal welfare legislation, operating animal adoption facilities, running programs to raise awareness concerning animal welfare issues, and assisting legislators and industry in developing animal welfare standards.

Harvey Fresh has been chosen because it represents a company whose advertisements about the welfare of the animals used in the production of their goods have been predominantly featured on mainstream Australian media, including television. There is limited existing research on marketing in the dairy industry in an Australian context. While there have been numerous studies on the marketing of dairy products, they have predominantly been in the context of other countries. Examples include studies exploring the marketing of dairy products in Ethiopia, Somalia and Sub-Saharan Africa generally (Debrah & Berhanu, 1991; Holden & Coppock, 1992; Little, 1994). There have also been global studies on the marketing of dairy products that have included analysis of Australia amongst many other countries (Manjunatha et al., 2013), as well as Australian studies that have focused on the marketing of food generally, which include an analysis of the dairy industry (Kelly et al., 2008). There was a recent study by Thorley (2014) that did focus on dairy marketing in Australia specifically. However, the study analysed issues such as cost, health, safety, taste and convenience. There was no mention of marketing based on animal welfare. There is clearly a need for more research on dairy marketing in Australia and specifically studies that focus on animal welfare and marketing.

Harvey Fresh has also been included because it is a clear and widely known example of a company which draws on the ideology of animal welfare to market its products. It is an example of a company which is able to charge higher prices for its products through marketing them as involving higher animal welfare standards. While there is some willingness amongst consumers to pay more for better animal welfare, as was noted earlier, media exposés have also led to some cynicism amongst the public about the ethical standards of products marketed as more ethical (Schröder & McEachern, 2004, p. 168).

In response to these concerns of companies "cashing in" on promoting their products as ethical without actually making significant changes to their production methods, value-based labelling formats such as quality-assured logos have developed. These logos differentiate products on a wide range of different categories, examples include free-range and organic (Schröder & McEachern, 2004, pp. 168-169). The RSPCA has been chosen as a prominent example of an organisation setting up such quality-assured logos in Australia through their animal welfare assurance schemes. Consumers may be more likely to purchase food from businesses such as Harvey Fresh that promote animal welfare-friendly products, if they are accompanied by a logo of approval from a government-funded non-profit organisation such as the RSPCA.

Another reason that the RSPCA has been chosen is to demonstrate that the promotion of animal welfare standards is not limited to private companies but is reinforced by other institutions, which assists in maintaining the dominance of the animal welfare perspective. Social institutions are the formal structures within society that can influence individuals towards certain ideologies. Examples include governments, businesses, the media and non-profit organisations. Individuals are most likely to adopt a certain ideology when it is consistently promoted across a wide range of institutions (Germov & Hornosty, 2009, p. 7). Animal welfare is not only promoted by businesses but it is also reinforced by governments, the media and non-profit organisations.

The government supports animal welfare through animal welfare laws as well as by funding non-profit animal welfare organisations such as the RSPCA but not animal rights organisations (RSPCA, 2012b; Pendergrast, 2015, pp. 104-105). Businesses, governments and well-resourced non-profit organisations, such as the RSPCA, dominate mainstream media coverage of animal issues. In contrast, more grassroots animal rights groups that challenge dominant concepts, such as humane slaughter, are rarely given a voice in the mainstream media, as they do not have the same resources or perceived legitimacy (Pendergrast, 2015, pp. 114-115). Focusing on the RSPCA, as a government-funded non-profit organisation that is regularly represented in the mainstream media, allows the analysis to explore the dominance of the animal welfare perspective across a wide range of institutions.

Consumers rely on both organisations to give them information about animal welfare when they consume animal-origin products (Schröder & McEachern, 2004, p. 170). The analysis of these two examples focuses on their packaging and advertising materials. It explores the utilisation and promotion of the ideology of animal welfare in the marketing of animal-origin products.

HARVEY FRESH

In the marketing of Harvey Fresh dairy products there is a strong and consistent theme of animal welfare (Harvey Fresh, 2013). Three aspects of animal welfare are important in this context: the animal welfare conditions being represented on packaging, the animal welfare conditions being portrayed in the brand's advertising content, and the actual animal welfare conditions on the farms of Harvey Fresh milk suppliers.

The packaging of Harvey Fresh products is limited in the amount of information it can provide. Harvey Fresh has chosen to present the majority of its dairy products in packaging with labels of a smiling young boy, with a backdrop of green pastures and cows grazing in large fields (Harvey Fresh, n.d.b). This imagery sends consumers the message that the images they are seeing are that of the source of the dairy products. The packaging does not alert the consumer to any harm to animals caused in the creation of this product. Rather, the consumer could be reassured that the cows from which the dairy product originates are roaming, free from any harm, on the green hills of Southwest Australia.

Video advertising used in the marketing of Harvey Fresh free-range milk offers more in-depth explanations to consumers of the conditions for the dairy cows. An example of this is a Harvey Fresh video advertisement which appeared regularly on Australian commercial television stations, and which was solely centred on an animal welfare theme (Harvey Fresh, 2013). The video is thirty seconds in duration and sends the message that "Harvey Fresh cows" are being raised in idyllic environments and conditions. During the thirty seconds, the viewer is shown a typical day of a Harvey Fresh cow. The imagery presented to consumers is that of cows roaming around green pastures with captions such as '10am personal training', 'midday mediation', '2pm hydrotherapy', and '4pm massage', likening the life of a cow creating Harvey Fresh products to that of a human attending a day spa retreat. At the end of the video, the consumer is invited to 'enjoy a taste of their good life' (Harvey Fresh, 2013).

Of course, this commercial is an idyllic representation and only reflects at best part of the life of a typical free-range dairy cow in an environment particularly aesthetic, and not necessarily representative of the norm. For example, dairy production also involves the slaughter of young male "bobby calves" because they do not produce milk and are therefore not profitable (RSPCA, 2011). The bobby calves are separated from their mothers and killed within a few days of birth (RSPCA, 2011). This is the case even in products with labels such as 'organic' (Animals Australia, 2017). Harvey Fresh omits discussion of these standard industry practices from its video advertisement, and other marketing, even though the content is strongly themed around the welfare of their animals.

Animal Rights Advocates Inc. (ARA), an animal rights organisation based in Western Australia, requested Harvey Fresh provide information on the welfare of their cows regarding three common welfare issues in dairy farming (Voiceless, 2015b). The response from Harvey Fresh is provided below.

Thank you for your email regarding our cows. In answer to your questions:

1. *What happens to the male cows that are born to the free-range dairy cows?*

Male cows are raised on farms or sold to other farmers [sic]

2. *What happens to the dairy cows after they stop producing milk?*

You would need to contact famers [sic] regarding this information.

3. *How are the dairy cows impregnated?*

You would need to contact famers [sic] regarding this information"

This response appears to demonstrate that the Harvey Fresh brand is interested in distancing itself from harmful practices in the supply chain. In the response, Harvey Fresh refers to the cows as 'our cows' but then immediately deflects responsibility for their welfare, stating that: 'You would need to contact famers [sic] regarding this information'. Harvey Fresh heavily relies on the theme of animal welfare in the marketing of its products, however in this case deflects responsibility for the welfare of the animals.

In fact, Harvey Fresh has been charged with misleading labelling twice. One of these misleading claims was stating that its cheese products were manufactured in Western Australia, when they were actually produced in Victoria (The Ethical Consumer Group, 2017). Specifically regarding animal welfare, Lactalis, a part of which, as was mentioned earlier, is Harvey Fresh, has received extremely poor evaluations of its animal welfare practices. The 2016 Business Benchmark on Farm Animal Welfare (BBFAW) ranked Lactalis in the lowest category, tier 6, with 1 being the best and 6 being the worst. Tier 6 refers to 'No Evidence [of] that [animal welfare] on the Business Agenda' (The Ethical Consumer Group, 2017).

Harvey Fresh's marketing represents a number of issues regarding companies profiting from perceptions of high animal welfare standards. Based on its reaction to the email published earlier, its animal welfare ranking from the BBFAW and its marketing content discussed, Harvey Fresh attempts to capitalise on an idealised version of animal welfare to drive consumers towards its products and possibly lead some to pay more for them, because of the promotion of higher welfare standards. Its idyllic portrayals of animal treatment also have the broader effect of perpetuating the idea of humane animal use, which plays a role in the widespread consumption of animal-origin products generally. There exists an economic interest in Harvey Fresh maintaining its image of a local and animal welfare conscious brand and this is reflected in its marketing content and brand communications. Harvey Fresh's use of the term "free-range" is particularly prone to misleading the public because it is not certified by an independent organisation (Schröder & McEachern, 2004, pp. 168-169).

RSPCA

In supermarkets in Western countries, branded animal welfare certifications are often presented to consumers at the point of selection of animal-origin products. These are intended to influence during the process of consumer product differentiation. Such certifications schemes are particularly important for those consumers sceptical about humane claims by businesses (Schröder & McEachern, 2004, pp. 168-169). In Australia, the independent animal welfare organisation and charity RSPCA is one of the significant providers of such information through its Approved Farming Scheme certifications. These certifications are placed on animal-origin products from producers with farming practices which are considered by the RSPCA to meet its animal welfare standards (RSPCA, 2016).

By allowing certain companies to use its logo on their packaging of turkey, pig, and chicken-origin products, the RSPCA declares that a level of consideration has been given to the welfare of the animal prior to slaughter for human consumption. Detailed information about the minimum standards of welfare required to attain this certification is provided on the RSPCA website, however not on the product labels. The labelling simply informs the consumer that the RSPCA has approved the farming practices of the producer by providing very basic information. For example, the RSPCA approved chicken packaging states: "Chickens from RSPCA approved barns have space to flap their wings and forage" (news.com.au, 2017). This labelling forms a significant part of the marketing strategy of approved chicken farms and processors, as aside from price, it could be argued there remains very few other aspects that can be promoted from a marketing and branding perspective to differentiate chicken meat products on supermarket shelves (Schröder & McEachern, 2004, p. 170).

The message to the consumer is that by selecting a product with the RSPCA certification, they are choosing the most humane product available and are making a choice in consideration of animal welfare factors. This draws on animal welfare ideology to differentiate one brand of animal-origin product from another. The message sent through this labelling is clear, visual and simple. For a consumer ready to prioritise animal-origin products with animal welfare factors considered, the certification makes it easy to make their choice without too much effort or investigation. Other studies have found that only a very small proportion of consumers will search the product for more detailed information about animal welfare conditions (Schröder & McEachern, 2004, p. 170). Therefore, it is likely that very few consumers would explore the issue further by checking the website for the detailed RSPCA Approved Farming Scheme Standards documents, made publicly available (see RSPCA, 2016).

These certifications have a significant part to play in the reinforcement of animal welfare ideology – the ideology that as long as animals are raised and slaughtered "humanely", animal-origin products are acceptable for human consumption. Every time a consumer chooses an RSPCA-certified product off a supermarket shelf, they exercise a behaviour pattern with animal welfare ideology at its centre. Products with this label may cost more, with individuals purchasing these products putting into practice their willingness to pay more for animal-origin products from animals that they believe have been raised humanely (Harper & Makatouni, 2002, pp. 287-289; Taylor & Signal, 2009, p. 351).

This certification also raises the question of economic drivers and interests in the reinforcement and perpetuation of animal welfare ideology. It is in the interest of the RSPCA, along with the certified farms and processing companies, that animal welfare ideology is perpetuated. Without the ideology being strongly present in consumer behaviour and the product selection process, the effectiveness of the marketing strategy of differentiating an animal-origin product as the "humane option" from the other available, is weakened. Just as an Australian supermarket chain, Coles Supermarkets, advertises that they stock some RSPCA-approved animal-origin products (Australia Online Catalogues, 2016), the RSPCA itself often invests in advertising claiming that animal welfare is at the core of its Approved Farming Scheme. One example of this type of advertising is a four minute *YouTube* video targeted at consumers on the chicken-origin products market (RSPCA, 2013). The video features a softly spoken narrator explaining how the chickens are raised with full animal welfare consideration, details how the RSPCA Approved Farming Scheme works, farmers discussing how much they are committed to the welfare of the birds they are raising, and imagery of chickens running around freely in barns (RSPCA, 2013).

The use and effectiveness of RSPCA Approved Farming Scheme certifications in the marketing of animal-origin products to consumers presents a challenge in shifting or changing the animal welfare ideology in the consumer base, especially while there continues to be strong economic interests in perpetuating and strengthening this. Animal rights activists have pointed to the harm inflicted on animals even under products certified by the RSPCA. For example, Animal Liberation Victoria has investigated the conditions of animals used to create products under RSPCA's Approved Farming Scheme. Animal Liberation Victoria (2017) claims that pig farms that have been approved by the RSPCA have "failed to provide every one of the 'five freedoms' animals are entitled to". Even when these five freedoms are ensured, the slaughter of animals is accepted as unproblematic by such animal welfare certification schemes (Bourke, 2009, p. 133; Taylor, 2005, p. 47; Signal & Taylor, 2006, p. 266).

DISCUSSION

Regardless of their effectiveness in practice, certified logos provided by organisations such as the RSPCA are seen as a method to prevent misleading claims from businesses (Schröder & McEachern, 2004, p. 168). Misleading conduct in the marketing of animal-origin products has not only been challenged by animal advocates, as has been outlined earlier, but also in consumer protection legal cases. The case of Australian Competition and Consumer Commission (ACCC) v C.I. & Co Pty Ltd [2010] FCA 1511 was the first case the ACCC brought against egg producers for misleading and deceptive conduct. The allegation was that C.I. & Co Pty Ltd, Antonio Pisano and Anna Angela Pisano misled consumers by marketing their eggs as "free-range" when the ACCC claimed that many of the eggs sold using this label were actually "caged eggs". The Court sided with the ACCC, describing the marketing as "a cruel deception on consumers who mostly seek out free-range eggs as a matter of principle, hoping to advance the cause of animal welfare by doing so" (Voiceless, 2015a, p. 29). The Federal Court fined Antonio Pisano $50,000 as well as prohibited the companies from continuing to misrepresent their products, required they publish an apology to all customers, and ordered Anna Angela Pisano to pay $15,000 towards the legal costs of the ACCC. While the Court acknowledged that this was a relatively small penalty, it was satisfied that this case would act as a deterrent for other deceptive marketing (Voiceless, 2015a, p. 29).

A key problem is that "free-range" is a widely used but also frequently misunderstood term (Harper & Makatouni, 2002, p. 287). While the free-range label may conjure up images similar to those represented in Harvey Fresh's marketing, the reality is often very different. Regarding eggs, the Australian Greens political party (The Greens, 2017) state that "in March 2016 state and federal consumer affairs ministers agreed a free-range standard that would allow stocking densities of up to 10,000 hens per hectare". As a result, they argue that: "Producers are cashing in on the higher prices while their hens suffer in conditions that are far from free-range" and "in some cases they are jammed into sheds with little room to move and limited or no access to the outdoors" (The Greens, 2017).

The solution presented by the Greens (2017) is to "pressure state and federal ministers to introduce a legislated standard for free-range eggs that meets consumer expectations" and in the meantime they encourage individuals to look for what they refer to as "genuine free-range" eggs. Suggestions include boycotting suppliers that also produce caged eggs, to avoid some of the problems outlined in the ACCC court case above, as well as buying eggs that are certified to have higher standards than what they see as the inadequate government standard for free-range (The Greens, 2017). Conversations about ensuring that products labelled as providing higher levels of animal welfare actually do so in reality are important in discouraging misleading marketing practices.

However, another important issue is that what is left out of most of the discussions on marketing, government regulation and certification schemes relating to animal welfare is animal rights perspectives that fundamentally challenge the slaughter of animals in these industries, not just their treatment prior to slaughter. For example, animal rights activists have pointed out standard industry practices that occur across the board, even in "genuine free-range" milk and egg production. Examples include the slaughter of males because they do not produce the desired product and females as soon as they are no longer producing enough to be profitable to the industry (Humane Myth.org, n.d.; Peaceful Prairie Sanctuary, 2012). Without such animal rights voices, the debate is generally confined to the best way to use and slaughter animals, with the notion of consuming animal-origin products in the first place rarely challenged. This animal rights versus welfare debate is a central one in the contemporary animal advocacy movement (Garner, 2006, p. 161; Taylor & Signal, 2009, p. 346; Signal & Taylor, 2006, p. 266). There are important discussions to be had about whether even very high levels of animal welfare are enough to meet our ethical obligations to other animals.

Animal welfare accepts human supremacy over other animals (Beers, 2006, p. 3; Munro, 2012, p. 170) but even the extent to which the consumption of products assumed to be of higher animal welfare standards is primarily motivated by concern for non-human animals at all is questionable. Harper and Makatouni (2002, pp. 288-289) found that health was the primary motivating factor for individuals choosing to consume organic animal-origin products. Animal welfare was merely an indicator of other, and what people saw as more important, considerations such as food quality. There is a widely held belief amongst companies producing animal products, and even animal advocates, that minimising stress (especially prior to slaughter) and generally better treatment of non-human animals lead to better quality meat (see American Meat Institute, 2007; Humane Society International & the World Society for the Protection of Animals, 2009). Schröder and McEachern (2004, p. 170) found that when choosing meat, animal welfare was not as important a consideration as many other factors, including appearance and price. Therefore, consumers choosing animal-origin products marketed as being more humane are often motivated at least as much by anthropocentric (human-centric) values as zoocentric values reflecting concern for other animals (Harper & Makatouni, 2002, pp. 288-289).

Nevertheless, from the point of view of advocating for non-human animals, there are some positives to discussions about the consumption of animal-origin products with higher welfare standards. Consumers generally avoid the link between meat and other animal-origin products and the animals involved in the creation of these products (Schröder & McEachern, 2004, p. 170). Therefore, discussions about the treatment of animals, particularly more critical discussions that look beyond marketing representations and into the reality of animal welfare, can be important in bridging the gap between consumption and production, by bringing the animals back into the equation. However, as noted previously, these discussions will only relate to challenging the slaughter of animals if animal rights perspectives are also brought into the conversation.

CONCLUSION

This chapter explored the dominance of the animal welfare perspective and how this is reflected and promoted in the marketing of animal-origin products. Such marketing is used by businesses such as Harvey Fresh and is also reinforced by government-funded non-profit organisations such as the RSPCA. Certification of products by such organisations legitimises the marketing of businesses which attempt to persuade consumers towards their products and also sometimes convince them to pay more, based on the promotion of high animal welfare standards. The reality for the animals used by these companies does not always live up to the marketing materials and there are often calls for consumers to avoid misleading marketing and instead choose "genuine free-range" animal-original products (The Greens, 2017).

There is widespread public debate about misleading marketing of animal-origin products, the inadequacies of government regulations concerning "free-range" as well as discussion about various certification schemes. All of these discussions are important in terms of allowing consumers to make informed choices. However, left out of most of the discussions on these issues are animal rights perspectives that fundamentally challenge the slaughter of animals in these industries. The growing move for individuals to attempt to consume animal-origin products of higher welfare standards not only fails to fundamentally challenge our current relationship with other animals but is also primarily motivated by other factors such as food quality, which are not related to animals at all.

The current dominance of the animal welfare perspective and the related widespread consumption of animal-origin products explored in this chapter is unsurprising, considering its promotion across a wide range of institutions including businesses, governments, the media and well-resourced non-profit organisations. Further research exploring the marketing of animal-origin products by other companies and different animal welfare certification schemes would be beneficial in providing more insight into this topic.

REFERENCES

American Meat Institute. (2007). *Meat matters: Animal welfare in the meat industry*. Retrieved from http://www.meatmattersinfo.org/ht/a/GetDocumentAction/i/8681

Animal Liberation Victoria. (2017). *Free range fraud*. Retrieved from http://freerangefraud.com/free-range-fraud/

Australia, A. (2017). What you never knew about dairy. Retrieved from http://www.animalsaustralia.org/issues/dairy.php

Australia Online Catalogues. (2016). Coles Catalogue Christmas 21-27 December 2016. Retrieved from: https://www.catalogueau.com/coles/coles-catalogue-christmas-21-december-2016/

Beers, D. L. (2006). *For the prevention of cruelty: The history and legacy of animal rights activism in the United States*. Athens, OH: Shallow Press. doi:10.1353/book.7001

Best, S., & Nocella, A. J. (2004). Behind the mask: Uncovering the animal liberation front. In S. Best & A. J. Nocella (Eds.), *Terrorists or freedom fighters? Reflections on the liberation of animals* (pp. 9–64). New York, NY: Lantern Press.

Bourke, D. (2009). The use and misuse of 'rights talk' by the animal rights movement. In P. J. Sankoff & S. White (Eds.), *Animal law in Australasia: A new dialogue* (pp. 128–150). Sydney, Australia: The Federation Press.

Cherry, E. (2010). Shifting symbolic boundaries: Cultural strategies of the animal rights movement. *Sociological Forum*, *25*(3), 450–475. doi:10.1111/j.1573-7861.2010.01191.x

Debrah, S., & Berhanu, A. (1991). *Dairy marketing in Ethiopia: Markets of first sale and producers' marketing patterns*. Addis Ababa, Ethiopia: International Livestock Centre for Africa.

Dunayer, J. (2001). *Animal equality: Language and liberation*. Derwood, MD: Ryce Pub.

Francione, G. (1996). *Rain without thunder: The ideology of the animal rights movement*. Philadelphia, PA: Temple University Press.

Francione, G. (2010). The abolition of animal exploitation. In G. Francione & R. Garner (Eds.), *The animal rights debate: Abolition or regulation?* New York, NY: Columbia University Press.

Franklin, A. (2007). Human-nonhuman animal relationships in Australia: An overview of results from the first national survey and follow-up case studies 2000-2004. *Society & Animals*, *15*(1), 7–27. doi:10.1163/156853007X169315

Freeman, C. P. (2013). Stepping up to the veggie plate: Framing veganism as living your values. In E. Plec (Ed.), *Perspectives on human-animal communication: Internatural communication* (pp. 93–112). New York, NY: Taylor and Francis.

Fresh, H. (2013). Harvey Fresh free-range milk [YouTube video]. Retrieved from https://www.youtube.com/watch?v=QNQK8EWOQko

Fresh, H. (n.d.a). Our story. Retrieved from http://www.harveyfresh.com.au/pages/Our-Story.html

Fresh, H. (n.d.b). Milk and dairy. Retrieved from http://www.harveyfresh.com.au/categories.php?category=Milk-%26-Dairy

Garner, R. (2006). Animal welfare: A political defense. *Journal of Animal Law and Ethics*, *1*, 161–174.

Germov, J., & Hornosty, J. (2009). Imagining health problems as social issues. In J. Germov (Ed.), *Second opinion: An introduction to health sociology* (pp. 3–24). New York, NY: Oxford University Press.

Harper, G. C., & Makatouni, A. (2002). Consumer perception of organic food production and farm animal welfare. *British Food Journal*, *104*(3), 287–299. doi:10.1108/00070700210425723

Holden, S. J., & Coppock, D. (1992). Effects of distance to market, season, and family wealth on pastoral dairy marketing in Ethiopia. *Journal of Arid Environments*, *23*(3), 321–334.

Humane Society International & the World Society for the Protection of Animals. (2009). Better quality, safer food: Animal welfare in meat production. Retrieved from http://media.animalsmatter.org/resources/casestudies/en/CaseStudy-HSI-Animal-Ag.pdf

Kelly, B., Bochynska, K., Kornman, K., & Chapman, K. (2008). Internet food marketing on popular children's websites and food product websites in Australia. *Public Health Nutrition*, *11*(11), 1180–1187. doi:10.1017/S1368980008001778 PMID:18298882

Kline, C., Murray, A., & Lancaster, E. (2012). Animal welfare approved – 2011 animal products survey results. East Carolina University. Retrieved from https://faunalytics.org/feature-article/animal-welfare-approved-2011-animal-products-survey-results/

Lactalis. (n.d.). The Latcalis Group. Retrieved from http://www.lactalis-international.com/en/the-lactalis-group.html

Leneman, L. (1999). No animal food: The road to veganism in Britain, 1909-1944. *Society & Animals*, *7*(3), 219–228. doi:10.1163/156853099X00095

Little, P. D. (1994). Maidens and milk markets: The sociology of dairy marketing in Southern Somalia. In E. Fratkin, K. A. Galvin, & E. A. Roth (Eds.), *African pastoralist systems: An integrated approach* (pp. 165–184). Boulder, CO: Lynne Rienner.

Manjunatha, A. V., Gana Shruthy, M. K., & Ramachandra, V. A. (2013). Global marketing systems in the dairy sector: A comparison of selected countries. *Indian Journal of Marketing*, *43*(10), 23–35. doi:10.17010/ijom/2013/v43/i10/38354

María, G. A. (2006). Public perception of farm animal welfare in Spain. *Livestock Science*, *103*(3), 250–256. doi:10.1016/j.livsci.2006.05.011

Munro, L. (2012). The animal rights movement in theory and practice: A review of the sociological literature. *Sociology Compass*, *6*(2), 166–181. doi:10.1111/j.1751-9020.2011.00440.x

Myth, H. org. (n.d.). *Deconstructing the myth of humane animal agriculture.* Retrieved from http://www.humanemyth.org/index.htm

News.com.au. (2016). *This Coles chicken has gangrene.* Retrieved from http://www.news.com.au/finance/business/retail/this-coles-chicken-has-gangrene/news-story/994f472fa624707b2939c1ffdeee5717

O'Sullivan, S. (2006). Conflict and coherence within the Australian animal protection movement. In *Proceedings of the Australasian Political Studies Association Conference*. University of Newcastle.

Pancia, A. (2017). Milk processor Harvey Fresh 'disappointed' dairy farmers turn back on pain share proposal. *ABC News*. Retrieved from http://www.abc.net.au/news/2017-05-05/processor-disappointed-dairy-farmers-turned-back-on-proposal/8499712http://www.abc.net.au/news/2017-05-05/processor-disappointed-dairy-farmers-turned-back-on-proposal/8499712

Parmalat. (2016). Parmalat Group. Retrieved from http://www.parmalat.com/en/about_us/parmalat_group/Parmalat%20Group%202016.pdf

Peaceful Prairie Sanctuary. (2012). *The "free-range" myth.* Retrieved from http://www.peacefulprairie.org/freerange1.html

Pendergrast, N. (2015). Live animal export, humane slaughter and media hegemony. *Animal Studies Journal*, *4*(1), 99–125.

Royal Society for the Prevention of Cruelty to Animals (RSPCA). (2011). *What happens to bobby calves?* Retrieved from http://kb.rspca.org.au/What-happens-to-bobby-calves_87.html

Royal Society for the Prevention of Cruelty to Animals (RSPCA). (2012a). *Corporate supporters.* Retrieved from http://www.rspca.org.au/what-we-do/about-us/who-supports-us/corporate-supporters.html

Royal Society for the Prevention of Cruelty to Animals (RSPCA). (2012b). How we govern ourselves. Retrieved from http://www.rspca.org.au/what-we-do/about-us/how-we-govern-ourselves/

Royal Society for the Prevention of Cruelty to Animals (RSPCA). (2013). What happens on an RSPCA approved meat chicken farm? [YouTube video]. Retrieved from https://www.youtube.com/watch?v=mtTLm9LF5Ns

Royal Society for the Prevention of Cruelty to Animals (RSPCA). (2016). *Impact report.* Retrieved from https://www.rspca.org.au/sites/default/files/2016-10-RSPCA-AFS-Impact-Report-web.pdf

Royal Society for the Prevention of Cruelty to Animals (RSPCA). (2017a). About us. Retrieved from https://www.rspca.org.au/what-we-do/about-us-0

Royal Society for the Prevention of Cruelty to Animals (RSPCA). (2017b). Our history. Retrieved from https://www.rspca.org.au/what-we-do/about-us/our-history

Sankoff, P. J. (2009). The welfare paradigm: Making the world a better place for animals? In P. J. Sankoff & S. White (Eds.), *Animal law in Australasia: A new dialogue* (pp. 7–34). Sydney, Australia: Federation Press.

Schröder, M. J. A., & McEachern, M. G. (2004). Consumer value conflicts surrounding ethical food purchase decisions: A focus on animal welfare. *International Journal of Consumer Studies*, *28*(2), 168–177. doi:10.1111/j.1470-6431.2003.00357.x

Signal, T. D., & Taylor, N. (2006). Attitudes to animals in the animal protection community Compared to a normative community sample. *Society & Animals*, *14*(3), 265–274. doi:10.1163/156853006778149181

Singer, P. (1975). *Animal liberation: A new ethics for our treatment of animals*. New York, NY: New York Review/Random House.

Singer, P. (2012). Personal interview with Peter Singer, Australian ethicist (Copy of the Transcript on File with the Authors).

Taylor, N. (2005). Luddites or limits? Animal rights activists' attitudes towards science. *Journal for Critical Animal Studies*, *3*(1), 46–61.

Taylor, N., & Signal, T. D. (2009). Willingness to pay: Australian consumers and "on the farm" welfare. *Journal of Applied Animal Welfare Science*, *12*(4), 345–359. doi:10.1080/10888700903163658 PMID:20183486

The Ethical Consumer Group. (2017). *Harvey Fresh*. Retrieved from http://guide.ethical.org.au/company/?company=316

The Greens. (2017). *Free-range eggs: Our truth in labelling toolkit*. Retrieved from http://greens.org.au/free-range

Thorley, V. (2014). 'There is absolutely no substitute for fresh milk': Dairy marketing in Australia, twentieth century. *International Journal of Liberal Arts and Social Science*, *2*(2), 1–14.

Voiceless. (2015a). *The animal law toolkit*. Retrieved from https://www.voiceless.org.au/voiceless-animal-law-toolkit-second-edition

Voiceless. (2015b). *Dairy cows*. Retrieved from https://www.voiceless.org.au/the-issues/dairy-cows

Wallerstein, I. (2003). Citizens all? Citizens some! The Making of the citizen. *Comparative Studies in Society and History*, *45*(04), 650–679. doi:10.1017/S0010417503000318

White, S. (2009). Exploring different philosophical approaches to animal protection in law. In P. J. Sankoff & S. W. White (Eds.), *Animal law in Australasia: A new dialogue* (pp. 79–107). Sydney, Australia: The Federation Press.

Wicks, D. (2004). Humans, food, and other animals: The vegetarian option. In J. Germov & L. Williams (Eds.), *A sociology of food & nutrition* (Vol. 2, pp. 263–287). Melbourne, Australia: Oxford University Press.

Williams, C. (2012). *The framing of animal cruelty by animal advocacy organizations* [Honors thesis]. University of Maine. Retrieved from http://digitalcommons.library.umaine.edu/honors/91

World Society for the Protection of Animals. (2011). Will Canadians vote with their hearts? Retrieved from http://www.humanespot.org/content/will-canadians-vote-their-hearts

Wrenn, C. L. (2011). Resisting the globalization of speciesism: Vegan abolitionism as a site for consumer-based social change. *Journal for Critical Animal Studies*, *9*(3), 9–27.

Yates, R. (2010). Language, power and speciesism. *Critical Sociology*, *3*, 11–19.

KEY TERMS AND DEFINITIONS

Animal Rights: Contests the concept of other animals being here for humans to use and slaughter; regardless of how "humanely" or otherwise this is done.

Animal Welfare: Strives for the humane use and slaughter of non-human animals.

Harvey Fresh: A company which sells dairy products, owned by The Lactalis Group, the largest dairy group in the world with production operations in forty-three countries worldwide.

Property Status of Non-Human Animals: The status of other animals as merely property under the law.

Sentience: Beings who are conscious and capable of experiencing suffering and pleasure, rather than objects.

Speciesism: Discrimination based on species.

The Australian Royal Society for the Prevention of Cruelty to Animals (RSPCA): A non-profit organisation and charity that advocates for animal welfare.

ENDNOTES

1. Throughout this chapter, the terms 'non-human animals', 'other animals' and 'animals' are used interchangeably; however, the importance of the terms 'non-human animals' and 'other animals' rather than 'animals' is certainly accepted, as using the term 'animals' to refer only to non-human animals reinforces the idea that humans are somehow separate to other animals, rather than simply being one species of animal. The decision to sometimes refer to non-human animals in this way was made in recognition of the practicalities of readability when the term is being used so often (for more on the term 'animals' and speciesist language, see: Yates, 2010, pp. 15-16; Dunayer, 2001, p. 10).
2. Throughout the chapter, when a point is taken from one of the interviews the authors conducted, this is indicated through the inclusion of 'interview' in the reference.

APPENDIX

Figure 1. Screenshot of Harvey Fresh's email response

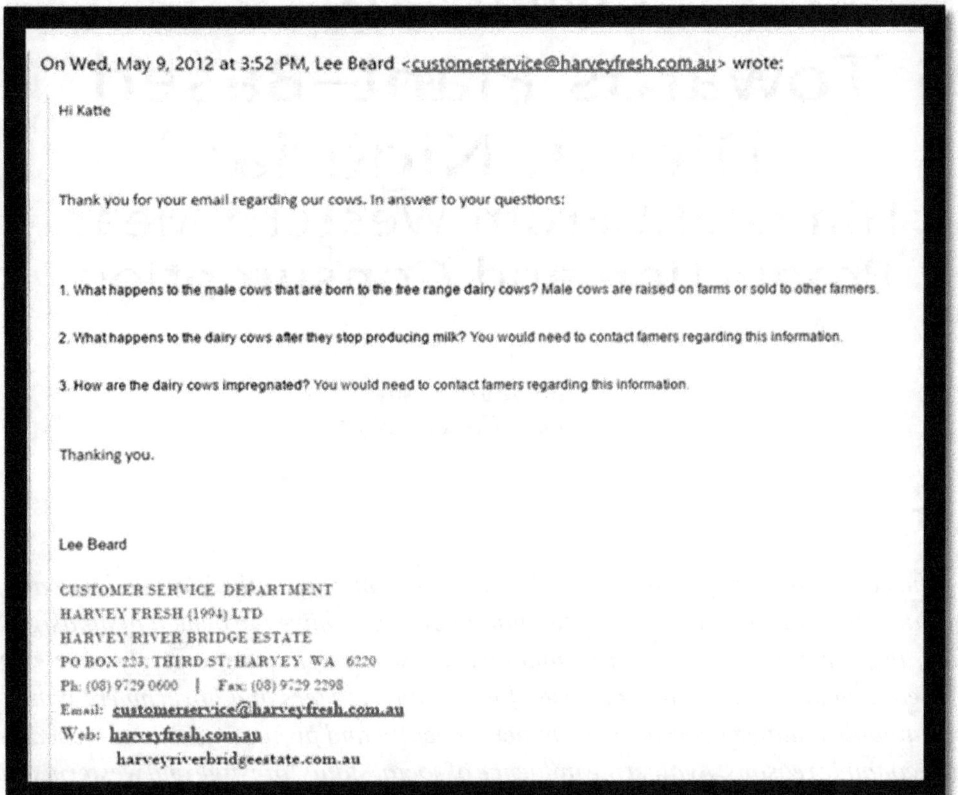

On Wed, May 9, 2012 at 3:52 PM, Lee Beard <customerservice@harveyfresh.com.au> wrote:

Hi Katie

Thank you for your email regarding our cows. In answer to your questions:

1. **What happens to the male cows that are born to the free range dairy cows?** Male cows are raised on farms or sold to other farmers.

2. **What happens to the dairy cows after they stop producing milk?** You would need to contact famers regarding this information.

3. **How are the dairy cows impregnated?** You would need to contact famers regarding this information.

Thanking you.

Lee Beard

CUSTOMER SERVICE DEPARTMENT
HARVEY FRESH (1994) LTD
HARVEY RIVER BRIDGE ESTATE
PO BOX 223, THIRD ST, HARVEY WA 6220
Ph: (08) 9729 0600 | Fax: (08) 9729 2298
Email: customerservice@harveyfresh.com.au
Web: harveyfresh.com.au
harveyriverbridgeestate.com.au

Chapter 16
Towards Plant-Based Diet in Nigeria:
Hindsight From Western Meat Production and Consumption

Emmanuel Ajadi
Juli Standard College, Nigeria

ABSTRACT

Considering the consequences of meat production and consumption in the West and globally, countries such as Nigeria with relatively low meat consumption per capita have the benefit of hindsight. However, if not checked, the current social structures and mechanisms, might progressively accelerate the consumption of meat and demand for animal-based food. Policy makers and government parastatals need to strike a sustainable balance between environmental health and promoting animal-based products for nutrition and economic reasons. Against the influence of social status, prestige and westernisation, people need to be responsible for their dietary choices supported by education and awareness. This chapter presents an overview of animal production and consumption in Nigeria to uncover unapparent factors and social drivers encouraging the livestock sector. Disproving the general assumption and misbeliefs that promoting plant-based diets might negatively affect developing countries, the localised implications on nutrition, health, environment and the Nigerian economy are weighed and clarified.

INTRODUCTION

The growing significance of plant-based diet around the world is becoming apparent in the light of food insecurity, health problems and environmental concerns (Gold & Porritt, 2004; Henning, 2011; Nordgren, 2012; Raphaely & Marinova, 2016). Many authors have argued the resource use benefits of plant-based relative to diets based on animal products (Henning, 2011; Pimentel & Pimentel, 2003; Raphaely & Marinova, 2014a; Yacoubou, 2009). To obtain the needed animal products such as meat, dairy and eggs, animals have to be reared and intensively fed. The unjustifiable land-use, water-use, and grain consump-

DOI: 10.4018/978-1-5225-4757-0.ch016

tion in the animal agriculture sector pose a threat to the continual existence of humans on earth (Singer & Mason, 2006; Raphaely & Marinova, 2014a). The environmental impacts of industrialised animal farming are also undeniable (Macrae, 2010; Pelletier & Tyedmers, 2010). Driven by the increasing human population and its excessive appetites for meat consumption, the growth of the animal agriculture sector has been accelerated to an unsustainable level for the planet (Raphaely & Marinova, 2014a). Human dietary choices, therefore, transcend individual interests. They concern human health (both public and personal), ecological health, the economy and even animal welfare. As emphasised by Raphaely and Marinova (2014a), individual choice of food has a cumulative impact on earth's sustainability.

Currently, the inordinate appetite of the western world for meat consumption has resulted in health problems such as obesity, diabetes, cardiovascular diseases, cancer and antibiotics resistance (Abioye-Kuteyi et al., 2004; Azevedo & Alla, 2008; Chan et al., 2011; Ferrucci et al., 2010); increase in greenhouse gases (GHGs) resulting in climate change (Goodland & Anhang, 2009; Raphaely & Marinova, 2014b; Stehfest et al., 2009; Steinfeld et al., 2006a); and a misappropriate use of land for animal agriculture (Lubowski et al., 2006; Thornton et al., 2011). The complications resulting from animal agriculture are expansive, for example, animal agriculture can be linked to the starvation experienced by about 1 billion hungry people in the world (FAO, 2015). The current grains production in the world is more than sufficient to feed about 9 billion population, however, these grains (which should have been consumed by humans) are been fed to animals which subsequently produce meat with a poor grain to meat ratio (Foer, 2009; Godfray et al., 2010; Henning, 2011; Pimentel & Pimentel, 2003; Yotopoulos, 1985). Beyond the unjustified grains to meat conversion ratio, meat production and consumption have also resulted in global inequality, as most of the meat produced from grains sourced across the globe is consumed by the western world (Raphaely & Marinova, 2014a). About 80% of the over I billion hungry population are distributed across developing nations (FAO, 2015; Andersen & Kuhn, 2014). Contrastingly, these developing nations, in most cases, grow sufficient grains to feed their human population but the grains are feed to livestock animals locally or through exportation (Godfray et al., 2010; Guyomard et al., 2013).

Considering the consequences of meat production and consumption in the western world and globally, developing countries such as Nigeria with currently relatively low meat consumption per capita have the benefit of hindsight, and can, therefore, promote plant-based diets. Unfortunately, the current social structures and/or mechanisms in Nigeria, if not checked, might progressively accelerate the consumption of meat and demand for animal-based food products. Both the public and the government need a change in orientation about the significance of animal-based products on the environment and for the economy. Policy makers and government parastatals must be able to strike a sustainable balance between ensuring environmental health and promoting animal based products for nutrition and economic reasons. Against the influence of social status, prestige and westernisation, individuals and families need to be responsible for their dietary choices. Notably, appropriate education and awareness are a powerful social tool which cannot be downplayed for people to be responsible and rightly choose their diets. Accordingly, this chapter discusses an overview of animal production and consumption in Nigeria to uncover some unapparent factors and social drivers that promote the livestock sector in this country. Disproving the general assumption and misbeliefs that promoting plant-based diets might negatively affect developing countries like Nigeria, the localised implications of plant-based diet on nutrition, health, environment and the Nigerian economy are weighed and clarified.

OVERVIEW OF ANIMAL PRODUCTION AND CONSUMPTION IN NIGERIA

Nigeria has a population of about 187 million people in 2016 (UNdata, 2016) and its annual meat consumption was 1485548 tonnes in 2014 (FAOSTAT, 2017)[1]. Although on a per capita basis, Nigeria's meat consumption is one of the lowest in the world – estimated at 5.9 kg per person per year in 2016 (OECD, 2017), in absolute terms the country is a large consumer of animal proteins in the sub-Sahara region. Major animals consumed and produced include cattle, sheep, goat, pig and poultry (Ogbeide, 2015). Beef, which is one of the highest meats consumed (Adetunji & Rauf, 2012), was predicted by the Nigeria Ministry of Agriculture in 2014 to have an increased consumption rate of about 280% by 2050 (Premium Times, 2014). However, meat production in Nigeria fluctuates and responds to price elasticities (Osho & Nazemzadeh, 2005). Consequently, the livestock sector is constantly fueled by the government and private agricultural organisations to meet up with local consumption demands (Adetunji & Rauf, 2012; Yatai, 2013). Although international market also drives meat production in Nigeria, local consumption is by far more significant (Bénard et al., 2010). Local consumption of meat and other animal-based products facilitates subsistence animal production which is still a significant method of animal production in Nigeria (Momoh & Ochaba, 2002). According to FAO (2005), Nigeria consumed more meats and animal products than its production level, indicating that the country imports more than exports to cover for the local consumption demands.

Most Nigerians lack adequate education on the nutritional, public health and environmental implications of meat consumption and they eat meat as much as their income permits (Adetunji & Rauf, 2012; Eboh & Boye, 2006; Makinde & Babalola, 2011; Osho & Nazemzadeh, 2005). Also, Adetunji and Rauf (2012) and Osho and Nazemzadeh (2005) noted that an increase in the price of a particular type of meat results in demand shift to other types (instead of reducing the overall meat consumption), which shows there is a craving for meat consumption amongst Nigerians. Despite unfavourable economic situations, the research by Makinde and Babalola (2011) involving 397 respondents in south-western Nigeria reveals about 84% are meat eaters (63% red meat eaters and 21% white meat eater). This figure shows that Nigerians' appetites for meat transcends pricing factors. It therefore demands reorientation to avoid trailing the western path of meat production and consumption and any associated negative public health and environmental consequences. Preserving traditional diets, including the consumption of beans, sorghum, brown rice, yams, plantains and vegetables, is a much better and healthier alternative to westernisation.

However, a different scenario is being actively pursued. Animal agriculture contributes about 5-6% of Nigeria's total Gross Domestic Product (GDP) and is seen by the government as a mechanism to reduce hunger, poverty and unemployment (Mshelbwala, 2013; Yatai, 2013). This view has resulted in an emerging era of industrialised animal farming. The highly profit-driven industrialised livestock production is based on limited technical know-how, advent of antibiotics usage, poor welfare reputation of abattoirs, overgrazing, land misappropriations and overall characterised as unhealthy ways of food provision for Nigeria (Alawa et al., 2011; Kabir et al., 2004; Nsofor & Iroegbu, 2012; Olatoye & Basiru, 2013; Steinfeld et al., 2006b). The precarious economy and technological status of Nigeria places it at a greater risk in coping with the attending problems of meat production and consumption. Such demand and promotion of animal production and consumption trends in Nigeria can potentially place the country on the same western path of excessive and inappropriate animal protein intake with expansive consequences.

SOME SOCIAL DRIVERS TO MEAT CONSUMPTION IN NIGERIA

Dietary choices and food habits are not exempt from the influence of social power. In fact, authors like Nordgren (2012) and Blades (2001) argued that social relationships can significantly affect what we eat. Some social orientations to the consumption of animal-based foods in Nigeria are discussed below.

Status and Prestige

Historically, meat consumption is believed to be a classy lineament of the affluent. This belief, for most colonized countries, is connected to the status definition introduced by the European colonizers. Colonized countries were made to believe that meat saturated colonizers' foods were superior to their native plant-based diets (Trigg, 2004). Consequently, individual or family food choices became an indicator of their social status and financial buoyancy. Sadly, most colonized African countries, including Nigeria, are still plagued with this meat consumption defined social status. This mentality explains why income level is directly linked to meat consumption in Nigeria. Osho and Nazemzadeh (2005) and Adetunji and Rauf (2012) in separate studies on meat consumption patterns in Nigeria affirm that demand for meat in Nigeria is very price elastic. As households' income increases, they accordingly tend to consume more meat. Meat consumption to most Nigerians is a sign of affluence and an indicator of financial capacity (Anyiro et al., 2013). So, many Nigerians consume meat for them not to be stigmatized as poor. The health and environmental implications are hardly considered once they can afford the price of the meat.

This link between meat consumption and socio-economic status in Nigeria has been noted in academic publications as far back as the 1980s. Kent (1987) (cited in Gomna and Rana, 2007) documented that animal-based foods are usually inaccessible to the poor and they, therefore, substitute meat with fish to at least cover up for their economic status. Relatedly, Gomna and Rana (2007) discovered that heads of households (culturally, household heads in Nigeria are treated with respect and reference) consume more animal-based food than other members of the household. This observation by Gomna and Rana (2007) buttressed and indicates the reference and prestige associated with meat eating in Nigeria.

Misguided Nutrition Knowledge and Government Sponsorship

Animal-based foods have been exaggeratedly paraded as a significantly unavoidable component of a nutritious diet (Jabbar et al., 1995; Murphy & Allen, 2003). It is generally believed that animal-based foods are the major sources of proteins and essential vitamins. However, recent studies have confirmed that informed combination of plant-based food can adequately supply human nutritional needs (Beverland, 2014; Raphaely & Marinova, 2016). Despite these recent findings and studies confirming the nutritional adequacy of plant-based diets and the potential problems associated with animal-based food production and consumption, meat consumption is still being indirectly promoted by government agencies and parastatals. The Nigerian government on several occasions has affirmed its commitment to promoting livestock production, canvassing intensification of livestock production as a solution to malnutrition and poverty (Ogbeh, 2016; Premium Times, 2014; Yatai, 2013). Clearly, increase in livestock production with supporting marketability policies by the government will contribute to the increasing demand of meat consumption in Nigeria. The public will be misguided and led to believe that livestock production and consumption are worthwhile.

Urbanisation and Westernisation

The influence of westernisation on developing countries cannot be overstated. Almost every aspect of life in Nigeria is directly or indirectly influenced by the western world, especially in this globalised age (Fasanmade et al., 2014; Mohammed, 2012). Through various advancements in media technologies and internet, the western ideas and culture are progressively overshadowing traditional cultures and lifestyles (Raphaely & Marinova, 2013; Scott, 2007). The diet of the western world, which is generally meat prone, is strongly pervading most developing nations (Goodland, 2001; Raphaely & Marinova, 2013). Naturally, African diets are rich in plant-based sources (Famodu et al., 1998), however, western influence is creating a significant shift towards animal-based diets. Liverpool-Tasie et al. (2016) argued that household diets in Nigeria are experiencing significant transformation due to westernisation. Alarmingly, it was noted that animal proteins account for about 20% of the average share of the household's budget while 10% is for fruits and vegetables. This finding is contrary to typical African diets which are normally saturated by plant proteins (Goodland, 2001; Raphaely & Marinova, 2013).

Moreover, urbanisation, which is one of the footprints of westernisation on developing countries (Kandala & Stranges, 2014), significantly contributes to an increased consumption of animal-based foods. According to Delgado (2003), per capita meat and milk consumption is rising fast in urbanising regions. While this increase in per capita consumption might be partly due to rapid income growth that comes with urbanisation, the availability and closeness to supermarkets and/or refined abattoirs also facilitate buying of meats and variety of animal-based food in Nigerian urban centres (Adetunji & Rauf, 2012; Ogbeide, 2015).

PROMOTING PLANT-BASED DIETS IN NIGERIA

Arguably, dietary choice is an immensely complex issue. Many factors such as psychological, sociological, biological, nutritional and recently environmental interplay to affect what we eat (Blades, 2001; Singer & Mason, 2006; Nestle, 1999). Also, dietary choices in Nigeria are greatly influenced by age, religion, and wealth (Adetunji & Rauf, 2012; Ibrahim, 2010). However, education and awareness of the significance of animal production and consumption remain a notable factor whose tentacles spread across other factors. Although many authors have argued the nutritional, health and environmental benefits of plant-based diet (Abiodun, 1991; Idogun et al., 2008; Ketiku et al., 2009; Makinde & Babalola, 2011; Raphaely & Marinova, 2016), studies by Ibrahim (2010) and Makinde and Babalola (2011) still show that there is need for improved appraisal towards vegetarianism or plant-based diets. This lag is due to lack of public knowledge about the implications of plant-based diets (Eboh & Boye, 2006; Ibrahim, 2010). Practice and affinity towards vegetarianism need to be improved for the health, environmental, and even economic benefit of Nigeria.

Essentially, human behaviours and habits are generally influenced by societal and individuals' perception of cost and benefits of an idea, action or behaviour (Australian Public Service Commission, 2007). Connectedly, public and individual perceptions are defined by social norms, government policies, promotions and public advertisements. These defining factors to public and individual perceptions significantly shape behaviours in society and can result in desired behavioural changes when appropriately manoeuvred. For example, Grier and Bryant (2005) noted that programs to promote socially beneficial behavioural change in public health are based on this principle of reorienting perception of cost and benefits, which is termed social marketing.

Social marketing involves providing appropriate information and setting appropriate environment from the bottom-up or consumers' perspectives on the cost and benefits of an idea or product (Donovan & Henley, 2003). Optimising the concepts of social marketing to change human behaviours is a viable tool towards promoting plant-based diets in Nigeria. This is because social marketing principles target people's orientations and interests (Donovan & Henley, 2003; Grier & Bryant, 2005). However, adequate and appropriate information is pivotal in changing people's orientation and promoting an idea, even good ones (Kotler et al., 2002). Studies by Abioye-Kuteyi et al. (2004) on the assessment of dietary knowledge in Nigeria confirmed that structured dietary advice significantly affects people's choice of food. Relatedly, Makinde and Babalola (2011) in a research analysing four dietary groups in south-western Nigeria, emphasised the important role of awareness and education in diet choices. Accordingly, useful and appropriate information remains pivotal towards promoting plant-based diets in Nigeria. Some informative implications of plant-based diet in Nigeria are discussed below.

Nutrition and Health Implications

In 2014, the World Health Organisation (WHO) documented that about 249,960 Nigerians died from cardiovascular disease (CVD), cancer and diabetes (WHO, 2014). These diseases, in most cases, have been substantially linked to dietary patterns. Makinde and Babalola (2011) affirm a progressive increase in CVD risk has dietary pattern moves from vegetarianism through lacto-ovo-vegetarianism to red meat eaters. Similarly, Chan et al. (2011) and Abioye-Kuteyi et al. (2004) justified the high-risk potential of meat eaters to carcinogenic disease and diabetes. In fact, some of these diseases are checked by plant-based dietary prescriptions (Abioye-Kuteyi et al., 2004; Idogun et al., 2008). Plant-based diets, therefore, offer an affordable platform to prevent personal pains and even communal implications of these animal-based diet related diseases. Also, combating these diseases might be unbearable for developing countries like Nigeria with emerging economy and primitive technological advancement.

Clearly, animal-based diets provide a good source of proteins, iron, zinc and vitamins such as Vitamin B12, B3, and B6 (Sanders, 1999). However, trends in diet-related diseases are showing a significant shift from nutrient deficiency to chronic diseases caused by dietary excesses, especially in meat consumption (Kandala & Stranges, 2014; Nestle, 1999). Studies and research have justified the adequacy of plant-based diets in supplying optimal human nutritional requirements (Nestle, 1999; Sanders, 1999). Meat, egg and dairy consumption, therefore, becomes an option rather than being essential as we are mythically made to believe. Although, as discussed by Sanders (1999), the case of developing nations might be an exemption because choices of food are restricted and exposure to wide variety of salads, vegetables, fruit, pulses, and nuts is limited. Consequently, vitamin B12 and iron might be a major concern in proposing plant-based diets in Nigeria. Notwithstanding, Nigerians can move towards a plant-based diet by embracing flexitarian dietary options (Raphaely & Marinova, 2014a) that enable them to meet their optimal nutritional needs while escaping the health problems associated with animal-based diets. A flexitarian diet implies keeping the consumption of animal-based products within the recommended limits or consuming animal-based products for required nutrition and not for affluence (Raphaely & Marinova, 2014a). Many plant-based food sources that are readily available in Nigeria have been analysed to be of high nutritional significance (Abiodun, 1991; Idogun et al., 2008; Ojofeitimi et al., 1984; Osundahunsi & Aworh, 2002).

Environmental Implications

The global and regional ecosystems are part of the major bearers of animal production for human consumption. Environmental studies have shown a considerable link between human food choices and the destruction of the natural resource base (land, water and air) that supports life (Raphaely & Marinova, 2014a; Stehfest et al., 2009). Diets rich on meat require more energy, water and land in comparison with plant-based diets. For example, 1kg of beef requires about 2,500 gallons of water to produce; animal-based diet requires more than 6 times the land needed to produce an equivalent vegetarian diet and 18 times the land needed for a vegan diet (Andersen & Kuhn, 2014). The demands of animal production for human consumption are significantly extensive for the environment.

Meeting the consumption demands for meat has resulted in uncontrolled grazing, especially in the Nigerian northern territories leading to aggravated environmental degradation (Asadu et al., 2004; Earth Policy Institue, 2012). Although, it is traditionally believed that livestock grazing has a restorative effect on farmlands, the current rate of grazing in Nigeria is questionable. Lal and Couper (1990) (cited in Asadu et al., 2004) observed that 4-8 cattle per hectare have a severe implication on soil compaction; the about 12 cattle per hectare practised in Nigeria (Federal Ministry of Environment of Nigeria, 2001) have much more impact. Overgrazing in Nigeria contributes significantly to erosion, desertification and bush fire (Federal Government of Nigeria, 2012; Ogbuene et al., 2012). Extensive grazing occupies about 20% of the total land area use for agricultural purposes (Federal Government of Nigeria, 2012). This livestock grazing land-use does not include the land used for livestock-grain plantations and the land used for other animal agriculture purposes. Relieving this significant amount of land used for animal production purposes by promoting plant-based diets can contribute to an improved land resource, biodiversity boost, and conserved natural terrain.

Based on a livestock population of about 300 million (Mshelbwala, 2013), Nigeria's livestock population produces over 120 billion tons of animal waste per year (estimated from the US production rate in Andersen and Kuhn, 2014). While it can be argued that this animal dung can be used as manure, it also contains toxic elements harmful to the environment and human health, especially when applied crudely (Asadu et al., 2004). Also, the global warming significance of methane gases released from such population of livestock is considerable (Arthur & Baidoo, 2011).

The closeness of most butcher houses in Nigeria to water bodies also aggravates the risk of water pollution (Akinro et al., 2009). UNdata (2016) shows that only about 64% of Nigerians have access to clean water, unchecked meat consumption will increase meat production and subsequently rob more people of access to clean water.

Economic Implications

Anderson (2014) argued that a sudden drive towards vegetarianism might result in a widespread socio-economic distress because the meat industry has been significantly entrenched into the economy. Indeed, a drive towards plant-based diet will have both positive and negative implications on the economy. The agriculture sector, of which animal agriculture carries a significant proportion, provides employment for about 65% of the Nigerian total population (Olajide et al., 2012). A shift towards plant-based diet will pose a considerable threat to the people whose livelihood depends on animal agriculture. Also, a reduction in demand for animal products consequent to a shift towards plant-based diets will affect the socio-economic status of many families, especially in the northern regions, whose primary means of asset accumulation are cattle and other livestock animals (Sansoucy et al., 1995). Therefore, unemployment and poverty might be some of the unwanted aftermaths of a shift towards plant-based diets in Nigeria.

On the other hand, a reduced animal agriculture will make a substantial amount of grains available for human consumption, which can greatly reduce hunger and poverty (Steinfeld et al., 2006b). Potential unemployment and poverty consequent to a shift towards plant-based diets should therefore not be an excuse to embrace the relatively greater complications from animal production and consumption. Importantly, the Nigerian government can focus on proactive policies to drive the transition to a more plant-based diet with minimal socio-economic implications.

Also, while indeed Nigeria exports animal agricultural products, FAO (2005), revealed that the net foreign trade in both live animals and other livestock products is in negative values. For example, the net trade in live animals and other livestock products was -1.1 million animal counts and -611,883 metric tons respectively (FAO, 2005). These figures indicate that the importation of animal products is significantly high in order to meet the Nigerians consumption rates. Therefore, facilitating plant-based diets in Nigeria will reflect in a reduction in imports of live animals and other livestock products, consequently boosting the internal economy. Optimal effort can then be channelled into cash crops (cocoa, rubber and cashew) from which Nigeria had significant earnings in the 1970s (Olajide et al., 2012).

CONCLUSION

The notable and oftentimes irreversible consequences of animal production and consumption are indisputable. Undoubtedly, the Western world is currently plagued with some of these avoidable animal-based diet related consequences such as obesity, cancer, CVD, antibiotics resistance and other health problems; increasing GHGs; and land misappropriation for animal agriculture. While developed countries are currently battling with these aftermaths, a developing country like Nigeria can learn from them and avoid the path of promoting animal origin food. The population of Nigeria is progressively increasing and a continual fueling of animal production and consumption to meet this increasing population might be disastrous. Plant-based diets can be embraced to afford a better life for current and future generations. Compared to animal-based foods, plant-based foods justify the land, water, energy and other resources used in their production. Apart from adequately meeting the essential nutritional requirements, plant-based foods also provide a remedial and escape route from CVD, cancer, diabetes and related health issues. Plant-based food is, therefore, an ecologically and environmentally wise dietary choice.

Arguably, the implications associated with food choices go beyond mere appetite satisfaction. An informed choice is important in the light of health, environmental and socio-economic implications. However, dietary choices in Nigeria are limited by appropriate knowledge and mostly driven by social status, prestige, westernisation and misguiding government support and sponsorships. Reorientation and information-based awareness, therefore, remain a pivotal consideration in promoting a plant-based diet in Nigeria. Nigerians need to be presented with clarifying information to adequately enable them to evaluate the costs and benefits of their dietary choices.

The implications of plant-based diets in Nigeria justify their viability in enhancing a healthy lifestyle and promoting an environmentally balanced economy. However, proactive polices are needed from government parastatals to efficiently drive the transition to more plant-based diets, with minimal unwanted economic effects. Also, the peculiar case of limited varieties of plant food in developing countries like Nigeria demands a guided transition to plant-based diets. Therefore, a fllexitarian diet which ensures a controlled consumption of animal-based food to its minimum, as required by health recommendations, is suggested.

REFERENCES

Abiodun, P. (1991). Use of soya-beans for the dietary prevention and management of malnutrition in Nigeria. *Acta Paediatrica (Oslo, Norway)*, *80*(s374), 175–182. doi:10.1111/j.1651-2227.1991.tb12021.x PMID:1957623

Abioye-Kuteyi, E., Ojofeitimi, E., Ijadunola, K., & Fasanu, A. (2004). Assessment of dietary knowledge, practices and control in type 2 diabetes in a Nigerian teaching hospital. *Nigerian Journal of Medicine*, *14*(1), 58–64. PMID:15832645

Adetunji, M., & Rauf, M. (2012). Analysis of household demand for meat in southwest, Nigeria. *Global Journal of Science Frontier Research (D)*, *12*(1), 15–22.

Akinro, A., Ologunagba, I., & Yahaya, O. (2009). Environmental implications of unhygienic operation of a city abattoir in Akure, Western Nigeria. *Journal of Engineering and Applied Sciences (Asian Research Publishing Network)*, *4*(9), 60–63.

Alawa, C. B., Etukudo-Joseph, I., & Alawa, J. N. (2011). A 6-year survey of pathological conditions of slaughtered animals at Zango abattoir in Zaria, Kaduna State, Nigeria. *Tropical Animal Health and Production*, *43*(1), 127–131. doi:10.1007/s11250-010-9664-5 PMID:20734135

Andersen, K., & Kuhn, K. (2014). *Cowspiracy: The sustainability secret*. US: A.U.M Films and First Spark Media.

Anderson, L. V. (2014). What if the whole world became vegetarian? *SBS Australia*. Retrieved from http://www.sbs.com.au/news/article/2014/05/04/what-if-whole-world-became-vegetarian

Anyiro, C., Ezeh, C., Osondu, C., & Madu, L. (2013). Meat consumption patterns among different income groups in Imo State, Nigeria. *Journal of Agriculture. Forestry and the Social Sciences*, *11*(1), 21–31.

Arthur, R., & Baidoo, M. F. (2011). Harnessing methane generated from livestock manure in Ghana, Nigeria, Mali and Burkina Faso. *Biomass and Bioenergy*, *35*(11), 4648–4656. doi:10.1016/j.biombioe.2011.09.009

Asadu, C. L., Ezeaku, P. I., & Nnaji, G. U. (2004). Land use and soil management situations in Nigeria: An analytical review of changes. *Outlook on Agriculture*, *33*(1), 27–37. doi:10.5367/000000004322877755

Australian Public Service Commission. (2007). *Changing behaviour: A public policy perspective*. Retrieved from http://www.apsc.gov.au/publications-and-media/archive/publications-archive/changing-behaviour

Azevedo, M., & Alla, S. (2008). Diabetes in sub-saharan Africa: Kenya, Mali, Mozambique, Nigeria, South Africa and Zambia. *International Journal of Diabetes in Developing Countries*, *28*(4), 101–108. doi:10.4103/0973-3930.45268 PMID:20165596

Bénard, C., Bonnet, B., & Guivert, B. (2010). Demand for farm animal products in Nigeria: An opportunity for Sahel countries. *Grain de Sel*, *51*(1), 14–15.

Beverland, M. B. (2014). Sustainable eating: Mainstreaming plant-based diets in developed economies. *Journal of Macromarketing*, *34*(3), 369–382. doi:10.1177/0276146714526410

Blades, M. (2001). Factors affecting what we eat. *Nutrition & Food Science*, *31*(2), 71–74. doi:10.1108/00346650110366982

Chan, D. S., Lau, R., Aune, D., Vieira, R., Greenwood, D. C., Kampman, E., & Norat, T. (2011). Red and processed meat and colorectal cancer incidence: Meta-analysis of prospective studies. *PLoS One*, *6*(6), e20456. doi:10.1371/journal.pone.0020456 PMID:21674008

Delgado, C. L. (2003). Rising consumption of meat and milk in developing countries has created a new food revolution. *The Journal of Nutrition*, *133*, 3907S–3910S. PMID:14672289

Donovan, R. J., & Henley, N. (2003). *Social marketing: Principles and practice*. Melbourne, Australia: IP communications.

Earth Policy Institue. (2012). *Livestock and human populations in Nigeria*. Retrieved from http://www.earth-policy.org/datacenter/xls/book_fpep_ch5_17.xlsx

Eboh, L. O., & Boye T. E., (2006). Nutrition knowledge and food choices of primary school pupils in the Niger Delta region, Nigeria. *Pakistan Journal of Nutrition*, *5*(4), 308–311. doi:10.3923/pjn.2006.308.311

Famodu, A. A., Osilesi, O., Makinde, Y. O., & Osonuga, O. A. (1998). Blood pressure and blood lipid levels among vegetarian, semi-vegetarian, and non-vegetarian native Africans. *Clinical Biochemistry*, *31*(7), 545–549. doi:10.1016/S0009-9120(98)00067-8 PMID:9812174

FAOSTAT. (2017). *Livestock primary*. Food and Agriculture Organisation of the United Nations. Retrieved from http://www.fao.org/faostat/en/#data/QL

Fasanmade, O., Odeniyi, I., Fasanmade, O., & Iwuala, S. (2014). Global challenges in health: Effect of westernization on the prevalence of diabetes mellitus in Nigeria. *Research Journal of Health Sciences*, *2*(2), 56–63.

Federal Government of Nigeria. (2012). *Nigeria's path to sustainable development through green economy. Country Report to the Rio+20 Summit*. Retrieved from http://www.ng.undp.org/content/nigeria/en/home/library/environment_energy/RioReport.html

Federal Ministry of Environment of Nigeria. (2001). *National action programme to combat desertification.* Retrieved from http://www.agrhymet.ne/portailCC/images/pdf/PANLCDNIGERIA.pdf

Ferrucci, L. M., Sinha, R., Ward, M. H., Graubard, B. I., Hollenbeck, A. R., Kilfoy, B. A., & Cross, A. J. et al. (2010). Meat and components of meat and the risk of bladder cancer in the NIH-AARP Diet and Health Study. *Cancer, 116*(18), 4345–4353. doi:10.1002/cncr.25463 PMID:20681011

Foer, J. S. (2009). *Eating animals.* New York, NY: Little, Brown & Company.

Food and Agriculture Organization of the United Nations (FAO). (2005). Livestock Sector Brief: Nigeria. Retrieved from http://www.fao.org/ag/againfo/resources/en/publications/sector_briefs/lsb_NGA.pdf

Food and Agriculture Organization of the United Nations (FAO). (2015). *The state of food insecurity in the world.* Rome, Italy: FAO.

Godfray, H. C. J., Beddington, J. R., Crute, I. R., Haddad, L., Lawrence, D., Muir, J. F., & Toulmin, C. et al. (2010). Food security: The challenge of feeding 9 billion people. *Science, 327*(5967), 812–818. doi:10.1126/science.1185383 PMID:20110467

Gold, M., & Porritt, J. (2004). *The global benefits of eating less meat.* Petersfield, UK: Compassion in World Farming Trust.

Gomna, A., & Rana, K. (2007). Inter-household and intra-household patterns of fish and meat consumption in fishing communities in two states in Nigeria. *British Journal of Nutrition, 97*(1), 145–152. doi:10.1017/S0007114507201734 PMID:17217570

Goodland, R. (2001). The westernization of diets: The assessment of impacts in developing countries. *Global Hunger Alliance.* Retrieved from http://globalhunger.net/GoodlandChina.pdf

Goodland, R., & Anhang, J. (2009). Livestock and climate change: What if the key actors in climate change are... cows, pigs, and chickens? *World Watch Magazine, 22*(6), 10–19.

Grier, S., & Bryant, C. A. (2005). Social marketing in public health. *Annual Review of Public Health, 26*(1), 319–339. doi:10.1146/annurev.publhealth.26.021304.144610 PMID:15760292

Guyomard, H., Manceron, S., & Peyraud, J.-L. (2013). Trade in feed grains, animals, and animal products: Current trends, future prospects, and main issues. *Animal frontiers, 3*(1), 14–18. doi:10.2527/af.2013-0003

Henning, B. G. (2011). Standing in Livestock's' Long Shadow': The ethics of eating meat on a small planet. *Ethics and the Environment, 16*(2), 63–93. doi:10.2979/ethicsenviro.16.2.63

Ibrahim, F. M. (2010). Coping appraisal and affinity towards vegetarianism among a group of civil servants of Oyo state, Nigeria. *Journal of Medicine and Medical Sciences, 1*(7), 273–279.

Idogun, E., Famodu, A., Olasunkanmi, L., Osilesi, O., & Adebawo, O. (2008). Effects of fruits and vegetables on electrolytes and blood pressure of hypertensive patients seen in Nigeria. *African Journal of Food, Agriculture, Nutrition and Development, 8*(3), 349–357. doi:10.4314/ajfand.v8i3.19197

Jabbar, M., Ehui, S., & Fitzhugh, H. (1995). The contribution of livestock to food security and sustainable development. Livestock development strategies for low income countries. *Proceedings of the Joint FAO/ ILRI Roundtable on Livestock Development Strategies for Low Income Countries, ILRI, Addis Ababa, Ethiopia, 27*. Retrieved from http://ageconsearch.umn.edu/bitstream/182946/2/1995-Livestck%20and%20 food%20security-Keynote%20paper-FAO%20Proc.pdf

Kabir, J., Umoh, V., Audu-Okoh, E., Umoh, J., & Kwaga, J. (2004). Veterinary drug use in poultry farms and determination of antimicrobial drug residues in commercial eggs and slaughtered chicken in Kaduna State, Nigeria. *Food Control*, *15*(2), 99–105. doi:10.1016/S0956-7135(03)00020-3

Kandala, N.-B., & Stranges, S. (2014). Geographic variation of overweight and obesity among women in Nigeria: A case for nutritional transition in Sub-Saharan Africa. *PLoS One*, *9*(6), e101103. doi:10.1371/ journal.pone.0101103 PMID:24979753

Kent, G. (1987). *Fish, food, and hunger. The potential of fisheries for alleviating malnutrition.* Boulder, CO: Westview Press.

Ketiku, A. O., Akinola, O. O., & Akinnawo, O. O. (2009). *Nutritional status and plasma lipid profile of vegetarian and non-vegetarian female adolescents at Ile-Ife, Nigeria.* Paper presented at the Annals of Nutrition and Metabolism. Retrieved from https://www.karger.com/Article/Pdf/248288

Kotler, P., Roberto, N., & Lee, N. (2002). *Social marketing: Improving the quality of life*. Thousand Oaks, CA: Sage Publications.

Lal, R., & Couper, D. C. (1990). Soil microvariability. In *Soils of the humid tropics* (pp. 45–49). Washington, DC: US National Research Council, National Academy of Sciences.

Liverpool-Tasie, L., Adjognon, S., & Reardon, T. (2016). Transformation of the food system in Nigeria and female participation in the Non-Farm Economy (NFE). *Paper presented at the 2016 Annual Meeting, Boston, Massachusetts*, July 31-August 2. Retrieved from http://ageconsearch.umn.edu/bitstream/236284/2/ AAEA_2016_FoodSystemTransformationNigeria_1.pdf

Lubowski, R. N., Vesterby, M., Bucholtz, S., Baez, A., & Roberts, M. J. (2006). Major uses of land in the United States, 2002. *Economic Information Bulletin*, 14. Retrieved from http://americandreamcoalition.org/openspace/MajorLandUse.pdf

Macrae, F. (2010, February 13). How being vegetarian does more harm to the environment than eating meat. *Daily Mail*. Retrieved from http://www.dailymail.co.uk/health/article-1250532/Being-vegetarian-does-harm-environment-eating-meat.html#ixzz45PTjJ0Uj

Makinde, Y., & Babalola, D. (2011). Diet and hypertension: A comparative analysis of four diet groups in South-Western Nigeria. *African Journal of Food, Agriculture, Nutrition and Development*, *11*(1). Retrieved from https://www.ajol.info/index.php/ajfand/article/view/65882. doi:10.4314/ajfand.v11i1.65882

Mohammed, U. (2012). Globalization and changing cultural values In Nigeria: Driving westernization to its zenith. *Ilorin Journal of Sociology, 4*(1). Retrieved from http://www.unilorin.edu.ng/ejournals/ index.php/index/search/authors/view?firstName=Mohammed&middleName=%2C&lastName=Usman&affiliation=&country=NG

Momoh, O., & Ochaba, A. (2002). Herd structure of Small-Holder goat production in Otukpo LGA of Benue State, Nigeria. *Nigerian Journal of Animal Science*, *5*(2). Retrieved from https://www.ajol.info/index.php/tjas/article/view/50133

Mshelbwala, G. M. (2013). National livestock policy focal point presentation – Nigeria. *Paper presented at the Side-meeting of NLPFPS on VET-GOV programme engagement/targetting and capacity building facilitation*. Retrieved from http://www.au-ibar.org/component/jdownloads/finish/67-vet-gov-presentations/1427-nigeria-national-livestock-policy-focal-point-presentation

Murphy, S. P., & Allen, L. H. (2003). Nutritional importance of animal source foods. *The Journal of Nutrition*, *133*, 3932S–3935S. PMID:14672292

Nestle, M. (1999). Animal v. plant foods in human diets and health: Is the historical record unequivocal? *The Proceedings of the Nutrition Society*, *58*(02), 211–218. doi:10.1017/S0029665199000300 PMID:10466159

Nordgren, A. (2012). Ethical issues in mitigation of climate change: The option of reduced meat production and consumption. *Journal of Agricultural & Environmental Ethics*, *25*(4), 563–584. doi:10.1007/s10806-011-9335-1

Nsofor, C. A., & Iroegbu, C. U. (2012). Antibiotic resistance profile of Escherichia coli isolated from apparently healthy domestic livestock in South-East Nigeria. *Journal of Cell and Animal Biology*, *6*(8), 129–135.

Ogbeh, A. (2016). Retreat on livestock and dairy development in Nigeria. Keynote address delivered by the Hon. Minister of Agriculture and Rural Development, Chief Audu Ogbeh. Retrieved from http://fmard.gov.ng/retreat-on-livestock-and-dairy-development-in-nigeria-keynote-address-delivered-by-the-hon-minister-of-agriculture-and-rural-development-chief-audu-ogbeh/

Ogbeide, O. A. (2015). Meat industry development in Nigeria: Implications of the consumers' perspective. *Agribusiness*, *1*(1), 59–75.

Ogbuene, E., Eze, H., & Adinna, E. (2012). The Impact of Overgrazing and Deforestation on Rainfall Variability in Northern Fringes of Nigeria. *Journal of Environmental Management and Safety*, *3*(3), 21–36.

Ojofeitimi, E., Afolabi, O., Fapojuwo, O., Grissom, F., & Oke, O. (1984). The use of black-eyed cowpeas, maize-gruel mixture ('ewa-ogi') in the treatment and prevention of infantile protein malnutrition. *Nutrition Reports International*, *30*, 841–851.

Olajide, O., Akinlabi, B., & Tijani, A. (2012). Agriculture resource and economic growth in Nigeria. *European Scientific Journal*, *8*(22), 103–115.

Olatoye, I. O., & Basiru, A. (2013). Antibiotic usage and oxytetracycline residue in African catfish (Clarias gariepinus) in Ibadan, Nigeria. *World Journal of Fish and Marine Sciences*, *5*(3), 302–309.

Organisation for Economic Co-operation and Development (OECD). (2017). *Meat consumption (indicator)*. doi: Retrieved from https://data.oecd.org/agroutput/meat-consumption.htm10.1787/fa290fd0-en

Osho, G., & Nazemzadeh, A. (2005). Consumerism: Statistical estimation of Nigeria meat demand. *Journal of International Business Research*, *4*(1), 69–79.

Osundahunsi, O. F., & Aworh, A. C. (2002). A preliminary study on the use of tempe-based formula as a weaning diet in Nigeria. *Plant Foods for Human Nutrition (Dordrecht, Netherlands)*, *57*(3/4), 365–376. doi:10.1023/A:1021805117084 PMID:12602942

Pelletier, N., & Tyedmers, P. (2010). Forecasting potential global environmental costs of livestock production 2000–2050. *Proceedings of the National Academy of Sciences of the United States of America*, *107*(43), 18371–18374. doi:10.1073/pnas.1004659107 PMID:20921375

Pimentel, D., & Pimentel, M. (2003). Sustainability of meat-based and plant-based diets and the environment. *The American Journal of Clinical Nutrition*, *78*, 660S–663S. PMID:12936963

Premium Times. (2014). Nigeria to increase beef consumption to 1.3 million tonnes by 2050 – Adesina. Retrieved from https://www.premiumtimesng.com/news/160843-nigeria-increase-beef-consumption-1-3-million-tonnes-2050-adesina.html

Raphaely, T., & Marinova, D. (2013). Flexitarianism: Traditional diets as social innovation for sustainability. *Visão Global*, *15*(1-2), 403–422.

Raphaely, T., & Marinova, D. (2014a). Flexitarianism: A more moral dietary option. *International Journal of Sustainable Society*, *6*(1-2), 189–211. doi:10.1504/IJSSOC.2014.057846

Raphaely, T., & Marinova, D. (2014b). Flexitarianism: Decarbonising through flexible vegetarianism. *Renewable Energy*, *67*, 90–96. doi:10.1016/j.renene.2013.11.030

Raphaely, T., & Marinova, D. (2016). *Impact of meat consumption on health and environmental sustainability*. Hershey, PA: IGI Global. doi:10.4018/978-1-4666-9553-5

Sanders, T. (1999). The nutritional adequacy of plant-based diets. *The Proceedings of the Nutrition Society*, *58*(2), 265–269. doi:10.1017/S0029665199000361 PMID:10466165

Sansoucy, R., Jabbar, M. A., Ehui, S., & Fitzhugh, H. (1995). The contribution of livestock to food security and sustainable development (Keynote Paper). Retrieved from http://www.fao.org/Wairdocs/ILRI/x5462E/x5462e04.htm

Scott, M. M. (2007). Westernization in sub-Saharan Africa: Facing loss of culture, knowledge, and environment [Master of Architecture Thesis]. Montana State University. Retrieved from http://scholarworks.montana.edu/xmlui/handle/1/2230

Singer, P., & Mason, J. (2006). *The ethics of what we eat: Why our food choices matter*. Emmaus, PA: Rodale.

Stehfest, E., Bouwman, L., Van Vuuren, D. P., Den Elzen, M. G., Eickhout, B., & Kabat, P. (2009). Climate benefits of changing diet. *Climatic Change*, *95*(1-2), 83–102. doi:10.1007/s10584-008-9534-6

Steinfeld, H., Gerber, P., Wassenaar, T., Castel, V., Rosales, M., & De Haan, C. (2006a). *Livestock's long shadow*. Rome, Italy: FAO.

Steinfeld, H., Wassenaar, T., & Jutzi, S. (2006b). Livestock production systems in developing countries: Status, drivers, trends. *World Organisation for Animal Health (OIE). Scientific and Technical Review*, *25*, 505–516. doi:10.20506/rst.25.2.1677 PMID:17094693

Thornton, P., Herrero, M., & Ericksen, P. (2011). *Livestock and climate change*. Livestock Exchange Issue Brief 3. International Livestock Research Institute. Retrieved from https://cgspace.cgiar.org/bitstream/handle/10568/10601/IssueBrief3.pdf

Trigg, H. (2004). Food choice and social identity in early colonial New Mexico. *Journal of the Southwest*, *46*(2), 223–252.

UNdata. (2016). *Country profile: Nigeria*. Retrieved from http://data.un.org/CountryProfile.aspx?crName=NIGERIA

World Health Organisation (WHO). (2014). Noncommunicable Diseases (NCD) Country Profiles. Retrieved from http://www.who.int/nmh/publications/ncd-profiles-2014/en/

Yacoubou, J. (2009). Save our water: The vegetarian way. *The Vegetarian Resource Group*. Retrieved from http://www.vrg.org/environment/water_brochure.php

Yatai, F. (2013). Boosting animal protein production in Nigeria. *The Tide*. Retrieved from http://www.thetidenewsonline.com/2013/11/04/boosting-animal-protein-production-in-nigeria/

Yotopoulos, P. A. (1985). Middle-income classes and food crises: The "new" food-feed competition. *Economic Development and Cultural Change*, *33*(3), 463–483. doi:10.1086/451474

KEY TERMS AND DEFINITIONS

Developing Country: A country which is not industrialised. Since 2016, the World Bank and the United Nations no longer use this term; instead countries are classified based on their per capita Gross National Income in the following categories: low-income, lower middle-income; upper middle-income and high-income economies.

Diet: Food and drink preferences to provide nutrition.

Flexitarianism: A dietary style characterised with reduced animal meat consumption and abundance of plant-based options.

Livestock Agriculture: Raising of farm animals for food production, including meat, eggs and dairy products.

Nutrition: The process of obtaining the necessary food for maintaining health and growth.

Sub-Saharan Africa: The region of the African continent located south of the Sahara Desert.

Westernisation: Adopting the culture of the West, it refers to cultures in Europe, United States of America, Canada, Australia, New Zealand and parts of Latin America.

ENDNOTES

1 There are inconsistencies in statistical data (e.g. demographic data) reported for Nigeria depending on the source used. Although the actual source used is quoted, the data should be treated only as informative.

Chapter 17
Insights Into Chinese Diets:
A Social Marketing Formative Study

Jashim Khan
University of Surrey, UK

Sharyn Rundle-Thiele
Griffith University, Australia

Gary Rivers
University of Surrey, UK

ABSTRACT

The rise in demand for beef in China is occurring at a time when red meat consumption is being discouraged by leading health authorities globally. Social marketing starts by understanding individuals and the social and built environment that they are a part of to gain actionable insights which can be used in policy and program action to change behaviours for the better. This chapter aims to understand why Chinese individuals consume red meat. Through ethnographic and systematic analysis of twenty-three selected users' postings over a six-month period on Meishi and Chinese Food Safety electronic message boards ("netnography"), an understanding is developed why affluent Chinese consumers buy imported beef products from international groceries. Acknowledging that obesity is a complex multi-factorial issue, environmental and social norms are considered to ensure a broader view is taken. Recommendations for social marketing are made.

INTRODUCTION

More than 60% of all deaths worldwide are attributed to non-communicable diseases (NCD) (WHO, 2013) which are linked to four behavioural risk factors, namely tobacco use, prejudicial use of alcohol, unhealthy eating and lack of physical activity. Cardiovascular disease, cancer, diabetes and chronic respiratory diseases are four widely recognized NCDs (Demaio et al., 2014). The impact of NCDs extends beyond individuals to societies and governments who bear increased healthcare expenditure costs in addition to economic losses. Over the next 15 years, in middle and low-income countries the economic

DOI: 10.4018/978-1-5225-4757-0.ch017

loss attributed to NCDs is estimated to amount to seven trillion dollars (Centers for Disease Control and Prevention, 2016). According to the World Health Organization (WHO, 2016) overweight and obesity indicated by raised body mass index (BMI) are a major risk factor for NCDs, including cardiovascular diseases (mainly heart disease and stroke), diabetes, musculoskeletal disorders (especially osteoarthritis – a highly disabling degenerative disease of the joints) and some cancers (including endometrial, breast, ovarian, prostate, liver, gallbladder, kidney and colon).

According to WHO (2016), obesity prevalence rates have more than doubled since 1980 and today an estimated 1.9 billion adults aged over 18 years are overweight placing an even greater proportion of the population at NCD risk. Of these, 600 million are obese (WHO, 2016). Overweight and obesity also extend to children with statistics indicating that 41 million children aged 5 years or less are overweight and obese (WHO, 2016). China, the context chosen for the study presented in this chapter, has an estimated population of 1.3 billion people and current WHO estimates indicate that 38.7% of adult Chinese men are overweight (WHO, 2016). Obesity occurs when energy intake from food and drink consumption is greater than energy expenditure through the body's metabolism and physical activity over a prolonged period, resulting in the accumulation of excess body fat.

Obesity is considered by WHO to be entirely preventable. However, it is important to acknowledge that obesity is a multi-factorial, wicked problem which requires adopting a wider focus that extends beyond the individuals who have accumulated excess body fat. There is an increasing understanding that combatting obesity requires multi-sector support ensuring that more conducive environments are built to encourage physical activity (Pang et al., 2017), attention is directed to product formulation and serving sizes through policy frameworks and more. The many factors contributing to obesity are best explained by the Foresight Obesity Map which displays factors contributing directly or indirectly. As a complex, interrelated web, together they prey on our inherent human vulnerabilities to gain weight. Energy imbalance is pictured at the core to highlight the process by which obesity occurs over time and more than 100 factors are organized into seven cross cutting themes. Food environment, biology, the activity environment, societal influences, individual psychology, physical activity and food consumption are all recognized as contributing to obesity.

A wide range of disparate fields and disciplines seek to deliver behavioural change. Examples of "behaviour change fields" include (but are not limited to) education, training, enforcement, infrastructure, technology, urban planning, community development, health promotion and social marketing (Tapp & Rundle-Thiele, 2016). While each discipline has evolved with its own unique theories, tools and techniques, there are also similarities between fields. Contemporary social marketing research and practice are characterized by broad thinking that ensures research extends beyond "individualistic" parameters and draws from a wider behavioural ecological system framework to enhance understanding of social markets (Brennan et al., 2016). In contrast to other behavioural change fields, social marketers seek to initially identify barriers preventing the desired behaviour from being undertaken. Within structural and social constraints identified social marketers then seek to understand how they can move and motivate change at the individual, social and built environment level based on available budget envelopes and timeframes.

Meat has a special place in Chinese diet and is one of the most important components of a daily meal. Burgeoning income and associated living conditions among middle and upper-middle class in China have contributed to demand for high quality imported red meat at a time when meat consumption is being discouraged by leading world health organizations such as WHO[1]. Etherington and Bardsley (1995) estimate the amount of money spent on meat products each week in China could be as much as a third of a household budget, indicating the importance attached to meat by Chinese households. Analysis of the Chinese market indicates that while demand for imported meat has increased, the domestic industry has prospered (Chang & Hsia, 2000). According to the United States Department of Agriculture, China's meat imports are predicted to rise ten-fold in the coming decades; for example, imports of beef, which come primarily from Oceania and Latin America are predicted to rise from 2010 to over 750,000 million tonnes by 2023/24 (Hansen and Gale, 2014). The same pattern is reflected in domestic meat production where China's share in world meat production rose to 29% in 2006, a level that is commensurate to China's share of the world's population (Li, 2009).

As noted by Schroeter and Azzam (1990), the Chinese meat industry includes production and meat processing (e.g. procurement of livestock from farms, slaughtering and processing of different parts channeled through various marketing and retail channels). John Hopkins Center for a Livable Future (2015) raises serious public health concerns for industry workers, rural communities, consumers of animal products and the general public. Sapkota et al. (2007) cautioned that the feed given to industrially-raised cattle is formulated to maximize production with feed ingredients containing antibiotic, arsenical drugs and other ingredients delivering harmful contaminants and antibiotic-resistant bacteria into the human food chain (Silbergeld et al., 2008). Further concerns are raised by Donham et al. (2007) who found that farm worker health is compromised through handling of toxic gases from animal waste and crowded, unsanitary conditions for animals which lead to transmission of diseases from animals to workers, who might then spread infections to their communities.

Chinese consumers who can afford high quality of meat are likely to shop in foreign retail outlets rather than traditional open-air markets, indicating affordability of imported beef influencing their purchase choice. China is a collectivist society that harvests social motives in consumption drive (Bagozzi et al., 2000; Chan & Lau, 2001); however, consumers are prepared to pay a premium price for quality (Shukla, 2015). Notwithstanding this, Guo et al. (2016, p. 221) posit that Chinese consumers continue to ignore the negative impact of consuming meat on the environment, which include "excessively high contributions to global greenhouse gas emissions, land and water pollution and depletion, antimicrobial resistance and negative impacts on human health".

This research seeks to examine potential factors that may impact beef consumption in China. Accordingly, we review the literature to identify pertinent social and environmental factors relevant to beef consumption to broaden understanding beyond individual Chinese consumers whose views are observed using netnography. Finally, we present the results of the study together with a discussion and our conclusion, including managerial implications and the limitations of the research.

METHODOLOGY

A mixed method study was employed. It comprised of a narrative review to identify individual, social and environmental factors influencing beef consumption in China and a netnographic study to observe consumer views and concerns about beef.

Study 1: The Narrative Review

In order to examine the social and surrounding food supply and other environmental factors contributing to beef consumption in China, we undertook a narrative review. It identified and synthesized a compilation of more than 20 years (since 1996) of empirical research on beef consumption in China.

Publications were extracted from the following databases: Emerald, Science Direct and Social Science Index. Abstracts were reviewed to determine the relevance of the papers (Aaker et al., 2012). The key words 'beef', 'meat', 'red meat', 'beef purchase', 'beef consumption', 'processed meat', 'pork', 'lamb'. 'chicken' or 'goat' were used; no language restrictions were applied. Further, we reviewed the references in the identified articles to find more relevant studies.

Study 2: Netnography

To examine reasons for buying imported beef, an ethnographic approach based on netnography (Kozinets, 2015) was employed. Netnography is suitable for open and public information available in online forums to understand and analyse consumers' needs and requirements. It adapts ethnographic research techniques to study communities online and ensures that consumer-centred data is obtained. Netnography is primarily based upon the observation of textual discourse – an important difference from balancing of discourse, and observed behaviour that occurs during in-person ethnography.

There are many advantages of netnography as it can take place anywhere as long as there is a computer with access to the internet saving time and money. Participants are not required to take part in the research and researchers can look for the information using available online data. In addition, since the respondents do not meet the researchers, the method is unobtrusive and affords greater privacy, which can also reduce biases that occur in self-reporting. However, the scope of the method can be narrow since it only focuses on the online groups limiting generalizability. Twenty-three user posts posted online over a six-month period on Meishi and Chinese Food Safety electronic message boards were studied.

STUDY 1 RESULTS: THE NARRATIVE REVIEW

Generally, when consumers purchase meat their selections are based on key attributes which include freshness, colour, packaging, convenience, price, inspection labels and organic certification (Shi, 2008). Similarly, Liu et al. (2007) found that consumers pay more attention to freshness, colour and textural attributes before purchasing. Previous research indicates that awareness of, and consumption of, meat is very limited in China (Zhou et al., 2013). Moreover, Grunert et al., (2011) argue Chinese consumers have little knowledge about environmental effects of meat farming, which is corroborated by other researchers (e.g. Thøgersen & Zhou, 2012). We note the Chinese government has recently begun to promote sustainable farming and health and food safety.

Affluence and Red Meat Consumption

China's fast and continued economic expansion has delivered personal income increases among urban dwellers (Guo et al., 2016). This rise in affluence has greatly enhanced purchasing power and demand for animal proteins including imported meat (Cao et al., 2013), which is believed to be of a higher quality than locally produced red meat. Rising purchasing power coupled with urbanisation has resulted in a growing demand for imported meat in China (Liu et al., 2009). Statistics indicate the largest share of households' food budgets, an estimated 29%, goes toward meat products (Dietrich, 2008) and this is growing (see Figure 1). As China moves from low to middle income in urban areas we can expect meat consumption to increase (Gao, Wailes & Cramer, 1996).

Figure 1. Relationship between income and consumption of beef

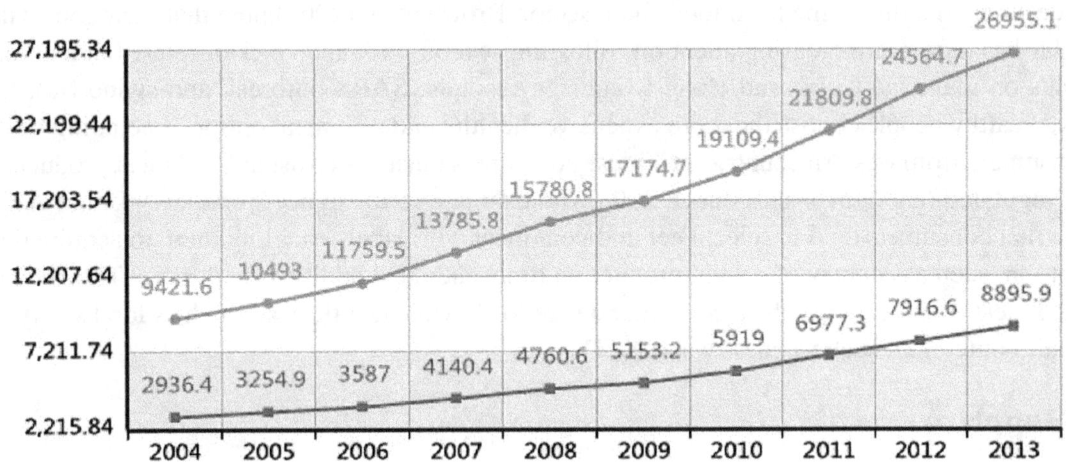

Quality Perceptions

Affluent Chinese consumers view meat quality as a crucial attribute to base their purchase decisions (Ortega et al., 2011). Liu et al. (2007) note that consumers prioritize meat quality, indicating a quality–price trade-off. Pan et al. (2012) indicate that consumers pay more attention to quality than price when income levels are higher. To meet high quality beef demands, Chinese consumers are buying imported beef. Generally, Australian and New Zealand beef is considered of higher quality, comprising mostly of grass-fed and some grain-fed beef (Hwang, 1993). Imported beef is sold in selected supermarkets (Walmart, Tesco, Sam's Club and Carrefour) delivering additional prestige perceptions.

As incomes increase Chinese consumers become more aware of and focused on quality attributes, such as country-of-origin of beef products indicating the growing importance of these attributes in the country's market. In China, beef supply is fragmented (Brown et al., 2002). Beef sold by farmers and individual vendors is considered lower quality and not comparable with certified beef supplied via international supermarkets. Chain supermarkets offer clean beef (typically imported) that is sold in a more secure food supply environment and the meat is considered a better source than open-air (flee) markets. Although consumers believe that beef sold in supermarkets has a higher profit margin for the seller, consumer preference for this type of outlet indicates Chinese consumers are more concerned about food safety and quality issues than they are about the price (Qing et al., 2014). Hence, rising incomes and a focus on quality and safety influence the choice between supermarket chains and locally produced markets.

Health Perceptions

Chinese consumers are largely unaware about the impact of meat consumption on their own health (e.g. acquiring cancer, heart disease, see Micha et al., 2013; Pan et al., 2012; Sinha et al., 2009). However, the country of origin plays a significant role in health perceptions (Shi et al., 2012). Rather health concerns are more short-term focused, centering attention on food safety, reflecting the diversity in the supply system in a developing country such as China. Chinese consumers often express concerns regarding food safety (Jonge et al., 2008). China is a country with considerable food safety problems and has faced a series of recent food scares. This has resulted in considerable consumer awareness of food safety issues and widespread distrust in the local food chain sector. Brown et al. (2002) note that meat food safety in particular has attracted increasing attention following several pork and chicken-related human disease outbreaks on mainland China and Hong Kong (for example, SARS outbreak and swine flu). Consequently, wealthy people choose the more expensive, healthy and safe meat options, including beef. Unlike consumers from western countries, Chinese consumers place less trust in local meat producers who are not regulated (e.g. James and Marks, 2008 who examined trust in beef products). Liu et al. (2007) indicate that consumers tend to select beef and goat meat with labels enabling them to acquire detailed information, such as country of origin, production time, chemical additives and more. The demand for imported meat (beef) is driven by a consumer desire to alleviate health risks, such as food safety, rather than health outcomes, such as obesity and NCDs.

Beef Supply

A series of globally recognised food safety scandals (e.g. the Husi scandal which involved the supply of expired beef to KFC, McDonalds and more) have brought increased awareness to China's inefficient certification and inspection system (Ortega et al., 2011; James, 2014). When selecting beef products, especially fresh beef sold by small vendors, consumers have few clues about its source, production process, suppliers or other information. The only way to acquire this information is through sellers' descriptions. Although big local supermarkets sell beef with labels providing detailed information, residents still have doubts regarding the beef quality. Quality concerns exist due to consumers' limited trust in government food certification and inspection systems. As a result, imported meat sold in global chain supermarkets is popular given that foreign certification, strict regulations and inspection systems are perceived to be reliable.

Suppliers are a crucial factor in the whole beef chain. Brown et al. (2002) suggest that within the Chinese beef industry, individual slaughterhouses, which account for almost 90% of all cattle suppliers in China, supply poor-quality, low-value beef to the mass beef market. These individual suppliers and abattoirs lack the advanced technology to maintain a sanitary and scientific breeding environment as well as a sound slaughter process. They cannot establish an advanced beef traceable system to ensure safe production. As a consequence, the quality of beef supplied by individual vendors is not trusted (Pan et al., 2012). There are scandals that some farmer slaughterers rely heavily on the use of chemicals (toxic pesticides) in their production systems to cope with various animal diseases. Indeed, sick cattle can be purchased in the Chinese market. This contributes to consumers' worries and distrust for domestic beef.

Social Influences

Lifestyle is a reflection of people's values, beliefs and habits and is considered to be an important social factor influencing purchasing behaviours (Song, 2011). Researchers have revealed that consumers with similar values and attitudes are likely to have similar preferences and behaviours in food consumption (Grunert et al., 2011). Kang et al. (2015) identified that consumers attach importance to health. However, as previously noted in terms of beef, Chinese consumers are more concerned with food safety. Research by Verbeke and Viaene (1999) suggested that safety-related attributes are a key element affecting consumers' choices. Some consumers care about animal welfare (Verbeke & Viaene, 2000); for instance, some refuse to purchase beef and other meat because they think feeding livestock for eating is not ethical.

The Growing Prominence of Convenience

Purchase and eating habits affect consumers' behaviour and so do the increasing busy lifestyles experienced by many. Meat products are popular as they are considered quick, easy and convenient to prepare (Capps et al., 1988). Recently, pre-cooked beef has become popular and constitutes a larger portion of overall meat consumption. In urban centers, people's fast paced lifestyle demands pre-cooked beef; which is perceived to deliver time saving. Further, research sponsored by the beef industry appears to support the opinion that consumers prefer lean beef marketing as healthier. Meat producers reduce the fat content in pre-cooked beef and offer consumers a lean "house brand" in addition to choice grades.

The Complex Interplay Between Economics and Beef Consumption

Socioeconomic status influences consumption behaviours (Lahelma et al., 1998). People in a similar social status grouping are likely to have similar consumption patterns and different groups have different patterns. For example, Steptoe and Wardle (2003) identify health differences: consumers in high socioeconomic status are more likely to exercise while those in low socioeconomic status are more likely to smoke. Importantly from a beef consumption perspective, people in the high socioeconomic status group take pride in introducing their expensive food items to their guests. For example, they would tell guests about the price of their beef, where they bought it in addition to quality markers such as country of orgin. Purchasing is a means to impress others and gain access to higher status (Danzer et al., 2014).

A broad range of environmental and social issues are contributing to trends in beef purchasing and consumption. Of note, is the limited awareness in China about the health effects of excessive meat consumption and poor local food production practices which are driving demand for imported beef. Taken together, prior research indicates a range of factors that have previously been associated with beef purchasing and consumption in China. Income and socioeconomic status are related to lifestyle and health consciousness, which in turn contribute to an increase in demand for quality beef that can be delivered through a trusted certified supply system. To date, research has taken a narrow view centering attention only on the Chinese consumers; consideration of the social and environmental factors underlying current consumption is important for actionable insights that can inform policy change.

STUDY 2 RESULTS: NETNOGRAPHY

The narrative analysis from blog post revealed themes relating to economic factors (income and price), social factors (safety and lifestyle) and environmental issues. Selected quotes (in italics below) show that in line with the factors observed in the narrative review, netnography revealed the role that economic development exerts. Comments indicate that as living standards rise Chinese consumers have larger budgets to spend on higher-priced food.

In recent years, my family prefers imported beef because of the increase income.

I have more wages than before, why not selecting imported beef regardless price difference?

Forum posts voiced that in general customers are not price-sensitive when purchasing beef and meat products. They tend to select imported beef with higher price because they can afford to, which alleviates food safety fears. Interestingly, imported beef prices are no longer higher compared with domestically produced beef.

I purchase much more imported beef than before since the price decreased in recent months.

The price of domestic beef has increased recently.

The price of imported beef is not that much more expensive than domestic beef now, sometimes it can be lower.

There are many social factors influencing consumers' behaviour towards beef consumption. Beef safety, compared to other food categories, is always of concern. Chinese consumers thought that imported beef is generally well qualified and safe compared with domestic beef.

Imported beef has better quality, especially Australia, New Zealand beef.

It is well known that imported beef must follow more strict standards, making it safer.

It is a very common phenomenon that imported and packed frozen meat is more popular.

It seems that domestic produced beef is still not so convincing. It is well known that imported beef from US has the best quality.

Imported beef is popular since developed countries have advanced technology to ensure better quality.

I think imported beef sold in big chain supermarkets is the best class.

Traditional beef countries have more experience in beef production.

It can be observed that Chinese residents showed their trust towards imported beef. It is believed that beef in developed countries, such as Australia, New Zealand and US, whose residents traditionally regard beef as a major category, are more experienced and own advanced technology in production. Pan et al. (2012) observed that most western countries have established traceable system in beef supply and other meat industries, enabling consumers to trace every element of their meat's production. China, on the other hand, still lacks the system to convince consumers about beef safety. Questions such as the origin of beef, what feed is used cannot be answered.

There are more potential safety problems regarding beef, especially domestically produced beef.

It is hard to identify where and how the beef is produced, we are not sure whether they add some harmful additives, it is horrible and I am afraid of eating domestic beef with many uncertainties.

In China, food safety issues happen quite frequently. Especially in recent years, with the development of new medias, more scandals are exposed.

Even KFC, McDonald's and other famous restaurant chains are exposed to use expired beef. Who can we trust in the market?

Targeted users showed their distrust in the domestic beef industry to some extent. Since they have increased consciousness regarding food safety, they tend to select traceable imported beef. Consequently, respondents' messages demonstrated that lifestyle may be contributing to imported beef consumption.

Imported precooked beef with labels is convenient and sanitary; therefore, it is becoming popular among customers.

Beef, compared with pork has low fat and high protein.

Beef is my first choice when I started to lose weight.

Due to the fast pace of life in urban areas, most young people will select convenience foods to save time. Therefore, imported pre-cooked beef in big chain supermarkets is increasing in popularity given advantages that include convenient, reduced cooking skills and, for young consumers, more time to do other activities. In addition, since people are becoming more concerned about health issues and trying to shift to healthy lifestyles, beef is regarded as a good alternative to pork. Food selection distinguishes different socio-economic classes; therefore, purchasing imported beef is also regarded as a way to demonstrate status.

When inviting guests, we will prepare the best food and introduce in details, like Australian steaks, French wine.

Buying imported beef is a symbolization of rich status, not only imported beef, but all imported goods.

When I visited my friends, buying imported beef as a gift looked more graceful and fancy.

Well qualified imported beef is sold in high end stores; I enjoy shopping in that environment rather than the open-air market.

In this case, imported beef is much more than meat or food. It is regarded as an upscale lifestyle symbol, enabling consumers to communicate status via the food served. By serving Australian steaks, a Chinese consumer can convey their wealth to their peers and family members.

Chinese consumers display high concern for personal and family safety when it comes to buying and consuming beef. The lack of awareness amongst Chinese consumers about environmental factors relating to meat production, livestock and cattle farming is evident. Respondents voiced concern for personal safety. For example, vendors have no refrigerating equipment to store meat, therefore, more germs are contained. One respondent triggered discussion about local butchers who slaughter sick cattle to get rid of the problem, hence passing substandard meat to local retailers. Another respondent explained that the *Shuanghui Meat Company is reported to use harmful additives in sausages.*

Even at on individual personal health level, there was no awareness of the extensive evidence about the contribution of meat consumption towards obesity, cancer and other non-communicable diseases. Furthermore, there was not acknowledgement of the national or international guidelines aiming at restricting red meat consumption. If the current understanding and perceptions about imported beef are not challenged, as income levels in China continue to grow, the negative impacts of increased beef consumption are going to be felt not only in this country but also globally. This is particularly worrying for the heavy environmental footprint related to beef.

A BROAD VIEW OF BEEF CONSUMPTION

Individual modifiable factors are evident in this study. Increase in income levels in Chinese households is fueling demand for beef, particularly imported beef in the absence of awareness of the detrimental health effects of excessive red meat consumption. Understanding the environmental impacts of food production and obesity risks from excessive red meat consumption are not prominent in the observed online discussions about beef consumption. Concerns relating to food safety and securing reliable meat supplies that will not harm in the short-term are more prominent when examining both consumer behaviour literature and comments posted on Internet forums. The lack of awareness of the detrimental health effects that excessive red meat consumption is an area which requires urgent action.

Social factors play an important role in Chinese beef consumption. One of the most important elements in meat purchasing is quality and prestigious foods. The netnographic study demonstrates the role that prestigious food products play in conveying Chinese wealth. Imported beef which is often certified and delivered via known food management systems is equated with quality and viewed as healthier than the one produced domestically. These are potentially dangerous perceptions given the size of China's population as they trigger increases in global production of beef – the meat with the worst environmental footprint which is also the most inefficient use of feed calories to be converted into human food (Eshel et al., 2014).

As incomes in China have increased more consumers are buying imported beef and this has delivered more competition, which in turn has lowered imported beef prices. The netnographic study delivered evidence that imported beef is now much cheaper in China compared to the past, which in turn stimulates demand for this meat. This aggravates the problems even further.

Health concerns among affluent consumers remain a crucial factor in determining food choice. Consumers are safety conscious and imported beef alleviates quality concerns. Imported beef products are under the control of comprehensive safety monitoring in all areas including production, slaughtering and packaging. Australia, New Zealand and the UK are examples of where beef production follows strict standards and offers traceable systems. Our result highlights that there are serious environmental and health risks associated with any meat consumption, although be it slightly different – immediate health risks associated with local meat and more long-term for imported meat. Whilst the Chinese style of meat consumption avoids the intake of processed meats (which is better than in the West), the increasing consumption of red meat in China is likely to cause western types of diseases, such as diabetes, obesity and cancers which were traditionally less common when the population of this country was adhering to its traditional diets.

There are different social marketing implications from this study. Most importantly, the lack of awareness about the health, environmental and climate change implications and risks from increased beef consumption requires urgent interventions which improve the level of information Chinese consumers have as well as influence their behaviour. Given China's size and its demand for beef, and red meat in general, the changes that occur in this country are of global significance. It is time for China's consumers to embrace the recommendations by the Chinese government for a decrease in red meat consumption (FIA Communications, 2016) and replace the immediate concerns about food safety with better long-term options.

REFERENCES

Aaker, A. D., Day, S. G., Kumar, V., & Leone, R. (2012). *Marketing research* (11th ed.). Hoboken, NJ: John Wiley & Sons.

Bagozzi, R. P., Wong, N., Abe, S., & Bergami, M. (2000). Cultural and situational contingencies and the theory of reasoned action: application to fast food restaurant consumption. *Journal of Consumer Psychology*, *9*(2), 97–106. doi:10.1207/S15327663JCP0902_4

Brennan, L., Previte, J., & Fry, M. L. (2016). Social marketing's consumer myopia: Applying a behavioural ecological model to address wicked problems. *Journal of Social Marketing*, *6*(3), 219–239. doi:10.1108/JSOCM-12-2015-0079

Brown, C. G., Longworth, J. W., & Waldron, S. (2002). Food safety and development of the beef industry in China. *Food Policy*, *27*(3), 269–284. doi:10.1016/S0306-9192(02)00017-9

Cao, L.-J., Tian, W.-M., Wang, J.-M., Malcolm, B., Liu, H.-B., & Zhau, Z.-Y. (2013). Recent food consumption trends in China and trade implications to 2020. *Australasian Agribusiness Review*, *21*, 2. Retrieved from http://www.agrifood.info/review/2013/Cao_et_al.pdf

Capps, O. Jr, Moen, D., & Branson, R. (1988). Consumer characteristics associated with the selection of lean meat products. *Agribusiness*, *4*(6), 549–557. doi:10.1002/1520-6297(198811)4:6<549::AID-AGR2720040605>3.0.CO;2-D

Centers for Disease Control and Prevention. (2016). *Economics of NCDs, injury and environmental health: Advancing evidence-based policies*. Retrieved from http://www.cdc.gov/

Chan, R. Y. K., & Lau, L. B. Y. (2001). Explaining green purchasing behavior: A cross-cultural study on American and Chinese consumers. *Journal of International Consumer Marketing*, *14*(2/3), 9–41.

Chang, H., & Hsia, C. (2000). Beef import market shares in Taiwan: Implications for Australia. *The Australian Journal of Agricultural and Resource Economics*, *44*(2), 217–231. doi:10.1111/1467-8489.00108

Cross, A. J., Leitzmann, M. F., Gail, M. H., Hollenbeck, A. R., Schatzkin, A., & Sinha, R. (2007). A prospective study of red and processed meat intake in relation to cancer risk. *PLoS Medicine*, *4*(12), e325. doi:10.1371/journal.pmed.0040325 PMID:18076279

Danzer, M. A., Dietz, B., Gatskova, K., & Schmillen, A. (2014). Showing off to the new neighbors? Income, socioeconomic status and consumption patterns of internal migrants. *Journal of Comparative Economics*, *42*(1), 230–245. doi:10.1016/j.jce.2013.05.002

Demaio, A. R., Nielsen, K. K., Tersbøl, B. P., Kallestrup, P., & Meyrowitsch, D. W. (2014). Primary health care: A strategic framework for the prevention and control of chronic non-communicable disease. *Global Health Action*, *7*(1), 24504. doi:10.3402/gha.v7.24504

Dietrich, J. (2008). Testing unitary and bargaining models of Chinese household food consumption. *Applied Financial Economics*, *18*(4-6), 397–410. doi:10.1080/09603100500399134

Donham, K. J., Wing, S., Osterberg, D., Flora, J. L., Hodne, C., Thu, K. M., & Thorne, P. S. (2007). Community health and socioeconomic issues surrounding concentrated animal feeding operations. *Environmental Health Perspectives*, *115*(2), 317–320. doi:10.1289/ehp.8836 PMID:17384786

Eshel, G., Shepon, A., Makov, T., & Milo, R. (2014). Land, irrigation water, greenhouse gas, and reactive nitrogen burdens of meat, eggs, and dairy production in the United States. *Proceedings of the National Academy of Sciences of the United States of America*, *111*(33), 11996–12001. doi:10.1073/pnas.1402183111 PMID:25049416

Etherington, D. J., & Bardsley, R. G. (1995). Enzymes in the meat industry. In G. A. Tucker & L. F. J. Woods (Eds.), *Enzymes in food processing* (pp. 144–189). London, UK: Blackie. doi:10.1007/978-1-4615-2147-1_5

Food Industry Asia (FIA) Communications. (2016). *New Chinese dietary guidelines: A reference for industry*. Retrieved from https://foodindustry.asia/new-chinese-dietary-guidelines-a-reference-for-industry

Gao, X., Wailes, E., & Cramer, G. (1996). A two-stage rural household demand analysis: Microdata evidence from Jiangsu Province, China. *American Journal of Agricultural Economics*, *78*(3), 604–613. doi:10.2307/1243278

Grunert, G. K., Perrea, T., Zhou, Y. F., Huang, G., Sørensen, B. T., & Krystallis, A. (2011). Is food-related lifestyle (FRL) able to reveal food consumption patterns in non-Western cultural environments? Its adaptation and application in urban China. *Appetite*, *56*(2), 357–367. doi:10.1016/j.appet.2010.12.020 PMID:21192995

Guo, X., Raphaely, T., & Marinova, D. (2016). China's growing meat demands: Implications for sustainability. In T. Raphaely & D. Marinova (Eds.), *Impact of meat consumption of health and environmental sustainability* (pp. 221–232). Hershey, PA: IGI Global. doi:10.4018/978-1-4666-9553-5.ch011

Hansen, J., & Gale, F. (2014). China in the next decade: Rising meat demand and growing imports of feed. United States Department of Agriculture. Retrieved from https://www.ers.usda.gov/amber-waves/2014/april/china-in-the-next-decade-rising-meat-demand-and-growing-imports-of-feed/

Hwang, T.-C. (1993). Meat expenditure pattern, forecast, and impact from liberalisation in Taiwan. *Journal of Agricultural Economics*, *54*(December), 117–164.

James, A. (2014). China arrests five over tainted meat. *Evening Standard*, July 23, Retrieved from http://web.a.ebscohost.com/ehost/detail/detail?vid=3&sid=fdad63be-967a-477a-b9a6-750d49b294ba%40sessionmgr4001&hid=4112&bdata=Jmxhbmc9emgtY24mc2l0ZT1laG9zdC1saXZl#db=nfh&AN=97167012

James, H. S. Jr, & Marks, L. A. (2008). Trust and distrust in biotechnology risks managers: Insights from the United Kingdom, 1996–2002. *AgBioForum*, *11*(2), 93–105.

John Hopkins Center for a Livable Future. (2015). Industrial food animal production in America: Examining the Impact of the Pew Commission's priority recommendations. Retrieved from https://www.jhsph.edu/research/centers-and-institutes/johns-hopkins-center-for-a-livable-future/_pdf/research/clf_reports/CLF-PEW-for%20Web.pdf

Jonge, J. D., Trijp, H. V., Goddard, E., & Frewer, J. (2008). Consumer confidence in the safety of food in Canada and the Netherlands: The validation of a generic framework. *Food Quality and Preference*, *19*(5), 439–451. doi:10.1016/j.foodqual.2008.01.002

Kaluza, J., Wolk, A., & Larsson, S. C. (2012). Red meat consumption and risk of stroke: A meta-analysis of prospective studies. *Stroke*, *43*(10), 2556–2560. doi:10.1161/STROKEAHA.112.663286 PMID:22851546

Kang, J., Jun, J., & Arendt, S. W. (2015). Understanding customers' healthy food choices at casual dining restaurants: Using the value–attitude–behavior model. *International Journal of Hospitality Management*, *48*, 12–21. doi:10.1016/j.ijhm.2015.04.005

Kozinets, R. V. (2015). *Netnography: Redefined*. London, UK: Sage. doi:10.1002/9781118767771.wbiedcs067

Lahelma, E., Pietinen, P., Roos, E., & Virtanen, M. (1998). Gender, socioeconomic status and family status as determinants of food behaviour. *Social Science & Medicine*, *46*(12), 1519–1529. doi:10.1016/S0277-9536(98)00032-X PMID:9672392

Li, J. P. (2009). Exponential growth, animal welfare, environmental and food safety impact: The case of China's livestock production. *Journal of Agricultural & Environmental Ethics*, *22*(3), 217–240. doi:10.1007/s10806-008-9140-7

Liu, H., Parton, K., Zhou, Z., & Cox, R. (2009). At-home meat consumption in China: An empirical study. *The Australian Journal of Agricultural and Resource Economics*, *53*(4), 485–501. doi:10.1111/j.1467-8489.2009.00463.x

Liu, X., Nelson, M., & Ibrahim, M. (2007). Analyzing consumer's calculation factors in the purchase decision of goat meat. *Journal of Food Distribution Research*, *38*(1), 196–202.

Micha, R., Michas, G., Lajous, M., & Mozaffarian, D. (2013). Processing of meats and cardiovascular risk: Time to focus on preservatives. *BMC Medicine*, *11*(1), 136. doi:10.1186/1741-7015-11-136 PMID:23701737

Ortega, D. L., Wang, H. H., Wu, L., & Olynk, N. J. (2011). Modeling heterogeneity in consumer preferences for select food safety attributes in China. *Food Policy*, *36*(2), 318–324. doi:10.1016/j.foodpol.2010.11.030

Pan, L., Tian, L., Cao, J. M., & Zhang, J. Y. (2012). 世界牛肉消费趋势及影响因素分析. *Zhongguo Xumu Zazhi*, *48*(16), 20–23.

Pang, B., Rundle-Thiele, S. R., & Kubacki, K. (2017). An empirical examination of the Ecological and Cognitive Active Commuting framework: A social marketing formative research study. *Health Education*, *117*(6), 581–598. doi:10.1108/HE-12-2016-0066

Qing, P., Xi, A., & Hu, W. (2014). Consumer preference for meat in China: A case study of Beijing. *Emerging Markets Finance and Trade*, 50(Sup2), 135-143.

Sapkota, A. R., Lefferts, L. Y., McKenzie, S., & Walker, P. (2007). What do we feed to food-production animals? A review of animal feed ingredients and their potential impacts on human health. *Environmental Health Perspectives*, *115*(5), 663–670. doi:10.1289/ehp.9760 PMID:17520050

Schroeter, J., & Azzam, A. (1990). Measuring market power in multi-product oligopolies: The US meat industry. *Applied Economics*, *22*(10), 1365–1376. doi:10.1080/00036849000000107

Shi, Y. X. (2008). 中国牛肉消费现状及其影响因素分析. *Farm Economic Management*, *4*, 53–55.

Shi, Z., Xu, P., Wang, Z., & Song, S. (2012). Willingness to pay for traceable pork: Evidence from Beijing, China. *China Agricultural Economic Review*, *4*(2), 200–215. doi:10.1108/17561371211224782

Shukla, P. (2015). Consumers in Asia buy luxuries for different reasons to the West. *The Conversation*. Retrieved from https://theconversation.com/consumers-in-asia-buy-luxuries-for-different-reasons-to-the-west-45069

Silbergeld, E. K., Graham, J., & Price, L. B. (2008). Industrial food animal production, antimicrobial resistance, and human health. *Annual Review of Public Health*, *29*(1), 151–169. doi:10.1146/annurev.publhealth.29.020907.090904 PMID:18348709

Sinha, R., Cross, A. J., Graubard, B. I., Letzmann, M. F., & Schatzkin, A. (2009). Meat intake and mortality: A prospective study of over half a million people. *Archives of Internal Medicine*, *169*(6), 562–571. doi:10.1001/archinternmed.2009.6 PMID:19307518

Song, L.F. (2011). 简述影响消费者购买行为的因素. *The Business Circular*, 24-25.

Steptoe, A., & Wardle, J. (2003). Socioeconomic differences in attitudes and beliefs about healthy lifestyles. *Journal of Epidemiology and Community Health*, *57*(6), 440–443. doi:10.1136/jech.57.6.440 PMID:12775791

Tapp, A., & Rundle-Thiele, S. R. (2016). Integrating social marketing into a multi-disciplinary environment behaviour change: Past present and future. In F. Spotswood (Ed.), *Beyond behaviour change: Key issues, interdisciplinary approaches and future directions* (pp. 135–156). Bristol, UK: The Policy Press.

Thøgersen, J., & Zhou, Y. (2012). Chinese consumers' adoption of a "green" innovation: The case of organic food. *Journal of Marketing Management*, *28*(3-4), 313–333. doi:10.1080/0267257X.2012.658834

Verbeke, W., & Viaene, J. (1999). Beliefs, attitude and behaviour towards fresh meat consumption in Belgium: Empirical evidence from a consumer survey. *Food Quality and Preference*, *10*(6), 437–445. doi:10.1016/S0950-3293(99)00031-2

Verbeke, W., & Viaene, J. (2000). Ethical challenges for livestock production: Meeting consumer concerns about meat safety and animal welfare. *Journal of Agricultural & Environmental Ethics*, *12*(2), 141–151. doi:10.1023/A:1009538613588

Vergnaud, A.-C., Norat, T., Romaguera, D., Mouw, T., May, A. M., Travier, N., & Peeters, P. H. et al. (2010). Meat consumption and prospective weight change in participants of the EPIC-PANACEA study. *The American Journal of Clinical Nutrition*, *92*(2), 398–407. doi:10.3945/ajcn.2009.28713 PMID:20592131

World Cancer Research Fund (WCRF) International. (2015). Continuous update project report: Diet, nutrition, physical activity and liver cancer. Retrieved from http://www.wcrf.org/sites/default/files/Liver-Cancer-2015-Report.pdf

World Health Organization (WHO). (2016). *Obesity and overweight*. Fact sheet. Retrieved from http://www.who.int/mediacentre/factsheets/fs311/en/

World Health Organization (WHO). (2013). Global action plan for the prevention and control of non-communicable diseases 2013-2020. Retrieved from www.who.int

Zhou, L.-J., Ying, G.-G., Liu, S., Zhang, R.-Q., Lai, H.-J., Chen, Z.-F., & Pan, C.-G. (2013). Excretion masses and environmental occurrence of antibiotics in typical swine and dairy cattle farms in China. *The Science of the Total Environment*, *444*, 183–195. doi:10.1016/j.scitotenv.2012.11.087 PMID:23268145

KEY TERMS AND DEFINITIONS

Body Mass Index (BMI): An index based on weight and height used to determine whether an adult person is underweight, within the healthy range, overweight or obese; it is an estimate of body fat and applied as a predictor for weight-related diseases such as high blood pressure, diabetes 2 and cardiovascular disease.

Food Safety: The condition of food being protected during production, preparation, handling, storing and supply from contamination, infection and other conditions which could affect the health of those consuming it.

Narrative Review: A review of scientific literature related to a topic or theme from a theoretical point of view, hence providing qualitative results.

Netnography: Derived from network and ethnography, the term refers to research based on online information to understand social interactions and experiences.

Non-Communicable Disease: A disease which is not caused by infection; examples include cancer, autoimmune diseases, cardiovascular disease and many others.

Quality: A characteristic which compares something or somebody against others; also used as a description of excellence.

Western Countries: Refers to United States of America, Canada, Australia, New Zealand and countries in Europe with the exception of the former Eastern Europe and Turkey.

ENDNOTE

1 A growing body of research suggests meat and animal products are detrimental to human health, with heart disease (Micha et al., 2013; Pan et al., 2012; Sinha et al 2009); stroke (Kaluza et al., 2012), type 2 diabetes (Pan et al., 2011), obesity (Vergnaud et al., 2010), cancers (Pan et al., 2012; Cross et al., 2007; WCRF International, 2015), and earlier death (Sinha et al., 2009) resulting from excessive red meat consumption.

Chapter 18
Marketing an Environmentally Sustainable Catering Model:
A Case Study of Medley Hall Residential College in Victoria, Australia

Emily Foenander
Swinburne University of Technology, Australia

Celia Green
Australian National University, Australia

Linda Portsmouth
Curtin University, Australia

Talia Raphaely
Curtin University, Australia

ABSTRACT

This chapter presents a novel case study of a diet sustainability model implemented at Medley Hall, an on-campus student accommodation facility at a university in Victoria, Australia. Diet sustainability refers to measures to minimise adverse environmental impacts attributable to food production. A qualitative evaluation of this initiative was conducted during 2016 including interviews with both residents and staff. The results depict a grass-roots initiative that evolved to become a deeply embedded component of organisational identity. Social marketing strategies were employed at multiple governance levels, including: (i) residents, (ii) staff and (iii) college. The evaluation data from this study provides indication of the key drivers of success in motivating consumers (residents) to engage with and embrace diet sustainability interventions and demonstrates the utility of community-based social marketing (CBSM) in informing such initiatives.

DOI: 10.4018/978-1-5225-4757-0.ch018

INTRODUCTION

In discussing a case study of an environmental sustainability intervention, this chapter demonstrates the utility of community-based social marketing (CBSM) in supporting reduced meat consumption policy implementation in localised, organisational contexts. Implementation of similar initiatives in a residential tertiary college has not been documented, nor evaluated, situating this case study as a novel insight into a nascent area. Sustainable dietary policy is an important component of broader environmental sustainability work.

This chapter presents a social marketing case study of a diet sustainability model at Medley Hall residential college, which included a central marketing message of reduced meat consumption as a more environmentally sustainable dietary behaviour. As this model emerged without pre-planned grounding in any social marketing theoretical perspective, retrospective consideration is given to its theoretical alignment. Based on this retrospective consideration, the social marketing model at Medley Hall (Medley model hereafter) is contextualised as an example of CBSM. The objectives of this chapter are to evaluate the Medley model against the CBSM evaluation framework of Lynes et al. (2014).

BACKGROUND

There are complex links between climate change, food systems and dietary choices, and with a rising world population it is anticipated that the global food system will experience a multitude of converging pressures over coming decades (Pearson et al., 2014). Food production and consumption require significant amounts of natural resources (land, water, minerals, energy) which in turn generate substantial greenhouse gas (GHG) emissions (Elferink et al., 2008). Spurred by large increases in global populations and more recently, rising affluence, food production more than doubled in the second half of the 20th century (Khan & Hanjra, 2009). This increased demand has placed unparalleled pressures on the environment, resulting in changes to climate systems, loss of biodiversity, land degradation and increased resource use (Ericksen et al., 2009).

Whether food is animal-based or plant-based has a large bearing on the amount of GHG emitted in its production life cycle. Livestock production has been shown to be especially GHG intensive, with the global livestock sector accounting for approximately 14.5% of all anthropogenic GHG emissions (Ripple et al., 2014). Globally the demand for meat is rising, with Steinfeld et al. (2006) predicting it to double by 2050 from the 1999/01 levels. This poses significant societal challenges given livestock production impacts on almost all elements of the environment, i.e. land, soil, water, air, biodiversity (de Vries & de Boer, 2010).

Sustainable Diets

Through its impact on the food system, climate change affects people's diets and nutritional status. Conversely, dietary choices and food systems affect GHG emissions, and consequently climate change. Greenhouse gas emissions from food production have been shown to be on par with emissions from the transport sector (Garnett, 2009) and a regional European analysis showed food accounting for 31% of the EU-25s total GHG impact (Tukker et al., 2006). Recently there have been a number of studies examining the association between dietary choices, food production systems, and the resultant impact on GHG emissions. The term "sustainable diet" used in the context of this chapter, refers to dietary models designed with an aim of minimising, where contextually practicable, adverse environmental food production impacts.

Joyce et al. (2014) conducted a systematic review of research modelling different dietary patterns and GHG emissions which revealed that the greater the reduction in animal-based foods, the lower the GHG emission impact. Reduced animal food production has the potential to decrease GHG emissions compared to technological mitigation or increased productivity measures (Hedenus et al., 2014; Popp et al., 2010), with the greatest GHG reduction potential achieved by a combined approach integrating both diet sustainability and other sustainability measures (Popp et al., 2010).

Social Marketing

Diet modelling studies shed light on the areas requiring policy change, particularly, reduced consumption of animal-based foods, but this research base does not provide much guidance on the form these interventions could take, or how change could be achieved at a population level (Joyce et al., 2014). The discipline of social marketing has garnered attention as a possible means by which to promote sustainable consumption. To a limited degree this has included the marketing of sustainable food choices. Environmental issues were first addressed by marketing scholars in the 1970s in concepts such as ecological marketing (Henion & Kinnear, 1976), the ecologically concerned consumer (Kardash, 1976), and the theory of responsible consumption (Fisk, 1973). These concepts have been viewed as a representing an environmentally-focused extension of social marketing, which maintains that marketing activities should focus not only on the interests of consumers and business shareholders, but be equally concerned with the welfare of society (Prothero, 1990).

However, these early conceptions were focused primarily on only a relatively small number of sectors (namely oil, cars and chemicals) and public behaviours (recycling, fuel saving) and as the oil shock issues of the decade diminished, they lost some momentum (Peattie & Peattie, 2009). In the late 1980s and early 1990s as attention returned to environmental issues, these concepts re-surfaced, variously being termed with labels such as green marketing or environmental marketing (Peattie & Peattie, 2009).

An early definition of green or environmental marketing (Polonsky, 1994) extended the concept from a mere promotion of products with a characteristic that decreases the risk of environmental harm (e.g. phosphate-free) to incorporate a more traditional understanding of commercial marketing. The definition included all "activities that generate and facilitate any exchanges intended to satisfy human needs to wants, such that the satisfaction of these needs and wants occurs with minimal detrimental impact on the natural environment" (Polonsky, 1994, p. 2). This revised definition could then be applied to services (e.g. eco-tours) and incorporated all aspects of the product or service such as packaging and the production processes used. Contemporaneously, an often-cited definition of social marketing by Andreasen (1994, p. 110) also applied commercial marketing techniques to "programs designed to influence the voluntary behaviour of target audience to improve their personal welfare and that of the society of which they are part". This definition remained relatively unchallenged for many years, focussing social marketing action onto individual voluntary behaviour change with a top-down approach in terms of selection of target audiences, targeted behaviours and program development.

Later thinkers in social marketing Donovan and Henley (2010), included the consideration of involuntary behaviours, recognising the role of the social and environmental determinants of health on an individual's behaviours. They conceptualised social marketing as working towards "socially desirable goals" (Donovan & Henley, 2010, p. 6) with goal selection informed by the UN Universal Declaration of Human Rights. Consideration of this newer understanding of social marketing assists this chapter's case study. At Medley Hall, voluntary behaviours became normalised within an environment in which policy development and implementation (in consultation with the target group) supported social change on-site.

Community-Based Social Marketing Evaluation

Community-based social marketing is a branch of social marketing developed by Doug McKenzie Mohr. The CBSM methodology is informed by social psychology research which indicates that effective behaviour change is made more likely when programs incorporate direct personal contact at a community level (McKenzie-Mohr, 2011) while reducing barriers and promoting the positive benefits of behaviour change (McKenzie-Mohr et al., 2012).

The Medley model exemplifies the fourth stage of the CBSM approach: piloting before broad scale community-wide implementation and evaluation. Earlier stages involve: 1) careful selection of behaviours; 2) identifying both the barriers to behaviour change and the benefits of action; and 3) developing appropriate strategies. Community-based social marketing strategies include direct contact in which personal appeals are made to gain commitment and develop new community norms (McKenzie-Mohr, 2011; McKenzie-Mohr et al., 2012). McKenzie-Mohr (2011) suggests sustained behaviour change that contributes to the development of social norms is more likely when commitment is freely volunteered, public, durable, and actively engages consumers at both individual and group levels.

Messages used to persuade people about the target behaviours should: capture attention; be specific, easy to remember and appropriate to the audience; use a credible source; emphasise losses which result from inaction; and provide personal or community goals (McKenzie-Mohr, 2011). The final requirement of CBSM is making the targeted behaviour easy to enact by reducing barriers to change which would include, for example, making sustainable food easily available. This case study demonstrates utilisation of these CBSM strategies to increase the target sustainable diet behaviour, namely increased consumption of plant-based foods.

Lynes et al. (2014) have built on McKenzie-Mohr's work to develop a 21-factor evaluation model for CBSM initiatives. These CBSM evaluation criteria address five key areas, adapted from McKenzie-Mohr (2011), including: (1) Selecting behaviours, (2) Identifying barriers and benefits, (3) Developing a strategy, (4) Conducting a pilot, and (5) Evaluating broad scale implementation. The benchmark criteria are retrospectively applied to the Medley Hall case study (Lynes et al., 2014).

MAIN FOCUS OF THE CHAPTER

Medley Hall is an on-campus student accommodation facility at a Victorian university in Australia with a capacity of housing 57 residents (Medley Hall, 2017d). The college markets itself as a socially inclusive, secular institution which values critical thinking, altruism, environmental awareness and sustainable living (Medley Hall, 2017b; Medley Hall, 2017c). From 2015, Medley introduced a 5:2 (vegetarian: meat option) catering model to promote environmentally sustainable dietary behaviour, including reduced meat consumption (Medley Hall, 2017a). The Medley Hall website summarises the environmental sustainability ethos inherent to its catering policy, stating: (1) the 5-day-per-week vegetarian meal schedule, (2) a commitment to sourcing animal products from free range and environmentally sustainable farmers, and (3) the aim to locally source produce wherever possible.

A research base focused on social marketing approaches effective in engaging communities in reduced consumption of animal products, as an environmental sustainability behaviour, has not yet been established. This chapter offers a contribution toward this research niche by presenting the Medley model of environmental sustainability as a CBSM case study.

METHODOLOGY

This evaluation involved a qualitative research design, including face-to-face interviews with Medley Hall residents (n = 12) and staff (n = 2), to explore the evolution of and consumer response(s) to the environmental sustainability model implemented onsite. The interviews were recorded and transcribed verbatim and then thematically analysed. This chapter contextualises these results against the 21-factor CBSM benchmark criteria of Lynes et al. (2014).

The resident population at Medley is inherently transient and dynamic, with an annual turnover period during which existing residents leave and new residents (generally new university students) join the college. Nine (64.28%) of participants were omnivores, while the remaining five (35.71%) identified as vegetarian. Some individuals who identified as vegetarian also reported occasional meat consumption and/or identified as 'Medletarian' (predominantly vegetarian at Medley and flexible consumers of meat when off-site).

RESULTS

The Evolution of the Medley Model

Staff and residents recalled initial environmental sustainability measures being focused on water usage, as a response to the devastating Australian drought conditions of 2006. The Medley of today has emerged following a thorough (1) governance, (2) architectural, and (3) catering policy transformation. Interviewees shared memories of a once unkempt building, with little sustainability infrastructure.

Sustainability efforts began with modest changes, including: placing bricks in on-site toilet cisterns to circumvent excess water flow problems, the installation of shower-use timers, and signs reminding residents to switch off electrical appliances when not in use. The generosity of philanthropic funding and university scholarship programs subsequently reduced pressure on the college budget, enabling its management to reallocate funds to planned sustainability measures, including innovation of the college catering policy.

As the model continued to evolve, innovative and sophisticated structural sustainability measures were implemented. Hydronic heating provides warmth during winter months, while a rock store underneath the building circulates air to insulate the entire site. Louvres and double-glazed windows have also been installed, and at the time of data collection, the college disclosed plans to install solar panels. Kitchen cellars have been converted to water storage bladders and toilets are flushed with rainwater. Gradually, a shift from serving "an awful lot of meat" to preparing fewer meat meals, to sourcing meat from suppliers practising environmentally conscious farming was initiated:

... we only serve meat here twice a week, so 21 meals a week are served here, but only two of them are meat meals.

Informal focus group discussions in the early phases on the model inception identified increased plant-based food consumption as the primary target behaviour within the Medley environmental sustainability intiative. The college governance initiated this decision-making process, and also informally consulted with residents to seek their responses and feedback about the proposed changes. Medley intake and induction staff advise all incoming students that the catering policy is a part of the broader on-site sustainability initiative at residency enquiry stage, and catering policy information is also freely available on the college website (Medley Hall, 2017a). The target audience in this campaign is self-selecting to be involved in this initiative, indicating the likelihood they are arriving with an openness and/or curiosity toward the target behaviour.

Community Based Social Marketing Thematic Analysis

The Medley Hall intervention was a grass-roots movement and the evaluation of the Medley model indicates that:

- Fifteen of the twenty-one benchmark criteria were met in full;
- One of the criteria was partially met;
- One criterion was unable to be (retrospectively) reported against, and
- Three criteria were not met.

Table 1 presents the evaluation results which are subsequently integrated with thematic analysis results, under sub-headings based on Lynes et al.'s (2014) five key CBSM domain reporting format.

CBSM Stage 1: Selecting Behaviours

As recommended by Lynes et al. (2014), from the point of model inception, the Medley Hall governance clearly identified its target audience – its residents – and clearly limited the number of target behaviours, focusing primarily on reduced meat consumption. Following informal focus group discussions at model inception stage, reduced meat consumption was identified as an appropriate target behaviour at Medley. The resident council members were consulted during planning, implementation and subsequent stages. With the number of behaviours to be addressed being limited, namely focused on reduced meat consumption, but they also included a limited number of day-to-day energy conservation behaviours, such as switching off appliances when not in use, and self-monitoring of shower times.

CBSM Stage 2: Identifying Barriers and Benefits

While initial focus groups were held to identify barriers and benefits, following these early planning stages, identification of barriers and benefits became a more informal process. At Medley, residents' ease of access to vegetarian food reduces barriers to the target behavior:

The only other thing with choice is that on meat nights sometimes there is a sign that says, vegetarians only. So the vegetarian options are only available to people listed as vegetarians.

Residents identified quality of vegetarian food at model inception as a barrier, noting that a previous catering company that no longer services Medley was inexperienced at preparing appetising vegetarian food and that this detracted from the appeal of the catered vegetarian options. Conversely, the catering company employed at the time of data collection was extensively praised for the consistent delivery of delicious vegetarian food.

Table 1. Medley case study results evaluated against the CBSM framework of Lynes et al. (2014)

CBSM Step	CBSM Benchmarks	Medley's Progress Toward Benchmark
✔ = *integrated in the Medley intervention* ⌂ = *partially integrated in the Medley intervention* ? = *unknown* X = *beyond the scope of this intervention*		
Step 1: Selecting Behaviours	1a. Clearly identifies target audience	✔ Target population is clearly defined – Medley Hall residents
	1b. Selects behaviours that are both non-divisible and end-state	✔ The target behaviour was reduced meat consumption
	1c. Evaluates list of selected behaviours for potential impact, penetration and probability	✔ In 2006 when Medley first adopted this behaviour, there was group consensus among staff that this was an appropriate target behaviour at this site. Resident council members were consulted during planning, implementation and subsequent stages.
	1d. Limits the number of behaviours to be addressed in the campaign	✔ This CBSM evaluation comprises one highly visible component of the Medley Hall sustainability intervention (meat consumption). Other target behaviours are limited to basic, day-to-day energy conservation behaviours, such as switching off appliances when not in use, and self-monitoring of shower-length.
Step 2. Identifying barriers and benefits	2a. Conducts research on barriers and benefits for each of the potential segments in the target group	✔ Initial focus groups were held to identify anticipated barriers and benefits. The model has evolved so that it now gathers feedback with regard to barriers and benefits more informally. Feedback from sub-groups or individuals within the resident cohort is communicated by individual residents or via student representatives. This feedback can be communicated to college governance at any time and reflects Medley's broader commitment to continuous quality improvement. College governance also ensure that meals catered on-site are nutritionally balanced.
	2b. Identifies and distinguishes between internal/external barriers and benefits for target audience	✔ Internal barriers and benefits were identified with the target audience via focus group discussions at the inception of the intervention. These have been monitored via informal feedback over the subsequent years. No external barriers were identified at the inception of the intervention or over the subsequent years. Medley Hall governance and the university as a whole were strong advocates of the initiative. There were no practical barriers to making and maintaining the reduced meat catering.

continued on following page

Table 1. Continued

CBSM Step	CBSM Benchmarks	Medley's Progress Toward Benchmark
Step 3. Developing a strategy	3a. Creates strategies that are appropriate for the barriers of the behaviour(s) being promoted and reduce the benefits of the behaviour(s) being discouraged	✔ This is inherent to the Medley model. Providing catered vegetarian meals 5 days per week is a strategy to address a number of barriers identified during initial focus groups in 2006, and confirmed via ongoing informal feedback over subsequent years. These barriers include: (i) uncertainty about planning nutritionally balanced vegetarian meal options, (ii) accessibility, (iii) education about the environmental, social and individual benefits of reduced meat consumption, and (iv) convenience. This catering model also encourages reduced meat consumption, by providing ease of access to information about the environmental, social and individual benefits of vegetarianism.
	3b. Integrates the six components of effective commitment tools	X Residents are not required to commit to the dietary practice of reduced meat consumption.
	3c. Develops prompts that take into account the four principles	✔ Vegetarian meals are labelled in the bain-marie. This is a point-of-decision prompt, particularly on the two days per week when meat options are offered to residents.
	3d. Engages well-known and well-respected people to be part of the campaign	✔ When interviewed in 2015, many Medley residents recounted a visit by renowned ethicist Peter Singer the year prior, who presented on-site on the topic of ethical vegetarianism/veganism. Medley regularly invites guest speakers to present on topics pertinent to the onsite target behaviours.
	3e. Encourages the use of norms that are visible and reinforced through personal contact	✔ As a consequence of the majority of residents participating in the 5:2 plant-based/meat-option catering model, reduced meat consumption became highly normalised within Medley Hall. Via participation in the daily ritual of eating in a communal dining hall, residents' exposure to their peers' reduced meat consumption was extensive.
	3f. Integrates effective communication tools	✔ This evaluation did not include content analysis of specific communication tools, however interviewees considered catering to be a permanent agenda item at both governance and resident meetings. Communication tools also included ethical vegetarianism documentary screening nights. Resident representatives provide communication liaison between staff and residents and residents are invited to provide feedback in a communication feedback book onsite.
	3g. Establishes appropriate incentives/ disincentives	? The evaluation design did not include assessment of incentives/ disincentives
	3h. Initiates convenience strategies that attempt to address external barriers	✔ Implementation of the 5:2 Medley catering policy made reduced meat consumption highly convenient for residents, by circumventing (i) overall time, (ii) food preparation, (iii) financial cost, and (iv) transport barriers for residents.
Step 4. Conducting a pilot	4a. Develops a pilot that can be compared with baseline measurements	✔ The Medley model emerged of an informal "grass-roots" pilot that has evolved to become embedded in college policy. X The researchers did not take baseline measures. ? Researchers did not enquire as to whether internal baseline measurements were taken by college governance.
	4b. Utilizes a control group	X A control group was not utilised
	4c. Applies a random assignment of target audience into each group being tested	X As above
	4d. Evaluates effectiveness of change directly rather than using self-reporting	X This was a qualitative and exploratory evaluation. As such, only self-report data was collected.
	4e. Focuses only on the strategies that can be implemented at a broad scale	✔ The Medley model provides a scalable dietary sustainability framework.
Step 5. Broad scale implementation	5a. Measures activity prior to implementation and at several points afterwards	△ During interviews, residents provided self-report feedback that they had reduced their meat consumption since living at Medley, however pre-post data was not collected. This was not a repeated measures evaluation design, however Medley governance may commission future evaluations.
	5b. Utilizes evaluation data to refine strategy and/or provide feedback	✔ Continuous quality improvement is a central feature of the Medley model and college governance are committed to refining the Medley model based on evaluation feedback.

As a grass-roots social marketing movement, assessment of barriers and benefits for resident sub-groups often occurred through consultation and discussion between residents and staff. College staff encourage and facilitate (i) resident involvement in decision making processes, and (ii) constructive feedback from residents. Thus, the identification of barriers and benefits for sub-groups of the resident body occurs as an ongoing function of continuous feedback loops between staff and residents.

CBSM Stage 3: Developing a Strategy

By implementing the 5:2 vegetarian catering model on-site, Medley Hall invited its resident body to engage in an achievable yet environmentally significant behavioural initiative. In line with recommendation from Lynes et al. (2014), the Medley model includes behaviour prompts that are visible (ease of access to vegetarian food), and prompts that focus on the encouragement of target behaviours including signs that indicate vegetarian food options at the on-site bain-marie.

Residents are not required to formally commit to the dietary practice of reduced meat consumption, but rather invited and encouraged to do so via exposure to diet sustainability information on-site. Participation is also encouraged via immersion in a resident community where reduced meat consumption, vegetarianism and veganism are normalised and observed daily, in the communal dining hall.

Medley has also engaged established experts to contribute to its campaign; most notably, ethicist and animal advocate Peter Singer. The address by Peter Singer in 2015, was explicitly cited as a catalyst of behaviour change by a number of non-vegetarian residents:

Yeah, so semester two Peter Singer came and spoke about three ethical reasons for veganism ... he outlaid his kind of utilitarian point of view and the environmental concern and I think also the concern for disparity in living standards was the third pillar of his argument. Following on from that there were quite a handful of people who were like, yeah, I've been challenged. I'm going to accept that. So, from that I kind of joined in. However, this year when we've gone to just two nights of meat initially I thought, oh well, I think I can continue to do full vegetarianism.

Residents reflected on the importance of being able to utilise communication channels such as student representatives, to express concerns and/or positive feedback. Examples included residents advising catering staff of preferred meal options, allergies and dietary requirements, and cultural food preferences. Interviewees reported that catering remains a permanent agenda item at both governance and resident meetings. Ethical vegetarianism documentary screening nights were also reported.

Catered meals are planned to meet dietary recommendation guidelines to provide residents with both nutritionally complete vegetarian and meat-optioned meals. Onsite resident kitchen facilities enable students to prepare meals (with or without meat) of their free choosing as frequently as they wish. Participation in the Medley model also appeared to have impacted some residents' subjective identity. The choice to identify as "*Medletarian*" exemplifies such identity influence:

... for me it felt like the right time to, I guess, be confronted with the importance of making that type of change and, I guess, empowered a bit to seek out those types of choices even when I'm away from college...

We have a term - Medletarian. So there are some people who eat vegetarian at Medley because it's so good and so easy and just there. But they would still eat meat at home for example.

Many residents who consume meat attributed reduction in their meat consumption, and changes in their attitudes, to the immersive experience of living at Medley. An on-site culture of non-judgemental, open-mindedness was also cited as inherent to model success and sustained behaviour change:

I think creating that kind of non-judgemental culture means that people are more likely to let their guard down a little bit …But I think the key thing is that…we don't want it to be an imposed thing, and that's the key, thing that we can attribute the success of what it currently is.

Both staff and students reflected on an empowered student voice at the college. Opportunities for student involvement in governance decisions related to catering were common. These feedback opportunities include a resident elected food representative, and a "feedback book" residents can write in.

I feel like it has a lot to do with the leadership, really. I really think that [deidentified's] voice and values is sort of the catalyst for a lot of the things that have been built. If we didn't have a leadership that cared so much about sustainable issues I don't think that the college necessarily would've made bounds and leaps in that direction, or had decided that that was a core principle.

CBSM Stage 4: Conducting a Pilot

The Medley model emerged as an informal pilot, which later evolved into an organisational policy. No baseline data measurements were taken or requested as a part of this evaluation. This model is a grassroots initiative and the scope of its evaluation is specifically qualitative and exploratory. For these reasons, only self-reported interview data was collected.

The results indicated that other residential colleges within the same university may be in the process of informally replicating the Medley model. Other residents also alluded to evidence of model contagion, having observed that the catering company Medley hires has begun catering for other (internal) residential colleges:

Certainly when you look at the food sort of things and increasing vegetarian options, a number of other of colleges have started to copy that as well, which I found really interesting.

At the university there's been a big push towards divestment. That's just student wide. So, I guess the knowledge of environmentally sustainable practices is around. But we are the only college that has a sustainability representative on the council.

[de-identified college] actually had the same catering company that we do. I believe [de-identified] College has as well, but [de-identified] as far as I'm aware started a lot of their environmental pushes after modelling some of the stuff that Medley had done a few years ago.

Residents cited increasing engagement between Medley and other colleges at the same university as an influence on model contagion. "Dinner swap" events were mentioned, during which approximately ten Medley residents are invited to dine at another college while non-Medley students dine at Medley.

Resident engagement with the Medley model offers evidence of the effectiveness of the pilot. Stage five of the CBSM evaluation (broad scale implementation) is yet to occur, however this preliminary evidence suggests that scalability of the Medley model would be possible and likely successful.

CBSM Stage 5: Evaluating Broad Scale Implementation

Early signs of model contagion have been reported, though no formal process of broad scale implementation had occurred at this university at the time of data collection. Broad-scale implementation cannot be evaluated based on existing data, however the positive resident response to the Medley model indicates scope for broad scale implementation and a potential for success.

While specific pre-implementation measures were not a part of the Medley campaign design, evaluation data included self-report feedback which indicated that most residents had reduced their meat consumption since living at Medley.

Resident Challenges

While a majority of residents interviewed expressed a positive attitude toward the Medley catering model, several liked the quality and taste of catered meals, but expressed desires for meat-optioned meals more than two nights per week. Other interviewees indicated a preference for an earlier version of the catering model – a reversed "5:2" model with catered meat options 5 days per week and exclusively vegetarian options only two days per week. Some interviewees indicated that if meat-eaters wish to eat meat at exclusively vegetarian catered meal-times, they prepare their own meat meals (on-site) and dine in the communal dining space as they please, however other interviewees conversely reported that this does not occur, and would be socially taboo at Medley.

While internal catering feedback channels attracted praise, some interviewees expressed the perspective that there is scope for governance to disseminate clearer and more comprehensive information about the theoretical basis of the catering policy, reflecting that many residents remained unclear about the ethical philosophy of reduced meat consumption. Inductions during Orientation-week were broached as a suggestion to offer new residents more background information. Residents also suggested posters to inform about the rationale for the catering policy and its broader environmental sustainability context.

DISCUSSION

The catering intervention implemented at Medley Hall is an innovative, community-based social marketing campaign for the reduction of animal origin food consumption as part of a broader, environmental sustainability ethos. To the knowledge of the authors, Medley is the first university residential college in Australia to implement a comprehensive diet sustainability model inclusive of an on-site catering strategy. By introducing a 5:2 plant-based:meat-option on-site catering model, Medley Hall marketed a highly accessible behaviour change campaign, with ample scope for individual tailoring. Residents who identify as vegans or vegetarians have the scope to choose plant-based catering options one-hundred percent of the time, while other residents who wish to engage with the model by adopting a behaviour of reduced meat consumption are provided with meat-options two-days per week.

The Medley catering policy emerged out of a broader environmental sustainability policy, in response to concerns about climate change, and based on existing evidence about the scope for sustainable dietary practices to positively impact anthropogenic climate change (Sustainable Development Commission, 2009, p. 4). It is important to acknowledge that the relationship between climate change and diet is bi-directional – climate change affects people's diets and nutritional status, and conversely dietary choices and food systems affect GHG emissions, and consequently climate change. No existing comprehensive guidelines or recommendations on the development of social marketing campaigns to promote the target behaviour of reduced meat consumption exist. By presenting the Medley Hall catering model of reduced meat consumption as a case study of a CBSM, this chapter also offers a contribution toward this research deficit.

The analysis of the evaluation results against a CBSM framework indicated that the Medley model met fifteen of the twenty-one campaign benchmark criteria, and partially met an additional one CBSM criteria (refer to Table 1). In considering the overwhelmingly positive resident responses to the Medley campaign, the results of this evaluation offer preliminary evidence that social marketing for reduced consumption of animal products can be effective.

Constructive feedback indicated that some residents who eat meat have found engaging in the behaviour of reduced meat consumption challenging while conversely, other meat-eaters explained that if they feel like consuming a vegetarian meal at a meat-optioned meal time, they experience a barrier, due to vegetarian meals being labelled as "vegetarian only" and only being available to residents listed as vegetarian. Key themes emergent in thematic analysis included: (1) a strong governance structure invested in the campaign, (2) target audience empowerment involvement in campaign development, maintenance and evolution, (3) freedom of choice of target audience, and (4) exposure to a clear ethical rationale for behaviour change.

Governance Investment in the Campaign

Interview feedback resoundingly echoed praise for the catalytic role an impassioned and committed governance structure has exerted over the Medley model. There was a strong belief among residents that the success of the campaign is largely attributable to support from the college governance, and also from the dedicated role of resident representatives in maintaining open and flowing communication feedback loops between staff and residents. Within the Medley model, residents have the scope to become involved in governance decision making and a diverse range of perspectives are respected and valued.

Target Audience Empowerment

Residents reflected on the importance of the work performed by elected resident representatives. The receptiveness of the college governance to feedback from its residents appeared to have nurtured an empowered student body, within which individuals feel heard and valued; even if disagreement arises. Examples of the successes of the communication feedback loops at Medley include caterers responding to feedback about: food preferences, food allergies, other dietary requirements, and cultural food preferences of Medley residents. At Medley, catering is an ongoing agenda item at both governance and resident meetings, further reflecting widespread internal engagement with this campaign.

Respect for Individual Freedom of Choice

A key reason attributed to the success of this initiative is a space for all voices, diverse perspectives and respectful debate on issues pertaining to environmental sustainability, such as diet and climate change. By providing residents with meals that are (i) nutritionally complete and environmentally sustainable based on the principles of ethical vegetarianism, Medley has made the target behaviour of reduced meat consumption both convenient and highly accessible. The ease with which residents are able to adopt the target behaviour is tempered with a key implicit factor – freedom of choice. By offering residents with (i) an ethical rationale for the target behaviour, (ii) ease of access to the target behaviour, and (iii) ensuring the target behaviour is enticing (all interviewees commended the quality of the catered food), Medley has provided the resources to motivate consumer change, however have not compelled or enforced this behaviour as a requirement. Residents are free to prepare meals (with or without meat) whenever they choose to, using on-site kitchen facilities, and/or to purchase food from the myriad local eateries. Some interviewees felt there was a social taboo at Medley against bringing self-prepared meat-meals to the communal dining area on vegetarian-only catered days, however other interviewees indicated this was not the case.

Despite having the opportunity to consume unlimited (self-prepared or externally-purchased) quantities of meat and other animal food origin products, the majority of meat-eaters interviewed expressed an acceptance or preference for the Medley catering model. Many meat-eaters cited the quality and taste of on-site vegetarian food as a key determinant of their initial openness to practising a predominantly vegetarian diet. Interviewees identified as vegans, vegetarians, meat-eaters or "medletarians".

Residents who identified as meat-eaters when arriving at Medley, but had since embraced the Medley model by identifying as either as vegetarians or medletarians, conveyed the importance of their freedom of choice in doing so. These residents expressed experiences of being philosophically challenged toward behaviour change, generally due to engagement with robust and well-substantiated ethical vegetarianism rationales they had been exposed to at the college.

Ethical Rationale for Behaviour Change

A range of behaviour prompts were informally embedded in the Medley model, including food labels to distinguish vegetarian and non-vegetarian options at meal times, open invitation for catering-related feedback from residents, and opportunity to participate in peer discussion on the ethical impacts of dietary choices. Information on ethical rationales for reduced meat consumption is displayed on the Medley website, cited by staff involved in intake and admission, and augmented during documentary screening nights on ethical vegetarianism, and eminent guest speakers.

Interviewees indicated that other residential colleges at the university had begun to replicate elements of the Medley model. While interviewees were not aware of any other cases of diet sustainability policy similar to Medley's 5:2 model, they reported general shifts at other colleges, toward increased vegetarian catering and/or employment of the same catering company.

Interviewees expressed the perspective that there is scope for governance to circulate more comprehensive information about the ethical basis of the catering policy, citing that a number of residents remained uncertain of this. Orientation-week inductions were suggested as a possible response to this.

CONCLUSION

The Medley Hall social marketing campaign for reduced meat consumption among college residents, is an exemplar of an emerging breed of informal and localised grass-roots social marketing initiatives. Such initiatives demonstrate the utility of alternative approaches to traditional formalised/top-down social marketing interventions. The marketing approach implemented at Medley, and other similar grass-roots approaches have unique scope to foster community ownership of the campaign and personal investment in the survival of the initiative as it evolves and grows as a part of the community where it was born.

REFERENCES

Andreasen, A. R. (1994). Social marketing: Its definition and domain. *Journal of Public Policy & Marketing*, *13*(1), 108–114.

de Vries, M., & de Boer, I. J. M. (2010). Comparing environmental impacts for livestock products: A review of life cycle assessments. *Livestock Science*, *128*(1-3), 1–11. doi:10.1016/j.livsci.2009.11.007

Donovan, R., & Henley, N. (2010). *Principles and practice of social marketing: An international perspective* (2nd ed.). Melbourne, Australia: IP Communications. doi:10.1017/CBO9780511761751

Elferink, E. V., Nonhebel, S., & Moll, H. C. (2008). Feeding livestock food residue and the consequences for the environmental impact of meat. *Journal of Cleaner Production*, *16*(12), 1227–1233. doi:10.1016/j.jclepro.2007.06.008

Ericksen, P. J., Ingram, J. S. I., & Liverman, D. M. (2009). Food security and global environmental change: Emerging challenges. *Environmental Science & Policy*, *12*(4), 373–377. doi:10.1016/j.envsci.2009.04.007

Fisk, G. (1973). Criteria for a theory of responsible consumption. *Journal of Marketing*, *37*(2), 24–31. doi:10.2307/1250047

Garnett, T. (2009). Livestock-related greenhouse gas emissions: Impacts and options for policy makers. *Environmental Science & Policy*, *12*(4), 491–503. doi:10.1016/j.envsci.2009.01.006

Hedenus, F., Wirsenius, S., & Johansson, D. J. A. (2014). The importance of reduced meat and dairy consumption for meeting stringent climate change targets. *Climatic Change*, *124*(1-2), 79–91. doi:10.1007/s10584-014-1104-5

Henion, K. E., & Kinnear, T. C. (Eds.). (1976). *Ecological marketing*. Chicago, IL: American Marketing Association.

Joyce, A., Hallett, J., Hannelly, T., & Carey, G. (2014). The impact of nutritional choices on global warming and policy implications: Examining the link between dietary choices and greenhouse gas emissions. *Energy and Emission Control Technologies*, *2*, 33–43. doi:10.2147/EECT.S58518

Kardash, W. J. (1976). Corporate responsibility and the quality of life: Developing the ecologically concerned consumer. In K. E. Henion, & T.C. (Eds), Ecological marketing (pp. 5-9). Chicago, IL: American Marketing Association.

Khan, S., & Hanjra, M. A. (2009). Footprints of water and energy inputs in food production – global perspectives. *Food Policy*, *34*(2), 130–140. doi:10.1016/j.foodpol.2008.09.001

Lynes, J., Whitney, S., & Murray, D. (2014). Developing benchmark criteria for assessing community-based social marketing programs: A look into Jack Johnson's "All at Once" campaign. *Journal of Social Marketing*, *4*(2), 111–132. doi:10.1108/JSOCM-08-2013-0060

McKenzie-Mohr, D. (2011). *Fostering sustainable behavior: An introduction to community-based social marketing* (3rd ed.). Gabriola Island, BC: New Society Publishers.

McKenzie-Mohr, D., Lee, N. R., Schultz, P. W., & Kotler, P. (2012). *Social marketing to protect the environment: What works*. Thousand Oaks, CA: Sage. doi:10.4135/9781483349466

Medley Hall. (2017a). *Great food*. Retrieved from http://www.boojum.com.au/medley/ what-we-offer/171/

Medley Hall. (2017b). *Home page*. Retrieved from http://www.boojum.com.au/medley/

Medley Hall. (2017c). *What we offer*. Retrieved from http://www.boojum.com.au/medley/ what-we-offer/

Medley Hall. (2017d). *Who we are*. Retrieved from http://www.boojum.com.au/medley/who-we-are/

Pearson, D., Friel, S., & Lawrence, M. (2014). Building environmentally sustainable food systems on informed citizen choices: Evidence from Australia. *Biological Agriculture and Horticulture*, *30*(3), 183–197. doi:10.1080/01448765.2014.890542

Peattie, K., & Peattie, S. (2009). Social marketing: A pathway to consumption reduction? *Journal of Business Research*, *62*(2), 260–268. doi:10.1016/j.jbusres.2008.01.033

Polonsky, M. J. (1994). An introduction to green marketing. *Electronic Green Journal*, *1*(2), 3. Retrieved from http://escholarship.org/uc/item/49n325b7

Popp, A., Lotze-Campen, H., & Bodirsky, B. (2010). Food consumption, diet shifts and associated non-CO_2 greenhouse gases from agricultural production. *Global Environmental Change, Governance. Complexity and Resilience*, *20*(3), 451–462.

Prothero, A. (1990). Green consumerism and the societal marketing concept: Marketing strategies for the 1990's. *Journal of Marketing Management*, *6*(2), 87–103. doi:10.1080/0267257X.1990.9964119

Ripple, W. J., Smith, P., Haberl, H., Montzka, S. A., McAlpine, C., & Boucher, D. H. (2014). Ruminants, climate change and climate policy. *Nature Climate Change*, *4*(1), 2–5. doi:10.1038/nclimate2081

Steinfeld, H., Gerber, P., Wassenaar, T., Castel, V., Rosales, M., & de Haan, C. (2006). *Livestock's long shadow: Environmental issues and options*. Rome, Italy: Food and Agriculture Organization of the United Nations.

Sustainable Development Commission. (2009). *Setting the table: Advice to government on priority elements of sustainable diets. Report*. London, UK: Sustainable Development Commission.

Tukker, A., Huppes, G., Guinée, J. B., Heijungs, R., de Koning, A., & van Oers, L. … Nielsen, P. (2006). Environmental impact of products (EIPRO) analysis of the life cycle environmental impacts related to the final consumption of the EU-25 (Technical Report Series, EUR 22284 EN). Retrieved from https://openaccess.leidenuniv.nl/handle/1887/11434

KEY TERMS AND DEFINITIONS

Evaluation: A systematic assessment of the merits of a particular initiative.

Marketing Campaign: Specially designed activities aimed at encouraging the use of particular products, services or promoting particular behaviours.

Medletarian: A Medley College resident consuming predominantly vegetarian food at Medley whilst being a flexible consumer of meat when off-site.

Orientation-Week: The week before commencement of semester studies at university when new students are welcomed and introduced to university life.

Pilot Study (Pilot): A small-scale study conducted to evaluate feasibility and appropriateness of a larger or full-scale implementation or research project.

Residential College: An organization which provides housing for university students within a community setting with shared meals and other activities which enhance university life.

Sustainable Diet: A diet which minimizes the environmental impact of the food consumed by humans.

Chapter 19
Consumption of Animal Products in Bulgaria:
The Case for Change

Septemvrina Kostova
University for National and World Economy, Bulgaria

Borislav Atanasov
University for National and World Economy, Bulgaria

Dora Marinova
Curtin University, Australia

ABSTRACT

This chapter analyses the trends in production and consumption of animal-based food products, including meat, dairy, eggs and fish, in Bulgaria between 2010 and 2015. Against decreasing population, the production of livestock, yogurt, packaged milk and cheese remained relatively stable or increased resulting in rises on a per capita basis. There was an overall 9% increase in meat consumption with 45% being pork and 72% of it being processed. This trend goes against international dietary recommendations and contributes to climate change and environmental deterioration. The consumer survey conducted in Sofia in 2017 shows limited awareness about these problems with price of meat being the dominant regulator of meat consumption. Nevertheless, there was an acknowledgement by more than half of the survey respondents that Bulgarians should cut their meat intake which is a good starting point for social marketing and encouragement to change consumption away from animal-based products.

INTRODUCTION

The food industry plays a significant role in Bulgaria's economy (Slavova, 2016). During 2010-2015, this economic sector of the country grew at a stable rate and its industrial output reached 15.2% in 2015 (NSI, 2017c) compared to 14.6% in 2011 (NSI, 2013). In 2015, the production of the Bulgarian food industry was worth BGN9.8 billion (NSI, 2017c) or US$5.87 billion, BGN7.9 billion or US$4.77 billion

DOI: 10.4018/978-1-5225-4757-0.ch019

were direct agricultural products, such as grains, fruits and vegetables, livestock and animal products (NSI, 2017a).

Industry decisions related to production volumes and efficiency are made in an economic environment which is often uncertain and volatile (Todorov & Smallbone, 2014) but also driven by consumer preferences. Such decisions pursue better development opportunities, niche markets and responding to demand and people's preferences as well as dealing with uncertainty and risk. The food sector in Bulgaria has increased the supply of some products in response to growing export opportunities and more aggressive penetration of foreign producers. This industry has rapidly adjusted to the economic conditions in Bulgaria.

The three main sectors of the Bulgarian food industry are: grain-related products, including bread (traditionally a staple commodity), meat and livestock products and other foods, including fruits, vegetables, sugar products and preserves. Following the transition to a market economy in the 1990s and later integration within the European Union, the food industry required significant restructuring related to values of outputs, assets, investment and management of human resources. In response to the low purchasing power of the Bulgarian consumers after the disintegration of the Eastern Block, producers sought price reductions at the expense of product quality, poor hygienic conditions in production and breaches in the technological requirements resulting in inconsistencies in taste, texture and other attributes (Slavova, 2016). With improvement in living standards in Bulgaria, nowadays the country's food sector has become more competitive domestically and internationally offering a variety of products, improved packaging and better sanitary conditions in production (Boeva, 2008).

Of particular interest to this chapter are the changes that occurred in Bulgaria during 2010–2015, after the country joined the expanded European Union (as of 1 January 2007) and opened its economy to western markets and influences. The traditional Bulgarian diet involves high consumption of bread and grain-based products, fruits and vegetables as well as limited intake of animal products, such as dairy, eggs and animal meat. According to the Bulgarian Orthodox Church, its followers should voluntarily abstain from the consumption of animal-based products for 200 days in a year which includes each Wednesday and each Friday as well as four extended periods of lent or fasting (Pravoslavie, 2009). This is seen as spiritual and physical manifestation of the individual's power against sinning and desire to do good. With the industrialisation of the country since the mid-1940s under a socialist development model and later the introduction of the market economy in the 1990s, many changes occurred in the Bulgarian diet which particularly affected the consumption of animal-based products. Such products have become a daily presence on the Bulgarian table. Although the consumption of animal-based foods in Bulgaria continues to be middle-of-the-range on a world scale, the country's population is certainly no longer following the prescribed 200 days per year of abstention. Hence, this dietary transition is contributing to climate change and global environmental deterioration as well as negatively impacting people's health.

After analysing the trends in the production of livestock products in Bulgaria, the chapter looks at national consumption patterns. The next section reports results from an exploratory survey which asked Bulgarian customers about the reasons for them to consume animal products. We then examine the marketing of animal-based products and discuss opportunities for interventions which educate and influence the Bulgarian consumer about the health and environmental co-benefits of keeping the intake of such foods within the limits prescribed by the traditional diet.

PRODUCTION TRENDS IN LIVESTOCK FOOD PRODUCTS

Since the late 1980s, the Bulgarian population has been declining due to low fertility rates – at around 1.53. and high emigration – more than 2 million Bulgarians now reside outside the country (EuroChicago, 2011) although the net migration in recent years is much lower than the rates experienced in the 1990s and 2000s (see Table 1). Between 2010 and 2015, the size of the country's population decreased by 3% to 7.2 million. Against this demographic profile, it would not be surprising for many food indicators to also manifest declining trends.

Table 2 shows the annual numbers of animals raised in Bulgaria during 2010-2015 for production of animal-based foods, including meat, dairy and eggs. During the period the numbers cattle, sheep, pigs, poultry and eggs remained relatively constant whilst the numbers of goats decreased by more than 22% and those of buffaloes increased with over 16% in 2015 compared to 2010. On a per capita basis, however, almost all numbers of livestock (with the exception of goats) as well as eggs increased in recent years (see Figure 1). This reflects the increased demand for animal-based products.

Although the number of slaughtered animals for red meat consumption overall decreased, on a per capita basis it remained relatively stable at around a third of animal per person per year during 2010-2015 (see Table 3). The number of slaughtered poultry fluctuated around 7.5 birds per person per year (see Table 4). Some of the largest Bulgarian companies for meat production were Bony and Agrotime for pork (Valkanov, 2013) and Pilko and Gradus-1 for poultry (Capital, 2017).

Table 1. Bulgarian population, 2010-2015

Year	Population [Thousands]	Population Index	Fertility Rate	Net Migration
2010	7396	100	1.57	24 190
2011	7348	99.4	1.51	4 795
2012	7306	98.8	1.50	2 512
2013	7265	98.2	1.48	1 108
2014	7224	97.7	1.53	2 112
2015	7178	97.1	1.53	4 247

Data sources: World Bank, 2017 and NSI, 2017b

Table 2. Livestock in Bulgaria, 2010-2015 (number of animals)

Year	Cattle	Buffaloes	Pigs	Sheep	Goats	Poultry [in Thousands]	Eggs [in Thousands]
2010	544 456	9 241	664 000	1 367 987	356 334	15 934	1 437 543
2011	557 641	9 887	608 266	1 454 617	341 362	14 656	1 185 041
2012	526 112	9 212	530 945	1 361 545	293 639	15 260	1 174 438
2013	575 584	9 964	586 418	1 369 578	289 308	13 214	1 194 623
2014	552 807	9 555	553 114	1 335 283	292 644	14 609	1 218 685
2015	550 200	10 800	600 100	1 331 900	276 900	15 600	1 285 779

Data source: NSI, 2017c

Table 3. Slaughtered food animals and poultry in Bulgaria, 2010-2015 (in thousand)

Year	Bovine	Pigs	Sheep	Buffaloes and Equidae	Goats	Poultry	Total	Per Capita Red Meat Animals	Per Capita Poultry
2010	138	925	1285	1	332	58463	61144	0.36	7.90
2011	147	1043	1099	1	338	54650	57278	0.36	7.44
2012	143	1033	1219	2	265	57105	59767	0.36	7.82
2013	131	1044	1007	2	226	52254	54664	0.33	7.19
2014	127	988	1084	2	234	53024	55459	0.34	7.34
2015	137	1043	980	1	173	53913	56247	0.33	7.51

Data source: NSI, 2017c

Figure 1. Per capita livestock animals and eggs in Bulgaria, 2010-2015
Data sources: NSI, 2017c and World Bank, 2017

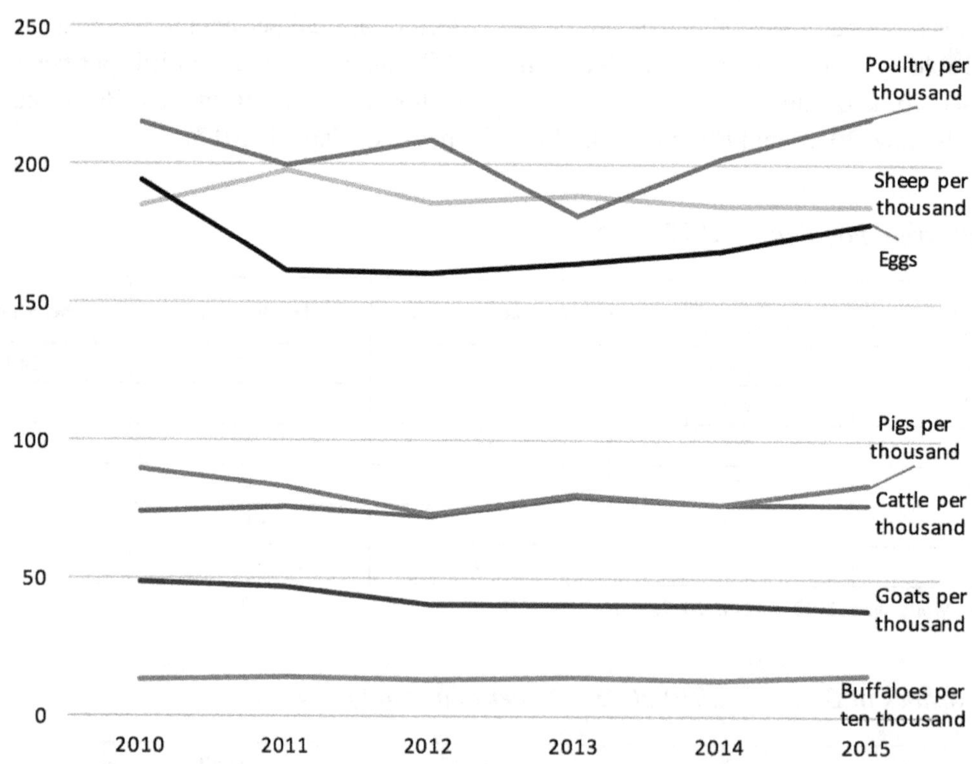

In the actual production, there was an overall decrease in red meat and poultry as well as in the per capita amounts (see Table 4) which dropped by 22% between 2010 and 2015. It appears that the Bulgarian population is gradually reducing meat production. This however is not indicative of shifts in the Bulgarian diet away from animal-based foods because of other livestock products, such as milk and cheese, as well as the balance between local production, exports and imports.

Between 2010 and 2015, the production of milk decreased by 10% overall and across most categories, namely cow, sheep and goat milk (see Table 5). Per capita total milk production also decreased (see Figure 2). There is however an increase in the last year of the period in the production of packaged milk, cream and natural yogurt products in the Bulgarian dairies (see Table 4). White cheese increased in the last two years and increases in 2015 were observed for semi-hard, processed and other cheeses (Table 6). On a per capita basis (see Figure 3), natural yogurt, packaged milk and processed and other cheeses marked an increase in the last year with the remaining dairy products being relatively stable. It should be noted however that less than half of all milk produced in Bulgaria (namely 47% in 2015) is processed in the country's dairies (NSI, 2017c) with the remaining amounts being consumed or sold directly by the producers making the overall production much higher.

With Bulgaria being part of the integrated European Union market, production alone does not provide a complete picture of the consumption trends in livestock-based foods in the country. In order to understand better the demand for animal proteins, consumption figures which take into account the balance between exports and imports help shed light on the changes in the Bulgarian consumer market.

Table 4. Production of meat in Bulgaria, 2010-2015

Year	Beef and Veal (t)	Pork (t)	Lamb and Mutton (t)	Buffalo and Equidae (t)	Goat (t)	Poultry (t)	Total Red Meat (t)	Total Meat (t)	Per Capita Red Meat (kg)	Per Capita Poultry (kg)	Per Capita Meat (kg)
2010	19 610	70 471	13 320	225	3 699	106 897	107 325	214 222	14.51	14.45	28.96
2011	20 887	72 506	11 812	131	4 116	103 834	109 452	213 286	14.90	14.13	29.03
2012	20 377	73 159	13 796	341	3 229	107 609	110 902	218 511	15.18	14.73	29.91
2013	19 106	72 905	10 599	260	2 218	98 388	85 982	203 476	11.84	13.54	25.38
2014	17 210	67 441	10 678	447	2 456	102 193	98 232	200 425	13.60	14.15	27.74
2015	18 548	69 259	9 907	168	1 770	91 296	71 197	190 948	9.92	12.72	22.64

Data sources: NSI, 2017c and World Bank, 2017

Table 5. Production of milk in Bulgaria, 2010-2015 (thousand litres)

Year	Cow Milk	Buffalo Milk	Sheep Milk	Goat Milk	Total
2010	1 091 612	7 688	82 127	58 707	1 240 134
2011	1 093 033	8 593	86 276	59 809	1 247 711
2012	1 061 198	7 830	84 447	51 830	1 205 305
2013	1 115 081	8 459	91 170	52 892	1 267 602
2014	1 070 613	8 593	72 442	43 267	1 194 915
2015	998 093	9 179	71 810	39 622	1 118 704

Data source: NSI, 2017c

Table 6. Production of dairy products in Bulgarian dairies, 2010-2015

Year	Packaged Milk (Thousand Litres)	Cream (t)	Natural Yoghurt (t)	Milk Fats (t)	Fresh Cheese, Including Curds (t)	White Cheese (t)	Semi-Hard Cheese (t)	Processed and Other Cheese (t)
2010	60 144	2 595	134 670	1 083	4 558	42 884	19 945	2 701
2011	65 298	2 465	118 027	1 130	4 070	44 263	19 507	1 753
2012	69 973	2 267	123 482	1 133	4 949	45 221	17 796	1 900
2013	68 453	2 135	120 881	1 112	4 613	42 344	20 138	2 194
2014	64 614	2 316	120 678	1 001	4 989	51 225	19 692	3 462
2015	74 493	2 429	128 404	974	3 907	51 089	20 079	4 507

Data source: NSI, 2017c

Figure 2. Per capita production of milk in Bulgaria, 2010-2015 (thousand litres)
Data sources: NSI, 2017c and World Bank, 2017

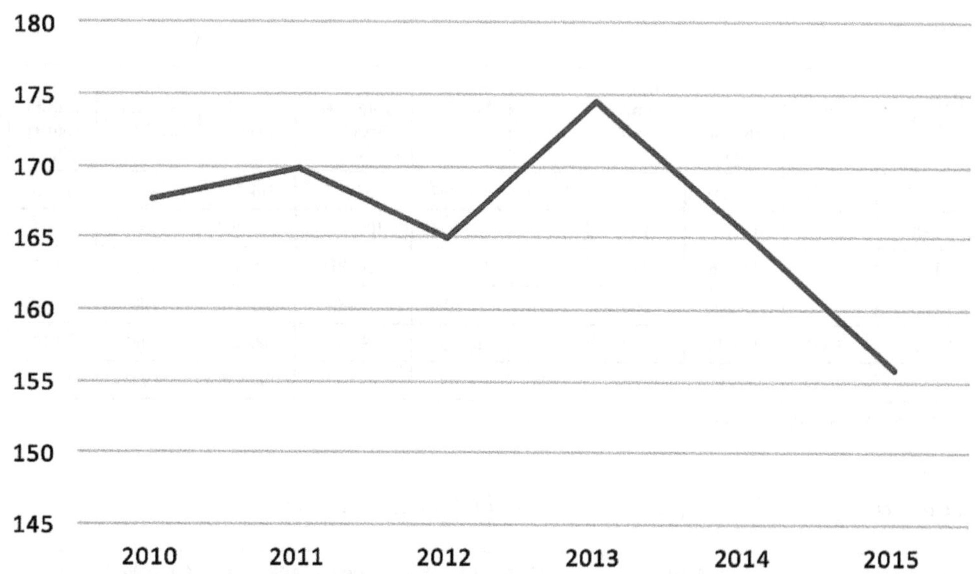

CONSUMPTION TRENDS IN ANIMAL-BASED FOOD PRODUCTS

Bulgaria both imports and exports all categories meat, with the trade balance being negative – more meat is imported than exported. This obviously means that domestic consumption exceeds local production. During 2010-2015, the overall per capita meat consumption increased by 9% (see Table 8) based on aggregate data (rather than on household survey data which tend to underestimate consumption). However, in the last few years of the analysed period, the overall consumption of all red meat other than pork and that of poultry decreased while pork consumption was on the rise – a 9.6% increase between 2010 and 2015. Pork represents a major part – on average around 45%, of all meats consumed in Bulgaria. The increased pork consumption includes meat per se (fresh and frozen) as well as processed meats, such as cold cuts, tinned meat, sausages, salami and other sub-products, which represent on average 72% of all Bulgarian pork consumption during this period (see Table 9).

Figure 3. Per capita production of dairy products in Bulgaria, 2010-2015
Data sources: NSI, 2017c and World Bank, 2017

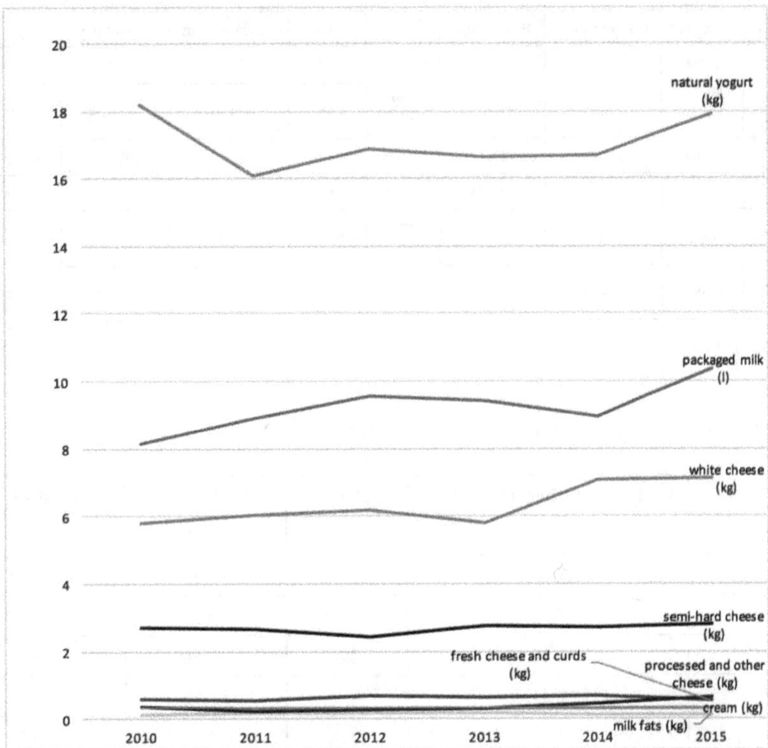

Despite the recent decrease in the consumed processed pork (see Table 9), its share is extremely high and unhealthy from a public health perspective given the recommendations of prestigious cancer research bodies that such meat should not be consumed at all (WCR/AICR, 2007). Moreover, the World Health Organisation classifies processed meat as category 1 carcinogenic (WHO, 2015). Consequently, Bulgarian consumers are adopting a dietary profile which is dangerous from a public health perspective. From a climate change point of view, the production of pork meat is associated with less greenhouse gas emissions compared to beef and veal but generates slightly higher emissions than poultry (Eshel et al., 2014). Nevertheless, it causes higher environmental pollution than plant-based options and the increase in the Bulgarian dietary preferences for pork results in negative ecological and climate change implications.

Dairy products and eggs also have a heavier environmental footprint than plant-based dietary choices. During the 2010-2015 period, the overall consumption of milk and eggs in Bulgaria fluctuated slightly (see Table 10). Per capita consumption of milk in particular decreased by 7% (see Table 11). The consumption of cheese products however was steadily on the increase registering a 69% growth by the end of the period. On a per capita basis, the growth at 74% is even more significant. This has serious implications for greenhouse gas emissions as cheese is the highest emitter from the group of dairy products and also has a heavier contribution to climate change compared to eggs and poultry. A shift towards more cheese and away from fruits and vegetables within the Bulgarian diet impacts negatively both human health and the wellbeing of the planet.

Table 7. Meat consumption in Bulgaria, 2010-2015 (tonnes)

Year	Red Meat Other Than Pork				Pork				Poultry			
	Production	Import	Export	Consumption	Production	Import	Export	Consumption	Production	Import	Export	Consumption
2010	36 854	28 867	7 784	57 937	70 471	95 341	1 728	164 084	106 897	81 289	45 636	142 550
2011	36 946	29 973	10 711	56 208	72 506	102 484	4 683	170 307	103 834	102 093	47 845	158 082
2012	37 743	27 170	8 565	56 348	73 159	96 524	4 808	164 875	107 609	109 238	46 673	170 174
2013	37 183	27 362	5 144	59 401	72 905	91 716	1 825	162 796	98 388	87 900	36 339	149 949
2014	30 791	28 538	5 825	53 504	67 441	108 337	1 711	174 037	102 193	98 244	41 355	159 082
2015	30 393	27 958	6 383	51 968	69 259	109 845	2 245	179 859	91 296	102 709	39 872	154 133

Data sources: NSI, 2017a and c

Table 8. Per capita meat consumption in Bulgaria, 2010-2015 (kg)

Year	Red Meat Other Than Pork	Pork	Red Meat	Poultry	Meat
2010	7.83	22.19	30.02	19.27	49.29
2011	7.65	23.18	30.83	21.51	52.34
2012	7.71	22.57	30.28	23.29	53.57
2013	8.18	22.41	30.58	20.64	51.22
2014	7.41	24.09	31.50	22.02	53.52
2015	7.24	25.06	32.30	21.47	53.77

Data sources: NSI, 2017a and c and World Bank, 2017

Table 9. Consumption of processed pork in Bulgaria, 2010-2015

Year	Domestic Consumption (t)	Per capita Consumption (kg)	Share of Total Per Capita Pork Consumption (%)
2010	121 259	16.40	74
2011	120 433	16.39	71
2012	123 843	16.95	75
2013	120 438	16.58	74
2014	118 119	16.35	68
2015	121 302	16.90	67

Data sources: NSI, 2017a and c

Recent years witnessed a large increase in the consumption of fish and fish products in Bulgaria – 28% overall, 97% in domestic production capacity and 32% on a per capita basis (see Table 12), triggered to a large extent by imports and the operation of 870 domestic fish farms. Although fish overall has a better environmental and health profile than livestock-based dietary choices, there are still issues related to whether fish is produced sustainably and the use of antibiotics to maintain the health of the commercial stock.

Table 10. Consumption of dairy products and eggs in Bulgaria, 2010-2015

Year	Milk (Thousand Litres)				Cheese, Curds, Semi Hard Cheese and Milk Fats (Tonnes)				Eggs (Thousands)			
	Production	Import	Export	Consumption	Production	Import	Export	Consumption	Production	Import	Export	Consumption
2010	1 240 134	92 788	11 652	1 321 270	50 143	11 575	24 285	37 433	1 437 543	60 000	188 516	1 309 327
2011	1 247 711	85 147	15 981	1 316 866	50 086	14 344	24 262	40 168	1 185 041	62 000	187 567	1 059 474
2012	1 205 305	73 367	22 270	1 256 402	52 070	19 599	24 004	47 665	1 174 438	81 516	160 033	1 095 921
2013	1 267 602	88 261	19 615	1 336 248	49 151	22 958	24 881	47 228	1 194 623	116 533	178 267	1 132 889
2014	1 194 915	79 470	15 309	1 259 076	59 676	24 142	30 692	53 126	1 218 685	89 783	221 300	1 087 168
2015	1 118 704	99 784	21 885	1 196 603	59 503	30 208	26 445	63 266	1 285 779	136 067	250 117	1 171 729

Data sources: NSI, 2017a and c

Table 11. Per capita consumption of dairy products and eggs in Bulgaria, 2010-2015

Year	Milk (l)	Cheese, Curds, Semi Hard Cheese and Milk Fats (kg)	Eggs
2010	178.65	5.06	177
2011	179.21	5.47	144
2012	171.97	6.52	150
2013	183.93	6.50	156
2014	174.29	7.35	150
2015	166.70	8.81	164

Data sources: NSI, 2017a and c and World Bank, 2017

Table 12. Fish and fish products consumption in Bulgaria, 2010-2015

Year	Production (t)	Import (t)	Export (t)	Consumption (t)	Per capita Consumption (kg)
2010	5 530	25 665	5 914	25 281	3.42
2011	5 531	23 601	4 663	24 469	3.33
2012	5 986	24 351	5 392	24 945	3.41
2013	9 674	25 308	5 432	29 550	4.07
2014	9 113	24 432	4 208	29 337	4.06
2015	10 873	26 381	4 821	32 433	4.52

Data sources: EAFA, 2017, NSI, 2017a and c and World Bank, 2017

From a global perspective, the consumption of animal products in Bulgaria is average (see Table 13). There are however some discrepancies between the data reported by international bodies, such as the United Nations Food and Agriculture Organisation (FAO) and the Bulgarian government agencies. For example, per capita meat supply in Bulgaria for 2013 (the latest available FAO data) is reported to be 58.36 (FAOSTAT, 2017) while data from Bulgarian agencies shows 51.22 kg per person per year (see Table 8). Irrespective of the accounting methodological differences, Bulgarians consume higher meat,

Table 13. Per capita consumption of animal food products in 2013, FAO and Bulgaria data (kg)

Product	Bulgarian National Data	FAO Data for Bulgaria	FAO Data for Europe	FAO Data for the World
Meat	51.22	58.36	80.78	45.46
Fish	4.07	6.97	21.91	19.17
Eggs	9.36*	8.36	12.99	9.19
Milk	183.93	155.71	215.11	90
Cheese	6.50	10.35	20.54	1.82

Data source: FAOSTAT, 2017 and Bulgarian sources used in tables above.
Note: *Estimated average weight of an egg is 60g.

milk and cheese quantities than the world's average but lower than those of Europe (see Table 13). Their egg consumption is similar to the world's average but lower than that of Europe and their fish intake is lower than the global and European averages.

Hence, on a global scale the Bulgarian diet contributes averagely to the challenges of climate change and environmental deterioration with the evidence showing that Bulgarians are no longer adhering to the tradition requiring them to abstain from the consumption of animal-based products for 200 days in the year. The high intakes of meat, milk and cheese are leaving a lot of opportunities for a switch to better dietary options. As for the most of the developed world, this is not an easy behavioural transition and the next section explores people's attitudes towards animal-based foods in order to understand the potential for social marketing of better plant-based alternatives.

SOFIA CONSUMER SURVEY

In 2017, a survey was conducted in the capital of Bulgaria Sofia in three international supermarket chain stores – Kaufland, Billa and Lidl, which have numerous outlets in the country. Since the 1990s, the Bulgarian retail sector has been marked with fierce competition that witnessed the penetration of multinational retailers and the demise of some domestic shops. The three chosen chain stores represent well the most common supermarket and hypermarket places where Sofia residents shop.

Convenience stores, which are usually small with a more limited range of goods and foods, are located within densely populated residential areas and have longer (often not restricted) opening hours. This format is very popular in Sofia. In order to capture these types of customers, the survey was also offered online on the Internet. Bulgaria has a 100% mobile and Internet area coverage and online communications are increasingly popular.

Bulgarian shopping habits have evolved from the uniform fixed prices of the socialist era to a sharp differentiation between those who opt for premium, mid-market and value or discounted groceries. The new "hybrid consumer" (Scott, 2014) who usually looks for cheap prices but occasionally buys more expensive products, e.g. for special occasions such as holidays and celebrations, is also becoming popular in Bulgaria. By combining a survey in large retailers and online, there was an opportunity to capture all categories of shoppers. With this research area being relatively new, there is a very limited number of previous international studies (e.g. Bogueva et al., 2017 conducted in Sydney, Australia) and none in Bulgaria.

From 200 randomly selected customers, 68 responded – 39 in the stores and 29 online, which represents a reasonable response rate of 34%. The survey was exploratory and the random voluntary self-selected sample is indicative of the basic characteristics of Bulgarian consumers. More women – 45 (66%), responded to the survey compared to 23 (34%) men. The survey's self-administered questionnaire contained questions about consumption of red meat, poultry, milk, cheese and yogurt. Given environmental, public health and ethical concerns associated with meat consumption (Raphaely & Marinova, 2016), the survey also asked the respondents' opinion about possible reduction.

Although an overwhelming majority of the exploratory sample (97%) consume red meat, many (41%) do this rarely, that is less than twice per week (see Table 14). Only a small fraction (3%) do not eat red meat. This frequency of consumption is less than that reported by Bogueva et al. (2017).

Economic considerations prevail in people's decisions about whether to eat meat (see Table 15) with almost half of the respondents (47%) finding meat to be expensive compared to other dietary options. Bulgaria still does not use factory farming and the red meat animals are predominantly free range which contributes to the high prices. Although more than half of the red meat consumed domestically nowadays is imported (54% in 2015, see Table 7), the prices reflect the Bulgarian conditions for animal husbandry. In many ways, they represent better the costs associated with meat and act as a social marketing mechanism towards lower consumption.

There is some understanding about red meat's impact on the environment with more than a quarter of the respondents (26%) being concerned about livestock's effect on climate change, land use and other ecological systems. A large section of the Bulgarian consumers however is not worried about livestock's impact on the environment (44%) or do not have any opinion about this (30%). There is lack

Table 14. Frequency in red meat consumption, Sofia survey

Frequency	Number	Percentage of Sample
Every day	1	1%
3-5 days per week	18	27%
Twice per week	19	28%
Less than twice per week	28	41%
Do not eat red meat	2	3%
Total	68	100%

Table 15. Reasons for level of red meat consumption, Sofia survey

Reason	Number	Percentage of Sample
Meat is expensive	32	47%
Meat represents higher social status and prestige	22	32.5%
Too much meat contributes to weight gain	7	10%
Eating meat is unhealthy	4	6%
Concern about animal welfare	2	3%
Meat is a symbol of masculinity	1	1.5%
Total	68	100%

of widespread information and awareness about these issues reaffirming the pricing mechanism as the one controlling red meat consumption.

Half of the survey respondents (50%) indicated their dietary preference for poultry meat because it is considered lighter, healthier and has a lower price. When asked directly whether they agree with the concept that people should eat less meat (red and poultry), 54% of the respondents provided a positive answer. The consumption of other animal-based products is also extremely popular in Bulgaria with 80% of the respondents consuming milk, 86% yogurt and 97% cheese. There was explicit preference for locally made products compared to imported brands, particularly for Bulgarian white brined cheese (feta) and yogurts containing the local lactobacillus bulgaricus.

Any dietary decisions we make are influenced by a wide range of social, cultural, economic, aesthetic, symbolic, moral, emotional and health-related values. In the case of Bulgaria, the price of meat in particular plays a very important role in directing consumer preferences. The retail sector itself, including the way food is packaged and presented, type of stores – department stores of multinational companies (Cliquet, 2000), local smaller grocery stores or neighbourhood convenience shops, advertising and other applied marketing techniques, is also influencing consumer behaviour. Demographic factors, such as population aging, consumer age, growth in income and changes in the household budget spent on meat and meat products, together with historical development (Flavian et al., 2002) similarly impact on purchasing behaviour and retailers use these in their marketing strategies. In this complex field of daily decision-making and negotiation with individual and public values, a new factor emerged related to the natural environment. Although the impact of this factor is relatively small according to the Sofia survey, there are already some signs that people see meat in particular as a product we should consume less.

There are many global problems associated with the consumption of animal-based products to which Bulgarians are contributing. In addition to direct risks for cancer, other non-communicable diseases, increased greenhouse gas emissions, pollution of soil, water and air, rearing livestock is an inefficient use of natural resources and land. For example, it is alarming that 70% of the earth's cultivable land is sowed with crops for animals, such as soya and other grain fodder, and not directly for human food (Meat Atlas, 2014). Meat production also poses disproportionately higher demands on water resources –1 kg of veal requires 15500 litres of water, the same quantity to grow 12 kg wheat, 61 kg potatoes or 118 kg carrots (Meat Atlas, 2014). Furthermore, the new industrial techniques for breeding cattle and poultry rely on the use of large quantities of harmful substances, including unabsorbed nitrates and phosphorous that percolate in the soil and reach the groundwater, and antibiotics which can lead to antimicrobial resistance (Meat Atlas, 2014).

Social marketing in food retailing and public spaces needs to change. There is a splendid opportunity to influence the Bulgarian consumers away from products which are detrimental to human and environmental health. Social media, such as Facebook and Twitter, can be used to spread simple messages to different people. There is also a role for nongovernment associations, clubs and foundations which can provide a space for their members to communicate the dangers posed to human health and the environment and gain support from friends and like-minded people about reducing the consumption of animal-based products. Other events that could be useful include special lectures delivered in schools, advertising the benefits from healthy eating, mass sport events with specialised rewards, articles in magazines, the Internet and social media, public forums and discussions. All these will influence the behaviour of the Bulgarian consumer.

CONCLUSION

The analysis of the Bulgarian livestock sector for the period 2010-2015 shows its dynamism in response to consumer demand and buying capacity. With the decreasing trend in the country's population, the numbers of reared cattle, sheep, pigs, poultry and produced eggs remained relatively stable during this period generating increases on a per capita basis. The per capita production of yogurt, packaged milk and cheese in the Bulgarian dairies also increased while that of milk dropped.

In order to understand better the consumption of animal-based products, the analysis of the net balance between domestic production, export and import shows an increase of 9% in the overall per capita meat consumption triggered by the rise in consumed pork which represents an average of around 45% of all meats eaten in Bulgaria during this period. Bulgarians consume red meat, poultry, milk and cheese in quantities that are above the world averages but below the average European intake. Processed red meat however occupies a large share in the Bulgarian diet (e.g. 72% of all consumed pork), which is of concern given the WHO's warning about its negative effects on human health.

From a customer perspective, the exploratory survey conducted in Sofia in 2017 shows that price is the main regulator restricting the presence of meat in people's diets. Only a fraction of the population, namely 26% based on this survey, are concerned about the environmental impacts of the food they eat, and meat in particular. Climate change is not high on the political and people's agenda in Bulgaria. With milk and cheese also prominent in the Bulgarian diet, the country is contributing towards global greenhouse gas emissions and environmental deterioration. The traditional recommendations for 200 days of abstinence from consuming animal-based products are long-forgotten. Almost all survey respondents, namely 97%, reported regular cheese intake. Moreover, the per capita consumption of cheese has been steadily increasing between 2010 and 2015.

Although largely determined by price, people's dietary choices are not entirely rational and respond to a mixture of emotional, social, health, nutritional and marketing messages. Food marketing, for example, brings together the food producer and the consumer through a chain of activities aimed at promoting the consumption of particular products. A large percentage of the Sofia survey respondents, namely 54%, were of the opinion that people in Bulgaria should cut their meat intake. This is an excellent starting point for social marketing campaigns that can facilitate a transition in consumer behaviour to achieve such reductions whilst improving the consumption of fruits, vegetables, grains, legumes, nuts and other plant-based foods. They can be an additional factor to price differentiations and other market-based mechanisms to sway consumer choices.

Government support is essential for success in changing consumer behaviour away from animal-based products. Given the existing evidence about the negative impacts of the consumption of these foods and the benefits from plant-based options (Raphaely and Marinova, 2016), the government should decouple its shorter-term role in promoting growth of the Bulgarian livestock industry from its wider responsibility in safeguarding public and environmental health.

In Bulgaria people have the choice to select from a vast range of nutritional and tasty options to satisfy their basic necessity to eat. Their dietary decisions however have wider implications for their own health, other living species and the state of the planet. When people are at liberty to select the food they eat, such as in Bulgaria, awareness building and information dissemination through social marketing are essential to achieve positive social and environmental benefits.

REFERENCES

Boeva, B. (2008). *International management* [in Bulgarian]. Sofia, Bulgaria: Stopanstvo.

Bogueva, D., Marinova, D., & Raphaely, T. (2017). Reducing meat consumption: The case for social marketing. *Asia Pacific Journal of Marketing and Logistics*, *29*(3), 477–500. doi:10.1108/APJML-08-2016-0139

Capital. (2017). *Six companies with more than 10 mln lv income from poultry* [in Bulgarian]. Retrieved from http://www.capital.bg/specialni_izdaniia/regal500plus/2015/12/22/2675141_shest_kompanii_s_nad_10_mln_lv_prihodi_ot_pileshko_meso/

Cliquet, G. (2000). Large format retailers. *Journal of Retailing and Consumer Services*, *4*(4), 183–195. doi:10.1016/S0969-6989(00)00017-5

Eshel, G., Shepon, A., Makov, T., & Milo, R. (2014). Land, irrigation water, greenhouse gas, and reactive nitrogen burdens of meat, eggs, and dairy production in the United States. [PNAS]. *Proceedings of the National Academy of Sciences of the United States of America*, *111*(33), 11996–12001. doi:10.1073/pnas.1402183111 PMID:25049416

EuroChicago. (2011). *Number of Bulgarians abroad (2011)* [in Bulgarian]. Retrieved from http://www.eurochicago.com/2012/04/v-tchuzhbina/

Executive Agency of Fisheries and Aquaculture (EAFA). (2017). *Operational* programmes. Retrieved from http://iara.government.bg/?page_id=15846&lang=en

FAOSTAT. (2017). *Food supply – livestock and fish primary equivalent*. Food and Agriculture Organization of the United Nations. Retrieved from http://www.fao.org/faostat/en/#data/CL

Flavian, C., Haberberg, A., & Polo, Y. (2002). Food retailing strategies in the European Union. A comparative analysis of the UK and Spain. *Journal of Retailing and Consumer Services*, *9*(3), 125–138. doi:10.1016/S0969-6989(01)00011-X

Meat Atlas. (2014). Facts and figures about the animals we eat. Berlin, Germany: Heinrich Böll Foundation and Brussels, Belgium: Friends of the Earth Europe. Retrieved from https://www.boell.de/sites/default/files/meat_atlas2014_kommentierbar.pdf

National Statistical Institute (NSI). (2013). *Statistical yearbook 2012*. Sofia, Bulgaria: NSI.

National Statistical Institute (NSI). (2017a). *Economic accounts for agriculture – annual data*. Republic of Bulgaria. Retrieved from http://www.nsi.bg/en/content/15323/метаданни/economic-accounts-agriculture-—annual-data

National Statistical Institute (NSI). (2017b). *International migration by age and sex*. Republic of Bulgaria. Retrieved from http://www.nsi.bg/en/content/6697/international-migration-age-and-sex

National Statistical Institute (NSI). (2017c). *Statistical yearbook 2016*. Sofia, Bulgaria: NSI.

Pravoslavie. (2009). *Lent in the Orthodox Church* [in Bulgarian]. Retrieved from http://www.pravoslavieto.com/docs/post/postite_v_BPC.htm#1

Raphaely, T., & Marinova, D. (Eds.). (2016). *Impact of meat consumption on health and environmental sustainability*. Hershey, PA: IGI Global. doi:10.4018/978-1-4666-9553-5

Scott, M. (2014, January 13). Hybrid consumers abandon mid-market retailers. *Forbes magazine*. Retrieved from http://www.forbes.com/sites/mikescott/2014/01/13/fybrid-consumers-abandon-mid-market-retailers/

Slavova, P. (2016). Conditions of productivity processes in a company of food industry in Bulgaria. *Procedia: Social and Behavioral Sciences*, *230*, 367–371. doi:10.1016/j.sbspro.2016.09.046

Todorov, K., & Smallbone, D. (2014). *Handbook of research on strategic management of small and medium enterprises*. Hershey, PA: Business Science Reference. doi:10.4018/978-1-4666-5962-9

Valkanov, N. (2013). *Analysis of the market for meat and meat products in Bulgaria* [in Bulgarian]. Institute for Market Economy. Retrieved from http://ime.bg/var/images/Meat_Market_2013.pdf

World Bank. (2017). *Public data: Population*. Retrieved from https://www.google.com.au/publicdata/explore?ds=d5bncppjof8f9_&met_y=sp_pop_totl&idim=country:BGR:GRC:SRB&hl=en&dl=en

World Cancer Research Fund and American Institute for Cancer Research (WCRF/AICR). (2007). *Food, nutrition, physical activity and the prevention of cancer: a global perspective*. Washington, DC: AICR.

World Health Organisation (WHO). (2015). *Q&A on the carcinogenicity of the consumption of red meat and processed meat*. Retrieved from http://www.who.int/features/qa/cancer-red-meat/en/

KEY TERMS AND DEFINITIONS

Abstention or Abstinence: Choosing to restrain consumption.

Exploratory Survey: A study based on a survey whose aim is to provide insights on a previously unexplored topic and which does not pursue statistical representativeness of the results.

Free Range Animals: Animals raised in conditions which allow them to roam freely in open air for at least part of the day; different countries have various regulations about the time and space available to the animals to be outdoors.

Hybrid Consumer: A consumer who generally seeks for cheap (value, budget, low-end, generic or discount) products and services but also opts for expensive (premium or high-end) options on particular occasions or for certain types of needs.

Lactobacillus Bulgaricus: One of several gram-positive bacteria used in the production of yogurt; it is found originally in the gastrointestinal tract of some animals living in Bulgaria but is also grown artificially, including one strain extracted from the leaves of the snowdrop flower.

Poultry: Animal flesh for human consumption which is lighter in colour when cooked and usually is associated with chickens, hens, turkeys, ducks and geese generally referred to as white meat.

Red Meat: Animal flesh for human consumption which is dark brown when cooked and usually associated with livestock animals, such as cattle, pigs, sheep, goats and buffaloes, but also with animals, such as camels, horses, kangaroos, dears, rabbits, emus and ostriches.

Chapter 20
Meat Marketing Dissonance:
A South African Case Study

Erin Hill
University of Cape Town, South Africa

Talia Raphaely
Curtin University, Australia

ABSTRACT

This chapter discusses a South African supermarket's print advertisement promoting meat consumption for a national public holiday. Meat consumption is portrayed as symbolic of and necessary for cultural belonging, participation and celebration. It is used to maximise profits by maintaining the distance between consumers and the realities of the power and violence perpetrated against the sentient life from which the "culturally" commodified meat product is sourced. National Heritage Day celebrates the demise of South Africa's history of domination, exploitation and discrimination and its bright present and future. The case study however illustrates that the marketing of meat as a cultural commodity reinforces hegemonic control and is contrary to what Heritage Day represents. It indicates a dangerous dissonance that encourages and endorses domination and violence against animals. Whilst the case study focuses on South Africa, hegemonic influence through visual commodification and marketing of meat is apparent in most western societies.

INTRODUCTION: HERITAGE DAY AND THE "BRAAI"

September 24th — Heritage Day in South Africa — is a national celebration of cultural diversity and democracy. It emphasises equality, hope, freedom and a bright future for all in light of the end of the country's oppressive history of Apartheid. Heritage Day, referred to as "Braai Day", is celebrated in a typically South African manner — outdoors with a big meal accompanied by alcohol and sport events. Meat consumption marketing for Heritage Day has ensured that the "Braai" and meat intake have become a prerequisite for participating in collective South African heritage and nationalism (Molefe, 2014). As such, Heritage Day has become interchangeable or synonymous with a certain hegemonic cultural

DOI: 10.4018/978-1-5225-4757-0.ch020

ritual — the braai, which is historically and paradoxically the cultural food preparation practice of the Afrikaans people (the architects of the apartheid regime, the antithesis of what Heritage Day celebrates).

The word "braai" is Afrikaans for grill, roast or fry and is a social gathering activity that involves cooking meat outdoors over a fire. Like many western holidays all over the world (including Christmas, Easter, Australia Day and American Thanksgiving), celebrating Heritage Day in a conventional, acceptable and socially understood manner has come to require the production and consumption of vast quantities of animal body parts and by-products in the form of meat, dairy, and eggs.

Meat mass-produced from animals raised in factory farms (the case in most countries, including South Africa) can be compared to the human rights abuse that dominated Apartheid, and extends back to the trade of African people as slaves prevalent up until the 19th century: "Africans captured and forced into slavery were often compared to animals in an effort to justify their treatment. They were called 'brutes' and 'beasts'. Their lives were considered expendable, and many died at the hands of their oppressors. The same oppressive mentality behind those actions leads to the slaughter of animals today" (PETA in Cooper, 2007).

Yet ironically, Heritage Day was established post-apartheid to celebrate the diversity of the South African nation and encourage respect, equality and unity. As Nelson Mandela (1994, p. 385) said: "The truth is that we are not yet free; we have merely achieved the freedom to be free, the right not to be oppressed. We have not taken the final step of our journey, but the first step on a longer and even more difficult road. For to be free is not merely to cast off one's chains, but to live in a way that respects and enhances the freedom of others". Marketing and consumption of meat, particularly meat produced from animals reared in factory farms, is by no explanation, living in a way that respects or enhances the freedom of others.

Historically, September 24th was a Zulu celebration commemorating its leader King Shaka. However, fears of promoting tribalism led to a compromise; the day was appropriated and merged into a bank holiday where all South Africans could respectfully celebrate the multiplicity of cultures, histories and heroes (Molefe, 2014). Although many cultures practice cooking meat outdoors over a fire in some form, the South African version of the braai has its roots in the Great Trek, an emigration of some 14,000 Afrikaans Boers (or farmers) in search of fresh pastures and in rebellion of British governance. The Great Trek is historically viewed as an important phase in the Western colonisation of South Africa, oppression of the indigenous peoples and the origin of Afrikaans nationhood and domination (de Klerk, 2009). While 1994 saw the dawn of democracy in South Africa, political decolonisation did not end the process of Western domination. The dominant political and economic system today remains mainly of Western origin. Despite its role in South Africa's history of Apartheid and oppression, and seemingly without considering the oppressive past of a very specific white man's ritual, Jan Scannell, otherwise known as Jan Braai, chose Heritage Day to spearhead a 2005 media campaign to promote and realise his ideal of unifying all South Africans around the braai (Molefe, 2014). Despite the fact that "the notion of a still-divided nation unifying around a shared love of grilled meat seemed both feeble and potentially offensive" (Mlambo in Moskin, 2016), the braai emerged as a tentative symbol of South African unity! Archbishop Desmond Tutu – patron of National Heritage Day, proclaimed the Braai as "one thing that can unite us irrespective of all the things that are trying to tear us apart" (Tutu in Moskin, 2016)

Language and visuals are used to maintain a dissonance between the braaivleis (grilled meat) and the fact that these ingredients are a by-product of a once living, sentient being, slaughtered for consumer gratification. The animal source and the experienced suffering are of little or no significance. Rather, the murder and destruction of life are used as a marketing mechanism with an emphasis on meat consumption. Retailers have picked up on the profit opportunities associated with Braai Day. Shops print and distribute pamphlets promoting meat purchases; selling not only the products but also the idea of a perfect Heritage Day celebration, which would be incomplete or unattainable without meat cooked over a fire.

'Ocularcentrism' – a perceptual and epistemological bias in Western cultures where vision is ranked over other senses (Chandler & Munday, 2011) is one of the main features of 21st century capitalism and the marketing on which it relies. Vision has been elevated to the primary way of knowing, reasoning and selling – for example: "I see", "seeing is believing" and "I'll believe it when I see it with me own eyes". Images and visual representations saturating the social world have become powerful mediators of discourse, relationships and domination. Advertising harnesses this visual influence to suit specific products and markets, everyone and everything are seen only in terms of commodity value (Garland-Thomson in Adams & Gruen, 2014, p. 26). Almost standardised advertisements present images of dead animal bodies as desirable food, inanimate commodities to use in celebration and for human fulfilment. Such pristine, cling-wrapped meat products disassociate from and subordinate the reality of slaughter normalising and endorsing a culture of animal consumption.

Commodification of life to maximise profit margins is clearly illustrated through a case study of a South African campaign marketing meat consumption and the braai (barbeque) culture as a requirement for participation in national commemoration and celebration. The meat is visually and semantically separated from its animal-person source and instead connected to celebration, nationhood and participation. By interchanging product sales with such cultural values, a physical and mental distance is safeguarded and maintained between consumers and the consumed.

CASE STUDY

One of South Africa's biggest supermarket chains circulated a meat marketing pamphlet for Heritage Day 2015 and subsequently does so annually. This is the case study for the chapter's discussion.

The Advertisement

The emphasis of the sales pitch in the advertisement focused on meat products at (supposedly) reasonable market prices. Consisting of a cover page, a centre spread and back page, below is the description of the advertisement:

- The cover page consisted of bold text saying: "SA has voted: the country's best boerewors is here!" (boerewors is an iconic farmers' sausage). This text is accompanied by a picture of the national flag and a background image of tomato relish, the hot coals of a fire and roosterbrood (a traditional South African bread originally baked over hot coals). The image comes into strong focus in the bottom half of the page with a large piece of cooked boerewors directly below the aforementioned text. Overlaying labels explain the product as "champion boerewors SA's No. 1" and the price. Another label alludes to the new recipe, and how the product is "just in time for Braai Day!" Towards the bottom of the cover is the supermarket's name and slogan.

- The centre spread has the same styling — large, bold text, flags and the meat products on offer. The central picture is the South African flag overlaid with bold text asserting "WHEN YOU'RE SUPPORTING THE BEST, YOU CAN'T BRAAI WITH ANYTHING LESS". Framing the very colourful flag are 11 different meat products cooked and placed on a variety of serving dishes, grill grids and wooden chopping boards. Text substantiates the images with prices and weight describing the product objectively, while adjectives such as exclusive, gourmet, famous, perfectly matured, hassle-free, tender, and authentic local delicacies embellish the products and appeal to the senses.
- The back page of the pamphlet is dedicated to liquor advertising. It is implied that no braai is complete without a big meal of animal food washed down with alcohol. The products advertised are predominantly typical male drinks – beer, whiskey, brandy, gin, and wine. There is also a competition to win a gas braai cooker with the purchase of this alcohol.

Discussion of Advertisement

The meat products are portrayed solely as ingredients not as dead and dismembered bodies. Every part of an advertisement such as this instills and maintains a physical and cognitive distance between the consumer and the source (Sheth & Parvatiyar, 1995, p. 259).

Masculinity

With the back page consisting solely of alcohol products, such advertisements imply a certain masculinity; power is attached to a male's consumption of food and alcohol and males are deemed the stronger sex through excessive consumption (Stibbe, 2004, p. 43). This supposedly simple advertisement perpetuates the triad of braaing, drinking alcohol and meat consumption as a normalised cultural ritual.

Selling Patriotism

Boerewors is a very local South African consumable. One of the products on offer is described as "Champion Boerewors", implying that to be a good South African requires to be a proud meat eater with copious consumption habits. National heritage, belonging, being a "Champion South African" become wrongly synonymous with a hegemonic idea of the new South Africa (Patricios, 2016). Diversity and democracy are thus celebrated with a ritual embedded in layers of suffering and oppression.

Given the oppression of the past, the bold text stating "SA has voted: the country's best boerewors is here!" alludes to the cherished democracy of South Africa where all citizens over age 18 have the right to vote. The word "voted" has connotations of democracy and objectivity implying that the meat-eating being promoted is an external, factual, crucial and agreed upon aspects of our society. Referring to the products as "the country's best" implies that South Africa is unified through meat eating. Advertising is flawed at the best of times; but in this case the message is problematic because it implies that equality and unity in the South African society go hand in hand with a ritual that inherently accepts the exploitation, submission, domination and consumption of other living beings (Patricios, 2016).

The layout of the centre spread is predominantly layered with photographs of meat and labels stating prices and bombarded with adjectives in the text. With the words "When you're supporting the best, you can't braai with anything less", the centrepiece is most striking. These words sit atop the colourful

South African flag – a strong symbol of the rainbow nation encouraging patriotism and participation, while the repeated use of the word "best" reinforces associations with quality. The labels are a mixture of English and Afrikaans imposing a specific heritage of white people (the oppressive ruling class for many years) in South Africa and making it interchangeable with the new supposedly diverse heritage. In this case it is the white man's braai symbolising white male domination and power, secured under Apartheid. Such advertising works to subliminally maintain hegemonic social structures and overlooks the painful history of black oppression. Compounding on this, equality and respect are supposedly celebrated by systematically distinguishing humans as a superior species, promoting and justifying the oppression and consumption of dead bodies in large quantities.

Seducing the Market

The food imagery is vivid and appeals to the senses. Warm lighting and ready-to-serve staging insinuate a comforting convenience. The meat products are surrounded by herbs, spices, marinades and numerous grilled lemons indicating flavour and implying taste. Ironically, while the photographs are intended to stimulate taste and desire, food photography often involves a great deal of non-consumable chemical enhancements to achieve the desired colour, consistency and texture as well as digital post-editing (Chapin, 2016). These staging, transforming and editing are symbolic of the constructed messages and artificiality of the advertisement.

The language supports and compliments the meat imagery using alluring, seductive adjectives to emphasise the product and its taste thereby maintaining dissonance from the flesh factor. It focusses on describing the current form as a commodity product with words like exclusive gourmet (ribs), famous (pork cuts), perfectly matured (beef cuts), hassle-free tender (spatchcock chicken) and authentic local delicacies. Even where the animal's life is referenced, it is in relation to how it enhances the food product — "100% Naturally Reared Home-Grown Lamb". The fact that the meat is "free-range", had a diet "free of animal by-products" and 'free of antibiotics & added hormones" conveys to consumers that the life of the sheep was directed specifically to satisfy their demands and preferences, not the comfort of the animal's life (Lusk et al., 2007).

Detached notions of meat such as beef, pork etc., have cultural and semantic meanings that are severed from the animal source; the animal is "de-animalised" and this conceptual transformation works in favour of species mastery and selective disassociation with certain animals, particularly animals that are presented as food (Soron, 2011). Francione calls this "moral schizophrenia" — where one can show affection towards certain animals, and yet hold others as 'things' (to eat or use) without acknowledging their sentient status (Francione, 2004, p. 108). The image of beef as a neat and orderly package sits in sharp contrast with the sadistic reality of the rearing and slaughtering process (Foer, 2009). In a study conducted by the University of Colorado, 85% of people who eat meat said they could not kill an animal illustrating a natural disinclination (Dorovskikh, 2015). Perhaps if consumers were more aware of the process they would be less inclined to support it. After all, "food and clothing choices are a further politicisation of the personal" (Twine, 2014, p. 400). While consumers are generally out of touch, workers in animal agribusiness are inundated in perturbing conditions with serious physical and psychological implications (Dillard, 2008).

Looking Past the Advertisement

Language can be used to justify destructive practices. Slavery was a legal and justified practice not too long ago because handlers pronounced that the slaves benefitted from their enslavement saying it saved them from a "barbaric life in Africa" (Wise, 2002, p. 12). Similarly, language plays an important role to mediate and justify the animal agribusiness industry.

Justifying the Industry

Language is the main mode of communication for humans and is therefore anthropocentric and speciesist by nature (Adami, 2013). A simple look at any website of meat manufacturers shows text to describe the virtuous intentions of the company. The overwhelming amount of text is a circumlocution attempt to disconnect and evade reality. Civility discourse uses euphemisms to shift the animal subject to object; dead carcasses are referred to as meat, abattoirs become processing plants, chickens become poultry, cows become beef, calves become veal, sheep become mutton, and collectively animals become livestock (Pickover, 2005). The practices are also redirected; animals are harvested, chickens' beaks are trimmed, and pigs' tails are docked. Things are framed differently so as to dismiss sentient value and promote the notion of humane slaughter.

The term "humane" – defined as "having or showing compassion or benevolence" (Oxford Dictionaries), is a strategy of good intentions but it works to veil brutal conditions. Calm animals treated well with respect and slaughtered in a painless, swift manner – the idyllic "humane" image, contrasts strongly with the harsh reality illustrated by numerous first-hand accounts. The industry not only affects the animals, but also consumer health, the environment, wildlife destruction, atmospheric pollution and employees' psychological wellbeing (Mason & Finelli 2006).

"Humane slaughter" has also been argued to be a racist extension of constructing white civility where western notions of mass operations justify the practices as civil and refined in comparison to other geographies; essentially, "the underlying message is that we kill our animals in a civilised way and they don't" (Wadiwel in Twine, 2014, p. 197). So, is it even possible for agribusiness to be "humane"? Is it just a means of distraction to settle human minds of the disturbing reality behind the industry? Animals who are kept in sheds, fed unnatural diets, deprived of sunlight and enough space to stretch, violently abused, "artificially inseminated" (raped) and eventually killed – all of these practices are classified as humane by the industry (City of Tshwane Metropolitan Municipality 2004). Even "free-range" produce is problematic. As it stands, there is no legislation stipulating requirements for "free-range" (Red Barn Free Range Chicken, n.d.). At best, there are associations that set practice guidelines but their first objective is to serve their members. Most "free-range" farmed animals are slightly better off than factory-farmed animals; however, they are still seen as a mechanical component, a means to maximum profit objectives (Southern African Poultry Association, 2012). "Free-range" is merely the lesser of two evils. The notion is used to put consumers' minds at ease so as to preserve the industry. It becomes an alternative marketing strategy.

Pickover (2005, 145) poses this question: "if you treat slaves humanely, does this make it justifiable?" Should the same not apply to human and nonhuman animals alike? Contrary to the industry position, a utilitarian viewpoint holds that the disadvantages do not outweigh the benefits that animal products offer. All this does is legitimise cruelty and exploitation. The notion of humane is a hollow illusion.

More Meat for the Men?

Looking again at the case study's Braai Day advert, another major issue is the hints of gendered consumption behaviours. On the right edge of the centre spread there is a ladies rump label, which infers that the rest of the products are by default male portions. A different standard for different sexes? More meat for the men? This touches on the common gendered assumptions that hold the task of braai-ing as the man's domain while women are confined to prepare more passive "plant-based" foods in the kitchen (Molefe, 2014). Contrary to progressive and liberal assertions, the marketing of Braai Day reasserts patriarchal roles. The braai entrenches sexual inequality because it is embedded in an image where cooking is deemed an inferior, female activity and men who cook are considered effeminate. However, the element of danger makes braai-ing meat over a fire the only exception to the rule (Stibbe, 2004). It relates back to a time when to attain meat mankind would have had to hunt and dismember an animal with only basic tools and then cook it over a fire. It is this risk factor that asserts male power in braai-ing (Stibbe, 2004). Molefe (2014) also refers to a different gendered history – where black women cooked for the family using fire. Yet this is not acknowledged in the majority of marketing campaigns. The hegemonic Braai Day message overlooks the experience of black as well as female histories (Molefe, 2014).

As with any branding the advertisement sells not just the product but the aligned lifestyle, values and status. A few of the meat products are accompanied by their brand logo – for example, Steakhouse Classic and Gourmet Ribs & Sosaties. Meat manufactures and retailers collaborate to promote the ideals of Heritage Day; however, the real agenda is to promote their own sales and profits. Braai Day comes to disguise what Hooks (2000, p. 19) calls the "white supremacist-capitalist-patriarchal class structure"; the force of domination which the braai epitomises. Molefe (2014) describes Braai Day as a "day of sponsored forgetting" when commemorating the past is blurred with an emphasis on consumption steeped in white supremacy and masked as "national heritage". Braai Day thus comes to embody intersectional oppression. It was not Jan Braai's intention to encroach on other histories and heritages but such oblivion leads to dangerous ambiguity; people buy into ideologies steeped in problematic histories without any awareness thereby maintaining hegemonic power hierarchies. Not only are people made complicit in perpetuating the silence and segregation of others but also, they are complicit in the silencing of the animals who lose their lives in the name of heritage and tradition.

The Function of Ideology

According to Marxism, ideology functions to maintain hierarchical group relations and the ruling elite's control of content and social discourse (Sidanius & Pratto, 1999). Much of the modern society was built on these principles of control with oppression mediated by socialisation. Brittan & Maynard (1984, p. 180) state: "All forms of oppression are expressed and reproduced at the ideological level as though they were a natural process". Images appear as objective informants and in this way normalise oppressive and power-driven agendas. Ideology operates as common sense, naturalised knowledge, and an everyday dynamic, and it is largely unconscious and collective (Brittan & Maynard, 1984). Oppression thus shapes how humans collectively approach and understand the social world. Yet to simply attribute racism, sexism and speciesism to collective phenomena justifies and reproduces oppressive circumstances. Discrimination – toward human or nonhuman beings, is collectively reproduced in social consciousness and a culture of violence upon one justifies violence upon another (WHO, 2009).

Pickover's (2005) book is one of the few sources regarding the treatment of animals in the South African context. She looks at human-to-animal interactions (use, abuse and protection) in South Africa situating it in the global context. Pickover draws parallels between Apartheid and animal abuse. Apartheid facilitated a process of justified objectification where "blackness" became a marker for a person's 'thing-like' condition, and thus the thing-like's labour could be exploited without regard for sentience. Similarly, the unsustainable increase in meat and dairy is part of a westernisation of 'food colonialism' — where the animal is also seen as 'thing-like' — a commodified source of food (Twine, 2014, p. 193).

The practice of meat eating exacerbates binaries of wealth and poverty by contributing to global hunger. Pickover (2005) describes animal-based agribusiness corporations as "the new agriculture colonialists". In South Africa around 50% of all grain produced is for animal feed. However, animal products are not environmentally efficient food sources - it requires more resources to grow an animal than what it can offer as a dismembered product (Humane Society International, n.d.). Considering the vast world hunger and water shortage problems, animal agriculture is inefficient (not to mention cruel) and only benefits a minority of shareholders at the cost of the environment, the animal beings and mass-deprived populations.

CHANGING COLLECTIVE CONSCIOUS

The most effective space for expanding one's moral circle is to target consumer choices as it literally and figuratively reveals what one 'buys into', what they accept and what they reject. For this reason, vegetarian and vegan lifestyles are encouraged by animal advocacy projects that call for utilitarianism. In an interview with race theorist George Yancy, animal rights philosopher Peter Singer refers to Steven Pinker's notion of "the expanding circle" in the argument for legal protection for non-human animals. Ideally if the law protected non-human animals these practices would come to an end but law change will not happen without a fundamental shift in the western collective mind-set (Yancy & Singer 2015). "The expanding circle" is based on the premise that human moral concerns are slowly growing to include other-than-human interests and will hopefully one day recognise the value of sentience beyond species.

Due to animal agribusiness, billions of non-human animals are constricted, mutilated and eventually killed each year, public health is compromised, natural habitats are destroyed to accommodate the industry, the environment is irrevocably polluted, and water sources are depleted and contaminated (Mason & Finelli, 2006). Vegan practices redirect habits and beliefs thus having the potential to change cultural and social norms and make void the warped messages delivered in marketing campaigns such as the Heritage Day advertisement. Studies show that a vegan diet provides for all the body's nutritional needs. The common misconception of protein deficiency is an industry myth. Sufficient protein levels come from only 8-10% of one's entire diet. According to the China Project, excess protein is linked to precancerous lesions and tumors (Marcus, 2001). For this reason, vegetarianism and specifically veganism is arguably the most effective means for an individual to oppose speciesist oppression, exploitation and all detrimental repercussions that come with the industry while promoting their own health (Gandhi in Pickover, 2005). Unfortunately, discourse on vegan universalism is colossally eclipsed by cultural and economic globalisation and excessive rates of meat and dairy consumption (Twine, 2014).

Braai-ing is not going to disappear from society. However, society would do well to spend more time reflecting on consumer choices, ideological motives and the implications of social "rituals", practices, traditions and heritage. Oblivion can be offensive and certain practices maintain patriarchal, oppressive ideological structures (Stibbe, 2004). Braai-ing on September 24th (and every other day of recreation) will continue but Jan Braai's campaign has done relatively little to bring different cultures together (The Economist, 2014). The country remains segregated in spite of dialogue of unifying the people of South Africa around the fire. Cultural and race lines are not clear-cut and many have appropriated braai-ing as a recreational and social gathering as celebrating heritage is not a bad thing in itself. However, braai-ing is not the country's only heritage, nor is it the result of a superior culture. Rather, it is embedded in a deeply misogynistic, oppressive and racist background. It is ethnocentric, anthropocentric and overlooks many narratives essentially celebrating the burning of copious amounts of flesh. More decolonial reflection, particularly in consumer culture, may help to mitigate the perpetuation of such social practices. Society should be encouraged to consider "the expanding circle" so as not to be ignorant of the deeper political ripples of seemingly innocent practices. It doesn't have to be a male task to make a fire. More importantly in terms of this discussion, it is not necessary to enslave, oppress, dominate, kill and consume other animals in order to celebrate human liberation, freedom and release from domination and oppression. In fact, such apparent celebration, only further entrenches that from which one is claiming release.

According to Buddhist beliefs, violence in the mind leads to violence expressed in the world. If we can change the way the human mind perceives other animals, perhaps we can change the human culture of exploiting other species purely as food to consume or for utilisation purposes. Conscientious vegan practices effectively prevent engagement in the widespread objectification and commodification of nonhuman animals. However, a vegan universalism seems unlikely in the foreseeable future. There is hope – as academics, environmentalists and activists continue to highlight the unsustainable environmental demand, cruelty and detrimental health effects – that there is a growth in conscious consumer choices not to purchase animal products. The more informed we are as consumers, the more likely we are to see the parallels between human and nonhuman animal sentience, turn away from the meat consumption industry and shift the dominant perspective that perceives the use and exploitation of nonhuman animals as a normal component of culture (Twine, 2014).

CONCLUSION

Seeing is not always believing — society is fed the stuff of market maintenance. Visual advertisements of meat as a commodity, a food source removed from sentience, suffering and death, subliminally reinforce and perpetuate domination, abuse, speciesism, sexism, racism and inequality. As the case study of meat and Heritage Day in South Africa illustrates, the use of such visuality portraying the braai as a symbol and in fact, prerequisite of unity, nationalism, belonging, participation and celebration of heritage leads to a disturbing dissonance. While the historical contexts may differ, this is arguably truer for western countries where consumption habits are not limited to availability and marketing campaigns are dictated by capitalist agendas. Without awareness of the cause of the dissonance and the implications from it, hegemonic inequality continues to be entrenched at the expense of animal beings, the environment and human wellbeing. Whilst Heritage Day has come to symbolise an ideal, utopian, diverse South Africa this symbolism veils the ideological (and physical) violence inherent in the braai activity.

REFERENCES

Adami, V. (2013). Culture, language and environmental rights: The anthropocentrism of English. *Pólemos Journal of Law. Literature and Culture*, *7*(12), 335–355.

Adams, C. J., & Gruen, L. (Eds.). (2014). *'Groundwork' in ecofeminism: Feminist interactions with other animals and the earth*. New York, NY: Bloomsbury.

Brittan, A., & Maynard, M. (1984). *Sexism, racism and oppression*. Oxford, UK: Blackwell.

Chandler, D., & Munday, R. (2011). *A dictionary of media and communication*. Oxford, UK: Oxford University Press. doi:10.1093/acref/9780199568758.001.0001

Chapin, A. (2016). WD-40 and microwaved tampons: Secrets of food photography revealed. *The Guardian*. Retrieved from https://www.theguardian.com/lifeandstyle/2016/jan/04/food-stylist-photography-tricks-advertising

City of Tshwane Metropolitan Municipality. (2004). *Local authority notice*. Retrieved from http://www.tshwane.gov.za/sites/business/Bylaws/Promulgated%20ByLaws%20Documents/ByLaw_KeepingAnimalsBirdsPoultry.pdf

Cooper, A. (2007). *Campaign for the abolition of animal slavery*. Retrieved from http://www.animalslavery.net/index.html

de Klerk, P. (2009). Was die Groot Trek werklik groot? 'n Historiografiese ondersok na di gevolge en betekenis van die Groot Trek. *Tydskrif vir Geesteswetenskappe*, *49*(4), 658–673.

Dillard, J. (2008). A slaughterhouse nightmare: Psychological harm suffered by slaughterhouse employees and the possibility of redress through legal reform. *Georgetown Journal on Poverty Law & Policy*, *15*, 391–408.

Dorovskikh, A. (2015. *Killing for a living: Psychological and physiological effects of alienation of food production on slaughterhouse workers* (Honours Thesis). Boulder, CO: University of Colorado.

Foer, J. S. (2009). *Eating animals*. London, UK: Hamish Hamilton.

Francione, G. L. (2004). Animals – property or person. In C. R. Sunstein & M. C. Nussbaum (Eds.), *Animal rights: Current debates and new directions* (pp. 108–142). Oxford, UK: Oxford University Press.

Hooks, B. (2000). *Feminist theory: From margins to centre*. London, UK: Pluto Press Humane Society International. (n.d.). *The impact of industrialized animal agriculture on world hunger*. Retrieved from http://www.fao.org/fileadmin/user_upload/animalwelfare/HSI--The%20Impact%20of%20Industrialized%20Animal%20Agriculture%20on%20World%20Hunger.pdf

Lusk, J. L., Norwood, F. B., & Prickett, R. W. (2007). *Consumer preferences for farm animal welfare: Results of a nationwide telephone survey*. Retrieved from http://cratefreefuture.com/pdf/American%20Farm%20Bureau-Funded%20Poll.pdf

Mandela, N. (1994). *The long walk to freedom: The autobiography of Nelson Mandela*. Boston, MA: Little, Brown and Company.

Marcus, E. (2001). *Vegan: The new ethics of eating* (2nd ed.). Ithaca, NY: McBook Press.

Mason, J., & Finelli, M. (2006). Brave new farm? In P. Singer (Ed.), *In defense of animals: The second wave* (pp. 104–122). Oxford, UK: Blackwell.

Molefe, T. O. (2014). *'National Braai Day' a day of forgetting*. Retrieved from http://www.news24.com/Columnists/TOMolefe/National-Braai-Day-a-day-of-forgetting-20140917

Moskin, J. (2016). South Africa: One nation united by the grill. *The New York Times*, May 23. Retrieved from https://www.nytimes.com/2016/05/25/dining/braai.html

Oxford Dictionaries. (2017). *Humane*. Retrieved from https://en.oxforddictionaries.com/definition/humane

Patricios, O. (2016). *Heritage Day or Braai Day? It's time to choose*. Retrieved from https://www.dailymaverick.co.za/opinionista/2016-10-05-heritage-day-or-braai-day-its-time-to-choose./#.WUFnaxOGMkg

Pickover, M. (2005). *Animal rights in South Africa*. Cape Town, South Africa: Double Storey Books.

Red Barn Free Range Chicken. (n.d.). *Just what is free range?* Retrieved from http://freerangechicken.co.za/2011/02/just-what-is-free-range/

Sheth, J. N., & Parvatiyar, A. (1995). Relationship marketing in consumer markets: Antecedents and consequences. *Journal of the Academy of Marketing Science*, *23*(4), 255–271. doi:10.1177/009207039502300405

Sidanius, J., & Pratto, F. (1999). *Social dominance: An intergroup theory of social hierarchy and oppression*. Cambridge, UK: Cambridge University Press. doi:10.1017/CBO9781139175043

Soron, D. (2011). Road kill: Commodity fetishism and structural violence. In J. Sanbonmatsu (Ed.), *Critical theory and animal liberation* (pp. 55–69). Plymouth, UK: Rowman & Littlefield.

Southern African Poultry Association. (2012). *Code of practice*. Retrieved from http://www.sapoultry.co.za/pdf-docs/code-practice-broilers.pdf

Stibbe, A. (2004). Health and the social construction of masculinity in Men's Health magazine. *Men and Masculinities*, *7*(1), 31–51. doi:10.1177/1097184X03257441

The Economist. (2014). *TG its Braai Day: The politics of great meat*. Retrieved from http://www.economist.com/news/middle-east-and-africa/21620249-politics-grilled-meat-tg-its-braai-day

Twine, R. (2014). Ecofeminism and veganism: Reviewing the question of universalism. In C. J. Adams & L. Gruen (Eds.), *Ecofeminism: Feminist interactions with other animals and the earth* (pp. 191–207). New York, NY: Bloomsbury.

Wise, S. M. (2002). *Drawing the line: Sentience and the case for animal rights*. Cambridge, UK: Perseus Books.

World Health Organisation (WHO). (2009). *Violence Prevention*. Retrieved from http://www.who.int/violence_injury_prevention/violence/norms.pdf

Yancy, G., & Singer, P. (2015). *Peter Singer: On racism, animal rights and human rights*. Retrieved from http://opinionator.blogs.nytimes.com/2015/05/27/peter-singer-on-speciesism-and-racism/?_r=1

KEY TERMS AND DEFINITIONS

Afrikaans: The mainly Dutch descendent white population (and their language) of South Africa.

Agribusiness: The business of agricultural production.

Barbeque: An outdoor device for grilling food.

Braa Day: National Heritage Day celebrated in South Africa.

Decolonial Thinking: A means of undoing social norms associated with Western colonisation and dominance.

Free-Range: Describes farm animals who have access to outdoor space.

Humane: Having or showing sympathy and compassion to other beings.

Section 4
New Meat Plant–Based Products and Alternatives

Chapter 21
Re-Thinking Meat:
How Climate Change Is Disrupting the Food Industry

Jeff Anhang
The World Bank Group, USA

ABSTRACT

This chapter describes how among vegetarian, vegan and animal advocates, it has been a common practice for many decades to cede the terms "meat" to livestock producers, and to ask people to sacrifice meat. Yet during those decades, global consumption of livestock products has exploded. People have often overlooked the fact that "meat" has been defined for centuries as an essential food that includes vegan versions, and plant-based meat has always been framed as equivalent or superior to animal-based meat. In fact, replacing animal-based foods with better alternatives is said to be the only pragmatic way to stop climate change quickly as needed. However, it is unlikely to happen through efforts to reduce meat consumption. It is much more likely to happen through efforts to disrupt meat production and consumption by making and marketing meat and other foods directly from plants.

INTRODUCTION

The invitation to write this chapter started with the following introductory claims: "Our understanding about the benefits and negatives related to the consumption of meat… is influenced by dietary habits and social norms but also by their marketing. There is however ample scientific evidence that excessive meat consumption is not good for the natural environment and can be detrimental to human health".

However, this chapter explains why the abovementioned claims are themselves detrimental. First, vegan food producers sometimes market their products as "meat" (Field Roast, 2017), and dictionaries define "meat" as an essential food that includes plant-based meat (Merriam Webster Dictionary, 2017); so a critique of "excessive meat consumption" is unnecessarily ambiguous if it does not specify whether the meat in question is animal-based or plant-based. Second, the abovementioned claims imply that moderate animal-based meat consumption could be good for the natural environment, when there is plenty of evidence to the contrary. Third, those claims wrongly imply that it could be good for the environment

DOI: 10.4018/978-1-5225-4757-0.ch021

for people to switch from consuming animal-based meat to consuming dairy products and eggs. Fourth, those claims suggest that advocating against excessive meat consumption could be successful, but this is contradicted by history. Fifth, those claims omit any reference to climate change, though plenty of evidence indicates that climate change is unique among environmental risks in being large-scale, transboundary, potentially irreversible, and potentially catastrophic in the near term.

While this chapter provides evidence to contradict the abovementioned claims and their implications, it also proposes ways in which some common views of animal- and plant-based meat might be constructively reassessed.

SHORT HISTORY OF "MEAT"

In English, the word "meat" was used in the early Middle Ages as a generic term to describe foods in general. Later in the Middle Ages, the word gradually became focused on various types of flesh used for food, including the flesh of vegetables (Online Etymology Dictionary, 2017). These days, food companies market products such as "grain meat" (Wegmans, 2017) and "nut meat" (Vegie Delights, 2017), practically always as being equivalent or superior to animal-based meat.

The phenomenon by which plant-based meat is considered equivalent or superior to animal-based meat is not new. Soyfoods started to be considered superior foods in China during the Han dynasty (206 BC–220 AD), when soy sprouts began to be used alternately as both food and medicine. During this period, the introduction of the hand-turned stone mill helped in developing and expanding the production of soymilk, fermented black soybeans, fermented soybean paste, soy sauce, and fermented tofu (Shurtleff et al., 2014).

Starting in the ninth century AD, a form of soymeat called Yuba was created from the film formed when soybeans are boiled; this began first in China and soon after in Japan (Tsutsumi & Tsutsui, 2009). Around the same time, soybean oil and cake – as well as tofu – also started to be created in China (Shurtleff et al., 2014). The earliest known document to use the word "tofu" was written by Tao Ku around the year 965 (Shurtleff et al., 2014). The document was called Qing Yilu – which translates to "Anecdotes, Simple and Exotic" – and it framed soyfoods as superior to animal-based foods. Several centuries later in China, an encyclopedic document entitled Jujia Biyong Shilei Quanji – which translates to "Essential Arts for Family Living" – described methods of making plant-based sausage using wheat gluten. From then through to modern times, soybeans have been rarely used in whole form in Asian cuisine (Shurtleff et al., 2014).

In modern times, disruption of one industry occurs after another has become prevalent. However, this was not always so. In fact, the history of meat shows that its production generally developed in phases of evolution and consolidation, rather than through rapid disruption.

Originally, in Paleolithic societies, people's success in hunting wild animals was never assured; shooting an arrow and missing the target was often as likely as success. As technology for hunting improved, success still was highly variable, notably dependent on seasonality, local climatic conditions, and the local availability of desired animals (Chiles & Fitzgerald, 2017). Later, after the transition from hunting to animal agriculture, animals were first used for draft labor, eggs, milk, wool, and soil fertilization more than for meat. Feed crops were generally considered too valuable to feed to animals. Livestock products were mainly reserved for rich people, and even for them, they often provided a minor contribution to diets overall (Chiles & Fitzgerald, 2017).

The evolution of democracy brought with it a positive political connotation when animal-based meat was taken up by the non-rich. At the same time, vegetarianism became denigrated as being for poor and/or non-Western people. However, vegetarianism was still common due to widespread poverty and the lack of industrialized processes to produce, process, refrigerate, and transport animal-based foods.

Industrialization of livestock production brought refrigeration, transportation, large-scale production, and reduced prices. It also meant that consumption of animal-based foods was no longer dependent on seasonality, local climatic conditions, and the local availability of desired animals. Animal-based foods became symbols of prosperity and health (Chiles & Fitzgerald, 2017). This occurred even though modern European genes may have favored vegetarianism (Ye et al., 2017). Yet while the size and marketing prowess of the livestock sector have increased year after year for many years, plant-based diets have persisted all over the world, even among people who do not live in poverty.

SACRIFICING MEAT

As described above, the origins of the word "meat" indicate that plant-based meat has long been a rival to animal-based meat. This suggests that there is no good reason for ceding the term "meat" to livestock producers and asking people to sacrifice meat. Indeed, since "meat" is commonly defined as an essential food, livestock producers would be expected to benefit by having a monopoly on the marketing of "meat". As evidence of this, a conglomerate representing livestock producers in the European Union has lobbied for the word "meat" to be reserved for animal-based products (Mammoser, 2017). Another tactic used by some livestock producers – and by some people who cannot imagine giving up animal-based meat – is to call plant-based meat "fake".

Yet plant-based meat need not involve any more processing than does whole-wheat bread, which nobody calls fake. In fact, plant-based meat has almost always been produced by artisanal methods – whereas animal-based meat has long been produced in developed economies primarily in factory settings, using hormones and antibiotics. Producers of plant-based meat never use hormones or antibiotics, and they also often avoid genetically modified organisms – which are rarely avoided in animal-based meat production. With that in mind, and given the long history of plant-based meat, animal-based meat could be considered less authentic than plant-based meat. In other words, animal-based meat could be considered an ersatz version of meat when compared to plant-based meat.

However, among vegetarian, vegan, and animal advocates, it has been common practice for many decades to cede the terms "meat" and "milk" to livestock producers, and to ask people to sacrifice meat and milk. Yet during those decades, global consumption of livestock products has exploded six-fold (Renner, 2014), twice as fast as human population growth. Further evidence for a case not to cede the term "meat" to livestock producers exists in a major trend to market plant-based meat for sustainability (Retail News Insider, 2014 and 2017). Therefore, some part of vegetarian, vegan, and animal advocacy might merit re-thinking.

Perhaps the most popular campaign that advocates for people to sacrifice meat is the Meatless Mondays campaign. By touting "meatless" eating in its name, the campaign overlooks the fact that dictionaries define meat as an essential food that includes vegan versions. The Meatless Mondays campaign prioritizes a prescription from medical authorities who have indicated that a 15 percent reduction in saturated fat is needed for good medical health (Kamila, 2011). According to the campaign, this can be fully achieved if people give up consuming meat just one day per week. However, by its name and otherwise, the

Meatless Mondays campaign fails to emphasize that dairy products often contain even more saturated fat per serving than does meat, and eggs too contain a significant amount of saturated fat; nor does the campaign indicate what change in consumption is needed for good climatic health.

For example, for consumers concerned about saturated fat, a fitness website has estimated that a 3.5-ounce fast-food hamburger contains approximately 4 grams of saturated fat (Myfitnesspal, 2017a). The same website has also estimated that 100 grams (equivalent to 3.5 ounces) of quiche Lorraine contains 8 grams of saturated fat. Yet the Meatless Mondays campaign can and does lead some people to switch from a hamburger to quiche Lorraine, which can worsen both public health and climate change.

If the Meatless Mondays campaign were to clarify that it frowns upon eggs and dairy products as well as animal-based meat, then it could potentially yield a 13 percent replacement of livestock products with better alternatives. Yet 13 percent less livestock products would be far less than the amount of replacement that is actually needed to reverse climate change – which is somewhere between 50 to 85 percent, depending on whose analysis is used (Goodland, 2014).

However, it seems unlikely that Meatless Mondays will ever yield even 13 percent less livestock products. After all, the campaign frames what is needed as a sacrifice, so the required action is likely to suffer the same fate as everything that promotes sacrifice – i.e., people who sacrifice livestock products one day are likely to crave them more the next day. Indeed, the Meatless Monday campaign anachronistically touts its basis in American rationing during World War I (Meatless Monday, 2017), after which a major expansion in meat production occurred in the U.S. (The National Provisioner, 2016). Yet no consumer product is successfully sold by pressing people to use it just one day a week. For example, consumers might be wary of choosing Pepsi Cola at all if its marketing promoted it as a one-day-a-week drink, conceding that Coca Cola remains the drink of choice the rest of the week.

In fact, while Meatless Mondays has expanded around the world since 2003, the worldwide consumption of livestock products did not fall in the subsequent decade; it rather continued to rise (Nierenberg & Reynolds, 2012). It continued to rise even during 2007-2012 which is especially striking when considering the wave of economic downturns in one region after another during this period. By comparison, in earlier times in history, the consumption of livestock products dropped markedly during economic downturns (Hawkins, 1974).

Actual trends in global meat consumption are surely more important than the trend of organizations to adopt Meatless Mondays. Perhaps the organizers of Meatless Mondays would achieve more success by framing alternatives to livestock products as better products, rather than a sacrifice. If alternatives to livestock products might seem hard to promote, then one might consider as an example the fact that bicycles may be hard to promote to car-lovers, but bike advocates normally do not frame bike-riding as a sacrifice.

The Meatless Monday campaign promotes sacrificing meat to reduce health risks, energy and water usage, and carbon emissions. Yet goals for such reductions are common in the case of many consumer products, and they usually do not motivate major action to replace any products. In contrast, emergencies normally motivate major action – and both the UN Intergovernmental Panel on Climate Change and the UN International Energy Agency have warned that greenhouse gas emissions must be reduced significantly by 2020 (Stromberg, 2012) or at the latest 2026 (Dechert, 2016), or else climate change may no longer be controllable. Therefore, climate change may be the most compelling motivation on which to dwell.

An alternative to the Meatless Mondays campaign is a campaign that has a similar but more sophisticated name, namely Meat Free Monday, founded and operated by three members of a famous family, Mary, Stella and Paul McCartney. By replacing "Meatless" with "Meat Free", they have moved from using a term that connotes taking something away to an expression that raises the idea of being free. Unlike the Meatless Mondays, the Meat Free Monday campaign was launched specifically to address climate change (Lean, 2014). The Meat Free Monday campaign has made it clear that it does not support switching from animal-based meat to eggs or dairy (e.g. Meat Free Monday, 2017b). Sometimes the Meat Free Monday campaign has clearly stated that it promotes "plant-based meats" (e.g. Meat Free Monday, 2017a).

So there are several ways in which the Meatless Monday campaign could easily improve itself to become more relevant – notably by using a more positive and climate-oriented approach to its advocacy; by clarifying that it does not support switching from animal-based meat to eggs or dairy; and by promoting plant-based meat.

In recent years, activists have promoted the idea of getting people to sacrifice animal-based meat by taxing it. Yet people who favor animal-based meat far outnumber those who do not, so it is likely to be political suicide for politicians to propose taxing animal-based meat in almost every jurisdiction in the world. Moreover, in any particular jurisdiction, taxing animal-based meat to combat climate change would contradict the fact that climate change can be managed effectively only with a global approach. Anyway, tax is generally imposed on an industry to get it to do something only when there is not a business case to do it – yet there is a business case for replacing livestock products with better alternatives (Goodland & Anhang, 2009).

A CASE TO REPLACE

A vivid example of how detrimental it can be to advocate for "less meat" was displayed during a meeting in 2015 where public comments were made on recommendations for U.S. dietary guidelines. Those comments can be seen and heard in a video of the meeting (Health.gov, 2015). A man representing McCormick Spices played to the crowd, saying: "let's spice up the guidelines!" He proposed that consumers would buy his company's products "not because they have to but because they want to". Some speakers at the meeting said they were attending on behalf of a broad coalition representing "millions of Americans" anxious for the dietary guidelines to incorporate recommendations for "less meat" to improve environmental sustainability. One couldn't help wondering who would win a contest between millions of "less meat" consumers *versus* hundreds of millions of meat consumers. Indeed, a number of speakers representing livestock interests spoke as if they represented the average consumer, and they pitched livestock products as center-of-the-plate foods in the most positive terms possible.

In contrast, none of those promoting "less meat" pitched anything easily perceived by an average consumer as center-of-the-plate foods. Instead, they pressed for meat to be replaced with things like "fruits and vegetables" and "more plants". They left it to the audience to puzzle over how vegetables and fruits might be something other than side dishes and desserts, and how a plant could be a center-of-the-plate food. Contradicting the claim by the "less meat" speakers that they spoke for a broad coalition, virtually all but one of them were clearly Caucasian. In contrast, many speakers outside that coalition were clearly African American, Asian American, and Hispanic American.

One speaker said "less meat" is needed because emissions of methane and nitrous oxide from livestock production "may double by 2070... making it impossible to meet climate change targets" and "Americans are eager for good science-based information". Yet according to the most prominent climate authorities, the world must significantly reduce greenhouse gases by 2020 (Stromberg, 2012) or at the latest 2026 (Dechert, 2016), or else climate change may no longer be controllable. So, the "less meat" speakers failed to define correctly what is needed. They also failed to explain that Americans cannot act to meet climate targets on their own. That is because greenhouse gas emissions and climate change are large-scale and do not respect borders. Climate targets can be met only if people in much more populous countries participate, especially China and India. Yet it is even less possible to sell "less meat" in China and India than it is in the U.S., as there is much less perception in those countries that there is an excess of meat consumption.

"Less meat" proponents also failed to talk about how widely-cited assessments of food and climate change by the Food and Agriculture Organization of the United Nations (FAO) and others have focused on *all* livestock production, not just meat production. Yet promotion of "less dairy products" and "less eggs" would be even less acceptable than "less meat" in China and India – particularly in India, where dairy products are especially preferred.

So, it seems that what is needed is some sort of positive, internationally acceptable marketing of center-of-the-plate and other vegan products. They could be called something like "Happy Better Vegan Foods". In part because positive marketing of center-of-the-plate products is already being undertaken by plant-based food producers who market products such as "grain meat" and "nut meat," it seems that recommendations for changing U.S. dietary guidelines were mistaken in prescribing "smaller meat portions" without qualifying them as animal-based meat portions.

If a term such as "Happy Better Vegan Foods" would be used, then what is needed could be framed as preferable, delicious center-of-the plate foods and vegan alternatives to dairy products and eggs. This could inspire consumers to choose what is needed not because of dietary guidelines, but because they want to – the holy grail prescribed by the man from McCormick Spices.

A variation on the "less meat" theme came from a speaker advocating for the "humane" raising of animals. She spoke of her concern for greenhouse gas emissions, saying: "The FAO has evidence to show that 14.5 percent of anthropogenic greenhouse gas emissions come from livestock production". Therefore, this speaker claimed, "there is an overwhelming case" to accept recommendations for "less meat". However, the FAO report that originated the cited 14.5 percent emissions estimate actually promotes more livestock production, to be facilitated by "technologies and practice currently used by the 10 percent of producers with the lowest emission intensity" (Gerber et al., 2013, p. xiii). The lowest emission intensity producers are those with the most confined operations – which means that they raise animals in the least humane way possible.

The FAO's livestock-climate analysis cited by the "less meat" speakers was used in the recommendations for "less meat" that they cited, but it elicited no criticism from them. Yet the FAO's livestock-climate analysis has been written by livestock specialists, not environmental specialists, and the organisation is just one of nineteen UN specialized agencies.

In contrast, Bill Gates (2013) argues for the replacement of most livestock products with better alternatives, referencing the work of environmental specialists employed by two other UN specialized agencies – the World Bank and International Finance Corporation (IFC) – who have explained how livestock account for much more greenhouse gas than the FAO asserts (Goodland & Anhang, 2009). One of those environmental specialists – Goodland (2012) published a critique of the FAO's partnership with the global livestock industry which appeared in The New York Times. Whether "less meat" activists use the FAO's analysis or not, if they otherwise want to address climate change properly, then they might serve themselves and others well by defining the key problem as being the need to reduce emissions significantly before climate tipping points occur, and by settling on a calculation of how much livestock reduction is needed to avoid those tipping points.

Our world is at stake, so there is an ethical need to act without worrying what policymakers or consumers might accept. In a past case, it turned out that such worrying was undue (Shaw & Stroup, 1995), and it similarly involved large-scale emissions that do not respect borders. Specifically, in the 1990s, environmentalists worried whether policymakers and consumers would accept (under the Montreal Protocol) eliminating coolants and aerosols that destroy the ozone layer. People loved their spray cans, refrigerators and air conditioners just as much as people today love consuming livestock products. Yet decisions were made to frame alternative products as positive things, and to talk about spray cans as much as refrigerators and air conditioners – and to define exactly what was needed – and it worked (Parry, 2011).

As with coolants and aerosols, it should not matter that "less meat" proponents are vastly outnumbered. So were Steve Jobs and Bill Gates long ago but they didn't tone down out of fear of what policymakers or consumers might accept. They just went ahead with marketing happier and better things – which made their competitors' products obsolete in only a few years – and the same can be done with Happy Better Vegan Foods.

The case promoted by "less meat" proponents at the meeting for public comments on the proposed U.S. dietary guidelines ended up not being reflected in new U.S. dietary guidelines. This might not be considered surprising. After all, Steve Jobs and Bill Gates didn't market fewer mainframe computers; instead they marketed Happier Better Cheaper Computers. Similarly, rather than promoting less meat, greater success might well come from promoting plant-based meat to replace animal-based meat.

PEAK LIVESTOCK

The FAO's report entitled "Livestock's Long Shadow" (Steinfeld et al., 2006) contemplates actions to manage a projected doubling in livestock production to feed the projected 9 billion people who will be alive in 2050. Specifically, "Livestock's Long Shadow" projects that "the production of meat will double between now and 2050" (Steinfeld et al., 2006, p. 388). Yet the FAO's projection is based on a presumed large-scale expansion of the livestock sector, which would lead to "further destruction of natural habitats like rainforests" and would "not solve food insecurity", according to the Soil Association (Soil Association, 2010, p. 8 and p. 3).

The FAO's projection presumes that it is possible for the livestock sector to continue expanding. In contrast, a projection that demand for animal products could decline through at least 2030 has been published by the International Food Policy Research Institute (IFPRI) in its report entitled "Feeding the Future's Changing Diets" (Msangi & Rosegrant, 2011). The IFPRI co-published with FAO a report 15 years ago that kicked off the "Livestock Revolution", projecting inevitably more livestock (Delgado et al., 1999). So, it is particularly striking to see the IFPRI now projecting such a different future.

In thinking about whether livestock production is bound to expand or contract, it is worthwhile noting that there are presently more than 173 billion animals raised for food each year (Chomping Climate Change, 2015). In fact, it has been said that replacing livestock products with better alternatives may be the only pragmatic strategy to reverse climate change before it is too late (Goodland, 2014). That is because livestock and feed production are estimated to occupy 45 percent of all land on earth (Thornton et al., 2011) – that's all land, both arable and non-arable, not excluding ice caps or mountaintops or anything else. Much of that 45 percent of all land was once forested, and could be forested again, yielding many more trees to absorb excess carbon from our atmosphere.

In 2006, the FAO published a report estimating that livestock were responsible for 18 percent of anthropogenic greenhouse gas emissions – yet that report prescribed no less livestock, but rather more factory farming: "The principle means of limiting livestock's impact on the environment must be... intensification" (Steinfeld et al., 2006, p. 236). That report's lead author and a co-author later wrote to confirm that prescription (Steinfeld & Gerber, 2010). The FAO subsequently published a 2013 report that reduced its livestock emissions estimate from 18 percent to 14.5 percent, and paired that estimate with prescriptions to facilitate 70 percent more livestock production by 2050 (Gerber et al., 2013).

However, livestock products can be replaced with better alternatives in order to reverse climate change before it's too late (Goodland, 2014). If livestock are not replaced with better alternatives voluntarily, then climate change is likely to force it. Notably, a one degree Celsius rise in temperature above optimum in a growing season causes a 10 percent decline in grain yields (Brown, 2011). This is already happening in some regions.

Spikes in the prices of grains used to feed animals have started to make animal-based meat production unprofitable. For example, at the start of 2017, it was forecast that the average U.S. pork producer would lose money for the year, after having been unprofitable in 2016, and before that in 2012-2013, and in 2008-2009 (Plain, 2017). The phenomenon of ongoing unprofitability has occurred in Chinese pork production (Day, 2015). In the U.S., the production of feedlot beef – the vast majority of beef in the U.S. – has been unprofitable for the past two years (Soderlin, 2017). Indeed, as of January 2017, few countries in the world could claim long-term profitability in cattle enterprises, even though beef prices rose to record highs in 2013-2014 (Behrendt & Weeks, 2017).

While poultry production may be profitable for now, poultry are expected to suffer the worst of any livestock under climate change, as they are particularly sensitive to temperature-associated environmental challenges, especially heat stress (Bhadauria at el., 2014). In fact, heat stress from climate change may have only just started to be felt. As conservative an organization as PriceWaterhouseCoopers (2012) has warned of a possible six degree Celsius rise in global temperature this century – that's a 10.8° Farenheit rise – which implies a 60 percent decline in agricultural outputs.

Energy specialists may aim for continued expansion of the fossil-fuel based sector until Peak Oil is reached– that is, when oil demand can no longer be satisfied as a result from a terminal decline in production (Heinberg, 2017). Livestock specialists may similarly aim for expansion of the livestock sector until "Peak Livestock" is reached. However, there are some notable differences between the oil and livestock industries. As the production of oil takes place underground and underwater, it is relatively unaffected by climate change. On the contrary, agriculture is more exposed to the impacts of climate change than any other industry as the production of livestock and crops to feed them takes place aboveground and largely outdoors. According to Chomping Climate Change (Admin, 2015): "Until recently, evidence was slim that climate change was causing dire hardship and large-scale die-offs in the raising of livestock and crops that feed them. However, there has recently been a noticeable spike in such hardships and die-offs all over the world". This has helped to create a point of inflection, whereby after many years of expansion of the livestock sector, there suddenly appears to be a trend favoring the replacement of animal-based foods with plant-based ones.

While a point of inflection seems to be taking hold (e.g., see Sciponi, 2016), projections are still commonly cited not only for a doubling in livestock production, but also for 70 percent more food; and in some places, it is even being noted that the FAO projects a potential need for 100 percent more food worldwide by 2050 (WFP, 2009). Yet such FAO projections have been called a "big fat lie" (Soil Association, 2010). After all, human population is not projected to increase by 70 percent or 100 percent by 2050.

The UN Population Division's medium-variant projection for human population in 2050 is 9.77 billion (up from around 7.55 billion in 2017), while its low-variant project for human population in 2050 is 8.8 billion (UN, 2017)[1]. This is 30 (medium-variant) or 17 (low-variant) percent more people than exist in 2017. If 17 to 30 percent more people exist in 2050 than today, then there is no obvious good reason why the world would need 70 percent more food. The UN Population Division has not expressed any opinion on whether its low- or medium-variant projection is more likely to be fulfilled. So even if nothing is done to reduce the incidence of overweight and obese people — and the most recent data indicates that a shocking 2.2 billion people are overweight or obese today (The GBD 2015 Obesity Collaborators, 2017) — it seems that between 25 and 30 percent more food would be needed in 2050, not 70 percent more food.

Yet the UN's projections do not factor in any potential for population contraction due to sea-level rise due to climate change (ENS, 2013). Sea-level rise driven by climate change is said to imperil 1700 cities in the U.S. alone, including New York, Boston, and Miami (Strauss, 2013). Much poorer cities across the world face a similar risk, which they are much less capable of managing (ENS, 2013). This suggests that fewer people may well exist in 2050 than today, which by itself should mean that the world would need less food, not more.

Whether or not fewer people exist in 2050 than today, disruptive climate events are already causing declines in agricultural output in every region of the world. These declines are projected to worsen over time in both magnitude and geographic scope. This is helping to create a new business case – connected to climate change – for making meat directly from crops, rather than from feeding many times the same amount of crops to animals.

Trends in the food industry have historically been supply-led, rather than demand-driven. For instance, food industry leaders – rather than consumers – have been responsible for such innovations as chicken nuggets, Big Macs, and bacon-wrapped pizza. In fact, supply-led trends are generally the norm in most categories of consumer products. For example, consumers did not (nor could they) originate trends favoring digital TVs, iPhones, or drones; those trends were originated by industry leaders. However, while consumers have not originated those trends, they have had the power to help drive or stop their spread. So, to drive a trend, it is essential to engage consumers.

Large-scale die-offs of livestock and feed crops due to climate change now provide extra reason for food industry leaders to be interested in replacing animal-based foods with plant-based ones. Food industry leaders have generally ignored vegetarian or vegan advocacy based on concerns over public health and animal rights – but they cannot ignore climate change. In other words, climate change is uniquely and unmistakably advancing a business case for disruption of the food industry.

CULTURE CHANGE?

While a business case connected to climate change is developing for making meat directly from plants rather than from animals, animal-rights activists rarely incorporate this in their advocacy. Instead, they generally advocate for a change in culture – otherwise known as "culture change" – whereby people in the future would reject the systemic aggression and violence used in raising and slaughtering animals to become food.

When animal-rights activists advocate for transformations in the age of climate change, it would seem ethically sound for them to recognize that culture change is normally generational, taking typically 50-100 years to achieve, under the best of circumstances, with reversals not uncommon (e.g., one can think of the "Dark Ages" or today's "Brexit"). So, activists working toward such culture change could be acting perversely, if they could better succeed with a climate strategy. An approach that seeks culture change might not only extend the misuse of animals for decades longer than under a climate change strategy, but could mean that activists would be resigning themselves to the possibility of extinction of much of life on earth.

Conversely, a strategy could better succeed by recognizing the origin and positive associations of the word "meat", and by aiming to disrupt rather than reduce its consumption. An interesting perspective on such a strategy has been enunciated by Ethan Brown, the founder and CEO of a company named "Beyond Meat". Mr. Brown said in a televised interview in 2014: "We've been having meat as humans for about 2.3 million years so there is a great familiarity with it, the way it crosses across the teeth, the way it bites, etc. and we don't want to walk away from that. You know, fried chicken tastes great. Steak tastes great. Let's just take the amino acid, the fats, from another source and recreate those so we can take an animal entirely out of the equation. I also think about what happened with the automotive sector where we had horse-drawn carriages, the internal combustion engine came along and basically obviated the need for the horse in that equation. We're trying to do the same with animal protein" (CBS This Morning, 2014). Mr. Brown also invoked climate change in that interview: "And here's an important statistic, so people have a certain hopelessness about climate change, they say: 'I don't know what to do?', but, in fact, 51 percent of greenhouse gas emissions can be attributed to livestock" (CBS This Morning, 2014).

In other words, the best strategy to address climate change – and to disrupt the meat industry – may involve engaging people to persuade them to do something that fits their existing priorities, rather than advocating something that requires them to change their priorities. Less meat or meatless diets, vegan diets and animal rights rank nowhere on most people's lists of priorities. Conversely, climate change is among the very top few priorities for many policymakers, industry leaders and other individuals across the world.

So, activists can implement a quick, global strategy of engaging people to learn how climate change imperils life on earth in the near term, but can be reversed through plant-based meat and other plant-based foods. Already, momentum has been building in efforts to replace animal-based foods with plant-based ones, often with references to climate change.

Companies that have tried sticking with animal agriculture have already started to go out of business (e.g., see Genoways, 2015), while financiers of plant-based food companies have started to become the envy of investors everywhere (Wortham & Miller, 2013). A similar phenomenon has occurred in every disrupted industry. For example, in many poor countries, about 20 years ago, only a few percent of people had telephones; a few years later, 25 percent had mobile access; a few years later, the figure was 70-80 percent (Sullivan, 2007). These days, analogue telephones and their manufacturers can scarcely be found anymore, anywhere in the world.

Surveys consistently show that consumers buy food items primarily on the basis of price and quality. Included in quality are ease and speed of preparation and delivery, cleanliness of retail outlets and good taste. Only a relatively small percentage of consumers have ever chosen foods on any other basis, and there is no sign that this will change anytime soon. While activists have a long track record of agitating for less or no meat, the results show more meat-eating year after year, not less.

Climate-friendliness is now sometimes included as part of marketing of food quality to consumers. Indeed, there is no practical alternative for consumers to reverse climate change – especially if it is true that livestock products are responsible for at least 51 percent of anthropogenic greenhouse gas emissions.

One reason why animal advocacy has not reduced global consumption of animal products is that most activists do not account for the way people normally decide to try different foods. Most people will happily experiment one meal at a time, and will then repeat if the new meal made them happy. In contrast, promoting a vegan/vegetarian diet will appear to most people as abrupt and radical as if McDonald's were to promote a "meatarian" diet. Instead, McDonald's has conquered one country after another by marketing "Happy Meals". In order to match or beat McDonald's success, animal advocates might do well to promote something even more positive, such as "Happier Meals" – marketing plant-based meat burgers as the best ones to choose any day of the week or year.

CONCLUSION

Authoritative projections indicate that climate change may no longer be reversible if emissions are not cut significantly by 2020 (Stromberg, 2012) or at the latest 2026 (Dechert, 2016). Yet according to the International Energy Agency, the amount of renewable energy infrastructure that is needed to stop climate change could only be fully developed long after 2026, and will cost at least $53 trillion (Kramer, 2013).

A faster and much more economical strategy begins with recognizing that livestock production accounts for at least half of human-caused greenhouse gas (De Schutter, 2014) and uses 45 percent of all land on earth (ILRI, 2011). Replacing livestock products with better alternatives offers a unique dual opportunity to reduce greenhouse gas emissions while freeing up land to enable more trees to capture excess atmospheric carbon.

Better alternatives to livestock products are generally made from grains and legumes, such as wheat, peas, sorghum and beans. Such foods are better than livestock products because any food that comes directly from a plant will generally be responsible for much less greenhouse gas than are livestock products. According to an article in Nature (Petherick, 2012), improvements in the way livestock are raised can achieve only 4 percent reduction in greenhouse gas emissions through 2030. That is much less reduction in emissions than every other industry is being called upon to achieve, and indeed is a trivial amount relative to what the food industry needs to accomplish (Goodland, 2013).

People can change their food choices literally overnight. That is a key reason why replacing animal-based foods with better alternatives is said to be the only pragmatic way to stop climate change quickly as needed. However, it is unlikely to happen through efforts to reduce meat consumption. It is much more likely to happen through efforts to disrupt meat production and consumption by making and marketing meat and other foods directly from plants.

REFERENCES

Behrendt, K., & Weeks, P. (2017). *How are global and Australian beef producers performing?* Meat & Livestock Australia. Retrieved from https://www.mla.com.au/globalassets/mla-corporate/prices--markets/documents/trends--analysis/agri-benchmark/revised_mla_agribenchmark-beef-results-report_jan-2017.pdf

Bhadauria, P., Kataria, J. M., Majumdar, S., Bhanja, S.K., & Divya, G.& Kolluri. (2014). Impact of hot climate on poultry production system-A review. *Journal of Poultry Science and Technology*, *2*(4), 56–63.

Brown, L. R. (2011). *World on the edge: How to prevent environmental and economic collapse*. New York, NY: Norton.

CBS This Morning. (2014). Beyond Meat CEO Ethan Brown on the benefits of meat substitutes. Retrieved from https://www.cbsnews.com/videos/beyond-meat-ceo-ethan-brown-on-the-benefits-of-meat-substitutes-2/

Chiles, R. M., & Fitzgerald, A. J. (2017). Why is meat so important in Western history and culture? A genealogical critique of biophysical and political-economic explanations. *Agriculture and Human Values*. Retrieved from https://link.springer.com/article/10.1007/s10460-017-9787-7 doi:10.1007/s10460-017-9787-7

Chomping Climate Change. (2014). Why it's a big fat lie that the world needs 70 percent more food by 2050. Retrieved from http://www.chompingclimatechange.org/updated-analysis/why-its-a-big-fat-lie-that-the-world-needs-70-percent-more-food-by-2050

Chomping Climate Change. (2015). Has climate change caused "Peak Livestock"? Retrieved from http://www.chompingclimatechange.org/updated-analysis/has-the-world-reached-peak-livestock/

Day, C. (2015). Smaller Chinese hog herd, opportunity for U.S. National Hog Farmer. Retrieved from http://www.nationalhogfarmer.com/marketing/smaller-chinese-hog-herd-opportunity-us

De Schutter, O. (2014). Ending hunger - the rich world holds the keys. *The Ecologist*, *25*(March). Retrieved from http://www.theecologist.org/blogs_and_comments/commentators/2333245/ending_hunger_the_rich_world_holds_the_keys.html

Dechert, S. (2016). *1.5 degree climate chances "Not dead yet," but gone within a decade*. Planetsave. Retrieved from http://planetsave.com/2016/09/24/1-5-degree-climate-chances-not-dead-yet-but-gone-within-a-decade

Delgado, C., Rosegrant, M., Steinfield, H., Ehui, S., & Courbois, C. (1999). *Livestock to 2020: The next food revolution*. Food, Agriculture and the Environment Discussion Paper 28. Washington D.C.: International Food Policy Research Institute (IFPRI), Food Agriculture Organization (FAO) and International Livestock Research Institute (ILRI).

Environment News Service (ENS). (2013). 10 Coastal cities at greatest flood risk as sea levels rise. Retrieved from http://ens-newswire.com/2013/09/03/10-coastal-cities-at-greatest-flood-risk-as-sea-levels-rise

Field Roast. (2017) FAQ. Retrieved from http://fieldroast.com/faq

Gates, B. (2013). *Food is ripe for innovation*. Mashable. Retrieved from http://mashable.com/2013/03/21/bill-gates-future-of-food/#n7CpGZPdiGqi

Genoways, T. (2015). *Fear in a handful of dust*. New Republic. Retrieved from https://newrepublic.com/article/121558/what-climate-change-doing-texas-cattle-ranch

Gerber, P. J., Steinfeld, H., Henderson, B., Mottet, A., Opio, C., Dijkman, J., . . . Tempio, G. (2013). Tackling climate change through livestock: A global assessment of emissions and mitigation opportunities. Food and Agriculture Organization of the United Nations (FAO), Rome, Italy.

Goodland, R. (2012). FAO yields to meat industry pressure on climate change. *New York Times*, 11 July. Retrieved from bittman.blogs.nytimes.com/2012/07/11/fao-yields-to-meat-industry-pressure-on-climate-change/?_r=0

Goodland, R. (2013). Lifting livestock's long shadow. *Nature Climate Change*, *3*(1), 2. doi:10.1038/nclimate1755

Goodland, R. (2014). How to reverse climate change before it's too late. *Meatanomics*. Retrieved from https://meatonomics.com/2014/09/04/how-to-reverse-climate-change-before-its-too-late

Goodland, R., & Anhang, J. (2009). Livestock and climate change: What if the key actors in climate change are... cows, pigs and chickens? *World Watch*, (November/December), 11–19. Retrieved from https://www.worldwatch.org/files/pdf/Livestock%20and%20Climate%20Change.pdf

Hawkins, A. (1974). *Tighten your belt: Food prices to soar with world demand. The Afro-American*, 10 August. Retrieved from https://news.google.com/newspapers?nid=2211&dat=19740810&id=uSomAAAAIBAJ&sjid=YP4FAAAAIBAJ&pg=1821,526870&hl=en

Health.gov. (2015). *Public meeting for oral testimony on the Scientific Report of the 2015 Dietary Guidelines Committee*. U.S. Office of Disease Prevention and Health Promotion. Retrieved from https://health.gov/DietaryGuidelines/2015/public-meeting.asp

Heinberg, R. (2017). *The Peak Oil President?* Post Carbon Institute. Retrieved from http://www.postcarbon.org/the-peak-oil-president

International Livestock Research Institute (ILRI). (2011). Livestock and climate change. Retrieved from https://www.ilri.org/node/6432

Kamila, A. Y. (2011). Natural foodie: Sebago Brewing Co. launches Meatless Monday menu. *Portland Press Herald*. Retrieved from http://www.pressherald.com/2011/06/29/sebago-brewing-co_-launches-meatless-monday-menu_2011-06-29

Kramer, S. (2013). $53 trillion of clean energy needed to meet global 2C target. Earthtechling. Retrieved from http://earthtechling.com/2015/11/53-trillion-of-clean-energy-needed-to-meet-global-2c-target

Lean, G. (2014). Sir Paul McCartney: Why I have a beef with meat-eating. *Telegraph*. Retrieved from http://www.telegraph.co.uk/news/earth/environment/globalwarming/11231472/Sir-Paul-McCartney-why-I-have-a-beef-with-meat-eating.html

Mammoser, G. (2017). Meat producers are concerned vegan bacon is deceiving consumers. *Vice*. Retrieved from https://munchies.vice.com/en_uk/article/aey4ba/the-way-you-eat-pizza-says-a-lot-about-you-according-to-body-language-experts

Meat Free Monday. (2017a). Mark Ruffalo and Lily Cole back #MFMclimatepledge in NYC. Retrieved from https://www.meatfreemondays.com/pledge-brunch-spotlights-un-climate-summit-pledge-campaign/

Meat Free Monday. (2017b). Vegan Quarter puts plant-based food centre stage. Retrieved from https://www.meatfreemondays.com/vegan-quarter-puts-plant-based-food-centre-stage/

Meatless Monday. (2017). History. Retrieved from http://www.meatlessmonday.com/about-us/history

Merriam Webster Dictionary. (2017). Meat. Retrieved from https://www.merriam-webster.com/dictionary/meat

Msangi, S., & Rosegrant, R. W. (2011). Feeding the future's changing diets: Implications for agriculture markets, nutrition and policy, 2020. *Paper presented at the Leveraging Agriculture for Improving Nutrition and Health Conference*, New Delhi, India. Retrieved from http://www.foresightfordevelopment.org/sobipro/download-file/46-953/54

Myfitnesspal. (2017a). Calories in hamburger fast food. Retrieved from http://www.myfitnesspal.com/food/calories/45914216

Myfitnesspal. (2017b). Calories in Traditionnelle Quiche Lorraine. Retrieved from http://www.myfitnesspal.com/food/calories/traditionnelle-quiche-lorraine-510312963

Nierenberg, D., & Reynolds, L. (2012). Disease and drought curb meat production and consumption. Vital Signs, Worldwatch Institute. Retrieved from http://vitalsigns.worldwatch.org/vs-trend/disease-and-drought-curb-meat-production-and-consumption

Online Etymology Dictionary. 2017. Meat (n.). Retrieved from http://www.etymonline.com/index.php?allowed_in_frame=0&search=meat

Parry, W. (2011). Climate success story: Saving the ozone layer. *Live Science*. Retrieved from https://www.livescience.com/17347-climate-success-montreal-protocol-ozone.html

Petherick, A. (2012). Light is cast on a long shadow. *Nature Climate Change*, *2*(10), 705–706. doi:10.1038/nclimate1703

Plain, R. (2017). More hogs and higher prices — unusual, but desirable. *National Hog Farmer*. Retrieved from http://www.nationalhogfarmer.com/marketing/more-hogs-and-higher-prices-unusual-desirable

PriceWaterhouseCoopers (PWC). (2012). *Too late for two degrees?* Retrieved from https://www.pwc.com/gx/en/sustainability/publications/low-carbon-economy-index/assets/pwc-low-carbon-economy-index-2012.pdf

Renner, M. (2014). Peak meat production strains land and water resources. *Vital Signs, Worldwatch Institute*. Retrieved from http://vitalsigns.worldwatch.org/vs-trend/peak-meat-production-strains-land-and-water-resources

Retail News Insider. (2014). *From lab to table: The future of food.* Retrieved from http://www.retailnewsinsider.com/2014/06/01/from-lab-to-table-the-future-of-food

Retail News Insider. (2017). *Supply solutions: Sourcing Sophistication for today's new retail landscape.* Retrieved from http://www.retailnewsinsider.com/2017/07/06/supply-solutions-sourcing-sophistication-for-todays-new-retail-landscape/

Sciponi, J. (2016). *Bill Gates and NY Met David Wright see money in meatless venture.* Fox Business. Retrieved from http://www.foxbusiness.com/features/2016/10/31/bill-gates-and-ny-met-david-wright-see-money-in-meatless-venture.htm

Shaw, J. S., & Stroup, R. L. (1995). *Should we worry about ozone?* National Center for Policy Analysis. Policy Report No. 191. Retrieved from http://www.ncpa.org/pdfs/st191.pdf

Shurtleff, W., Huang, H. T., & Aoyagi, A. (2014). *History of soyfoods in China and Taiwan, and in Chinese cookbooks, restaurants, and Chinese work with soyfoods outside China. Extnsively annotated bibliography and sourcebook.* Lafayette, CA: Soyinfo Center.

Soderlin, B. (2017). *More cattle, lower prices: Ranchers and feeders hope consumers respond by buying more beef.* Omaha World. Retrieved from http://www.omaha.com/money/more-cattle-lower-prices-ranchers-and-feeders-hope-consumers-respond/article_f7dd3bbc-2b41-5c05-a5e7-4f55a24483a1.html

Soil Association. (2010). *Telling porkies: The big fat lie about doubling food production.* Bristol, UK: Soil Association. Retrieved from http://stopogm.net/sites/stopogm.net/files/webfm/plataforma/Telling-Porkies.pdf

Steinfeld, H., & Gerber, P. (2010). Livestock production and the global environment: Consume less or produce better? *Proceedings of the National Academy of Sciences of the United States, 107*(43), 18237–18238. doi:10.1073/pnas.1012541107 PMID:20935253

Steinfeld, H., Gerber, P., Wassenaar, T., Castel, V., Rosales, M., & de Haan, C. (2006). *Livestock's long shadow: environmental issues and options.* Rome, Italy: Food Agriculture Organisation.

Strauss, B. H. (2013). Rapid accumulation of committed sea-level rise from global warming. *Proceedings of the National Academy of Sciences of the United States, 110*(34), 13699–13700. doi:10.1073/pnas.1312464110 PMID:23898210

Stromberg, J. (2012). Climate change tipping point: research shows that emission reductions must occur by 2020. Smithsonian.com. Retrieved from http://www.smithsonianmag.com/science-nature/climate-change-tipping-point-research-shows-that-emission-reductions-must-occur-by-2020-162222340

Sullivan, N. P. (2007). *You can hear me now: How microloans and cell phones are connecting the world's poor to the global economy.* San Francisco, CA: Jossey-Bass.

The GBD 2015 Obesity Collaborators. (2017). Health effects of overweight and obesity in 195 countries over 25 years. *The New England Journal of Medicine, 377*, 13-27.

The National Provisioner. (2016). Meat industry timeline: 1917-1941. Retrieved from http://www.provisioneronline.com/articles/103508-meat-industry-timeline-1917-1941

Thornton, P., Herrero, M., & Ericksen, P. (2011). *Livestock and climate change. Livestock Exchange Issue Brief, 3*. Nairobi, Kenya: International Livestock Research Institute. Retrieved from https://cgspace.cgiar.org/bitstream/handle/10568/10601/IssueBrief3.pdf

Tsutsumi, A., & Tsutsui, N. (2009). Yuba ~ it's a traditional healthy food. The Kyoto Project. Retrieved from http://thekyotoproject.org/english/yubaits-a-traditional-healthy-food

United Nations. (2017). *World population prospects 2017*. Retrieved from https://esa.un.org/unpd/wpp/

Vegie Delights. (2017). Products: Nutmeat. Retrieved from www.vegiedelights.com.au/product/nutmeat

Wegmans. (2017). Field Roast: Grain Meat Sausages, Vegetarian, Smoked Apple Sage. Retrieved from https://www.wegmans.com/products/natures-marketplace/frozen-foods/sausage/grain-meat-sausages-vegetarian-smoked-apple-sage.html

World Food Programme (WFP). (2009). *World must double food production by 2050: FAO chief*. Retrieved from https://www.wfp.org/content/world-must-double-food-production-2050-fao-chief

Wortham, J., & Miller, C. (2013, April 28). Venture capitalists are making bigger bets on food start-ups. *New York Times*. Retrieved from http://www.nytimes.com/2013/04/29/business/venture-capitalists-are-making-bigger-bets-on-food-start-ups.html

Ye, K, Gao, F., Wang, D., Bar-Yosef, O., & Keinan, A. (2017). Dietary adaptation of FADS genes in Europe varied across time and geography. *Nature Ecology & Evolution, 1*, 0167. doi:10.1038/s41559-017-0167

KEY TERMS AND DEFINITIONS

Animal-Based Meat: Food that consists of animal flesh.

Disruption: Appearance of disturbances, problems or alternatives which interrupt the usual course of an event, activity or process.

Meat Free Monday: A campaign launched by Paul, Mary and Stella McCartney to address climate change by promoting the consumption of plant-based foods on Monday.

Meatless Monday: A non-profit initiative and global movement to cut the consumption of meat on Monday.

Peak Livestock: The moment in time when livestock production reaches its peak and is consequently reduced due to factors beyond the control of the producers, such as lower demand or climate change disruptions.

Plant-Based Meat: Food that consists of flesh from plants.

Yuba: A form of soymeat created from the film formed when soybeans are boiled.

ENDNOTE

1 The United Nations low-variant population projection is for 10.6 billion people in 2050 or 40 percent more people than in 2017. This does not justify a 70 percent increase in food demand either.

Chapter 22
Marketing Meat Alternatives:
Meat Myths and Their Replication in Advertising for Plant-Based Meat

Malte B. Rödl
The University of Manchester, UK

ABSTRACT

Meat alternatives have been proposed as one solution to decrease meat consumption and thus its negative effects on individuals and the environment. Using three meat myths identified in literature on meat consumption—meat eating is normal, natural, and necessary—this chapter discusses how they emerge in six selected print adverts: (1) normal: dishes containing meat alternatives are portrayed as traditional, perpetuating normality; (2) natural: the myth that it is natural to eat meat is not explicitly opposed, but bypassed; (3) necessary: meat alternatives are portrayed as even more necessary for good health than meat. The author proposes changes to neutralise these meat myths; but they are unlikely to be adopted by advertising due to its commercial goals. Although meat alternatives are theoretically preferable over meat (and can help individual transitions to vegetarianism), their marketing perpetuates meat myths, and may therefore reinforce a meat-centred culture.

INTRODUCTION

Meat is a centrepiece of Western culture, deeply entangled with the structure and culture of our society (Leroy & Praet, 2015), and despite many negative criticisms, is consumed on a frequent basis (Holm & Møhl, 2000). Those negative criticisms are mainly related to the impact of meat consumption on individual health (Battaglia Richi et al., 2015), the impacts of animal farming on the environment (Steinfeld et al., 2006), and animal welfare (Verbeke & Viaene, 2000). Meat alternatives, i.e. commercial products that are meant to replace meat, are proposed as suitable to solve these issues conveniently for some consumers (Hoek, 2010; Wild et al., 2014), while others prefer foods without any reference to meat (Elzerman, Boekel, & Luning, 2013).

DOI: 10.4018/978-1-5225-4757-0.ch022

Due to their increased prevalence in British and Western diets (Beckett, 2013; Elzerman et al., 2013), this chapter aims to contribute to the sparse understanding of the cultural context of meat alternatives (see Nath & Prideaux, 2011). More specifically, this chapter explores how advertising for meat alternatives deals with meat myths, which are understood here as widely-held beliefs about why meat eating is justified (Joy, 2009).

The chapter proceeds as follows. Firstly, meat alternatives are defined, followed by a summary of the state of current knowledge on these products. The main section of this chapter introduces myth in relation to meat, and the three meat myths, discusses the role and context of advertising, and then proceeds with investigating selected adverts along the myths. The discussion aims at finding solutions and recommendations for advertising of meat alternatives. Lastly, future research pathways are highlighted, and the chapter is concluded.

The main aim of this contribution is to investigate whether meat myths can be found in the marketing for meat alternatives, and to which extent they are embedded into their marketing strategy. Secondary aims are an introduction to the state of knowledge on meat alternatives, and a discussion for how to remove the identified myths from advertising for meat alternatives. The author acknowledges the clear significant positive impacts of meat alternatives, and as such, the findings are not intended to condemn meat alternatives themselves. Rather, it is their marketing and perpetuation of meat myths that is under scrutiny for their potential negative cultural impacts.

BACKGROUND

Meat alternatives—sometimes also called meat substitutes, meat analogs, vegetarian meat, or similar (Sadler, 2004)—are meat-like food products. They are "something that looks, tastes, and feels like meat" (Zorpette, 2013, p. 64), that "should have a certain resemblance to meat in order to replace meat on the plate" (Hoek, Boekel, Voordouw, & Luning, 2011, p. 371). Other definitions propose meat alternatives to have "approximately the same taste, appearance, and texture of a related food made from meat, poultry, fish or shellfish … [while their] nutritional value is, in general, approximately equal to (or sometimes greater than) that of the related food, including essential vitamin B-12" (Shurtleff & Aoyagi, 2014, p. 5), or as "products that fulfil consumer demands of healthy and tasty products which both replace the function of meat in a dish and contribute a similar high protein nutritional value" (Wild et al., 2014, p. 45).

All these various definitions describe food items which relate to meat in ways that consumers can observe; including sensory aspects and experiences, the function of meat in meals, as well as nutrition and health. Consumers were found to understand novel products as relating to established ones on the basis of 'similarities' and 'analogies'; similarities are shared attributes, such as colour or texture, analogies are shared relations, such as goals or scripts (Michaut, 2004). This chapter understands meat alternatives as commercial products which are portrayed as sharing attributes, such as physical properties, or their product name with meat, or sharing relations, such as their function for nutrition or in a meal.

Being generally proposed as a viable alternative to the issues of excessive meat consumption (Hoek, 2010; Wild et al., 2014), research describes the consumption of meat alternatives as healthier (Sadler, 2004) and more environmentally-friendly than meat: carbon emissions are found equal or lower to that of chicken and fish, and substantially lower than those of pigs or cattle. Land use requirements are lower than those of all meats (Nijdam, Rood, & Westhoek, 2012). Among meat alternatives, different ingredients and production methods lead to different footprints, with soy-meal-based meat alternatives appearing the most environmental-friendly option (Smetana, Mathys, Knoch, & Heinz, 2015). Meat alternatives are commonly produced from soybeans and other pulses (tofu, tempeh, or via protein isolates as textured vegetable protein), wheat (in form of gluten, for example as seitan), fungi (Quorn™), vegetables, or a combination of those; products often also contain eggs (as a binder), milk, and occasionally rice, as well as emulsifiers or stabilisers (Davies & Lightowler, 1998; Shurtleff & Aoyagi, 2014).

Meat alternatives are consumed more frequently by young, female, and affluent people (Beckett, 2013; Hoek, Luning, Stafleu, & Graaf, 2004). They were found to have lifestyle and health attitudes in between those of meat eaters and vegetarians (Hoek et al., 2004). Consumers of meat alternatives mostly avoid meat because they wish to reduce or stop consumption of red meats for health, environmental or animal-welfare reasons (Beckett, 2013). Research indicated that health reasons appear to be of primary importance for partial avoidance of meat, while complete avoidance is more often found to be related to sustainability and animal welfare (Izmirli & Phillips, 2011; Tobler, Visschers, & Siegrist, 2011). Barriers to meat consumption are taste, which is sometimes perceived to be bland, uniform or not meat-like enough, unfamiliarity with the product, and price (Elzerman et al., 2013; Beckett, 2013). Hoek et al. (2011) found that people consuming less meat substitutes wanted them to be more similar to meat. Positive aspects are reported to be health, ethics, and easy preparation (Elzerman et al., 2013; Hoek et al., 2011a). For individuals wanting to become vegetarian, meat alternatives were found helpful as a transition aid, especially in context of meat-centred gatherings, such as barbecues, Christmas, or Thanksgiving (Nath & Prideaux, 2011).

In an experiment which made consumers eat meat alternatives on a regular basis, they were evaluated better over time (Hoek et al., 2013). Meals containing meat alternatives are evaluated more positively when they resemble a commonly-known dish (Elzerman, Hoek, Boekel, & Luning, 2015), whereas when eaten separately, consumers emphasise taste and texture more (Elzerman, Hoek, Boekel, & Luning, 2011). Meat alternatives are rated more similar to their models when resembling processed meat products which have lost their original meat-like appearance (Hoek et al., 2011).

MEAT MYTHS IN MARKETING OF MEAT ALTERNATIVES

Along the aim of this book, this contribution investigates the marketing of meat alternatives in relation to meat myths; for this, meat myths (using "the three N's of justification" by Joy, 2009) are examined in six selected print adverts for meat alternatives found in *The Vegetarian*. Such investigation is relevant as meat alternatives become more important in British diets, while an analysis of these products in a critical cultural context is missing (Nath & Prideaux, 2011).

This section begins with summarising myths and their application to meat, and introduces the three meat myths. The advertising of meat alternatives and the origins of the used examples are then discussed. Finally, the three meat myths are discussed using selected examples of advertisements.

Meat and Myths

Myths in society surround sensitive and emotional discourses or practices and can carry values, beliefs, or ideals; they are essentially free from criticism by providing the symbolic foundations of society (Bouchard, 2013). Although objectively debatable, myths give an idea of what is subjectively good or bad to do or to think; in this way they combine seeming dichotomies of reason and emotion, or truth and falsehood.

Bouchard (2013) further describes myths in society as unquestionable, archetypic, and instrumental for society. Myths provide path-dependent links between past, present, and future (Ritzer, 2007). Myths are a common part of modern culture (Barthes, 1957) and used frequently as a tool to analyse advertising (Cronin, 2004). Advertised myths were also found reiterated by consumers (Thompson, 2004).

Meat consumption can be understood as such myth. It has played a central role for the development of social systems, rituals, and traditions in human culture (Leroy & Praet, 2015), while these links continue to persist (Fiddes, 1992). In a society where many people consume meat (Beckett, 2013), meat eaters were found to feel attacked by the mental presence of non-meat eaters (Rothgerber, 2014), underlining that it is unquestionable as such. Thus, vegetarians face challenges to communicate their diet (Romo & Donovan-Kicken, 2012), to continue participating in social gatherings which are often meat-centred (Kleine & Hubbert, 1993; Nath & Prideaux, 2011), and to maintain relations to their family and friends (Beardsworth & Keil, 1992).

Some researchers have linked the terms 'meat' and 'myths': Clark (1991) refers to meat myths in the context of misconceptions about nutrition and health regarding meat; Bogueva & Phau (2016) identify six meat myths on the basis of marketing in Australia; Joy (2009) describes meat myths as common justifications for meat consumption, identifying three on the basis of theoretical work and consumer interviews. In order to identify meat myths in marketing, Joy's set of meat myths was chosen to guide this investigation, as it is the most consumer-orientated.

The three myths, termed "the three N's of justification", are: "eating meat is *normal*, *natural*, and *necessary*" (Joy, 2009, p. 96, emphasis in original). Piazza et al. (2015) added 'nice' to this list, and found that more than 83%-91% of justifications can be related to these four guilt-alleviating categories. As advertising is probably always about something 'nice', only the former three 'myths' are discussed in the following analysis. Their main constituents are as follows:

- **Meat Consumption Is Normal:** Because meat is ubiquitous, readily available, and part of every-day life, customs, and traditions.
- **Meat Consumption Is Natural:** Because it is historical, divine, and "biologically irrefutable" (Joy, 2009, p.109).
- **Meat Consumption Is Necessary:** Because it is main requirement for human health, and animal containment, and an economic imperative.

Advertising for Meat Alternatives

Adverts mediate products from producer to consumer. While advertising resonates with consumers' desires, these desires are equally shaped by advertising (Fowles, 1996). However, an analysis of adverts may neither reflect what the advertiser thinks, nor what consumers perceive or understand of it (Janks, 1997).

The three mentioned meat myths are understood here as the basis of society's attachment to meat. Meat alternatives may currently not achieve the same mythical status as meat, yet they provide an alternative basis for the myths. The market for meat alternatives comprises meat eaters who like to cut down on meat for various reasons, as well as of vegetarians who like the taste or social aspect of meat. Therefore, advertising for meat alternatives is likely to repeat what consumers like about meat, and may selectively relay meat myths in order to match the consumers' altered consciousness.

While vegetarian ready meals were advertised frequently, there were fewer for meat alternatives. This may be due to the lower advertising expenditure for meat alternatives. Expensive TV advertising (and thus most of the marketing expenditure) has come from the leading brand Quorn, and also from runner-up Linda McCartney (Beckett, 2013). For other companies, print advertising, below-the-line marketing, and word-of-mouth are the most popular marketing means. Given the targeted market and the small budget of specialist manufacturers, print advertising is generally found in small or specialist magazines (Soininen, 2011; Winther, 2004).

Adverts found in *The Vegetarian*, the members' magazine of the Vegetarian Society of England, are used to discuss the three meat myths. The readership of the magazine is largely female, vegetarian, and is interested in cooking (Vegetarian Society, 2017). Adverts for meat alternatives were identified on the basis of their meat-like designation (e.g., burger, fillet) in issues from 1990 to 2016; the selection of illustrative examples aimed, as much as possible, to present different perspectives on the myth. Bibliographic data for these adverts can be found in the Appendix to this chapter.

Normality

The first myth is about meat eating being normal: normal to be bought in the supermarket, normal at the daily dinner table, and normal as part of festive events and social gatherings (Joy, 2009). As certain brands are available in all major retailers, and others in many health food shops, this section will only discuss meat as a normal dish. An advert, printed in 1993, for a meat-free "*Toad in the Hole*" from *Haldane Foods Group's Vegetable Feasts* replicates this normality.

A toad in the hole is a traditional British dish in which sausages are baked in batter (Davidson, 2014). The depicted white dinner plate is filled with vegetables and potatoes in foreground and background, while the main part of the plate is taken up by a golden brown, crispy-looking object, in which the shape of four sausages can be observed underneath the layer of batter. To the author, it looks like a classic British meat dish; only the context of the magazine and the word "vegetarian" in the main text show that this is not a traditional, meat-based *Toad in the Hole*.

The advertising text affirms this view: this dish is "a traditional favourite" and "a real family favourite", making the dish not only a guarantor for a great dinner with the family, but also a keeper of traditions, which resonates culinary identity. This advert does not challenge the myth of normality, but replicates and extends it to include vegetarian imitates of traditional meals.

A two-page advertising feature by *Quorn* "for a sophisticated vegetarian Christmas" (printed in 2002, see Figure 1) attempts the opposite by claiming to emancipate families from a turkey-dependency:

When it was first launched, the Quorn Roast provided a much-needed centrepiece to the turkey-less Christmas lunch in many households. It was certainly much appreciated by those dining with meat-eating families, as a vegetarian option which was both satisfying and easy to prepare.

By being a "much-needed" foodstuff, the centrality of meat to dining traditions is criticised, while it simultaneously claims to have helped breaking them. It has been shown before that meat alternative products can fulfil an important role for individuals changing their diet (Nath & Prideaux, 2011). That individuals could change whole dining traditions however may be questioned, as research found that new vegetarians prepared food for themselves during festive meals, while still preparing meat for others to maintain social tranquility (Kleine & Hubbert, 1993).

Figure 1. Advertisement for Quorn products
Source: © 2002 Quorn Foods. Used with permission.

The next paragraph in the advert discusses the versatility of the product for cooks, where it was found "delicious simply sliced", such as meat, but also "as a versatile ingredient in a wide variety of other dishes"; three recipes accompany this description with the following remark:

These inspiring new recipes developed by The Vegetarian Society's Cordon Vert [Cookery] School ensure Quorn products' position on the most elegant dining tables in the land this Christmas.

These recipes—for *quenelles* (cf. Harris, 1991), *en papillote* (cf. Hesser, 1999), and *roast puffs*—are originally fish or meat-based. Food at special occasions, according to the myth of normality, has to contain meat. So, even if the consumer is not aware that the recipes are traditionally animal-based, the claim that they help to "ensure Quorn products' position on the most elegant dining tables" seems to perpetuate it. Nonetheless, by being home-made and partially of foreign origin, the recipes bring variety, and can be appreciated by vegetarian consumers' search for something "satisfying and easy to prepare".

The two adverts discussed in this section approached the normality of meat from opposing angles: while the first advert closely replicated a traditional British dish, introduced it as meat-free, and claimed to be widely available, the second advert argued that vegetarian consumers need an alternative for turkey and other meat-centred Christmas meals. However, the proposed alternatives are originally meat dishes as well. In these examples, the meat myth is overcome by providing functionally equal, traditional or exciting dishes, which promise satisfaction and easy preparation; so instead of questioning the myth of normality, the advert extends it to encompass meat alternatives.

Naturalness

Meat consumption is seen as natural for historical, religious or biological reasons. According to Joy (2009), the biological part of this myth builds on ideas of supremacy over animals. While this meat myth itself was not repeated in the screened advertising, a few adverts from around the millennium depict animals; two of these are discussed here looking at the human-animal-relationship.

Firstly, an advert promoting meat-free *Streaky Strips* and *Back Bacon* of the American brand *Morningstar Farms* (printed in 2001, see Figure 2): in a drawn picture, the front half of a happy-looking pink pig stands in a field with green grass, the background depicts a hill with a few trees and blue sky. Right next to the pig's snout, white printed letters say: "Relax boys, the heat's off", appearing with quotation marks, as if the advertisers wanted to quote the pig. On the bottom of the page, uppercase letters state: "THE GREAT TASTE OF BACON WITHOUT THE PIG", and a longer text on top reads:

To stay healthy, who says you have to give up the taste of your favourite bacon butty? Time to wake up to meat-free Streaky Strips and Back Bacon from Morningstar Farms. Two delicious alternatives to bacon. Unashamedly high on taste. Super low in cholesterol — that means good news for you (and even better news for pigs).

This text confirms meat eaters' ideas about "the great taste of bacon", but also draws explicit lines to the animal-origin of this product, without hiding meat behind linguistic lines found in English language (i.e. "pig" as the animal, "pork" as the meat, see Evans & Miele, 2012). The advert implies that pigs would be happier—may live in grassland or nature—if they were not killed, but not that these animals ceased to exist. However, the framing suggests that consumers can save individual pig lives; this may be seen similar to some consumers feeling entitled to eat meat because they see themselves on top of the food chain (Graça, Calheiros, & Oliveira, 2015). Understanding meat alternatives as a technology, this account can be seen as part of an ecological modernisation discourse; by bringing the animal back to nature, it restores or advances 'nature' through technological progress (Hajer, 1996), while the human remains in power over animals (Stepaniak & Messina, 1998).

An advert by *Redwood Wholefoods* printed in 2003 depicts a large drawing of what is subtitled "the codfish". A dark red stamp saying "extinct?" is placed in the top right part of the picture, while in uppercase letters the advert suggests: "IT NEED NOT BE THIS WAY", and thus questioning overfishing. However, instead of appealing to people to stop eating fish, the advert proposes an alternative by advertising "fish style fingers" that have "all the taste of the ocean but [are] totally free from fish". A longer text on the bottom of the page reads:

Figure 2. Advertisement for Morningstar Farm's bacon substitutes
Source: © 2001 Kellogg Company. Reprinted with permission of the copyright owner, Kellogg Company. Morningstar Farms is a trademark of Kellogg NA Co.

Great for veggies and vegans, they're good news too for people who'd rather not eat fish because they're worried about over-fishing — and the threat it causes to cod and hake stocks.

While among "veggies and vegans" there may be people who would appreciate the replication of fish flavours, the rationale for the 'over-fishing conscious' portrays over-fishing and its threat to fish stocks as a problem; on the contrary, eating the individual fish seems acceptable. Despite the possibility of some people rejecting fish for the enjoyment of others, the argument here is not to stop eating fish completely; instead, fish should be eaten carefully to avoid overfishing, and fish-like products should be consumed otherwise, in order to not miss out on the taste.

The argumentation shifts the focus of concern away from the animal, and makes fish stocks a vulnerable resource requiring careful management; this 'resourcification' of living organisms was found to be a common strategy in reports on climate change and food security (Arcari, 2017). Again, technology is proposed to solve issues of concern: management of a tasty yet finite resource.

Both adverts see meat eating as a pleasurable and tasty experience, but not as natural. Confronting consumers with negative impacts on animals and ecosystems, the adverts offer an alternative product with similar taste but without the animal: a technology that can solve this dilemma (Hajer, 1996). The adverts ask the consumer to decide about organisms and ecosystems, making them part of humanity's power to shape the world (Stibbe, 2001) rather than taking care of it (Donovan & Adams, 2007).

Necessity

The third myth revolves around the necessity of meat consumption for human health, to contain animals, or as an economic imperative (Joy, 2009); the latter two arguments could not be found in the advertising, while a good deal of adverts seem to equate meat consumption to a good diet, sometimes by including reference to protein. An example for this is an advertisement by *Linda McCartney Foods* printed in 1992; this text-heavy advert frames its products not only as to "look and taste like traditional meat dishes", but also presents itself as healthy: "All the nourishment you need — without the meat!" The health section of the advert elucidates that the products contain a lot of protein, but it is unclear whether this is "all the nourishment" people need:

With Linda McCartney's range there's no need to worry that you're missing out on protein. By using Textured Vegetable Protein as a main ingredient, each dish contains as much protein as meat (if not more). And as an added health benefit, TVP contains a great deal less fat, has no cholesterol and is lower in calories than most meats.

When presenting what their foods are made of, namely TVP, a comparison to meat is possible: pure TVP contains more than twice as much protein as raw lean beef, and with far less fat (Davies & Lightowler, 1998; Sadler, 2004). While meat and protein do not represent the entirety of necessary nutrients (Achterberg, McDonnell, & Bagby, 1994), the statement "all the nourishment you need" refers to the myth of necessity reflected in consumer beliefs that meat is essential for the human body. The advert then elaborates that TVP has a high protein content, and the last sentence describes "an *added* health benefit"; this means, the superiority of meat nutrition is unchallenged, but TVP is framed as even healthier. Albeit not stated explicitly, the context suggests that the mentioned contents fat, cholesterol, and calories may be nutritionally disadvantageous (cf. Chizzolini, Zanardi, Dorigoni, & Ghidini, 1999; Rampone & Reynolds, 1988), and TVP may be even healthier. However, consumers are required to have knowledge about this. The advert thus reaffirms the myth of necessity, while branding the advertised products as healthier meat and without educating on health.

An advert by *Grassington's* (printed in 2008) promotes two 'beef style', and one 'chicken style' product. In bullet points is claimed that the products are "low in fat", or "an excellent source of complete protein", and the displayed product packaging highlights low fat and salt content along with the contained calorie information. The catchphrase: "Be one of the first to try a NEW meat substitute which tastes as good as it looks!" and a large picture of the 'chicken style fillet' product is depicted in a corner. A short paragraph reads:

Grassington's Gardein not only tastes great, but is made from a nutritious blend of beans, vegetables and grains, grown naturally on the farm, slow cooked to have the authentic taste and texture of premium lean meat.

'Gardein'—a portmanteau of garden and protein—is the name of the used protein ingredient and is subtitled "Farm grown protein"; it is made from extruded soy protein and wheat gluten (Food Processing, 2004). The advert ties the product strongly to both meat and nutrition: the products, through being likened to 'premium lean meat', are constructed as a high-quality meat substitute; the 'naturally grown' and 'slow cooked' plant ingredients emphasise the connection between farm and fork, whilst covering the industrial processing needed to produce the products (see Davies & Lightowler, 1998). The nutrition claims build on positive and negative attributes of meat which are known to the consumer: protein, fat, calories, salt. The nutritional value of the included grains, vegetables, and beans are not emphasised further in their own right. Therefore, meat remains the central point of reference to both experience and nutrition, whilst plants are only utilised to make the product appear a rooted farm product.

Both adverts depict the nutrition of their products relative to meat: rather than good nutrition, they discussed 'better-than-meat' nutrition, in which plants are used to make the product appear more natural. By presenting the products as healthier or as healthy as meat, meat is perpetuated as the baseline, reaffirming that meat is necessary for humans.

SOLUTIONS AND RECOMMENDATIONS

In the previous section, the existence of three meat myths in print advertising for meat alternatives was investigated. These myths dealt with normality, naturalness, and necessity of meat consumption for humans. Given their diverse scopes, the issues and possible solutions to neutralise their influence on meat myths will be discussed separately.

The first advertisement example depicted a replication of a traditional meat dish, echoing the myth that meat eating is normal. The second example claimed to be part of emancipating Christmas dinner from meat, yet its recipes were based on meat and fish dishes. When considering that meat alternatives were defined above as sharing scripts and goals with meat, replication of meat dishes with meat alternatives is thus justified. They extend the myth of normality to non-animal yet meat-like products. Meat alternatives may become part of a slightly modified status quo, making it easy to switch away from animal flesh, but more challenging to switch to a non-meat diet. However, in case meat-like ingredients are generic enough, encouragement to cook creatively with these, such as seen in the second advert, may still be desirable as it suggests to replace traditional meals; this may lead to genuinely free-to-chose food at rituals, traditions, and formerly meat-centred gatherings.

The second myth is that meat eating is natural. While most adverts did not feature animals and thus muted any discussion about the myth, the two examples bypassed an explicit discussion of the topic. Therefore, the basis for the meat myth, the implied power of humans over animals, was discussed (Joy, 2009; Stepaniak & Messina, 1998). Hinting at the undesirability of animal-origin food, both examples suggest technological progress (i.e. the meat alternative) to reconcile good taste and moral consciousness: consumers were coerced into a choice about continued consumption of the animal-based product or a similar, non-animal-flesh alternative. By making the animal's fate part of human decision, it perpetuates the idea of human power over animals. McDonagh & Prothero (1997) demand that advertising discussing environmental issues should also point out the underlying power relations in this system, for example, between humans and animals. With such a limited number of examples, it is difficult to assess the favourability of including animals in meat alternatives or not.

The last two adverts were discussed on the basis of meat as a necessity for the human diet. Both were found to build up their nutrition-claims on the basis of meat, essentially branding themselves as healthier meat. While this indirectly damages the status of meat as a superior nutritional source, it does not criticise meat as a necessity in human diet. Instead, the meat myth is amended, framing meat alternatives as even healthier than meat. However, healthy nutrition or a healthy diet was not discussed in the adverts, which leaves myth-believing consumers as dependent on meat alternatives as they were on meat before. Unfortunately, it seems unlikely that adverts for meat alternatives would educate in this way, as this would emancipate their consumers towards independence from the 'nutritional superiority' claimed by the advertising.

As adverts do exactly what they are supposed to do—make a certain group of consumers aware of a product that matches their needs and worldview—general critique and reasonable solutions for advertisers are difficult to imagine. Instead, more consumer education and changing traditions may be necessary to emancipate them from the meat myths. As the market for meat alternatives provides a product that shares attributes and relations (and thus allows easy adjustment of the meat myths internalised by consumers), emancipation from meat myths would mean that meat alternatives became just like meat, only without animal flesh.

FUTURE RESEARCH DIRECTIONS

While current academic literature on meat alternatives is largely concerned with investigating benefits, uptake, and consumer acceptance, this contribution discussed meat myths in advertising for meat alternatives. As only a few examples from a long period were selected, further analyses of more recent adverts, temporal changes, or differences in between the various brands could lead to better understanding of the topic. A more systematic analysis, especially guided by the data rather than by meat myths, may provide additional insights building on these initial findings.

Further, the analysis is no statement on the state of mind of manufacturers or consumers. An investigation of the causes and effects of the findings is necessary to understand how meat myths could become stabilised or alleviated through their selective recreation in (advertising for) meat alternatives; this can be done, for example, by looking at how they manifest in consumer discourse or what role they play for product development in the industry.

CONCLUSION

Given the rapid growth of the meat alternatives market and increasing full or partial rejection of meat in individual diets, this topic is highly relevant. The analysis highlighted how the meat myths were extended, bypassed, or amended: the example adverts suggest animal-free but meat-based practices, perpetuate an imbalance between humans and animals, and they base good nutrition on meat. They do not educate consumers on the diversity of tasty and fancy vegetable-based foods, on genuinely meat-free foods and issues of animal agriculture, or on good health; instead, they re-entrench consumer dependence on supposedly normal, natural and necessary food away from animal-based meat towards meat alternatives. Therefore, it may at least be questionable, whether—in their current form—they deserve to be seen as a generally desirable solution. If the findings prove to be consistent throughout the discourse surrounding meat alternatives, these products may not only be evaluated positively by their consumers (for example as transition aid for meat reducers, or a saviour for meat-liking vegetarians); they would also entrench meat-eaters further into the meat myths.

With a belief in technology to solve society's problems as conveniently as possible, and a system based on selling highly value-added goods, it is unlikely that advertising for meat alternatives would change these patterns. However, while the wider implications and societal manifestations of the findings are yet to be explored, none of them can discredit the positive and quantifiable environmental, animal welfare, and health impacts of meat substitution.

REFERENCES

Achterberg, C., McDonnell, E., & Bagby, R. (1994). How to put the food guide pyramid into practice. *Journal of the American Dietetic Association, 94*(9), 1030–1035. doi:10.1016/0002-8223(94)92198-9 PMID:8071485

Arcari, P. (2017). Normalised, human-centric discourses of meat and animals in climate change, sustainability and food security literature. *Agriculture and Human Values, 34*(1), 69–86. doi:10.1007/s10460-016-9697-0

Barthes, R. (1957). *Mythologies*. Paris, France: Seuil.

Battaglia Richi, E., Baumer, B., Conrad, B., Darioli, R., Schmid, A., & Keller, U. (2015). Health risks associated with meat consumption: A review of epidemiological studies. *International Journal for Vitamin and Nutrition Research, 85*(1-2), 70–78. doi:10.1024/0300-9831/a000224 PMID:26780279

Beardsworth, A., & Keil, T. (1992). The vegetarian option: Varieties, conversions, motives and careers. *The Sociological Review, 40*(2), 253–293. doi:10.1111/j.1467-954X.1992.tb00889.x

Beckett, A. (2013). *Meat-free and free-from foods (Market Research Report)*. Mintel.

Bogueva, D., & Phau, I. (2016). Meat myths and marketing. In T. Raphaely & D. Marinova (Eds.), *Impact of meat consumption on health and environmental sustainability* (pp. 264–276). Hershey, PA: IGI Global. doi:10.4018/978-1-4666-9553-5.ch015

Bouchard, G. (2013). For a new sociology of social myths. *Revue Européenne Des Sciences Sociales, 51*(1), 95-120.

Chizzolini, R., Zanardi, E., Dorigoni, V., & Ghidini, S. (1999). Calorific value and cholesterol content of normal and low-fat meat and meat products. *Trends in Food Science & Technology, 10*(4–5), 119–128. doi:10.1016/S0924-2244(99)00034-5

Clark, N. (1991). Nutrition and fitness. *The Physician and Sportsmedicine, 19*(1), 31–34. doi:10.1080/00913847.1991.11702123 PMID:27422190

Cronin, A. M. (2004). *Advertising myths; The half-lives of images and commodities*. London, UK: Routledge.

Davidson, A. (2014). *Toad in the hole. In The Oxford Companion to Food* (p. 822). Oxford, UK: Oxford University Press.

Davies, J., & Lightowler, H. (1998). Plant-based alternatives to meat. *Nutrition & Food Science*, *98*(2), 90–94. doi:10.1108/00346659810201050

Donovan, J., & Adams, C. J. (2007). *The feminist care tradition in animal ethics: A reader*. New York, NY: Columbia University Press.

Elzerman, J. E., Hoek, A. C., van Boekel, M. A. J. S., & Luning, P. A. (2011). Consumer acceptance and appropriateness of meat substitutes in a meal context. *Food Quality and Preference*, *22*(3), 233–240. doi:10.1016/j.foodqual.2010.10.006

Elzerman, J. E., Hoek, A. C., van Boekel, M. J. A. S., & Luning, P. A. (2015). Appropriateness, acceptance and sensory preferences based on visual information: A web-based survey on meat substitutes in a meal context. *Food Quality and Preference*, *42*, 56–65. doi:10.1016/j.foodqual.2015.01.010

Elzerman, J. E., van Boekel, M. A. J. S., & Luning, P. A. (2013). Exploring meat substitutes: Consumer experiences and contextual factors. *British Food Journal*, *115*(5), 700–710. doi:10.1108/00070701311331490

Evans, A. B., & Miele, M. (2012). Between food and flesh: How animals are made to matter (and not matter) within food consumption practices. *Environment and Planning. D, Society & Space*, *30*(2), 298–314. doi:10.1068/d12810

Fiddes, N. (1992). *Meat: A natural symbol (Reprinted)*. London, UK: Routledge.

Fowles, J. (1996). *Advertising and popular culture*. Thousand Oaks, CA: Sage.

Graça, J., Calheiros, M. M., & Oliveira, A. (2015). Attached to meat? (Un)Willingness and intentions to adopt a more plant-based diet. *Appetite*, *95*, 113–125. doi:10.1016/j.appet.2015.06.024 PMID:26148456

Hajer, M. A. (1996). Ecological modernisation as cultural politics. In S. Lash, B. Szerszynski, & B. Wynne (Eds.), *Risk, environment and modernity: Towards a new ecology* (pp. 246–268). London, UK: Sage.

Harris, A. P. (1991, 4 August). Fare of the country; delicate pike quenelles, a Lyons Tradition. *The New York Times*. Retrieved from http://www.nytimes.com/1991/08/04/travel/fare-of-the-country-delicate-pike-quenelles-a-lyons-tradition.html

Hesser, A. (1999, 19 May). The envelope, please: Cooking en papillote. *The New York Times*. Retrieved from http://www.nytimes.com/1999/05/19/dining/the-envelope-please-cooking-en-papillote.html?mcubz=3

Hoek, A. C. (2010). *Will novel protein foods beat meat? Consumer acceptance of meat substitutes – a multidisciplinary research approach* [Doctoral thesis]. Wageningen University. Retrieved from http://edepot.wur.nl/15997

Hoek, A. C., Elzerman, J. E., Hageman, R., Kok, F. J., Luning, P. A., & Graaf, C. D. (2013). Are meat substitutes liked better over time? A repeated in-home use test with meat substitutes or meat in meals. *Food Quality and Preference*, *28*(1), 253–263. doi:10.1016/j.foodqual.2012.07.002

Hoek, A. C., Luning, P. A., Stafleu, A., & de Graaf, C. (2004). Food-related lifestyle and health attitudes of Dutch vegetarians, non-vegetarian consumers of meat substitutes, and meat consumers. *Appetite, 42*(3), 265–272. doi:10.1016/j.appet.2003.12.003 PMID:15183917

Hoek, A. C., Luning, P. A., Weijzen, P., Engels, W., Kok, F. J., & de Graaf, C. (2011). Replacement of meat by meat substitutes. A survey on person- and product-related factors in consumer acceptance. *Appetite, 56*(3), 662–673. doi:10.1016/j.appet.2011.02.001 PMID:21315123

Hoek, A. C., van Boekel, M. A., Voordouw, J., & Luning, P. A. (2011). Identification of new food alternatives: How do consumers categorize meat and meat substitutes? *Food Quality and Preference, 22*(4), 371–383. doi:10.1016/j.foodqual.2011.01.008

Holm, L., & Møhl, M. (2000). The role of meat in everyday food culture: An analysis of an interview study in Copenhagen. *Appetite, 34*(3), 277–283. doi:10.1006/appe.2000.0324 PMID:10888291

Izmirli, S., & Phillips, C. J. C. (2011). The relationship between student consumption of animal products and attitudes to animals in Europe and Asia. *British Food Journal, 113*(3), 436–450. doi:10.1108/00070701111116482

Janks, H. (1997). Critical discourse analysis as a research tool. *Discourse (Abingdon), 18*(3), 329–342. doi:10.1080/0159630970180302

Joy, M. (2009). *Why we love dogs, eat pigs, and wear cows: An introduction to carnism*. Berkley, CA: Conari Press.

Kleine, S. S., & Hubbert, A. R. (1993). How do consumers acquire a new food consumption system when it is vegetarian? In L. McAlister & M. L. Rothschild (Eds.), *Advances in consumer research* (Vol. 20, pp. 196–201). Provo, UT: Association for Consumer Research.

Leroy, F., & Praet, I. (2015). Meat traditions. The co-evolution of humans and meat. *Appetite, 90*, 200–211. doi:10.1016/j.appet.2015.03.014 PMID:25794684

McDonagh, P., & Prothero, A. (1997). Leap-frog marketing: The contribution of ecofeminist thought to the world of patriarchal marketing. *Marketing Intelligence & Planning, 15*(7), 361–368. doi:10.1108/02634509710193190

Michaut, A. M. (2004). *Consumer response to innovative products: With application to foods.* (Doctoral thesis). Wageningen University. Retrieved from http://edepot.wur.nl/121564

Nath, J., & Prideaux, D. (2011). The civilised burger: Meat alternatives as a conversion aid and social instrument for Australian vegetarians and vegans. *Australian Humanities Review, 51*, 135–151.

Nijdam, D., Rood, T., & Westhoek, H. (2012). The price of protein: Review of land use and carbon footprints from life cycle assessments of animal food products and their substitutes. *Food Policy, 37*(6), 760–770. doi:10.1016/j.foodpol.2012.08.002

Piazza, J., Ruby, M. B., Loughnan, S., Luong, M., Kulik, J., Watkins, H. M., & Seigerman, M. (2015). Rationalizing meat consumption. The 4Ns. *Appetite, 91*, 114–128. doi:10.1016/j.appet.2015.04.011 PMID:25865663

Processing, F. (2004). Two next-generation analogues better simulate full muscle texture. *Food Processing, 65*(8), 38.

Rampone, A. J., & Reynolds, P. J. (1988). Obesity: Thermodynamic principles in perspective. *Life Sciences, 43*(2), 93–110. doi:10.1016/0024-3205(88)90286-X PMID:3292870

Ritzer, G. (Ed.). (2007). Myth. *Blackwell Encyclopedia of Sociology Online*. Retrieved from http://www.sociologyencyclopedia.com/public/search?query=myth

Romo, L. K., & Donovan-Kicken, E. (2012). "Actually, I Don't Eat Meat": A multiple-goals perspective of communication about vegetarianism. *Communication Studies, 63*(4), 405–420. doi:10.1080/10510974.2011.623752

Rothgerber, H. (2014). Efforts to overcome vegetarian-induced dissonance among meat eaters. *Appetite, 79*, 32–41. doi:10.1016/j.appet.2014.04.003 PMID:24727102

Sadler, M. J. (2004). Meat alternatives —- market developments and health benefits. *Trends in Food Science & Technology, 15*(5), 250–260. doi:10.1016/j.tifs.2003.09.003

Shurtleff, W., & Aoyagi, A. (2014). *History of meat alternatives (965 CE to 2014): Extensively annotated bibliography and sourcebook*. Retrieved from www.soyinfocenter.com/pdf/179/MAL.pdf

Smetana, S., Mathys, A., Knoch, A., & Heinz, V. (2015). Meat alternatives: Life cycle assessment of most known meat substitutes. *The International Journal of Life Cycle Assessment, 20*(9), 1254–1267. doi:10.1007/s11367-015-0931-6

Soininen, K. (2011). *Meat-free and free-from foods - UK - September 2011. Market Research Report*. Mintel.

Steinfeld, H., Gerber, P., Wassenaar, T. D., Castel, V., Rosales, M., & de Haan, C. (2006). *Livestock's long shadow: Environmental issues and options*. Rome, Italy: Food and Agriculture Organization of the United Nations.

Stepaniak, J., & Messina, V. (1998). *The vegan sourcebook*. Los Angeles, CA: Lowell House.

Stibbe, A. (2001). Language, power and the social construction of animals. *Society & Animals, 9*(2), 145–161. doi:10.1163/156853001753639251

Thompson, C. J. (2004). Marketplace mythology and discourses of power. *The Journal of Consumer Research, 31*(1), 162–180. doi:10.1086/383432

Tobler, C., Visschers, V. H. M., & Siegrist, M. (2011). Eating green. Consumers' willingness to adopt ecological food consumption behaviors. *Appetite, 57*(3), 674–682. doi:10.1016/j.appet.2011.08.010 PMID:21896294

Vegetarian Society. (2017). *Advertising in The Vegetarian*. Retrieved from https://www.vegsoc.org/advertising

Verbeke, W. A. J., & Viaene, J. (2000). Ethical challenges for livestock production: Meeting consumer concerns about meat safety and animal welfare. *Journal of Agricultural & Environmental Ethics, 12*(2), 141–151. doi:10.1023/A:1009538613588

Wild, F., Czerny, M., Janssen, A. M., Kole, A. P., Zunabovic, M., & Domig, K. J. (2014). The evolution of a plant-based alternative to meat: From niche markets to widely accepted meat alternatives. *Agro Food Industry Hi-Tech, 25*(1), 45–49.

Winther, A. (2004). *Meat-free foods - UK - December 2004. Market Research Report.* Mintel.

Zorpette, G. (2013). Muscling out meat. *IEEE Spectrum, 50*(6), 64–70. doi:10.1109/MSPEC.2013.6521036

KEY TERMS AND DEFINITIONS

Meat Alternative: A manufactured food item which aims to be similar to meat by pointing out shared attributes and relations; a meat substitute, meat analogue, vegetarian meat, vegan meat.

Myth: A rigid and widely-held belief about a sensitive topic in society which is difficult to criticise and is hardly mutable.

Myth of Naturalness: Justifies meat consumption because it has always been this way, religion says so, or because humans are meant to eat meat.

Myth of Necessity: Justifies meat consumption because it is a main requirement for human health, an economic imperative, and needed to keep animals contained.

Myth of Normality: Justifies meat consumption because meat is available everywhere and part of everyday life, rituals, and traditions.

Substitute: A product which can replace another product as it has similar attributes or functions; an alternative or replacement.

Textured Vegetable Protein (TVP): A fibrous, largely tasteless, meat-like product obtained from the extrusion of soya protein; TVP is a registered trademark by Archer Daniels Midland, but is often used in a more generic way.

APPENDIX

Table 1. Overview of adverts from used in the analysis in order of appearance

Brand	Issue	Product	Catchphrase
Vegetable Feasts	Spring 1993, p.2	ready meal	*Try our new Toad in the Hole. You'd have to be hopping mad not to.*
Quorn	Winter 2002, p.34–35	pate, pieces, roast	*Quorn™... for a sophisticated vegetarian Christmas*
Morningstar Farms	Spring 2001, p.13	bacon, strips	*THE GREAT TASTE OF BACON WITHOUT THE PIG*
Redwood	Spring 2003, p.64	fingers	*IT NEED NOT BE THIS WAY*
Linda McCartney Foods	Mar 1992, p.12	various	*"Try this ... another good reason not to eat meat"*
Grassington's	Winter 2008, p.23	balls, fillet, steak	*Be one of the first to try our* NEW meat substitute *which tastes as good as it looks!*

Chapter 23
New Meat Without Livestock

Kurt Schmidinger
University of Vienna, Austria

Diana Bogueva
Curtin University, Australia

Dora Marinova
Curtin University, Australia

ABSTRACT

This chapter summarizes the global problems associated with livestock production and meat consumption and shows solution strategies through replacing animal products with plant-based alternatives. The positive effects of plant-based alternatives on human health and the environment are reviewed together with approaches for reducing world hunger. Psychological strategies for nutritional transitions towards more sustainable consumption patterns and criteria for market success of meat alternatives are presented. This is followed by an overview of meat alternatives – from soy[1], lupine or wheat based, to bleeding burgers and artificial intelligence concepts. Marketing strategies and best practice policy suggestions complete the chapter.

INTRODUCTION

Global mass production of livestock and the consumption of animal products are the major cause of a wide range of serious problems – environmental, health-related, concerning animal welfare and world nutrition. Environmentally, livestock production is a, or the, leading factor in land use, water consumption, pollution, rainforest destruction, climate change, loss of biodiversity and soil erosion (Steinfeld et al., 2006). The main reason for most of these problems is the inefficiency of livestock, where the largest share of the feed calories is used in the animals' metabolism and converted to excrements instead of food for human consumption. Such lengthened food chains, namely plant to animal to human, are heavily inefficient in resource use compared to short food chains, namely plant to human (see Figure 1). This inefficiency also explains why mass production of livestock is associated with world hunger (see later for more detail).

DOI: 10.4018/978-1-5225-4757-0.ch023

Most of the 70 billion animals (excluding sea creatures) produced annually for food consumption live in confined conditions raising severe concerns for their welfare. Although animal welfare is beyond the scope of this chapter, it is a major consideration for the wellbeing of all living beings on this planet. Intensive livestock production is a major risk factor for new global pandemics originating from industrial types of facilities as well as for antibiotic resistances while excessive consumption of meat, eggs and dairy is associated with lifestyle diseases, such as obesity, type 2 diabetes, cancer and heart disease (Schmidinger, 2012).

Given the convincing evidence about the negative impacts of animal-based dietary choices (Raphaely & Marinova, 2016), the question arises how to make consumers consume less of such food and whether a meat-free future is possible. This chapter explores plant-based alternatives to meat and other animal products together with strategies to encourage their acceptability. It also outlines criteria for market success which can trigger positive responses from the consumers and beneficial outcomes.

MAKING CONSUMERS EAT LESS ANIMAL PRODUCTS

Promoting plant-based food diets has a solid environmental and especially health case and is increasingly finding space in the EU countries. This is the case in the food guidelines of Sweden (Fischer et al., 2016), France (ANSES France, 2017), the UK Eatwell Guide (Public Health England, 2017) and Germany (DGE, 2017). Producing, distributing, selling and promoting meat is a seriously lucrative business, which relies heavily on the well-established forms of animal mass production at a minimum cost for the producer and especially on the ever-increasing consumption of meat and other foods of animal origin. The existing marketing and advertising efforts aim at bolstering further the intake of animal-based proteins (Bogueva and Phau, 2016). This is despite the clear evidence about the positive consequences, for both human health and the environment, of dietary changes toward healthier and more sustainable plant-based intake (Raphaely and Marinova, 2016; Bogueva et al., 2017; Springmann et al., 2016) and meat alternatives (Schmidinger, 2012). A major shift is clearly necessary.

In principle, a shift could be achieved with existing foods which do not contain animal products, but new plant-based innovations can assist such a transition and make it more realistic (Aiking and de

Figure 1. Livestock's long food chain

Note: Lengthening the food chain by livestock production leads to a loss of a big share of calories from plants within the metabolism of the farmed animals, only a small share of the plant calories is converted to animal products, the major share is converted to excrements and lost for human nutrition.

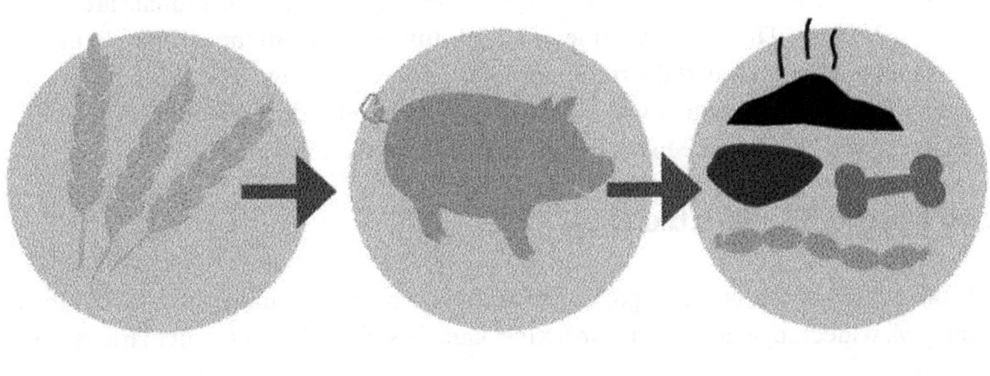

Boer, 2006). As it stands, at the moment the consumption of new alternatives has a long way to cut across existing habits before achieving mass popularity globally. Within any given society, the majority of people tend to adhere to an average diet. In traditional societies, this diet uses more plant-based ingredients, but globalisation triggers widespread westernisation of consumer tastes and with it higher intake of animal products (Hossain, 2016). Furthermore, improvements in people's earning capacity in developing countries also result in preferences for animal-based food (Raphaely & Marinova, 2014). On the other hand, people are influenced by the food choices made by others – relatives, friends, peers, celebrities, as well as advertising, availability and accessibility of products.

Stability/Energy Minimum Hypothesis

The *Stability/Energy Minimum Hypothesis* is a model derived from the theory of Balluch (2009). Adapted to nutritional aspects it shows the need for concerted actions instead of relying only on behaviour changes by billions of individuals.

The basic assumption of this hypothesis is that most individuals in a society try to live in a way that requires least effort or minimum energy. In Figure 2 this is represented by the trough, the area around the minimum of the curve. Applied to eating habits, this means that people tend to eat what is cheap, widely available, socially accepted and tastes well. In industrialised societies, this overwhelmingly involves animal-based products. Living as a vegan, an individual might be excluded from eating in certain restaurants. It may also cause stressful situations when attending business lunches or being invited for dinner or barbecue where vegan options are not served. Furthermore, it may cost more energy and longer shopping times to find the right foods. When abroad in a country with a foreign language, it will be harder to identify all ingredients of food products or dishes. It could be harder for vegetarian parents to find all-day school places offering a varied vegetarian menu for their children. Furthermore, for the children it might cost more energy to avoid becoming an outsider by not joining their friends in going to fast-food restaurants and eating non-vegetarian burgers.

Many individuals who originally were willing to change, tend to "save energy" and revert back to behaviour that makes their lives easier and matches that of the majority of the society to which they belong. In Figure 2, the red minimum represents the behaviour which requires the minimum energy associated with heavy use of animal-based foods in industrialised societies. The right side from the curve's minimum represents a more sustainable/ethical diet, while the left side is a less sustainable diet. Both require more individual energy than adhering to the average diet of a western society. The problem of minimum energy arises from both sides of the curve. A vegan or vegetarian diet is an example from the more sustainable right hand-side of the curve. Eating dogs may be acceptable in some parts of the world (see Figure 3), but would require more energy in the West where such animals are considered pets and domestic companions. This is an example of a less ethical diet from the left hand-side of the curve.

Living outside the trough around the minimum of the curve (see Figure 2) costs energy and requires more effort than following the nutritional mainstream. Such individuals need a lot of motivation and perseverance not to roll back and keep their position stable in the long term.

Shifting to a More Sustainable Diet

In Figure 4, the trough of the curve is pushed to the right, towards a more sustainable form of eating within a society. A wider range of new and attractive plant-based foods offered in markets, supermarkets,

Figure 2. Stability/energy minimum hypothesis in industrialised countries

Note: This graph shows how much energy an individual needs to keep up a certain diet. The political and economic system shape the curve. The trough (in red) is the minimum energy area. Outside the minimum, the individuals have to invest perpetual energy not to "roll back" into the trough, so their position is not stable.

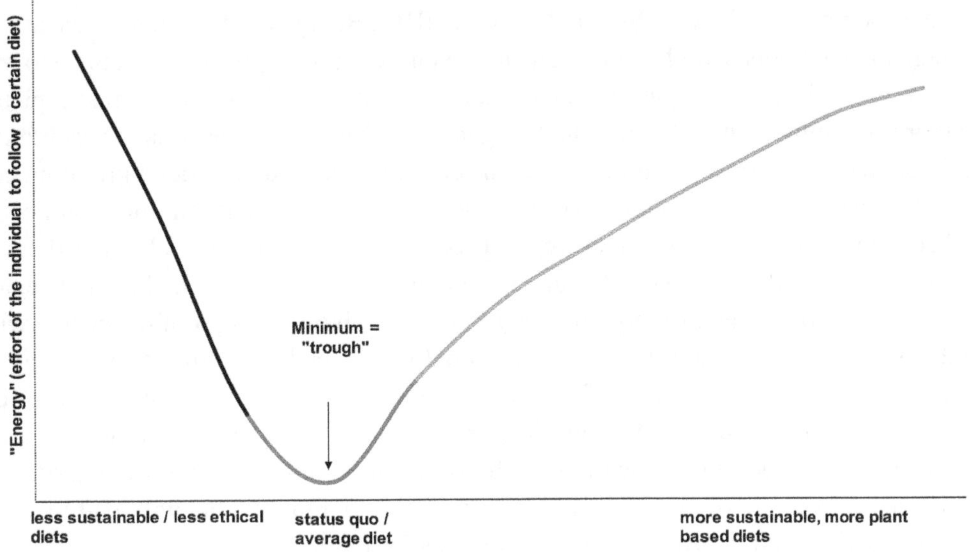

Figure 3. Dog meat sold in the streets of Hanoi, Vietnam, March 2017

shops, restaurants and canteens can help push the trough towards a more sustainable consumption if these new choices become easily available, cheaper and their marketing is successful. The reminder of the chapter presents ideas how to make possible and pleasant to eat more sustainably, which pushes the minimum energy trough to the right and with it the majority of individuals in a society towards a more sustainable nutrition.

Figure 5 shows a further variation of this model taken from Schmidinger (2012). In it, communities within a society define their own, more sustainable "rules" of nutrition, and the process of adhering to these agreements leads to social acceptance and affirmation creating local troughs in the right part of the curve. Examples are the vegan movements in Europe or the US since 2012 – it has become trendy to live without animal products (e.g. Harvard Medical School, 2016). Being part of such movements and adhering to their vegan agreements form local troughs in the curve on the right of the status quo minimum.

Let's use the example of the vegan movement and illustratively draw an optimistic picture for its future. The more like-minded people form such vegan groupings, the easier it is for each individual to stick to the lifestyle of the group. Figuratively, the more individuals such a social grouping consists of, the more "weight" will be exerted on the curve and the deeper such a local minimum will become. The markets will respond with new varieties of vegan products and food offers, labelling them as vegan. Politics will change due to the influence of vegan voters; the media will react, making the vegan lifestyle even more attractive, and the vegan energy minimum (the trough on the right of the curve) will become deeper and deeper. Such local minimums could eventually also lead to a shift of the energy minimum to the right as shown in Figure 4. Ideally if the more sustainable local minimums become deeper than the current minimum, many individuals from the current trough will roll over to the new minimum to the right of the curve. This will make the old trough disappear with not many individuals there and less weight and the curve from the old minimum will go directly up. Finally, this will lead to a new trough further right than before, and thus a more sustainable diet is achieved.

If broad target groups of people or even the majority of society are to shift to the right of the respective curves as postulated by the Stability/Energy Minimum-Hypothesis, many actions would be required. Given the seriousness of the problems associated with the consumption of animal-based products, it is

Figure 4. Push to a more sustainable diet
Note: Changed conditions in a society (e.g. food markets, political actions etc.) can push the energy minimum to the right, to a more sustainable diet

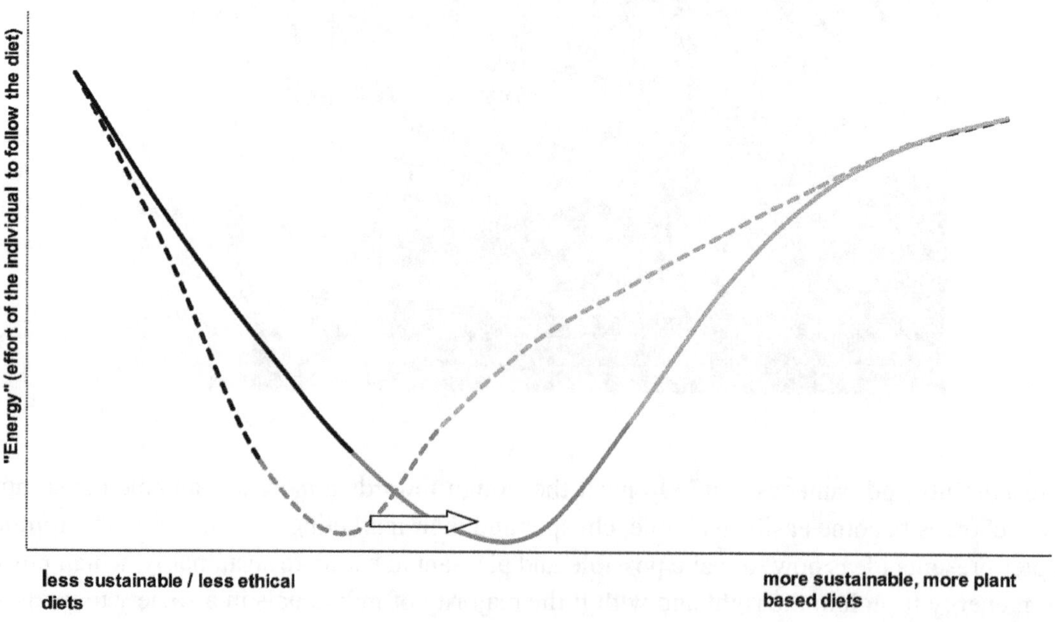

Figure 5. Push to a more sustainable diet

Note: Local minimums might also attract groups of individuals to practise a more sustainable diet. The more popular such a diet becomes, the deeper and relatively more stable the local minimums are. An optimum final consequence might be that such a new local minimum becomes deeper than the original minumum, making people roll over from the old to the new (more sustainable) minimum trough as shown in Figure 4.

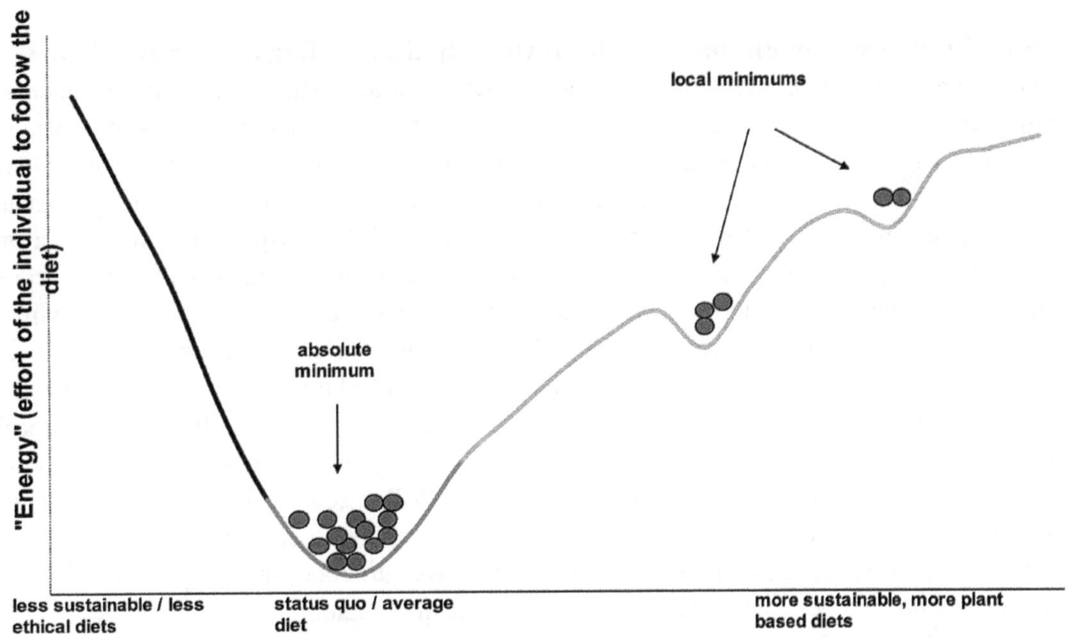

important that such a transition occurs smoothly with wide social acceptance. People however are generally reluctant to make drastic changes in their diets, even when their personal health is threatened (Blanchard et al., 2008). What criteria should the new plant-based food options fulfil? What requirements should the new plant-based alternatives to animal products, including alternatives to beef, veal, pork, poultry, lamb, mutton, venison, eggs and dairy products, satisfy to be accepted by the majority of consumers? Would even cultured meat grown in vitro in labs become an acceptable alternative? The section below lays out criteria for the success of alternatives to animal products in order to shift the average consumer diet towards more sustainable nutrition.

SUCCESS CRITERIA FOR ALTERNATIVES TO ANIMAL PRODUCTS

The original definition of "meat" refers to the core of a food as distinctive to its husk, shell or to a drink (Merriam–Webster, 2017). More recently however the word "meat" began to be associated with the flesh of an animal used for food. Irrespective of the term's etymology, what is important in this day and age is to break the largely spread assumption that when we eat meat we need to consume animal-based products. We need to reclaim the word together with encouraging food choices healthier for consumers and the planet. Hence, we refer to the entire spectrum of sustainable food options which do not involve livestock as the *new meat*. This includes traditional fruit and vegetables, classical products using tofu as well as new plant-based products, such as vegetarian sausages and soy mince, and meats produced in laboratory conditions. They all share the common characteristic of being animal-free food products.

In order for the new meat to be socially acceptable and to become a preferred option for consumers, it needs to satisfy several criteria. Below is a list of five main criteria informed by the work of Molnár (1989), de Boer and Hoek (2006) and Schmidinger (2012) developed predominantly for western consumers and individuals who are in a position to make food choices.

1. **Sensual Properties and Flavour – Taste, Texture, Satiety Feeling and Aroma:** In the perception of the majority of people within society, the flavour of alternatives to animal products should completely satisfy their preferences. Textures can be fibre-like – such as in meat products, gel-like – such as in yoghurt, coagulated – such as in cheese, and so on (O'Kane, 2006). Hence the alternatives to animal products must fulfil various texture tasks. Meat-like sensory properties and luxury aspects are relevant for plant-based alternatives with higher protein content in a product improving satiety sensations (Hoek, 2006). For example, favoured properties for vegetarian meat products are: brown, soft, smooth, crispy, seasoned, spicy and meat-like flavour (Elzerman, 2006).
2. **Price:** Alternatives to animal products should be affordable, preferably cheaper than the livestock-based products. The lengthened food chain and the losses of plant food calories through metabolism make animal products costly in principle. Model calculations for pea-based meat alternatives show that they should be cheaper than pork (Apaiah, 2006). Applications for the byproducts of, for example, pea- or soy-based meat alternatives exist (Willemsen, 2006), but should be economically optimised. Efficient alternatives to the byproducts of livestock production, such as leather, gelatine or pet food, need to be found (Willemsen & Apaiah, 2006), although many already exist while others need to be improved and made economically viable.
3. **Marketing, Target Groups and Advertising:** Alternatives to animal products should appeal to a wide target group, not only to vegans, vegetarians or health-conscious people! In fact, the target should be the general or average consumer. Information about new foods should "evoke feelings like comfort, familiarity, happiness, ease, low price and popularity" (Goodland & Anhang, 2009, p. 17). Advertising campaigns should "pitch the theme of eating all week long a line of food products that is tasty, easy to prepare and includes a superfood, such as soy" that will enrich the consumers' lives (Goodland and Anhang, 2009, p. 17). Availability in supermarket and discount stores as well as advertising, especially at the point of sale, are essential and have massive room for improvement (Ruiz, 2007). Also, plant-based alternatives should be placed side by side on the same shelf with livestock products to achieve the same exposure to consumers (Goodland and Anhang, 2009).
4. **Health:** Fruits and vegetables have numerous health benefits and their consumption should continue to be encouraged. The new plant-based foods should also be healthier than the animal products in an overall health appraisal. This should be valid at a personal level as well as being a public health consideration. Their use could minimise the risk of formation of new pandemics, antibiotic resistance (Raphaely et al., 2016) and development of salmonella, E. coli and other infections (Review of Antimicrobial Resistance, 2015). They should also be able to outperform animal products in terms of personal health issues. With reference to cultured meat, for example, it should be possible to optimise the fatty acid or amino acid composition of the final product and leave out cholesterol, Neu5GC and other unwanted compounds, making a healthier meat than those currently existing.
5. **Shelf Life and Hygiene:** Existing plant-based meat-, egg- or dairy-alternatives typically have a longer shelf-life than their equivalent livestock products – a fact that easily can be verified in any supermarket. For example, dried products, such as textured vegetable protein (TVP) chunks, have shelf lives of a year or longer. In fact, manufacturers of meat products use plant-based solutions as

a natural way to extend shelf life, control bacteria development and improve food safety (Pelligrini, 2014). With the majority of foodborne diseases originating from animal products, plant-based foods carry lower risk and hence, their shelf life is longer representing weighty advantages for the consumer and the food industry alike.

PRODUCTS MAKING THE CHANGE POSSIBLE

There is plenty of more or less well-known plant-based alternatives to meat, milk and eggs on the market, but certain innovations – recent or still being developed, could have a bright future. Some common or promising livestock-free solutions are presented below. The focus is on meat alternatives (sometimes even difficult to distinguish visually as shown in Figure 6), but similar innovations are also available to replace egg or dairy products.

Classic Plant-Based Meat Alternatives

The most common base materials for meat alternatives are wheat gluten (also called seitan) and soy-based ingredients, such as tofu and textured soy protein (abbreviated as TSP or TVP), also called soy meat. Seitan is obtained simply by rinsing wheat dough and washing out the starch until the protein components gliadin and glutenin are isolated from the wheat. Tofu is a worldwide well-known traditional Asian foodstuff, where a coagulant (traditionally nigari salt) is added to soy milk and the resulting protein solids are pressed into a desired form. Soy meat is produced using hot extrusion of defatted soy proteins, resulting in expanded high protein chunks, nuggets, strips, grains and other shapes. The fibrous, insoluble, porous soy meat can soak up water or other liquids a multiple of its own weight.

Figure 6. Plant based chicken drumsticks

Unlike tofu, seitan and even more soy meat show consistencies which are remarkably similar to the stringy fibres that make up animal-based meat. Often, you find products made of mixes of soy- and wheat-based protein ingredients. The disadvantage of this mix is that these products are not suitable for consumer groups suffering from soy allergies or gluten intolerance (coeliac disease). For the other consumers, such mixes represent perfect meat-like textures as well as optimised protein contents and quality. The protein quality can be explained by the fact that the profiles of the essential amino acids contained in soy and wheat complete each other well and compensate the deficiencies of their individual amino acid profiles.

Another classical plant-based meat alternative is tempeh which has a very old tradition in Indonesia. Controlled fermentation of soaked, hulled, hacked and damped soybeans with a Rhizopus mold binds them together into a compact, firm white patty form. The protein content makes tempeh a suitable ingredient for meat alternatives, whereas its texture is not meat-like. Experiments to produce tempeh based on barley and oats instead of soy have also been made (Swedish-Research-Council, 2008).

Other Meat Alternatives

These ingredients are innovative, some already available on the market, others on the way to being commercialised. The list of such alternatives is long and expanding in response to rising consumer interest, mainly from vegans and vegetarians. Below is a selection of such new meats.

Quorn, based on the so called Mycoprotein, is a commercially successful meat alternative range introduced by the English company Marlow Foods. Mycoprotein is a fermented fungus which is processed and textured to produce meat alternatives. Quorn products include steaks, burgers, chicken breasts as well as sliced meats and ready meals. It is marketed in European countries, USA, South Africa and Australia.

Sweet lupines have become another, increasingly popular base ingredient for meat or dairy alternatives, especially in Europe. Meatless was one of the first companies to use lupine-based fibres for the production of meat substitutes. The already completed Like Meat project funded by the European Union similarly used lupines as one of its experimental base materials.

Sprouted soybeans are used commercially, even though on a small scale, especially by the Hungarian company Yaso. Rice protein and pea protein have also been introduced for the production of meat alternatives together with vegetable fibres used by companies like Wiefleisch or the former company Proviand, taken over by the German veggie meat specialist Like Meat.

Using fresh mushrooms could be another option, as the company Fresh'shrooms has shown. Algae similarly holds huge potential for meat alternatives. Nuts (e.g. pecans) and garbanzo beans are the main ingredients for meat alternatives produced by Neat.

Science-Intensive Plant-Based Alternatives

This category of new meats includes innovations underpinned by scientific work which aims at reproducing the appearance of animal products to our senses A plant-based, perfect *bleeding beef burger* is the flagship of Impossible Foods in the USA, using heme (haem) from plants as a "bloody" juice. The burger exhibits a meat-like exterior fulfilling the equation: plants + science = meat. With funding from Google and Bill Gates (Woods, 2015), the company was able to create plant-based meats that give people the texture, flavour, aroma, taste and nutritional benefits of animal meat, without the negative health and environmental impacts of livestock products (Belvedere, 2016; Herships, 2016; Fellet, 2015; Gates, 2013).

The Not Company in Chile also explores path-breaking ways. Currently it focuses on dairy alternatives, but the same ideas will be applied to meat analogues. The company uses Guiseppe – the smartest food scientist on earth, who studies the perceptions about foods by humans (Sunder, 2016). However, Giuseppe is not a person, but an artificial intelligence robot that replicates the taste, texture and even smell of animal-based products by copying their molecular structure. Guiseppe uses plant-based ingredients for its food creations with the aim to achieve high nutritional values with low ecological impacts. Unlike humans, Giuseppe's knowledge is ever-increasing as the robot never forgets anything it has learned.

Real Meat of the Future out of the Lab

Besides plant-based meat alternatives, there are even more futuristic approaches. The concept is called *in vitro* meat or cultured meat, and the process is in principle as follows. Starting cells are taken painlessly from live animals; they are put into plant-based culture media, including growth factors, where they start to proliferate and grow independently from the animal. This all should happen in large bioreactors which can be monitored and controlled. To achieve a fibrous and three-dimensional texture, various concepts are applied – using edible scaffolds to which the cells could attach, 3-D-printing to print meat or electrical stimulation on the cells as a training to build muscle-like fibres.

Mark Post and his team in the Netherlands were the first to produce a burger in vitro, with financial support from the Google founder Sergey Brin. The burger was presented in 2013 in London and while still extremely expensive at an estimated cost of around US$ 300,000, it was a striking achievement (Shen, 2013). Memphis Meats recently produced several cultured meat balls. Modern Meadow are US-based projects also working on cultured meat. In Israel, Supermeat with Yaakov Nahmias and the Kitchen FoodTech Hub similarly pursue cultured meat efforts. The list of organisations and initiatives which are active in this domain includes New Harvest, the Good Food Institute, Future Food and the Modern Agriculture Foundation. They are making good progress with a lot of publicly available information.

MARKETING OF FUTURE FOOD ALTERNATIVES

Currently worldwide there exist many plant-based meat alternatives and plant-based protein products – enough to fill up a meatless butcher shop. The producers are concentrated mainly in (Shurtleff & Aoyagi, 2014; Schmidinger, 2012): USA and Canada in North America, Germany, the Netherland, UK, Italy, Czech Republic, Austria, France and Hungary in Europe, Australia and New Zealand in the Asia Pacific, Taiwan, China and Thailand in Asia, Brazil and Argentina in South America. Meat alternatives are projected to be soon stretched out of their niche market segment and as per the Allied Market Research (2016) forecast this trend is going to grow substantially offering many business opportunities (The Economist, 2017). Similarity to animal flesh-food composition, appearance and flavour is one reason for these plant-based food alternatives starting to make their way and gradually becoming popular amongst consumers. Another reason is their improved performance in relation to human health – they are cholesterol-free, have lower risks for numerous chronic diseases, such as cancer and cardiovascular disease. They also perform better in response to environmental concerns. In countries, such as USA, Germany and UK, these new meat alternatives are gaining good market shares and are no longer limited to a display at the back shelves of the supermarket. Nevertheless, the new meat alternatives still require more intense and competitive market strategies to establish themselves in the consumers' mind and to break out of their niche label into the mainstream.

Marketing strategies used by new meat producers usually follow the traditional mix around the 4P – product, promotion, place and price (Luca & Suggs, 2010; Thackeray & McCormack Brown, 2010), focused on increasing awareness about the existence of new cutting edge innovative plant-based products and promoting them among consumers. Some however are utilising novel approaches. Injecting culturally relevant concepts which resonate with people, through social media (e.g. Facebook) into brand communication was used by the advertising campaign of Alternative Meat Co (2017). The campaign ridiculed the Lambasador used by livestock advertisers to create a cultural identity of the multicultural Australian society around eating lamb on Australia Day. Alternative Meat Co used a mocking advertisement highlighting the increasing number of Australians who represent the changing food trends towards reduced meat consumption. The advertisement encourages people to try an alternative, e.g. vegetables, on Australia Day in line with the social trend away from animal-based products. This online advertisement received more than 1.1 million views, 13.5 thousand shares, 11 thousand likes and 5 thousand comments (Australian Meat Co, 2017). Tofurky can replace the turkeys traditionally consumed on Thanksgiving in USA (Shurtleff and Aoyagi, 2014).

Endorsement by celebrities is a marketing strategy employed by the California-based start-up Impossible Foods (Woods, 2015; Belvedere, 2016; Herships, 2016; Fellet, 2015). Promoting famous vegetarians who symbolise strength and masculinity is also a good way to increase the attractiveness of new meats. The list of names includes Mike Tyson – the undisputed heavyweight boxer champion, Carl Lewis – the nine-time Olympic gold medallist athlete, Brendan Brazier – the Ironman triathlete, Daniel Sturridge – premier league club Liverpool footballer, Serena and Venus Williams – the superstar tennis players and athletes, and many others.

Sensing the consumer shift to protein alternatives, major global meat producers are keen to stay in the game by participating in the new meats market. Tyson Foods in USA acquired a 5 percent share in the plant-based protein food manufacturer Beyond Meat. Similarly, the German meat packer company Rügenwalder Mühl and the Canadian Maple Leaf Foods are tailoring their marketing strategies to establish a strong platform in the plant-based proteins market (Strom, 2016).

A major component of the attractiveness of animal meat is its taste, smell, textural properties, fibrous structure, deliciousness and juicy mouth-feel – attributes stated by Australian Sydney residents (Bogueva et al., 2017). Using new meats' resemblance to these qualities can be a successful marketing strategy for a transition to healthier, environmentally better and morally higher diets.

The qualities of the new meats will continue to improve and their prices will become increasingly compatible. Any marketing and advertising campaigns will need to use this to reform and rebrand the consumer perceptions about food. However, there is a role for government and other institutions to play in supporting and facilitating these changes.

Against the ample evidence about the need to move towards healthier and environmentally respectful dietary patterns, the new meats alternatives are perfect novelties that must be supported as a trendy shift. Instead of lagging behind, government bodies should take an active stance and start developing and disseminating official dietary guidelines and recommendations, embedding health and sustainability objectives and creating policies fostering them (Fischer et al, 2016).

In addition to financial support for the new meats and removal of any funding benefiting the livestock sector (Hamilton, 2016; Di Croce et al. 2016), the government needs to engage in promoting the alternatives. In a similar way to dealing with tobacco and cigarettes, this should include freeing up the public advertising space from undesired messages and instigating social marketing of better alternatives. New meat options should be made available in public institutions, such as school canteens, hospitals and promoted in supermarkets, foodcourts and restaurants. Marketing strategies using the 4S model – sustainability, strength, self-confidence and sharing (Bogueva et al., 2017) can encourage transitioning to more sustainable diets.

WORLD HUNGER AND FOOD ALTERNATIVES

Although nearly half a billion people in the world identify themselves as vegetarians (Meat Atlas, 2014), the consumption of animal products continues to be strong in Western countries, including Australia, USA and Europe. Moreover, traditional diets are changing in places such as China and India exacerbating the seriousness of the climate change challenges (Myers & Kent, 2003; Vidal, 2013; Yu, 2015). Adding to this is the world's hunger problem of 1 billion people, among them 3 million children and 20 million people dying from starvation each year (Lappé & Collins, 2015). Global hunger will not be resolved by using the inefficient lengthened plant–to animal–to human food chains.

As seen in Figure 1, the losses of calories for global nutrition due to livestock production are enormous – 36 percent of the global cereal harvests (Schmid & Goldhofer, 2016) as well as 70 to 75 percent of the global soy harvests (Brack et al., 2016) are used for livestock. In 2016, 320 million tonnes of meat have been produced (FAO, 2016). According to Alexander et al. (2017), 1060 million tonnes of feed from crops plus 440 million tonnes of forage crops (e.g. alfalfa and forage maize) plus additional grass from grassland make up just 240 million tonnes of animal products in dry matter.

An average German person wastes about 400 kg of plant food just by eating meat. This is based on an average of 7 to 8 calories of plant-based feed to produce 1 calorie of meat (an estimate based on Smil, 2002 and Garnett, 2009). Milk and eggs are not even included in these figures. This waste of food for meat consumption alone is much higher than the annual 179 kg of wasted food per capita in the EU from private households, producers, supermarkets and gastronomy all together (European Commission, 2010)! The world produces more than enough to feed all humans on the planet Earth but not through inefficient food chains.

In response to the myriad of negative consequences triggered by livestock products, many are opting for plant-based alternatives (Market and Markets, 2016; Roy Morgan Research, 2016). This is also where the future of food lies and the quicker the transition, the better will be the outcomes for all.

CONCLUSION

The consumption of animal-based products is associated with serious impacts on human health, the natural environment and world hunger. The Stability/Energy Minimum hypothesis explains people's dominant eating behaviour as the one which conforms with the majority preferences within the society, circle of friends or at home and requires the least effort. A push towards more sustainable dietary choices needs to be facilitated by making plant-based options attractive in terms of flavours, textures, price, availability and varieties. By satisfying the five criteria related to taste, cost, health, shelf life and marketing, the alternatives to animal-based products can find their way into society and contribute to the creation of new more sustainable minimum energy conditions that encourage better health and environment related options.

As diets are expressed as a personal choice, the new meats based on fruit, vegetables, plants, TPV, cultured meat and other innovations can enrich the options available to the consumers who opt to exclude animal-based products from their dietary preferences. When wisely and properly marketed, these new meat food products will help shift the average diet and make it more sustainable. On a global scale this will free up a lot of waste associated with the current inefficient lengthened food chain, which feeds livestock first before feeding people, and allow world hunger to be eliminated. The future of food lies in many plant-based innovations as well as other options away from livestock products. Meat without livestock is the alternative we need to embrace if we are to dream for a brighter future.

ACKNOWLEDGMENT

The second and third authors acknowledge the contribution of an Australian Government Research Training Program Scholarship in supporting this research.

REFERENCES

Agence nationale de sécurité sanitaire de l'alimentation, de l'environnement et du travail (ANSES). (2017, January 24). *ANSES updates its food consumption guidelines for the French population*. French Agency for Food, Environmental and Occupational Health & Safety. Retrieved from https://www.anses.fr/en/content/anses-updates-its-food-consumption-guidelines-french-population

Aiking, H., & de Boer, J. (2006). Transition feasibility and implications for stakeholders. In H. Aiking, H., J. de Boer, & J. Vereijken (Eds.), Sustainable protein production and consumption: Pigs or peas? (pp. 193-215). Dordrecht, Netherlands: Springer. doi:10.1007/1-4020-4842-4_7

Alexander, P., Brown, C., Arneth, A., Finnigan, J., Moran, D., & Rounsevell, M. D. A. (2017). Losses, inefficiencies and waste in the global food system. *Agricultural Systems*, *153*, 190–200. doi:10.1016/j.agsy.2017.01.014 PMID:28579671

Allied Market Research. (2016). *Meat substitute market by product type (tofu, tempeh, textured vegetable protein, quorn, seitan), source (soy, wheat, mycoprotein), category (frozen, refrigerated, shelf-stable): Global opportunity analysis and industry forecast, 2014 - 2020*. Retrieved from https://www.alliedmarketresearch.com/meat-substitute-market

Alternative Meat Co. (2017, January 12). *Dave Hughes addresses Australia*. Alternative Meat Co (AMC) Facebook Page. Retrieved https://www.facebook.com/altmeatco/videos/1856335437973845/

Apaiah, R. K. (2006). Methodology for chain design. In H. Aiking, J. de Boer, & J. Vereijken (Eds.), *Sustainable protein production and consumption: Pigs or peas?* (pp. 79–85). Dordrecht, Netherlands: Springer.

Balluch, M. (2009). *Widerstand in der Demokratie - ziviler Ungehorsam und konfrontative Kampagnen*. Vienna, Austria: Promedia Druck- und VerlagsgesmbH Wien.

Belvedere, M. (2016, August 1). *We tried the plant-based "impossible burger" that's backed by Bill Gates*. CNBC. Retrieved from http://www.cnbc.com/2016/07/29/impossible-burger-our-test-tube-meat-tastes-great.html

Blanchard, C. M., Courneya, K. S., & Stein, K. (2008). Cancer survivors' adherence to lifestyle behavior recommendations and associations with health-related quality of life: Results from the American Cancer Society's SCS-II. *Journal of Clinical Oncology, 26*(13), 2198–2204. doi:10.1200/JCO.2007.14.6217 PMID:18445845

Bogueva, D., Marinova, D., & Raphaely, T. (2017). Reducing meat consumption: The case for social marketing. *Asia Pacific Journal of Marketing and Logistics, 29*(3), 477–500. doi:10.1108/APJML-08-2016-0139

Bogueva, D., & Phau, I. (2016). Meat myths and marketing. In T. Raphaely & D. Marinova (Eds.), *Impact of meat consumption on health and environmental sustainability* (pp. 264–276). Hershey, PA: IGI Global. doi:10.4018/978-1-4666-9553-5.ch015

Brack, D., Glover, A., & Wellesley, L. (2016). *Agricultural commodity supply chains: Trade, consumption and deforestation*. London, UK: The Royal Institute of International Affairs, Chatham House.

de Boer, J., & Hoek, A. (2006). Social desirability: Consumer aspects. In H. Aiking, J. de Boer, & J. Vereijken (Eds.), *Sustainable protein production and consumption: Pigs or peas?* (pp. 99–127). Dordrecht, Netherlands: Springer. doi:10.1007/1-4020-4842-4_4

Deutsche Gesellschaft für Ernährung (DGE). (2017). Der Wissenschaft verpflichtet – Ihr Partner für Essen und Trinken (The science – Your partner for eating and drinking). Retrieved from https://www.dge.de

Di Croce, P., Lymbery, P., Dibb, S., Hameleers, R., Wates, J., & Renshaw, N. … Martin, F. (2016). Letter to the Commissioner for Agriculture and Rural Development, European Commission of 10 November 2016. Retrieved from https://www.foeeurope.org/sites/default/files/agriculture/2016/meat-letter-hogan.pdf

Elzerman, H. (2006). Substitution of meat by NPFs: Sensory properties and contextual factors. In H. Aiking, J. de Boer, & J. Vereijken (Eds.), *Sustainable protein production and consumption: Pigs or peas?* (pp. 116–123). Dordrecht, Netherlands: Springer.

European Commission. (2010). *Preparatory study on food waste across EU 27*. Retrieved from http://ec.europa.eu/environment/archives/eussd/pdf/bio_foodwaste_report.pdf

Fellet, M. (2015). A fresh take on fake meat. Can scientists deliver a meatless burger that tastes good and will not harm the planet? *ACS Central Science, 1*(7), 347–349. doi:10.1021/acscentsci.5b00307 PMID:27162992

Fischer, C., & Garnett, T. (2016). *Plates, pyramids and planets*. FAO and FCRN, University of Oxford. Retrieved from http://www.fao.org/3/a-i5640e.pdf

Food and Agriculture Organisation of the United Nations (FAO). (2016). Food outlook: Biannual report on global food markets. Retrieved from http://www.fao.org/3/a-i6198e.pdf

Garnett, T. (2009). Livestock-related greenhouse gas emissions: Impacts and options for policy makers. *Environmental Science & Policy*, *12*(4), 491–503. doi:10.1016/j.envsci.2009.01.006

Gates, B. (2013, March 18). *Future of food.* The Gates Notes. Blog of Bill Gates. Retrieved from https://www.gatesnotes.com/About-Bill-Gates/Future-of-Food

Goodland, R. & Anhang, J. (2009). Livestock and climate change. *Worldwatch Institute Magazine*, November/December, 11-19.

Hamilton, J. (2016, December 7). *Common agricultural policy: Why is the EU pushing meat?* Honey Colony. Retrieved from https://www.honeycolony.com/article/common-agricultural-policy/

Harvard Medical School. (2016). *Becoming a vegetarian.* Harvard Health Publications. Retrieved from https://www.health.harvard.edu/staying-healthy/becoming-a-vegetarian

Herships, S. (2016, September 23). *A veggie burger that 'bleeds' might convince some carnivores to eat green.* Public Radio International "The World". Retrieved from https://www.pri.org/stories/2016-09-23/veggie-burger-bleeds-might-convince-some-carnivores-eat-green

Hoek, A. (2006). Substitution of meat by NPFs: Factors in consumer choice. In H. Aiking, J. de Boer, & J. Vereijken (Eds.), *Sustainable protein production and consumption: Pigs or peas?* (pp. 110–116). Dordrecht, Netherlands: Springer.

Hossain, A. (2016). Sustainable food consumption: A mission almost impossible because of the West. In T. Raphaely & D. Marinova (Eds.), *Impact of meat consumption on health and environmental sustainability* (pp. 255–263). Hershey, PA: IGI Global. doi:10.4018/978-1-4666-9553-5.ch014

Lappé, F. M., & Collins, J. (2015). *World hunger: Ten myths.* New York, NY: Grove Press.

Luca, N., & Suggs, S. (2010). Strategies for the social marketing mix: A systematic review. *Social Marketing Quarterly*, *16*(4), 122–149. doi:10.1080/15245004.2010.522767

Markets and Markets. (2016). *Meat substitutes market by type (tofu & tofu ingredients, tempeh, textured vegetable protein, seitan, quorn), source (soy-based, wheat-based, mycoprotein), category (frozen, refrigerated), and region – global forecast to 2022.* Markets and Markets. Retrieved from http://www.marketsandmarkets.com/Market-Reports/meat-substitutes-market-979.html

Meat Atlas. (2014). *Facts and figures about the animals we eat.* Berlin, Germany: Heinrich Böll Foundation and Brussels, Belgium: Friends of the Earth Europe. Retrieved from https://www.boell.de/sites/default/files/meat_atlas2014_kommentierbar.pdf

Merriam–Webster. (2017). *Meat.* Retrieved from https://www.merriam-webster.com/dictionary/meat

Molnár, P. J. (1989). A theoretical model to describe food quality. *Journal of Food Quality*, *12*(1), 1–11. doi:10.1111/j.1745-4557.1989.tb00305.x

Myers, N., & Kent, J. (2003). New consumers: The influence of affluence on the environment. *Proceedings of the National Academy of Sciences of the United States of America*, *100*(8), 4963–4968. doi:10.1073/pnas.0438061100 PMID:12672963

O'Kane, F. E. (2006). NPF Texture formation. In H. Aiking, J. de Boer, & J. Vereijken (Eds.), *Sustainable protein production and consumption: Pigs or peas?* (pp. 62–66). Dordrecht, Netherlands: Springer.

Pelligrini, M. (2014). *Extending shelf-life in protein products, naturally*. The Natural Provisioner. Retrieved from http://www.provisioneronline.com/articles/100955-extending-shelf-life-in-protein-products-naturally

Public Health England. (2017). *A quick guide to the government healthy eating recommendations*. Nutrition Advice Team, Public Health England. Retrieved from https://www.gov.uk/government/uploads/system/uploads/attachment_data/file/595133/A_quick_guide_to_govt_healthy_eating.pdf

Raphaely, T., & Marinova, D. (2014). Flexitarianism: A more moral dietary option. *International Journal of Sustainable Society*, *6*(1/2), 189–211. doi:10.1504/IJSSOC.2014.057846

Raphaely, T., & Marinova, D. (Eds.). (2016). *Impact of meat consumption on health and environmental sustainability*. Hershey, PA: IGI Global. doi:10.4018/978-1-4666-9553-5

Raphaely, T., Marinova, D., & Marinova, M. (2016). Antibiotics and the livestock sector. In T. Raphaely & D. Marinova (Eds.), *Impact of meat consumption on health and environmental sustainability* (pp. 178–200). Hershey, PA: IGI Global. doi:10.4018/978-1-4666-9553-5.ch009

Review on Antimicrobial Resistance. (2015). *Antimicrobials in agriculture and the environment: Reducing unnecessary use and waste*. Retrieved from https://amr-review.org/sites/default/files/Antimicrobials%20in%20agriculture%20and%20the%20environment%20-%20Reducing%20unnecessary%20use%20and%20waste.pdf

Roy Morgan Research. (2016). *The slow, but steady rise of Vegetarianism in Australia*. Retrieved from http://www.roymorgan.com/findings/vegetarianisms-slow-but-steady-rise-in-australia-201608151105

Ruiz, M. (2007). *Ausblick und Chancen des Vegetarismustrends im Lebensmittelhandel*. (Master thesis). Vienna, Austria: FH Corporate Governance and Management

Schmid, W., & Goldhofer, H. (2016). *Agrarmärkte 2016: 2 Getreide*. Retrieved from http://www.lfl.bayern.de/mam/cms07/iem/dateien/02_getreide__by_.pdf

Schmidinger, K. (2012). *Worldwide alternatives to animal derived foods – overview and evaluation models - solutions to global problems caused by livestock*. (Doctoral dissertation). Vienna, Austria: University of Natural Resources and Life Sciences.

Shen, A. (2013). Why we should stop obsessing over how expensive the world's first test-tube hamburger is. *ThinkProgress*. Retrieved from https://thinkprogress.org/why-we-should-stop-obsessing-over-how-expensive-the-worlds-first-test-tube-hamburger-is-c4e7011f52f4/

Shurtleff, W., & Aoyagi, A. (2014). History of meat alternatives (965CE to 2014): Extensively annotated bibliography and sourcebook. *Soyinfo Center*. Retrieved from http://www.soyinfocenter.com/pdf/179/MAL.pdf

Smil, V. (2002). Worldwide transformation of diets, burdens of meat production and opportunities for novel food proteins. *Enzyme and Microbial Technology*, *30*(3), 105–311. doi:10.1016/S0141-0229(01)00504-X

Springmann, M., Godfray, H. C. J., Rayner, M., & Scarborough, P. (2016). Analysis and valuation of the health and climate change cobenefits of dietary change. [PNAS]. *Proceedings of the National Academy of Sciences of the United States of America, 113*(15), 4146–4151. doi:10.1073/pnas.1523119113 PMID:27001851

Steinfeld, H., Gerber, P., Wassenaar, T., Castel, V., Rosales, M., & de Haan, C. (2006). Livestock's long shadow: Environmental issues and options. Rome, Italy: Food and Agriculture Organization of the United Nations (FAO).

Strom, S. (2016, 10 October). Tyson Foods, a meat leader, invests in protein alternatives. *The New York Times*. Retrieved from https://www.nytimes.com/2016/10/11/business/tyson-foods-a-meat-leader-invests-in-protein-alternatives.html?_r=0

Sunder, K. (2016). Meet the world's smartest food scientist: GIUSEPPE. Biotechin Asia. Retrieved from https://biotechin.asia/2016/02/16/meet-the-worlds-smartest-food-scientist-guiseppe/

Swedish Research Council. (2008, May 30). New vegetarian food with several health benefits. *ScienceDaily*. Retrieved from https://www.sciencedaily.com/releases/2008/05/080528095627.htm

Thackeray, R., & McCormack Brown, K. (2010). Creating successful price and placement strategies for social marketing. *Health Promotion Practice, 11*(2), 166–168. doi:10.1177/1524839909360892 PMID:20400655

The Economist. (2017, 2 February). *The market for alternative-protein products*. Retrieved from https://www.economist.com/news/business/21716076-plant-based-meat-products-have-made-it-menus-and-supermarket-shelves-market

Vidal, J. (2013, 14 April). Climate change: How a warming world is a treat to our food supplies. *The Guardian*. Retrieved from https://www.theguardian.com/environment/2013/apr/13/climate-change-threat-food-supplies

Willemsen, F. (2006). Options for non-protein fractions. In H. Aiking, J. de Boer, & J. Vereijken (Eds.), *Sustainable protein production and consumption: Pigs or peas?* (pp. 86–91). Dordrecht, Netherlands: Springer.

Willemsen, F., & Apaiah, R. (2006). Combined chains. In H. Aiking, J. de Boer, & J. Vereijken (Eds.), *Sustainable protein production and consumption: Pigs or peas?* (pp. 166–175). Dordrecht, Netherlands: Springer.

Woods, B. (2015, 14 May). *Bill Gates bets on growing demand for sustainable foods*. CNBC.com. Retrieved from http://www.cnbc.com/2015/05/14/hampton-creek-and-impossible-foods-technology.html

Yu, X. (2015). Meat consumption in China and its impact on international food security: Status quo, trends, and policies. *Journal of Integrative Agriculture, 14*(6), 989–994. doi:10.1016/S2095-3119(14)60983-7

KEY TERMS AND DEFINITIONS

Cultured Meat: Meat grown in vitro in laboratories which does not involve the slaughter of animals.

Meat Alternative: A substance with a high protein content used to replace animal flesh as food.

New Meat: Covers the entire spectrum of traditional and new food options which do not involve livestock.

Shelf Life: The recommended time for the sale of a food product.

Stability/Energy Minimum Hypothesis: A model which explains eating behaviour as a process conforming with the majority preferences in a society.

Textured Vegetable Protein (TVP): Dried vegetable matter with a high protein content by-product of extracting soybean oil used as a new meat in vegetarian and vegan food products.

World Hunger: Inefficient use and distribution of food resources, including feeding livestock instead of directly feeding people.

ENDNOTE

1 The terms soy and soya refer to the same bean – a legume type, with the preferred spelling in the USA being "soy" and in Europe – "soya". We have opted to use "soy" in this chapter; however, all products described here may also appear in the literature and on the market as "soya".

Conclusion

IT'S TIME

In 1852, Victor Hugo wrote that it is impossible to resist the invasion of ideas as they are more powerful than all armies in the world (Hugo, 2005). The book that you have just finished reading is about the power of ideas in changing humans' perceptions about animal proteins and shifting their behaviour towards plant-based foods. Only people themselves – be it in western countries or in nations where the prosperity of population is constantly improving – can make the choice to follow diets which are low in animal-origin foods. There is a role that governments and international collaboration can play – through legislation, commitments and treaties, for protecting human and environmental health whilst fighting the realities of climate change. The livestock industry itself may also be looking for solutions to reduce the impact of its products on the planet, but the moral challenge about taking life away from a sentient being when alternatives exist will remain. Doctors, nutritionists and toxicologists are vigourously researching and spreading information about the negative consequences from excessive consumption of animal products and the benefits of plant-based options. All these armies of people who are trying to influence or control human behaviour are likely to remain powerless until the ideas that eating meat and other animal-origin foods is wrong, conquer the world.

The message of all contributors to this book is that it is time for these new ideas to penetrate our knowledge and behaviour for personal benefits but also for the common good. By understanding the psychology of why we eat meat, the need for change given the challenges of climate change, generation of waste, soil and water contamination, threats to human health as well as how stupid 21st century people can still be, the book lays the grounds for the need of innovative ways of communicating the new ideas. We have presented a suite of tools and approaches to spread information, promote and even impose plant-based options covering flexitarianism, taxation, the use of social networks, traditional wisdom, redefining masculinity and challenging the notion of luxury. From a time perspective, we have looked both, into the past and the moral ethics of people who are now considered geniuses, as well as into the future by re-conceptualising what we call "meat" and describing some of the new and upcoming food products. The seven case studies extend across six countries (Australia, Bulgaria, China, Nigeria, South Africa and Turkey) and four continents. They all analyse the challenges of weaning people away from their attachment to animal-based foods, some even report success.

By arguing the case for the impact social marketing can have on people and their food-related behaviour, this book opens the door for the new ideas to become a reality – a safer, more gentle and loving reality for all of us who inhabit this beautiful planet. Thank you for reading and sharing with us the new ideas whose time has arrived.

Dora Marinova
Curtin University, Australia

Diana Bogueva
Curtin University, Australia

Talia Raphaely
Curtin University, Australia

REFERENCES

Hugo, V. (2005). Histoire d'un crime [History of a crime]. Paris, France: Mondial (originally published 1879)

Compilation of References

Aaker, A. D., Day, S. G., Kumar, V., & Leone, R. (2012). *Marketing research* (11th ed.). Hoboken, NJ: John Wiley & Sons.

Aarestrup, F. (2012). Get pigs off antibiotics. *Nature, 486*(7404), 465–466. doi:10.1038/486465a PMID:22739296

Aarestrup, F. M. (2000). Characterization of glycopeptide-resistant enterococcus faecium (GRE) from broilers and pigs in Denmark: Genetic evidence that persistence of GRE in pig herds is associated with coselection by resistance to macrolides. *Journal of Clinical Microbiology, 38*, 2774–2777. PMID:10878086

Aarestrup, F. M. (2009). Occurrence of glycopeptide resistance among enterococcus faecium isolates from conventional and ecological poultry farms. *Microbial Drug Resistance (Larchmont, N.Y.), 1*(3), 255–257. doi:10.1089/mdr.1995.1.255 PMID:9158784

Aarestrup, F. M., Jensen, V. F., Emborg, H. D., Jacobsen, E., & Wegener, H. C. (2010). Changes in the use of antimicrobials and the effects on productivity of swine farms in Denmark. *American Journal of Veterinary Research, 71*(7), 726–733. doi:10.2460/ajvr.71.7.726 PMID:20594073

Abete, I., Romaguera, D., Vieira, A. R., Lopez de Munain, A., & Norat, T. (2014). Association between total, processed, red and white meat consumption and all-cause, CVD and IHD mortality: A meta-analysis of cohort studies. *British Journal of Nutrition, 112*(5), 762–775. doi:10.1017/S000711451400124X PMID:24932617

Abiodun, P. (1991). Use of soya-beans for the dietary prevention and management of malnutrition in Nigeria. *Acta Paediatrica (Oslo, Norway), 80*(s374), 175–182. doi:10.1111/j.1651-2227.1991.tb12021.x PMID:1957623

Abioye-Kuteyi, E., Ojofeitimi, E., Ijadunola, K., & Fasanu, A. (2004). Assessment of dietary knowledge, practices and control in type 2 diabetes in a Nigerian teaching hospital. *Nigerian Journal of Medicine, 14*(1), 58–64. PMID:15832645

Achterberg, C., McDonnell, E., & Bagby, R. (1994). How to put the food guide pyramid into practice. *Journal of the American Dietetic Association, 94*(9), 1030–1035. doi:10.1016/0002-8223(94)92198-9 PMID:8071485

Adami, V. (2013). Culture, language and environmental rights: The anthropocentrism of English. *Pólemos Journal of Law. Literature and Culture, 7*(12), 335–355.

Adams, C. J. (2006). *The sexual politics of meat: A feminist-vegetarian critical theory*. New York, NY: Continuum.

Adams, C. J., & Calarco, M. (2016). Derrida and the sexual politics of meat. In A. Potts (Ed.), *Meat culture* (pp. 31–53). Leiden, UK: Brill. doi:10.1163/9789004325852_003

Adams, C. J., & Gruen, L. (Eds.). (2014). *'Groundwork' in ecofeminism: Feminist interactions with other animals and the earth*. New York, NY: Bloomsbury.

Adetunji, M., & Rauf, M. (2012). Analysis of household demand for meat in southwest, Nigeria. *Global Journal of Science Frontier Research (D), 12*(1), 15–22.

Agence nationale de sécurité sanitaire de l'alimentation, de l'environnement et du travail (ANSES). (2017, January 24). *ANSES updates its food consumption guidelines for the French population.* French Agency for Food, Environmental and Occupational Health & Safety. Retrieved from https://www.anses.fr/en/content/anses-updates-its-food-consumption-guidelines-french-population

Ahn, K. (2014). *What geniuses actually eat?* Retrieved from https://food-hacks.wonderhowto.com/how-to/real-brain-food-what-geniuses-actually-eat-part-1-0156531/

Aiello, L. C. (1997). Brains and guts in human evolution: The expensive tissue hypothesis. *Brazilian Journal of Genetics, 20*(1), 141–148. Retrieved from http://www.scielo.br/scielo.php?script=sci_arttext&pid=S0100-84551997000100023 doi:10.1590/S0100-84551997000100023

Aiking, H., & de Boer, J. (2006). Transition feasibility and implications for stakeholders. In H. Aiking, H., J. de Boer, & J. Vereijken (Eds.), Sustainable protein production and consumption: Pigs or peas? (pp. 193-215). Dordrecht, Netherlands: Springer. doi:10.1007/1-4020-4842-4_7

Ajzen, I. (1991). The theory of planned behavior. *Organizational Behavior and Human Decision Processes, 50*(2), 179–211. doi:10.1016/0749-5978(91)90020-T

Akgungor, S., Miran, B., & Abay, C. (2010). Consumer willingness to pay for organic food in urban Turkey. *Journal of International Food & Agribusiness Marketing, 22*(3-4), 299–313. doi:10.1080/08974431003641455

Akinro, A., Ologunagba, I., & Yahaya, O. (2009). Environmental implications of unhygienic operation of a city abattoir in Akure, Western Nigeria. *Journal of Engineering and Applied Sciences (Asian Research Publishing Network), 4*(9), 60–63.

Aksoy, T. (2014). Turkish organic poultry sector: General evaluation and lessons from successful practices. *Paper presented at the Practitioners' Track, IFOAM Organic World Congress 2014, 'Building Organic Bridges.'* Retrieved from http://orgprints.org/24161/

Alawa, C. B., Etukudo-Joseph, I., & Alawa, J. N. (2011). A 6-year survey of pathological conditions of slaughtered animals at Zango abattoir in Zaria, Kaduna State, Nigeria. *Tropical Animal Health and Production, 43*(1), 127–131. doi:10.1007/s11250-010-9664-5 PMID:20734135

Alexander, D. D., Bylsma, L. C., Vargas, A. J., Cohen, S. S., Doucette, A., Mohamed, M., & Fryzek, J. P. et al. (2016). Dairy consumption and CVD: A systematic review and meta-analysis. *British Journal of Nutrition, 115*(4), 737–750. doi:10.1017/S0007114515005000 PMID:26786887

Alexander, D. D., Miller, P. E., Vargas, A. J., Weed, D. L., & Cohen, S. S. (2016). Meta-analysis of egg consumption and risk of coronary heart disease and stroke. *Journal of the American College of Nutrition, 35*(8), 704–716. doi:10.1080/07315724.2016.1152928 PMID:27710205

Alexander, P., Brown, C., Arneth, A., Finnigan, J., Moran, D., & Rounsevell, M. D. A. (2017). Losses, inefficiencies and waste in the global food system. *Agricultural Systems, 153*, 190–200. doi:10.1016/j.agsy.2017.01.014 PMID:28579671

Ali, S. M. (2015) *Meat: The opium of the 21st century* (2nd rev. ed.). Hamburg, Germany: Books on Demand.

Allan, N. E., Appleby, P. N., Davey, G. K., & Key, T. J. (2000). Hormones and diet: Low insulin-like growth factor-I but normal bioavailable androgens in vegan man. *British Journal of Cancer, 83*(1), 95–97. PMID:10883675

Allegretti, G., & Hartz-Karp, J. (2017). Participatory budgeting: a methodological approach to address sustainability challenges. In J. Hartz-Karp & D. Marinova (Eds.), *Methods for sustainability research* (pp. 203–216). Cheltenham, UK: Edward Elgar. doi:10.4337/9781786432735.00024

Allen, M. (2015). *Short-lived promise? The science and policy of cumulative and short-lived climate pollutants (Oxford Martin Policy Paper)*. Oxford, UK: Oxford University. Retrieved from http://www.oxfordmartin.ox.ac.uk/publications/view/1960

Allen, M. R., Frame, D. J., Huntingford, C., Jones, C. D., Lowe, J. A., Meinshausen, M., & Meinshausen, N. (2009). Warming caused by cumulative carbon emissions towards the trillionth tonne. *Nature*, *458*(7242), 1163–1166. doi:10.1038/nature08019 PMID:19407800

Alleyne, R. (2011, February 8). Food for thought – diet does boost your intelligence. *The Telegraph*. Retrieved from: http://www.telegraph.co.uk/news/health/news/8308726/Food-for-thought-diet-does-boost-your-intelligence.html

Allied Market Research. (2016). *Meat substitute market by product type (tofu, tempeh, textured vegetable protein, quorn, seitan), source (soy, wheat, mycoprotein), category (frozen, refrigerated, shelf-stable): Global opportunity analysis and industry forecast, 2014 - 2020*. Retrieved from https://www.alliedmarketresearch.com/meat-substitute-market

Alternative Meat Co. (2017, January 12). *Dave Hughes addresses Australia*. Alternative Meat Co (AMC) Facebook Page. Retrieved https://www.facebook.com/altmeatco/videos/1856335437973845/

American Meat Institute. (2007). *Meat matters: Animal welfare in the meat industry*. Retrieved from http://www.meat-mattersinfo.org/ht/a/GetDocumentAction/i/8681

Andersen, K., & Kuhn, K. (2014). *Cowspiracy: The sustainability secret*. US: A.U.M Films and First Spark Media.

Anderson, L. V. (2014). What if the whole world became vegetarian? *SBS Australia*. Retrieved from http://www.sbs.com.au/news/article/2014/05/04/what-if-whole-world-became-vegetarian

Andreasen, A. R. (1994). Social marketing: Its definition and domain. *Journal of Public Policy & Marketing*, *13*(1), 108–114.

Andreasen, A. R. (1995). *Marketing social change: Changing behaviour to promote health, social development, and the environment*. San Francisco, CA: Jossey-Bass.

Andreasen, A. R. (2002). Marketing social marketing in the social change marketplace. *Journal of Public Policy & Marketing*, *21*(1), 3–13. doi:10.1509/jppm.21.1.3.17602

Andreasen, N. C. (2011). A journey into chaos: Creativity and the unconscious. *Mens Sana Monographs*, *9*(1), 42–53. doi:10.4103/0973-1229.77424 PMID:21694961

Animal Liberation Front. (2006). *Meat-eating is an unsustainable luxury*. Retrieved from http://www.animalliberation-front.com/Practical/Health/MeatNotSustainable.htm

Animal Liberation Victoria. (2017). *Free range fraud*. Retrieved from http://freerangefraud.com/free-range-fraud/

Anyiro, C., Ezeh, C., Osondu, C., & Madu, L. (2013). Meat consumption patterns among different income groups in Imo State, Nigeria. *Journal of Agriculture. Forestry and the Social Sciences*, *11*(1), 21–31.

Apaiah, R. K. (2006). Methodology for chain design. In H. Aiking, J. de Boer, & J. Vereijken (Eds.), *Sustainable protein production and consumption: Pigs or peas?* (pp. 79–85). Dordrecht, Netherlands: Springer.

Apostolidis, C., & McLeay, F. (2016). Should we stop meating like this? Reducing meat consumption through substitution. *Food Policy*, *65*, 74–89. doi:10.1016/j.foodpol.2016.11.002

Appleby, P. N., Davey, G. K., & Key, T. J. (2002). Hypertension and blood pressure among meat eaters, fish eaters, vegetarians and vegans in EPIC-Oxford. *Public Health Nutrition*, *5*(5), 645–654. doi:10.1079/PHN2002332 PMID:12372158

Arcari, P. (2017). Normalised, human-centric discourses of meat and animals in climate change, sustainability and food security literature. *Agriculture and Human Values*, *34*(1), 69–86. doi:10.1007/s10460-016-9697-0

Archer, D., Eby, M., Brovkin, V., Ridgwell, A., Cao, L., Mikolajewicz, U., & Tokos, K. et al. (2009). Atmospheric lifetime of fossil fuel carbon dioxide. *Annual Review of Earth and Planetary Sciences*, *37*(1), 117–134. doi:10.1146/annurev.earth.031208.100206

Aristotle. (1999). *Politics* (B. Jowett, Trans.). Kitchener, ON: Batoche Books. (Original work published 4th century BC). Retrieved from http://socserv2.mcmaster.ca/~econ/ugcm/3ll3/aristotle/Politics.pdf

Arlington, K. (2016, August 18). Why The Economist says Sydney is no longer one of the world's 10 most liveable cities. *The Sydney Morning Herald*. Retrieved from http://www.smh.com.au/nsw/the-heightened-perceived-threat-of-terrorism-affects-sydneys-liveability-20160817-gqv8kf.html

Arneth, A., Sitch, S., Pongratz, J., Stocker, B. D., Ciais, P., Poulter, B., & Zaehle, S. et al. (2017). Historical carbon dioxide emissions caused by land-use changes are possibly larger than assumed. *Nature Geoscience*, *10*(2), 79–84. doi:10.1038/ngeo2882

Arno, A., & Thomas, S. (2016). The efficacy of nudge theory strategies in influencing adult dietary behaviour: A systematic review and meta-analysis. *BMC Public Health*, *16*(1), 1–11. doi:10.1186/s12889-016-3272-x PMID:27475752

Arthur, R., & Baidoo, M. F. (2011). Harnessing methane generated from livestock manure in Ghana, Nigeria, Mali and Burkina Faso. *Biomass and Bioenergy*, *35*(11), 4648–4656. doi:10.1016/j.biombioe.2011.09.009

Asadu, C. L., Ezeaku, P. I., & Nnaji, G. U. (2004). Land use and soil management situations in Nigeria: An analytical review of changes. *Outlook on Agriculture*, *33*(1), 27–37. doi:10.5367/000000004322877755

Aschemann-Witzel, J. (2015). Consumer perception and trends about health and sustainability: Trade-offs and synergies of two pivotal issues. *Current Opinion in Food Science*, *3*, 6–10. doi:10.1016/j.cofs.2014.08.002

Asch, S. E. (1956). Studies of independence and conformity: A minority of one against a unanimous majority. *Psychological Monographs*, *70*(9), 1–70. doi:10.1037/h0093718

Ascui, F., & Lovell, H. (2011). As frames collide. *Accounting. Auditing and Accountability*, *24*, 978–999. doi:10.1108/09513571111184724

Asher, K., Green, C., Gutbrod, H., Jewell, M., Hale, G., & Bastian, B. (2014). Study of current and former vegetarians and vegans. *Faunalytics*. Retrieved from https://faunalytics.org/feature-article/hrc-study-of-current-and-former-vegetarians-and-vegans/

Ashmore, M. R. (2005). Assessing the future global impacts of ozone on vegetation. *Plant, Cell & Environment*, *28*(8), 949–964. doi:10.1111/j.1365-3040.2005.01341.x

Astrup, A., Rice Bradley, B., Brenna, J., Delplanque, B., Ferry, M., & Torres-Gonzalez, M. (2016). Regular-fat dairy and human health: A synopsis of symposia presented in Europe and North America (2014–2015). *Nutrients*, *8*(8), 463. doi:10.3390/nu8080463 PMID:27483308

Atkinsonová, R. L., Atkinson, R. C., Smith, E. E., Bem, D. J., & Nolen-Hoeksema, S. (1995). Psychologie [Psychology]. Praha, Czech Republic: Victoria Publishing.

Audsley, E., Brander, M., Chatterton, J., Murphy-Bokern, D., Webster, C., & Williams, A. (2009). How low can we go? An assessment of greenhouse gas emissions from the UK food system and the scope to reduce them by 2050. *WWF-UK*. Retrieved from https://dspace.lib.cranfield.ac.uk/handle/1826/6503

Aune, D., Chan, D. S., Vieira, A. R., Navarro Rosenblatt, D. A., Vieira, R., Greenwood, D. C., & Norat, T. et al. (2013). Red and processed meat intake and risk of colorectal adenomas: A systematic review and meta-analysis of epidemiological studies. *Cancer Causes & Control, 24*(4), 611–627. doi:10.1007/s10552-012-0139-z PMID:23380943

Aune, D., Keum, N., Giovannucci, E., Fadnes, L. T., Boffetta, P., Greenwood, D. C., & Norat, T. et al. (2016a). Nut consumption and risk of cardiovascular disease, total cancer, all-cause and cause-specific mortality: A systematic review and dose-response meta-analysis of prospective studies. *BMC Medicine, 14*(1), 207. doi:10.1186/s12916-016-0730-3 PMID:27916000

Aune, D., Keum, N., Giovannucci, E., Fadnes, L. T., Boffetta, P., Greenwood, D. C., & Norat, T. et al. (2016b). Whole grain consumption and risk of cardiovascular disease, cancer, and all cause and cause specific mortality: Systematic review and dose-response meta-analysis of prospective studies. *BMJ (Clinical Research Ed.), 353*, i2716. doi:10.1136/bmj.i2716 PMID:27301975

Aune, D., Navarro Rosenblatt, D. A., Chan, D. S., Vieira, A. R., Vieira, R., Greenwood, D. C., & Norat, T. et al. (2015). Dairy products, calcium, and prostate cancer risk: A systematic review and meta-analysis of cohort studies. *The American Journal of Clinical Nutrition, 101*(1), 87–117. doi:10.3945/ajcn.113.067157 PMID:25527754

Austin, D. W. (2008). Hyper-Masculinity and Disaster: Gender Role Construction in the Wake of Hurricane Katrina. *Allacademic*. Retrieved from http://www.allacademic.com/meta/p241530_index.html

Australia Online Catalogues. (2016). Coles Catalogue Christmas 21-27 December 2016. Retrieved from: https://www.catalogueau.com/coles/coles-catalogue-christmas-21-december-2016/

Australia, A. (2017). What you never knew about dairy. Retrieved from http://www.animalsaustralia.org/issues/dairy.php

Australian Bureau of Statistics (ABS). (2016). *Australian Health Survey: Consumption of food groups from the Australian Dietary Guidelines, Australia 2011-12* (Catalogue number 4364.0.55.012). Canberra, Australia: ABS. Retrieved from http://www.ausstats.abs.gov.au/ausstats/subscriber.nsf/0/12E8766EBAB492B0CA257FAF001A3CFD/$File/43640do002_20112012.pdf

Australian Bureau of Statistics (ABS). (2017). *Population clock*. Retrieved from http://www.abs.gov.au/ausstats/abs%40.nsf/94713ad445ff1425ca25682000192af2/1647509ef7e25faaca2568a900154b63?OpenDocument

Australian Council of Social Services (ACOSS). (2013). *Tax reform: purpose, principles and process*. Strawberry Hills, Australia: ACOSS. Retrieved from http://www.acoss.org.au/wp-content/uploads/2015/06/Tax_reform_ACOSS_August_2013.pdf

Australian Institute of Health and Welfare (AIHW). (2017). *Cancer in Australia 2017*. Canberra, Australia: AIHW. Retrieved from http://www.aihw.gov.au/WorkArea/DownloadAsset.aspx?id=60129559144

Australian Public Service Commission. (2007). *Changing behaviour: A public policy perspective*. Retrieved from http://www.apsc.gov.au/publications-and-media/archive/publications-archive/changing-behaviour

Australian Taxation Office (ATO). (2016). GST status of food items. Australian Government. Retrieved from https://www.ato.gov.au/business/gst/in-detail/your-industry/food/gst-food-guide/?anchor=H4#H4

Australian War Memorial. (n.d.). Rationing of food and clothing during the Second World War. Retrieved from https://www.awm.gov.au/articles/encyclopedia/homefront/rationing

Azadbakht, L., & Esmaillzadeh, A. (2009). Red meat intake is associated with metabolic syndrome and the plasma C-reactive protein concentration in women. *The Journal of Nutrition, 139*(2), 335–339. doi:10.3945/jn.108.096297 PMID:19074209

Azevedo, M., & Alla, S. (2008). Diabetes in sub-saharan Africa: Kenya, Mali, Mozambique, Nigeria, South Africa and Zambia. *International Journal of Diabetes in Developing Countries*, *28*(4), 101–108. doi:10.4103/0973-3930.45268 PMID:20165596

Babić, S., Mutavdžić, D., Ašperger, D., Horvat, A. J. M., & Kaštelan-Macan, M. (2006). Determination of veterinary pharmaceuticals in production wastewater by HPTLC-Videodensitometry. *Chromatographia*, *65*(1-2), 105–110. doi:10.1365/s10337-006-0109-2

Babio, N., Sorlí, M., Bulló, M., Basora, J., Ibarrola-Jurado, N., Fernández-Ballart, J., & Salas-Salvadó, J. et al. (2012). Association between red meat consumption and metabolic syndrome in a Mediterranean population at high cardiovascular risk: Cross-sectional and 1-year follow-up assessment. *Nutrition, Metabolism, and Cardiovascular Diseases*, *22*(3), 200–207. doi:10.1016/j.numecd.2010.06.011 PMID:20875949

Bae, S., Ulrich, C. M., Neuhouser, M. L., Malysheva, O., Bailey, L. B., Xiao, L., & Caudill, M. A. et al. (2014). Plasma choline metabolites and colorectal cancer risk in the women's health initiative observational study. *Cancer Research*, *74*(24), 7442–7452. doi:10.1158/0008-5472.CAN-14-1835 PMID:25336191

Bagozzi, R. P., Wong, N., Abe, S., & Bergami, M. (2000). Cultural and situational contingencies and the theory of reasoned action: application to fast food restaurant consumption. *Journal of Consumer Psychology*, *9*(2), 97–106. doi:10.1207/S15327663JCP0902_4

Bähr, C. C. (2015). Greenhouse gas taxes on meat products: A legal perspective. *Transnational Environmental Law*, *4*(01), 153–179. doi:10.1017/S2047102515000011

Bai, H., Qian, Y., Shi, B., Li, G., Fan, Y., Wang, Z., & Liu, L. et al. (2013). The association between fish consumption and risk of renal cancer: A meta-analysis of observational studies. *PLoS One*, *8*(11), e81939. doi:10.1371/journal.pone.0081939 PMID:24312383

Bailey, C. (2013, June 6). 9 brain foods that will improve your focus and concentration. A life of productivity. *A Life of Productivity*. Retrieved from http://alifeofproductivity.com/9-brain-foods-that-will-boost-your-ability-to-focus/

Bailey, R., Froggatt, A., & Wellesley, L. (2014). *Livestock – Climate Change's Forgotten Sector: Global Public Opinion on Meat and Dairy Consumption*. Chatham House, Energy, Environment and Resources. Retrieved from https://www.chathamhouse.org/sites/files/chathamhouse/field/field_document/20141203LivestockClimateChangeForgottenSectorBaileyFroggattWellesleyFinal.pdf

Bailey, R., Froggatt, A., & Wellesley, L. (2014). *Livestock – climate change's forgotten sector: Global public opinion on meat and dairy consumption*. London, UK: Energy, Environment and Resources, Chatham House. Retrieved from http://www.chathamhouse.org/sites/files/chathamhouse/field/field_document/20141203LivestockClimateChangeBaileyFroggattWellesleyUpdate.pdf

Balcombe, J. (2010). *Second nature: The inner lives of animals*. New York, NY: Palgrave Macmillan.

Balluch, M. (2009). *Widerstand in der Demokratie - ziviler Ungehorsam und konfrontative Kampagnen*. Vienna, Austria: Promedia Druck- und VerlagsgesmbH Wien.

Bandera, E. V., Kushi, L. H., Moore, D. F., Gifkins, D. M., & McCullough, M. L. (2007). Consumption of animal foods and endometrial cancer risk: A systematic literature review and meta-analysis. *Cancer Causes & Control*, *18*(9), 967–988. doi:10.1007/s10552-007-9038-0 PMID:17638104

Bao, J., Sherwood, S. C., Alexander, L. V., & Evans, J. P. (2017). Future increases in extreme precipitation exceed observed scaling rates. *Nature Climate Change*, *7*(2), 128–132. doi:10.1038/nclimate3201

Barker, P. (1998). Creativity and psychic distress in artists, writers and scientists: Implications for emergent models of psychiatric nursing practice. *Journal of Psychiatric and Mental Health Nursing*, *5*(2), 109–117. doi:10.1046/j.1365-2850.1998.00103.x PMID:9661412

Barnard, N. D., Gloede, L., Cohen, J., Jenkins, D. J., Turner-McGrievy, G., Green, A. A., & Ferdowsian, H. (2009). A low-fat vegan diet elicits greater macronutrient changes, but is comparable in adherence and acceptability, compared with a more conventional diabetes diet among individuals with type 2 diabetes. *Journal of the American Dietetic Association*, *109*(2), 263–272. doi:10.1016/j.jada.2008.10.049 PMID:19167953

Barnard, N. D., Scialli, A. R., Turner-McGrievy, G., & Lanou, A. J. (2004). Acceptability of a low-fat vegan diet compares favorably to a step II diet in a randomized, controlled trial. *Journal of Cardiopulmonary Rehabilitation*, *24*(4), 229–235. doi:10.1097/00008483-200407000-00004 PMID:15286527

Baron, R., Montgomery, W. D., & Tuladhar, S. (2009). *An analysis of black carbon mitigation as a response to climate change*. Washington, DC: Copenhagen Consensus Center. Retrieved from http://www.copenhagenconsensus.com/sites/default/files/ap_black_carbon_baron_montgomery_tuladhar_v.4.0.pdf

Barthes, R. (1957). *Mythologies*. Paris, France: Seuil.

Battaglia Richi, E., Baumer, B., Conrad, B., Darioli, R., Schmid, A., & Keller, U. (2015). Health risks associated with meat consumption: A review of epidemiological studies. *International Journal for Vitamin and Nutrition Research*, *85*(1-2), 70–78. doi:10.1024/0300-9831/a000224 PMID:26780279

Baur, G. (2008). *Farm sanctuary: Changing hearts and minds about animals and food*. New York, NY: Simon & Schuster.

BBC News. (2012, November 10). *Denmark to abolish tax on high-fat foods*. Retrieved from http://www.bbc.com/news/world-europe-20280863

BBC. (2014). Life on the front line. World War I. Retrieved from http://www.bbc.co.uk/schools/0/ww1/26247563

Beardsworth, A., & Keil, T. (1992). The vegetarian option: Varieties, conversions, motives and careers. *The Sociological Review*, *40*(2), 253–293. doi:10.1111/j.1467-954X.1992.tb00889.x

Beauvois, J. L., & Joule, E. V. (1996). *A radical dissonance theory*. London, UK: Taylor and Francis.

Beckett, A. (2013). *Meat-free and free-from foods (Market Research Report)*. Mintel.

Beers, D. L. (2006). *For the prevention of cruelty: The history and legacy of animal rights activism in the United States*. Athens, OH: Shallow Press. doi:10.1353/book.7001

Behavioural Insights Team. (2017). In partnership with Cabinet Office. Retrieved from http://www.behaviouralinsights.co.uk

Behrendt, K., & Weeks, P. (2017). *How are global and Australian beef producers performing?* Meat & Livestock Australia. Retrieved from https://www.mla.com.au/globalassets/mla-corporate/prices--markets/documents/trends--analysis/agri-benchmark/revised_mla_agribenchmark-beef-results-report_jan-2017.pdf

Bekoff, M. (2007). *The emotional lives of animals: A leading scientist explores animal joy, sorrow, and empathy – and why they matter*. Novato, CA: New World Library.

Belloni, M. L. (1994). A mundialização da cultura. *Sociedade e Estado*, *9*(1/2), 35–53.

Belvedere, M. (2016, August 1). *We tried the plant-based "impossible burger" that's backed by Bill Gates*. CNBC. Retrieved from http://www.cnbc.com/2016/07/29/impossible-burger-our-test-tube-meat-tastes-great.html

Bénard, C., Bonnet, B., & Guivert, B. (2010). Demand for farm animal products in Nigeria: An opportunity for Sahel countries. *Grain de Sel, 51*(1), 14–15.

Bendell, J., & Kleanthous, A. (2007). *Deeper luxury*. London, UK: WWF-UK.

Bennett, E., & Gough, B. (2012). In pursuit of leanness: The management of appearance, affect and masculinities within a men's weight loss forum. *Health, 17*(3), 284–299. doi:10.1177/1363459312454149 PMID:22815334

Benson, G. J., & Rollin, B. E. (Eds.). (2008). *The well-being of farm animals: Challenges and solutions*. Ames, IA: Blackwell Publishing.

Berndsen, M., & Van der Pligt, J. (2004). Ambivalence towards meat. *Appetite, 42*(1), 71–78. doi:10.1016/S0195-6663(03)00119-3 PMID:15036785

Bernstein, A. M., Sun, Q., Hu, F. B., Stampfer, M. J., Manson, J. E., & Willett, W. C. (2010). Major dietary protein sources and risk of coronary heart disease in women. *Circulation, 122*(9), 876–883. doi:10.1161/CIRCULATIONAHA.109.915165 PMID:20713902

Best, S., & Nocella, A. J. (2004). Behind the mask: Uncovering the animal liberation front. In S. Best & A. J. Nocella (Eds.), *Terrorists or freedom fighters? Reflections on the liberation of animals* (pp. 9–64). New York, NY: Lantern Press.

Beverland, M. B. (2014). Sustainable eating: Mainstreaming plant-based diets in developed economies. *Journal of Macromarketing, 34*(3), 369–382. doi:10.1177/0276146714526410

Beyaz Et Sanayıcılerı ve Damızlıkçıları Bırlığı Derneğı (BESD-BİR). (2015). *Olağan genel kurul toplantısı sunumu* [Presentation of 17th Ordinary General Assembly Meeting] Retrieved from http://www.besd-bir.org/assets/documents/SaitKocaGKSUNUMU.pdf

Bhadauria, P., Kataria, J. M., Majumdar, S., Bhanja, S.K., & Divya, G.& Kolluri. (2014). Impact of hot climate on poultry production system-A review. *Journal of Poultry Science and Technology, 2*(4), 56–63.

Bhattacarya, U. (1971). *Banglar Baul o Baul gaan*. Kolkata, India: Oriental Book Company.

Bhopal, V., Bola, G., Bottoms, I., Bromilow, J., Casson, L., & Hebditch, R. … Zeidler, M. (2013). *Zero carbon Britain: Rethinking the future*. Aberystwyth, UK: Centre for Alternative Technology. Retrieved from http://www.zerocarbonbritain.org/images/pdfs/ZCBrtflo-res.pdf

Bisarya, S., & Patil, D. (1993). Determination of salicylic acid and phenol (ppm level) in effluent from aspirin plant. *Research and Industry, 38*, 170–172.

Biswas, T., Garnett, S. P., Pervin, S., & Rawal, L. B. (2017). The prevalence of underweight, overweight and obesity in Bangladeshi adults: Data from a national survey. *PLoS One, 12*(5), e0177395. doi:10.1371/journal.pone.0177395 PMID:28510585

Blades, M. (2001). Factors affecting what we eat. *Nutrition & Food Science, 31*(2), 71–74. doi:10.1108/00346650110366982

Blanchard, C. M., Courneya, K. S., & Stein, K. (2008). Cancer survivors' adherence to lifestyle behavior recommendations and associations with health-related quality of life: Results from the American Cancer Society's SCS-II. *Journal of Clinical Oncology, 26*(13), 2198–2204. doi:10.1200/JCO.2007.14.6217 PMID:18445845

Blasing, T. J. (2013). *Recent greenhouse gas concentrations*. Oak Ridge, TN: Carbon Dioxide Information Analysis Centre; Retrieved from http://cdiac.ornl.gov/pns/current_ghg.html

Blom, M., Schroten, A., de Bruyn, S., & Rooijers, F. (2010). *Limits to green? Greening tax system in the Netherlands.* Delft, the Netherlands: CE Delft. Retrieved from http://www.ce.nl/publicatie/limits_to_green_elements_of_a_green_tax_system/1026

Boeva, B. (2008). *International management* [in Bulgarian]. Sofia, Bulgaria: Stopanstvo.

Bøgh, K. L., & Madsen, C. B. (2016). Food allergens: Is there a correlation between stability to digestion and allergenicity? *Critical Reviews in Food Science and Nutrition, 56*(9), 1545–1567. doi:10.1080/10408398.2013.779569 PMID:25607526

Bogueva, D., Marinova, D., & Raphaely, T. (2017). (forthcoming). Red meat consumption and social marketing interventions promoting appetite for change. *International Journal of Food Engineering, 3*(2).

Bogueva, D., Marinova, D., & Raphaely, T. (2017). Reducing meat consumption: The case for social marketing. *Asia Pacific Journal of Marketing and Logistics, 29*(3), 477–500. doi:10.1108/APJML-08-2016-0139

Bogueva, D., & Phau, I. (2016). Meat myths and marketing. In T. Raphaely & D. Marinova (Eds.), *Impact of meat consumption on health and environmental sustainability* (pp. 264–276). Hershey, PA: IGI Global. doi:10.4018/978-1-4666-9553-5.ch015

Bogueva, D., Raphaely, T., Marinova, D., & Marinova, M. (2017). Sustainability social marketing. In J. Hartz-Karp & D. Marinova (Eds.), *Methods for sustainability research* (pp. 280–291). Cheltenham, UK: Edward Elgar. doi:10.4337/9781786432735.00030

Bonafini, S., Antoniazzi, F., Maffeis, C., Minuz, P., & Fava, C. (2015). Beneficial effects of $ω$-3 PUFA in children on cardiovascular risk factors during childhood and adolescence. *Prostaglandins & Other Lipid Mediators, 120*, 72–79. doi:10.1016/j.prostaglandins.2015.03.006 PMID:25834924

Bond, T. C., Doherty, S. J., Fahey, D. W., Forster, P. M., Berntsen, T., DeAngelo, B. J., & Zender, C. S. et al. (2013). Bounding the role of black carbon in the climate system: A scientific assessment. *Journal of Geophysical Research, D, Atmospheres, 118*(11), 5380–5552. doi:10.1002/jgrd.50171

Borgi, L., Curhan, G. C., Willett, W. C., Hu, F. B., Satija, A., & Forman, J. P. (2015). Long-term intake of animal flesh and risk of developing hypertension in three prospective cohort studies. *Journal of Hypertension, 33*(11), 2231–2238. doi:10.1097/HJH.0000000000000722 PMID:26237562

Borreli, L. (2016, April 18). Mind wandering origins: Creative thinking is influenced by family genes, personality traits. *Medical Daily.* Retrieved from http://www.medicaldaily.com/creative-thinking-personality-traits-mind-wandering-family-genes-382323

Bosland, M. C., Oakley-Girvan, L., & Whittemore, A. S. (1999). Dietary fat, calories and prostate cancer risk. *Journal of the National Cancer Institute, 91*(6), 489–491. doi:10.1093/jnci/91.6.489 PMID:10088612

Bouchard, G. (2013). For a new sociology of social myths. *Revue Européenne Des Sciences Sociales, 51*(1), 95-120.

Boundless. (n.d.) *Second Industrial Revolution.* Retrieved from https://www.boundless.com/definition/second-industrial-revolution/

Bourdieu, P. (1997). *Sobre a televisão* (M. L. Machado, Trans.). Rio de Janeiro, RJ: Jorge Zahar.

Bourke, D. (2009). The use and misuse of 'rights talk' by the animal rights movement. In P. J. Sankoff & S. White (Eds.), *Animal law in Australasia: A new dialogue* (pp. 128–150). Sydney, Australia: The Federation Press.

Bouvard, V., Loomis, D., Guyton, K. Z., Gross, Y., El Ghissassi, F., Benbrahim-Tallaa, L., & Straif, K. et al. (2015). Carcinogenicity of consumption of red and processed meat. *The Lancet Oncology*, *16*(16), 1599–1600. doi:10.1016/S1470-2045(15)00444-1 PMID:26514947

Bouwman, L., Goldewijk, K. K., Van Der Hoek, K. W., Beusen, A. H., Van Vuuren, D. P., Willems, J., & Stehfest, E. (2013). Exploring global changes in nitrogen and phosphorus cycles in agriculture induced by livestock production over the 1900-2050 period. *Proceedings of the National Academy of Sciences of the United States of America*, *110*(52), 20882–20887. doi:10.1073/pnas.1012878108 PMID:21576477

Boyd, d. (2014). *It's complicated: The social lives of networked teens*. New Have, NY: Yale University Press.

Brack, D., Glover, A., & Wellesley, L. (2016). *Agricultural commodity supply chains: Trade, consumption and deforestation*. London, UK: The Royal Institute of International Affairs, Chatham House.

Bradley, P. M., Journey, C. A., Button, D. T., Carlisle, D. M., Clark, J. M., Mahler, B. J., & VanMetre, P. C. et al. (2016). Metformin and other pharmaceuticals widespread in wadeable streams of the southeastern United States. *Environmental Science & Technology Letters*, *3*(6), 243–249. doi:10.1021/acs.estlett.6b00170

Brenkert, G. G. (2008). *Marketing ethics*. Oxford, UK: Blackwell Publishing.

Brennan, L., Previte, J., & Fry, M. L. (2016). Social marketing's consumer myopia: Applying a behavioural ecological model to address wicked problems. *Journal of Social Marketing*, *6*(3), 219–239. doi:10.1108/JSOCM-12-2015-0079

Breyer, M. (2016, December 15). Eating this is linked to brain health and intelligence in older adults. *Tree Hugger*. Retrieved from https://www.treehugger.com/health/eating-linked-brain-health-and-intelligence-older-adults.html

Briggs, A. D. M., Kehlbacher, A., Tiffin, R., Garnett, T., Rayner, M., & Scarborough, P. (2013). Assessing the impact on chronic disease of incorporating the societal cost of greenhouse gases into the price of food: An econometric and comparative risk assessment modelling study. *BMJ Open*, *3*(10), e003543. doi:10.1136/bmjopen-2013-003543 PMID:24154517

Briggs, A. D. M., Kehlbacher, A., Tiffin, R., & Scarborough, P. (2016). Simulating the impact on health of internalising the cost of carbon in food prices combined with a tax on sugar-sweetened beverages. *BMC Public Health*, *16*(107), 1–14. PMID:26837190

Brittan, A., & Maynard, M. (1984). *Sexism, racism and oppression*. Oxford, UK: Blackwell.

Brown, C. G., Longworth, J. W., & Waldron, S. (2002). Food safety and development of the beef industry in China. *Food Policy*, *27*(3), 269–284. doi:10.1016/S0306-9192(02)00017-9

Brown, K. D., Kulis, J., Thomson, B., Chapman, T. H., & Mawhinney, D. B. (2006). Occurrence of antibiotics in hospital, residential, and dairy effluent, municipal wastewater, and the Rio Grande in New Mexico. *The Science of the Total Environment*, *366*(2-3), 772–783. doi:10.1016/j.scitotenv.2005.10.007 PMID:16313947

Brown, L. (2009). *Plan B 4.0: Mobilizing to save civilization*. New York, NY: W.W. Norton & Company.

Brown, L. R. (2011). *World on the edge: How to prevent environmental and economic collapse*. New York, NY: Norton.

Brügger, P. (2008). Os novos meios de comunicação: Uma antítese da educação ambiental? In C. Loureiro, P. Layrargues, & R. Castro (Eds.), *Educação ambiental: Repensando o espaço da cidadania* (4th ed., pp. 143–177). São Paulo, SP: Cortez.

Brügger, P. (2013). Especismo na TV: Um olhar abolicionista sobre o programa "Pelo Mundo". *Brazilian Animal Rights Journal*, *8*(13), 121–165. doi:10.9771/rbda.v8i13.8638

Brügger, P. (2016). Educação e televisão: O leão Cecil no programa Sem Fronteiras, Globo News. *Brazilian Animal Rights Journal*, *11*(21), 169–199. doi:10.9771/rbda.v11i21.16504

Brügger, P., Marinova, D., & Raphaely, T. (2016). Animal production and consumption: An ethical educational approach. In T. Raphaely & D. Marinova (Eds.), *Impact of meat consumption on health and environmental sustainability* (pp. 295–312). Hershey, PA: IGI Global. doi:10.4018/978-1-4666-9553-5.ch017

Bryngelsson, D., Hedenus, F., Johansson, D. J. A., Azar, C., & Wirsenius, S. (2017). How do dietary choices influence the energy-system cost of stabilizing the climate? *Energies*, *10*(2), 182. doi:10.3390/en10020182

Bubolz, M. M., & Sontag, M. S. (1993). Human ecology theory. In P. G. Boss, W. J. Doherty, R. LaRossa, W. R. Schumm, & S. K. Steinmetz (Eds.), *Sourcebook of family theories and methods: A conceptual approach* (pp. 419–448). New York, NY: Plenum Press. doi:10.1007/978-0-387-85764-0_17

Bucher, T., Collins, C., Rollo, M. E., McCaffrey, T. A., De Vlieger, N., Van der Bend, D., & Perez-Cueto, F. J. A. et al. (2016). Nudging consumers towards healthier choices: A systematic review of positional influences on food choice. *British Journal of Nutrition*, *115*(12), 2252–2263. doi:10.1017/S0007114516001653 PMID:27185414

Business, H. T. (2015). Kaç kişi Facebook'ta? [How many people are on Facebook?]. Retrieved from http://www.businessht.com.tr/teknoloji/haber/1123980-kac-kisi-facebookta

Buzby, J. C., & Hyman, J. (2012). Total and per capita value of food loss in the United States. *Food Policy*, *37*(5), 561–570. doi:10.1016/j.foodpol.2012.06.002

Caini, S., Masala, G., Gnagnarella, P., Ermini, I., Russell-Edu, W., Palli, D., & Gandini, S. (2016). Food of animal origin and risk of non-Hodgkin lymphoma and multiple myeloma: A review of the literature and meta-analysis. *Critical Reviews in Oncology/Hematology*, *100*, 16–24. doi:10.1016/j.critrevonc.2016.02.011 PMID:26921971

Calaprice, A. (2010). *The expanded quotable Einstein*. Retrieved from https://ivu.org/history/northam20a/einstein.html

Cambridge Declaration on Consciousness. (2012). Retrieved from http://fcmconference.org/img/CambridgeDeclarationOnConsciousness.pdf

Campbell-Arvai, V., Arvai, J., & Kalof, L. (2014). Motivating sustainable food choices: The role of nudges, value orientation, and information provision. *Environment and Behavior*, *46*(4), 453–475. doi:10.1177/0013916512469099

Cao, L.-J., Tian, W.-M., Wang, J.-M., Malcolm, B., Liu, H.-B., & Zhau, Z.-Y. (2013). Recent food consumption trends in China and trade implications to 2020. *Australasian Agribusiness Review*, *21*, 2. Retrieved from http://www.agrifood.info/review/2013/Cao_et_al.pdf

Capital. (2017). *Six companies with more than 10 mln lv income from poultry* [in Bulgarian]. Retrieved from http://www.capital.bg/specialni_izdaniia/regal500plus/2015/12/22/2675141_shest_kompanii_s_nad_10_mln_lv_prihodi_ot_pileshko_meso/

Capps, O. Jr, Moen, D., & Branson, R. (1988). Consumer characteristics associated with the selection of lean meat products. *Agribusiness*, *4*(6), 549–557. doi:10.1002/1520-6297(198811)4:6<549::AID-AGR2720040605>3.0.CO;2-D

Carballo, M., Esperón, F., Sacristán, C., González, M., Vázquez, B., Aguayo, S., & Torre, A. (2013). Occurrence of tetracycline residues and antimicrobial resistance in gram negative bacteria isolates from cattle farms in Spain. *Advances in Bioscience and Biotechnology*, *4*(2), 295–303. doi:10.4236/abb.2013.42A040

Carr, P. R., Walter, V., Brenner, H., & Hoffmeister, M. (2016). Meat subtypes and their association with colorectal cancer: Systematic review and meta-analysis. *International Journal of Cancer*, *138*(2), 293–302. doi:10.1002/ijc.29423 PMID:25583132

Carvalho, P. N., Basto, M. C. P., Almeida, C. M. R., & Brix, H. (2014). A review of plant–pharmaceutical interactions: From uptake and effects in crop plants to phytoremediation in constructed wetlands. *Environmental Science and Pollution Research International*, *21*(20), 11729–11763. doi:10.1007/s11356-014-2550-3 PMID:24481515

Castanon, J. I. R. (2007). History of the use of antibiotic as growth promoters in European poultry feeds. *Poultry Science*, *86*(11), 2466–2471. doi:10.3382/ps.2007-00249 PMID:17954599

CBS This Morning. (2014). Beyond Meat CEO Ethan Brown on the benefits of meat substitutes. Retrieved from https://www.cbsnews.com/videos/beyond-meat-ceo-ethan-brown-on-the-benefits-of-meat-substitutes-2/

Center for Disease Dynamics, Economics & Policy (CDDEP). (2015). State of the world's antibiotics, 2015. Washington, DC: CDDEP.

Centers for Disease Control and Prevention. (2016). *Economics of NCDs, injury and environmental health: Advancing evidence-based policies*. Retrieved from http://www.cdc.gov/

Centre for Generational Kinetics. (2016). *An intro to generations*. Retrieved from http://genhq.com/faq-info-about-generations/

Chan, D. S., Lau, R., Aune, D., Vieira, R., Greenwood, D. C., Kampman, E., & Norat, T. (2011). Red and processed meat and colorectal cancer incidence: Meta-analysis of prospective studies. *PLoS One*, *6*(6), e20456. doi:10.1371/journal.pone.0020456 PMID:21674008

Chandler, D., & Munday, R. (2011). *A dictionary of media and communication*. Oxford, UK: Oxford University Press. doi:10.1093/acref/9780199568758.001.0001

Chang, H., & Hsia, C. (2000). Beef import market shares in Taiwan: Implications for Australia. *The Australian Journal of Agricultural and Resource Economics*, *44*(2), 217–231. doi:10.1111/1467-8489.00108

Chan, R. Y. K., & Lau, L. B. Y. (2001). Explaining green purchasing behavior: A cross-cultural study on American and Chinese consumers. *Journal of International Consumer Marketing*, *14*(2/3), 9–41.

Chapin, A. (2016). WD-40 and microwaved tampons: Secrets of food photography revealed. *The Guardian*. Retrieved from https://www.theguardian.com/lifeandstyle/2016/jan/04/food-stylist-photography-tricks-advertising

Chapman, G., Kumar, K., Fraser, C., & Gaber, F. (1997). *Environmentalism and the mass media: The North-South divide*. London, UK: Routledge. doi:10.4324/9780203443514

Chen, G.-C., Lv, D.-B., Pang, Z., & Liu, Q.-F. (2013). Red and processed meat consumption and risk of stroke: A meta-analysis of prospective cohort studies. *European Journal of Clinical Nutrition*, *67*(1), 91–95. doi:10.1038/ejcn.2012.180 PMID:23169473

Chen, M., Cooper, V. I., Deng, J., Amatya, P. L., Ambrus, D., Dong, S., & Patel, J. et al. (2015). Occurrence of pharmaceuticals in Calgary's wastewater and related surface water. *Water Environment Research*, *87*(5), 414–424. doi:10.2175/106143015X14212658614199 PMID:26460461

Chen, M., Li, Y., Sun, Q., Pan, A., Manson, J. E., Rexrode, K. M., & Hu, F. B. et al. (2016). Dairy fat and risk of cardiovascular disease in 3 cohorts of US adults. *The American Journal of Clinical Nutrition*, *104*(5), 1209–1217. doi:10.3945/ajcn.116.134460 PMID:27557656

Cherry, E. (2010). Shifting symbolic boundaries: Cultural strategies of the animal rights movement. *Sociological Forum*, *25*(3), 450–475. doi:10.1111/j.1573-7861.2010.01191.x

Chevalier, M., & Mazzalovo, G. (2012). *Luxury brand management: A world of privilege* (2nd ed.). Singapore: John Wiley & Sons. doi:10.1002/9781119199168

Chiles, R. M., & Fitzgerald, A. J. (2017). Why is meat so important in Western history and culture? A genealogical critique of biophysical and political-economic explanations. *Agriculture and Human Values*. Retrieved from https://link.springer.com/article/10.1007/s10460-017-9787-7 doi:10.1007/s10460-017-9787-7

Chizzolini, R., Zanardi, E., Dorigoni, V., & Ghidini, S. (1999). Calorific value and cholesterol content of normal and low-fat meat and meat products. *Trends in Food Science & Technology, 10*(4–5), 119–128. doi:10.1016/S0924-2244(99)00034-5

Cho, C. E., Taesuwan, S., Malysheva, O. V., Bender, E., Tulchinsky, N. F., Yan, J., & Caudill, M. A. et al. (2017). Trimethylamine-*N*-oxide (TMAO) response to animal source foods varies among healthy young men and is influenced by their gut microbiota composition: A randomized controlled trial. *Molecular Nutrition & Food Research, 61*(1), 1600324. doi:10.1002/mnfr.201600324 PMID:27377678

Chomping Climate Change. (2014). Why it's a big fat lie that the world needs 70 percent more food by 2050. Retrieved from http://www.chompingclimatechange.org/updated-analysis/why-its-a-big-fat-lie-that-the-world-needs-70-percent-more-food-by-2050

Chomping Climate Change. (2015). Has climate change caused "Peak Livestock"? Retrieved from http://www.chompingclimatechange.org/updated-analysis/has-the-world-reached-peak-livestock/

Chunhui, Z., Liangliang, W., Xiangyu, G., & Xudan, H. (2016). Antibiotics in WWTP discharge into the Chaobai River, Beijing. *Archives of Environmental Protection, 42*(4). doi:10.1515/aep-2016-0036

Ciais, P., Sabine, C., Bala, G., Bopp, L., Brovkin, V., & Canadell, J. … Thornton, P.K. (2013). Carbon and other biogeochemical cycles. In *Climate Change 2013: The Physical Science Basis. Contribution of Working Group 1 to the Fifth Assessment Report of the Intergovernmental Panel on Climate Change.* Intergovernmental Panel on Climate Change (IPCC). Retrieved from https://www.ipcc.ch/pdf/assessment-report/ar5/wg1/WG1AR5_Chapter06_FINAL.pdf

City of Tshwane Metropolitan Municipality. (2004). *Local authority notice.* Retrieved from http://www.tshwane.gov.za/sites/business/Bylaws/Promulgated%20ByLaws%20Documents/ByLaw_KeepingAnimalsBirdsPoultry.pdf

Clark, N. (1991). Nutrition and fitness. *The Physician and Sportsmedicine, 19*(1), 31–34. doi:10.1080/00913847.1991.11702123 PMID:27422190

Clifton, P. M. (2011). Protein and coronary heart disease: The role of different protein sources. *Current Atherosclerosis Reports, 13*(6), 493–498. doi:10.1007/s11883-011-0208-x PMID:21912836

Cliquet, G. (2000). Large format retailers. *Journal of Retailing and Consumer Services, 4*(4), 183–195. doi:10.1016/S0969-6989(00)00017-5

Cohen, D. A., & Babey, S. H. (2012). Contextual influences on eating behaviours: Heuristic processing and dietary choices. *Obesity Reviews, 13*(9), 766–779. doi:10.1111/j.1467-789X.2012.01001.x PMID:22551473

Cole, M., & Steward, K. (2014). *Our children and other animals: The cultural construction of human-animal relations in childhood.* Farnham, UK: Ashgate.

Commonwealth of Australia. (2009). *Australia's future tax system.* Canberra, Australia: Attorney-General's Department. Retrieved from https://taxreview.treasury.gov.au/content/downloads/final_report_part_1/00_AFTS_final_report_consolidated.pdf

Connelly, T. (2016, July 22). New man about town – "Traditional masculinity is dead", says new research. *The Drum*. Retrieved from http://www.thedrum.com/news/2016/07/22/new-man-about-town-traditional-masculinity-dead-says-new-research

Conrad, K., Flay, B., & Hill, D. (1992). Why children start smoking cigarettes: Predictors of onset. *British Journal of Addiction, 87*(12), 1711–1724. doi:10.1111/j.1360-0443.1992.tb02684.x PMID:1490085

Contois, E. J. H. (2013). *Gender and dieting. Encyclopedia of Food and Agricultural Ethics*. Springer. doi:Retrieved from https://link.springer.com/referenceworkentry/10.1007/978-94-007-6167-4_472-1#page-1 doi:10.1007/97894-007-6167-4_472-1

Cooper, A. (2007). *Campaign for the abolition of animal slavery*. Retrieved from http://www.animalslavery.net/index.html

Coreil, J., Bryant, C. A., & Henderson, J. N. (2001). *Social and behavioural foundations of public health*. Thousand Oaks, CA: Sage.

Cormack, L. (2016, June 5). Australia is the third-fastest growing vegan market in the world. *The Sydney Morning Herald*. Retrieved from http://www.smh.com.au/business/consumer-affairs/australia-is-the-thirdfastest-growing-vegan-market-in-the-world-20160601-gp972u.html

Corner, A., & Randall, A. (2011). Selling climate change? The limitations of social marketing as a strategy for climate change public engagement. *Global Environmental Change, 21*(3), 1005–1014. doi:10.1016/j.gloenvcha.2011.05.002

CountryEconomy. (n.d.). *Government budget deficit*. Retrieved from http://countryeconomy.com/deficit

Coutinho, F. H., Pinto, L. H., Vieira, R. P., Martins, O. B., Salloto, G. R. B., & Santoro, D. O. … Cardoso, A.M. (2013). Antibiotic resistance in aquatic environments of Rio de Janeiro, Brazil. In I. Ahmad, & M.A. Dar (Eds.), Perspectives in water pollution (pp. 1-22). Rijeka, Croatia: InTech.

Cox, M. S., McLure, C. E., & Neumark, F. (2009). Taxation. In *Encyclopaedia Britannica*. Retrieved from https://www.britannica.com/topic/taxation

Cox, P. (2002). *You don't need meat*. New York, NY: St. Martin's Press.

Craig, W., & Mangles, A. (2009). Position of the American Dietetic Association: Vegetarian diets. *Journal of the American Dietetic Association, 109*(7), 1266–1282. doi:10.1016/j.jada.2009.05.027 PMID:19562864

Crawshaw, P. (2007). Governing the healthy male citizen: Men, masculinity, and popular health in Men's Health magazine. *Social Science & Medicine, 65*(8), 1606–1618. doi:10.1016/j.socscimed.2007.05.026 PMID:17628269

Cribb, J. (2010). *The coming famine: The global food crisis and what we can do to avoid it*. Berkeley, CA: University of California Press.

Cronin, A. M. (2004). *Advertising myths; The half-lives of images and commodities*. London, UK: Routledge.

Cross, A. J., Ferrucci, L. M., Risch, A., Graubard, B. I., Ward, M. H., Park, Y., & Sinha, R. et al. (2010). A large prospective study of meat consumption and colorectal cancer risk: An investigation of potential mechanisms underlying this association. *Cancer Research, 70*(6), 2406–2414. doi:10.1158/0008-5472.CAN-09-3929 PMID:20215514

Cross, A. J., Leitzmann, M. F., Gail, M. H., Hollenbeck, A. R., Schatzkin, A., & Sinha, R. (2007). A prospective study of red and processed meat intake in relation to cancer risk. *PLoS Medicine, 4*(12), e325. doi:10.1371/journal.pmed.0040325 PMID:18076279

Cuéllar, A. D., & Webber, M. E. (2010). Wasted food, wasted energy: The embedded energy in food waste in the United States. *Environmental Science & Technology, 44*(16), 6464–6469. doi:10.1021/es100310d PMID:20704248

Cui, C. W., Ji, S. L., & Ren, H. Y. (2006). Determination of steroid estrogens in wastewater treatment plant of a controceptives producing factory. *Environmental Monitoring and Assessment*, *121*(1-3), 409–419. doi:10.1007/s10661-005-9139-8 PMID:16758282

da Silva, F. B., Jelic, A., López-Serna, R., Mozeto, A. A., Petrovic, M., & Barceló, D. (2011). Occurrence and distribution of pharmaceuticals in surface water, suspended solids and sediments of the Ebro river basin, Spain. *Chemosphere*, *85*(8), 1331–1339. doi:10.1016/j.chemosphere.2011.07.051 PMID:21880345

Dagevos, H. (2016). Exploring flexitarianism: Meat reduction in a meat-centred food culture. In T. Raphaely & D. Marinova (Eds.), *Impact of meat consumption on health and environmental sustainability* (pp. 233–243). Hershey, PA: IGI Global. doi:10.4018/978-1-4666-9553-5.ch012

Dagevos, H., & Voordouw, J. (2013). Sustainability and meat consumption: Is reduction realistic? *Sustainability: Science, Practice, and Policy*, *9*, 60–69.

Danzer, M. A., Dietz, B., Gatskova, K., & Schmillen, A. (2014). Showing off to the new neighbors? Income, socioeconomic status and consumption patterns of internal migrants. *Journal of Comparative Economics*, *42*(1), 230–245. doi:10.1016/j.jce.2013.05.002

Danziger, P. N. (2005). *Let them eat cake: Marketing luxury to the masses—as well as the classes*. Chicago, IL: Dearborn Trade Publishing.

Dasgupta, S. (1976). *Obscure religious cults*. Kolkata, India: Firma KLM.

Dauchet, L., Amouyel, P., & Dallongeville, J. (2005). Fruit and vegetable consumption and risk of stroke: A meta-analysis of cohort studies. *Neurology*, *65*(8), 1193–1197. doi:10.1212/01.wnl.0000180600.09719.53 PMID:16247045

Dauchet, L., Amouyel, P., & Dallongeville, J. (2009). Fruits, vegetables and coronary heart disease. *Nature Reviews. Cardiology*, *6*(9), 599–608. doi:10.1038/nrcardio.2009.131 PMID:19652655

Dauchet, L., Amouyel, P., Hercberg, S., & Dallongeville, J. (2006). Fruit and vegetable consumption and risk of coronary heart disease: A meta-analysis of cohort studies. *The Journal of Nutrition*, *136*, 2588–2593. PMID:16988131

Davidson, A. (2014). *Toad in the hole. In The Oxford Companion to Food* (p. 822). Oxford, UK: Oxford University Press.

Davies, J., & Lightowler, H. (1998). Plant-based alternatives to meat. *Nutrition & Food Science*, *98*(2), 90–94. doi:10.1108/00346659810201050

Dawkins, M. (2017). Animal welfare and efficient farming: Is conflict inevitable? *Animal Production Science*, *57*, 201–208.

Dawson, H. C., & Phelan, M. (Eds.). (2016). *Language files material for an instruction to language and linguistics* (12th ed.). Columbus, OH: The Ohio State University.

Day, C. (2015). Smaller Chinese hog herd, opportunity for U.S. National Hog Farmer. Retrieved from http://www.nationalhogfarmer.com/marketing/smaller-chinese-hog-herd-opportunity-us

De Bakker, E., & Dagevos, H. (2012). Reducing meat consumption in today's consumer society: Questioning the citizen-consumer gap. *Journal of Agricultural & Environmental Ethics*, *25*(6), 877–894. doi:10.1007/s10806-011-9345-z

De Boer, J. (2006). Socio-cultural potential. In H. Aiking, J. de Boer, & J. Vereijken (Eds.), *Sustainable protein production and consumption: Pigs or peas?* (pp. 103–110). Dordrecht, the Netherlands: Springer.

De Boer, J., & Aiking, H. (2017). Pursuing a low meat diet to improve both health and sustainability: How can we use the frames that shape our meals? *Ecological Economics*, *142*, 238–248. doi:10.1016/j.ecolecon.2017.06.037

de Boer, J., & Hoek, A. (2006). Social desirability: Consumer aspects. In H. Aiking, J. de Boer, & J. Vereijken (Eds.), *Sustainable protein production and consumption: Pigs or peas?* (pp. 99–127). Dordrecht, Netherlands: Springer. doi:10.1007/1-4020-4842-4_4

de Goede, J., Soedamah-Muthu, S. S., Pan, A., Gijsbers, L., & Geleijnse, J. M. (2016). Dairy consumption and risk of stroke: A systematic review and updated dose-response meta-analysis of prospective cohort studies. *Journal of the American Heart Association*, *5*(5), e002787. doi:10.1161/JAHA.115.002787 PMID:27207960

de Jonge, J., van der Lans, I. A., & van Trijp, H. C. (2015). Different shades of grey: Compromise products to encourage animal friendly consumption. *Food Quality and Preference*, *45*, 87–99. doi:10.1016/j.foodqual.2015.06.001

de Klerk, P. (2009). Was die Groot Trek werklik groot? 'n Historiografiese ondersok na di gevolge en betekenis van die Groot Trek. *Tydskrif vir Geesteswetenskappe*, *49*(4), 658–673.

de Koning, L., Fung, T. T., Liao, X., Chiuve, S. E., Rimm, E. B., Willett, W. C., & Hu, F. B. et al. (2011a). Low-carbohydrate diet scores and risk of type 2 diabetes in men. *The American Journal of Clinical Nutrition*, *93*(4), 844–850. doi:10.3945/ajcn.110.004333 PMID:21310828

de Oliveira Otto, M. C., Alonso, A., Lee, D. H., Delclos, G. L., Bertoni, A. G., Jiang, R., & Nettleton, J. A. et al. (2012a). Dietary intakes of zinc and heme iron from red meat, but not from other sources, are associated with greater risk of metabolic syndrome and cardiovascular disease. *The Journal of Nutrition*, *142*(3), 526–533. doi:10.3945/jn.111.149781 PMID:22259193

De Schutter, O. (2014). Ending hunger - the rich world holds the keys. *The Ecologist*, *25*(March). Retrieved from http://www.theecologist.org/blogs_and_comments/commentators/2333245/ending_hunger_the_rich_world_holds_the_keys.html

de Vries, M., & de Boer, I. J. M. (2010). Comparing environmental impacts for livestock products: A review of life cycle assessments. *Livestock Science*, *128*(1–3), 1–11. doi:10.1016/j.livsci.2009.11.007

Debrah, S., & Berhanu, A. (1991). *Dairy marketing in Ethiopia: Markets of first sale and producers' marketing patterns*. Addis Ababa, Ethiopia: International Livestock Centre for Africa.

Dechert, S. (2016). *1.5 degree climate chances "Not dead yet," but gone within a decade*. Planetsave. Retrieved from http://planetsave.com/2016/09/24/1-5-degree-climate-chances-not-dead-yet-but-gone-within-a-decade

Deci, E. L., & Ryan, R. M. (1985). *Intrinsic motivation and self-determination in human behavior*. New York, NY: Plenum. doi:10.1007/978-1-4899-2271-7

Delahoyde, M., & Despenich, S. C. (1994). Creating meat-eaters: The child as advertising target. *Journal of Popular Culture*, *28*(1), 135–149. doi:10.1111/j.0022-3840.1994.2801_135.x

Delgado, C., Rosegrant, M., Steinfield, H., Ehui, S., & Courbois, C. (1999). *Livestock to 2020: The next food revolution*. Food, Agriculture and the Environment Discussion Paper 28. Washington D.C.: International Food Policy Research Institute (IFPRI), Food Agriculture Organization (FAO) and International Livestock Research Institute (ILRI).

Delgado, C. L. (2003). Rising consumption of meat and milk in developing countries has created a new food revolution. *The Journal of Nutrition*, *133*, 3907S–3910S. PMID:14672289

Demaio, A. R., Nielsen, K. K., Tersbøl, B. P., Kallestrup, P., & Meyrowitsch, D. W. (2014). Primary health care: A strategic framework for the prevention and control of chronic non-communicable disease. *Global Health Action*, *7*(1), 24504. doi:10.3402/gha.v7.24504

Department of Climate Change and Energy Efficiency (DCCEE). (2012a). *Australian national greenhouse accounts national inventory report 2009*. Canberra, Australia: DCCEE. Retrieved from http://www.climatechange.gov.au/~/media/publications/greenhouse-acctg/national-inventory-report-2009-vol1.pdf

Department of Climate Change and Energy Efficiency (DCCEE). (2012b). *National inventory report (NIR) 2010 Australian national greenhouse accounts, The Australian Government: Submission to the United Nations Framework Convention on Climate Change*. Canberra, Australia: DCCEE. Retrieved from http://www.climatechange.gov.au/en/publications/greenhouse-acctg/national-inventory-report-2010.aspx

Department of Health and Human Services/Department of Agriculture (DHHS/USDA). (2015). *Scientific report of the 2015 dietary guidelines advisory committee*. Washington, DC. First print, February. Retrieved from https://ods.od.nih.gov/pubs/2015_DGAC_Scientific_Report.pdf

Despain, D. (2012, December 2). Why you can all stop saying meat eating fueled evolution of larger brains right now. *Evolving Health*. Retrieved from: http://evolvinghealthscience.blogspot.com.au/2012/12/why-you-can-all-stop-saying-meat-eating.html

Deutsche Gesellschaft für Ernährung (DGE). (2017). Der Wissenschaft verpflichtet – Ihr Partner für Essen und Trinken (The science – Your partner for eating and drinking). Retrieved from https://www.dge.de

Devaney, E. (2005). A plan for men's health. *Mid Western Health Board*. Retrieved from http://www.lenus.ie/hse/handle/10147/45737

Dhont, K., Hodson, G., Costello, K., & MacInnis, C. C. (2014). Social dominance orientation connects prejudicial human–human and human–animal relations. *Personality and Individual Differences*, *61-62*, 104–108. doi:10.1016/j.paid.2013.12.020

Di Croce, P., Lymbery, P., Dibb, S., Hameleers, R., Wates, J., & Renshaw, N. … Martin, F. (2016). Letter to the Commissioner for Agriculture and Rural Development, European Commission of 10 November 2016. Retrieved from https://www.foeeurope.org/sites/default/files/agriculture/2016/meat-letter-hogan.pdf

Diaz, R. J., & Rosenberg, R. (2008). Spreading dead zones and consequences for marine ecosystems. *Science*, *321*(5891), 926–929. doi:10.1126/science.1156401 PMID:18703733

Dibb, S., & Fitzpatrick, I. (2014). *Let's talk about meat: Changing dietary behaviour for the 21st century*. Eating Better. Retrieved from http://www.eating-better.org/uploads/Documents/Let'sTalkAboutMeat.pdf?utm_source=FCRN+Mailing&utm_campaign=dc14cb3104-RSS_%2A%7CRSSFEED%3ADATE%3Aj+F+Y%7C%2A&utm_medium=email&utm_term=0_a29d7fdc4d-dc14cb3104-330057737

Dietitians of Canada. (2014). *Healthy eating guidelines for vegans*. Retrieved from http://www.dietitians.ca/Downloads/Factsheets/Guidlines-for-Vegans.aspx

Dietrich, A. (2014). The mythconception of the mad genius. *Frontiers in Psychology*, *5*, 79. doi:10.3389/fpsyg.2014.00079 PMID:24616710

Dietrich, J. (2008). Testing unitary and bargaining models of Chinese household food consumption. *Applied Financial Economics*, *18*(4-6), 397–410. doi:10.1080/09603100500399134

Diliberti, N., Bordi, P. L., Conklin, M. T., Roe, L. S., & Rolls, B. J. (2004). Increased portion size leads to increased energy intake in a restaurant meal. *Obesity Research*, *12*(3), 562–568. doi:10.1038/oby.2004.64 PMID:15044675

Dillard, J. (2008). A slaughterhouse nightmare: Psychological harm suffered by slaughterhouse employees and the possibility of redress through legal reform. *Georgetown Journal on Poverty Law & Policy*, *15*, 391–408.

Dimock, E. C. Jr. (1966). *The place of the hidden moon*. Chicago, IL: The University of Chicago.

Dinç, N.T. (2017, June 3). Personal interview.

Djousse, L., Khawaja, O. A., & Gaziano, J. M. (2016). Egg consumption and risk of type 2 diabetes: A meta-analysis of prospective studies. *The American Journal of Clinical Nutrition*, *103*(2), 474–480. doi:10.3945/ajcn.115.119933 PMID:26739035

Dong, Y., & Wu, G. (2016). Lack of association of poultry and eggs intake with risk of non-Hodgkin lymphoma: A meta-analysis of observational studies. *European Journal of Cancer Care*. doi:10.1111/ecc.12546 PMID:27405484

Donham, K. J., Wing, S., Osterberg, D., Flora, J. L., Hodne, C., Thu, K. M., & Thorne, P. S. (2007). Community health and socioeconomic issues surrounding concentrated animal feeding operations. *Environmental Health Perspectives*, *115*(2), 317–320. doi:10.1289/ehp.8836 PMID:17384786

Donovan, R. J., & Henley, N. (2003). *Social marketing: Principles and practice*. Melbourne, Australia: IP communications.

Donovan, J., & Adams, C. J. (2007). *The feminist care tradition in animal ethics: A reader*. New York, NY: Columbia University Press.

Donovan, R. J., & Henley, N. (2010). *Principles and practice of social marketing: An international perspective*. Cambridge, UK: Cambridge University Press. doi:10.1017/CBO9780511761751

Donovan, R., & Henley, N. (2003). *Social marketing: Principles and practice*. Melbourne, Australia: IP Communications.

Doran-Browne, N. A., Eckard, R. J., Behrendt, R., Ross, S., & Kingwell, R. S. (2015). Nutrient density as a metric for comparing greenhouse gas emissions from food production. *Climatic Change*, *129*(1-2), 73–87. doi:10.1007/s10584-014-1316-8

Dorovskikh, A. (2015. *Killing for a living: Psychological and physiological effects of alienation of food production on slaughterhouse workers* (Honours Thesis). Boulder, CO: University of Colorado.

Douglas, M., & Gross, J. (1981). Food and culture: Measuring the intricacy of rule system. *Social Sciences Information. Information Sur les Sciences Sociales*, *20*(1), 1–35. doi:10.1177/053901848102000101

Drijfhout, S., Bathiany, S., Beaulieu, C., Brovkin, V., Claussen, M., & Huntingford, C. ... Swingedouw, D. (2015). Catalogue of abrupt shifts in Intergovernmental Panel on Climate Change climate models. *Proceedings of the National Academy of Sciences* (pp. E5777–E5786).

Dunayer, J. (2001). *Animal equality: Language and liberation*. Derwood, MD: Ryce Pub.

Dunkley, C. S. (2014). Global warming: How does it relate to poultry? *Caes.uga*. Retrieved from https://secure.caes.uga.edu/extension/publications/files/pdf/B%201382_4.PDF

Dunn, R. (2012). *Human ancestors were nearly all vegetarians*. Retrieved from https://blogs.scientificamerican.com/guest-blog/human-ancestors-were-nearly-all-vegetarians

Duyum, S. (2016). *Turkey: Poultry and poultry products semi-annual*. Global Agricultural Information Network (GAIN) Report TR-6014. Retrieved from https://gain.fas.usda.gov/Recent%20GAIN%20Publications/Poultry%20and%20Poultry%20Products%20Semi-Annual_Ankara_Turkey_3-23-2016.pdf

Earth Policy Institue. (2012). *Livestock and human populations in Nigeria*. Retrieved from http://www.earth-policy.org/datacenter/xls/book_fpep_ch5_17.xlsx

Eboh, L. O., & Boye T. E., (2006). Nutrition knowledge and food choices of primary school pupils in the Niger Delta region, Nigeria. *Pakistan Journal of Nutrition*, *5*(4), 308–311. doi:10.3923/pjn.2006.308.311

Eckard, R. J., Grainger, C., & De Klein, C. A. M. (2010). Options for the abatement of methane and nitrous oxide from ruminant production: A review. *Livestock Science*, *130*(1), 47–56. doi:10.1016/j.livsci.2010.02.010

Eckel, R. H., Jakicic, J. M., Ard, J. D., Hubbard, V. S., de Jesus, J. M., Lee, I-M., … Yanovski, S. Z. (2013). 2013 AHA/ACC guideline on lifestyle management to reduce cardiovascular risk: A report of the American College of Cardiology/American Heart Association Task Force on Practice Guidelines. https://<ALIGNMENT.qj></ALIGNMENT>10.1161/01.cir.0000437740.48606.d1

Elephant Journal. (2011). The world's greatest geniuses are vegetarians! Retrieved from https://www.elephantjournal.com/2011/02/the-worlds-greatest-geniuses-are-vegetarians/

Elferink, E. V., Nonhebel, S., & Moll, H. C. (2008). Feeding livestock food residue and the consequences for the environmental impact of meat. *Journal of Cleaner Production*, *16*(12), 1227–1233. doi:10.1016/j.jclepro.2007.06.008

Elgin, D. (2010). Voluntary simplicity: Toward a way of life that is outwardly simple, inwardly rich (2nd rev. ed.). New York, NY: Harper.

Elias, N. (2006). *O procesu civilizace: Sociogenetické a psychogenetické studie* [On the process of civilization: Sociogenetic and psychogenetic investigations]. Praha, Czech Republic: Argo.

Elliott, G., Rundle-Thiele, S., & Waller, D. (2014). *Marketing* (3rd ed.). Milton, Australia: Wiley.

Ellulu, M. S., Khaza'ai, H., Abed, Y., Rahmat, A., Ismail, P., & Ranneh, Y. (2015). Role of fish oil in human health and possible mechanism to reduce the inflammation. *Inflammopharmacology*, *23*(2-3), 79–89. doi:10.1007/s10787-015-0228-1 PMID:25676565

Elzerman, H. (2006). Substitution of meat by NPFs: Sensory properties and contextual factors. In H. Aiking, J. de Boer, & J. Vereijken (Eds.), *Sustainable protein production and consumption: Pigs or peas?* (pp. 116–123). Dordrecht, Netherlands: Springer.

Elzerman, J. E., Hoek, A. C., van Boekel, M. A. J. S., & Luning, P. A. (2011). Consumer acceptance and appropriateness of meat substitutes in a meal context. *Food Quality and Preference*, *22*(3), 233–240. doi:10.1016/j.foodqual.2010.10.006

Elzerman, J. E., Hoek, A. C., van Boekel, M. J. A. S., & Luning, P. A. (2015). Appropriateness, acceptance and sensory preferences based on visual information: A web-based survey on meat substitutes in a meal context. *Food Quality and Preference*, *42*, 56–65. doi:10.1016/j.foodqual.2015.01.010

Elzerman, J. E., van Boekel, M. A. J. S., & Luning, P. A. (2013). Exploring meat substitutes: Consumer experiences and contextual factors. *British Food Journal*, *115*(5), 700–710. doi:10.1108/00070701311331490

Emborga, H., Ersbøll, A. K., Heuera, O. E., & Wegenera, H. C. (2001). The effect of discontinuing the use of antimicrobial growth promoters on the productivity in the Danish broiler production. *Preventive Veterinary Medicine*, *50*(1-2), 53–70. doi:10.1016/S0167-5877(01)00218-5 PMID:11448495

Emel, J., & Hawkins, R. (2010). Is it really easier to imagine the end of the world than the end of industrial meat? *Human Geographies*, *3*(2), 35–48.

English Oxford Living Dictionaries. (2017). *Definition of genius in English: Genius.* Retrieved from https://en.oxforddictionaries.com/definition/genius

English, O. L. D. (2017). *Dictionary.* Oxford University Press. Retrieved from https://en.oxforddictionaries.com

Enticott, G., & Vanclay, F. (2011). Scripts, animal health and biosecurity: The moral accountability of farmers' talk about animal health risks. *Health Risk & Society*, *13*(4), 293–309. doi:10.1080/13698575.2011.575456

Environment News Service (ENS). (2013). 10 Coastal cities at greatest flood risk as sea levels rise. Retrieved from http://ens-newswire.com/2013/09/03/10-coastal-cities-at-greatest-flood-risk-as-sea-levels-rise

Environmental Protection Agency (EPA). (2016). Inventory of US greenhouse gas emissions and sinks: 1990-2014. Washington, DC: EPA. Retrieved from https://www.epa.gov/sites/production/files/2016-04/documents/us-ghg-inventory-2016-main-text.pdf

Erb, K.-H., Lauk, C., Kastner, T., Mayer, A., Theurl, M. C., & Haberl, H. (2016). Exploring the biophysical option space for feeding the world without deforestation. *Nature Communications*, *7*, 11382. doi:10.1038/ncomms11382 PMID:27092437

Ergin, E. A., & Ozsacmaci, B. (2011). Turkish consumers' perceptions and consumption of organic foods. *African Journal of Business Management*, *5*(3), 910–914.

Ericksen, P. J., Ingram, J. S. I., & Liverman, D. M. (2009). Food security and global environmental change: Emerging challenges. *Environmental Science & Policy*, *12*(4), 373–377. doi:10.1016/j.envsci.2009.04.007

Eshel, G., & Martin, P. A. (2006). Diet, energy, and global warming. *Earth Interactions*, *10*(9), 1–17. doi:10.1175/EI167.1

Eshel, G., Shepon, A., Makov, T., & Milo, R. (2014). Land, irrigation water, greenhouse gas, and reactive nitrogen burdens of meat, eggs, and dairy production in the United States. *Proceedings of the National Academy of Sciences of the United States of America*, *111*(33), 11996–12001. doi:10.1073/pnas.1402183111 PMID:25049416

Etherington, D. J., & Bardsley, R. G. (1995). Enzymes in the meat industry. In G. A. Tucker & L. F. J. Woods (Eds.), *Enzymes in food processing* (pp. 144–189). London, UK: Blackie. doi:10.1007/978-1-4615-2147-1_5

EuroChicago. (2011). *Number of Bulgarians abroad (2011)* [in Bulgarian]. Retrieved from http://www.eurochicago.com/2012/04/v-tchuzhbina/

European Commission. (2010). *Preparatory study on food waste across EU 27*. Retrieved from http://ec.europa.eu/environment/archives/eussd/pdf/bio_foodwaste_report.pdf

European Commission. (2017). *VAT rates applied in the Member States of the European Union*. Retrieved from http://ec.europa.eu/taxation_customs/sites/taxation/files/resources/documents/taxation/vat/how_vat_works/rates/vat_rates_en.pdf

Evans, A. B., & Miele, M. (2012). Between food and flesh: How animals are made to matter (and not matter) within food consumption practices. *Environment and Planning. D, Society & Space*, *30*(2), 298–314. doi:10.1068/d12810

Executive Agency of Fisheries and Aquaculture (EAFA). (2017). *Operational* programmes. Retrieved from http://iara.government.bg/?page_id=15846&lang=en

Facebook. (2015, 6 November). Facebook Accessibility (Facebook message). Retrieved from https://www.facebook.com/accessibility/posts/997008960342829

Falk, D., Lepore, F. E., & Noe, A. (2013). The cerebral cortex of Albert Einstein: A description and preliminary analysis of unpublished photographs. *Brain*, *136*(4), 1304–1327. doi:10.1093/brain/aws295 PMID:23161163

Famodu, A. A., Osilesi, O., Makinde, Y. O., & Osonuga, O. A. (1998). Blood pressure and blood lipid levels among vegetarian, semi-vegetarian, and non-vegetarian native Africans. *Clinical Biochemistry*, *31*(7), 545–549. doi:10.1016/S0009-9120(98)00067-8 PMID:9812174

FAOSTAT. (2003). *Global and regional food consumption patterns and trends*. Retrieved from http://www.fao.org/docrep/005/AC911e/ac911e05.htm

FAOSTAT. (2017). *Food supply – livestock and fish primary equivalent*. Food and Agriculture Organization of the United Nations. Retrieved from http://www.fao.org/faostat/en/#data/CL

FAOSTAT. (2017). *Livestock primary*. Food and Agriculture Organisation of the United Nations. Retrieved from http://www.fao.org/faostat/en/#data/QL

FAOSTAT. (2017). *Livestock primary*. Food and Agriculture Organization of the United Nations. Retrieved from http://www.fao.org/faostat/en/#data/QL

Farm Sanctuary. (2017). *Farm sanctuary*. Retrieved from https://www.farmsanctuary.org/

Farvid, M. S., Cho, E., Chen, W. Y., Eliassen, A. H., & Willett, W. C. (2014a). Adolescent meat intake and breast cancer risk. *International Journal of Cancer*, *136*(8), 1909–1920. doi:10.1002/ijc.29218 PMID:25220168

Farvid, M. S., Cho, E., Chen, W. Y., Eliassen, A. H., & Willett, W. C. (2014b). Dietary protein sources in early adulthood and breast cancer incidence: Prospective cohort study. *BMJ (Clinical Research Ed.)*, *348*, g3437. doi:10.1136/bmj.g3437 PMID:24916719

Fasanmade, O., Odeniyi, I., Fasanmade, O., & Iwuala, S. (2014). Global challenges in health: Effect of westernization on the prevalence of diabetes mellitus in Nigeria. *Research Journal of Health Sciences*, *2*(2), 56–63.

Federal Government of Nigeria. (2012). *Nigeria's path to sustainable development through green economy. Country Report to the Rio+20 Summit*. Retrieved from http://www.ng.undp.org/content/nigeria/en/home/library/environment_energy/RioReport.html

Federal Ministry of Environment of Nigeria. (2001). *National action programme to combat desertification*. Retrieved from http://www.agrhymet.ne/portailCC/images/pdf/PANLCDNIGERIA.pdf

Fellet, M. (2015). A fresh take on fake meat. Can scientists deliver a meatless burger that tastes good and will not harm the planet? *ACS Central Science*, *1*(7), 347–349. doi:10.1021/acscentsci.5b00307 PMID:27162992

Fendley, S. (2015, 3 November). What does the Twitter heart mean? *ClearPivot*. Retrieved from https://www.clearpivot.com/blog/what-does-the-twitter-heart-mean

Ferrucci, L. M., Sinha, R., Ward, M. H., Graubard, B. I., Hollenbeck, A. R., Kilfoy, B. A., & Cross, A. J. et al. (2010). Meat and components of meat and the risk of bladder cancer in the NIH-AARP Diet and Health Study. *Cancer*, *116*(18), 4345–4353. doi:10.1002/cncr.25463 PMID:20681011

Feskens, E. J. M., Sluik, D., & van Woudenbergh, G. J. (2013). Meat consumption, diabetes, and its complications. *Current Diabetes Reports*, *13*(2), 298–306. doi:10.1007/s11892-013-0365-0 PMID:23354681

Fessler, D. M. T., & Navarrete, C. D. (2003). Meat is good to taboo: Dietary proscriptions as a product of the interaction of psychological mechanisms and social processes. *Journal of Cognition and Culture*, *3*(1), 1–40. doi:10.1163/156853703321598563

Festinger, L. (1962). *A theory of cognitive dissonance* (Vol. 2). Stanford, UK: Stanford University Press.

Fick, J., Söderström, H., Lindberg, R. H., Phan, C., Tysklind, M., & Larsson, D. G. J. (2009). Contamination of surface, ground, and drinking water from pharmaceutical production. *Environmental Toxicology and Chemistry*, *28*(12), 2522–2527. doi:10.1897/09-073.1 PMID:19449981

Fiddes, N. (1991). *Meat: A natural symbol*. London, UK: Routledge.

Fiddes, N. (1992). *Meat: A natural symbol (Reprinted)*. London, UK: Routledge.

Fiddes, N. (1994). Social aspects of eating meat. *The Proceedings of the Nutrition Society*, *53*(02), 272–280. doi:10.1079/PNS19940032 PMID:7972141

Field Roast. (2017) FAQ. Retrieved from http://fieldroast.com/faq

Filimonau, V., Lemmer, C., Marshall, D., & Bejjani, G. (2017). 'Nudging' as an architect of more responsible consumer choice in food service provision: The role of restaurant menu design. *Journal of Cleaner Production*, *144*, 161–170. doi:10.1016/j.jclepro.2017.01.010

Financial Times. (2016). *Big business identifies appetite for plant-based milk*. Retrieved from https://www.ft.com/content/7df72c04-491a-11e6-8d68-72e9211e86ab

Fischer, C., & Garnett, T. (2016). *Plates, pyramids and planets*. FAO and FCRN, University of Oxford. Retrieved from http://www.fao.org/3/a-i5640e.pdf

Fishbein, M., & Ajzen, I. (1975). *Belief, attitude, intention, and behavior: An introduction to theory and research*. Reading, MA: Addison-Wesley.

Fisk, G. (1973). Criteria for a theory of responsible consumption. *Journal of Marketing*, *37*(2), 24–31. doi:10.2307/1250047

Flacelière, R. (2002). *Daily life in Greece at the time of Pericles*. London, UK: Phoenix Press.

Flavian, C., Haberberg, A., & Polo, Y. (2002). Food retailing strategies in the European Union. A comparative analysis of the UK and Spain. *Journal of Retailing and Consumer Services*, *9*(3), 125–138. doi:10.1016/S0969-6989(01)00011-X

Florida News Group. (n.d.). *Eminent scientists and inventors on vegetarianism*. Vegetarian Era. Retrieved from http://www.godsdirectcontact.org/eng/news/160/vg5.htm

Florit, L., & Sbardelati, C. (2016). Intensive speciesism regions in Brazil: Ethical and social stains in territories supplying global meat markets. In T. Raphaely & D. Marinova (Eds.), *Impact of meat consumption on health and environmental sustainability* (pp. 277–294). Hershey, PA: IGI Global. doi:10.4018/978-1-4666-9553-5.ch016

Foer, J. S. (2009). *Eating animals*. New York, NY: Little, Brown & Company.

Foley, J. A., Ramankutty, N., Brauman, K. A., Cassidy, E. S., Gerber, J. S., Johnston, M., & Zaks, D. P. M. et al. (2011). Solutions for a cultivated planet. *Nature*, *478*(7369), 337–342. doi:10.1038/nature10452 PMID:21993620

Food and Agriculture Organisation of the United Nations (FAO). (2016). Food outlook: Biannual report on global food markets. Retrieved from http://www.fao.org/3/a-i6198e.pdf

Food and Agriculture Organisation of the United Nations (FAO). (2017). *FAOSTAT*. Retrieved from http://www.fao.org/faostat/en/#data/QA and http://www.fao.org/faostat/en/#data/QL

Food and Agriculture Organisation of the United Nations (FAO). (2017). *Food outlook: Biannual report on global food markets*. Rome, Italy: FAO. Retrieved from http://www.fao.org/3/a-i7343e.pdf

Food and Agriculture Organisation of the United Nations (FAO). (n.d.). FAOSTAT Gateway. Retrieved from http://faostat3.fao.org/faostat-gateway/go/to/home/E

Food and Agriculture Organization of the United Nations (FAO). (2005). Livestock Sector Brief: Nigeria. Retrieved from http://www.fao.org/ag/againfo/resources/en/publications/sector_briefs/lsb_NGA.pdf

Food and Agriculture Organization of the United Nations (FAO). (2006). Livestock's long shadow: Environmental issues and options. Rome, Italy: FAO. Retrieved from http://www.fao.org/docrep/010/a0701e/a0701e00.HTM

Food and Agriculture Organization of the United Nations (FAO). (2011). *Antibiotics in farm animal production: Public health and animal welfare*. Rome, Italy: FAO.

Food and Agriculture Organization of the United Nations (FAO). (2011). *Global food losses and food waste—extent, causes and prevention*. Rome, Italy: FAO.

Food and Agriculture Organization of the United Nations (FAO). (2013). *Food wastage footprint: Impacts on natural resources*. Summary Report. Retrieved from http://www.fao.org/docrep/018/i3347e/i3347e.pdf

Food and Agriculture Organization of the United Nations (FAO). (2014). *Animal Production and Health: Meat Consumption*. Agriculture and Consumer Protection Department. Retrieved from http://www.fao.org/ag/againfo/themes/en/meat/background.html

Food and Agriculture Organization of the United Nations (FAO). (2015). *The state of food insecurity in the world*. Rome, Italy: FAO.

Food and Drug Administration (FDA). (2016). *2015 Summary Report on antimicrobials sold or distributed in for use in food-producing animals*. Department of Health and Human Services. Retrieved from https://www.fda.gov/downloads/ForIndustry/UserFees/AnimalDrugUserFeeActADUFA/UCM534243.pdf

Food Industry Asia (FIA) Communications. (2016). *New Chinese dietary guidelines A reference for industry*. Retrieved from https://foodindustry.asia/new-chinese-dietary-guidelines-a-reference-for-industry

Food Industry Asia (FIA) Communications. (2016). *New Chinese dietary guidelines: A reference for industry*. Retrieved from https://foodindustry.asia/new-chinese-dietary-guidelines-a-reference-for-industry

Forster, P., Ramaswamy, V., Artaxo, P., Berntsen, T., Betts, R., & Fahey, D. W. … Van Dorland, R. (2007). Changes in atmospheric constituents and in radiative forcing. In S. Soloman, D. Qin, M. Manning, M. Marquis, K. Averyt, & M.M.B. Tignor (Eds.), Climate change 2007: The physical science basis. contribution of Working Group I to the Fourth Assessment Report of the Intergovernmental Panel on Climate Change. Cambridge, UK: Cambridge University Press.

Forthofer, M. S., & Bryant, C. A. (2000). Using audience-segmentation techniques to tailor health behavior change strategies. *American Journal of Health Behavior*, *24*(1), 36–43. doi:10.5993/AJHB.24.1.6

Forzieri, G., Feyen, L., Russo, S., Vousdoukas, M., Alfieri, L., Outten, S., & Cid, A. et al. (2016). Multi-hazard assessment in Europe under climate change. *Climatic Change*, *137*(1–2), 105–119. doi:10.1007/s10584-016-1661-x

Fowler, D. (2008). *Ground-level ozone in the 21st century: Future trends, impacts and policy implications. Science Policy Report 15/08*. London, UK: Royal Society. Retrieved from https://royalsociety.org/~/media/Royal_Society_Content/policy/publications/2008/7925.pdf

Fowles, J. (1996). *Advertising and popular culture*. Thousand Oaks, CA: Sage.

Fox, N. J., Davidson, R. S., Marion, G., & Hutchings, M. R. (2015). Modelling livestock parasite risk under climate change. *Advances in Animal Biosciences*, *6*(1), 32–34. doi:10.1017/S204047001400048X

Francione, G. (1996). *Rain without thunder: The ideology of the animal rights movement*. Philadelphia, PA: Temple University Press.

Francione, G. (2000). *Introduction to animal rights: Your child or the dog?* Temple, PA: Temple University Press.

Francione, G. (2004). Animals: Property or persons? In C. Sunstein & M. Nussbaum (Eds.), *Animal rights: Current debates and new directions* (pp. 108–142). New York, NY: Oxford University Press.

Francione, G. (2010). The abolition of animal exploitation. In G. Francione & R. Garner (Eds.), *The animal rights debate: Abolition or regulation?* New York, NY: Columbia University Press.

Francione, G. L. (2004). Animals – property or person. In C. R. Sunstein & M. C. Nussbaum (Eds.), *Animal rights: Current debates and new directions* (pp. 108–142). Oxford, UK: Oxford University Press.

Franklin & Marshall College. (2008). *Franklin's favorite foods*. The Benjamin Franklin Tercentenary. Retrieved from http://www.benfranklin300.org/etc_article_foods.htm

Franklin, A. (1999). *Animals and modern cultures: A sociology of human–animal relations in modernity*. London, UK: Sage.

Franklin, A. (2007). Human-nonhuman animal relationships in Australia: An overview of results from the first national survey and follow-up case studies 2000-2004. *Society & Animals*, *15*(1), 7–27. doi:10.1163/156853007X169315

Fraser, G. E. (2009). Vegetarian diets: What do we know of their effects on common chronic diseases? *The American Journal of Clinical Nutrition*, *89*(5), 1607S–1612S. doi:10.3945/ajcn.2009.26736K PMID:19321569

Fraser, G. E., & Shavlik, D. J. (2001). Ten years of life: Is it a matter of choice? *Archives of Internal Medicine*, *161*(13), 1645–1652. doi:10.1001/archinte.161.13.1645 PMID:11434797

Freedman, M. R., & Brochado, C. (2010). Reducing portion size reduces food intake and plate waste. *Obesity (Silver Spring, Md.)*, *18*(9), 1864–1866. doi:10.1038/oby.2009.480 PMID:20035274

Freeman, C. P. (2013). Stepping up to the veggie plate: Framing veganism as living your values. In E. Plec (Ed.), *Perspectives on human-animal communication: Internatural communication* (pp. 93–112). New York, NY: Taylor and Francis.

Freire, N. A. (2014). When luxury advertising adds the identitary value of luxury: A semiotic analysis. *Journal of Business Research*, *67*(12), 2666–2675. doi:10.1016/j.jbusres.2014.04.004

French, J. (2011). When nudging is not enough. *Journal of Social Marketing*, *1*(2), 154–162. doi:10.1108/20426761111141896

Fresco, L. O. (2016). *Meat necessity and luxury, hamburgers in paradise: The stories behind the food we eat*. Princeton, NJ: Princeton University Press. doi:10.1515/9781400873319

Fresh, H. (2013). Harvey Fresh free-range milk [YouTube video]. Retrieved from https://www.youtube.com/watch?v=QNQK8EWOQko

Fresh, H. (n.d.a). Our story. Retrieved from http://www.harveyfresh.com.au/pages/Our-Story.html

Fresh, H. (n.d.b). Milk and dairy. Retrieved from http://www.harveyfresh.com.au/categories.php?category=Milk-%26-Dairy

Friedman, S. M. (1991). Two decades of the environmental beat. In C. I. LaMay & E. E. Dennis (Eds.), *Media and the environment* (pp. 17–28). Washington, DC: Island Press.

Fry, M. M., Naik, V., West, J. J., Schwarzkopf, M. D., Fiore, A. M., Collins, W. J., & Zeng, G. et al. (2012). The influence of ozone precursor emissions from four world regions on tropospheric composition and radiative climate forcing. *Journal of Geophysical Research*, *117*(D7). doi:10.1029/2011JD017134

Fuchs, D., Di Guilio, A., Glaab, K., Lorek, S., Maniates, M., Princen, T., & Røpke, I. (2016). Power: The missing link in sustainable consumption and absolute reductions research and action. *Journal of Cleaner Production*, *132*, 298–307. doi:10.1016/j.jclepro.2015.02.006

Fung, T. T., Hu, F. B., Hankinson, S. E., Willett, W. C., & Holmes, M. D. (2011). Low-carbohydrate diets, dietary approaches to stop hypertension-style diets, and the risk of postmenopausal breast cancer. *American Journal of Epidemiology*, *174*(6), 652–660. doi:10.1093/aje/kwr148 PMID:21832271

Fung, T. T., van Dam, R. M., Hankinson, S. E., Stampfer, M., Willett, W. C., & Hu, F. B. (2010). Low-carbohydrate diets and all-cause and cause-specific mortality: Two cohort studies. *Annals of Internal Medicine*, *153*(5), 289–298. doi:10.7326/0003-4819-153-5-201009070-00003 PMID:20820038

Fury, A. (2016, January 14). Men's grooming is now a multi-billion pound worldwide industry. *The Independent*. Retrieved from http://www.independent.co.uk/life-style/fashion/features/mens-grooming-is-now-a-multi-billion-pound-worldwide-industry-a6813196.html

Gans, J., King, S., Stonecash, R. E., Byford, M., Libich, J., & Mankiw, N. G. (2013). *Principles of economics* (6th ed.). South Melbourne, Australia: Victoria Cengage Learning.

Gao, L., Hu, J., Zhang, X., Wei, L., Li, S., Miao, Z., & Chai, T. (2015). Application of swine manure on agricultural fields contributes to extended-spectrum β-lactamase-producing Escherichia coli spread in Tai'an, China. *Frontiers in Microbiology*, *6*, 1–7. doi:10.3389/fmicb.2015.00313 PMID:25926828

Gao, M., Sun, K., Guo, M., Gao, H., Liu, K., Yang, C., & Liu, N. et al. (2015). Fish consumption and n-3 polyunsaturated fatty acids, and risk of hepatocellular carcinoma: Systematic review and meta-analysis. *Cancer Causes & Control*, *26*(3), 367–376. doi:10.1007/s10552-014-0512-1 PMID:25534918

Gao, X., Wailes, E., & Cramer, G. (1996). A two-stage rural household demand analysis: Microdata evidence from Jiangsu Province, China. *American Journal of Agricultural Economics*, *78*(3), 604–613. doi:10.2307/1243278

García Molinos, J., Halpern, B. S., Schoeman, D. S., Brown, C. J., Kiessling, W., Moore, P. J., & Burrows, M. T. et al. (2016). Climate velocity and the future global redistribution of marine biodiversity. *Nature Climate Change*, *6*(1), 83–88. doi:10.1038/nclimate2769

Garcia-Fernandez, E., Rico-Cabanas, L., Rosgaard, N., Estruch, R., & Bach-Faig, A. (2014). Mediterranean diet and cardiodiabesity. *Revista de Nutrição*, *6*(9), 3474–3500. PMID:25192027

García-Galán, M. J., Garrido, T., Fraile, J., Ginebreda, A., Díaz-Cruz, M. S., & Barceló, D. (2010). Simultaneous occurrence of nitrates and sulfonamide antibiotics in two ground water bodies of Catalonia (Spain). *Journal of Hydrology (Amsterdam)*, *383*(1–2), 93–101. doi:10.1016/j.jhydrol.2009.06.042

Gardetti, M. A., & Justo, R. (2017). Sustainable luxury fashion: The entrepreneurs' vision. In M. A. Gardetti (Ed.), *Sustainable management of luxury* (pp. 347–360). Singapore: Springer. doi:10.1007/978-981-10-2917-2_16

Garner, R. (2006). Animal welfare: A political defense. *Journal of Animal Law and Ethics*, *1*, 161–174.

Garnett, T. (2014). Changing what we eat: A call for research and action on widespread adoption of sustainable healthy eating. *Food Climate Research Network*. Retrieved from http://www.fcrn.org.uk/sites/default/files/fcrn_wellcome_gfs_changing_consumption_report_final.pdf

Garnett, T. (2009). Livestock-related greenhouse gas emissions: Impacts and options for policy makers. *Environmental Science & Policy*, *12*(4), 491–503. doi:10.1016/j.envsci.2009.01.006

Garnett, T. (2011). Where are the best opportunities for reducing greenhouse gas emissions in the food system (including the food chain)? *Food Policy*, *36*, S23–S32. doi:10.1016/j.foodpol.2010.10.010

Gasser, T., Guivarch, C., Tachiiri, K., Jones, C. D., & Ciais, P. (2015). Negative emissions physically needed to keep global warming below 2 °C. *Nature Communications*, *6*, 7958. doi:10.1038/ncomms8958 PMID:26237242

Gates, B. (2013). *Food is ripe for innovation*. Mashable. Retrieved from http://mashable.com/2013/03/21/bill-gates-future-of-food/#n7CpGZPdiGqi

Gates, B. (2013, March 18). *Future of food.* The Gates Notes. Blog of Bill Gates. Retrieved from https://www.gatesnotes.com/About-Bill-Gates/Future-of-Food

Gathirua-Mwangi, W. G., & Zhang, J. (2014). Dietary factors and risk for advanced prostate cancer. *European Journal of Cancer Prevention, 23*(2), 96–109. doi:10.1097/CEJ.0b013e3283647394 PMID:23872953

Gattario, K. H., Frisén, A., Fuller-Tyszkiewicz, M., Ricciardelli, L. A., Diedrichs, P. C., Yager, Z., & Smolak, L. (2015). How is men's conformity to masculine norms related to their body image? Masculinity and muscularity across Western countries. *Psychology of Men & Masculinity, 16*(3), 337–347. doi:10.1037/a0038494

Gelb, M. J. (2004). *How to think like Leonardo da Vinci: Seven steps to genius every day.* New York, NY: Bantam Dell.

Generational Differences Chart. (n.d.). *West Midland Family Center.* Retrieved from http://www.wmfc.org/uploads/GenerationalDifferencesChart.pdf

Genoways, T. (2015). *Fear in a handful of dust.* New Republic. Retrieved from https://newrepublic.com/article/121558/what-climate-change-doing-texas-cattle-ranch

Gerber, P. J., Steinfeld, H., Henderson, B., Mottet, A., Opio, C., & Dijkman, J. … Tempio, G. (2013). *Tackling climate change through livestock: A global assessment of emissions and mitigation opportunities.* Rome, Italy: FAO. Retrieved from http://www.fao.org/docrep/018/i3437e/i3437e.pdf

Gerber, P. J., Steinfeld, H., Henderson, B., Mottet, A., Opio, C., Dijkman, J., . . . Tempio, G. (2013). Tackling climate change through livestock: A global assessment of emissions and mitigation opportunities. Food and Agriculture Organization of the United Nations (FAO), Rome, Italy.

Germov, J., & Hornosty, J. (2009). Imagining health problems as social issues. In J. Germov (Ed.), *Second opinion: An introduction to health sociology* (pp. 3–24). New York, NY: Oxford University Press.

Gifford, R. (2007). Environmental psychology: Principles and practice. Colville, WA: Optimal books.

Gijsbers, L., Ding, E. L., Malik, V. S., de Goede, J., Geleijnse, J. M., & Soedamah-Muthu, S. S. (2016). Consumption of dairy foods and diabetes incidence: A dose-response meta-analysis of observational studies. *The American Journal of Clinical Nutrition, 103*(4), 1111–1124. doi:10.3945/ajcn.115.123216 PMID:26912494

Giles, G., & Ireland, P. (1997). Diet, nutrition and prostate cancer. *International Journal of Cancer. Supplement, 10*(S10), 13–17. doi:10.1002/(SICI)1097-0215(1997)10+<13::AID-IJC5>3.0.CO;2-C PMID:9209014

Gill, R., Henwood, K., & McLean, C. (2005). Body projects and the regulation of normative masculinity. *Body & Society, 11*(1), 37–62. doi:10.1177/1357034X05049849

Giubilini, A. (2017). Why we should tax meat that contains antibiotics. *The Conversation.* Retrieved from https://theconversation.com/why-we-should-tax-meat-that-contains-antibiotics-75721

Godart, F., & Seong, S. (2014). Is sustainable fashion possible? In M. A. Gardetti & A. L. Torres (Eds.), *Sustainability luxury: Managing social and environmental performance in iconic brands* (pp. 12–27). Sheffield, UK: Greenleaf Publishing. doi:10.9774/GLEAF.9781783530625_3

Godfray, H. C. J., Beddington, J. R., Crute, I. R., Haddad, L., Lawrence, D., Muir, J. F., & Toulmin, C. et al. (2010). Food security: The challenge of feeding 9 billion people. *Science, 327*(5967), 812–818. doi:10.1126/science.1185383 PMID:20110467

Goffman, E. (1959). *The presentation of self in everyday life.* New York, NY: Anchor Books.

Goldberg, M. E. (1995). Social marketing: Are we fiddling while Rome burns? *Journal of Consumer Psychology*, *4*(4), 347–370. doi:10.1207/s15327663jcp0404_03

Gold, M., & Porritt, J. (2004). *The global benefits of eating less meat*. Petersfield, UK: Compassion in World Farming Trust.

Gómez-Pinilla, F. (2008). Brain foods: The effects of nutrients on brain function. *Nature Reviews. Neuroscience*, *9*(7), 568–578. doi:10.1038/nrn2421 PMID:18568016

Gomna, A., & Rana, K. (2007). Inter-household and intra-household patterns of fish and meat consumption in fishing communities in two states in Nigeria. *British Journal of Nutrition*, *97*(1), 145–152. doi:10.1017/S0007114507201734 PMID:17217570

Goodland, R. & Anhang, J. (2009). Livestock and climate change. *Worldwatch Institute Magazine*, November/December, 11-19.

Goodland, R. (2001). The westernization of diets: The assessment of impacts in developing countries. *Global Hunger Alliance*. Retrieved from http://globalhunger.net/GoodlandChina.pdf

Goodland, R. (2012). FAO yields to meat industry pressure on climate change. *New York Times*, 11 July. Retrieved from bittman.blogs.nytimes.com/2012/07/11/fao-yields-to-meat-industry-pressure-on-climate-change/?_r=0

Goodland, R. (2014). How to reverse climate change before it's too late. *Meatanomics*. Retrieved from https://meatonomics.com/2014/09/04/how-to-reverse-climate-change-before-its-too-late

Goodland, R., & Anhang, J. (2009). Livestock and climate change: What if the key actors in climate change are … cows, pigs, and chickens? *World Watch*, November/December. Retrieved from http://www.worldwatch.org/files/pdf/Livestock%20and%20Climate%20Change.pdf

Goodland, R., & Anhang, J. (2009). Livestock and climate change: What if the key actors in climate change are… cows, pigs and chickens? *World Watch Magazine*, November/December, 10-19. Retrieved from http://www.worldwatch.org/files/pdf/Livestock%20and%20Climate%20Change.pdf

Goodland, R. (2013). Lifting livestock's long shadow. *Nature Climate Change*, *3*(1), 2. doi:10.1038/nclimate1755

Goodland, R., & Anhang, J. (2009). Livestock and climate change: What if the key actors in climate change are... cows, pigs and chickens? *World Watch*, (November/December), 11–19. Retrieved from https://www.worldwatch.org/files/pdf/Livestock%20and%20Climate%20Change.pdf

Goodland, R., & Anhang, J. (2009). Livestock and climate change: What if the key actors in climate change are... cows, pigs, and chickens? *World Watch Magazine*, *22*(6), 10–19.

Gough, B. (2007). "Real men don't diet": An analysis of contemporary newspaper representations of men, food and health. *Social Science & Medicine*, *64*(2), 326–337. doi:10.1016/j.socscimed.2006.09.011 PMID:17070972

Gough, B., & Conner, M. T. (2006). Barriers to healthy eating among men: A qualitative analysis. *Social Science & Medicine*, *62*(2), 387–395. doi:10.1016/j.socscimed.2005.05.032 PMID:16011867

Graça, J., Calheiros, M. M., & Oliveira, A. (2015). Attached to meat? (Un)Willingness and intentions to adopt a more plant-based diet. *Appetite*, *95*, 113–125. doi:10.1016/j.appet.2015.06.024 PMID:26148456

Grace Communications Foundation. (2017). *Waste management*. Retrieved from http://www.sustainabletable.org/906/waste-management

Gráda, Ó. C. (2009) Famine: A short history, Princeton, NJ: Princeton University Press.

Graham, T., & Abrahamse, W. (2017). Communicating the climate impacts of meat consumption: The effect of values and message framing. *Global Environmental Change*, *44*, 98–108. doi:10.1016/j.gloenvcha.2017.03.004

Gravert, C., & Kurz, V. (2017). Nudging à la carte: A field experiment on food choice. Working Paper in Economics, No. 690. Gothenburg, Sweden: University of Gothenburg, Department of Economics.

Greenpeace Mediterranean. (2017a). *Biz kimiz?* [Who are we?]. Retrieved from http://www.greenpeace.org/turkey/tr/about/

Greenpeace Mediterranean. (2017b). *Başarılar* [Success stories] Retrieved from http://www.greenpeace.org/turkey/tr/about/history/basarilar/

Greenpeace Mediterranean. (2017c). *Acil cevap bekleniyor* [Urgent reply expected]. Retrieved from https://imza.greenpeace.org/yumurtakapi

Green, R. E., Newton, I. A. N., Shultz, S., Cunningham, A. A., Gilbert, M., Pain, D. J., & Prakash, V. (2004). Diclofenac poisoning as a cause of vulture population declines across the Indian subcontinent. *Journal of Applied Ecology*, *41*(5), 793–800. doi:10.1111/j.0021-8901.2004.00954.x

Greger, M. (2010). Eliminating the #1 cause of death. *NutritionFacts.org*. Retrieved from https://nutritionfacts.org/video/eliminating-the-1-cause-of-death/

Greger, M. (2013). Survival of the firmest: Erectile dysfunction and death. *NutritionFacts.org*. Retrieved from https://nutritionfacts.org/video/survival-of-the-firmest-erectile-dysfunction-and-death/

Grier, S., & Bryant, C. A. (2005). Social marketing in public health. *Annual Review of Public Health*, *26*(1), 319–339. doi:10.1146/annurev.publhealth.26.021304.144610 PMID:15760292

Grivetti, L., & Applegate, E. A. (1997). From Olympia to Atlanta: A cultural-historical perspective on diet and athletic training. *The Journal of Nutrition*, *127*(5), 860S–868S. PMID:9164253

Grunert, G. K., Perrea, T., Zhou, Y. F., Huang, G., Sørensen, B. T., & Krystallis, A. (2011). Is food-related lifestyle (FRL) able to reveal food consumption patterns in non-Western cultural environments? Its adaptation and application in urban China. *Appetite*, *56*(2), 357–367. doi:10.1016/j.appet.2010.12.020 PMID:21192995

Guertin, K. A., Li, X. S., Graubard, B. I., Albanes, D., Weinstein, S. J., Goedert, J. J., & Sinha, R. et al. (2017). Serum trimethylamine n-oxide, carnitine, choline and betaine in relation to colorectal cancer risk in the Alpha Tocopherol and Beta Carotene Study. *Cancer Epidemiology, Biomarkers & Prevention*, *26*(6), 945–952. doi:10.1158/1055-9965.EPI-16-0948 PMID:28077427

Gunduz, O., & Bayramoglu, Z. (2011). Consumer's willingness to pay for organic chicken meat in Samsun province of Turkey. *Journal of Animal and Veterinary Advances*, *10*(3), 334–340. doi:10.3923/javaa.2011.334.340

Guo, X., Raphaely, T., & Marinova, D. (2016). China's growing meat demands: Implications for sustainability. In T. Raphaely & D. Marinova (Eds.), *Impact of meat consumption of health and environmental sustainability* (pp. 221–232). Hershey, PA: IGI Global. doi:10.4018/978-1-4666-9553-5.ch011

Gupta, S. (2016). Brain food: Clever eating. *Nature*, *531*(7592), S12–S13. doi:10.1038/531S12a PMID:26934519

Gustavsson, J., Cederberg, C., Sonesson, U., van Otterdijk, R., & Meybeck, A. (2011). Global food losses and food waste: Extent, causes and prevention. *Food and Agriculture Organization of the United Nations*, *38*. doi:10.1098/rstb.2010.0126

Guyomard, H., Manceron, S., & Peyraud, J.-L. (2013). Trade in feed grains, animals, and animal products: Current trends, future prospects, and main issues. *Animal frontiers*, *3*(1), 14–18. doi:10.2527/af.2013-0003

Hajer, M. A. (1996). Ecological modernisation as cultural politics. In S. Lash, B. Szerszynski, & B. Wynne (Eds.), *Risk, environment and modernity: Towards a new ecology* (pp. 246–268). London, UK: Sage.

Hall, K. D., Guo, J., Dore, M., & Chow, C. C. (2009). The progressive increase of food waste in America and its environmental impact. *PLoS One*, *4*(11), e7940. doi:10.1371/journal.pone.0007940 PMID:19946359

Hallström, E., Carlsson-Kanyama, A., & Börsjesson, P. (2015). Environmental impact of dietary change: A systematic review. *Journal of Cleaner Production*, *91*, 1–11. doi:10.1016/j.jclepro.2014.12.008

Halton, T. L., Liu, S., Manson, J. E., & Hu, F. B. (2008). Low-carbohydrate-diet score and risk of type 2 diabetes in women. *The American Journal of Clinical Nutrition*, *87*(2), 339–346. PMID:18258623

Hamilton, J. (2016, December 7). *Common agricultural policy: Why is the EU pushing meat?* Honey Colony. Retrieved from https://www.honeycolony.com/article/common-agricultural-policy/

Hansen, J., & Gale, F. (2014). China in the next decade: Rising meat demand and growing imports of feed. United States Department of Agriculture. Retrieved from https://www.ers.usda.gov/amber-waves/2014/april/china-in-the-next-decade-rising-meat-demand-and-growing-imports-of-feed/

Hansen, T. H., Gøbel, R. J., Hansen, T., & Pedersen, O. (2015). The gut microbiome in cardio-metabolic health. *Genome Medicine*, *7*(1), 33. doi:10.1186/s13073-015-0157-z PMID:25825594

Haq, M. E. (1975). *A history of Sufi-ism in Bengal*. Dhaka, Bangladesh: Asiatic Book Society of Bangladesh.

Hardy, K., Brand-Miller, J., Brown, K. D., Thomas, M. G., & Copeland, L. (2015). The importance of dietary carbohydrate in human evolution. *The Quarterly Review of Biology*, *90*(3), 251–268. doi:10.1086/682587 PMID:26591850

Haring, B., Gronroos, N., Nettleton, J. A., Wyler von Ballmoos, M. C., Selvin, E., & Alonso, A. (2014). Dietary protein intake and coronary heart disease in a large community based cohort: Results from the Atherosclerosis Risk in Communities (ARIC) Study. *PLoS One*, *9*(10), e109552. doi:10.1371/journal.pone.0109552 PMID:25303709

Harper, G. C., & Makatouni, A. (2002). Consumer perception of organic food production and farm animal welfare. *British Food Journal*, *104*(3), 287–299. doi:10.1108/00070700210425723

Harris, A. P. (1991, 4 August). Fare of the country; delicate pike quenelles, a Lyons Tradition. *The New York Times*. Retrieved from http://www.nytimes.com/1991/08/04/travel/fare-of-the-country-delicate-pike-quenelles-a-lyons-tradition.html

Hartmann, C., & Siegrist, M. (2017). Consumer perception and behaviour regarding sustainable protein consumption: A systematic review. *Trends in Food Science & Technology*, *61*, 11–25. doi:10.1016/j.tifs.2016.12.006

Hartz-Karp, J., & Weymouth, R. (2017). Deliberative democracy – democratic renewal capable of addressing sustainability. In J. Hartz-Karp & D. Marinova (Eds.), *Methods for sustainability research* (pp. 113–128). Cheltenham, UK: Edward Elgar. doi:10.4337/9781786432735.00017

Harvard Medical School. (2016). *Becoming a vegetarian*. Harvard Health Publications. Retrieved from https://www.health.harvard.edu/staying-healthy/becoming-a-vegetarian

Harwatt, H., Sabaté, J., Eshel, G., Soret, S., & Ripple, W. (2017). Substituting beans for beef as a contribution toward US climate change targets. *Climatic Change*. doi:10.1007/s10584-017-1969-1

Hashmi, G. (2017). Redefining the essence of sustainable luxury management: The slow value creation model. In M. A. Gardetti (Ed.), *Sustainable management of luxury: Environmental footprints and eco-design of products and processes* (pp. 4–27). Singapore: Springer Nature. doi:10.1007/978-981-10-2917-2_1

Hastings, G. (2003). Competition in social marketing. *Social Marketing Quarterly*, *9*(3), 6–10. doi:10.1080/15245000309109

Hastings, G., & Saren, M. (2003). The critical contribution of social marketing: Theory and application. *Marketing Theory*, *3*(3), 305–322. doi:10.1177/147059310333005

Havlicek, J., & Lenochova, P. (2006). The effect of meat consumption on body odour attractiveness. *Chemical Senses*, *31*(8), 747–752. doi:10.1093/chemse/bjl017 PMID:16891352

Hawkins, A. (1974). *Tighten your belt: Food prices to soar with world demand. The Afro-American*, 10 August. Retrieved from https://news.google.com/newspapers?nid=2211&dat=19740810&id=uSomAAAAIBAJ&sjid=YP4FAAAAIBAJ&pg=1821,526870&hl=en

Health & Fitness Advisory. (2013). Is red meat bad for your brain? Retrieved from http://www.fitnessadvisory.org/2013/09/04/is-red-meat-bad-for-your-brain/

Health Council of the Netherlands. (2011). *Guidelines for a healthy diet: The ecological perspective*. The Hague, the Netherlands: Health Council of the Netherlands. Retrieved from https://www.gezondheidsraad.nl/sites/default/files/201108E.pdf

Health.gov. (2015). *Public meeting for oral testimony on the Scientific Report of the 2015 Dietary Guidelines Committee*. U.S. Office of Disease Prevention and Health Promotion. Retrieved from https://health.gov/DietaryGuidelines/2015/public-meeting.asp

Hearn, J., Blagojević, M., & Harrison, K. (Eds.). (2013). *Rethinking transnational men: Beyond, between and within nations*. London: Taylor & Francis.

Hedenus, F., Wirsenius, S., & Johansson, D. J. A. (2014). The importance of reduced meat and dairy consumption for meeting stringent climate change targets. *Climatic Change*, *124*(1-2), 79–91. doi:10.1007/s10584-014-1104-5

Heilman, K. M. (2016). Possible brain mechanisms of creativity. *Archives of Clinical Neuropsychology*, *31*(4), 285–296. doi:10.1093/arclin/acw009 PMID:27001974

Heinberg, R. (2017). *The Peak Oil President?* Post Carbon Institute. Retrieved from http://www.postcarbon.org/the-peak-oil-president

Hektoen, H., Berge, J. A., Hormazabal, V., & Yndestad, M. (1995). Persistence of antibacterial agents in marine sediments. *Aquaculutre*, *133*(3-4), 175–184. doi:10.1016/0044-8486(94)00310-K

Henion, K. E., & Kinnear, T. C. (Eds.). (1976). *Ecological marketing*. Chicago, IL: American Marketing Association.

Hennigs, N., Wiedmann, K. P., Klarmann, C., & Behrens, S. (2013b). Sustainability as part of the luxury essence: Delivering value through social and environmental excellence. *Journal of Corporate Citizenship*, *52*(11), 25–35. doi:10.9774/GLEAF.4700.2013.de.00005

Henning, B. G. (2011). Standing in Livestock's' Long Shadow': The ethics of eating meat on a small planet. *Ethics and the Environment*, *16*(2), 63–93. doi:10.2979/ethicsenviro.16.2.63

Hennings, N., Wiedmann, K. P., & Klarmann, C. (2013a). Consumer value perception of luxury goods: A cross cultural and cross industry comparison. In K. P. Wiedmann & N. Hennings (Eds.), *Luxury marketing: A challenge for theory and practice* (pp. 77–100). Gabler, Germany: Springer. doi:10.1007/978-3-8349-4399-6_5

Herculano-Houzel, S. (2012). The remarkable, yet not extraordinary, human brain as a scaled-up primate brain and its associated cost. *Proceedings of the National Academy of Sciences of the United States of America*, *109*(Suppl. 1), 10661–10668. doi:10.1073/pnas.1201895109 PMID:22723358

Herrero, M., Havlík, P., Valin, H., Notenbaert, A., Rufino, M. C., & Thornton, P. K., … Obersteiner, M. (2013). Biomass use, production, feed efficiencies, and greenhouse gas emissions from global livestock systems. *Proceedings of the National Academy of Sciences of the United States of America*, 110, 20888–20893. doi:10.1073/pnas.1308149110

Herrero, M., Henderson, B., Havlík, P., Thornton, P. K., Conant, R. T., Smith, P., & Stehfest, E. et al. (2016). Greenhouse gas mitigation potentials in the livestock sector. *Nature Climate Change*, *6*(5), 452–461. doi:10.1038/nclimate2925

Herships, S. (2016, September 23). *A veggie burger that 'bleeds' might convince some carnivores to eat green*. Public Radio International "The World". Retrieved from https://www.pri.org/stories/2016-09-23/veggie-burger-bleeds-might-convince-some-carnivores-eat-green

Hesser, A. (1999, 19 May). The envelope, please: Cooking en papillote. *The New York Times*. Retrieved from http://www.nytimes.com/1999/05/19/dining/the-envelope-please-cooking-en-papillote.html?mcubz=3

Heuer, H., Schmitt, H., & Smalla, K. (2011). Antibiotic resistance gene spread due to manure application on agricultural fields. *Current Opinion in Microbiology*, *14*(3), 236–243. doi:10.1016/j.mib.2011.04.009 PMID:21546307

Hirshon, B. (2017). *Big heads*. American Association for the Advancement of Science (AAAS). Retrieved from http://sciencenetlinks.com/science-news/science-updates/big-heads/

Hoek, A. C. (2010). *Will novel protein foods beat meat? Consumer acceptance of meat substitutes – a multidisciplinary research approach* [Doctoral thesis]. Wageningen University. Retrieved from http://edepot.wur.nl/15997

Hoek, A. (2006). Substitution of meat by NPFs: Factors in consumer choice. In H. Aiking, J. de Boer, & J. Vereijken (Eds.), *Sustainable protein production and consumption: Pigs or peas?* (pp. 110–116). Dordrecht, Netherlands: Springer.

Hoek, A. C., Elzerman, J. E., Hageman, R., Kok, F. J., Luning, P. A., & Graaf, C. D. (2013). Are meat substitutes liked better over time? A repeated in-home use test with meat substitutes or meat in meals. *Food Quality and Preference*, *28*(1), 253–263. doi:10.1016/j.foodqual.2012.07.002

Hoek, A. C., Luning, P. A., Weijzen, P., Engels, W., Kok, F. J., & de Graaf, C. (2011). Replacement of meat by meat substitutes. A survey on person- and product-related factors in consumer acceptance. *Appetite*, *56*(3), 662–673. doi:10.1016/j.appet.2011.02.001 PMID:21315123

Hoek, A. C., Luning, P. A., Weijzen, P., Engels, W., Kok, F. J., & De Graaf, C. (2011). Replacement of meat by meat substitutes: A survey on person- and product-related factors in consumer acceptance. *Appetite*, *42*, 265–272. doi:10.1016/j.appet.2003.12.003 PMID:21315123

Hoek, A. C., Pearson, D., James, S. W., Lawrence, M. A., & Friel, S. (2017a). Shrinking the food-print: A qualitative study into consumer perceptions, experiences and attitudes towards healthy and environmentally friendly food behaviours. *Appetite*, *108*, 117–131. doi:10.1016/j.appet.2016.09.030 PMID:27686818

Hoek, A. C., Pearson, D., James, S. W., Lawrence, M. A., & Friel, S. (2017b). Healthy and environmentally sustainable food chpoices: Consumer responses to point-of-purchase actions. *Food Quality and Preference*, *58*, 94–106. doi:10.1016/j.foodqual.2016.12.008

Hoek, A. C., van Boekel, M. A., Voordouw, J., & Luning, P. A. (2011). Identification of new food alternatives: How do consumers categorize meat and meat substitutes? *Food Quality and Preference*, *22*(4), 371–383. doi:10.1016/j.foodqual.2011.01.008

Hoekstra, A. Y. (2013). *The water footprint of modern consumer society*. London, UK: Earthscan from Routledge.

Holden, S. J., & Coppock, D. (1992). Effects of distance to market, season, and family wealth on pastoral dairy marketing in Ethiopia. *Journal of Arid Environments*, *23*(3), 321–334.

Holm, L., & Møhl, M. (2000). The role of meat in everyday food culture: An analysis of an interview study in Copenhagen. *Appetite*, *34*(3), 277–283. doi:10.1006/appe.2000.0324 PMID:10888291

Hooks, B. (2000). *Feminist theory: From margins to centre*. London, UK: Pluto Press Humane Society International. (n.d.). *The impact of industrialized animal agriculture on world hunger*. Retrieved from http://www.fao.org/fileadmin/user_upload/animalwelfare/HSI--The%20Impact%20of%20Industrialized%20Animal%20Agriculture%20on%20World%20Hunger.pdf

Hopwood, B., Mellor, M., & O'Brien, G. (2005). Sustainable development: Mapping different approaches. *Sustainable Development*, *13*(1), 38–52. doi:10.1002/sd.244

Hormes, J. M., Rozin, P., Green, M. C., & Fincher, K. (2013). Reading a book can change your mind, but only some changes last for a year: Food attitude changes in readers of The Omnivore's Dilemma. *Frontiers in Psychology*, *4*, 778. doi:10.3389/fpsyg.2013.00778 PMID:24198795

Hosie, R. (2016). Flexitarianism predicted as key food trend for 2017. *The Independent*, 9 December. Retrieved from http://www.independent.co.uk/life-style/food-and-drink/flexitarianism-predicted-as-key-food-trend-for-2017-vegetarian-less-meat-a7465156.html

Hossain, A. (1995). *Mazar culture in Bangladesh* [PhD thesis]. Perth, Australia: Murdoch University.

Hossain, A. (2016). Sustainable food consumption: A mission almost impossible because of the West. In T. Raphaely & D. Marinova (Eds.), *Impact of meat consumption on health and environmental sustainability* (pp. 255–263). Hershey, PA: IGI Global. doi:10.4018/978-1-4666-9553-5.ch014

Howarth, R. W. (2014). A bridge to nowhere: Methane emissions and the greenhouse gas footprint of natural gas. *Energy Science & Engineering*, *2*(2), 47–60. doi:10.1002/ese3.35

Huang, R.-X., Duan, Y.-Y., & Hu, J.-A. (2015). Fish intake and risk of liver cancer: A meta-analysis. *PLoS One*, *10*(1), e0096102. doi:10.1371/journal.pone.0096102 PMID:25615823

Huggler, J. (2017). Discord in Angela Merkel's government after environment ministry bans meat at official functions. *The Telegraph*, 21 February. Retrieved from http://www.telegraph.co.uk/news/2017/02/21/discord-angela-merkels-government-environment-ministry-bans/

Hughes, L., Rickards, L. A., Steffen, W., Stock, P., & Rice, M. (2016). *On the frontline: Climate change & rural communities*. Sydney, Australia: Climate Council of Australia. Retrieved from https://www.climatecouncil.org.au/uploads/564abfd96ebac5cbc6cf45de2f17e12d.pdf

Hugo, V. (2005). Histoire d'un crime [History of a crime]. Paris, France: Mondial (originally published 1879)

Humane Society International & the World Society for the Protection of Animals. (2009). Better quality, safer food: Animal welfare in meat production. Retrieved from http://media.animalsmatter.org/resources/casestudies/en/CaseStudy-HSI-Animal-Ag.pdf

Husic, M., & Cicic, M. (2009). Luxury consumption factors. *Journal of Fashion Marketing and Management*, *13*(2), 231–245. doi:10.1108/13612020910957734

Hwang, T.-C. (1993). Meat expenditure pattern, forecast, and impact from liberalisation in Taiwan. *Journal of Agricultural Economics*, *54*(December), 117–164.

Ibrahim, F. M. (2010). Coping appraisal and affinity towards vegetarianism among a group of civil servants of Oyo state, Nigeria. *Journal of Medicine and Medical Sciences*, *1*(7), 273–279.

Idogun, E., Famodu, A., Olasunkanmi, L., Osilesi, O., & Adebawo, O. (2008). Effects of fruits and vegetables on electolytes and blood pressure of hypertensive patients seen in Nigeria. *African Journal of Food, Agriculture, Nutrition and Development*, *8*(3), 349–357. doi:10.4314/ajfand.v8i3.19197

Intergovernmental Panel on Climate Change (IPCC). (2014). Climate change 2014: Synthesis report. Fifth Assessment Report. Retrieved from http://www.ipcc.ch/report/ar5/syr/

International Livestock Research Institute (ILRI). (2011). Livestock and climate change. Retrieved from https://www.ilri.org/node/6432

Ireland, C. (2008). Eating meat led to smaller stomachs, bigger brains. *Harvard Gazette*, 3 April. Retrieved from http://news.harvard.edu/gazette/story/2008/04/eating-meat-led-to-smaller-stomachs-bigger-brains/

Islam, M. (1985). *Folklore, pulse of the people: in the context of Indic folklore*. New Delhi, India: Naurang Rai Concept Publishing Company.

Iwamoto, D. K., & Smiler, A. P. (2013). Alcohol makes you macho and helps you make friends: The role of masculine norms and peer pressure in adolescent boys' and girls' alcohol use. *Substance Use & Misuse*, *48*(5), 371–378. doi:10.3109/10826084.2013.765479 PMID:23421386

Izmirli, S., & Phillips, C. J. C. (2011). The relationship between student consumption of animal products and attitudes to animals in Europe and Asia. *British Food Journal*, *113*(3), 436–450. doi:10.1108/00070701111116482

Jabbar, M., Ehui, S., & Fitzhugh, H. (1995). The contribution of livestock to food security and sustainable development. Livestock development strategies for low income countries. *Proceedings of the Joint FAO/ILRI Roundtable on Livestock Development Strategies for Low Income Countries, ILRI, Addis Ababa, Ethiopia, 27*. Retrieved from http://ageconsearch.umn.edu/bitstream/182946/2/1995-Livestck%20and%20food%20security-Keynote%20paper-FAO%20Proc.pdf

Jafari, T., Fallah, A. A., & Azadbakht, L. (2013). Role of dietary n-3 polyunsaturated fatty acids in type 2 diabetes: A review of epidemiological and clinical studies. *Maturitas*, *74*(4), 303–308. doi:10.1016/j.maturitas.2013.01.008 PMID:23384976

Jalil, A. (1993). *Diverse aspects of folk literature (in Bangla)*. Dhaka, Bangladesh: Bangla Academy.

James, A. (2014). China arrests five over tainted meat. *Evening Standard*, July 23, Retrieved from http://web.a.ebscohost.com/ehost/detail/detail?vid=3&sid=fdad63be-967a-477a-b9a6-750d49b294ba%40sessionmgr4001&hid=4112&bdata=Jmxhbmc9emgtY24mc2l0ZT1laG9zdC1saXZl#db=nfh&AN=97167012

James, H. S. Jr, & Marks, L. A. (2008). Trust and distrust in biotechnology risks managers: Insights from the United Kingdom, 1996–2002. *AgBioForum*, *11*(2), 93–105.

Janks, H. (1997). Critical discourse analysis as a research tool. *Discourse (Abingdon)*, *18*(3), 329–342. doi:10.1080/0159630970180302

Jaslow, R. (2012, August 22). Survey: "Digital peer pressure" fuelling drug, alcohol use in high school students. *SBS News*. Retrieved from http://www.cbsnews.com/news/survey-digital-peer-pressure-fueling-drug-alcohol-use-in-high-school-students/

Jauk, E., Neubauer, A. C., Dunst, B., Fink, A., & Benedek, M. (2015). Gray matter correlates of creative potential: A latent variable voxel-based morphometry study. *NeuroImage*, *1*(111), 312–320. doi:10.1016/j.neuroimage.2015.02.002 PMID:25676914

JBPV's Blog. (2009). *Folklores – the heart of Bangladeshi culture and heritage (Part One)*. Retrieved from https://jbpv.wordpress.com/2009/10/17/folklores-the-heart-of-bangladeshi-culture-and-heritage/

Jechalke, S., Heuer, H., Siemens, J., Amelung, W., & Smalla, K. (2014). Fate and effects of veterinary antibiotics in soil. *Trends in Microbiology*, *22*(9), 536–545. doi:10.1016/j.tim.2014.05.005 PMID:24950802

Jevrejeva, S., Jackson, L. P., Riva, R. E. M., Grinsted, A., & Moore, J. C. (2016). Coastal sea level rise with warming above 2°C. In *Proceedings of the National Academy of Sciences of the United States of America*, *113*(47), 13342–13347. doi:10.1073/pnas.1605312113 PMID:27821743

Jiang, G., Li, B., Liao, X., & Zhong, C. (2016). Poultry and fish intake and risk of esophageal cancer: A meta-analysis of observational studies. *Asia Pacific Journal of Clinical Oncology*, *12*(1), e82–e91. doi:10.1111/ajco.12114 PMID:23910094

Jiang, P., Jiang, Z., Shen, K., & Yue, Y. (2014). Fish intake and ovarian cancer risk: A meta-analysis of 15 case-control and cohort studies. *PLoS One*, *9*(4), e94601. doi:10.1371/journal.pone.0094601 PMID:24732053

John Hopkins Center for a Livable Future. (2015). Industrial food animal production in America: Examining the Impact of the Pew Commission's priority recommendations. Retrieved from https://www.jhsph.edu/research/centers-and-institutes/johns-hopkins-center-for-a-livable-future/_pdf/research/clf_reports/CLF-PEW-for%20Web.pdf

Johnson, E. J., Shu, S. B., Dellaert, B. G. C., Fox, C., Goldstein, D. G., Häubl, D. G., & Weber, E. U. et al. (2012). Beyond nudges: Tools of a choice architecture. *Marketing Letters*, *23*(2), 487–504. doi:10.1007/s11002-012-9186-1

Jonge, J. D., Trijp, H. V., Goddard, E., & Frewer, J. (2008). Consumer confidence in the safety of food in Canada and the Netherlands: The validation of a generic framework. *Food Quality and Preference*, *19*(5), 439–451. doi:10.1016/j.foodqual.2008.01.002

Joyce, C. (2010). Food for thought: Meat-based diet made us smarter (Special series: The human edge). *NPR*. Retrieved from http://www.npr.org/2010/08/02/128849908/food-for-thought-meat-based-diet-made-us-smarter

Joyce, A., Hallett, J., Hannelly, T., & Carey, G. (2014). The impact of nutritional choices on global warming and policy implications: Examining the link between dietary choices and greenhouse gas emissions. *Energy and Emission Control Technologies*, *2*, 33–43. doi:10.2147/EECT.S58518

Joy, M. (2011). *Why we love dogs, eat pigs, and wear cows: An introduction to carnism*. Berkley, CA: Conari press.

Kabir, J., Umoh, V., Audu-Okoh, E., Umoh, J., & Kwaga, J. (2004). Veterinary drug use in poultry farms and determination of antimicrobial drug residues in commercial eggs and slaughtered chicken in Kaduna State, Nigeria. *Food Control*, *15*(2), 99–105. doi:10.1016/S0956-7135(03)00020-3

Kahleova, H., Matoulek, M., Malinska, H., Oliyarnik, O., Kazdova, L., Neskudla, T., & Pelikanova, T. et al. (2011). Vegetarian diet improves insulin resistance and oxidative stress markers more than conventional diet in subjects with Type 2 diabetes. *Diabetic Medicine*, *28*(5), 549–559. doi:10.1111/j.1464-5491.2010.03209.x PMID:21480966

Kahn, J. S. (2011). Feminist therapy for men: Challenging assumptions and moving forward. *Women & Therapy*, *34*(1-2), 59–76. doi:10.1080/02703149.2011.532458

Kalof, L., Dietz, T., Stern, P. C., & Guagnano, G. A. (1999). Social psychological and structural influences on vegetarian beliefs. *Rural Sociology*, *64*(3), 500–511. doi:10.1111/j.1549-0831.1999.tb00364.x

Kaluza, J., Wolk, A., & Larsson, S. C. (2012). Red meat consumption and risk of stroke: A meta-analysis of prospective studies. *Stroke*, *43*(10), 2556–2560. doi:10.1161/STROKEAHA.112.663286 PMID:22851546

Kamila, A. Y. (2011). Natural foodie: Sebago Brewing Co. launches Meatless Monday menu. *Portland Press Herald*. Retrieved from http://www.pressherald.com/2011/06/29/sebago-brewing-co_-launches-meatless-monday-menu_2011-06-29

Kandala, N.-B., & Stranges, S. (2014). Geographic variation of overweight and obesity among women in Nigeria: A case for nutritional transition in Sub-Saharan Africa. *PLoS One*, *9*(6), e101103. doi:10.1371/journal.pone.0101103 PMID:24979753

Kang, D. H., Gupta, S., Rosen, C., Fritz, V., Singh, A., Chander, Y., & Rohwer, C. et al. (2013). Antibiotic uptake by vegetable crops from manure-applied soils. *Journal of Agricultural and Food Chemistry*, *61*(42), 9992–10001. doi:10.1021/jf404045m PMID:24106840

Kang, J., Jun, J., & Arendt, S. W. (2015). Understanding customers' healthy food choices at casual dining restaurants: Using the value–attitude–behavior model. *International Journal of Hospitality Management*, *48*, 12–21. doi:10.1016/j.ijhm.2015.04.005

Kapferer, J. N. (1997). *Strategic brand management: Creating and sustaining brand equity long term* (2nd ed.). London, UK: Kogan Page.

Kapferer, J. N., & Bastien, V. (2009). The specificity of luxury management: Turning marketing upside down. *Journal of Brand Management*, *16*(5/6), 311–322. doi:10.1057/bm.2008.51

Kapferer, J. N., & Bastien, V. (2010). *The luxury strategy: Break the rules of marketing to build luxury brands*. London, UK: Kogan Page.

Kardash, W. J. (1976). Corporate responsibility and the quality of life: Developing the ecologically concerned consumer. In K. E. Henion, & T.C. (Eds), Ecological marketing (pp. 5-9). Chicago, IL: American Marketing Association.

Karim, A. (1980). *The Bauls of Bangladesh*. Kushtia, Bangladesh: Lalon Academy.

Karvelas, P. (2012, December 26). Peer pressure key to drug use. *The Australian*. Retrieved from http://www.theaustralian.com.au/news/health-science/peer-pressure-key-to-drug-use/news-story/8bf6a201c01e365c31c5b8dc8ea0c8a7

Kateman, B. (Ed.). (2017). *The reducetarian solution: How the surprisingly simple act of reducing the amount of meat in your diet can transform your health and the planet*. New York, NY: TarcherPerigee.

Katz, D. L., & Meller, S. (2014). Can we say what diet is best for health? *Annual Review of Public Health*, *35*(1), 83–103. doi:10.1146/annurev-publhealth-032013-182351 PMID:24641555

Kaye, L. (2014). Should we view meat as a luxury? *Triplepundit*. Retrieved from http://www.triplepundit.com/2014/10/meat-as-a-luxury/

Kaye, L. (2014, 29 October) Should we view meat as a luxury? Triple Pundit: People, Planet, Profit. Retrieved from http://www.triplepundit.com/2014/10/meat-as-a-luxury/

Kearney, J. (2010). Food consumption trends and drivers. *Philosophical Transactions of the Royal Society of London. Series B, Biological Sciences*, *365*(1554), 2793–2807. doi:10.1098/rstb.2010.0149 PMID:20713385

Kelischek, N. (2011). Energy budget of nitrogen use in the United States. *Journal of Student Research in Environmental Science at Appalachian*, *1*(1), 32–35. Retrieved from http://pimlico.phys.appstate.edu/JSRESA/kelischek.1-1.pdf

Kelly, B., Bochynska, K., Kornman, K., & Chapman, K. (2008). Internet food marketing on popular children's websites and food product websites in Australia. *Public Health Nutrition*, *11*(11), 1180–1187. doi:10.1017/S1368980008001778 PMID:18298882

Kemp, S. (2016). *Digital in 2016*. Retrieved from https://www.slideshare.net/wearesocialsg/digital-in-2016

Kent, G. (1987). *Fish, food, and hunger. The potential of fisheries for alleviating malnutrition*. Boulder, CO: Westview Press.

Kéri, S. (2009). Genes for psychosis and creativity: A promoter polymorphism of the neuregulin 1 gene is related to creativity in people with high intellectual achievement. *Psychological Science*, *20*(9), 1070–1073. doi:10.1111/j.1467-9280.2009.02398.x PMID:19594860

Ketiku, A. O., Akinola, O. O., & Akinnawo, O. O. (2009). *Nutritional status and plasma lipid profile of vegetarian and non-vegetarian female adolescents at Ile-Ife, Nigeria.* Paper presented at the Annals of Nutrition and Metabolism. Retrieved from https://www.karger.com/Article/Pdf/248288

Keum, N., Lee, D. H., Marchand, N., Oh, H., Liu, H., Aune, D., & Giovannucci, E. L. et al. (2015). Egg intake and cancers of the breast, ovary and prostate: A dose–response meta-analysis of prospective observational studies. *British Journal of Nutrition*, *114*(7), 1099–1107. doi:10.1017/S0007114515002135 PMID:26293984

Keyman, F. (2006). *Türkiye'de sivil toplumun serüveni: İmkânsızlıklar içinde bir vaha* [Adventure of civil society in Turkey? An oasis in impossibility]. Ankara, Turkey: Sivil Toplum Geliştirme Merkezi Yayınları.

Keyzer, M. A., Merbis, M. D., Pavel, I. F. P. W., & van Wesenbeeck, C. F. A. (2005). Diet shifts towards meat and the effects on cereal use: Can we feed the animals in 2030. *Ecological Economics*, *55*(2), 187–202. doi:10.1016/j.ecolecon.2004.12.002

Khan, M., Hossain, A., & Marinova, D. (2015). Traditional sustainability accounting principles in Bangladesh. *World Journal of Social Sciences*, *5*, 201–210.

Khan, S., & Hanjra, M. A. (2009). Footprints of water and energy inputs in food production – global perspectives. *Food Policy*, *34*(2), 130–140. doi:10.1016/j.foodpol.2008.09.001

Kim, A. E., Lundgreen, A., Wolff, R. K., Fejerman, L., John, E. M., Torres-Mejía, G., & Stern, M. C. et al. (2016). Red meat, poultry, and fish intake and breast cancer risk among Hispanic and Non-Hispanic white women: The Breast Cancer Health Disparities Study. *Cancer Causes & Control*, *27*(4), 527–543. doi:10.1007/s10552-016-0727-4 PMID:26898200

Kim, E., Coelho, D., & Blachier, F. (2013). Review of the association between meat consumption and risk of colorectal cancer. *Nutrition Research (New York, N.Y.)*, *33*(12), 983–994. doi:10.1016/j.nutres.2013.07.018 PMID:24267037

King, L. (2009, December 30). *Peer pressure is what made me use drugs and alcohol.* Drugfree.org. Retrieved from https://drugfree.org/parent-blog/peer-pressure-is-what-made-me-use-drugs-and-alcohol/

King, A. D., Karoly, D. J., & Henley, B. J. (2017). Australian climate extremes at 1.5°C and 2°C of global warming. *Nature Climate Change*, *7*(6), 412–416. doi:10.1038/nclimate3296

Kirschke, S., Bousquet, P., Ciais, P., Saunois, M., Canadell, J. G., Dlugokencky, E. J., & Zeng, G. et al. (2013). Three decades of global methane sources and sinks. *Nature Geoscience*, *6*(10), 813–823. doi:10.1038/ngeo1955

Kleine, S. S., & Hubbert, A. R. (1993). How do consumers acquire a new food consumption system when it is vegetarian? In L. McAlister & M. L. Rothschild (Eds.), *Advances in consumer research* (Vol. 20, pp. 196–201). Provo, UT: Association for Consumer Research.

Kline, C., Murray, A., & Lancaster, E. (2012). Animal welfare approved – 2011 animal products survey results. East Carolina University. Retrieved from https://faunalytics.org/feature-article/animal-welfare-approved-2011-animal-products-survey-results/

Klöckner, C. A. (2013). A comprehensive model of the psychology of environmental behavior—A meta-analysis. *Global Environmental Change*, *23*(5), 1028–1038. doi:10.1016/j.gloenvcha.2013.05.014

Kluger, J. (2016). Sorry vegans: Here's how meat-eating made us human. *Time*. Retrieved from http://time.com/4252373/meat-eating-veganism-evolution/

Knight, E. L., Stampfer, M. J., Hankinson, S. E., Spiegelman, D., & Curhan, G. C. (2003). The impact of protein intake on renal function decline in women with normal renal function or mild renal insufficiency. *Annals of Internal Medicine, 138*(6), 460–467. doi:10.7326/0003-4819-138-6-200303180-00009 PMID:12639078

Knutti, R., Rogelj, J., Sedláček, J., & Fischer, E. M. (2016). A scientific critique of the two-degree climate change target. *Nature Geoscience, 9*(1), 13–18. doi:10.1038/ngeo2595

Koca, A. (2013). Türkiye'deki Twitter kullanıcılarının sayısı 9.6 milyona ulaştı [Twitter users in Turkey reached 9.6 million]. Retrieved from http://webrazzi.com/2013/02/12/twitter-turkiye-istatistikleri-2013/

Koger, S. M., & Winter, D. D. (2011). The psychology of environmental problems: Psychology for sustainability (3rd ed.). New York, NY: Psychology Press.

Kohák, E. (2000). *Zelená svatozář: Kapitoly z ekologické etiky* (Green halo: Chapters in ecological ethics]. Praha, Check Republic: Slon.

Kopp, R.E., Shwom, R.L., Wagner, G., & Yuan, J. (2016). Tipping elements and climate–economic shocks: Pathways toward integrated assessment. *Earth's Future*, 4(8). doi:10.1002/2016EF000362

Korn, C. (2014, October 16). How gut bacteria ensure a healthy brain – and could play a role in treating depression. *The Conversation.* Retrieved from https://theconversation.com/how-gut-bacteria-ensure-a-healthy-brain-and-could-play-a-role-in-treating-depression-33041

Kotler, P. (1972). A generic concept of marketing. *Journal of Marketing, 36*(2), 46–54. doi:10.2307/1250977

Kotler, P., & Lee, N. (2008). *Social marketing: Influencing behaviors for good* (4th ed.). Thousand Oaks, CA: Sage.

Kotler, P., & Lee, N. (2008). *Social marketing: Influencing behaviours for good* (3rd ed.). Thousand Oaks, CA: Sage.

Kotler, P., & Roberto, N. (1989). *Social marketing. Strategies for changing public behavior.* New York, NY: Free Press.

Kotler, P., Roberto, N., & Lee, N. (2002). *Social marketing: Improving the quality of life.* Thousand Oaks, CA: Sage Publications.

Kotler, P., & Zaltman, G. (1971). Social marketing: An approach to planned social change. *Journal of Marketing, 35*(3), 3–12. doi:10.2307/1249783 PMID:12276120

Kozinets, R. V. (2015). *Netnography: Redefined.* London, UK: Sage. doi:10.1002/9781118767771.wbiedcs067

Kramer, S. (2013). $53 trillion of clean energy needed to meet global 2C target. Earthtechling. Retrieved from http://earthtechling.com/2015/11/53-trillion-of-clean-energy-needed-to-meet-global-2c-target

Kristiansson, E., Fick, J., Janzon, A., Grabic, R., Rutgersson, C., Weijdegard, B., & Larsson, D. G. et al. (2011). Pyrosequencing of antibiotic-contaminated river sediments reveals high levels of resistance and gene transfer elements. *PLoS One, 6*(2), e17038. doi:10.1371/journal.pone.0017038 PMID:21359229

Kromhout, D., & de Goede, J. (2014). Update on cardiometabolic health effects of ω-3 fatty acids. *Current Opinion in Lipidology, 25*(1), 85–90. doi:10.1097/MOL.0000000000000041 PMID:24345990

Kubberød, E., Ueland, O., Rodbotten, M., Westad, F., & Risvik, E. (2002). Gender specific preferences and attitudes towards meat. *Food Quality and Preference, 13*(5), 285–294. doi:10.1016/S0950-3293(02)00041-1

Kumar, K., Gupta, C. S., Chander, Y., & Singh, A. K. (2005). Antibiotic use in agriculture and its impact on the terrestrial environment. *Advances in Agronomy, 87*, 1–54. doi:10.1016/S0065-2113(05)87001-4

Kummu, M., de Moel, H., Porkka, M., Siebert, S., Varis, O., & Ward, P. J. (2012). Lost food, wasted resources: Global food supply chain losses and their impacts on freshwater, cropland, and fertiliser use. *The Science of the Total Environment, 438*, 477–489. doi:10.1016/j.scitotenv.2012.08.092 PMID:23032564

Lactalis. (n.d.). The Latcalis Group. Retrieved from http://www.lactalis-international.com/en/the-lactalis-group.html

Lahelma, E., Pietinen, P., Roos, E., & Virtanen, M. (1998). Gender, socioeconomic status and family status as determinants of food behaviour. *Social Science & Medicine, 46*(12), 1519–1529. doi:10.1016/S0277-9536(98)00032-X PMID:9672392

Lal, R., & Couper, D. C. (1990). Soil microvariability. In *Soils of the humid tropics* (pp. 45–49). Washington, DC: US National Research Council, National Academy of Sciences.

Lane, A. (2014). *A taxing approach to choice: How behavioural taxes deliver perverse outcomes*. Institute of Public Affairs. Retrieved from https://ipa.org.au/portal/uploads/IPA_Paper-A_taxing_approach_to_choice-Feb_2014.pdf

LaPiere, R. T. (1934). Attitude versus action. *Social Forces, 13*(2), 230–237. doi:10.2307/2570339

Lappé, F. M., & Collins, J. (2015). *World hunger: Ten myths*. New York, NY: Grove Press.

Larsson, D. G., de Pedro, C., & Paxeus, N. (2007). Effluent from drug manufactures contains extremely high levels of pharmaceuticals. *Journal of Hazardous Materials, 148*(3), 751–755. doi:10.1016/j.jhazmat.2007.07.008 PMID:17706342

Larsson, S. C., & Orsini, N. (2014). Red meat and processed meat consumption and all-cause mortality: A meta-analysis. *American Journal of Epidemiology, 179*(3), 282–289. doi:10.1093/aje/kwt261 PMID:24148709

Larsson, S., Crippa, A., Orsini, N., Wolk, A., & Michaëlsson, K. (2015). Milk consumption and mortality from all causes, cardiovascular disease, and cancer: A systematic review and meta-analysis. *Nutrients, 7*(9), 7749–7763. doi:10.3390/nu7095363 PMID:26378576

Lauterborn, B. (1990). New marketing litany: Four Ps passé: C-words take over. *Advertising Age, 61*(4), 26.

Laxminarayan, R., Van Boeckel, T., & Teillant, A. (2015). *The economic costs of withdrawing antimicrobial growth promoters from the livestock sector* (Vol. 78). Paris, France: OECD Publishing. doi:10.1787/18156797

Lean, G. (2014). Sir Paul McCartney: Why I have a beef with meat-eating. *Telegraph*. Retrieved from http://www.telegraph.co.uk/news/earth/environment/globalwarming/11231472/Sir-Paul-McCartney-why-I-have-a-beef-with-meat-eating.html

Lee, A. (2014, 28 August) The battle to feed Tommy: New exhibition looks at the diet of a WW1 soldier. *Express*. Retrieved from http://www.express.co.uk/news/world-war-1/502452/The-Battle-to-feed-Tommy-The-diet-of-a-WW1-soldier

Lee, Y. Y., & Derakhshan, M. H. (2013). Environmental and lifestyle risk factors of gastric cancer. *Archives of Iranian Medicine, 16*(6), 358–365. PMID:23725070

Lefebvre, R. C., & Flora, J. A. (1988). Social marketing and public health intervention. *Health Education Quarterly, 15*(3), 299–315. doi:10.1177/109019818801500305 PMID:3056876

Lehner, M., Mont, O., & Heiskanen, E. (2016). Nudging – a promising tool for sustainable consumption behaviour? *Journal of Cleaner Production, 134*, 166–177. doi:10.1016/j.jclepro.2015.11.086

Le, L. T., & Sabaté, J. (2014). Beyond meatless, the health effects of vegan diets: Findings from the Adventist cohorts. *Nutrients, 6*(6), 2131–2147. doi:10.3390/nu6062131 PMID:24871675

Leneman, L. (1999). No animal food: The road to veganism in Britain, 1909-1944. *Society & Animals, 7*(3), 219–228. doi:10.1163/156853099X00095

Lenton, T. M., Held, H., Kriegler, E., Hall, J. W., Lucht, W., Rahmstorf, S., & Schellnhuber, H. J. (2008). Tipping elements in the Earth's climate system. *Proceedings of the National Academy of Sciences of the United States of America*, *105*(6), 1786–1793. doi:10.1073/pnas.0705414105 PMID:18258748

Leroy, F., & Praet, I. (2015). Meat traditions. The co-evolution of humans and meat. *Appetite*, *90*, 200–211. doi:10.1016/j.appet.2015.03.014 PMID:25794684

Leutgeb, V., Ille, R., Wabnegger, A., Schienle, A., Schöggl, H., Weber, B., & Fink, A. et al. (2016). Creativity and borderline personality disorder: Evidence from a voxel-based morphometry study. *Cognitive Neuropsychiatry*, *21*(3), 242–255. doi:10.1080/13546805.2016.1182904 PMID:27174566

Lewis, S., & Maslin, M. (2015). Defining the Anthropocene. *Nature*, *519*(7542), 171–180. doi:10.1038/nature14258 PMID:25762280

Li, J. P. (2009). Exponential growth, animal welfare, environmental and food safety impact: The case of China's livestock production. *Journal of Agricultural & Environmental Ethics*, *22*(3), 217–240. doi:10.1007/s10806-008-9140-7

Li, M., Fan, Y., Zhang, X., Hou, W., & Tang, Z. (2014). Fruit and vegetable intake and risk of type 2 diabetes mellitus: Meta-analysis of prospective cohort studies. *BMJ Open*, *4*(11), e005497. doi:10.1136/bmjopen-2014-005497 PMID:25377009

Lin, A. Y. C., & Tsai, Y. (2009). Occurrence of pharmaceuticals in Taiwan's surface waters: Impact of waste streams from hospitals and pharmaceutical production facilities. *The Science of the Total Environment*, *407*(12), 3793–3802. doi:10.1016/j.scitotenv.2009.03.009 PMID:19345984

Lin, A. Y., Yu, T., & Lin, C. (2008). Pharmaceutical contamination in residential, industrial, and agricultural waste streams: Risk to aqueous environments in Taiwan. *Chemosphere*, *74*(1), 131–141. doi:10.1016/j.chemosphere.2008.08.027 PMID:18829065

Ling, J. C., Franklin, B. A. K., Lindsteadt, J. F., & Gearon, S. A. N. (1992). Social marketing: Its place in public health. *Annual Review of Public Health*, *13*(1), 341–362. doi:10.1146/annurev.pu.13.050192.002013 PMID:1599593

Lipinski, B., Hanson, C., Lomax, J., Kitinoja, L., Waite, R., & Searchinger, T. (2013). *Reducing food loss and waste* (Working Paper). World Resource Institute. Retrieved from http://pdf.wri.org/reducing_food_loss_and_waste.pdf

Lippi, G., Mattiuzzi, C., & Cervellin, G. (2016). Meat consumption and cancer risk: A critical review of published meta-analyses. *Critical Reviews in Oncology/Hematology*, *97*, 1–14. doi:10.1016/j.critrevonc.2015.11.008 PMID:26633248

Little, P. D. (1994). Maidens and milk markets: The sociology of dairy marketing in Southern Somalia. In E. Fratkin, K. A. Galvin, & E. A. Roth (Eds.), *African pastoralist systems: An integrated approach* (pp. 165–184). Boulder, CO: Lynne Rienner.

Liu, H., Parton, K., Zhou, Z., & Cox, R. (2009). At-home meat consumption in China: An empirical study. *The Australian Journal of Agricultural and Resource Economics*, *53*(4), 485–501. doi:10.1111/j.1467-8489.2009.00463.x

Liu, X., Nelson, M., & Ibrahim, M. (2007). Analyzing consumer's calculation factors in the purchase decision of goat meat. *Journal of Food Distribution Research*, *38*(1), 196–202.

Liverman, D., & Kapadia, K. (2010). Food systems and the global environment: An overview. In J. Ingram, P. Ericksen, & D. Liverman (Eds.), *Food Security and Global Environmental Change* (pp. 3–24). London, UK: Earthscan.

Liverpool-Tasie, L., Adjognon, S., & Reardon, T. (2016). Transformation of the food system in Nigeria and female participation in the Non-Farm Economy (NFE). *Paper presented at the 2016 Annual Meeting, Boston, Massachusetts*, July 31-August 2. Retrieved from http://ageconsearch.umn.edu/bitstream/236284/2/AAEA_2016_FoodSystemTransformationNigeria_1.pdf

Li, Y., Zhou, C., Zhou, X., & Li, L. (2013). Egg consumption and risk of cardiovascular diseases and diabetes: A meta-analysis. *Atherosclerosis*, *229*(2), 524–530. doi:10.1016/j.atherosclerosis.2013.04.003 PMID:23643053

Llonch, P., Haskell, M. J., Dewhurst, R. J., & Turner, S. P. (2017). Current available strategies to mitigate greenhouse gas emissions in livestock systems: An animal welfare perspective. *Animal*, *11*(2), 274–284. doi:10.1017/S1751731116001440 PMID:27406001

Longmire, A., Taylor, C., & Wedderburn-Bisshop, G. (2014). *Land use: Agriculture and forestry discussion paper*. Melbourne, Australia: Beyond Zero Emissions; Melbourne Sustainable Society Institute. Retrieved from http://bze.org.au/land-use-agriculture-and-forestry/

Loughnan, S., Haslam, N., & Bastian, B. (2010). The role of meat consumption in the denial of moral status and mind to meat animals. *Appetite*, *55*(1), 156–159. doi:10.1016/j.appet.2010.05.043 PMID:20488214

Lubowski, R. N., Vesterby, M., Bucholtz, S., Baez, A., & Roberts, M. J. (2006). Major uses of land in the United States, 2002. *Economic Information Bulletin*, 14. Retrieved from http://americandreamcoalition.org/openspace/MajorLandUse.pdf

Luca, F., Perry, G. H., & Di Rienzo, A. (2010). Evolutionary adaptations to dietary changes. *Annual Review of Nutrition*, *30*(1), 291–314. doi:10.1146/annurev-nutr-080508-141048 PMID:20420525

Luca, N., & Suggs, S. (2010). Strategies for the social marketing mix: A systematic review. *Social Marketing Quarterly*, *16*(4), 122–149. doi:10.1080/15245004.2010.522767

Lucan, S., Barg, F., Karasz, A., Palmer, C., & Long, J. (2012). Concepts of healthy diet among urban, low-income, African Americans. *Journal of Community Health*, *37*(4), 754–762. doi:10.1007/s10900-011-9508-x PMID:22101636

Lu, L., Xun, P., Wan, Y., He, K., & Cai, W. (2016). Long-term association between dairy consumption and risk of childhood obesity: A systematic review and meta-analysis of prospective cohort studies. *European Journal of Clinical Nutrition*, *70*(4), 414–423. doi:10.1038/ejcn.2015.226 PMID:26862005

Lundqvist, J., De Fraiture, C., & Molden, D. (2008). *Saving water: From field to fork – curbing losses and wastage in the food chain. SIWI Policy Brief*. Stockholm, Sweden: Stockholm International Water Institute.

Lupton, D. (1996). *Food, the body and the self*. London, UK: Sage.

Lusk, J. L., Norwood, F. B., & Prickett, R. W. (2007). *Consumer preferences for farm animal welfare: Results of a nation-wide telephone survey*. Retrieved from http://cratefreefuture.com/pdf/American%20Farm%20Bureau-Funded%20Poll.pdf

Lu, W., Chen, H., Niu, Y., Wu, H., Xia, D., & Wu, Y. (2016). Dairy products intake and cancer mortality risk: A meta-analysis of 11 population-based cohort studies. *Nutrition Journal*, *15*(1), 91. doi:10.1186/s12937-016-0210-9 PMID:27765039

Lynes, J., Whitney, S., & Murray, D. (2014). Developing benchmark criteria for assessing community-based social marketing programs: A look into Jack Johnson's "All at Once" campaign. *Journal of Social Marketing*, *4*(2), 111–132. doi:10.1108/JSOCM-08-2013-0060

Macdiarmid, J. L., Douglas, F., & Campbell, J. (2015). Eating like there's no tomorrow: Public awareness of the environmental impact of food and reluctance to eat less meat as part of a sustainable diet. *Appetite*, *96*, 487–493. doi:10.1016/j.appet.2015.10.011 PMID:26476397

MacFadyen, L., Stead, M., & Hastings, G. (1999). A synopsis of social marketing. Institute for Social Marketing. Retrieved from http://www.qihub.scot.nhs.uk/media/162221/social_marketing_synopsis.pdf

Macrae, F. (2010, February 13). How being vegetarian does more harm to the environment than eating meat. *Daily Mail.* Retrieved from http://www.dailymail.co.uk/health/article-1250532/Being-vegetarian-does-harm-environment-eating-meat.html#ixzz45PTjJ0Uj

Mahalik, J. R., Locke, B. D., Ludlow, L. H., Diemer, M. A., Scott, R. P. J., Gottfried, M., & Freitas, G. (2003). Development of the conformity to masculine norms inventory. *Journal of Men and Masculinity, 4*(1), 3–25. doi:10.1037/1524-9220.4.1.3

Maibach, E. W., Maxfield, A., Ladin, K., & Slater, M. (1996). Translating health psychology into effective health communication: The American Healthstyles Audience Segmentation Project. *Journal of Health Psychology, 1*(3), 261–277. doi:10.1177/135910539600100302 PMID:22011991

Maio, G. R., Verplanken, B., Manstead, A. S., Stroebe, W., Abraham, C., Sheeran, P., & Conner, M. (2007). Social psychological factors in lifestyle change and their relevance to policy. *Social Issues and Policy Review, 1*(1), 99–137. doi:10.1111/j.1751-2409.2007.00005.x

Makinde, Y., & Babalola, D. (2011). Diet and hypertension: A comparative analysis of four diet groups in South-Western Nigeria. *African Journal of Food, Agriculture, Nutrition and Development, 11*(1). Retrieved from https://www.ajol.info/index.php/ajfand/article/view/65882. doi:10.4314/ajfand.v11i1.65882

Malik, V. S., Li, Y., Tobias, D. K., Pan, A., & Hu, F. B. (2016). Dietary protein intake and risk of type 2 diabetes in US men and women. *American Journal of Epidemiology, 183*(8), 715–728. doi:10.1093/aje/kwv268 PMID:27022032

Mammoser, G. (2017). Meat producers are concerned vegan bacon is deceiving consumers. *Vice*. Retrieved from https://munchies.vice.com/en_uk/article/aey4ba/the-way-you-eat-pizza-says-a-lot-about-you-according-to-body-language-experts

Mandela, N. (1994). *The long walk to freedom: The autobiography of Nelson Mandela*. Boston, MA: Little, Brown and Company.

Manjunatha, A. V., Gana Shruthy, M. K., & Ramachandra, V. A. (2013). Global marketing systems in the dairy sector: A comparison of selected countries. *Indian Journal of Marketing, 43*(10), 23–35. doi:10.17010/ijom/2013/v43/i10/38354

Manning, M., & Reisinger, A. (2011). Broader perspectives for comparing different greenhouse gases. *Philosophical Transactions of the Royal Society A: Mathematical, Physical and Engineering Sciences, 369*(1943), 1891–1905. doi:10.1098/rsta.2010.0349 PMID:21502165

Manoff, R. K. (1985). *Social marketing: A new imperative for public health*. New York, NY: Praeger.

Manthiou, A., Kang, J., Chiang, L., & Tang, L. (2016). Investigating the effects of memorable experiences: An extended model of script theory. *Journal of Travel & Tourism Marketing, 33*(3), 362–379. doi:10.1080/10548408.2015.1064055

Marcus, E. (1998). *Vegan: The new ethics of eating*. Ithaca, NY: McBooks Press.

Marcuse, H. (1968). *One-dimensional man: Studies in the ideology of advanced industrial society*. Boston, MA: Beacon Press.

María, G. A. (2006). Public perception of farm animal welfare in Spain. *Livestock Science, 103*(3), 250–256. doi:10.1016/j.livsci.2006.05.011

Marinova, D., & Raphaely, D. (2017) Impact of vegetarian diets on the environment. In W. Craig, W. (Ed.), Vegetarian nutrition and wellness (forthcoming). Boca Raton, FL: CRC Press/Taylor and Francis.

Markets and Markets. (2016). *Meat substitutes market by type (tofu & tofu ingredients, tempeh, textured vegetable protein, seitan, quorn), source (soy-based, wheat-based, mycoprotein), category (frozen, refrigerated), and region – global forecast to 2022.* Markets and Markets. Retrieved from http://www.marketsandmarkets.com/Market-Reports/meat-substitutes-market-979.html

Marsh, K., Saunders, A., & Zeuschner, C. (2016). Red meat and health: Evidence regarding red meat, health, and chronic disease risk. In T. Raphaely & D. Marinova (Eds.), *Impact of meat consumption on health and environmental sustainability* (pp. 131–177). Hershey, PA: IGI Global. doi:10.4018/978-1-4666-9553-5.ch008

Martinez, J. L. (2009). Environmental pollution by antibiotics and by antibiotic resistance determinants. *Environmental Pollution, 157*(11), 2893–2902. doi:10.1016/j.envpol.2009.05.051 PMID:19560847

Martin, P., & Williams, J. (2011). Renegotiating farmers' social licence. In *Defending the Social Licence of Farming: Issues, challenges and new directions for agriculture* (pp. 195–202). Melbourne, Australia: CSIRO Publishing.

Marushka, L., Batal, M., David, W., Schwartz, H., Ing, A., Fediuk, K., & Chan, H. M. et al. (2017). Association between fish consumption, dietary omega-3 fatty acids and persistent organic pollutants intake, and type 2 diabetes in 18 First Nations in Ontario, Canada. *Environmental Research, 156*, 725–737. doi:10.1016/j.envres.2017.04.034 PMID:28482294

Marx, K. (1887). Capital: A critique of political economy (Vol. 1, F. Engels Ed., S. Moore, & E. Aveling, trans.). Moscow, Russia: Progress Publishers. (Original work published 1867).

Maslin, M. A., Shultz, S., & Trauth, M. H. (2015). A synthesis of the theories and concepts of early human evolution. *Philosophical Transactions of the Royal Society of London. Series B, Biological Sciences, 370*(1663), 20140064. doi:10.1098/rstb.2014.0064 PMID:25602068

Mason, J., & Finelli, M. (2006). Brave new farm? In P. Singer (Ed.), *In defense of animals: The second wave* (pp. 104–122). Oxford, UK: Blackwell.

Mason, P., & Lang, T. (2017). *Sustainable diets: How ecological nutrition can transform consumption and the food system.* London, UK: Earthscan.

Masson, J. M. (2014). *Beasts: What animals can teach us about the origins of good and evil.* New York, NY: Bloomsbury.

Mathijs, E. (2015). Exploring future patterns of meat consumption. *Meat Science, 109*, 112–116. doi:10.1016/j.meatsci.2015.05.007 PMID:26002118

Mayfield, L. E., Bennett, R. M., Tranter, R. B., & Wooldridge, M. J. (2007). Consumption of welfare-friendly food products in Great Britain, Italy and Sweden, and how it may be influenced by consumer attitudes to, and behaviour towards, animal welfare attributes. *International Journal of Sociology of Agriculture and Food, 15*(3), 59–73.

Mayseless, N., Eran, A., & Shamay-Tsoory, S. G. (2015). Generating original ideas: The neural underpinning of originality. *NeuroImage, 116*, 232–239. doi:10.1016/j.neuroimage.2015.05.030 PMID:26003860

Mayseless, N., Uzefovsky, F., Shalev, I., Ebstein, R. P., & Shamay-Tsoory, S. G. (2013). The association between creativity and 7R polymorphism in the dopamine receptor D4 gene (DRD4). *Frontiers in Human Neuroscience, 7*, 502. doi:10.3389/fnhum.2013.00502 PMID:23986684

McAllister, P. (2009). *Manthropology: The science of the inadequate modern male.* Sydney, Australia: Hachette Australia.

McAlpine, C. A., Etter, A., Fearnside, P. M., Seabrook, L., & Laurance, W. F. (2009). Increasing world consumption of beef as a driver of regional and global change: A call for policy action based on evidence from Queensland (Australia), Colombia and Brazil. *Global Environmental Change, 19*(1), 21–33. doi:10.1016/j.gloenvcha.2008.10.008

McCrindle Research. (2012). Generations defined. Retrieved from http://mccrindle.com.au/resources/Generations-Defined-Sociologically.pdf

McDaniel, J. (1989). *The madness of the saints: Ecstatic religion in Bengal*. Chicago, IL: University of Chicago Press.

McDonagh, P., & Prothero, A. (1997). Leap-frog marketing: The contribution of ecofeminist thought to the world of patriarchal marketing. *Marketing Intelligence & Planning*, *15*(7), 361–368. doi:10.1108/02634509710193190

McEachran, A. D., Blackwell, B. R., Hanson, J. D., Wooten, K. J., Mayer, G. D., Cox, S. B., & Smith, P. N. (2015). Antibiotics, bacteria, and antibiotic resistance genes: Aerial transport from cattle feed yards via particulate matter. *Environmental Health Perspectives*, *123*, 337–343. PMID:25633846

McEvoy, C. T., Temple, N., & Woodside, J. V. (2012). Vegetarian diets, low-meat diets and health: A review. *Public Health Nutrition*, *15*(12), 2287–2294. doi:10.1017/S1368980012000936 PMID:22717188

McGregor, A., & Houston, D. (2017). Cattle in the Anthropocene: Four propositions. *Transactions of the Institute of British Geographers*, *6/30*. doi:10.1111/tran.12193

McKee, N. (1992). *Social mobilisation and social marketing*. Pennang, Malaysia: Southbound.

McKenzie-Mohr, D. (2013). *Fostering sustainable behavior: An introduction to community-based social marketing*. Gabriola Island, BC: New society publishers.

McKenzie-Mohr, D., Lee, N. R., Schultz, P. W., & Kotler, P. (2012). *Social marketing to protect the environment: What works*. Thousand Oaks, CA: Sage. doi:10.4135/9781483349466

McLuhan, M. (1964). *Understanding media*. London: Routledge.

McMahon, D. M. (2013). *Divine fury: A history of genius*. New York, NY: Basic Books.

McMahon, J. (2016). Paris Agreement portends a reckoning for meat and dairy. *Forbes*. Retrieved from https://www.forbes.com/sites/jeffmcmahon/2016/01/01/paris-agreement-will-impact-meat-and-dairy/#3106b4cc446b

McMichael, A. J., Powles, J. W., Butler, C. D., & Uauy, R. (2007). Food, livestock production, energy, climate change, and health. *Lancet*, *370*(9594), 1253–1263. doi:10.1016/S0140-6736(07)61256-2 PMID:17868818

McMichael, A., & Bambrick, H. (2005). Meat consumption trends and health: Casting a wider risk assessment net. *Public Health Nutrition*, *8*(04), 348–356. doi:10.1079/PHN2005742 PMID:15975177

Meadows, D. (1991). Changing the world through the information sphere. In C. Lamay & E. Dennis (Eds.), *Media and the environment* (pp. 67–79). Washington, DC: Island Press.

Meat Atlas. (2014). Facts and figures about the animals we eat. Berlin, Germany: Heinrich Böll Foundation and Brussels, Belgium: Friends of the Earth Europe. Retrieved from https://www.boell.de/sites/default/files/meat_atlas2014_kommentierbar.pdf

Meat Free Monday. (2017a). Mark Ruffalo and Lily Cole back #MFMclimatepledge in NYC. Retrieved from https://www.meatfreemondays.com/pledge-brunch-spotlights-un-climate-summit-pledge-campaign/

Meat Free Monday. (2017b). Vegan Quarter puts plant-based food centre stage. Retrieved from https://www.meatfreemondays.com/vegan-quarter-puts-plant-based-food-centre-stage/

Meatless Monday. (2017). History. Retrieved from http://www.meatlessmonday.com/about-us/history

Medley Hall. (2017a). *Great food*. Retrieved from http://www.boojum.com.au/medley/ what-we-offer/171/

Medley Hall. (2017b). *Home page*. Retrieved from http://www.boojum.com.au/medley/

Medley Hall. (2017c). *What we offer*. Retrieved from http://www.boojum.com.au/medley/ what-we-offer/

Medley Hall. (2017d). *Who we are*. Retrieved from http://www.boojum.com.au/medley/who-we-are/

Mekonnen, M. M., & Hoekstra, A. Y. (2010). The green, blue and grey water footprint of farm animals and animal products.: Vol. 1. *Main report*. Delft, the Netherlands: UNESCO. Retrieved from http://waterfootprint.org/media/downloads/Report-48-WaterFootprint-AnimalProducts-Vol1.pdf

Melendez, S. (2010). *How to strengthen your brain*. Griffin, GA: Melendez Publishing International.

Melina, V., Craig, W., & Levin, S. (2016). *Position of the Academy of Nutrition and Dietetics: Vegetarian diets*. Retrieved from http://www.eatrightpro.org/~/media/eatrightpro%20files/practice/position%20and%20practice%20papers/position%20papers/vegetarian-diet.ashx

Melina, V., Craig, W., & Levin, S. (2016). Position of the Academy of Nutrition and Dietetics: Vegetarian Diets. *Journal of the Academy of Nutrition and Dietetics*, *116*(12), 1970–1980. doi:10.1016/j.jand.2016.09.025 PMID:27886704

Mendes, J. (2017, June 23). *Eating bacon shown to reduce sperm in man*. Virility protocol. Retrieved from http://virilityprotocol.com/bacon-shown-reduce-sperm-men/

Merriam Webster Dictionary. (2017). Meat. Retrieved from https://www.merriam-webster.com/dictionary/meat

Merriam-Webster. (2009), Luxury. Retrieved from http://www.merriam-webster.com/dictionary/luxury

Merriam–Webster. (2017). *Meat*. Retrieved from https://www.merriam-webster.com/dictionary/meat

Mertens, E., Van 't Veer, P., Hiddink, G. J., Steijns, J. M. J. M., & Kuijsten, A. (2016). Operationalising the health aspects of sustainable diets: A review. *Public Health Nutrition*, *20*(04), 739–757. doi:10.1017/S1368980016002664 PMID:27819199

Messerli, F. H. (2012). Chocolate consumption, cognitive function, and Nobel laureate. *The New England Journal of Medicine*, *367*(16), 1562–1564. doi:10.1056/NEJMon1211064 PMID:23050509

Meybeck, A., & Gitz, V. (2017). Sustainable diets within sustainable food systems. *The Proceedings of the Nutrition Society*, *76*(01), 1–11. doi:10.1017/S0029665116000653 PMID:28195528

Micha, R., Khatibzadeh, S., Shi, P., Andrews, K. G., Engell, R. E., & Mozaffarian, D. (2015). Global, regional and national consumption of major food groups in 1990 and 2010: A systematic analysis including 266 country-specific nutrition surveys worldwide. *BMJ Open*, *5*(9), e008705. doi:10.1136/bmjopen-2015-008705 PMID:26408285

Micha, R., Michas, G., Lajous, M., & Mozaffarian, D. (2013). Processing of meats and cardiovascular risk: Time to focus on preservatives. *BMC Medicine*, *11*(1), 136. doi:10.1186/1741-7015-11-136 PMID:23701737

Micha, R., Michas, G., & Mozaffarian, D. (2012). Unprocessed red and processed meats and risk of coronary artery disease and type 2 diabetes–an updated review of the evidence. *Current Atherosclerosis Reports*, *14*(6), 515–524. doi:10.1007/s11883-012-0282-8 PMID:23001745

Micha, R., Wallace, S. K., & Mozaffarian, D. (2010). Red and processed meat consumption and risk of incident coronary heart disease, stroke, and diabetes mellitus: A systematic review and meta-analysis. *Circulation*, *121*(21), 2271–2283. doi:10.1161/CIRCULATIONAHA.109.924977 PMID:20479151

Michaut, A. M. (2004). *Consumer response to innovative products: With application to foods*. (Doctoral thesis). Wageningen University. Retrieved from http://edepot.wur.nl/121564

Miller, C. A., Corbin, K. D., da Costa, K. A., Zhang, S., Zhao, X., Galanko, J. A., & Zeisel, S. H. et al. (2014). Effect of egg ingestion on trimethylamine-N-oxide production in humans: A randomized, controlled, dose-response study. *The American Journal of Clinical Nutrition, 100*(3), 778–786. doi:10.3945/ajcn.114.087692 PMID:24944063

Millner, J. (2015, September 23). The secret to man's intelligence? POTATOES: Humans evolved large brains because our ancestors ate starchy carbohydrates. *Daily Mail Australia*. Retrieved from http://www.dailymail.co.uk/sciencetech/article-3189454/The-secret-man-s-intelligence-POTATOES-Humans-evolved-large-brains-ancestors-ate-starchy-carbohydrates.html#ixzz4qTO6KgWA

Miranowski, J. (2002) Energy Consumption in U.S. Agriculture. Presentation for Farm Foundation. Retrieved from https://www.farmfoundation.org/projects/documents/miranowski.ppt

Mitra, S. K. (Ed.). (1979). *Lalon Fakir: Kabi a kavya*. Kolkata, India: Pustak Bipani.

Mohammed, U. (2012). Globalization and changing cultural values In Nigeria: Driving westernization to its zenith. *Ilorin Journal of Sociology, 4*(1). Retrieved from http://www.unilorin.edu.ng/ejournals/index.php/index/search/authors/view?firstName=Mohammed&middleName=%2C&lastName=Usman&affiliation=&country=NG

Molefe, T. O. (2014). *'National Braai Day' a day of forgetting*. Retrieved from http://www.news24.com/Columnists/TOMolefe/National-Braai-Day-a-day-of-forgetting-20140917

Molnár, P. J. (1989). A theoretical model to describe food quality. *Journal of Food Quality, 12*(1), 1–11. doi:10.1111/j.1745-4557.1989.tb00305.x

Momoh, O., & Ochaba, A. (2002). Herd structure of Small-Holder goat production in Otukpo LGA of Benue State, Nigeria. *Nigerian Journal of Animal Science, 5*(2). Retrieved from https://www.ajol.info/index.php/tjas/article/view/50133

Money-Zine. (2017). 2017 *State Sales Tax Rates*. Retrieved from http://www.money-zine.com/financial-planning/tax-shelter/state-sales-tax-rates/

Morioka, M. (2013). A phenomenological study of "Herbivore Men". *The Review of Life Studies, 4*, 1–20.

Moskin, J. (2016). South Africa: One nation united by the grill. *The New York Times*, May 23. Retrieved from https://www.nytimes.com/2016/05/25/dining/braai.html

Mottet, A., Henderson, B., Opio, C., Falcucci, A., Tempio, G., Silvestri, S., & Gerber, P. J. et al. (2017). Climate change mitigation and productivity gains in livestock supply chains: Insights from regional case studies. *Regional Environmental Change, 17*(1), 129–141. doi:10.1007/s10113-016-0986-3

Mouritsen, O. G. (2016). Deliciousness of food and a proper balance in fatty acid composition as means to improve human health and regulate food intake. *Flavour (London), 5*(1), 1. doi:10.1186/s13411-016-0048-2

Msangi, S., & Rosegrant, R. W. (2011). Feeding the future's changing diets: Implications for agriculture markets, nutrition and policy, 2020. *Paper presented at the Leveraging Agriculture for Improving Nutrition and Health Conference*, New Delhi, India. Retrieved from http://www.foresightfordevelopment.org/sobipro/download-file/46-953/54

Mshelbwala, G. M. (2013). National livestock policy focal point presentation – Nigeria. *Paper presented at the Side-meeting of NLPFPS on VET-GOV programme engagement/targetting and capacity building facilitation*. Retrieved from http://www.au-ibar.org/component/jdownloads/finish/67-vet-gov-presentations/1427-nigeria-national-livestock-policy-focal-point-presentation

Mujtaba, S., & Musavi, L. (2000). *God and his attributes: Lessons on Islamic doctrine* (H. Algar, Trans.). Potomac, MD: Islamic Education Centre.

Munro, L. (2012). The animal rights movement in theory and practice: A review of the sociological literature. *Sociology Compass, 6*(2), 166–181. doi:10.1111/j.1751-9020.2011.00440.x

Murcott, A. (1982). The cultural significance of food and eating. *The Proceedings of the Nutrition Society, 41*(2), 203–210. doi:10.1079/PNS19820031 PMID:7111265

Murphy, S. P., & Allen, L. H. (2003). Nutritional importance of animal source foods. *The Journal of Nutrition, 133*, 3932S–3935S. PMID:14672292

Mutiyar, P. K., & Mittal, A. K. (2014). Occurrences and fate of selected human antibiotics in influents and effluents of sewage treatment plant and effluent-receiving river Yamuna in Delhi (India). *Environmental Monitoring and Assessment, 186*(1), 541–557. doi:10.1007/s10661-013-3398-6 PMID:24085621

Myers, D. G., & Spencer, S. J. (2001). *Social psychology* (Canadian edition). Toronto, Canada: McGraw-Hill Ryerson.

Myers, N., & Kent, J. (2003). New consumers: The influence of affluence on the environment. *Proceedings of the National Academy of Sciences of the United States of America, 100*(8), 4963–4968. doi:10.1073/pnas.0438061100 PMID:12672963

Myfitnesspal. (2017a). Calories in hamburger fast food. Retrieved from http://www.myfitnesspal.com/food/calories/45914216

Myfitnesspal. (2017b). Calories in Traditionnelle Quiche Lorraine. Retrieved from http://www.myfitnesspal.com/food/calories/traditionnelle-quiche-lorraine-510312963

Myth, H. org. (n.d.). *Deconstructing the myth of humane animal agriculture.* Retrieved from http://www.humanemyth.org/index.htm

Nardone, A., Ronchi, B., Lacetera, N., Ranieri, M. S., & Bernabucci, U. (2010). Effects of climate changes on animal production and sustainability of livestock systems. *Livestock Science, 130*(1), 57–69. doi:10.1016/j.livsci.2010.02.011

Nash, M., & Phillipov, M. (2014). Introduction to the special issue. Eating like a "man": Food and the performance and regulation of masculinities. *Women's Studies International Forum, 44*, 205–208. doi:10.1016/j.wsif.2014.03.007

Nath, J., & Prideaux, D. (2011). The civilised burger: Meat alternatives as a conversion aid and social instrument for Australian vegetarians and vegans. *Australian Humanities Review, 51*, 135–151.

National Health and Medical Research Council (NHMRC). (2013). *Australian dietary guidelines.* Canberra, Australia: NHMRC and Department of Health and Ageing, Australian Government.

National Health and Medical Research Council (NHMRC). (2013). Australian Dietary Guidelines. Canberra, Australia: NHMRC. Retrieved from https://www.eatforhealth.gov.au/sites/default/files/files/the_guidelines/n55_australian _dietary_guidelines.pdf

National Health and Medical Research Council (NHMRC). (2013). *Australian Dietary Guidelines.* Canberra, Australia: NHMRC. Retrieved from https://www.nhmrc.gov.au/_files_nhmrc/file/publications/n55_australian_dietary_guidelines1.pdf

National Museum of Natural History (NMNH). (2017). *Brains.* Retrieved from http://humanorigins.si.edu/human-characteristics/brains

National Social Marketing Centre (NSMC). (2011). *What is social marketing?* Retrieved from http://www.nsmcentre.org.uk/content/what-social-marketing-1

National Statistical Institute (NSI). (2013). *Statistical yearbook 2012.* Sofia, Bulgaria: NSI.

National Statistical Institute (NSI). (2017a). *Economic accounts for agriculture – annual data*. Republic of Bulgaria. Retrieved from http://www.nsi.bg/en/content/15323/метаданни/economic-accounts-agriculture-—annual-data

National Statistical Institute (NSI). (2017b). *International migration by age and sex*. Republic of Bulgaria. Retrieved from http://www.nsi.bg/en/content/6697/international-migration-age-and-sex

National Statistical Institute (NSI). (2017c). *Statistical yearbook 2016*. Sofia, Bulgaria: NSI.

Naylor, R., Steinfeld, H., Falcon, Q., Galloway, J., Smil, V., Bradford, E., & Mooney, H. et al. (2005). Agriculture: Losing the links between livestock and land. *Science*, *310*(5754), 1621–162. doi:10.1126/science.1117856 PMID:16339432

Nenova, S. (2015). *Ancient meals and eating habits*. Part 1 Greeks. Retrieved from http://www.ancientworldalive.com/single-post/2015/06/03/Ancient-meals-and-eating-habit-Part-1-Greeks

Nestle, M. (1999). Animal v. plant foods in human diets and health: Is the historical record unequivocal? *The Proceedings of the Nutrition Society*, *58*(02), 211–218. doi:10.1017/S0029665199000300 PMID:10466159

News.com.au. (2016). *This Coles chicken has gangrene*. Retrieved from http://www.news.com.au/finance/business/retail/this-coles-chicken-has-gangrene/news-story/994f472fa624707b2939c1ffdeee5717

Nierenberg, D., & Reynolds, L. (2012). Disease and drought curb meat production and consumption. Vital Signs, Worldwatch Institute. Retrieved from http://vitalsigns.worldwatch.org/vs-trend/disease-and-drought-curb-meat-production-and-consumption

Nijdam, D., Rood, T., & Westhoek, H. (2012). The price of protein: Review of land use and carbon footprints from life cycle assessments of animal food products and their substitutes. *Food Policy*, *37*(6), 760–770. doi:10.1016/j.foodpol.2012.08.002

Nisbet, E. G., Dlugokencky, E. J., & Bousquet, P. (2014). Methane on the rise—again. *Science*, *343*(6170), 493–495. doi:10.1126/science.1247828 PMID:24482471

Nordgren, A. (2012). Ethical issues in mitigation of climate change: The option of reduced meat production and consumption. *Journal of Agricultural & Environmental Ethics*, *25*(4), 563–584. doi:10.1007/s10806-011-9335-1

Nsofor, C. A., & Iroegbu, C. U. (2012). Antibiotic resistance profile of Escherichia coli isolated from apparently healthy domestic livestock in South-East Nigeria. *Journal of Cell and Animal Biology*, *6*(8), 129–135.

Nuttal, J. (2007). *An introduction to philosophy*. Cambridge, UK: Polity Press.

O'Kane, F. E. (2006). NPF Texture formation. In H. Aiking, J. de Boer, & J. Vereijken (Eds.), *Sustainable protein production and consumption: Pigs or peas?* (pp. 62–66). Dordrecht, Netherlands: Springer.

O'Sullivan, S. (2006). Conflict and coherence within the Australian animal protection movement. In *Proceedings of the Australasian Political Studies Association Conference*. University of Newcastle.

Ocak, H. (2017). "Greenpeace'e tavuk davası" [Chicken case to Greenpeace]. Cumhuriyet. Retrieved from http://www.cumhuriyet.com.tr/haber/cevre/656945/Greenpeace_e_tavuk_davasi.html

Oehlenschläger, J. (2012). Seafood: Nutritional benefits and risk aspects. *International Journal for Vitamin and Nutrition Research*, *82*(3), 168–176. doi:10.1024/0300-9831/a000108 PMID:23258397

Ogbeh, A. (2016). Retreat on livestock and dairy development in Nigeria. Keynote address delivered by the Hon. Minister of Agriculture and Rural Development, Chief Audu Ogbeh. Retrieved from http://fmard.gov.ng/retreat-on-livestock-and-dairy-development-in-nigeria-keynote-address-delivered-by-the-hon-minister-of-agriculture-and-rural-development-chief-audu-ogbeh/

Ogbeide, O. A. (2015). Meat industry development in Nigeria: Implications of the consumers' perspective. *Agribusiness*, *1*(1), 59–75.

Ogbuene, E., Eze, H., & Adinna, E. (2012). The Impact of Overgrazing and Deforestation on Rainfall Variability in Northern Fringes of Nigeria. *Journal of Environmental Management and Safety*, *3*(3), 21–36.

Oikkonen, J., Kuusi, T., Peltonen, P., Raijas, P., Ukkola-Vuoti, L., Karma, K., & Järvelä, I. et al. (2016). Creative activities in music--a genome-wide linkage analysis. *PLoS One*, *11*(2), e0148679. doi:10.1371/journal.pone.0148679 PMID:26909693

Ojofeitimi, E., Afolabi, O., Fapojuwo, O., Grissom, F., & Oke, O. (1984). The use of black-eyed cowpeas, maize-gruel mixture ('ewa-ogi') in the treatment and prevention of infantile protein malnutrition. *Nutrition Reports International*, *30*, 841–851.

Olajide, O., Akinlabi, B., & Tijani, A. (2012). Agriculture resource and economic growth in Nigeria. *European Scientific Journal*, *8*(22), 103–115.

Olatoye, I. O., & Basiru, A. (2013). Antibiotic usage and oxytetracycline residue in African catfish (Clarias gariepinus) in Ibadan, Nigeria. *World Journal of Fish and Marine Sciences*, *5*(3), 302–309.

Oliffe, J. L., Bottorff, J. L., Sharp, P., Caperchione, C. M., Johnson, S. T., Healy, T., & Errey, S. et al. (2015). Healthy eating and active living: Rural-based working men's perspectives. *American Journal of Men's Health*. doi:10.1177/1557988315619372 PMID:26669775

Oluyege, J. O., Oluwaniyi, T. T., & Ijasan, O. C. (2015). Composition of antibiotic resistant bacteria from irrigated vegetable farmland. *Journal of Microbiology Research (Rosemead, Calif.)*, *5*(5), 161–168.

Online Etymology Dictionary. 2017. Meat (n.). Retrieved from http://www.etymonline.com/index.php?allowed_in_frame=0&search=meat

Opotow, S. (1990). Moral exclusion and injustice: An introduction. *The Journal of Social Issues*, *46*(1), 1–20. doi:10.1111/j.1540-4560.1990.tb00268.x

Opotow, S. (1993). Animals and the scope of justice. *The Journal of Social Issues*, *49*(1), 71–85. doi:10.1111/j.1540-4560.1993.tb00909.x

Opotow, S. (1994). Predicting protection: Scope of justice and the natural world. *The Journal of Social Issues*, *50*(3), 49–63. doi:10.1111/j.1540-4560.1994.tb02419.x

Opotow, S. (2001). Reconciliation in times of impunity: Challenges for social justice. *Social Justice Research*, *14*(2), 149–170. doi:10.1023/A:1012888902705

Opotow, S., & Weiss, L. (2000). New ways of thinking about environmentalism: Denial and the process of moral exclusion in environmental conflict. *The Journal of Social Issues*, *56*(3), 475–490. doi:10.1111/0022-4537.00179

Oregon State University (OSU). (2012). *Trophic issues*. Retrieved from http://people.oregonstate.edu/~muirp/trophic.htm

Organisation for Economic Co-operation and Development (OECD). (2015). *Towards green growth? Tracking progress. Four years of the Green Growth Strategy*. Paris, France: OECD Green Growth Studies; doi:10.1787/9789264234437-

Organisation for Economic Co-operation and Development (OECD). (2017). *Meat consumption (indicator)*. doi: Retrieved from https://data.oecd.org/agroutput/meat-consumption.htm10.1787/fa290fd0-en

Organisation for Economic Cooperation and Development (OECD). (2017). *Meat consumption (indicator)*. Retrieved from; doi:10.1787/fa290fd0-

Orlich, M. J., & Fraser, G. E. (2014). Vegetarian diets in the Adventist Health Study 2: A review of initial published findings. *The American Journal of Clinical Nutrition, 100*(Suppl. 1), 353S–358S. doi:10.3945/ajcn.113.071233 PMID:24898223

Orlich, M. J., Singh, P. N., Sabaté, J., Jaceldo-Siegl, K., Fan, J., Knutsen, S., & Fraser, F. et al. (2014). Vegetarian dietary patterns and mortality in Adventist Health Study 2. *JAMA Internal Medicine, 173*(13), 1230–1238. doi:10.1001/jamainternmed.2013.6473 PMID:23836264

Ortega, D. L., Wang, H. H., Wu, L., & Olynk, N. J. (2011). Modeling heterogeneity in consumer preferences for select food safety attributes in China. *Food Policy, 36*(2), 318–324. doi:10.1016/j.foodpol.2010.11.030

Osho, G., & Nazemzadeh, A. (2005). Consumerism: Statistical estimation of Nigeria meat demand. *Journal of International Business Research, 4*(1), 69–79.

Osundahunsi, O. F., & Aworh, A. C. (2002). A preliminary study on the use of tempe-based formula as a weaning diet in Nigeria. *Plant Foods for Human Nutrition (Dordrecht, Netherlands), 57*(3/4), 365–376. doi:10.1023/A:1021805117084 PMID:12602942

Ouellette, J. A., & Wood, W. (1998). Habit and intention in everyday life: The multiple processes by which past behavior predicts future behavior. *Psychological Bulletin, 124*(1), 54–74. doi:10.1037/0033-2909.124.1.54

Oxford Dictionaries. (2017). *Humane.* Retrieved from https://en.oxforddictionaries.com/definition/humane

Oxford Latin Dictionary. (1992). Oxford, UK: Oxford University Press.

Ozdemir, B. P. (2012). Social media as a tool for online advocacy campaigns: Greenpeace Mediterranean's anti genetically engineered food campaign in Turkey. *Global Media Journal, 5*(2), 23–39.

Pacifici, M., Visconti, P., Butchart, S. H. M., Watson, J. E. M., Cassola, F. M., & Rondinini, C. (2017). Species' traits influenced their response to recent climate change. *Nature Climate Change, 7*(3), 205–208. doi:10.1038/nclimate3223

Palmqvist, R., & Santavirta, N. (2006). What friends are for: The relationship between body image, substance use, and peer influence among Finnish adolescents. *Journal of Youth and Adolescence, 35*(2), 203–217. doi:10.1007/s10964-005-9017-2

Pamir, B. (2004). Ben kesinlikle tavuk yemem [I definitely do not eat chicken] Retrieved from http://arsiv.sabah.com.tr/2004/11/01/gun101.html

Pan, A., Sun, Q., Bernstein, A. M., Manson, J. E., Willett, W. C., & Hu, F. B. (2013). Changes in red meat consumption and subsequent risk of type 2 diabetes mellitus: Three cohorts of US men and women. *JAMA Internal Medicine, 173*(14), 1328–1335. doi:10.1001/jamainternmed.2013.6633 PMID:23779232

Pan, A., Sun, Q., Bernstein, A. M., Schulze, M. B., Manson, J. E., Stampfer, M. J., & Hu, F. B. et al. (2012). Red meat consumption and mortality: Results from 2 prospective cohort studies. *Archives of Internal Medicine, 172*(7), 555–563. doi:10.1001/archinternmed.2011.2287 PMID:22412075

Pancia, A. (2017). Milk processor Harvey Fresh 'disappointed' dairy farmers turn back on pain share proposal. *ABC News*. Retrieved from http://www.abc.net.au/news/2017-05-05/processor-disappointed-dairy-farmers-turned-back-on-proposal/8499712http://www.abc.net.au/news/2017-05-05/processor-disappointed-dairy-farmers-turned-back-on-proposal/8499712

Pang, B., Rundle-Thiele, S. R., & Kubacki, K. (2017). An empirical examination of the Ecological and Cognitive Active Commuting framework: A social marketing formative research study. *Health Education, 117*(6), 581–598. doi:10.1108/HE-12-2016-0066

Pan, L., Tian, L., Cao, J. M., & Zhang, J. Y. (2012). 世界牛肉消费趋势及影响因素分析. *Zhongguo Xumu Zazhi, 48*(16), 20–23.

Papargyropoulou, E., Lozano, R., & Steinberger, K., J., Wright, N., & bin Ujang, Z. (. (2014). The food waste hierarchy as a framework for the management of food surplus and food waste. *Journal of Cleaner Production, 76*, 106–115. doi:10.1016/j.jclepro.2014.04.020

Parasecoli, F. (2006). Feeding hard bodies: Food and masculinities in men's fitness magazines. *Food & Foodways, 13*(1-2), 17–37. doi:10.1080/07409710590915355

Parmalat. (2016). Parmalat Group. Retrieved from http://www.parmalat.com/en/about_us/parmalat_group/Parmalat%20Group%202016.pdf

Parry, W. (2011). Climate success story: Saving the ozone layer. *Live Science*. Retrieved from https://www.livescience.com/17347-climate-success-montreal-protocol-ozone.html

Patel, P. S., Forouhi, N. G., Kuijsten, A., Schulze, M. B., van Woudenbergh, G. J., Ardanaz, E., & Wareham, N. J. et al. (2012). The prospective association between total and type of fish intake and type 2 diabetes in 8 European countries: EPIC-InterAct Study. *The American Journal of Clinical Nutrition, 95*(6), 1445–1453. doi:10.3945/ajcn.111.029314 PMID:22572642

Patricios, O. (2016). *Heritage Day or Braai Day? It's time to choose*. Retrieved from https://www.dailymaverick.co.za/opinionista/2016-10-05-heritage-day-or-braai-day-its-time-to-choose./#.WUFnaxOGMkg

Patrick, V. M., & Hagtvedt, H. (2015). Luxury branding. In D. J. MacInnis, C. W. Park, & J. W. Priester (Eds.), *Handbook of Brand Relationships* (pp. 267–280). New York, NY: Routledge.

Pawankar, R. (2014). Allergic diseases and asthma: A global public health concern and a call to action. *The World Allergy Organization Journal, 7*(1), 12. doi:10.1186/1939-4551-7-12 PMID:24940476

Peaceful Prairie Sanctuary. (2012). *The "free-range" myth*. Retrieved from http://www.peacefulprairie.org/freerange1.html

Pearson, D., Friel, S., & Lawrence, M. (2014). Building environmentally sustainable food systems on informed citizen choices: Evidence from Australia. *Biological Agriculture and Horticulture, 30*(3), 183–197. doi:10.1080/01448765.2014.890542

Pease, B. (2010). *Undoing privilege: Unearned advantage in a divided world*. London, UK: Zed Books.

Peattie, K., & Collins, A. (2009). Guest editorial: Perspectives on sustainabel consumption. *International Journal of Consumer Studies, 33*(2), 107–112. doi:10.1111/j.1470-6431.2009.00758.x

Peattie, K., & Peattie, S. (2009). Social marketing: A pathway to consumption reduction? *Journal of Business Research, 62*(2), 260–268. doi:10.1016/j.jbusres.2008.01.033

Pecl, G. T., Araújo, M. B., Bell, J. D., Blanchard, J., Bonebrake, T. C., Chen, I.-C., … Williams, S. E. (2017). Biodiversity redistribution under climate change: Impacts on ecosystems and human well-being. *Science*, 355(6332). doi:10.1126/science.aai9214

Pedersen, J. A., Soliman, M., & Suffet, I. H. (2005). Human pharmaceuticals, hormones, and personal care product ingredients in runoff from agricultural fields irrigated with treated wastewater. *Journal of Agricultural and Food Chemistry, 53*(5), 1625–1632. doi:10.1021/jf049228m PMID:15740050

Pelletier, N., & Tyedmers, P. (2010). Forecasting potential global environmental costs of livestock production 2000-2050. *Proceedings of the National Academy of Sciences of the United States of America*, *107*(43), 18371–18374. doi:10.1073/pnas.1004659107 PMID:20921375

Pelligrini, M. (2014). *Extending shelf-life in protein products, naturally*. The Natural Provisioner. Retrieved from http://www.provisioneronline.com/articles/100955-extending-shelf-life-in-protein-products-naturally

Pendergrast, N. (2015). Live animal export, humane slaughter and media hegemony. *Animal Studies Journal*, *4*(1), 99–125.

People for the Ethical Treatment of Animals (PETA). (2017). *Tax meat*. Retrieved from http://www.peta.org/features/tax-meat/

Petherick, A. (2012). Light is cast on a long shadow. *Nature Climate Change*, *2*(10), 705–706. doi:10.1038/nclimate1703

Pew Research Center. (2017, January 12). *Social media fact sheet*. Retrieved from http://www.pewinternet.org/fact-sheet/social-media/

Pham, N. M., Mizoue, T., Tanaka, K., Tsuji, I., Tamakoshi, A., Matsuo, K., & Tanaka, K. et al. (2014). Meat consumption and colorectal cancer risk: An evaluation based on a systematic review of epidemiologic evidence among the Japanese population. *Japanese Journal of Clinical Oncology*, *44*(7), 641–650. doi:10.1093/jjco/hyu061 PMID:24842864

Phau, I., & Prendergast, G. (2000). Consuming luxury brands: The relevance of the "rarity principle". *Journal of Brand Management*, *7*(5), 366–375. doi:10.1057/bm.2000.26

Phillips, P. J., Smith, S. G., Kolpin, D. W., Zaugg, S. D., Buxton, H. T., Furlong, E. T., & Stinson, B. et al. (2010). Pharmaceutical formulation facilities as sources of opioids and other pharmaceuticals to wastewater treatment plant effluents. *Environmental Science & Technology*, *44*(13), 4910–4916. doi:10.1021/es100356f PMID:20521847

Piazza, J., Ruby, M. B., Loughnan, S., Luong, M., Kulik, J., Watkins, H. M., & Seigerman, M. (2015). Rationalizing meat consumption. The 4Ns. *Appetite*, *91*, 114–128. doi:10.1016/j.appet.2015.04.011 PMID:25865663

Pickover, M. (2005). *Animal rights in South Africa*. Cape Town, South Africa: Double Storey Books.

Pifer, L., Shimizu, K., & Pifer, R. (1994). Public attitudes toward animal research: Some international comparisons. *Society & Animals*, *2*(2), 95–113. doi:10.1163/156853094X00126 PMID:11654358

Pimentel, D., & Pimentel, M. (2003). Sustainability of meat-based and plant-based diets and the environment. *The American Journal of Clinical Nutrition*, *78*, s660–s663. PMID:12936963

Pimentel, D., & Pimentel, M. H. (2008). *Food, energy, and society* (3rd ed.). Boca Raton, FL: CRC Press.

Plain, R. (2017). More hogs and higher prices — unusual, but desirable. *National Hog Farmer*. Retrieved from http://www.nationalhogfarmer.com/marketing/more-hogs-and-higher-prices-unusual-desirable

Pluhar, E. B. (2010). Meat and morality: Alternatives to factory farming. *Journal of Agricultural & Environmental Ethics*, *23*(5), 455–468. doi:10.1007/s10806-009-9226-x

Pohjolainen, P., Tapio, P., Vinnari, M., Jokinen, P., & Räsänen, P. (2016). Consumer consciousness on meat and the environment – Exploring differences. *Appetite*, *101*, 37–45. doi:10.1016/j.appet.2016.02.012 PMID:26873454

Pollack, H. (2015). Ordering your steak well-done can impact your brain health. *Munchies*, 9 April. Retrieved from https://munchies.vice.com/en_us/article/ypxbe5/ordering-your-steak-well-done-can-impact-your-brain-health

Pollan, M. (2006). *The omnivore's dilemma*. New York, NY: The Penguin Press.

Pollard, C. M., Daly, A., Moore, M., & Binns, C. W. (2013). Public say food regulatory policies to improve health in Western Australia are important: Population survey results. *Australian and New Zealand Journal of Public Health, 37*(5), 475–482. doi:10.1111/1753-6405.12128 PMID:24090332

Polonsky, M. J. (1994). An introduction to green marketing. *Electronic Green Journal, 1*(2), 3. Retrieved from http://escholarship.org/uc/item/49n325b7

Popp, A., Lotze-Campen, H., & Bodirsky, B. (2010). Food consumption, diet shifts and associated non-CO_2 greenhouse gases from agricultural production. *Global Environmental Change, Governance. Complexity and Resilience, 20*(3), 451–462.

Popper, K., & Condry, J. (1995). *Televisão: Um perigo para a democracia* (M. Carvalho, Trans.). Lisboa, Portugal: Gradiva.

Population Reference Bureau (PRB). (2016). *World population data sheet 2014.* Retrieved from http://www.prb.org/Publications/Datasheets/2014/2014-world-population-data-sheet.aspx

Postman, N. (1993). *Technopoly: The surrender of culture to technology.* New York, NY: Vintage Books/Random House.

Povey, R., Wellens, B., & Conner, M. (2001). Attitudes towards following meat, vegetarian and vegan diets: An examination of the role of ambivalence. *Appetite, 37*(1), 15–26. doi:10.1006/appe.2001.0406 PMID:11562154

Prakash, V. (1999). Status of vultures in Keoladeo national park, Bharatpur, Rajasthan, with special reference to population crash in Gyps species. *Journal of the Bombay Natural History Society, 96*, 365–378.

Prakash, V., Green, R. E., Pain, D. J., Ranade, S. P., Saravanan, S., Prakash, N., & Cunningham, A. A. et al. (2007). Recent changes in populations of resident *Gyps* vultures in India. *Journal of the Bombay Natural History Society, 104*, 129–135.

Prakash, V., Pain, D. J., Cunningham, A. A., Donald, P. F., Prakash, N., Verma, A., & Rahmani, A. R. et al. (2003). Catastrophic collapse of Indian white-backed *Gyps bengalensis* and long-billed *Gyps indicus* vulture populations. *Biological Conservation, 109*(3), 381–390. doi:10.1016/S0006-3207(02)00164-7

Pravoslavie. (2009). *Lent in the Orthodox Church* [in Bulgarian]. Retrieved from http://www.pravoslavieto.com/docs/post/postite_v_BPC.htm#1

Premium Times. (2014). Nigeria to increase beef consumption to 1.3 million tonnes by 2050 – Adesina. Retrieved from https://www.premiumtimesng.com/news/160843-nigeria-increase-beef-consumption-1-3-million-tonnes-2050-adesina.html

PriceWaterhouseCoopers (PWC). (2012). *Too late for two degrees?* Retrieved from https://www.pwc.com/gx/en/sustainability/publications/low-carbon-economy-index/assets/pwc-low-carbon-economy-index-2012.pdf

Princen, T. (2005). *The logic of sufficiency.* Cambridge, MA: MIT Press.

Princen, T., Manno, J., & Martin, P. (Eds.). (2015). *Ending the fossil fuel era.* Cambridge, MA: MIT Press. doi:10.7551/mitpress/9780262028806.001.0001

Principles of Marketing. (2010). University of Minnesota Libraries Publishing. Retrieved from http://open.lib.umn.edu/principlesmarketing/

Processing, F. (2004). Two next-generation analogues better simulate full muscle texture. *Food Processing, 65*(8), 38.

Prothero, A. (1990). Green consumerism and the societal marketing concept: Marketing strategies for the 1990's. *Journal of Marketing Management, 6*(2), 87–103. doi:10.1080/0267257X.1990.9964119

Prusty, S., Kundu, S. S., & Kumar Sharma, V. (2017). Nutrient utilization and methane emissions in Murrah buffalo calves fed on diets with different methanogenic potential. *Livestock Science, 202*, 89–95. doi:10.1016/j.livsci.2017.05.023

Public Health England. (2017). *A quick guide to the government healthy eating recommendations*. Nutrition Advice Team, Public Health England. Retrieved from https://www.gov.uk/government/uploads/system/uploads/attachment_data/file/595133/A_quick_guide_to_govt_healthy_eating.pdf

Qing, P., Xi, A., & Hu, W. (2014). Consumer preference for meat in China: A case study of Beijing. *Emerging Markets Finance and Trade*, 50(Sup2), 135-143.

Raghunathan, R., Naylor, R. W., & Hoyer, W. D. (2006). The unhealthy – tasty intuition and its effects on taste inferences, enjoyment, and choice of food product. *Journal of Marketing*, *70*(4), 170–184. doi:10.1509/jmkg.70.4.170

Rahman, S., Islam, M. T., & Alam, D. S. (2014). Obesity and overweight in Bangladeshi children and adolescents: A scoping review. *BioMed Central (BMC). Public Health*, *14*, 70. doi:10.1186/1471-2458-14-70 PMID:24450958

Rajneesh, B. (1977). *The beloved: Songs of the Baul mystics* (Vol. 1). Pune, India: Rajneesh Foundation.

Ralston, R. A., Truby, H., Palermo, C. E., & Walker, K. Z. (2014). Colorectal cancer and nonfermented milk, solid cheese, and fermented milk consumption: A systematic review and meta-analysis of prospective studies. *Critical Reviews in Food Science and Nutrition*, *54*(9), 1167–1179. doi:10.1080/10408398.2011.629353 PMID:24499149

Rampone, A. J., & Reynolds, P. J. (1988). Obesity: Thermodynamic principles in perspective. *Life Sciences*, *43*(2), 93–110. doi:10.1016/0024-3205(88)90286-X PMID:3292870

RAND Corporation. (2016). *The global economic costs of antimicrobial resistance*. Retrieved from https://www.rand.org/blog/2016/05/the-global-economic-costs-of-amr.html

Raphaely, T., & Marinova, D. (2015). Here's an idea to chew over: GST reform should add meat to the tax buffet. *The Conversation*. Retrieved from https://theconversation.com/heres-an-idea-to-chew-over-gst-reform-should-add-meat-to-the-tax-buffet-45160

Raphaely, T., & Marinova, D. (2013). Flexitarianism: Traditional diets as social innovation for sustainability. *Visão Global*, *15*(1-2), 403–422.

Raphaely, T., & Marinova, D. (2014). Flexitarianism: A more moral dietary option. *International Journal of Sustainable Society*, *6*(1/2), 189–211. doi:10.1504/IJSSOC.2014.057846

Raphaely, T., & Marinova, D. (2014b). Flexitarianism: Decarbonising through flexible vegetarianism. *Renewable Energy*, *67*, 90–96. doi:10.1016/j.renene.2013.11.030

Raphaely, T., & Marinova, D. (2016). *Impact of meat consumption on health and environmental sustainability*. Hershey, PA: IGI Global. doi:10.4018/978-1-4666-9553-5

Raphaely, T., Marinova, D., & Marinova, M. (2016). Antibiotics and the livestock sector. In T. Raphaely & D. Marinova (Eds.), *Impact of meat consumption on health and environmental sustainability* (pp. 178–200). Hershey, PA: IGI Global. doi:10.4018/978-1-4666-9553-5.ch009

Rapier. (2010, January 26). The price of energy. *Forbes*. Retrieved from https://www.forbes.com/sites/energysource/2010/01/26/the-price-of-energy/#25cf888f67b1

Ray, D. K., Mueller, N. D., West, P. C., & Foley, J. A. (2013). Yield trends are insufficient to double global crop production by 2050. *PLoS One*, *8*(6), e66428. doi:10.1371/journal.pone.0066428 PMID:23840465

Red Barn Free Range Chicken. (n.d.). *Just what is free range?* Retrieved from http://freerangechicken.co.za/2011/02/just-what-is-free-range/

Reeser, T. W. (2010). *Masculinities in theory: An introduction.* Chichester, UK: Wiley- Blackwell. doi:10.1002/9781444317312

Reganold, J. P., & Wachter, J. M. (2016). Organic agriculture in the 21st century. *Nature Plants, 2*(2), 15221. doi:10.1038/nplants.2015.221 PMID:27249193

Regan, T. (2004). *Empty cages: Facing the challenge of animal rights.* Lanham, MD: Rowman & Littlefield Publishers.

Reid, M. A., Marsh, K. A., Zeuschner, C. L., Saunders, A. V., & Baines, S. K. (2013). Meeting the nutrient reference values on a vegetarian diet. *The Medical Journal of Australia, 199*(4 Suppl), S33–S40. PMID:25369927

Reinders, M. J., Huitink, M., Coosje Dijkstra, S., Maaskant, A. J., & Heijnen, J. (2017). Menu-engineering in restaurants: Adapting portion sizes on plates to enhance vegetable consumption – a real life experiment. *The International Journal of Behavioral Nutrition and Physical Activity, 14*(1), 1–11. doi:10.1186/s12966-017-0496-9 PMID:28424081

Reisch, L. A., Sunstein, C. R., & Gwozdz, W. (2017). Viewpoint: Beyond carrots and sticks: Europeans support health nudges. *Food Policy, 69*, 1–10. doi:10.1016/j.foodpol.2017.01.007

Renner, M. (2014). Peak meat production strains land and water resources. *Vital Signs, Worldwatch Institute.* Retrieved from http://vitalsigns.worldwatch.org/vs-trend/peak-meat-production-strains-land-and-water-resources

Renner, M. (2015). Peak meat production strains land and water resources. Vital Signs: The trends that are shaping our future, 22. The Worldwatch Institute. Retrieved from http://www.worldwatch.org/peak-meat-production-strains-land-and-water-resources-1

Retail News Insider. (2014). *From lab to table: The future of food.* Retrieved from http://www.retailnewsinsider.com/2014/06/01/from-lab-to-table-the-future-of-food

Retail News Insider. (2017). *Supply solutions: Sourcing Sophistication for today's new retail landscape.* Retrieved from http://www.retailnewsinsider.com/2017/07/06/supply-solutions-sourcing-sophistication-for-todays-new-retail-landscape/

Rettner, R. (2009). *Why are human brains so big?* Live Science. Retrieved from: https://www.livescience.com/5540-human-brains-big.html

Reuter, M., Roth, S., Holve, K., & Hennig, J. (2006). Identification of first candidate genes for creativity: A pilot study. *Brain Research, 1069*(1), 190–197. doi:10.1016/j.brainres.2005.11.046 PMID:16403463

Review on Antimicrobial Resistance. (2015). *Antimicrobials in agriculture and the environment: Reducing unnecessary use and waste.* Retrieved from https://amr-review.org/sites/default/files/Antimicrobials%20in%20agriculture%20and%20the%20environment%20-%20Reducing%20unnecessary%20use%20and%20waste.pdf

Richard, C., Cristall, L., Fleming, E., Lewis, E. D., Ricupero, M., Jacobs, R. L., & Field, C. J. (2017). Impact of egg consumption on cardiovascular risk factors in individuals with type 2 diabetes and at risk for developing diabetes: A systematic review of randomized nutritional intervention studies. *Canadian Journal of Diabetes, 41*(4), 453–463. doi:10.1016/j.jcjd.2016.12.002 PMID:28359773

Richman, E. L., Kenfield, S. A., Stampfer, M. J., Giovannucci, E. L., Zeisel, S. H., Willett, W. C., & Chan, J. M. (2012). Choline intake and risk of lethal prostate cancer: Incidence and survival. *The American Journal of Clinical Nutrition, 96*(4), 855–863. doi:10.3945/ajcn.112.039784 PMID:22952174

Ridley, L. (2010). What's inside the brain of a genius? *BBC Science Focus Magazine.* Retrieved from http://www.sciencefocus.com/feature/tech/whats-inside-brain-genius

Ripple, W. J., Smith, P., Haberl, H., Montzka, S. A., McAlpine, C., & Boucher, D. H. (2014). Ruminants, climate change and climate policy. *Nature Climate Change*, *4*(1), 1–4.

Risebrough, R. W. (2004). Population collapses of three species of *Gyps* vultures in the Indian Subcontinent: An overview. In R. D. Chancellor & B. U. Meyburg (Eds.), *Raptors worldwide* (pp. 197–214). Budapest, Hungary: WWGBP/MME.

Ritzer, G. (Ed.). (2007). Myth. *Blackwell Encyclopedia of Sociology Online*. Retrieved from http://www.sociologyencyclopedia.com/public/search?query=myth

Rizzo, N. S., Sabaté, J., Jaceldo-Siegl, K., & Fraser, G. E. (2011). Vegetarian dietary patterns are associated with a lower risk of metabolic syndrome: The adventist health study 2. *Diabetes Care*, *34*(5), 1225–1227. doi:10.2337/dc10-1221 PMID:21411506

Roberts, P. (2008). *The end of food*. New York, NY: Houghton Mifflin Harcourt.

Robey-Graham, A. K. (2008). Generational comparisons and contrasts chart. Retrieved from http://www.napavalley.edu/people/jhall/Documents/Generational%20Chart.pdf

Rockström, J., Steffen, W., Noone, K., Persson, A., Chapin, F. S. III, Lambin, E. F., & Foley, J. A. et al. (2009). A safe operating space for humanity. *Nature*, *461*, 472–475. doi:10.1038/461472a

Rodayan, A., Afana, S., Segura, P. A., Sultana, T., Metcalfe, C. D., & Yargeau, V. (2016). Linking drugs of abuse in wastewater to contamination of surface and drinking water. *Environmental Toxicology and Chemistry*, *35*(4), 843–849. doi:10.1002/etc.3085 PMID:26190693

Rogelj, J., Schaeffer, M., Meinshausen, M., Shindell, D. T., Hare, W., & Klimont, Z., … Schellnhuber, H. J. (2014). Disentangling the effects of CO2 and short-lived climate forcer mitigation. In *Proceedings of the National Academy of Sciences* (Vol. 111, pp. 16325-16330).

Rogers, E. M. (2010). *Diffusion of innovations* (4th ed.). New York, NY: Simon and Schuster.

Rojas-Downing, M. M., Nejadhashemi, A. P., Harrigan, T., & Woznicki, S. A. (2017). Climate change and livestock: Impacts, adaptation, and mitigation. *Climate Risk Management*, *16*, 145–163. doi:10.1016/j.crm.2017.02.001

Romm, C. (2014). The World War II campaign to bring organ meats to the dinner table. *Atlantic (Boston, Mass.)*, *25*(September). Retrieved from https://www.theatlantic.com/health/archive/2014/09/the-world-war-ii-campaign-to-bring-organ-meats-to-the-dinner-table/380737/

Romo, L. K., & Donovan-Kicken, E. (2012). "Actually, I Don't Eat Meat": A multiple-goals perspective of communication about vegetarianism. *Communication Studies*, *63*(4), 405–420. doi:10.1080/10510974.2011.623752

Rosell, M., Appleby, P., Spencer, E., & Key, T. (2006). Weight gain over 5 years in 21,966 meat-eating, fish-eating, vegetarian, and vegan men and women in EPIC-Oxford. *International Journal of Obesity*, *30*(9), 1389–1396. doi:10.1038/sj.ijo.0803305 PMID:16534521

Rossi, M. A., & Tierno, P. (2009). A dimensão econômica da teoria política aristotélica. *Lua Nova*, *77*(77), 179–204. doi:10.1590/S0102-64452009000200006

Rothgerber, H. (2012). Real men don't eat (vegetable) quiche: Masculinity and the justification of meat consumption. *Psychology of Men & Masculinity*, *14*(4), 363–375. doi:10.1037/a0030379

Rothgerber, H. (2014). Efforts to overcome vegetarian-induced dissonance among meat eaters. *Appetite*, *79*, 32–41. doi:10.1016/j.appet.2014.04.003 PMID:24727102

Rothschild, M. L. (1999). Carrots, sticks and promises: A conceptual framework for the management of public health and social issue behaviors. *Journal of Marketing*, *63*(4), 24–37. doi:10.2307/1251972

Roy Morgan Research. (2016). The slow but steady rise of vegetarianism in Australia. Retrieved from http://www.roymorgan.com/findings/vegetarianisms-slow-but-steady-rise-in-australia-201608151105

Roy Morgan Research. (2016). *The slow, but steady rise of Vegetarianism in Australia*. Retrieved from http://www.roymorgan.com/findings/vegetarianisms-slow-but-steady-rise-in-australia-201608151105

Royal Society for the Prevention of Cruelty to Animals (RSPCA). (2011). *What happens to bobby calves?* Retrieved from http://kb.rspca.org.au/What-happens-to-bobby-calves_87.html

Royal Society for the Prevention of Cruelty to Animals (RSPCA). (2012a). *Corporate supporters*. Retrieved from http://www.rspca.org.au/what-we-do/about-us/who-supports-us/corporate-supporters.html

Royal Society for the Prevention of Cruelty to Animals (RSPCA). (2012b). How we govern ourselves. Retrieved from http://www.rspca.org.au/what-we-do/about-us/how-we-govern-ourselves/

Royal Society for the Prevention of Cruelty to Animals (RSPCA). (2013). What happens on an RSPCA approved meat chicken farm? [YouTube video]. Retrieved from https://www.youtube.com/watch?v=mtTLm9LF5Ns

Royal Society for the Prevention of Cruelty to Animals (RSPCA). (2016). *Impact report*. Retrieved from https://www.rspca.org.au/sites/default/files/2016-10-RSPCA-AFS-Impact-Report-web.pdf

Royal Society for the Prevention of Cruelty to Animals (RSPCA). (2017a). About us. Retrieved from https://www.rspca.org.au/what-we-do/about-us-0

Royal Society for the Prevention of Cruelty to Animals (RSPCA). (2017b). Our history. Retrieved from https://www.rspca.org.au/what-we-do/about-us/our-history

Rozin, P. (2006). The integration of biological, social, cultural and psychological influences on food choice. In R. Shepherd & M. Raats (Eds.), *Psychology of food choice* (Vol. 3, pp. 19–40). Oxfordshire, UK: CABI. doi:10.1079/9780851990323.0019

Rozin, P., Hormes, J. M., Faith, M. S., & Wansink, B. (2012). Is meat male? A quantitative, multi-method framework to establish metaphoric relationships. *The Journal of Consumer Research*, *39*(3), 629–643. doi:10.1086/664970

Ruby, M. B., & Heine, S. J. (2011). Meat, morals and masculinity. *Appetite*, *56*(2), 447–450. doi:10.1016/j.appet.2011.01.018 PMID:21256169

Ruiz, M. (2007). *Ausblick und Chancen des Vegetarismustrends im Lebensmittelhandel*. (Master thesis). Vienna, Austria: FH Corporate Governance and Management

Rutgersson, C., Fick, J., Marathe, N., Kristiansson, E., Janzon, A., Angelin, M., & Larsson, D. G. et al. (2014). Fluoroquinolones and qnr genes in sediment, water, soil, and human fecal flora in an environment polluted by manufacturing discharges. *Environmental Science & Technology*, *48*(14), 7825–7832. doi:10.1021/es501452a PMID:24988042

Ryan, R. M., & Deci, E. L. (2000). Self-determination theory and the facilitation of intrinsic motivation, social development, and well-being. *The American Psychologist*, *55*(1), 68–78. doi:10.1037/0003-066X.55.1.68 PMID:11392867

Ryder, R. (2005). All beings that feel pain deserve human rights - Equality of the species is the logical conclusion of post-Darwin morality. *The Guardian*. Retrieved from http://www.guardian.co.uk/uk/2005/aug/06/animalwelfare

Sabaté, J. (2003). The contribution of vegetarian diets to health and disease: A paradigm shift? *The American Journal of Clinical Nutrition*, *78*(3 Suppl.), 502S–507S. PMID:12936940

Sachs, J. (2017). The meat lobby, the politicians, and U.S. nutrition. In B. Kateman (Ed.), *The reducetarian solution: How the surprisingly simple act of reducing the amount of meat in your diet can transform your health and the planet* (pp. 103–106). New York, NY: TarcherPerigee.

Sadler, M. J. (2004). Meat alternatives — market developments and health benefits. *Trends in Food Science & Technology, 15*(5), 250–260. doi:10.1016/j.tifs.2003.09.003

Sage, C. (2012). *Environment and food.* London, UK: Routledge.

Sage, C. (2014). Making and un-making meat: Cultural boundaries, environmental thresholds and dietary transgressions. In M. K. Goodman & C. Sage (Eds.), *Food transgressions: Making sense of contemporary food politics* (pp. 181–203). Farnham, UK: Ashgate.

Sağlıklı Tavuk Bilgi Platformu. (2016) Platform hakkında [About the platform]. Retrieved from http://www.sagliklitavuk.org/platform-hakkinda

Sagoe, D. (2014). *Anabolic steroid use is not just about bodybuilding.* The Conversation. *Health & Medicine, 15*(July). Retrieved from http://theconversation.com/anabolic-steroid-use-is-not-just-about-bodybuilding-29180

Salehi, M., Moradi-Lakeh, M., Salehi, M. H., Nojomi, M., & Kolahdooz, F. (2013). Meat, fish, and esophageal cancer risk: A systematic review and dose-response meta-analysis. *Nutrition Reviews, 71*(5), 257–267. doi:10.1111/nure.12028 PMID:23590703

SALESmanago. (2015). *Advertising: the smiling carrion? How Oliviero Toscani Destroyed 5 Foundations of Marketing.* Retrieved from http://blog.salesmanago.com/marketing-automation-2/advertising-the-smiling-carrion-how-oliviero-toscani-destroyed-5-foundations-of-marketing/

Samraj, A., Pearce, O. M. T., Läubli, H., Crittenden, A. N., Bergfeld, A. K., & Banda, K. … Varki, A. (2015). A red meat-derived glycan promotes inflammation and cancer progression. *Proceedings of the National Academy of Sciences of the United States of America*, 112, 542-547. doi:10.1073/pnas.1417508112

Samuelsen, O. B., Torsvik, V., & Ervik, A. (1992). Long-range changes in oxytetracycline concentration and bacterial resistance towards oxytetracycline in a fish farm sediment after medication. *The Science of the Total Environment, 114*, 25–36. doi:10.1016/0048-9697(92)90411-K PMID:1594922

Sanderson, H., Fricker, C., Brown, R. S., Majury, A., & Liss, S. N. (2016). Antibiotic resistance genes as an emerging environmental contaminant. *Environmental Reviews, 24*(2), 205–218. doi:10.1139/er-2015-0069

Sanders, T. (1999). The nutritional adequacy of plant-based diets. *The Proceedings of the Nutrition Society, 58*(2), 265–269. doi:10.1017/S0029665199000361 PMID:10466165

Sankoff, P. J. (2009). The welfare paradigm: Making the world a better place for animals? In P. J. Sankoff & S. White (Eds.), *Animal law in Australasia: A new dialogue* (pp. 7–34). Sydney, Australia: Federation Press.

Sansoucy, R., Jabbar, M. A., Ehui, S., & Fitzhugh, H. (1995). The contribution of livestock to food security and sustainable development (Keynote Paper). Retrieved from http://www.fao.org/Wairdocs/ILRI/x5462E/x5462e04.htm

Sans, P., & Combris, P. (2015). World meat consumption patterns: An overview of the last fifty years (1961-2011). *Meat Science, 109*, 106–111. doi:10.1016/j.meatsci.2015.05.012 PMID:26117396

Santamaria, C. (2015). *Plant-based food experiment* (unpublished student research paper for the Social Psychology course). Psychology Department, University of New York in Prague. Retrieved from http://humanimal.cz/texty_soubory/plant-based_food_experiment-santamaria.pdf

Sapkota, A. R., Lefferts, L. Y., McKenzie, S., & Walker, P. (2007). What do we feed to food-production animals? A review of animal feed ingredients and their potential impacts on human health. *Environmental Health Perspectives*, *115*(5), 663–670. doi:10.1289/ehp.9760 PMID:17520050

Sariozkan, S., Yalcin, C., Cevger, Y., Aral, Y., & Sipahi, C. (2009). The financial impacts of the avian influenza outbreaks on Turkish table egg producers. *World's Poultry Science Journal*, *65*(01), 91–96. doi:10.1017/S0043933909000075

Sarmah, A. K., Meyer, M. T., & Boxall, A. B. A. (2006). A global perspective on the use, sales, exposure pathways, occurrence, fate and effects of veterinary antibiotics (VAs) in the environment. *Chemosphere*, *65*(5), 725–759. doi:10.1016/j.chemosphere.2006.03.026 PMID:16677683

Saunois, M., Jackson, R. B., Bousquet, P., Poulter, B., & Canadell, J. G. (2016). The growing role of methane in anthropogenic climate change. *Environmental Research Letters*, *11*(12), 120207. doi:10.1088/1748-9326/11/12/120207

Scarborough, P., Appleby, P. N., Mizdrak, A., Briggs, A. D. M., Travis, R. C., Bradbury, K. E., & Key, T. J. (2014). Dietary greenhouse gas emissions of meat-eaters, fish-eaters, vegetarians and vegans in the UK. *Climatic Change*, *125*(2), 179–192. doi:10.1007/s10584-014-1169-1 PMID:25834298

Schank, R., & Abelson, R. (1977). *Scripts plans goals and understanding: An inquiry into human knowledge structures.* Mahwah, NJ: Lawrence Erlbaum Associates.

Schewe, R. L., & Stuart, D. (2017). Why don't they just change? Contract farming, informational influence, and barriers to agricultural climate change mitigation. *Rural Sociology*, *82*(2), 226–262. doi:10.1111/ruso.12122

Schiebinger, L. (1993). *Nature's body: Gender in the making of modern science.* Boston, MA: Beacon Press.

Schlechtweg, H. P. (1996). Media frames and environmental discourse: The case of "Focus: Logjam". In J. Cantrill & C. Overac (Eds.), *The symbolic Earth: Discourse and our creation of the environment* (pp. 257–277). Lexington, KY: The University Press of Kentucky.

Schmid, W., & Goldhofer, H. (2016). *Agrarmärkte 2016: 2 Getreide.* Retrieved from http://www.lfl.bayern.de/mam/cms07/iem/dateien/02_getreide__by_.pdf

Schmidinger, K. (2012). *Worldwide alternatives to animal derived foods – overview and evaluation models - solutions to global problems caused by livestock.* (Doctoral dissertation). Vienna, Austria: University of Natural Resources and Life Sciences.

Schmidinger, K., Bogueva, D., & Marinova, D. (2018this volume). New meat without livestock. In D. Bogueva, D. Marinova, & T. Raphaely (Eds.), *Social marketing and its influence on animal-based products.* Hershey, PA: IGI Global.

Schoenemann, P. T. (2006). Evolution of the size and functional areas of the human brain. *Annual Review of Anthropology*, *35*(1), 379–406. doi:10.1146/annurev.anthro.35.081705.123210

Schösler, H., de Boer, J., & Boersema, J. J. (2012). Can we cut out the meat of the dish?: Constructing consumer-oriented pathways towards meat substitution. *Appetite*, *58*(1), 39–47. doi:10.1016/j.appet.2011.09.009 PMID:21983048

Schröder, M. J. A., & McEachern, M. G. (2004). Consumer value conflicts surrounding ethical food purchase decisions: A focus on animal welfare. *International Journal of Consumer Studies*, *28*(2), 168–177. doi:10.1111/j.1470-6431.2003.00357.x

Schroeter, J., & Azzam, A. (1990). Measuring market power in multi-product oligopolies: The US meat industry. *Applied Economics*, *22*(10), 1365–1376. doi:10.1080/00036849000000107

Schwartz, J. (2002, December 16). Supersize American dream: Expensive? I'll take it. *The New York Times*, 8.

Schwartz, S. H. (1977). Normative influences on altruism. *Advances in Experimental Social Psychology, 10*, 221–279. doi:10.1016/S0065-2601(08)60358-5

Schwarzer, S. (2012). *Growing greenhouse gas emissions due to meat production*. Geneva, Switzerland: UNEP Global Environmental Alert Service (GEAS). Retrieved from http://www.unep.org/pdf/UNEP-GEAS_OCT_2012.pdf

Schwietzke, S., Sherwood, O. A., Bruhwiler, L. M. P., Miller, J. B., Etiope, G., Dlugokencky, E. J., & Tans, P. P. et al. (2016). Upward revision of global fossil fuel methane emissions based on isotope database. *Nature, 538*(7623), 88–91. doi:10.1038/nature19797 PMID:27708291

Schwingshackl, L., Hoffmann, G., Schwedhelm, C., Kalle-Uhlmann, T., Missbach, B., Knüppel, S., & Boeing, H. (2016). Consumption of dairy products in relation to changes in anthropometric variables in adult populations: A Systematic review and meta-analysis of cohort Studies. *PLoS One, 11*(6), e0157461. doi:10.1371/journal.pone.0157461 PMID:27310919

Scientific Advisory Committee on Nutrition (SACN). (2010). *Iron and health*. London, UK: TSO. Retrieved from https://www.gov.uk/government/uploads/system/uploads/attachment_data/file/339309/SACN_Iron_and_Health_Report.pdf

Sciponi, J. (2016). *Bill Gates and NY Met David Wright see money in meatless venture*. Fox Business. Retrieved from http://www.foxbusiness.com/features/2016/10/31/bill-gates-and-ny-met-david-wright-see-money-in-meatless-venture.htm

Scott, M. (2014, January 13). Hybrid consumers abandon mid-market retailers. *Forbes magazine*. Retrieved from http://www.forbes.com/sites/mikescott/2014/01/13/fybrid-consumers-abandon-mid-market-retailers/

Scott, M. M. (2007). Westernization in sub-Saharan Africa: Facing loss of culture, knowledge, and environment [Master of Architecture Thesis]. Montana State University. Retrieved from http://scholarworks.montana.edu/xmlui/handle/1/2230

Šedová, I., Slovák, Ľ., & Ježková, I. (2016). Coping with unpleasant knowledge: Meat eating among students of environmental studies. *Appetite, 107*, 415–424. doi:10.1016/j.appet.2016.08.102 PMID:27554181

Seo, Y., Choi, J., Kim, S., Min, H., & Jung, Y. (2007). Prioritizing environmental risks of veterinary antibiotics based on the use and the potential to reach environment. *Korean Journal of Soil Science and Fertility, 40*(1), 43–50.

Serpell, J., & Paul, E. (2003). Pets and the development of positive attitudes to animals. In A. Manning & J. Serpell (Eds.), *Animals and human society: Changing perspectives* (pp. 127–144). London, UK: Taylor & Francis.

Sexton, A. (2016). Alternative proteins and the (non)stuff of "meat". *Gastronomica, 16*(3), 66–78. doi:10.1525/gfc.2016.16.3.66

Shamay-Tsoory, S. G., Adler, N., Aharon-Peretz, J., Perry, D., & Mayseless, N. (2011). The origins of originality: The neural bases of creative thinking and originality. *Neuropsychologia, 49*(2), 178–185. doi:10.1016/j.neuropsychologia.2010.11.020 PMID:21126528

Shang, X., Scott, D., Hodge, A. M., English, D. R., Giles, G. G., Ebeling, P. R., & Sanders, K. M. (2016). Dietary protein intake and risk of type 2 diabetes: Results from the Melbourne Collaborative Cohort Study and a meta-analysis of prospective studies. *The American Journal of Clinical Nutrition, 104*(5), 1352–1365. doi:10.3945/ajcn.116.140954 PMID:27629053

Shapiro, P. (2016). Feasting from the federal trough: how the meat, egg and dairy industries gorge on taxpayer dollars while fighting modest rules. In T. Raphaely, & D. Marinova (Eds), Impact of meat consumption on health and environmental sustainability (pp. 244-254). Hershey, PA: IGI Global. doi:10.4018/978-1-4666-9553-5.ch013

Shaw, J. S., & Stroup, R. L. (1995). *Should we worry about ozone?* National Center for Policy Analysis. Policy Report No. 191. Retrieved from http://www.ncpa.org/pdfs/st191.pdf

Shen, A. (2013). Why we should stop obsessing over how expensive the world's first test-tube hamburger is. *Think-Progress*. Retrieved from https://thinkprogress.org/why-we-should-stop-obsessing-over-how-expensive-the-worlds-first-test-tube-hamburger-is-c4e7011f52f4/

Sheth, J. N., & Parvatiyar, A. (1995). Relationship marketing in consumer markets: Antecedents and consequences. *Journal of the Academy of Marketing Science*, *23*(4), 255–271. doi:10.1177/009207039502300405

Shi, B., Cao, X., Chen, Q., Zhuang, K., & Qiu, J. (2017). Different brain structures associated with artistic and scientific creativity: A voxel-based morphometry study. *Scientific Reports*, *21*, 42911. doi:10.1038/srep42911 PMID:28220826

Shields, S., & Orme-Evans, G. (2015). The impacts of climate change mitigation strategies on animal welfare. *Animals (Basel)*, *5*(2), 361–394. doi:10.3390/ani5020361 PMID:26479240

Shine, K. P. (2012). The global warming potential—the need for an interdisciplinary retrial. *Climatic Change*, *96*(4), 467–472. doi:10.1007/s10584-009-9647-6

Shiva, V. (2005). *Earth democracy: Justice, sustainability and peace*. Cambridge, UK: South End Press.

Shi, Y. X. (2008). 中国牛肉消费现状及其影响因素分析. *Farm Economic Management*, *4*, 53–55.

Shi, Y., Yu, P.-W., & Zeng, D.-Z. (2015). Dose–response meta-analysis of poultry intake and colorectal cancer incidence and mortality. *European Journal of Nutrition*, *54*(2), 243–250. doi:10.1007/s00394-014-0705-0 PMID:24788671

Shi, Z., Xu, P., Wang, Z., & Song, S. (2012). Willingness to pay for traceable pork: Evidence from Beijing, China. *China Agricultural Economic Review*, *4*(2), 200–215. doi:10.1108/17561371211224782

Shoemaker, J., & Schrag, D. (2013). The danger of overvaluing methane's influence on future climate change. *Climatic Change*, *120*(4), 903–914. doi:10.1007/s10584-013-0861-x

Shukla, P. (2015). Consumers in Asia buy luxuries for different reasons to the West. *The Conversation*. Retrieved from https://theconversation.com/consumers-in-asia-buy-luxuries-for-different-reasons-to-the-west-45069

Shurtleff, W., & Aoyagi, A. (2014). *History of meat alternatives (965 CE to 2014): Extensively annotated bibliography and sourcebook*. Retrieved from www.soyinfocenter.com/pdf/179/MAL.pdf

Shurtleff, W., & Aoyagi, A. (2014). History of meat alternatives (965CE to 2014): Extensively annotated bibliography and sourcebook. *Soyinfo Center*. Retrieved from http://www.soyinfocenter.com/pdf/179/MAL.pdf

Shurtleff, W., Huang, H. T., & Aoyagi, A. (2014). *History of soyfoods in China and Taiwan, and in Chinese cookbooks, restaurants, and Chinese work with soyfoods outside China. Extnsively annotated bibliography and sourcebook*. Lafayette, CA: Soyinfo Center.

Sidanius, J., & Pratto, F. (1999). *Social dominance: An intergroup theory of social hierarchy and oppression*. Cambridge, UK: Cambridge University Press. doi:10.1017/CBO9781139175043

Siervo, M., Lara, J., Chowdhury, S., Ashor, A., Oggioni, C., & Mathers, J. C. (2015). Effects of the Dietary Approach to Stop Hypertension (DASH) diet on cardiovascular risk factors: A systematic review and meta-analysis. *British Journal of Nutrition*, *113*(1), 1–15. doi:10.1017/S0007114514003341 PMID:25430608

Sifferlin, A. (2012, May 21). Fat in red meat and butter may hurt your brain. *Time Magazine*. Retrieved from http://healthland.time.com/2012/05/21/fat-in-red-meat-and-butter-may-hurt-your-brain/?iid=hl-main-lede#ixzz1vWWNx67G

Signal, T. D., & Taylor, N. (2006). Attitudes to animals in the animal protection community Compared to a normative community sample. *Society & Animals*, *14*(3), 265–274. doi:10.1163/156853006778149181

Sik, B. (2016). Dünyayı tüketmek: Kümes hayvancılığı odağında endüstriyel hayvancılık sektörü [Consuming the world: Livestock industry with a focus on poultry farming]. Retrieved from http://www.greenpeace.org/turkey/Global/turkey/report/2016/dunyayi-tuketmek.pdf

Silbergeld, E. K., Graham, J., & Price, L. B. (2008). Industrial food animal production, antimicrobial resistance, and human health. *Annual Review of Public Health*, *29*(1), 151–169. doi:10.1146/annurev.publhealth.29.020907.090904 PMID:18348709

Silverstein, M. J., & Fiske, N. (2003). *Trading up: The new American luxury*. New York, NY: Portfolio Penguin Group.

Silvertown, J. (2015). Have ecosystem services been oversold? *Trends in Ecology & Evolution*, *30*(11), 641–648. doi:10.1016/j.tree.2015.08.007 PMID:26437632

Simon, N. S. (2005). Loosely bound oxytetracycline in riverine sediments from two tributaries of the Chesapeake Bay. *Environmental Science & Technology*, *39*(10), 3480–3487. doi:10.1021/es049039k PMID:15952351

Singer, P. (2009). Animal liberation: The definitive classic of the animal movement (updated ed.). New York, NY: HarperCollins.

Singer, P. (2012). Personal interview with Peter Singer, Australian ethicist (Copy of the Transcript on File with the Authors).

Singer, P. (1975). *Animal liberation: A new ethics for our treatment of animals*. New York, NY: New York Review/Random House.

Singer, P., & Mason, J. (2006). *The ethics of what we eat: Why our food choices matter*. New York, NY: Rodale.

Singh, P. N., Sabaté, J., & Fraser, G. E. (2003). Does low meat consumption increase life expectancy in humans? *The American Journal of Clinical Nutrition*, *78*(3 Suppl.), 526S–532S. PMID:12936945

Singh, S., Singh, P. P., Roberts, L. R., & Sanchez, W. (2013). Chemopreventive strategies in hepatocellular carcinoma. *Nature Reviews. Gastroenterology & Hepatology*, *11*(1), 45–54. doi:10.1038/nrgastro.2013.143 PMID:23938452

Sinha, R., Cross, A. J., Graubard, B. I., Letzmann, M. F., & Schatzkin, A. (2009). Meat intake and mortality: A prospective study of over half a million people. *Archives of Internal Medicine*, *169*(6), 562–571. doi:10.1001/archinternmed.2009.6 PMID:19307518

Slavova, P. (2016). Conditions of productivity processes in a company of food industry in Bulgaria. *Procedia: Social and Behavioral Sciences*, *230*, 367–371. doi:10.1016/j.sbspro.2016.09.046

Smetana, S., Mathys, A., Knoch, A., & Heinz, V. (2015). Meat alternatives: Life cycle assessment of most known meat substitutes. *The International Journal of Life Cycle Assessment*, *20*(9), 1254–1267. doi:10.1007/s11367-015-0931-6

Smil, V. (2013). Should humans eat meat? [Excerpt]. *Scientific American*. Retrieved from https://www.scientificamerican.com/article/should-humans-eat-meat-excerpt/

Smil, V. (2002). Worldwide transformation of diets, burdens of meat production and opportunities for novel food proteins. *Enzyme and Microbial Technology*, *30*(3), 305–311. doi:10.1016/S0141-0229(01)00504-X

Smil, V. (2004). Improving efficiency and reducing waste in our food system. *Environmental Sciences*, *1*(1), 17–26. doi:10.1076/evms.1.1.17.23766

Smil, V. (2013). *Should we eat meat evolution and consequences of modern carnivory*. Chichester, UK: Wiley-Blackwell. doi:10.1002/9781118278710

Smith, O. (2017, 14 May) Revealed: The nation that eats the least meat per capita. *The Telegraph*. Retrieved from http://www.telegraph.co.uk/travel/maps-and-graphics/world-according-to-meat-consumption/

Smith, P., Nayak, D., Linthorst, G., Peters, D., & Bucquet, C. (2016). *Science-based GHG emissions targets for agriculture and forestry commodities*. University of Aberdeen, ECOFYS; PBL Netherlands Environmental Assessment Agency. Retrieved from http://www.pbl.nl/sites/default/files/cms/publicaties/pbl-2016-science-based-greenhouse-gas-emissions-targets-for-agriculture-and-forestry-commodities-2856.pdf

Smith, E. R., Mackie, D. M., & Claypool, H. M. (2014). *Social Psychology*. New York, NY: Psychology Press.

Smith, F. A., Doughty, C. E., Malhi, Y., Svenning, J.-C., & Terborgh, J. (2016). Megafauna in the Earth system. *Ecography*, *39*(2), 99–108. doi:10.1111/ecog.02156

Smith, K. R., Desai, M. A., Rogers, J. V., & Houghton, R. A. (2013). Joint CO_2 and CH_4 accountability for global warming. *Proceedings of the National Academy of Sciences of the United States of America*, *110*(31), E2865–E2874. doi:10.1073/pnas.1308004110 PMID:23847202

Smithsonian. (2010). *Milestones in human evolution*. Newsdesk: Newsroom of the Smithsonian, Retrieved from http://newsdesk.si.edu/factsheets/milestones-human-evolution

Smith, W. A. (2000). Social marketing: An evolving definition. *American Journal of Health Behavior*, *24*(1), 11–17. doi:10.5993/AJHB.24.1.3

Smith, W. A. (2006). Social marketing: An overview of approach and effects. *Injury Prevention*, *12*(Suppl. 1), i38–i43. doi:10.1136/ip.2006.012864 PMID:16788110

Sobal, J. (2005). Men, meat, and marriage: Models of masculinity. *Food & Foodways*, *13*(1-2), 135–158. doi:10.1080/07409710590915409

Soderlin, B. (2017). *More cattle, lower prices: Ranchers and feeders hope consumers respond by buying more beef*. Omaha World. Retrieved from http://www.omaha.com/money/more-cattle-lower-prices-ranchers-and-feeders-hope-consumers-respond/article_f7dd3bbc-2b41-5c05-a5e7-4f55a24483a1.html

Sofi, F., Macchi, C., Abbate, R., Gensini, G. F., & Casini, A. (2014). Mediterranean diet and health status: An updated meta-analysis and a proposal for a literature-based adherence score. *Public Health Nutrition*, *17*(12), 2769–2782. doi:10.1017/S1368980013003169 PMID:24476641

Soil Association. (2010). *Telling porkies: The big fat lie about doubling food production*. Bristol, UK: Soil Association. Retrieved from http://stopogm.net/sites/stopogm.net/files/webfm/plataforma/TellingPorkies.pdf

Soininen, K. (2011). *Meat-free and free-from foods - UK - September 2011. Market Research Report*. Mintel.

Song, L.F. (2011). 简述影响消费者购买行为的因素. *The Business Circular*, 24-25.

Song, J., Su, H., Wang, B., Zhou, Y., & Guo, L.-L. (2014). Fish consumption and lung cancer risk: Systematic review and meta-analysis. *Nutrition and Cancer*, *66*(4), 539–549. doi:10.1080/01635581.2014.894102 PMID:24707954

Soron, D. (2011). Road kill: Commodity fetishism and structural violence. In J. Sanbonmatsu (Ed.), *Critical theory and animal liberation* (pp. 55–69). Plymouth, UK: Rowman & Littlefield.

Southern African Poultry Association. (2012). *Code of practice*. Retrieved from http://www.sapoultry.co.za/pdf-docs/code-practice-broilers.pdf

Souza, R. G. M., Gomes, A. C., Naves, M. M. V., & Mota, J. F. (2015). Nuts and legume seeds for cardiovascular risk reduction: Scientific evidence and mechanisms of action. *Nutrition Reviews*, *73*(6), 335–347. doi:10.1093/nutrit/nuu008 PMID:26011909

Special Eurobarometer 442. (2015). *Attitudes of Europeans toward animal welfare.* Brussels, Belgium: European Commission. Retrieved from http://ec.europa.eu/COMMFrontOffice/PublicOpinion/index.cfm/ResultDoc/download/DocumentKy/71348

Spiller, A., & Nitzko, S. (2015). Peak meat: The role of meat in sustainable consumption. In L.A. Reisch & J. Thøgersen (Eds.), Handbook of research on sustainable consumption (pp. 192-208). Cheltenham: Edward Elgar.

Spooner, B. (2016). Food Waste and Food Security in a Globalizing World. In *Food Waste Across the Supply Chain: A US Perspective on a Global Problem* (pp. 73–85). University of Pennsylvania.

Springmann, M., Godfray, H. C., Rayner, M., & Scarborough, P. (2016). Analysis and valuation of the health and climate change cobenefits of dietary change. *Proceedings of the National Academy of Sciences of the United States of America*, *113*(15), 4146–4151. doi:10.1073/pnas.1523119113 PMID:27001851

Springmann, M., Mason-D'Croz, D., Robinson, S., Weibe, K., Godfray, H. C. J., Rayner, M., & Scarborough, P. (2017). Mitigation potential and global health impacts from emissions pricing of food commodities. *Nature Climate Change*, *7*(1), 69–76. doi:10.1038/nclimate3155

Stalder, T., Barraud, O., Casellas, M., Dagot, C., & Ploy, M.-C. (2012). Integron involvement in environmental spread of antibiotic resistance. *Frontiers in Microbiology*, *3*, 1–14. doi:10.3389/fmicb.2012.00119 PMID:22509175

Stambaugh, J. E. (1988). *The ancient Roman city*. Baltimore, MD: Johns Hopkins University Press.

Stead, M., Gordon, R., Angus, K., & McDermott, L. (2007). A systematic review of social marketing effectiveness. *Health Education*, *107*(2), 126–191. doi:10.1108/09654280710731548

Steenhuis, I. H., Leeuwis, F. H., & Vermeer, W. M. (2010). Small, medium, large or supersize: Trends in food portion sizes in the Netherlands. *Public Health Nutrition*, *13*(06), 852–857. doi:10.1017/S1368980009992011 PMID:19912675

Stefan, A. (2012). *Fear appeals in social marketing* [Thesis]. Aarhus University. Retrieved from http://citeseerx.ist.psu.edu/viewdoc/download?doi=10.1.1.471.9334&rep=rep1&type=pdf

Steg, L., & de Groot, J. I. M. (2012). Environmental values. In S. D. Clayton (Ed.), *The Oxford handbook of environmental and conservation psychology* (pp. 81–92). Oxford, UK: Oxford University Press.

Stehfest, E., Bouwman, L., van Vuuren, D. P., den Elzen, M. G., Eickhout, B., & Kabat, P. (2009). Climate benefits of changing diet. *Climatic Change*, *95*(1–2), 83–102. doi:10.1007/s10584-008-9534-6

Steinfeld, H., Gerber, P., Wassenaar, T., Castel, V., Rosales, M., & de Haan, C. (2006). Livestock's long shadow: Environmental issues and options. Rome, Italy: Food and Agriculture Organization of the United Nations (FAO).

Steinfeld, H., & Gerber, P. (2010). Livestock production and the global environment: Consume less or produce better? *Proceedings of the National Academy of Sciences of the United States*, *107*(43), 18237–18238. doi:10.1073/pnas.1012541107 PMID:20935253

Steinfeld, H., Gerber, P., Wassenaar, T., Castel, V., Rosales, M., & de Haan, C. (2006). *Livestock's long shadow: environmental issues and options*. Rome, Italy: Food Agriculture Organisation.

Steinfeld, H., Gerber, P., Wassenaar, T., Castel, V., Rosales, M., & de Haan, C. (2006). *Livestock's long shadow: Environmental issues and options*. Rome, Italy: Food and Agriculture Organization of the United Nations; Retrieved from http://www.fao.org/docrep/010/a0701e/a0701e00.HTM

Steinfeld, H., Gerber, P., Wassenaar, T., Castel, V., Rosales, M., & De Haan, C. (2006a). *Livestock's long shadow*. Rome, Italy: FAO.

Steinfeld, H., Wassenaar, T., & Jutzi, S. (2006b). Livestock production systems in developing countries: Status, drivers, trends. *World Organisation for Animal Health (OIE). Scientific and Technical Review*, *25*, 505–516. doi:10.20506/rst.25.2.1677 PMID:17094693

Stepaniak, J., & Messina, V. (1998). *The vegan sourcebook*. Los Angeles, CA: Lowell House.

Steptoe, A., & Wardle, J. (2003). Socioeconomic differences in attitudes and beliefs about healthy lifestyles. *Journal of Epidemiology and Community Health*, *57*(6), 440–443. doi:10.1136/jech.57.6.440 PMID:12775791

Stern, P. C. (2000). New environmental theories: Toward a coherent theory of environmentally significant behavior. *The Journal of Social Issues*, *56*(3), 407–424. doi:10.1111/0022-4537.00175

Stern, P. C., Dietz, T., Abel, T. D., Guagnano, G. A., & Kalof, L. (1999). A value-belief-norm theory of support for social movements: The case of environmentalism. *Human Ecology Review*, *6*(2), 81–97.

Stibbe, A. (2001). Language, power and the social construction of animals. *Society & Animals*, *9*(2), 145–161. doi:10.1163/156853001753639251

Stibbe, A. (2004). Health and the social construction of masculinity in "Men's health" magazine. *Men and Masculinities*, *7*(1), 31–51. doi:10.1177/1097184X03257441

Stocker, T., Qin, D., Plattner, G.-K., & Tignor, M. (2013). *Climate change 2013, The physical science basis. Contribution of Working Group I to the Fifth Assessment Report of the Intergovernmental Panel on Climate Change*. IPCC. Retrieved from https://www.ipcc.ch/report/ar5/wg1/

Stoll-Kleemann, S., & Schmidt, U. J. (2017). Reducing meat consumption in developed and transition countries to counter climate change and biodiversity loss: A review of influence factors. *Regional Environmental Change*, *17*(5), 1261–1277. doi:10.1007/s10113-016-1057-5

Stradling, C., Hamid, M., Fisher, K., Taheri, S., & Thomas, N. (2013). A review of dietary influences on cardiovascular health: Part 1: the role of dietary nutrients. *Cardiovascular & Hematological Disorders Drug Targets*, *13*(3), 1–34. PMID:24304234

Strauss, B. H. (2013). Rapid accumulation of committed sea-level rise from global warming. *Proceedings of the National Academy of Sciences of the United States*, *110*(34), 13699–13700. doi:10.1073/pnas.1312464110 PMID:23898210

Strom, S. (2016, 10 October). Tyson Foods, a meat leader, invests in protein alternatives. *The New York Times*. Retrieved from https://www.nytimes.com/2016/10/11/business/tyson-foods-a-meat-leader-invests-in-protein-alternatives.html?_r=0

Stromberg, J. (2012). Climate change tipping point: research shows that emission reductions must occur by 2020. Smithsonian.com. Retrieved from http://www.smithsonianmag.com/science-nature/climate-change-tipping-point-research-shows-that-emission-reductions-must-occur-by-2020-162222340

Stuart, D., & Schewe, R. L. (2016). Constrained choice and climate change mitigation in US agriculture: Structural barriers to a climate change ethic. *Journal of Agricultural & Environmental Ethics*, *29*(3), 369–385. doi:10.1007/s10806-016-9605-z

Sullivan, N. P. (2007). *You can hear me now: How microloans and cell phones are connecting the world's poor to the global economy*. San Francisco, CA: Jossey-Bass.

Sunder, K. (2016). Meet the world's smartest food scientist: GIUSEPPE. Biotechin Asia. Retrieved from https://biotechin.asia/2016/02/16/meet-the-worlds-smartest-food-scientist-guiseppe/

Sundin, S. (2011). Make it do – meat and cheese rationing in World War II. WWII novels by Sarah Sundin. Retrieved from http://www.sarahsundin.com/make-it-do-meat-and-cheese-rationing-in-world-war-ii-2/

Sun, J., Chen, Q., Zhang, Q., Li, Y., Li, H., Wei, D., & Qiu, J. et al. (2016). Training your brain to be more creative: Brain functional and structural changes induced by divergent thinking training. *Human Brain Mapping*, *37*(10), 3375–3387. doi:10.1002/hbm.23246 PMID:27159407

Sustainable Development Commission. (2009). *Setting the table: Advice to government on priority elements of sustainable diets. Report*. London, UK: Sustainable Development Commission.

Swedish Research Council. (2008, May 30). New vegetarian food with several health benefits. *ScienceDaily*. Retrieved from https://www.sciencedaily.com/releases/2008/05/080528095627.htm

Tagore, R. (1970). *The religion of man*. London, UK: Allen & Unwin.

Takata, Y., Shu, X.-O., Gao, Y.-T., Li, H., Zhang, X., Gao, J., & Zheng, W. et al. (2013). Red meat and poultry intakes and risk of total and cause-specific mortality: Results from cohort studies of Chinese adults in Shanghai. *PLoS One*, *8*(2), e56963. doi:10.1371/journal.pone.0056963 PMID:23451121

Tamplin, H. (2016). *Veganuary campaign urges people to go vegan for a month*. Retrieved from http://metro.co.uk/2016/11/06/veganuary-campaign-urges-people-to-go-vegan-for-a-month-6238419

Tapp, A., & Rundle-Thiele, S. R. (2016). Integrating social marketing into a multi-disciplinary environment behaviour change: Past present and future. In F. Spotswood (Ed.), *Beyond behaviour change: Key issues, interdisciplinary approaches and future directions* (pp. 135–156). Bristol, UK: The Policy Press.

Tapsell, L. C. (2015). Fermented dairy food and CVD risk. *British Journal of Nutrition*, *113*(S2), S131–S135. doi:10.1017/S0007114514002359 PMID:26148916

Tarimsal Ekonomí ve Polítíka Gelіştírme Enstítüsü (TEPGE). (2014). *Ürün raporu: Kümes hayvancılığı* [Product report: Poultry farming]. Retrieved from http://arastirma.tarim.gov.tr/tepge/Lists/Haber/Attachments/18/KANATLI_URUN_RAPORU_2014.pdf

Tas, M., Balci, M., Yüksel, A., & Sahin Yesilçubuk, N. (2015). Consumer awareness, perception and attitudes towards genetically modified foods in Turkey. *British Food Journal*, *117*(5), 1426–1439. doi:10.1108/BFJ-01-2014-0047

Taylor, N. (2005). Luddites or limits? Animal rights activists' attitudes towards science. *Journal for Critical Animal Studies*, *3*(1), 46–61.

Taylor, N., & Signal, T. D. (2009). Willingness to pay: Australian consumers and "on the farm" welfare. *Journal of Applied Animal Welfare Science*, *12*(4), 345–359. doi:10.1080/10888700903163658 PMID:20183486

Tekiner, İ. H., & Özpınar, H. (2016). Occurrence and characteristics of extended spectrum beta-lactamases-producing Enterobacteriaceae from foods of animal origin. *Brazilian Journal of Microbiology*, *47*(2), 444–451. doi:10.1016/j.bjm.2015.11.034 PMID:26991276

Tesla, N. (1900, June). The problem of increasing human energy. *The Century Illustrated Monthly Magazine*. Retrieved from https://books.google.com.au/books?id=v-GZLL15Pb4C&printsec=frontcover&source=gbs_ge_summary_r&cad=0#v=onepage&q&f=false

Thackeray, R., & McCormack Brown, K. (2010). Creating successful price and placement strategies for social marketing. *Health Promotion Practice*, *11*(2), 166–168. doi:10.1177/1524839909360892 PMID:20400655

Thaler, R. H., & Sunstein, C. R. (2008). *Nudge: Improving decisions about health, wealth, and happiness*. New Haven, CT: Yale University Press.

Thaler, S., Zessner, M., Mayr, M. M., Haider, T., Kroiss, H., & Rechberger, H. (2013). Impacts of human nutrition on land use, nutrient balances and water consumption in Austria. *Sustainability of Water Quality and Ecology*, *1-2*, 24–39. doi:10.1016/j.swaqe.2014.04.003

The Economist. (2014). *TG its Braai Day: The politics of great meat*. Retrieved from http://www.economist.com/news/middle-east-and-africa/21620249-politics-grilled-meat-tg-its-braai-day

The Economist. (2017, 2 February). *The market for alternative-protein products*. Retrieved from https://www.economist.com/news/business/21716076-plant-based-meat-products-have-made-it-menus-and-supermarket-shelves-market

The Ethical Consumer Group. (2017). *Harvey Fresh*. Retrieved from http://guide.ethical.org.au/company/?company=316

The Free Library. (2004). *Famines through history*. Scholastic, Inc. Retrieved from https://www.thefreelibrary.com/Famines+through+history-a0114325996

The GBD 2015 Obesity Collaborators. (2017). Health effects of overweight and obesity in 195 countries over 25 years. *The New England Journal of Medicine*, 377, 13-27.

The Greens. (2017). *Free-range eggs: Our truth in labelling toolkit*. Retrieved from http://greens.org.au/free-range

The National Provisioner. (2016). Meat industry timeline: 1917-1941. Retrieved from http://www.provisioneronline.com/articles/103508-meat-industry-timeline-1917-1941

The Phrase Finder. (2017). *The meaning and origin of the expression: Genius is one percent inspiration, ninety-nine percent perspiration*. Retrieved from https://www.phrases.org.uk/meanings/genius-is-one-percent-perspiration-ninety-nine-percent-perspiration.html

The Richest. (2017). *Top 10 vegetarian or vegan athletes*. Retrieved from http://www.therichest.com/sports/other-sports/top-10-vegetarian-or-vegan-athletes/

Thøgersen, J., & Zhou, Y. (2012). Chinese consumers' adoption of a "green" innovation: The case of organic food. *Journal of Marketing Management*, *28*(3-4), 313–333. doi:10.1080/0267257X.2012.658834

Thomas, K. (1991). *Man and the natural world: Changing attitudes in England 1500–1800*. London, UK: Penguin Books.

Thomas, M. (2015). Are vegans the same as vegetarians? The effect of diet on perceptions of masculinity. *Appetite*, *97*, 79–86. doi:10.1016/j.appet.2015.11.021 PMID:26593101

Thompson, C. J. (2004). Marketplace mythology and discourses of power. *The Journal of Consumer Research*, *31*(1), 162–180. doi:10.1086/383432

Thorley, V. (2014). 'There is absolutely no substitute for fresh milk': Dairy marketing in Australia, twentieth century. *International Journal of Liberal Arts and Social Science*, 2(2), 1–14.

Thornton, P., Herrero, M., & Ericksen, P. (2011). *Livestock and climate change*. Livestock Exchange Issue Brief 3. International Livestock Research Institute. Retrieved from https://cgspace.cgiar.org/bitstream/handle/10568/10601/IssueBrief3.pdf

Thornton, P., Herrero, M., & Ericksen, P. (2011). *Livestock and climate change. Livestock Exchange Issue Brief, 3*. Nairobi, Kenya: International Livestock Research Institute. Retrieved from https://cgspace.cgiar.org/bitstream/handle/10568/10601/IssueBrief3.pdf

Tobler, C., Visschers, V. H. M., & Siegrist, M. (2011). Eating green. Consumers' willingness to adopt ecological food consumption behaviors. *Appetite*, *57*(3), 674–682. doi:10.1016/j.appet.2011.08.010 PMID:21896294

Todorov, K., & Smallbone, D. (2014). *Handbook of research on strategic management of small and medium enterprises*. Hershey, PA: Business Science Reference. doi:10.4018/978-1-4666-5962-9

Tomkins, S. S. (1962). Affect imagery consciousness (Vol. 1). New York, NY: Springer.

Tomley, F. M., & Shirley, M. W. (2009). Livestock infectious diseases and zoonoses. *Philosophical Transaction of the Royal Society B*, *364*(1530), 2637–2642. doi:10.1098/rstb.2009.0133 PMID:19687034

Toth, J. D., & Dou, Z. (2016). Wasted food, wasted resources: Land, irrigation water, and nutrients associated with food wastage in the U.S. In Z. Dou, J. D. Ferguson, D. T. Galligan, A. M. Kelly, S. M. Finn, & R. Giegengack (Eds.), *Food waste across the supply chain: A US perspective on a global problem* (pp. 57–71). Ames, IO: Council for Agricultural Science and Technology.

Toussaint-Samat, M. (2009). *A history of food*. Chichester, UK: John Wiley & Sons.

Trigg, H. (2004). Food choice and social identity in early colonial New Mexico. *Journal of the Southwest*, *46*(2), 223–252.

Tsai, S. (2005). Impact of personal orientation on luxury-brand purchase value. *International Journal of Market Research*, *47*(4), 429–454.

Tsampiras, C., & Overy, N. (2016). Why cutting meat from your diet could be a revolutionary act. *The Conversation*. Retrieved from https://theconversation.com/why-cutting-meat-from-your-diet-could-be-a-revolutionary-act-69904

Tschakert, P. (2015). 1.5°C or 2°C: A conduit's view from the science-policy interface at COP20 in Lima, Peru. *Climate Change Responses*, *2*(1), 3. doi:10.1186/s40665-015-0010-z

Tse, G., & Eslick, G. D. (2014). Egg consumption and risk of GI neoplasms: Dose–response meta-analysis and systematic review. *European Journal of Nutrition*, *1*(7), 1581–1590. doi:10.1007/s00394-014-0664-5 PMID:24500371

Tsutsumi, A., & Tsutsui, N. (2009). Yuba ~ it's a traditional healthy food. The Kyoto Project. Retrieved from http://thekyotoproject.org/english/yubaits-a-traditional-healthy-food

Tukker, A., Huppes, G., Guinée, J. B., Heijungs, R., de Koning, A., & van Oers, L. … Nielsen, P. (2006). Environmental impact of products (EIPRO) analysis of the life cycle environmental impacts related to the final consumption of the EU-25 (Technical Report Series, EUR 22284 EN). Retrieved from https://openaccess.leidenuniv.nl/handle/1887/11434

Türkiye Üçüncü Sektör Vakfı (TÜSEV). (2011). *Türkiye'de sivil toplum: Bir dönüm noktası* [Civil society in Turkey: A turning point]. İstanbul, Turkey: TÜSEV Yayınları.

Turkle, S. (2011). *Alone together: Why we expect more from technology and less from each other*. New York, NY: Basic Books.

Turner, S. (2012). What did Einstein, Gandhi & Benjamin Franklin all have in common? *Elephantjournal.com*. Retrieved from https://www.elephantjournal.com/2012/02/what-did-einstein-gandhi-benjamin-franklin-all-have-in-common/

Turner, L., Mermelstein, R., & Flay, B. (2004). Individual and contextual influences on adolescent smoking. *Annals of the New York Academy of Sciences*, *1021*(1), 175–197. doi:10.1196/annals.1308.023 PMID:15251888

Turner-McGrievy, G. M., Davidson, C. R., Wingard, E. E., Wilcox, S., & Frongillo, E. A. (2015). Comparative effectiveness of plant-based diets for weight loss: A randomized controlled trial of five different diets. *Nutrition (Burbank, Los Angeles County, Calif.)*, *31*(2), 350–358. doi:10.1016/j.nut.2014.09.002 PMID:25592014

Twine, R. (2010). *Animals as biotechnology--ethics, sustainability and critical animal studies*. London, UK: Earthscan.

Twine, R. (2014). Ecofeminism and veganism: Reviewing the question of universalism. In C. J. Adams & L. Gruen (Eds.), *Ecofeminism: Feminist interactions with other animals and the earth* (pp. 191–207). New York, NY: Bloomsbury.

Uddin, M. (1978). *Hara moni* (Vol. 7). Dhaka, Bangladesh: Bangla Academy.

Uehleke, R., & Hüttel, S. (2016). The hypothetical free-rider deficit. In *The demand for farm animal welfare labeled meat: 56th Annual Conference, Bonn, Germany, September 28-30*. German Association of Agricultural Economists (GEWISOLA). Retrieved from http://ageconsearch.umn.edu/record/244866

UNdata. (2016). *Country profile: Nigeria*. Retrieved from http://data.un.org/CountryProfile.aspx?crName=NIGERIA

Unger, N., Shindell, D., Koch, D., & Streets, D. (2008). Air pollution radiative forcing from specific emissions sectors at 2030. *Journal of Geophysical Research*, *113*(D2), D02306. doi:10.1029/2007JD008683

United Nations (UN). (2015). Transforming our world: The 2030 Agenda for Sustainable Development. Retrieved from https://sustainabledevelopment.un.org/post2015/transformingourworld

United Nations Educational Scientific and Cultural Organization (UNESCO). (2008). *Baul songs*. Retrieved from http://www.unesco.org/culture/ich/RL/00107

United Nations Environment Program (UNEP). (2016). Food systems and natural resources. A Report of the Working Group on Food Systems of the International Resource Panel. Retrieved from https://www.dropbox.com/sh/bhhivquadq7ycnd/AAAIl8mVW9GCiOyGwk71At_ra?dl=0&preview=UNEP_Food+systems+and+natural+resources_summary_web.pdf

United Nations Environment Program and World Meteorological Office (UNEP/WMO). (2011). *Integrated assessment of black carbon and tropospheric ozone: Summary for decision makers*. UNEP/WM. Retrieved from http://www.unep.org/dewa/Portals/67/pdf/Black_Carbon.pdf

United Nations. (2017). *World population prospects 2017*. Retrieved from https://esa.un.org/unpd/wpp/

United States Department of Agriculture (USDA). (2014). 2012 Census of Agriculture: Farm and Ranch Irrigation Survey 2013. USDA Census of Agriculture. Retrieved from https://www.agcensus.usda.gov/Publications/2012/Online_Resources/Farm_and_Ranch_Irrigation_Survey/

United States Department of Agriculture (USDA). (2015). 2014 Land values and cash rents: Cropland and pasture. National Agriculture Statistics Service (NASS) Highlights. Retrieved from https://www.nass.usda.gov/Publications/Highlights/2014_LandValues_CashRents/LVCR.pdf

United States Department of Agriculture (USDA). (n.d.) ChooseMyPlate.gov. Retrieved from https://www.choosemyplate.gov/

United States Geological Survey (USGS). (2016). The water content of things: How much water does it take to grow a hamburger? Retrieved from https://water.usgs.gov/edu/activity-watercontent.php

United States Geological Survey (USGS). (2017). Contaminants of emerging concern in the environment. *Environmental Health – Toxic Substances Hydrology Program*. Retrieved from http://toxics.usgs.gov/investigations/cec/index.php

Valkanov, N. (2013). *Analysis of the market for meat and meat products in Bulgaria* [in Bulgarian]. Institute for Market Economy. Retrieved from http://ime.bg/var/images/Meat_Market_2013.pdf

Van Boeckel, T. P., Brower, C., Gilbert, M., Grenfell, B. T., Levin, S. A., & Robinson, T. P., … Laxminarayan, R. (2015). Global trends in antimicrobial use in food animals. *Proceedings of the National Academy of Sciences of the United States of America*, *112*, 5649-5654. doi:10.1073/pnas.1503141112

van den Wijngaard, M. (1997). *Reinventing the sexes: the biomedical construction of femininity and masculinity (Race, gender, and science)*. Bloomington, IN: Indiana University Press.

Van Dijck, J. (2013). *The culture of connectivity: A critical history of social media*. New York, NY: Oxford University Press. doi:10.1093/acprof:oso/9780199970773.001.0001

Van Dingenen, R., Dentener, F. J., Raes, F., Krol, M. C., Emberson, L., & Cofala, J. (2009). The global impact of ozone on agricultural crop yields under current and future air quality legislation. *Atmospheric Environment*, *43*(3), 604–618. doi:10.1016/j.atmosenv.2008.10.033

van Dooren, C., & Kramer, G. (2012). Food patterns and dietary recommendations in Spain, France and Sweden: Healthy people, healthy planet. *LiveWell for life*. Retrieved from http://www.livewellforlife.eu/wp-content/uploads/2012/05/LiveWell_A4-Food-Patterns-Report_web.pdf

Van Dooren, C., Douma, A., Aiking, H., & Vellinga, P. (2017). Proposing a novel index reflecting both climate impact and nutritional impact of food products. *Ecological Economics*, *131*, 389–398. doi:10.1016/j.ecolecon.2016.08.029

van Hoven, B., & Hopkins, P. (2009). Masculinities. In R. Kitchin & N. Thrift (Eds.), *International Encyclopedia of Human Geography* (pp. 492–496). Oxford, UK: Elsevier. doi:10.1016/B978-008044910-4.00970-6

Van Loo, E. J., Hoefkens, C., & Verbeke, W. (2017). Healthy, sustainable and plant-based eating: Perceived (mis) match and involvement-based consumer segments as targets for future policy. *Food Policy*, *69*, 46–57. doi:10.1016/j.foodpol.2017.03.001

van Marle, M. J. E., Field, R. D., van der Werf, G. R., Estrada de Wagt, I. A., Houghton, R. A., Rizzo, L. V., & Tsigaridis, K. et al. (2017). Fire and deforestation dynamics in Amazonia (1973-2014). *Global Biogeochemical Cycles*, *31*(1), 24–38. doi:10.1002/2016GB005445 PMID:28286373

Vanhonacker, F., Van Loo, E. J., Gellynck, X., & Verbeke, W. (2013). Flemish consumer attitudes towards more sustainable food choices. *Appetite*, *62*, 7–16. doi:10.1016/j.appet.2012.11.003 PMID:23195711

Vaske, J. J., & Donnelly, M. P. (1999). A value-attitude-behavior model predicting wildland preservation voting intentions. *Society & Natural Resources*, *12*(6), 523–537. doi:10.1080/089419299279425

Vaughan, A. (2013, December 20). Tax meat to cut methane emissions, say scientists. *The Guardian*. Retrieved from https://www.theguardian.com/environment/2013/dec/20/tax-meat-cut-methane-emissions-scientists

Vegetarian Society. (2017). *Advertising in The Vegetarian*. Retrieved from https://www.vegsoc.org/advertising

Vegie Delights. (2017). Products: Nutmeat. Retrieved from www.vegiedelights.com.au/product/nutmeat

Velasquez, M. T., Ramezani, A., Manal, A., & Raj, D. S. (2016). Trimethylamine N-Oxide: The good, the bad and the unknown. *Toxins*, *8*(11), 326. doi:10.3390/toxins8110326 PMID:27834801

Velema, E., Vyth, E. L., & Steenhuis, I. H. (2017). Using nudging and social marketing techniques to create healthy worksite cafeterias in the Netherlands: Intervention development and study design. *BMC Public Health*, *17*(1), 1–9. doi:10.1186/s12889-016-3927-7 PMID:28077114

Verain, M. C. D., Sijtsema, S. J., Dagevos, H., & Antonides, G. (2017). Attribute segmentation and communication effects on healthy and sustainable consumer diet intentions. *Sustainability*, *9*(5), 1–19. doi:10.3390/su9050743

Verain, M., Dagevos, H., & Antonides, G. (2015). Flexitarianism: A range of sustainable food styles. In L. A. Reisch & J. Thøgersen (Eds.), *Handbook of research on sustainable consumption* (pp. 209–223). Cheltenham: Edward Elgar. doi:10.4337/9781783471270.00023

Verbeke, W., & Vackier, I. (2005). Individual determinants of fish consumption: Application of the theory of planned behaviour. *Appetite*, *44*(1), 67–82. doi:10.1016/j.appet.2004.08.006 PMID:15604034

Verbeke, W., & Viaene, J. (1999). Beliefs, attitude and behaviour towards fresh meat consumption in Belgium: Empirical evidence from a consumer survey. *Food Quality and Preference*, *10*(6), 437–445. doi:10.1016/S0950-3293(99)00031-2

Verbeke, W., & Viaene, J. (2000). Ethical challenges for livestock production: Meeting consumer concerns about meat safety and animal welfare. *Journal of Agricultural & Environmental Ethics*, *12*(2), 141–151. doi:10.1023/A:1009538613588

Vergnaud, A.-C., Norat, T., Romaguera, D., Mouw, T., May, A. M., Travier, N., & Peeters, P. H. et al. (2010). Meat consumption and prospective weight change in participants of the EPIC-PANACEA study. *The American Journal of Clinical Nutrition*, *92*(2), 398–407. doi:10.3945/ajcn.2009.28713 PMID:20592131

Vermeer, W. M., Steenhuis, I. H., & Poelman, M. P. (2014). Small, medium, large or supersize?: The development and evaluation of interventions targeted at portion size. *International Journal of Obesity*, *38*, 13–18. doi:10.1038/ijo.2014.84 PMID:25033959

Vermeulen, S. J., Campbell, B. M., & Ingram, J. S. I. (2012). Climate change and food systems. *Annual Review of Environment and Resources*, *37*(1), 195–222. doi:10.1146/annurev-environ-020411-130608

Veterinary Medicines Directorate (VMD). (2015). UK veterinary antibiotic resistance and sales surveillance report. Surrey, UK: VMD. Retrieved from https://www.gov.uk/government/uploads/system/uploads/attachment_data/file/582341/1051728-v53-UK-VARSS_2015.pdf

Vidal, J. (2013, 14 April). Climate change: How a warming world is a treat to our food supplies. *The Guardian*. Retrieved from https://www.theguardian.com/environment/2013/apr/13/climate-change-threat-food-supplies

Voiceless. (2015a). *The animal law toolkit*. Retrieved from https://www.voiceless.org.au/voiceless-animal-law-toolkit-second-edition

Voiceless. (2015b). *Dairy cows*. Retrieved from https://www.voiceless.org.au/the-issues/dairy-cows

Wallerstein, I. (2003). Citizens all? Citizens some! The Making of the citizen. *Comparative Studies in Society and History*, *45*(04), 650–679. doi:10.1017/S0010417503000318

Wallin, A., Di Giuseppe, D., Orsini, N., Patel, P. S., Forouhi, N. G., & Wolk, A. (2012). Fish consumption, dietary long-chain n-3 fatty acids, and risk of type 2 diabetes: Systematic review and meta-analysis of prospective studies. *Diabetes Care*, *35*(4), 918–929. doi:10.2337/dc11-1631 PMID:22442397

Walsh, R., & Tzelepis, F. (2007). Adolescents and tobacco use: Systematic review of qualitative research methodologies and partial synthesis of findings. *Substance Use & Misuse*, *42*(8), 1269–1321. doi:10.1080/10826080701204904 PMID:17674235

Wang, W., Wu, Y., & Zhang, D. (2016). Association of dairy products consumption with risk of obesity in children and adults: A meta-analysis of mainly cross-sectional studies. *Annals of Epidemiology*, *26*(12), 870–882.e2. doi:10.1016/j.annepidem.2016.09.005 PMID:27756684

Wang, X., Lin, X., Ouyang, Y. Y., Liu, J., Zhao, G., Pan, A., & Hu, F. B. (2015). Red and processed meat consumption and mortality: Dose-response meta-analysis of prospective cohort studies. *Public Health Nutrition*, *19*(5), 1–13. PMID:26143683

Wang, X., Lin, X., Ouyang, Y. Y., Liu, J., Zhao, G., Pan, A., & Hu, F. B. (2016). Red and processed meat consumption and mortality: Dose–response meta-analysis of prospective cohort studies. *Public Health Nutrition*, *19*(5), 893–905. doi:10.1017/S1368980015002062 PMID:26143683

Wang, Y.-Z., Wu, Q.-J., Zhu, J., & Wu, L. (2015). Fish consumption and risk of myeloma: A meta-analysis of epidemiological studies. *Cancer Causes & Control*, *26*(9), 1307–1314. doi:10.1007/s10552-015-0625-1 PMID:26156047

Wansink, B. (2006). *Mindless eating: Why we eat more than we think*. New York, NY: Bantam Books.

Wansink, B., Just, D. R., & Payne, C. R. (2009). Mindless eating and healthy heuristics for the irrational. *The American Economic Review*, *99*(2), 165–169. doi:10.1257/aer.99.2.165

Watkinsona, A. J., Murbyd, E. J., Kolpine, D. W., & Costanzof, S. D. (2009). The occurrence of antibiotics in an urban watershed: From wastewater to drinking water. *The Science of the Total Environment*, *407*(8), 2711–2723. doi:10.1016/j.scitotenv.2008.11.059 PMID:19138787

Watts, N., Adger, W. N., Agnolucci, P., Blackstock, J., Byass, P., Cai, W., & Costello, A. et al. (2015). Health and climate change; policy responses to protect public health. *Lancet*, *386*(10006), 1861–1914. doi:10.1016/S0140-6736(15)60854-6 PMID:26111439

Webb, S. H. (1998). *On God and dogs: A Christian theology of compassion for animals*. Oxford, UK: Oxford University Press.

Wedderburn-Bisshop, G., Longmire, A., & Rickards, L. A. (2015). Neglected transformational responses: Implications of excluding short lived emissions and near-term projections in greenhouse gas accounting. *The International Journal of Climate Change: Impacts and Responses*, *7*(3), 11–27.

Wegerer, J. (2014, January 2). Nutrition and dementia: Foods that may induce memory loss & increase Alzheimer's. *Alzheimers.net*. Retrieved from http://www.alzheimers.net/2014-01-02/foods-that-induce-memory-loss/

Wegmans. (2017). Field Roast: Grain Meat Sausages, Vegetarian, Smoked Apple Sage. Retrieved from https://www.wegmans.com/products/natures-marketplace/frozen-foods/sausage/grain-meat-sausages-vegetarian-smoked-apple-sage.html

Weiner, E. (2016). *Gastronomy of genius: History's great minds and the foods that fueled them*. NPR. Retrieved from http://www.npr.org/sections/thesalt/2016/03/11/469543237/the-gastronomy-of-genius-food-and-drink-that-inspired-great-minds

Weinstein, N. D. (1988). The precaution adoption process. *Health Psychology*, *7*(4), 355–386. doi:10.1037/0278-6133.7.4.355 PMID:3049068

Wellesley, L., Happer, C., & Froggatt, A. (2015). *Changing climate, Changing diets: Pathways to lower meat consumption*. London, UK: Chatham House Report. Retrieved from https://www.chathamhouse.org/sites/files/chathamhouse/publications/research/CHHJ3820%20Diet%20and%20climate%20change%2018.11.15_WEB_NEW.pdf

Wellesley, L., Happer, C., & Froggatt, A. (2015, November). *Changing climate, changing diets: Pathways to lower meat consumption*. Chatham House Report. Retrieved from https://www.chathamhouse.org/sites/files/chathamhouse/publications/research/CHHJ3820%20Diet%20and%20climate%20change%2018.11.15_WEB_NEW.pdf

Wellesley, L., Happer, C., & Froggatt, A. (2015). *Changing climate, changing diets: Pathways to lower meat consumption*. London, UK: Chatham House.

Wells, K. (2015). *Australian food and drink*. Australian Government. Retrieved from http://www.australia.gov.au/about-australia/australian-story/austn-food-and-drink

White, S. (2009). Exploring different philosophical approaches to animal protection in law. In P. J. Sankoff & S. W. White (Eds.), *Animal law in Australasia: A new dialogue* (pp. 79–107). Sydney, Australia: The Federation Press.

White, S., & Cordell, D. (2015). Global phosphorus security – diet, sustainability and food for thought. In K. Soeters (Ed.), *Meat the future: How cutting meat consumption can feed billions more* (pp. 75–86). Amsterdam, the Netherlands: Nicholaas G Pierson Foundation.

Whole Foods Market. (2017). *Whole Foods Market serves up top 10 trends for 2017*. Retrieved from http://media.wholefoodsmarket.com/news/whole-foods-market-serves-up-top-10-trends-for-2017

Wicker, A. W. (1969). Attitudes versus actions: The relationship of verbal and overt behavioral responses to attitude objects. *The Journal of Social Issues*, *25*(4), 41–78. doi:10.1111/j.1540-4560.1969.tb00619.x

Wicks, D. (2004). Humans, food, and other animals: The vegetarian option. In J. Germov & L. Williams (Eds.), *A sociology of food & nutrition* (Vol. 2, pp. 263–287). Melbourne, Australia: Oxford University Press.

Wiedemann, S., McGahan, E., Murphy, C., & Yan, M. (2016). Resource use and environmental impacts from beef production in eastern Australia investigated using life cycle assessment. *Animal Production Science*, *56*(5), 882–894. doi:10.1071/AN14687

Wiedmann, K. P., Hennigs, N., & Siebels, A. (2007). Measuring consumers' luxury value perception: A crosscultural framework. *Academy of Marketing Science Review*, *7*(7), 333–361.

Wild, F., Czerny, M., Janssen, A. M., Kole, A. P., Zunabovic, M., & Domig, K. J. (2014). The evolution of a plant-based alternative to meat: From niche markets to widely accepted meat alternatives. *Agro Food Industry Hi-Tech*, *25*(1), 45–49.

Wilkie, R. (2017). Animals as sentient commodities. In L. Kalof (Ed.), *The Oxford handbook of animal studies* (pp. 279–301). Oxford, UK: Oxford University Press.

Wilks, J. (2011). *Animal rights and 19th century antivivisection – was Charles Darwin the catalyst?* Retrieved from https://makinghistoryatmacquarie.wordpress.com/2011/11/22/animal-rights-and-19th-century-antivivisection-was-charles-darwin-the-catalyst/

Willard, B. E. (2006). The American story of meat. *Journal of Popular Culture*, *6*, 105–118.

Willemsen, F. (2006). Options for non-protein fractions. In H. Aiking, J. de Boer, & J. Vereijken (Eds.), *Sustainable protein production and consumption: Pigs or peas?* (pp. 86–91). Dordrecht, Netherlands: Springer.

Willemsen, F., & Apaiah, R. (2006). Combined chains. In H. Aiking, J. de Boer, & J. Vereijken (Eds.), *Sustainable protein production and consumption: Pigs or peas?* (pp. 166–175). Dordrecht, Netherlands: Springer.

Williams, C. (2012). *The framing of animal cruelty by animal advocacy organizations* [Honors thesis]. University of Maine. Retrieved from http://digitalcommons.library.umaine.edu/honors/91

Wilson, B. (2017). Wisdom from Margaret Mead. In B. Kateman (Ed.), *The reducetarian solution: How the surprisingly simple act of reducing the amount of meat in your diet can transform your health and the planet* (pp. 148–150). New York, NY: TarcherPerigee.

Winter, D. D. N., & Koger, S. M. (2009). *The psychology of environmental problems*. Prague, Czech Republic: Portál.

Winther, A. (2004). *Meat-free foods - UK - December 2004. Market Research Report*. Mintel.

Wise, S. (2004). Animal rights, one step at a time. In C. Sunstein & M. Nussbaum (Eds.), *Animal rights: Current debates and new directions* (pp. 19–49). New York, NY: Oxford University Press.

Wise, S. M. (2002). *Drawing the line: Sentience and the case for animal rights*. Cambridge, UK: Perseus Books.

Withey, A. (2015, December 23). Beards, masculinity and history. Dr Alan Withey blog. Retrieved from https://dralun.wordpress.com/2015/12/23/beards-masculinity-and-history/

Withnall, A. (2016, April 27). Denmark Ethics Council calls for tax on red meat to fight 'ethical problem' of climate change. *The Independent*. Retrieved from http://www.independent.co.uk/news/world/europe/denmark-ethics-council-calls-for-tax-on-red-meat-to-fight-ethical-problem-of-climate-change-a7003061.html

Wolchover, N. (2012). Will people really be forced to stop eating meat? *Livescience.com*. Retrieved from http://www.livescience.com/22814-meat-eating-vegetarianism.html

Wollenbergera, L., Halling-Sùrensenb, B., & Kusk, K. O. (2000). Acute and chronic toxicity of veterinary antibiotics to Daphnia Magna. *Chemosphere*, *40*(7), 723–730. doi:10.1016/S0045-6535(99)00443-9 PMID:10705550

Wood, M. (2008). Applying commercial marketing theory to social Marketing: A tale of 4Ps (and a B). *Social Marketing Quarterly*, *14*(1), 76–85. doi:10.1080/15245000701856877

Woods, B. (2015, 14 May). *Bill Gates bets on growing demand for sustainable foods*. CNBC.com. Retrieved from http://www.cnbc.com/2015/05/14/hampton-creek-and-impossible-foods-technology.html

World Bank. (2016). State and trends of carbon pricing. Washington, DC: World Bank Group. Retrieved from http://documents.worldbank.org/curated/en/598811476464765822/State-and-trends-of-carbon-pricing

World Bank. (2017). *GDP per capita (current US$)*. Retrieved from http://data.worldbank.org/indicator/NY.GDP.PCAP.CD

World Bank. (2017). *Public data: Population*. Retrieved from https://www.google.com.au/publicdata/explore?ds=d5bncppjof8f9_&met_y=sp_pop_totl&idim=country:BGR:GRC:SRB&hl=en&dl=en

World Cancer Research Fund (WCRF) International. (2015). Continuous update project report: Diet, nutrition, physical activity and liver cancer. Retrieved from http://www.wcrf.org/sites/default/files/Liver-Cancer-2015-Report.pdf

World Cancer Research Fund and American Institute for Cancer Research (WCRF/AICR). (2007). *Food, nutrition, physical activity and the prevention of cancer: a global perspective*. Washington, DC: AICR.

World Cancer Research Fund and American Institute for Cancer Research (WCRF/AICR). (2007). *Food, nutrition, physical activity and the prevention of cancer: A global perspective*. Washington, DC: AICR.

World Cancer Research Fund and American Institute for Cancer Research (WCRF/AICR). (2007). Food, nutrition, physical activity, and the prevention of cancer: A global perspective. Retrieved from http://www.aicr.org/assets/docs/pdf/reports/Second_Expert_Report.pdf

World Food Programme (WFP). (2009). *World must double food production by 2050: FAO chief*. Retrieved from https://www.wfp.org/content/world-must-double-food-production-2050-fao-chief

World Health Organisation (WHO). (2009). *Violence Prevention*. Retrieved from http://www.who.int/violence_injury_prevention/violence/norms.pdf

World Health Organisation (WHO). (2014). Noncommunicable Diseases (NCD) Country Profiles. Retrieved from http://www.who.int/nmh/publications/ncd-profiles-2014/en/

World Health Organisation (WHO). (2015). *Q&A on the carcinogenicity of the consumption of red meat and processed meat*. Retrieved from http://www.who.int/features/qa/cancer-red-meat/en/

World Health Organisation (WHO). (2017). WHO | *Noncommunicable diseases*. Retrieved from http://www.who.int/mediacentre/factsheets/fs355/en/

World Health Organization & Foodborne Disease Burden Epidemiology Reference Group (WHO/FDBERG). (2015). *WHO estimates of the global burden of foodborne diseases: Foodborne disease burden epidemiology reference group 2007-2015*. Retrieved from http://apps.who.int/iris/bitstream/10665/199350/1/9789241565165_eng.pdf?ua=1

World Health Organization (WHO). (2005). *The Bangkok charter for health promotion in a globalized world*. Geneva, Switzerland: WHO. Retrieved from www.who.int/healthpromotion/conferences/6gchp/bangkok_charter/en/

World Health Organization (WHO). (2012). The evolving threat of antimicrobial resistance: Options for action. Geneva, Swizerland: WHO.

World Health Organization (WHO). (2013). Global action plan for the prevention and control of noncommunicable diseases 2013-2020. Retrieved from www.who.int

World Health Organization (WHO). (2015). Q&A on the carcinogenicity of the consumption of red meat and processed meat. Retrieved from http://www.who.int/features/qa/cancer-red-meat/en/

World Health Organization (WHO). (2016). *Antimicrobial resistance*. Retrieved from http://www.who.int/mediacentre/factsheets/fs194/en

World Health Organization (WHO). (2016). *Obesity and overweight*. Fact sheet. Retrieved from http://www.who.int/mediacentre/factsheets/fs311/en/

World Meteorological Organisation (WMO). (2016). *The global climate in 2011-2015*. Geneva, Switzerland: WMO. Retrieved from http://ane4bf-datap1.s3-eu-west-1.amazonaws.com/wmocms/s3fs-public/1179_EN.pdf

World Society for the Protection of Animals. (2011). Will Canadians vote with their hearts? Retrieved from http://www.humanespot.org/content/will-canadians-vote-their-hearts

World Wild Fund for Nature (WWF). (2016). *Living planet report 2016; Summary*. Gland, Switzerland: WWF. Retrieved from: http://awsassets.panda.org/downloads/lpr_living_planet_report_2016_summary.pdf

Wortham, J., & Miller, C. (2013, April 28). Venture capitalists are making bigger bets on food start-ups. *New York Times*. Retrieved from http://www.nytimes.com/2013/04/29/business/venture-capitalists-are-making-bigger-bets-on-food-start-ups.html

Wrenn, C. L. (2011). Resisting the globalization of speciesism: Vegan abolitionism as a site for consumer-based social change. *Journal for Critical Animal Studies*, *9*(3), 9–27.

Wrots, C. (2016). What do geniuses eat? Here's Nikola Tesla's diet. *Onedio*. Retrieved from https://onedio.co/content/heres-genius-inventor-nikola-teslas-nutrition-diet-11938

Wu, G. (2016). Dietary protein intake and human health. *Food & Function*, *7*(3), 1251–1265. doi:10.1039/C5FO01530H PMID:26797090

Wu, J., Zeng, R., Huang, J., Li, X., Zhang, J., Ho, J., & Zheng, Y. (2016). Dietary protein sources and incidence of breast cancer: A dose-response meta-analysis of prospective studies. *Nutrients*, *8*(11), 730. doi:10.3390/nu8110730 PMID:27869663

Wu, K., Spiegelman, D., Hou, T., Albanes, D., Allen, N. E., Berndt, S. I., & Smith-Warner, S. A. et al. (2016). Associations between unprocessed red and processed meat, poultry, seafood and egg intake and the risk of prostate cancer: A pooled analysis of 15 prospective cohort studies. *International Journal of Cancer*, *138*(10), 2368–2382. doi:10.1002/ijc.29973 PMID:26685908

Wymer, W. (2010). Rethinking the boundaries of social marketing: Activism or advertising? *Journal of Business Research*, *63*(2), 99–103. doi:10.1016/j.jbusres.2009.02.003

Wymer, W. (2011). Developing more effective social marketing strategies. *Journal of Social Marketing*, *1*(1), 17–31. doi:10.1108/20426761111104400

Wynes, S., & Nicholas, K. A. (2017). The climate mitigation gap: Education and government recommendations miss the most effective individual actions. *Environmental Research Letters*, *12*(7), 1–10. doi:10.1088/1748-9326/aa7541

Xu, B., Sun, J., Sun, Y., Huang, L., Tang, Y., & Yuan, Y. (2013). No evidence of decreased risk of colorectal adenomas with white meat, poultry, and fish intake: A meta-analysis of observational studies. *Annals of Epidemiology*, *23*(4), 215–222. doi:10.1016/j.annepidem.2012.12.016 PMID:23375344

Xu, R., Wang, Q., & Li, L. (2015). A genome-wide systems analysis reveals strong link between colorectal cancer and trimethylamine N-oxide (TMAO), a gut microbial metabolite of dietary meat and fat. *BMC Genomics*, *16*(Suppl. 7), S4. doi:10.1186/1471-2164-16-S7-S4 PMID:26100814

Yacoubou, J. (2009). Save our water: The vegetarian way. *The Vegetarian Resource Group*. Retrieved from http://www.vrg.org/environment/water_brochure.php

Yancy, G., & Singer, P. (2015). *Peter Singer: On racism, animal rights and human rights*. Retrieved from http://opinionator.blogs.nytimes.com/2015/05/27/peter-singer-on-speciesism-and-racism/?_r=1

Yatai, F. (2013). Boosting animal protein production in Nigeria. *The Tide*. Retrieved from http://www.thetidenewsonline.com/2013/11/04/boosting-animal-protein-production-in-nigeria/

Yates, R. (2010). Language, power and speciesism. *Critical Sociology*, *3*, 11–19.

Ye, K, Gao, F., Wang, D., Bar-Yosef, O., & Keinan, A. (2017). Dietary adaptation of FADS genes in Europe varied across time and geography. *Nature Ecology & Evolution*, *1*, 0167. doi:10.1038/s41559-017-0167

Yi, A. X., Leung, K. M. Y., Lam, M. H. W., Lee, J. S., & Giesy, J. P. (2012). Review of measured concentrations of triphenyltin compounds in marine ecosystems and meta-analysis of their risks to humans and the environment. *Chemosphere*, *89*(9), 1015–1025. doi:10.1016/j.chemosphere.2012.05.080 PMID:22704212

Yoon, H., Benamouzig, R., Little, J., François-Collange, M., & Tomé, D. (2000). Systematic review of epidemiological studies on meat, dairy products and egg consumption and risk of colorectal adenomas. *European Journal of Cancer Prevention*, *9*(3), 151–164. doi:10.1097/00008469-200006000-00002 PMID:10954254

York, R., & Gossard, M. (2004). Cross-national meat and fish consumption: Exploring the effects of modernization and ecological context. *Ecological Economics*, *48*(3), 293–302. doi:10.1016/j.ecolecon.2003.10.009

Yotopoulos, P. A. (1985). Middle-income classes and food crises: The "new" food-feed competition. *Economic Development and Cultural Change*, *33*(3), 463–483. doi:10.1086/451474

Yu, X. (2015). Meat consumption in China and its impact on international food security: Status quo, trends, and policies. *Journal of Integrative Agriculture*, *14*(6), 989–994. doi:10.1016/S2095-3119(14)60983-7

Yu, X.-F., Zou, J., & Dong, J. (2014). Fish consumption and risk of gastrointestinal cancers: A meta-analysis of cohort studies. *World Journal of Gastroenterology*, *20*(41), 15398–15412. doi:10.3748/wjg.v20.i41.15398 PMID:25386090

Zabelina, D. L., Colzato, L., Beeman, M., & Hommel, B. (2016). Dopamine and the creative mind: Individual differences in creativity are predicted by interactions between dopamine genes DAT and COMT. *PLoS One*, *11*(1), e0146768. doi:10.1371/journal.pone.0146768 PMID:26783754

Zalasiewicz, J. (2015). Epochs: Disputed start dates for Anthropocene. *Nature*, *520*, 436. doi:10.1038/520436b

Zandstra, E. H., Stubenitsky, K., De Graaf, C., & Mela, D. J. (2002). Effects of learned flavour cues on short-term regulation of food intake in a realistic setting. *Physiology & Behavior*, *75*(1-2), 83–90. doi:10.1016/S0031-9384(01)00647-3 PMID:11890956

Zevallos, Z. (2014, November 28). *Sociology of gender*. The Other Sociologist. Retrieved from https://othersociologist.com/sociology-of-gender/

Zhang, L., Qiao, L., Chen, Q., Yang, W., Xu, M., & Yao, X. (1532). … Yang, D. (2016). Gray matter volume of the lingual gyrus mediates the relationship between inhibition function and divergent thinking. *Frontiers in Psychology*, *7*. doi:10.3389/fpsyg.2016.01532

Zhao, L.-G., Sun, J.-W., Yang, Y., Ma, X., Wang, Y.-Y., & Xiang, Y.-B. (2016). Fish consumption and all-cause mortality: A meta-analysis of cohort studies. *European Journal of Clinical Nutrition*, *70*(2), 155–161. doi:10.1038/ejcn.2015.72 PMID:25969396

Zheng, J., Huang, T., Yu, Y., Hu, X., Yang, B., & Li, D. (2012). Fish consumption and CHD mortality: An updated meta-analysis of seventeen cohort studies. *Public Health Nutrition*, *15*(4), 725–737. doi:10.1017/S1368980011002254 PMID:21914258

Zheng, J.-S., Huang, T., Yang, J., Fu, Y.-Q., & Li, D. (2012). Marine N-3 polyunsaturated fatty acids are inversely associated with risk of type 2 diabetes in Asians: A systematic review and meta-analysis. *PLoS One*, *7*(9), e44525. doi:10.1371/journal.pone.0044525 PMID:22984522

Zhou, L.-J., Ying, G.-G., Liu, S., Zhang, R.-Q., Lai, H.-J., Chen, Z.-F., & Pan, C.-G. (2013). Excretion masses and environmental occurrence of antibiotics in typical swine and dairy cattle farms in China. *The Science of the Total Environment*, *444*, 183–195. doi:10.1016/j.scitotenv.2012.11.087 PMID:23268145

Zhou, Y., Tian, C., & Jia, C. (2012). Association of fish and n-3 fatty acid intake with the risk of type 2 diabetes: A meta-analysis of prospective studies. *British Journal of Nutrition*, *108*(03), 408–417. doi:10.1017/S0007114512002036 PMID:22857650

Zhu, Y.-G., Johnson, T. A., Su, J.-Q., Qiao, M., Guo, G.-X., & Stedtfeld, R. D., … Tiedje, J.M. (2013). Diverse and abundant antibiotic resistance genes in Chinese swine farms. *Proceedings of the National Academy of Sciences of the United States of America*, *110*, 3435-3440. doi:10.1073/pnas.1222743110

Zhu, H.-C., Yang, X., Xu, L.-P., Zhao, L.-J., Tao, G.-Z., Zhang, C., & Sun, X.-C. et al. (2014). Meat consumption is associated with esophageal cancer risk in a meat- and cancer-histological-type dependent manner. *Digestive Diseases and Sciences*, *59*(3), 664–673. doi:10.1007/s10620-013-2928-y PMID:24395380

Zink, K. D., & Lieberman, D. E. (2016). Impact of meat and Lower Palaeolithic food processing techniques on chewing in humans. *Nature*, *531*(7595), 500–503. doi:10.1038/nature16990 PMID:26958832

Ziolkowska, J. R. (2015). Shadow price of water for irrigation – a case of the High Plains. *Agricultural Water Management*, *153*, 20–31. doi:10.1016/j.agwat.2015.01.024

Ziolkowska, J. R. (2017). Economic and environmental costs of agricultural food losses and waste in the US. *International Journal of Food Engineering*, *3*(2), 140–145.

Zorpette, G. (2013). Muscling out meat. *IEEE Spectrum*, *50*(6), 64–70. doi:10.1109/MSPEC.2013.6521036

zur Hausen, H. (2012). Red meat consumption and cancer: Reasons to suspect involvement of bovine infectious factors in colorectal cancer. *International Journal of Cancer*, *130*(11), 2475–2483. doi:10.1002/ijc.27413 PMID:22212999

About the Contributors

Diana Bogueva has more than 20 years of international communication and media experience as a professional radio journalist working with several worldwide recognised news media, including the Bulgarian National Radio, Bulgarian Section of BBC, London and Special Broadcasting Services (SBS), Sydney, Australia. She is currently working for SBS radio as a program producer and is Director of Market Research with Sydney Focus Groups. Diana completed her PhD studies at Curtin University, Australia, focusing on meat consumption, social marketing and sustainability. She is a member of the International Federations of Journalists and a Wood Badge member of the World Scout Organization.

Dora Marinova is the Director of the Curtin University Sustainability Policy Institute. Dora has over 400 referred publications and has successfully supervised 50 PhD. She served as a member of National Health and Medical Research Council's Panel on Centres of Research Excellence in Population Health. Her research interests cover innovation models, including the evolving global green system of innovation and the emerging area of sustainometrics. Together with Talia Raphaely, Dora co-edited the book *Impact of Meat Consumption on Health and Environmental Sustainability* which was awarded World Best Book at the prestigious 22nd Gourmand Awards.

Talia Raphaely, originally from Cape Town, South Africa, has 30 years of experience in behavioural and attitudinal change, communications and diverse media, sustainability awareness and conscientiousness, collaboration and partnership building for sustainability. She has worked with multicultural and heterogeneous groups in diverse organizational settings, including academia, media, research-based organisations, government bodies, non-government organisations, community-based organisations and industry. Talia is a University Associate at Curtin University in Perth, Australia and undertakes sustainability consultancy research. The book she co-edited with Dora Marinova *Impact of Meat Consumption on Health and Environmental Sustainability* won World Best Book at the prestigious 22nd Gourmand Awards.

* * *

Emmanuel Ajadi (1990-2017) was a young enthusiastic sustainability researcher who sought to find viable pathways to drive the world towards sustainable development. With keen interest in food sustainability, equitability between the developed and developing world in resources management, and respect for traditional and indigenous values, Emmanuel had a Master degree from Curtin University, worked as a tutor at Juli Standard College and shared a deep love for his native African continent. The chapter included in this book is the last contribution before his life was cut short.

Ahmad Ni'matullah Al-Baarri works at Diponegoro University, Faculty of Animal and Agricultural Sciences, Food Technology Department, Semarang, Indonesia. Ahmad is widely published and is the Editor-in-Chief of the Journal of Applied Food Technology.

Jeff Anhang is an environmental specialist at the World Bank Group's International Finance Corporation (IFC) where he assesses environmental and social risks and opportunities in projects proposed for financing, and advises companies on managing those risks and opportunities. He helped establish a public accountability mechanism for IFC and improve its environmental and social footprint. In collaboration with Robert Goodland, the World Bank's first ecologist, Jeff worked on environmental assessment of agriculture. Their widely cited 2009 article "Livestock and Climate Change", published by the Worldwatch Institute, argued the business case for replacing livestock products with better alternatives to address climate change.

Usha K. Aravind is a Research Coordinator, Advanced Centre of Environmental Studies and Sustainable Development, Mahatma Gandhi University Campus, Kottayam, India. She holds a Master's degree (University of Pune, India) and PhD (Cochin University of Science and Technology, Kerala). Usha conducted post-doctoral research at the Katholieke Universiteit Leuven, Belgium, and Technical University of Eindhoven, Holland. Her research covers nano-architecture of polysaccharides, proteins, polypeptides, polymers on membrane surfaces enhancing their separation ability for water pollutants, green technological routes for removing contaminants, water sensors. Usha was awarded 7 major projects and has 40 journal publications, a book chapter and 150 conference papers.

Charuvial T. Aravindakumar has a Master in chemistry and PhD from the University of Pune. He was a Post-Doctoral Fellow at Katholieke Universiteit Leuven, Belgium, Max-Planck-Institut für Strahlenchemie, Mülheim, Germany and Vrije Universiteit Amsterdam, Holland, and a visiting professor at the University of Paris (E) Marne-la-Vallée, France. He is a professor at the School of Environmental Sciences and Dean of the Faculty of Environmental & Atmospheric Sciences, Mahatma Gandhi University. His research interests are: screening of emerging pollutants, oxidation and membrane technologies for water purification, polar research, mass spectrometry and spectroscopy. He has 75 journal publications and 200 conference papers.

Borislav Atanasov is an Assistant Professor at the University of National and World Economy in Sofia, Bulgaria where he also completed his PhD in 2012. His PhD thesis analysed customers' purchasing behaviour in relation to fast-moving consumer goods. Borislav's research interests are in the areas of prices and pricing, including levying with the value added tax (VAT) the pricing mechanisms in tourism, private labels trade and role of trade for employment.

Md Abul Azad works for Royal Perth Hospital, Western Australia and is a PhD candidate at the Curtin University Sustainability Policy (CUSP) Institute, Australia. He has a Master in Business Studies and Bachelor of Commerce (with Honours) from Rajshahi University, Bangladesh and Diploma in Hospitality Management from Southern Cross University, Australia. His research interests relate to preservation of heritage sites in Bangladesh, sustainability and heritage tourism.

Paula Brügger is a Professor, Ecology and Zoology Department, Santa Catarina Federal University, Brazil, where she coordinates the Ecological Justice Observatory. Her undergraduate studies were in biology, Master's degree in education and PhD in environment and society. Paula's research interests include environmental and abolitionist education, representations of nature and nonhuman animals in the media, ethical/epistemological implications of mechanistic paradigms in vivisection, and ecological, ethical, social and economic dimensions of industrial livestock processes. She has authored two books and was Director of Education of the Animal Abolitionist Institute. Since 2008, Paula is a columnist for the Animal Rights News Agency, Brazil.

Jessica Lynn Campbell received her Master's in English-Technical Communication Degree from the University of Central Florida. She has a Bachelor's Degree in Psychology from the University of Wisconsin-River Falls. Jessica is an expert and experienced technical communicator, author and multi-media manager having been published on multiple media platforms, including print and online. Her scholarly interests include health and medical communications, technical communication, digital spaces and online connectivity, online sociality and digital marketing. Jessica can be reached at jessica.campbell@embarqmail.com or 407-810-7542.

Hans Dagevos (PhD) is senior scientist at Wageningen University & Research in the Netherlands. He approaches and analyses the world of food from the perspective of the sociology of consumption. This has resulted in numerous publications ranging from scholarly papers and research reports, books and book chapters, to book reviews and weblogs that he (co)authored and (co)edited. His latest research interests, next to reduction of meat consumption and food transition towards sustainable diets, are in the fields of social innovation, circular consumption, and sustainable food policy.

Emily Foenander works on interdisciplinary research at the Centre for Social Impact, Swinburne University of Technology where she is a Senior Research Assistant. She is also completing a Master of Applied Psychology (Community Psychology) at Victoria University. Emily's research focuses on program evaluation, social equity, social impact and environmental psychology.

Celia Green is a PhD candidate at the National Centre for Epidemiology and Population Health, the Australian National University. Her PhD examines how different welfare state models influence the policy process using a cross-country analysis of Australian and Swedish government policy responses to the issue of sustainable diets. Celia is also a Research Fellow at the University of New South Wales Canberra where she conducts social and health policy research. Her particular area of interest lies in the application of political science theories to social and health policy issues to gain better understanding of how to create more impactful policy changes.

Nicholas (Nick) Hardersen is currently a Master's degree candidate in Environmental Sustainability at the Department of Geography and Environmental Sustainability, University of Oklahoma. He received his BA in Environmental Sustainability with special distinction also from the University of Oklahoma. His research interests include food waste, sustainable agriculture, alternative food networks and urban agriculture.

Erin Hill is a young, female, South African, (but above all else) human artist and researcher. Much of her work deals with the relationship between humans and the environment. She is interested in subtle violence, particularly in pervasive consumer culture and how this filters into the family space as the site of socialisation. Her work relies heavily on visual examples to illustrate such ideas. Erin's main objective is to disrupt quiet social norms of inequality and trauma that tend to go unnoticed, particularly the anthropocentric notion that non-human animals are mere mechanisms for humankind's hedonistic purposes.

Amzad Hossain is a university associate at the Curtin University Sustainability Policy (CUSP) Institute, Australia and a guest teacher at the Institute of Environmental Science, Rajshahi University, Bangladesh. His interests cover research in indigenous culture, values education, self-reliance, appropriate technology, climate change and spirituality with relevance to individual, social, technological and environmental sustainability. He has published over 100 research papers, including 20 popular articles on the mystic Baul tradition of Bangladesh. Amzad has a MCom from Rajshahi University, MA (by research) in religious studies from Deakin University, Australia and two PhDs (in Anthropology and in Sustainability) from Murdoch University, Australia. Senior Fellow (Teaching) in Marketing with University of Surrey, UK.

Jashmin Khan holds a doctorate in business marketing from AUT University, New Zealand. His current research looks at experimental consumer behaviour in new digital environments with particular interest in how mobile devices influence consumption and inform online-mobile education. He is also an honorary lecturer in marketing with University of Liverpool, and a visiting professor of marketing with Ramkhamhaeng University, Thailand. His work appears in *Journal of Business Research, Journal of Economic Psychology, Association for Consumer Research; Journal of Business and Economics, and International Business and Economic Review*.

Septemvrina Kostova is a Professor at the University of National and World Economy (UNWE) in Sofia, Bulgaria. She holds a PhD in retail management and her research interests are in the area of marketing and retailing, including strategic models and vintage fashion, as well as the future of jobs and skills. Septemvrina teaches in retail economics and she has also held the position of Head of Department, Retail Management, UNWE. She is a long-distance and marathon runner athlete with many national, European and world titles to her name.

Kate Marsh is an Advanced Accredited Practicing Dietitian and Credentialled Diabetes Educator, with a PhD, Master of Nutrition and Dietetics, BSc (University of Sydney) and a Graduate Certificate in Diabetes Education and Management (University of Technology Sydney). Kate works in private practice with interests in vegetarian nutrition and plant-based diets, dietary and lifestyle management of diabetes and polycystic ovary syndrome. She has published peer-review papers on vegetarian/plant-based nutrition and regularly speaks on these topics. Kate is a board member and Fellow of the Australasian Society for Lifestyle Medicine and convenor of the Dietitians Association of Australia Vegetarian Discussion Group.

Sarah McGrath holds a Master of Science in addition to a Graduate Certificate in Sustainability and Climate Policy, awarded by Curtin University. She has worked in both private and public sectors in Australia in commercial management roles, having started her career in finance and accounting. Today Sarah is an independent researcher and consultant based in Paris, France, where she works with non-governmental organisations and think-tanks in the areas of social innovation and environmental conservation.

Sayedul Islam Montu is a PhD candidate at the Curtin University Sustainability Policy (CUSP) Institute, Australia. He has a Bachelor (with Honours) and Master of Science degrees in chemistry from the University of Dhaka, Bangladesh. His research interests relate to the role of traditional knowledge in Bangladesh and the influence of Bangladeshi gurus, including Bauls, on politicians and other prominent personalities.

B. Pınar Özdemir is associate professor at Ankara University, Faculty of Communication, Department of Public Relations and Advertising. She is the co-author of the first history of public relations book in Turkey. Her major research areas are history of public relations, public relations campaigns and digital public relations. Pinar has several published articles, book chapters and books.

Nick Pendergrast received his PhD in Sociology at Curtin University in 2014. His thesis applied sociological theories on social movements and organisations to the animal advocacy movement in Australia and USA. He taught Sociology and Anthropology at Curtin University and currently teaches Sociology at the University of Melbourne. In 2014 Nick was nominated for a Guild Excellence in Teaching Award. As a part of the Institute for Critical Animal Studies (Oceania) collective, he has organised Critical Animal Studies conferences around Australia. He has published widely on Critical Animal Studies, human/non-human relations, the media, social movements and social change.

Ian Phau is a Professor in Marketing at Curtin University, Australia and Editor-0in-Chief for the Asia Pacific Journal of Marketing and Logistics. His expertise are in management consulting and market research in the luxury fashion industry in Europe and Asia including portfolios for Hugo Boss, Araluen Botanic Park, Prada, Shiseido, AirAsia and BlackBerry. His research focusses on luxury branding, country image and advertising appeals. Ian has extensive teaching experience in UK, Singapore, Hong Kong, Malaysia and Singapore.

Jeeva M. Philip received her MSc (Environment Science and Management) from the School of Environmental Sciences, Mahatma Gandhi University, Kottayam, Kerala, India. She worked as Junior Research Fellow at the Centre for Water Resources Development and Management, Kozhikode, Kerala, India and has research experience in environmental impact assessment studies. Since 2014, Jeeva is pursuing her PhD at the School of Environmental Sciences, Mahatma Gandhi University, Kottayam, Kerala, India in the field of screening of emerging contaminants in drinking water and its degradation studies. She is a co-author of "Emerging Contaminants in Indian Environmental Matrices: A review", published in *Chemosphere*.

Linda Portsmouth is a Senior Lecturer in Health Promotion in the School of Public Health at Curtin University in Perth, Western Australia. She teaches, researches and supervises postgraduate research students in health promotion strategies and methods with a speciality in health communication, media materials development and social marketing. Linda also consults on the evaluation of community-based health promotion programs via Curtin's Collaboration for Evidence, Research and Impact in Public Health. She holds a Master of Health Communication and a PhD in social marketing.

Machiel J. Reinders (PhD) is senior scientist at Wageningen University & Research in the Netherlands. His research focuses on consumer behaviour with regard to sustainable and healthy food products, strategies for food marketing, and consumer response to food innovations and new technologies. He has published his work extensively in international peer-reviewed journals including *Food Quality and Preference*, *Trends in Food Science and Technology*, *Journal of Product Innovation Management* and *Journal of Business Research.*

Lauren Rickards is a Senior Lecturer at RMIT University, Melbourne. At RMIT, Lauren co-leads the Climate Change and Resilience research program at the Centre for Urban Research, conducts research on the social dimensions of environmental change, including the intersection of climate, carbon, land, food and water issues, and teaches a popular course Climate Change Responses. A human geographer with a background in consulting on agriculture and sustainability issues, Lauren co-leads the Institute of Australian Geographers' Hazards Risk and Disasters study group and is an editor for the journals *Dialogues in Human Geography* and *Resilience: International Policies, Practices and Discourses.*

Gary Rivers is Associate Dean of the China-based Surrey International Institute (SII)), University of Surrey, UK. His research interests cover international education, human resources, organizational behaviour, marketing and buyer behaviour. With 20-year involvement with Transnational Education programmes, he has extensive management knowledge. Gary's previous roles include Deputy Head of International Programmes and Director of China projects, Curtin University, Australia and Head of Department, Australian College of Kuwait. He has a PhD from the University of Western Australia, is a member of the Academy of Management (USA) and a fellow of the Higher Education Association (UK).

Malte B. Rödl received his Master's degree in Industrial Ecology from Chalmers University of Technology, Gothenburg, Sweden, in 2015 as part of the Erasmus Mundus MIND programme. Afterwards, he started his PhD at, and generously funded by, the Sustainable Consumption Institute at The University of Manchester. His research revolves around the relations of meat and meat alternatives in a cultural context.

Sharyn Rundle-Thiele is Director, Social Marketing at Griffith University and Editor-in-Chief, Journal of Social Marketing. Drawing on her commercial marketing background Sharyn's research focuses on applying marketing tools and techniques to change behaviour for the better. Selected current projects include changing adolescent attitudes towards drinking alcohol (see www.blurredminds.com.au/students), increasing healthy eating and physical activity to combat obesity, reducing food waste and delivering change in wide variety of settings. Sharyn's research is published in more than 120 books, book chapters and journal papers.

Angela Vince Saunders is an Accredited Practising Dietitian, holds Master of Arts in Leadership and Management (Health Services) and BSc in Dietetics (Loma Linda University). She is Senior Dietitian at Sanitarium Health and Wellbeing. Her 30+ years of work focusses on plant-based diets and the evidence related to improving health, longevity and reducing chronic diseases. Angela is a board member of Nutrition Australia (NSW), member of the General Conference Nutrition Council (Washington, DC) and moderator of the Dietitians Association of Australia Vegetarian Discussion Group. She edited and contributed to the Medical Journal of Australia supplement "Is a Vegetarian Diet Adequate?".

Kurt Schmidinger, graduated geophysicist from Graz University of Technology, Austria and doctor in food science from Vienna University, Austria, works for various animal protection and vegetation and environmental associations, software development companies and is a project leader of www.futurefood.org in Austria, Europe. As a geophysicist, food scientist and animal protectionist, Kurt Schmidinger is interested in the global consequences of human nutritional habits, climatic stability of food, global livestock farming and global meat consumption including environment and climate, world food, human health and animal welfare.

Iveta Šedová is currently a PhD candidate in the Department of Environmental Studies at the Masaryk University in Brno, the Czech Republic. The working title of her thesis is "The relationship of environmentally engaged humans to animals: discrepancies between their attitudes and behavior". In 2016, she published with colleagues the article *Coping with unpleasant knowledge: Meat eating among students of environmental studies*. Her research interests include critical animal studies, psychology of meat eating, cognitive dissonance and coping strategies of meat-eaters. She is vegan and animal rights activist.

İsmail Hakkı Tekiner has a BSc in Chemical Engineering from the Middle East Technical University. He worked for Turkish and multinational companies as engineer, process supervisor and module leader. In 2016, İsmail completed his PhD in Food Engineering at İstanbul Aydın University. He is currently an academic at Istanbul Gelişim University. His major interests cover food safety, nutrition and nutrigenetics. He has 36 refereed publications, a TV programme "Climate Change and Food Safety" and is Editorial Board member of TASAM, Journal of Applied Food Technology, Journal of Advanced Nutrition and Human Metabolism, and International Journal of Nanomaterials, Nanotechnology and Nanomedicine.

Tereza Vandrovcová has a PhD in Sociology from the Faculty of Arts, Charles University in Prague, Czech Republic. Her book "Animal as an Experimental Object: A Sociological Reflection" (in Czech) was published in 2011. She teaches Social Psychology at the University of New York in Prague (UNYP) and Introduction to Animal Studies at UNYP, Charles University in Prague and Masaryk University in Brno. Her research interests include critical animal studies, psychology of meat eating, social psychology, bioethics, qualitative methodology and sociology of science.

Gerard Wedderburn-Bisshop worked as a Principal Scientist with Queensland Government Natural Resources, monitoring broadscale deforestation. He co-authored the Beyond Zero Emissions' Land Use Plan, a plan to take Australia's land use and agriculture emissions beyond zero, and works with NGO World Preservation Foundation, focussing on deforestation, land degradation and biodiversity loss. Since 2015 he has been working with the land use team on the Zero Emissions Byron project and the forthcoming Zero Emissions Tweed project.

Carol Zeuschner is an Accredited Practicing Dietitian, with a Master of Science (Nutrition and Dietetics) and BSc from the University of Wollongong. Carol is employed at the Sydney Adventist Hospital as Director of Support Services and is responsible for a wide range of patient services, including Allied Health and Food Services. She has extensive insight into the challenges of maximising nutrition for patients and has presented internationally on menu management systems. Carol has a keen interest in vegetarian nutrition and is an active member of the Dietitians Association of Australia. She has contributed to many review papers on vegetarian nutrition.

Jadwiga (Jad) R. Ziolkowska is an Assistant Professor and Environmental Economist, Department of Geography and Environmental Sustainability, University of Oklahoma. She was a post-doctoral scholar, University of California at Berkeley and EU Marie Curie Fellow, 7th Framework Program. Jad was also a researcher at University of Texas at Austin. Her PhD and Habilitation, both in agricultural economics, are from Humboldt University, Berlin. She authored 3 books and 40+ articles and book chapters. Jad specializes in natural resource, environmental, bioenergy, agricultural economics, and sustainable resource management. Her current research is on water management, desalination, economics of food waste, biofuels and drought implications.

Index

O

P

Q

R

S

T

U

V

W

Y

www.ingramcontent.com/pod-product-compliance
Lightning Source LLC
LaVergne TN
LVHW062107300926
849161LV00010B/2389

* 9 7 8 1 5 2 2 5 4 7 5 7 0 *